LEMON-AID
USED CARS
AND MINIVANS
2003

LEMON-AID
USED CARS
AND MINIVANS
2003

PHIL EDMONSTON

Published in 2002 by Stoddart Publishing Co. Limited
895 Don Mills Road, 400-2 Park Centre, Toronto, Ontario M3C 1W3

www.stoddartpub.com

To order Stoddart books please contact General Distribution Services
Tel. (416) 213-1919   Fax (416) 213-1917
Email cservice@genpub.com

10 9 8 7 6 5 4 3 2 1

National Library of Canada Cataloguing in Publication Data

Edmonston, Louis-Philippe, 1944–
Lemon-aid used cars and minivans
Annual.
2003–
Continues: Edmonston, Louis-Philippe, 1944– . Lemon-aid used cars,
ISSN 1485-1121.
ISSN 1701-6908
ISBN 0-7737-6279-5 (2003 edition)

1. Used Cars—Purchasing—Periodicals. 2. Vans—Purchasing—
Periodicals I. Title.
TL162.E3398   629.222'2'05   C2002-900797-6

Cover design: Bill Douglas @ The Bang
Text design: Kinetics Design & Illustration
Editing, proofreading, and typesetting:
Colborne Communications

THE CANADA COUNCIL | LE CONSEIL DES ARTS
FOR THE ARTS | DU CANADA
SINCE 1957 | DEPUIS 1957

We acknowledge for their financial support of our publishing program the Canada Council, the Ontario Arts Council, and the Government of Canada through the Book Publishing Industry Development Program (BPIDP).

Printed and bound in Canada

Contents

Key Documents ix

Introduction THREE DECADES OF DECEIT AND PROGRESS 1

Part One BUY THE BEST, FOR LESS **3**
Why Canadians Buy Used 7
Choosing the Right Seller 12
Paying the Right Price 18
Financing Choices 19
Dealer Scams 20
Private Scams 23
Summary to Saving Money and Keeping Safe 24

Part Two LEMONS AND LAWYERS! **25**
Four Ways to Get Your Money Back 26
Warranties 27
How Long Should a Part or Repair Last? 43
Three Steps to a Settlement 48
Safety and Performance Defects: Step-by-Step Resolution 53
Going to Court 61
Key Court Decisions 63
Paint and Body Defects 64
Repairs 70
Secret Warranties 70
False Advertising 72
Damages (Punitive) 72

Part Three CAR AND MINIVAN RATINGS **75**
Finding a Good Vehicle 75
Definitions of Terms 75

Small Cars **86**

DaimlerChrysler	88	**General Motors/**		**Mazda**	133
Neon	88	**Suzuki**	117	323, Protegé	133
		Firefly, Metro,			
Ford	94	Sprint/Swift	117	**Nissan**	137
Escort, ZX2	94			Sentra	137
Focus	99	**Honda**	119		
		Civic, del Sol	119	**Subaru**	140
General Motors	101			Impreza, Forester,	
Cavalier/Sunfire		**Hyundai**	127	Loyale	140
(Sunbird)	101	Accent	127	Legacy, Outback	144
Saturn S-series,		Elantra	130		
L-series	109				

Suzuki	148	**Toyota**	150	**Volkswagen**	160
Esteem	148	Corolla	150	Cabrio, Golf, Jetta	160
		Echo	155		
		Paseo	157		
		Tercel	158		

Medium Cars   165

Acura	167	Bonneville, Cutlass,		**Nissan**	232
1.6, 1.7L EL	167	Cutlass Supreme,		Altima	232
CL-Series	168	Delta 88, Grand Prix,			
Integra	171	Intrigue, LeSabre,		**Toyota**	235
		Lumina, Malibu,		Camry, Solara	235
DaimlerChrysler	174	Monte Carlo, Regal	204		
Breeze, Cirrus,		Century, Ciera	213	**Volkswagen**	242
Stratus	174			New Beetle	242
		Honda	218	Passat	245
Ford	181	Accord	218		
Contour, Mystique	181				
Sable, Taurus	185	**Hyundai**	225		
		Sonata	225		
General Motors	199				
Achieva (Calais),		**Mazda**	228		
Grand Am, Skylark	199	626, MX-6	228		

Large Cars/Wagons   249

DaimlerChrysler	251	**Ford**	257	**General Motors**	265
300M, Concorde,		Cougar,		Caprice, Impala SS,	
Intrepid, LHS, New		Thunderbird	257	Roadmaster	265
Yorker, Vision	251	Crown Victoria,			
		Grand Marquis	262		

Luxury Cars   268

Acura	272	**Ford/Lincoln**	286	Cadillac Concours,	
RL	272	Continental, LS,		DeVille, Fleetwood	
TL	274	Mark VII, Mark VIII,		(FWD)	306
		Town Car	286		
Audi	277			**Infiniti**	309
90, A4, A6 (100),		**General Motors**	293	G20, I30, J30, Q45	309
A8, S6, TT Coupe	277	98 Regency, Park			
		Avenue	293	**Lexus**	315
BMW	281	Aurora, Riviera	296	ES 300, GS 300,	
3 Series, 5 Series,		Cadillac Brougham,		LS 400, SC 400	315
M Series, Z3	281	Fleetwood (RWD)	300		
		Cadillac Catera,		**Mazda**	320
		Eldorado, Seville	302	Millenia	320

Mercedes-Benz   323
300 series, 400 series,
500 series, E-Class   323
C-Class   326

Nissan   328
Maxima   328

Saab   332
900, 9000, 9-3, 9-5   332

Toyota   335
Avalon   335

Volvo   338
850, C70, S40, S70,
V40, V70   338
900 series, S80, S90,
V90   344

Sports Cars   348
DaimlerChrysler   350
Avenger, Sebring   350
Laser, Talon   354

Ford   357
Mustang   357
Probe   363

General Motors   366
Camaro, Firebird,
Trans Am   366
Corvette   372

Honda   377
Prelude   377

Hyundai   380
Tiburon   380

Mazda   382
Miata   382
MX-3, Precidia   384

Nissan   385
200SX   385
240SX   387

Toyota   388
Celica   388

Minivans   391
DaimlerChrysler   394
Caravan, Voyager,
Grand Caravan,
Grand Voyager,
Town & Country   394
PT Cruiser   408

Ford   412
Windstar   412

Ford/Nissan   424
Villager, Quest   424

General Motors   429
Astro, Safari   429
Lumina, Lumina APV,
Montana, Silhouette,
Trans Sport,
Venture   433

Honda   439
Odyssey   439

Mazda   445
MPV   445

Toyota   448
Sienna, Previa   448

Appendix I HELPFUL INTERNET INFO SITES   454

**Appendix II GOOD BUYS FOR A BAD ECONOMY:
"BEATERS," "ORPHANS," AND "CHICK MAGNETS"**   460

Cars
Acura Vigor   461
Checker   461–462
Chrysler Dart, Valiant, Duster, Scamp, Diplomat, Caravelle, Newport,
New Yorker Fifth Avenue, Gran Fury, 2000GTX, Stealth   462
Ford Maverick, Comet, Fairmont, Zephyr, Tracer, Mustang, Capri,
Cougar, Thunderbird, Torino, Marquis, Grand Marquis, LTD, LTD
Crown Victoria, Festiva, Probe   462

General Motors Chevette, Acadian, Nova, Ventura, Skylark, Phoenix, Spectrum, Camaro, Firebird, Malibu, LeMans, Century, Regal, Cutlass, Monte Carlo, Grand Prix, Bel Air, Impala, Caprice, Roadmaster, Laurentian, Catalina, Parisienne, LeSabre, Bonneville, Delta 88   463
Mazda MX-3, MX-6, 929, RX-7   463–464
Nissan Micra, Pulsar, NX, Stanza, 300ZX   464–465
Subaru Justy   465
Toyota early models, Celica, MR2, Cressida, Supra   465–466
Volvo 240 Series, 700 Series   466

Pickups
Mazda B-series; Nissan King Cab; Toyota Pickup, T100   467–468

Sport-Utilities
Jeep CJ, Wagoneer; Toyota Land Cruiser   468–469

Minivans and Wagons
Chrysler Colt/Summit/Vista; Ford Aerostar; Nissan Multi, Axxess   469–471

Appendix III LEMON-PROOFING BEFORE YOU BUY   472

Honda 1988–95 Civic head gasket leaks—bulletin   121
Honda 1988–2000 Civic rear suspension noise—bulletin   124
Honda 1996–2000 Civic harsh shifts—bulletin   125
Honda 2001 Civic free PCM replacement—bulletin   126
Hyundai 1995–2001 transaxle temperature sensor—bulletin   129
Hyundai poor shifting—bulletin   129
Hyundai 1996–99 transmission leak—bulletin   132–133
Mazda 1995–98 Protegé, Miata inoperative AC—bulletin   136
Toyota 1998–2000 Corolla brake pad vibration—bulletin   154
Volkswagen 2000–01 worn brake pads—bulletin   163
Chrysler 1995–96 Breeze, Cirrus, Stratus water leaks—bulletin   178
Chrysler 1995–98 Breeze, Cirrus, Stratus AC failure—bulletin   178–179
Chrysler 1995–98 Breeze, Cirrus, Stratus steering noise—bulletin   179
Ford 1995–99 Contour, Mystique brake noise—bulletin   183
Ford 1998–99 Contour, Mystique, Cougar exhaust odour—bulletin   184
Ford 1986–95 transmission defect—bulletin   187–188
Ford 1994–98 transmission defect—bulletin   188
Ford 1988–96 engine overheating—bulletin   189
Paint-delaminated Ford Taurus—photo   190
Ford 1996–97 Taurus, Sable harsh shifting—bulletin   196
Ford 1996–2001 Taurus, Sable inoperative windows—bulletin   197
Ford 2000–2001 Taurus, Sable fuel odour—bulletin   198
GM 1995–2000 brake rotor warranty   210–211
GM 2001 poor shifting—bulletin   216
GM 1997–2001 Century faulty shift lever—bulletin   217
Honda 1999–2000 Accord torque converter—bulletin   224
Toyota 1997–98 Camry steering noise—bulletin   240–241
Ford 1996–97 Mustang, Cougar, F-Series coolant leaks—letter   362
Chrysler 1996 minivans radar stalling—bulletin   396
Chrysler 1996–2001 minivans suspension noise—bulletin   404
Chrysler 1996–2001 minivans rusted/frozen brakes—bulletin   405–406
Chrysler 1997–2001 minivans rear brake noise—bulletin   406–407
Chrysler 2001 transmission surge/sag—bulletin   411
Ford 1999–2000 Windstar spark knock—bulletin   422–423
Toyota 1996–2001 engine oil sludge—bulletin   450
Toyota 1997–2001 Sienna, Camry, Avalon water leaks—bulletin   453

Key Documents

The following photos, charts, documents, memos, court filings and decisions, and service bulletins are included in this index so that you can easily find and photocopy whichever document will prove helpful in your dealings with automakers, government agencies, dealers, or service managers. Most of the service bulletins outline repairs or replacements that should be done for free.

Introduction THREE DECADES OF DECEIT AND PROGRESS
Chrysler AC 7-year secret warranty   2

Part One BUY THE BEST, FOR LESS
Windstar lemon protest—photo   3
Firestone tire blowout—photo   4
Faulty Ford, Chrysler, and GM transmissions—bulletins   5–7

Part Two LEMONS AND LAWYERS
Saskatchewan GM paint judgment   25
New Brunswick angry Chrysler owners—photo   25
Ford 1996–98 trucks, vans, and Windstar coolant loss—bulletin   31–32
Honda Accord window defects—bulletin   33
Firestone Affinity tire sidewall splitting—photo   42
Estimated part durability—chart   44
Used car or minivan complaint letter/fax/email   50
Secret warranty claim letter/fax/email   51
Woman injured from inadvertent airbag deployment—photo   53
Ford 1996 Windstar engine head gasket failure—judgment   67

Part Three CAR AND MINIVAN RATINGS
NHTSA Corvette steering lockup complaints   78–79
Sample *Red Book* prices   81
Mercury Mountaineer ad   82
Value of options for 1994–2001—chart   83
Chrysler 1995–99 engine head gaskets—bulletin   91–92
Chrysler 1998–99 trunk leaks—bulletin   93
Ford 1997–98 Escort engine oil leak—bulletin   96–97
Ford 1997–98 Escort cooling fan, no-starts—bulletin   97
Ford 2000–01 Focus interior water leaks—bulletin   100
GM 1985–2000 snow in rear brakes—bulletin   105
GM 1999–2000 no Third or Fourth gear—bulletin   107
GM 2000–01 inaccurate fuel gauge—bulletin   107–108
GM 1994–96 Saturn engine head gaskets—letter   113
GM 1996–98 Saturn hard starts, inoperative lights—bulletin   114
GM 2000–01 Saturn steering wheel shake—bulletin   115–116

Three Decades of Deceit and Progress

We're back. And marking our thirtieth year in print with sales of just over a million copies.

Not a great deal has changed over the past thirty years. Many vehicles are still unsafe and unreliable, Firestone/Bridgestone still makes lousy tires, rear-drives are seen as the next innovative milestone, and nostalgia cars (Chrysler's PT Cruiser, Ford's Thunderbird, and the VW New Beetle) are all the rage.

Fortunately, vehicles are more crashworthy and fuel efficient. But even these small improvements have been wiped out by failure-prone airbags, ABS brakes that don't brake, and "Godzilla" SUVs and pickups.

Lemon-Aid Used Cars and Minivans 2003 is unlike any other auto book on the market. It's a uniquely Canadian owner's manual that pulls no punches in disclosing what's a fair price for a used vehicle, which cars and minivans are lemons, which repairs are the automakers' responsibility, and which scams you should avoid. Paying a fair price is even more crucial this year: the bottom has fallen out of the lease and rental-car market, and 0 percent new-car financing has driven used prices down and made many off-lease vehicles and used rentals veritable bargains—if you know what to buy and how to use depreciation timing to your advantage.

My goal for over 30 years has been to keep ownership costs low and make automakers and dealers more honest and accountable—even as they hire lawyers and PR flacks to plead that wrong is right and that safety, like their own integrity, is relative. This guide continues a tradition of publicizing abusive auto industry practices and providing hard-to-get information that may save your life, or at least protect your wallet. *Lemon-Aid*'s information comes from owners who buy and drive these vehicles, not travel-junket-junkie, free-car-mongering car columnists. Our database includes Canadian and U.S. sources and is refined throughout the year with input from owner complaints, automaker whistleblowers, lawsuits, judgments, confidential technical service bulletins (TSBs), and independent garages.

Lemon-Aid was the first book to blow the whistle on Firestone "killer" tires, the Ford Explorer's safety-related problems, and the rising number of factory-related defects found in both Asian and American cars and minivans. We were also first off the mark in exposing GM's failure-prone anti-lock brakes; Chrysler's defective paint and biodegradable automatic transmissions and brakes; Ford Windstar's coil spring, engine and automatic transmission failures; and Toyota's and Honda's minivan transmission defects. Interestingly, following *Lemon-Aid*'s intervention, Chrysler and Ford paid hundreds of previously rejected owner claims and extended their warranties.

ADDENDUM TO BASIC WARRANTY

The following applies to 1993 through 1997 New Yorker, LHS, Concorde, Intrepid, Vision and Grand Cherokee vehicles equipped with factory-installed air conditioning:

> *The Basic Warranty coverage for the air conditioner evaporator has been extended to 7 years or 115,000 kilometres, whichever occurs first, from the vehicle's warranty start date.*

> *This extended coverage applies to all owners of the vehicle. All of the other warranty terms apply to this extension.*

AD9502-B

We suggest that you keep this addendum card in your warranty information booklet.

 CHRYSLER CANADA

You are looking at a rare piece of written evidence, showing Chrysler will pay for an AC failure—long after the original warranty has elapsed.

The 2003 edition has many more surprises in store for readers. It combines test results with owner feedback to provide a critical comparison of many cars and minivans sold during the past three decades. If improvements and additional safety features don't justify the higher costs of newer models (most don't), we say so. Safer, more reliable, and often cheaper alternatives are given for each vehicle, and reliability and crashworthiness ratings are shown for each model year. Finally, in response to the hard economic times we are facing, this year's guide includes a helpful appendix that rates the best vehicles available for buyers with a limited budget.

Lemon-Aid Used Cars and Minivans 2003 makes use of many more internal technical service bulletins than previous editions. We have found that having the service bulletin proof in hand works wonders in getting refunds for the correction of factory-related defects that are too often passed on as normal maintenance. I know divulging these confidential bulletins rankles many service managers and automakers, but keeping them secret only perpetuates a fraud on the motoring public.

It's time for this deception to end.

Phil Edmonston
March 2002

PART ONE

Buy the Best, for Less

1

How To Be a Millionaire

"Thirty-seven percent of millionaires buy used cars, which is one reason why they're so well off."

Getting Rich in America
Dwight R. Lee and Richard B. McKenzie

Since 1996, new-car prices have moderated, creating a large reservoir of bargain-priced used cars. And as we enter into 2002, used prices continue to decline in response to an uncertain economy, volatile fuel costs, new-car rebates, and low-percentage financing programs. There are lots of other reasons why now is a great time to buy a used car or minivan. First, there's not as much junk out there as there once was. Vehicles are safer, more fuel efficient, and loaded with extra convenience and performance features. Second, there are a lot of inexpensive models to choose from, because many good-quality vehicles are just coming off their 3-year leases, and dealers have slashed the unrealistically high trade-in values used to keep monthly lease payments small. Third, rental-car agencies, hit hard by reduced tourism and business travel, are flooding the market with their inventory as they cut operating costs.

Yes, prices are much lower, but you'll still have to do your homework if you want to get a good deal. Be especially wary of unsafe and unreliable cars and minivans lurking on the market—despite their lowered prices, they will make you rue the day you bought them (Ford's Windstar and Chrysler's Neon come to mind).

The Ford Windstar is one of the worst minivans ever made: if the tranny doesn't get you, the engine, front coil springs, brakes, or heater core will.

Garbage in, garbage out

I've spent almost 33 years battling automakers and dealers who lie through their teeth as they try to convince customers that their vehicles are well made, and that defects are caused mainly by the proverbial nut behind the wheel, poor maintenance, or abusive driving. That's why the auto industry has such a lousy reputation—car owners know better. The average Canadian has personally experienced (or knows someone who has) the lying, cheating, and stealing that's so rampant at all levels of the automotive manufacturing and marketing process.

Firestone wasn't an aberration; it was a microcosm of what goes on throughout the industry. Ford tried to push it under the rug with a secret warranty (see Part Two, "Secret Warranties"), paying off Explorer owners in Venezuela and Saudi Arabia who had tire failures. When the media discovered the cover-up, Ford lied to customers and officials alike, saying either that they weren't aware of the failures or that it was all Firestone's fault.

Both Firestone and Ford lied to their customers over the dangers inherent in Firestone-equipped Explorers. Although Ford's CEO Jac Nasser was booted out of the company following the fiasco, the two companies are in talks to renew their partnership.

This dishonesty and poor quality control has always existed. When I founded the Automobile Protection Association (APA) in Montreal in the fall of 1969, American Motors was giving out free television sets with the purchase of its failure-prone Eagle sport-utility (actually, the television sets lasted longer than the Eagle); Volkswagen had a monopoly on hazardous, poorly heated, and sluggish Beetles; Ford was churning out biodegradable cars and trucks (and denying they had a secret "J-67" warranty to cover rust repairs); Firestone was dragged, kicking and screaming, into announcing the recall of 11 million tires for catastrophic tread separation (in the late '70s); and Chrysler's entire product line was "rain-challenged"—stalling and leaking in wet weather due to faulty ballast resistors. Imagine, when the first guides were written a few years after the APA's founding, a good, 3-year-old Mustang could be had for less than $2,000; the average price now tops $10,000.

Japanese and European cars imported into Canada during the '70s were junk—as thousands of owners of rust-cankered and unreliable VWs, Hondas, Toyotas, and Nissans will confirm. Yet they got a toehold in the North American car market because the Big Three's products were worse—and they still are. Seizing the opportunity, foreign automakers smartened up within a remarkably short period of time. They quickly built reliable and durable cars and trucks and offered them fully loaded and reasonably priced.

Meanwhile, American automakers continued pumping out dangerous and unreliable junk through the '90s—these included GM's Chevy Vega, Firenza, and Fiero, as well as early Saturns, Cavaliers, Sunbirds, and the Lumina APV minivan; Chrysler's Omni, Horizon, Dynasty, Imperial, Concorde, Neon, and post-'90 minivans; and Ford's Pinto, Bobcat, Tempo, Topaz, Taurus, Sable, Contour, Mystique (mistake?), Merkur, Bronco, Explorer, and Windstar.

Today, Detroit's Big Three quality control is about where Japanese automakers' was in the mid-'70s. Where the gap hasn't narrowed (and a case can be made that it's actually gotten wider) is in engine, automatic transmission, airbag, and anti-lock brake reliability, as well as fit and finish.

Want proof not even your dealer's service manager can deny? Take a look at the following three confidential internal service bulletins depicting serious automatic transmission problems with Chrysler, Ford, and GM cars and minivans. Note how the Big Three automakers have allowed the same defect to be carried over year after year.

Ford's "Biodegradable" Aluminum Transmissions

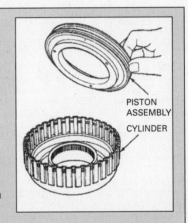

Subject: Forward Piston Change
Application: Ford   Date: 1995
Forward Piston Change
• No forward or reverse engagement.
• Delayed forward and/or reverse engagement.
• Shifts out of gear when coming to a stop.

All of these complaints can be attributed to a cracked or broken forward piston clutch. There have been three different versions of the aluminum piston in this location (the original plus two updates). Problems with cracking still persist.

PISTON ASSEMBLY

CYLINDER

A steel version of this part has been released that should prevent this from happening. The Ford part number is F4DZ-7A262-A. The aluminum piston should always be replaced with the steel piston.

Failures with Ford's aluminum forward piston clutch affect most of the company's products made since 1986, though complaints on the most recent models target mainly the Taurus, Sable, and Windstar. In February 2002, Ford executives promised me that the company would give "goodwill" refunds on a case-by-case basis to new- or used-vehicle owners (1995–99) who had been previously denied compensation for this defect.

Chrysler's "Limping" Transmissions

NO: 18-24-95   Date: Jun. 23, 1995   GROUP: Veh. Performance

Subject: Improved Transmission Shift Quality

Models:		
	1989-1995	(AA) Acclaim/Sprit/LeBaron Sedan
	1989-1993	(AC) Dynasty/New Yorker/New Yorker Salon
	1990-1993	(AG) Daytona
	1990-1994	(AJ) LeBaron Coupe/LeBaron Convertible
	1993-1994	(AP) Sundance/Shadow/Shadow Convertible
	1990-1991	(AQ) Chrysler TC
	1989-1995	(AS) Caravan/Voyager/Town & Country
	1990-1992	(AY) Imperial/New Yorker Fifth Avenue
	1993-1995	(ES) Chrysler Voyager (European Market)
	**1995	(FJ) Sebring/Avenger/Talon**
	1995	(JA) Cirrus/Stratus
	1993-1995	(LH) Concorde/Intrepid/Vision/LHS/New Yorker

NOTE: THIS BULLETIN APPLIES TO VEHICLES EQUIPPED WITH THE 41TE OR 42LE TRANSAXLE. SYMPTOM/CONDITION: 1992 AC. & AY VEHICLES BUILT AFTER FEB. 15, 1992 (MDH 02-15-XX). **1995 FJ VEHICLES** AND ALL OTHER 1993-1995 SUBJECT VEHICLES BUILT BEFORE OCT. 24, 1994, (MDH 10-24-XX) ARE VEHICLES EQUIPPED WITH AN ELECTRONICALLY MODULATED CONVERTOR CLUTCH (EMCC). Vehicles that operate at speeds where EMCC usage is engaged (vehicle speeds 34 – 41 MPH) may experience early deterioration of the transmission fluid (15,000 – 30,000 miles), exhibit a pronounced shudder during EMCC operation, harsh upshifts/downshifts, and/or harsh torque converter engagements. Performing REPAIR PROCEDURE # 2, which includes updates to the Transmission Control Module (TCM) calibration and eliminates EMCC, will resolve these symptoms/conditions. However, if an overheat condition is identified by the PCM or TCM, EMCC operation will be temporarily enabled.

ALL 1995 FJ VEHICLES AND ALL OTHER 1989-1995 SUBJECT VEHICLES BUILT BEFORE OCT. 24, 1994 (MDH 10-24-XX).

The TCM calibration used in the 1995 model year 41TE and 42LE TCM is being made available for all vehicles dating back to the 1989 model year. The shift quality improvements and default issues that will be corrected by the new TCM calibration are:

1. COASTDOWN TIP-IN BUMP: Vehicle is decelerated almost to a stop (less than 8 MPH), then the driver tips back into the throttle to accelerate, a noticeable bump may be felt.
2. COASTDOWN SHIFT HARSHNESS: Harsh coastdown shifts on some 4-3, 3-2, 2-1 downshifts.
3. 1995 LH WITH 42LE TRANSAXLE – SLUGGISHNESS/LACK OF RESPONSE: On some early 1995 LH vehicles built prior to Oct. 24, 1994, a perceived lack of power or transmission responsiveness may be encountered under normal operating conditions. The transmission may not release the converter clutch as desired with increased throttle. This occurs in 4th gear 35–50 MPH.
4. 1989-1994 WITH 41TE & 42LE TRANSAXLES: Harsh shifts and/or vehicle shudder during 3-2 or 2-1 kickdowns at speeds less than 25 MPH.
5. 1993 WITH 41TE TRANSAXLE: Harsh 3-4 upshifts may occur, especially at highway speeds, while using the speed control.
6. 1989-1994 WITH 41TE TRANSAXLE – HARSH/DELAYED GARAGE SHIFTS: Delay is less than 2 seconds and the shift is harsh after the brief delay. NOTE: Delays greater than 2 seconds are caused by transmission hardware malfunction, i.e., valve body, pump, failed lip seals, or malfunctioning PRNDL or neutral start switch.
7. EARLY 1993 WITH 41TE & 42LE TRANSAXLE – INTERMITTENT SPEED CONTROL DROP OUT: The new service calibration change corrects this condition (this condition was also covered in Technical Service Bulletin 08-09-93 dated Mar. 12, 1993).
8. 1989-1993 WITH 41TE & 42LE TRANSAXLES: New fault code 35 (failure to achieve pump prime) has been added for improved diagnostic capability, and fault codes 21, 22 and 24 are desensitized to reduce erroneous limp-in conditions.

Chrysler's problems are caused by both hardware and computer software glitches that affect almost its entire product line. Owners of 1996–99 vehicles should claim a "goodwill" repair refund from Chrysler. Hundreds of Chrysler claimants have received compensation up to 75 percent of the repair amount on vehicles not exceeding 100,000 miles (160,000 kilometres) when the transmission failed (see Part Two).

GM's "Neutral" Transmissions

Bulletin No.: 67-71-64   Date: February, 1997
Subject: Intermittent Neutral or Loss of Drive at Highway Speeds
or from Fourth Gear (Replace Control Valve Body Assembly)

Models: 1995–96 Buick Skylark Regal, Century, Park Avenue, Riviera, LeSabre • 1997 Buick
Skylark, Regal, Century, LeSabre • 1995 Cadillac DeVille • 1995–96 Chevrolet Beretta, Corsica,
Lumina APV, Lumina, Monte Carlo • 1997 Chevrolet Lumina, Monte Carlo, Venture • 1995–96
Oldsmobile Cutlass Ciera, Cutlass Cruiser, LSS, Ninety Eight, Ninety Eight Regency, Eighty Eight,
Achieva, Silhouette, Cutlass Supreme • 1997 Oldsmobile Eighty Eight, Achieva, Cutlass Supreme,
LSS, Silhouette • 1995–97 Pontiac Bonneville, Grand Am, Trans Sport, Grand Prix with HYDRA-
MATIC 4T60-E Transaxle (RPO M13)

Condition: Some owners may comment about an intermittent, neutral condition while driving at
highway speeds or intermittent neutral from fourth gear.

Cause: The 3–2 Manual Downshift valve may be sticking intermittently.

How's this for a scary scenario: you're cruising down the highway or in city traffic and the
transmission of your 1995–97 GM front-drive car or minivan drops into "neutral." Another traffic
fatality blamed on driver's error?

You can reduce your risk of buying a lemon by getting a vehicle recommended in this guide that has some of the original warranty still in effect. This protects you from some of the costly defects that are bound to crop up shortly after your purchase. The warranty allows you to make one final inspection before it expires and requires both the dealer and the automaker to compensate you for all warrantable defects found at that time.

Why Canadians Buy Used

Canadian car buyers are cheap, unpretentious, and faithful. We don't have short love affairs—with cars or trucks. We are very reluctant to trade in a vehicle or abandon a model that suits our needs. In fact, almost 47 percent of Canadians keep cars and trucks nine years or more, says Toronto-based industry analyst Dennis DesRosiers. We are also more conservative than Americans in our vehicle choice, with 86 percent of CAA's 2000 annual survey respondents stating they would buy the same vehicle again. And, confirming our *société distincte* status—at least to Americans—we love block heaters and minivans throughout Canada, particularly Subaru AWDs in Quebec.

Through the '90s, the popularity of used vehicles went up substantially in Canada. Why? Because, according to the Royal Bank, the average Canadian's take-home pay didn't keep pace with the rising cost of purchasing and owning a new vehicle. And Canadians are wary of dealers selling used cars. Of the almost 20 percent of the estimated 17 million vehicles on our roads that change hands each year, 70 percent are estimated to be private sales. Here are some of the main reasons why Canadians prefer buying used vehicles:

1. Less initial cash outlay, slower vehicle depreciation, "secret" warranty repair refunds, and better and cheaper parts availability
New-vehicle prices have moderated somewhat over the past few years, but they're still quite high—the Automotive Industries Association of Canada (AIA) pegs the average cost of a new truck at almost $28,000. Insurance is another wallet-buster, costing about $4,000 a year for young drivers. And once you add financing costs, maintenance, taxes, and a host of other expenses, CAA calculates the yearly outlay for a medium-sized car at over $8,252, or 36.7 cents/km; trucks or SUVs may run you about 10 cents/km more. For a comprehensive, though depressing, comparative analysis (cars vs. trucks, minivans, SUVs, etc.) of all the costs involved over a 1- to 10-year period, access Alberta's consumer information website at *www1.agric.gov.ab.ca/app09/carcostcalc*.

Want to pay less *and* legally avoid paying tax? Buy privately. You'll pay at least 10 percent less than the dealer's price and you may avoid the 7 percent federal Goods and Services Tax (GST) that applies in some provinces to dealer sales only.

Be practical. When buying a used car or minivan, keep in mind you're simply buying transportation and function. You want no-surprise handling; a comfortable ride; reliable performance; and interior, cargo, and passenger capacity. Because you only need about one-half the cash or credit required for a new vehicle, it's easy to see that you won't have to invest as much money in a depreciating investment. You may even be fortunate enough to forgo a loan.

Depreciation savings
If someone were to ask you to invest in stocks or bonds guaranteed to be worth about half their initial purchase value after four to five years, you'd probably head for the door. But this is exactly the trap you're falling into when you buy a new vehicle that could depreciate 20 percent in the first year and 15 percent each year thereafter (minivans and other specialty vehicles, like sport-utilities and trucks, depreciate more slowly). Here's what a new car or minivan in Ontario would cost:

Cost (New)

Purchase price	$28,000
Federal GST (7%)	$1,960
Provincial tax (8%)	$2,240
Total price	$32,200

When you buy used, the situation is altogether different. That same vehicle can be purchased four years later, in good condition, and with much of the manufacturer's warranty remaining, for one-half to two-thirds of its original cost. Look at what happens to the price:

Cost (Used)

Purchase price (four years old, 80,000 km)	$14,000
No GST (if sold privately)	—
Provincial tax (8%)	$1,120
Total price	$15,120

In this example, the used-vehicle buyer saves $14,000 on the selling price, $1,960 in federal taxes, and $1,120 in provincial taxes, and gets a reliable, guaranteed set of wheels. Furthermore, the depreciation "hit" will be much less in the ensuing years.

Secret warranty payouts
Believe it or not, some free repairs—like those related to Honda and Acura emissions problems—are authorized up to 14 years or 240,000 km (150,000 miles) under automaker "goodwill" programs. And if Ford reaches an agreement in settlement talks for its stall-prone 1983–95 ignition modules, owners of almost 5 million vehicles will get free module replacements up to 19 years or 160,000 km (100,000 miles). Still, most secret warranty extensions hover around the 5- to 10-year mark and seldom cover vehicles exceeding 160,000 km (100,000 miles). This benchmark includes engine and transmission defects affecting Chrysler minivans, Ford's Windstar, and Toyota V6 head gasket and engine oil sludge problems (1997–2001 models). Ford's 1995–98 Windstars carry a little-known 10-year warranty extension covering front coil spring breakage, and a free tire replacement, if punctured (see page 38).

Knowing which after-warranty repairs will be reimbursed can cut your maintenance costs dramatically. Incidentally, automakers and dealers claim that there are no secret warranties—that they are all expressed in service bulletins. Although this is technically correct, the sources that supply these bulletins are somewhat obscure to most vehicle owners, and the bulletins seldom state flat-out that the factory goofed.

Parts
Even when parts costs aren't deliberately boosted by American auto manufacturers, prices are unacceptably high. According to the Alliance of American Insurers, the price of original equipment replacement parts needed to rebuild a vehicle is over three times the original retail price. Last year's study discovered that rebuilding a 2000 Honda Accord cost a whopping $68,065.93 (U.S.), versus a retail list price of only $22,365.00 (U.S.). No labour was included in the estimate.

Generally, a new gasoline-powered car or minivan can be expected to run, relatively trouble-free, at least 200,000–240,000 km in its lifetime, and a diesel-powered vehicle can easily triple those figures. Some repairs will crop up at regular intervals, and along with preventive maintenance, your yearly running costs should average about $700–$800. Buttressing the argument that vehicles get cheaper to operate the longer you keep them, the U.S. Department of Transportation points out that the average vehicle requires one or more major repairs after every five years of use. However, once these repairs are done, it can then be run relatively trouble-free for another five years or more. In fact, the further west you go in Canada, the longer owners keep their vehicles—an average of 10 years or more in some provinces.

Time is on your side in other ways, too. Three years after a model's launching, the replacement-parts market usually catches up to consumer demand. Dealers stock larger inventories, and parts wholesalers and independent parts manufacturers expand their output. Used replacement parts are unquestionably easier to come by, through bargaining with local garages or through a careful search of auto wreckers' yards or the Internet. A reconditioned or used part usually costs one-third to one-half the price of a new part. There's generally no difference in the quality of reconditioned mechanical components, and they're often guaranteed for as long as, or longer than, new ones. In fact, some savvy shoppers use the ratings in Part Three of this guide to see which parts have a short life and then buy those parts from retailers that give lifetime warranties on their brakes, exhaust systems, tires, batteries, etc.

Also, buying from discount outlets or independent garages, or ordering through mail order houses, can save you big bucks (30–35 percent) on the cost of new parts and another 15 percent on labour when compared with dealer charges. Costco is another good example of savings realized through independent retailers. The retailer sells competitively priced replacement tires and offers free rotation, balancing, and other inspections during the life of the tire.

Body parts are a different story, however. Although car company repair parts cost 60 percent more than certified generic aftermarket parts, buyers would be wise to buy only original equipment manufacturer (OEM) parts supplied by automakers in order to get body panels that fit well, protect better in collisions, and have maximum rust resistance, says *Consumer Reports* in its February 1999 study. Although insurance appraisers often substitute cheaper, lower-quality aftermarket body parts in collision repairs, *Consumer Reports* found that 71 percent of those policyholders who requested OEM parts got them with little or no hassle. It suggests that consumers complain to their provincial Superintendent of Insurance if OEM parts aren't provided. If that doesn't produce the desired results, take out a small claims action or file a class action similar to the one recently won in the state of Illinois against State Farm.

With some European models, you can count on a lot of aggravation and expense caused by the unacceptably slow distribution of parts and the high markup. Because these companies have a quasi-monopoly on replacement parts, there are few independent suppliers you can turn to for help. And junkyards, the last-chance repository for inexpensive car parts, are unlikely to carry foreign parts for vehicles more than three years old or manufactured in small numbers.

Finding parts for Japanese and domestic cars and vans is hardly a problem, though, due to the large number of vehicles produced, the presence of hundreds of independent suppliers, the ease with which relatively simple parts can be interchanged from one model to another, and the large reservoir of used parts stocked by junkyards.

Auto clubs listed on the Internet are often helpful sources for parts that are otherwise unobtainable. Club members trade and sell specialty parts, keep a list of where rare parts can be found, and are usually well-informed as to where independent parts suppliers are located. Most car enthusiast magazines will put you in touch with auto clubs and suppliers of hard-to-find parts.

2. Lower insurance rates

The difference in annual insurance costs between a new minivan or truck and a used one may be only a few hundred dollars, but by carefully negotiating the deductible, the smart shopper can further reduce insurance premiums by another couple hundred dollars. For example, as a vehicle gets older, the amount of the deductible should increase. It may reach a maximum of $500 per collision. As the deductible increases, the annual premium for collision coverage decreases.

The Vehicle Insurance Information Centre of Canada at *www.vicc.com* lists which vehicles have the highest collision, comprehensive, and theft claim rates and cost the most to insure. The Centre can also be reached at 1-800-761-6703 or 416-445-5912.

3. Fewer "hidden" defects

Have your choice checked out by an independent mechanic (for $75–$100) before paying for a used vehicle. This examination before purchase protects you against any hidden defects the vehicle may have. It's also a tremendous negotiating tool, since you can use the cost of any needed repairs to bargain down the purchase price.

It's easier to get permission to have the vehicle inspected if you promise to give the seller a copy of the inspection report should you decide not to buy it. If you still can't get permission to have the vehicle inspected elsewhere, walk away from the deal, no matter how tempting the selling price. The seller is obviously trying to put something over on you. Ignore the standard excuses that the vehicle isn't insured, the licence plates have expired, or the vehicle has a dead battery.

Smart customers will want to get answers to the following questions before paying a penny for any used vehicle: What did it first sell for and what is its present value? How much of the original warranty is left? How many times has the vehicle been recalled for safety-related defects? Are parts easily available? Does the vehicle have a history of costly performance-related defects that can be corrected under a secret warranty, through a safety recall campaign, or with an upgraded part? (See Part Three, "Secret Warranties/Service Tips/TSBs.")

4. Litigation is quick, easy, and relatively inexpensive

A multitude of federal and provincial consumer protection laws go far beyond whatever protection may be offered by the standard new-vehicle warranty. Furthermore, buyers of used vehicles don't usually have to conform to any arbitrary rules or service guidelines to get this protection.

Let's say you do get stuck with a vehicle that's unreliable, has undisclosed accident damage, or doesn't perform as promised. Most small claims courts have a jurisdiction limit of $3,000–$10,000, which should cover the cost of repairs or compensate you if the vehicle is taken back. That way, any dispute between buyer and seller can be settled within a few months, without lawyers or excessive court costs. Furthermore, you're not likely to face a battery of lawyers standing in for the automaker and dealer. Actually, you may not have to face a judge, since many cases are settled through court-imposed mediators at a pre-trial meeting, usually scheduled a month or two after filing.

Choosing the Right Seller

When to buy

Used-car dealers and private sellers are generally easier to deal with in the winter. Although they have fewer vehicles available, they usually offer lower prices and are less hard-nosed in bargaining. This is partly because they see fewer customers and partly because used vehicles generally show their worst characteristics during the winter months. On the other hand, in fall and spring, new-car dealer stocks of good quality trade-ins and off-lease returns are at their highest level, and private sellers are more active. Prices will be higher, but there will be a greater choice of vehicles available.

Private sellers

Private sellers are your best source for a cheap and reliable used vehicle, because you're on an equal bargaining level with a vendor who isn't trying to profit from your inexperience. This translates into a golden opportunity to negotiate a fair price, which isn't common in many dealer transactions.

Apart from newspaper classified ads, you can track down deals and get a good idea of prices through the following:

- word of mouth
- grocery store bulletin boards
- specialty publications (e.g., *Auto Trader*, *Auto Mart*, or *Buy and Sell Bargain Hunter*)
- the *Canadian Red Book* or the Provincial Automobile Dealers Association *Black Book*
- free Internet price guides (see Appendix I)

The best way to determine the price range for a particular model is to read the publications or surf the websites listed in Appendix I before you buy the vehicle. This will give you a reasonably good idea of the top asking price. Remember, no seller expects to get his or her asking price, be it a dealer or private party. As with price reductions on home listings, a 10–20 percent reduction on the advertised price is common with private sellers. Dealers usually won't cut more than 10 percent off their advertised price.

Find out which published used-car guide is the accepted standard in your area of the country. The *Red Book* and *Black Book* serve Canadian dealers, while the *Kelley Blue Book* and *Edmunds Price Guide* are two of the most popular American guides, offering comprehensive ratings and prices, gratis, through the Internet. You can visit the *Kelley Blue Book* at *www.kbb.com* or Edmunds at *www.edmunds.com*.

Don't be surprised to find that many national price guides have an eastern Ontario–Quebec price bias. They often list unrealistically low prices compared with what you'll actually see in the eastern and western provinces and in rural areas, where good used cars are often sold for outrageously high prices or simply passed down through the family.

Be wary

As a buyer, you should get a printed sales agreement, even if it's just handwritten, that includes a clause stating there are no outstanding traffic violations or liens against the vehicle. It doesn't make a great deal of difference whether the car will be purchased "as is" or as certified under provincial regulation. A vehicle sold as safety "certified" can still be dangerous to drive or turn into a lemon. The certification process can be sabotaged if a minimal number of components are checked, the mechanic is incompetent, or the instruments are poorly calibrated. "Certified" is not the same as having a warranty to protect you from engine seizure or transmission failure. Certified means only that the vehicle has met minimum safety standards on the day tested.

Make sure the vehicle is lien-free and has not been damaged in a flood or written off after an accident. Flood damage can be hard to see. However, it impairs ABS, power steering, and airbag functioning (deployment is 10 times slower).

Canada has become a haven for rebuilt U.S. wrecks. Write-offs are also shipped from provinces where there are stringent disclosure regulations to provinces where there are lax rules—if rules exist at all. Ron Giblin of the Canadian Insurance Crime Prevention Bureau (ICPB) told the *Toronto Sun* that ICPB members voluntarily reported 26,709 salvaged vehicles in 1996 in Ontario alone. He estimates the true figure is about double that number.

If you suspect your vehicle is a rebuilt wreck from the States or was once a taxi, use Carfax (*www.carfax.com*; tel.: 1-888-422-7329) to carry out a background check to see if the vehicle has been part of a fleet, wrecked, has flood damage, is stolen, or shows incorrect mileage on the odometer. The $20 fee by telephone is cut to $14.95 (U.S.) if the order is placed via the Internet. A typical search takes only a few minutes and most Canadian provinces are included in the database. The search will also turn up vehicles that were trucked across the border as "parts" and then sold to resellers. An initial, free search on the Internet will confirm whether or not your vehicle is listed in the database.

In most provinces, you can do a lien and registration search yourself. If a lien does exist, you should contact the creditor(s) listed to find out whether any debts have been paid. If a debt is outstanding, you should arrange with the vendor to pay the creditor the outstanding balance. If the debt is larger than the purchase price of the car, it's up to you to decide whether or not you wish to complete the deal. If the seller agrees to clear the title personally, make sure that you receive a written relinquishment of title from the creditor before paying any money to the vendor. Make sure the title doesn't show an "R" for "restored," since this indicates the vehicle was written off as a total loss and may not have been properly repaired.

Even if all documents are in order, ask the seller to show you the vehicle's original sales contract and a few repair bills in order to ascertain how well it was maintained. The bills will show you if the odometer was turned back, and will also indicate which repairs are still guaranteed. If none of these can be found, run (don't walk!) away. If the contract shows that the car was financed, verify that the loan was paid. If you're still not sure that the vehicle is free of liens, ask your bank or credit union manager to check for you. If no clear answer is forthcoming, look for something else.

Repossessed vehicles

Repossessed vehicles are usually bad buys. They are often found at auctions, but they're sometimes sold by finance companies and banks as well. Fortunately, courts have held that these institutions are legally responsible for defects found in what they sell. Also, their deep pockets and abhorrence of bad publicity means you'll likely get your money back if you make a bad buy from a lending institution. The biggest problem with repossessed vans, sport-utilities, and pickups, in particular, is that they were likely abused or neglected by their financially troubled owners. Although you rarely get to test-drive or closely examine these vehicles, a local dealer may be able to produce a vehicle maintenance history by running the VIN through its manufacturer's database.

Cross-border shopping

It's very unlikely that you'll save money if you purchase a used vehicle in the U.S. and register it in Canada. But free trade in the other direction is booming. Automakers often sell their cars for less in Canada than they do in the States. This has created a "gray market" of buyers who purchase their new vehicles in Canada and register them in the United States. In fact, Dave Lawrence, Toronto Metro Credit Union's auto consultant, tells me that American dealers often siphon off the Ontario area's supply of good used vehicles by overbidding for Canadian cars and selling them at a profit in the U.S. Another consequence is that some manufacturers, like Honda USA, are denying owners warranty coverage as a means to discourage cross-border bargain-hunting and appease their U.S. dealers. Honda says, however, it's only targeting people trying to beat the system; Canadian owners who are suddenly transferred to the States or have other valid reasons for relocating won't be denied warranty.

Another risk: safety and pollution control regulations differ considerably between the two countries and it may be impossible to upgrade your used vehicle to Canadian standards. Transport Canada estimates that 15–20 percent of American vehicles can't meet Canadian standards, no matter how they're modified. To find out which ones pass muster, download Transport Canada's list of vehicles approved for import from its website at *www.tc.gc.ca/roadsafety* or call the Registrar of Imported Vehicles at 1-800-511-7755.

Buyers of used vehicles from the U.S. should also be wary of the fact that U.S. vehicles' odometers register in miles instead of kilometres and are likely to have the mileage rolled back—CNW Marketing/Research, a U.S. consulting firm, says 1 in 12 cars has its odometer rolled back about one-third of its actual mileage. Buyers usually have little effective legal recourse to get their money back, due to the distances involved and unclear title history.

If you do decide to import a used vehicle from the U.S., use the Carfax service mentioned previously to check the vehicle's past history, and ask an independent dealer selling that make of vehicle to pull the warranty and repair history on the car through its VIN number.

Rental and leased vehicles

The second-best choice for getting a good used vehicle is a rental company or leasing agency. Due to a slumping economy, Budget, Hertz, Avis, and National are selling, at cut-rate prices, vehicles that have one to two years of service and approximately 40,000–60,000 km. These rental companies will gladly provide a vehicle's complete history and allow an independent inspection by a qualified mechanic of the buyer's choice, as well as arrange competitive financing.

Rental vehicles are generally well maintained, sell for a few thousand dollars more than privately sold vehicles, and come with strong guarantees, like Budget's 30-day money-back guarantee or optional extended warranty. Rental car companies also usually settle customer complaints without much hassle so as not to tarnish their image with rental customers.

Vehicles that have just come off a 3- or 5-year lease are much more competitively priced, generally have less mileage, and are usually as well maintained as rental vehicles. You're also likely to get a better price if

you buy directly from the lessee rather than going through the dealership or an independent agency, but remember, you won't have the
dealer's leverage to extract post-warranty "goodwill" repairs from the
automaker.

New-car dealers

Most used-car buyers prefer to deal with private sellers. In fact, the
Federation of Automobile Dealer Associations of Canada states that 20
years ago, 86 percent of used cars were sold by new-car dealers—today
that number is less than 25 percent, due mainly to the GST, which has
driven buyers into the arms of private sellers.

Nevertheless, new-car dealers aren't a bad place to pick up a good used
car or minivan. Prices are 20 percent higher than those for vehicles sold
privately, but 0 percent new-vehicle plans are trimming used values dramatically. Plus, dealers are insured against selling stolen vehicles or
vehicles with finance owing or other liens. They also usually allow
prospective buyers to have the vehicle inspected by an independent
garage, offer a much wider choice of models, and have their own repair
facilities to do warranty work. Additionally, if there's a possibility of getting post-warranty "goodwill" compensation from the manufacturer,
your dealer can provide additional leverage, particularly if he's a fran-
chisee for the model you have purchased. Finally, if things do go terribly
wrong, dealers have "deeper pockets" than private sellers, so there's a
better chance of getting paid should a court judgment be won against
the firm.

"Certified" vehicles

Try to get a vehicle that the dealer has had certified by an auto association or an automaker, and that has had the required repairs carried out.
In Alberta, the Alberta Motor Association (AMA) will perform a vehicle
inspection at a dealer's request. On each occasion, the AMA gives a
written report to the dealer that identifies potential and actual problems,
required repairs, and serious defects.

Automakers have begun to refurbish and certify used vehicles sold by
their dealers. They guarantee the vehicle's mechanical fitness and provide a warranty where length depends on the age of the vehicle. But
these vehicles don't come cheap, mainly because manufacturers force
their dealers to bring them up to better-than-average condition before
certifying them. The higher price can be reduced by choosing an older
certified model, or amortized by keeping the vehicle longer.

Used-car leasing

Not a good idea for new or used vehicles. Leasing has been touted as a
method of making the high cost of vehicle ownership more affordable.
Don't you believe it: leasing is generally costlier than an outright purchase, and for most people the pitfalls far outweigh any advantages. If

you must lease, do so for the shortest time possible and make sure the lease is closed-ended (meaning that you walk away from the vehicle when the lease period ends). Also, make sure there's a maximum mileage allowance of at least 25,000 km a year and that the charge per excess kilometre is no higher than 8–10 cents.

Used-car dealers

Used-car dealers usually sell their vehicles for a bit less than what new-car dealers charge. However, their vehicles may be worth a lot less, because they don't get the first pick of top-quality trade-ins. Many independent urban dealerships are marginal operations that can't invest much money in reconditioning their vehicles, which are often collected from auctions and new-car dealers reluctant to sell the vehicles to their own customers. And used-car dealers don't always have repair facilities to honour what warranties they do provide. Often, their credit terms are easier (but more expensive) than those offered by franchised new-car dealers.

That said, used-car dealers operating in small towns are an entirely different breed. These small, often family-run businesses recondition and resell cars and trucks that usually come from within their community. Routine servicing is often done in-house and more complicated repairs are subcontracted out to specialized garages nearby. These small outlets survive by word-of-mouth advertising and would never last long if they didn't deal fairly with local townsfolk. On the other hand, their prices will likely be higher than elsewhere, due to the better quality of used vehicles they offer and the cost of reconditioning and repairing under warranty what they sell.

Auctions

You need patience and smarts to pick up anything worthwhile at an auction. Government auctions—places where the mythical $50 Jeep is sold—are fun to attend but are risky ventures. You can't determine the condition of the vehicles put up for bid, and government employees often pick over the stock before you ever see it.

To attend commercial auctions, however, is to swim with the piranhas. Many are fronts for used-car lots. They are frequented by "ringers" who bid up the prices and professional dealers who pick up cheap, worn-out vehicles unloaded by new-car dealers and independents. There are no guarantees, cash is required, and quality is apt to be as low as the price. Remember, too, that auction purchases are subject to provincial and federal sales taxes, the auction's sales commission (3–5 percent), and in some cases an administrative fee of $25–$50.

If you are interested in shopping at an auto auction, remember that certain days are reserved for dealers only, so call ahead. You'll find the vehicles locked in a compound, but you should have ample opportunity to inspect them and, in some cases, take a short drive around the property before the auction begins.

Paying the Right Price

Even though prices have moderated considerably, get ready for "sticker shock" when pricing the more popular used minivans, sport-utilities, vans, and pickups—some of these vehicles depreciate very little, and it's easy to get stuck with a cheap one that's been abused through hard off-roading or lack of care. Furthermore, even those vehicles with worse-than-average reliability ratings, like the Ford Taurus and Chrysler minivans, still command higher-than-average resale prices for the simple reason that they're popular, though not as popular as they once were.

If you don't want to pay too much when buying used, you've got the following four alternatives.

- Buy an older vehicle. Choose one that's five years old or more and has a good reliability and durability record. Buy extra protection with an extended warranty. The money you save from the extra years' depreciation and lower insurance premiums will more than make up for the extra warranty cost.
- Look for off-lease vehicles sold privately by owners who want more than what their dealer is offering. If you can't find what you're looking for in the local classified ads, put in your own ad asking for lessees to contact you if they're not satisfied with their dealer's offer.
- Buy a vehicle that's depreciated more than average simply because of its bland styling, lack of high-performance features, or discontinuation. For example, many of the Japanese entry-level compacts like the Nissan Sentra cost less to own than their flashier American-made counterparts, yet are more reliable and equally functional for most driving chores.
- Buy a cheaper twin or re-badged model like a Ford Probe, Chrysler Colt, or Nissan Quest. They offer Japanese high quality and usually share the same basic design, appearance, dimensions, and mechanical components.

Prices and price scams will vary

In spite of what many guide books say (including *Lemon-Aid*), the values for used sport-utilities, minivans, vans, and pickups are hard to nail down. Their volatility is due in part to roller-coaster fuel prices and a slowing economy.

There are several price guidelines, however, and dealers use the one that will make the most profit on each transaction. The most common price quoted is the *Red Book*, which shows the price the vehicle is worth when sold at full retail price (similar to the manufacturer's suggested retail price, or MSRP). The wholesale price, thousands of dollars less, is more likely what the dealer paid. Never mind that few people ever pay the MSRP; the fact that it's there is sufficient reason for most dealers to charge the higher rate. Both price indicators leave considerable room for the dealer's profit margin and some extra padding—inflated preparation charges and administration fees that shouldn't exist for a used vehicle.

Just as with new vehicles, dealers know that last-minute add-on charges are the way to stick it to you just before the contract is signed. Therefore, they try to extort extra profits through preparation and documentation fees and extra handling charges that give you nothing in return. Patiently await management's approval of the vehicle's bottom-line price, and then reject these add-on charges.

Financing Choices

No one should spend more than 30 percent of his or her annual gross income on the purchase of a new or used vehicle. By keeping the initial cost low, the purchaser may be able to pay mostly in cash. This can be an effective bargaining tool to use with private sellers, but dealers are less impressed by cash sales because they lose their kickback from the finance companies.

Credit unions
A credit union is the preferred place to borrow money at low interest rates and with easy repayment terms. You'll have to join the credit union or have an account with it before the loan is approved. You'll also probably have to come up with a larger down payment relative to what other lending institutions require.

In addition to giving you reasonable loan rates, credit unions help car buyers in a number of other ways. Toronto's Metro Credit Union (*www.metrocu.com*), for example, has a CarFacts Centre, which provides free, objective advice on car shopping, purchasing, financing, and leasing. CarFacts advisors provide free consultations in person or by phone. This includes:

- fact sheets on all aspects of buying new or used vehicles;
- a circulating library of vehicle buying and vehicle maintenance books and magazines;
- computerized analysis of different buying, leasing, and borrowing options;
- *Red Book* used-car price quotations; and
- dealer invoice price quotations on any make or model of new vehicle, at $20 each.

Banks
Interest rates, at 2.75 percent, are at their lowest level in 40 years, and banks want your business.

In your quest for a bank loan, keep in mind that the Internet offers help for people who need an auto loan and want quick approval but don't like to face a banker. The Bank of Montreal, the first Canadian bank to allow car buyers to post loan applications on its website (*www.bmo.com*), promises to send a loan response within a few minutes.

The service is available to any web surfer, including those who aren't current Bank of Montreal customers. Most other banks, credit unions, and
caisses populaires have a similar Internet approval procedure.

Dealers

Dealers can finance the cost of a used vehicle at rates that compete with
those of banks and finance companies. This is because they get substantial rebates from lenders and agree to take back the vehicle if the creditor
defaults on the loan. Some dealers mislead their customers into thinking
they can get financing at rates far below the prime rate. Actually, the
dealer jacks up the base price of the vehicle to compensate for the lower
interest charges.

Dealer Scams

Used vehicles are subject to the same deceptive sales practices deployed
by dealers who sell new vehicles. One of the more common tricks is to
not identify the previous owner because the vehicle either was used commercially or had been written off as a total loss from an accident. It's also
not uncommon to discover that the mileage has been turned back, particularly if the vehicle was part of a company's fleet. These scams can be
thwarted if you demand the name of the vehicle's previous owner as a
prerequisite to purchasing the vehicle.

It would be impossible to list all the dishonest tricks employed in
used-vehicle sales. As soon as the public is alerted to one scheme,
crooked sellers use other, more elaborate frauds. Nevertheless, under
industry-financed provincial compensation funds, buyers can get substantial refunds if defrauded by a dealer.

Here are some of the more common fraudulent practices you're likely
to encounter.

Failing to declare full purchase price

Here's where your own greed will do you in. A tactic used almost exclusively by small, independent dealers and some private sellers, the buyer
is told that he or she can pay less sales tax by listing a lower selling price
on the contract. But what if the vehicle turns out to be a lemon or the
sales agent has falsified the model year or mileage? The hapless buyer is
offered a refund on the fictitious purchase price indicated on the contract. If the buyer wanted to take the dealer to court, it's quite unlikely
that he or she would get any more than the contract price. Moreover,
both the buyer and dealer could be prosecuted for making a false declaration to avoid paying sales tax.

Phony private sales ("curbsiders")

Individuals sell about three times as many used vehicles as dealers. Some
crooked dealers have agents pose as private sellers in order to get a better

price for their cars and to avoid paying GST and giving a warranty. This scam is easy to detect if the seller can't produce the original sales contract or show some repair bills made out in his or her own name. You can usually identify a car dealer in the want ads section of the newspaper— just check to see if the same telephone number is repeated in many different ads. Sometimes you can trip up a curbsider by requesting information on the phone, without identifying the specific vehicle. If the seller asks you which car you are considering, you know you're dealing with a dealer.

Most new-car dealers get very angry when one of these scamming teams hits town. Unfortunately they don't get angry enough, because they continue to sell used cars at wholesale prices to curbsiders who they know are stealing their business and cheating consumers and tax authorities. Talk about hypocrisy, eh?

Curbsiders are particularly active in the west, buying cars at wholesale prices from dealers, legitimate auto auctions, and junkyards (many written off as total losses). They then place private classified ads in B.C. and Alberta papers, sell their stock, and leave town.

If you get taken by one of these scam artists, don't hesitate to sue the publication carrying the ad through small claims court for allowing this rip-off artist to operate.

"Free-exchange" privilege

Dealers get a lot of sales mileage out of this deceptive offer. The dealer offers to exchange any defective vehicle for any other vehicle in stock. What really happens, though, is that the dealer won't have *anything else* selling for the same price and so will demand a cash bonus for the exchange...or you may get that dubious privilege of exchanging one lemon for another.

"Money-back" guarantee

Once again, the purchaser feels safe in buying a used car with this kind of guarantee, because what could be more honest than a money-back guarantee? Dealers using this technique often charge exorbitant handling charges, rental fees, or mechanical repair costs to the customer who's bought one of these vehicles and then returned it.

"50/50" guarantee

This means that the dealer will pay half the repair costs over a limited period of time. It's a fair offer if an independent garage does the repairs. If not, the dealer can always inflate the repair costs to double their actual worth and write up a bill for that amount (a scam sometimes used in "goodwill" settlements). The buyer winds up paying the full price of repairs that would probably have been much cheaper at an independent garage. The best kind of used-vehicle warranty is 100 percent with full coverage for a fixed term, even if that term is relatively short.

"As is" cars

Buying a vehicle "as is" usually means that you're aware of mechanical defects, you're prepared to accept the responsibility for any damage or injuries caused by the vehicle, and all costs to fix it shall be paid by you. However, the courts have held that the "as is" clause is not a blank cheque to cheat buyers and therefore must be interpreted in light of the seller's true intent. That is, was there an attempt to deceive the buyer by including this clause? Did the buyer really know what the "as is" clause could do to his or her future legal rights? It's also been held that the courts may consider oral representations ("parole evidence") that were never written into the formal contract. So, if a seller makes claims as to the fine quality of the used vehicle, these claims can be used as evidence. Courts generally ignore "as is" clauses when the vehicle has been intentionally misrepresented, when the dealer is the seller, or when the defects are so serious that the seller is presumed to have known of their existence. Private sellers are usually given more credibility than dealers or their agents.

Odometer tampering

In theory, dealers face hefty fines and even imprisonment if caught altering the mileage of any vehicle they sell, but in practice, few odometer tampering cases make it to court because intent to defraud is so difficult to prove. Usually, independent outfits are hired to pick up the vehicle or visit the dealership and "fix" the odometer, a practice allowed under Canadian federal and provincial laws. With new cars used as demonstrators, service managers routinely disable the odometer until the vehicle is put up for sale. Demand that the dealer put the mileage figure on the contract and give you the name and address of the previous owner as well as all repair receipts. It would be smart to ask the same things of a private seller.

Misrepresentation

Used vehicles can be misrepresented in a variety of ways. A used airport commuter minivan may be represented as having been used by a Sunday school class. A mechanically defective pickup that's been rebuilt after several major accidents may have plastic filler in the body panels to muffle the rattles or hide rust damage, heavy oil in the motor to stifle the clanks, and cheap retread tires to eliminate the thumps. Your best protection against these dirty tricks is to have the vehicle's quality completely verified by an independent mechanic before completing the sale. Of course, you can still cancel the sale if you only learn of the misrepresentation after taking the vehicle home, but your chances dwindle as time passes.

Private Scams

A lot of space in this guide has been used to describe how used-car dealers and scam artists cheat uninformed buyers. Of course, private individuals can be dishonest too. In either case, protect yourself at the outset by keeping your deposit small and getting as much information as possible about the vehicle you're considering. Then, after a test drive, you may sign a written agreement to purchase the vehicle and give a deposit of sufficient value to cover the seller's advertising costs, subject to cancellation if the automobile fails its inspection. After you've taken these precautions, watch out for the following private sellers' tricks.

Used vehicles that are stolen or have finance owing

Many used vehicles are sold privately without free title because the original auto loan was never repaid. You can avoid being cheated by asking for proof of purchase and payment from a private seller. Be especially wary of any individual who offers to sell a used vehicle for an incredibly low price. Check the sales contract to determine who granted the original loan and call the lender to see if it's been repaid. Place a call to the provincial Ministry of Transportation to ascertain whether the car is registered in the seller's name. Find out if a finance company is named as beneficiary on the auto insurance policy. Finally, call up the original dealer to determine whether there are any outstanding claims.

In Ontario, an inexpensive Used Vehicle Information Package (mandatory for private sellers) will alert buyers to any problems with the title, but in other provinces, buyers don't have access to this information. Generally, you have to contact the provincial office that registers property and pay a small fee for a computer printout that may or may not be accurate. You'll be asked for the current owner's name and the car's VIN, which is usually found on the driver's side of the dashboard.

There are two high-tech ways to get the goods on the seller. First, have a dealer of that particular model run a "vehicle history" check through the automaker's on-line network. This will tell you who the previous owners and dealers were, what warranty and recall repairs were carried out, and what other free repair programs may still apply. Second, you could use Carfax (*www.carfax.com*; tel.: 1-888-422-7329) to carry out a background check.

Seller, protect thyself (!)

Now, one last word on protecting yourself from legal liability if you are selling a vehicle to a private individual. *Toronto Sun* business and consumer columnist Maryanna Lewyckyj tells of one case where a driver sold his clunker for $250; six months later he was sued by Liberty Mutual Insurance for $30,000 in damages caused by the subsequent owner. Apparently, the new owner never changed the registration. Normally, once you take the tags and give the buyer a bill of sale, you're no longer the registered owner. Nonetheless, go down to the registry office yourself to make sure the title has changed. As long as you're still listed as the owner of record, you could be sued by an insurance company for damages arising from an accident.

Summary to Saving Money and Keeping Safe

You can get a good used vehicle at a reasonable price—it just takes lots of patience and homework. You can further protect yourself by becoming thoroughly familiar with your legal rights as outlined in Part Two and buying a vehicle recommended in Part Three. Following is a summary of the steps to take to keep your risk to a minimum:

1. Buy a full-sized, rear-drive delivery van and convert it yourself instead of opting for a more expensive, smaller, less powerful minivan.
2. Trade in your vehicle if the GST and PST reduction is more than the potential profit of selling privately.
3. Sell to a private party.
4. Buy from a private party, rental car outlet, or dealer (in that order).
5. Use an auto broker to save time and money.
6. Buy a *Lemon-Aid*-recommended vehicle for depreciation, parts, and service savings.
7. Buy a 3- or 4-year-old vehicle with lots of original warranty that can be transferred (35–50 percent savings over a new vehicle).
8. Choose a vehicle that's crashworthy and cheap to insure.
9. Carefully inspect Japanese-built vehicles that have reached their fifth year (engine head gasket, CV joints, steering box, and front brakes).
10. Don't buy an extended warranty for a particular model year unless it's recommended you do so in *Lemon-Aid*.
11. Have repairs done by independent garages offering lifetime warranties.
12. Install used or reconditioned parts.
13. Keep all the previous owners' repair bills to facilitate warranty claims and to help mechanics know what's already been replaced or repaired.
14. Upon delivery, adjust mirrors to eliminate blind spots and adjust head restraints to prevent your head from snapping back in the event of a collision. On airbag-equipped vehicles, move the seat backward more than half its travel distance and sit at least a foot away from the airbag housing. Ensure that the airbag, spare tire, and tire jack haven't been removed.
15. Make sure the dealer and automaker have your name in their computers as the new owner of record. Ask for a copy of your vehicle's history, stored in the same computers.

PART TWO

Lemons and Lawyers!

2

Here Comes the Judge

"In my opinion most people in Saskatchewan grow up with cars and are familiar with cars. I think it is common knowledge that the original paint on cars normally lasts in excess of 15 years and that rust becomes a problem before the paint fails.... It is clear from the evidence of Frank Nemeth (independent body shop manager) that the delamination is a factory defect. His evidence was not seriously challenged. I find that the factory paint should not suffer a delamination defect for at least 15 years and that this factory defect breached the warranty that the paint was of acceptable quality and was durable for a reasonable period of time."

Judge H. G. Dirauf, Saskatchewan Provincial Court
Maureen Frank v. General Motors of Canada Limited
October 17, 2001

Nipping that lemon in the bud

Runzheimer Consultants says that one out of every ten American vehicles produced by the Detroit Big Three is a "lemon." I would guess that owners of Ford vehicles with faulty automatic transmissions and engine head gaskets, as well as the New Brunswick, British Columbia, Alberta, and Saskatchewan CLOGs (Chrysler Lemon Owners Groups), would put the number at a higher figure.

Court documents say Chrysler, Ford, and GM skipped the primer coat on many 1986–97 vehicles to save $15 per unit.

If you've bought an unsafe tire or a lemon, or if you've been forced to pay for repairs to correct factory-induced defects, this section's for you. It's intended to help you get your money back—without going to court or getting frazzled by the dealer's broken promises or "benign neglect." But if going to court is your only recourse, you'll find the jurisprudence you need to get an out-of-court settlement or to win your case without spending a fortune on lawyers and research.

Four Ways to Get Your Money Back

Remember the "money-back" guarantee? Well, with the exception of Saturn, automakers are reluctant to offer any warranty that requires them to take back a defective new car or minivan. Nevertheless, our provincial consumer protection laws have filled the gap so that now any sales contract for a new or used vehicle can be cancelled—or free repairs can be ordered—if the vehicle

- is misrepresented;
- is unfit for the purpose for which it was purchased;
- hasn't been reasonably durable, considering how well it was maintained, the mileage driven, and the type of driving done (particularly applicable to engine, transmission, and paint defects); or
- was covered by a secret warranty, without your knowledge.

Here's what the four legal concepts enumerated above mean in real-life situations: if the seller says that a minivan can pull a 900 kg (2,000 lb.) trailer and you discover that it can barely tow half that weight, you can cancel the contract for misrepresentation. The same principle applies to a seller's exaggerated claims concerning a vehicle's fuel economy or reliability, as well as to "demonstrators" that are in fact used cars with false (rolled-back) odometer readings.

Be wary of "hearsay"
It's essential that printed evidence and/or witnesses (relatives are not excluded) are available to confirm that a false representation actually occurred, that a part is failure prone, or that its replacement is covered by a secret warranty. Stung by an increasing number of small claims court defeats, automakers are now asking small claims court judges to disallow evidence from *Lemon-Aid*, service bulletins, or memos on the pretext that it's hearsay (not proven), unless confirmed by an independent mechanic or unless the document is recognized by the automaker or dealer's representative at trial. This is why you should bring in an independent garage mechanic or body expert to buttress your allegations. Sometimes, though, the service manager or company representative will make key admissions if questioned closely by you, a court mediator, or the trial judge. Some questions to ask: Is this a common

problem? Do you recognize this service bulletin? Is there a case-by-case "goodwill" plan covering this repair? This kind of questioning can be particularly effective if you call for the exclusion of witnesses until they're called (let them mill around outside the courtroom wondering what their colleagues have said).

Automakers often blame owners for having pushed their vehicle beyond its limits. Therefore, when you seek to set aside the contract or get a repair reimbursed, it's essential that you get the testimony of an independent mechanic and co-workers in order to prove that the vehicle's poor performance isn't caused by negligent maintenance or abusive driving.

The reasonable durability claim is your ace in the hole. It's probably the easiest allegation to prove, since all automakers have benchmarks as to how long body components, trim and finish, and mechanical and electronic parts should last (see the durability chart on page 44). Vehicles are expected to be reasonably durable and merchantable. What is reasonably durable depends on the price paid, kilometres driven, the purchaser's driving habits, and how well the vehicle was maintained by the owner. Judges carefully weigh all these factors in awarding compensation or cancelling a sale.

Whatever the reason you use to get your money back, don't forget to conform to the "reasonable diligence" rule that requires you to file suit within a reasonable time after purchase, or after you've discovered the defect or learned that the vehicle was misrepresented. If there have been no negotiations with the dealer or automaker, this period cannot exceed a few months. If either the dealer or the automaker has been promising to correct the defects for some time or has carried out repeated unsuccessful repairs, the delay for filing the lawsuit can be extended.

Refunds for other expenses

It's a lot easier to get the automaker to pay to replace a defective part than it is to obtain compensation for a missed day of work or a ruined vacation. Manufacturers hate to pay for consequential expenses under the basic warranty, supplementary warranty, or extended warranty because they can't control the amount of the refund. (Towing expenses, however, are usually accepted.) Courts are more generous, having ruled that all expenses (damages) flowing from a problem covered by a warranty or service bulletin are the manufacturer's/dealer's responsibility under both common law (all provinces except Quebec) and Quebec civil law. Fortunately, when legal action is threatened—usually through small claims court—automakers quickly back down from their refusal to pay consequential damage claims.

Warranties

The manufacturer's or dealer's warranty is a written legal promise that a vehicle will be reasonably reliable, subject to certain conditions.

Regardless of the number of subsequent owners, this promise remains in force as long as the warranty's original time/kilometre limits haven't expired. Unfortunately, these warranties are full of so many loopholes ("You abused the car; it was poorly maintained; it's normal wear and tear.") that they may be useless when a vehicle breaks down.

Thankfully, car owners get another kick at the can. As clearly stated in *Frank v. GM*, every vehicle sold new or used in Canada is also covered by an *implied* warranty—a collection of federal and provincial laws and regulations that protect you from hidden defects, misrepresentation, and a host of other scams. Furthermore, Canadian law presumes that car dealers, unlike private sellers, are aware of the defects present in the vehicles they sell. That way, they can't just pass the ball to the automakers and walk away from the dispute.

Treacherous tires

Tires aren't usually covered by car manufacturers' warranties (except for GM and Ford), and are warranted instead by the tiremaker on a pro-rated basis. This isn't such a good deal, because the manufacturer is making a profit by charging you the full list price. If you were to buy the same replacement tire from a discount store you'd likely pay less, without the pro-rated rebate.

But consumers have gained additional rights following Bridgestone/Firestone's massive recall in 2001 of its defective ATX II and Wilderness tires. Due to the confusion and chaos surrounding Firestone's handling of the recall, Ford's 575 Canadian dealers stepped into the breach and replaced the tires for any equivalent tires dealers had in stock. No questions asked.

This is an important precedent that tears down the traditional wall separating tire manufacturers from automakers in product liability claims. In essence, whoever sells the product can now be held liable for damages. In the future, Canadian consumers will have an easier time holding the dealer, automaker, and tire manufacturer liable, not just for recalled products, but for any defect that affects the safety or reasonable durability of that product.

This is particularly true now that the Supreme Court of Canada (*Winnipeg Condominium v. Bird Construction* [1995] 1S.C.R.85) has ruled that defendants are liable in negligence for any designs that resulted in a risk to the public for safety or health. The Supreme Court reversed a long-standing policy and provided the public with a new cause of action that had not existed before in Canada. Prior to this Supreme Court ruling, companies dodged liability for falling bridges and crashing planes by warranty exclusion and "entire-agreement" contract clauses. In the Winnipeg Condominium case, the Supreme Court held that repairs made to prevent serious damage or accident could be claimed from the designer/builder for the cost of repair in tort, from any subsequent purchaser. Consumers with tire- or other safety-related claims would be wise to insert this court decision (with explanation) in their claim letter and mail or fax it to the automaker's legal affairs or product liability department. A copy of the claim letter should also be deposited with the clerk of the small claims court if you have to use that recourse.

Warranty rights and wrongs

Safety restraints such as airbags and safety belts have warranty coverage extended for the lifetime of the vehicle, following an agreement made between U.S. automakers and importers. In Canada, though, many automakers try to dodge this responsibility, alleging that they are separate entities, distinct from their American counterparts. That distinction is both disingenious and dishonest, and wouldn't likely hold up in small claims court—probably the reason why most automakers relent when threatened with legal action.

Aftermarket products and services—such as gas-saving gadgets, rust-proofing, and paint protectors—can render the manufacturer's warranty invalid, so make sure you're in the clear before purchasing any optional equipment or services from an independent supplier.

How fairly a warranty is applied is more important than how long it remains in effect. Once you know the normal wear rate for a mechanical component or body part, you can demand proportional compensation when you get less than normal durability—no matter what the original warranty said.

Some dealers tell customers that they need to have original equipment parts installed in order to maintain their warranty. A variation on this theme requires that routine servicing—including tune-ups and oil changes (with a certain brand of oil)—be done by the selling dealer, or the warranty is invalidated.

Nothing could be further from the truth.

Canadian law stipulates that whoever issues a warranty cannot make that warranty conditional on the use of any specific brand of motor oil, oil filter, or any other component, unless it's provided to the customer free of charge.

Sometimes dealers will do all sorts of minor repairs that don't correct the problem, and then after the warranty runs out they'll tell you that major repairs are needed. You can avoid this nasty surprise by repeatedly bringing in your vehicle to the dealership before the warranty ends. During each visit, insist that a written work order include the specific nature of the problem as *you* see it and that the work order carry the notation that this is the second, third, or fourth time the same problem has been brought to the dealer's attention. Write it down yourself, if need be. This allows you to show a pattern of non-performance by the dealer during the warranty period and establishes that it's a serious and chronic problem. When the warranty expires, you have the legal right to demand that it be extended on those items consistently reappearing on your handful of work orders. *Lowe v. Fairview Chrysler* (see page 71) is an excellent judgment that reinforces this important principle.

A retired GM service manager gave me another effective tactic to use when you're not sure a dealer's warranty "repairs" will actually correct the problem for a reasonable period of time after the warranty expires. Here's what he says you should do:

> When you pick up the vehicle after the warranty repair has been done, hand the service manager a note to be put in your file that says you appreciate the warranty repair, however, you intend to return and ask for further warranty coverage if the problem reappears before a reasonable amount of time has elapsed—even if the original warranty has expired. A copy of the same note should be sent to the automaker.... Keep your copy of the note in the glove compartment as cheap insurance against paying for a repair that wasn't fixed correctly the first time.

Extended (supplementary) warranties

Supplementary warranties providing extended coverage may be sold by the manufacturer, dealer, or an independent third party, and are automatically transferred when the vehicle is sold. They cost between $1,000 and $1,500, and should be purchased only if the vehicle you're buying is off its original warranty, if it has a reputation for being unreliable or expensive to service (see Part Three), or if you're reluctant to use the small claims courts when factory-related trouble arises. Don't let the dealer pressure you into deciding right away.

Generally, you can purchase an extended warranty anytime during the period in which the manufacturer's warranty is in effect, or, in some cases, shortly after buying the vehicle from a used-car dealer. An automaker's supplementary warranty is the best choice but will likely cost about a third more than warranties sold by independents. And in some parts of the country, notably British Columbia, dealers have a quasi-monopoly on selling warranties, with little competition from the independents.

Because up to 60 percent of the warranty's cost represents dealer markup, dealers love to sell extended warranties, whether you need them or not. Out of the remaining 40 percent comes the sponsor's administration costs and profit margin, calculated at another 15 percent. What's left to pay for repairs is a minuscule 25 percent of the original amount. The only reason why automakers and independent warranty companies haven't been busted for operating this warranty Ponzi scheme is because only half of the car buyers who purchase extended service contracts actually use them.

It's often difficult to collect on supplementary warranties because independent companies frequently go out of business or limit the warranty's coverage through subsequent mailings. Both situations are covered by provincial laws. If the bankrupt warrantee company's insurance policy won't cover your claim, take the dealer to small claims court and ask for the repair cost and the refund of the original warranty payment. Your argument for holding the dealer responsible is a simple one: by accepting a commission for acting as an agent of the defunct company, the dealer took on the obligations of the company as well. As for limiting the coverage after you have bought the warranty policy: this is illegal, and it allows you to sue both the dealer and the warranty company for a refund of both the warranty and repair costs.

Emissions control warranties

These little-publicized warranties can save you big bucks if major engine or exhaust components fail prematurely. They come with all new vehicles and cover major components of the emissions control system for up to 8 years/130,000 km. Unfortunately, although owners' manuals vaguely mention the emissions warranty, most don't specify which parts are covered. Fortunately, the U.S. Environmental Protection Agency has intervened on several occasions with hefty fines against Chrysler and Ford and ruled that all major motor and fuel-system components are covered. These include fuel metering, ignition spark advance, restart, evaporative emissions, positive crankcase ventilation, engine electronics (computer modules), and catalytic converters, as well as hoses, clamps, brackets, pipes, gaskets, belts, seals, and connectors. Canada, however, has no government definition, and it's up to each manufacturer and the small claims courts to decide which components are covered.

Many of the confidential technical service bulletins listed in Part Three show parts failures that are covered under the emissions warranty even though motorists are routinely charged for their replacement. The following example, applicable to Ford's 1996–98 cars, minivans, vans, and trucks, shows the automaker will pay for major repairs to correct the loss of engine coolant or engine oil contaminated with coolant. Unfortunately, few owners will ever see these bulletins, and will end up paying for repairs that are really Ford's responsibility.

Coolant Loss/Engine Oil Contamination, 3.8L, 4.2L

Article No. 99 - 20 - 7
10/04/99
^ COOLING SYSTEM - 3.8L - UNDETERMINED LOSS OF COOLANT
^ COLLING SYSTEM - 4.2L - UNDETERMINED LOSS OF COOLANT
^ ENGINE - 3.8L - ENGINE OIL CONTAMINATED WITH COOLANT
^ ENGINE - 4.2L - ENGINE OIL CONTAMINATED WITH COOLANT

FORD:
1996-1997   THUNDERBIRD
1996-1998   MUSTANG, WINDSTAR
1997-1998   E-150, E-250, F-150

MERCURY:
1996-1997   COUGAR
This TSB article is being republished in its entirety to correct the front cover/water pump bolt torque values and the Front Cover Gasket Part Number.

ISSUE
Engine coolant may be leaking into the engine oil on some vehicles. The internal coolant leak may be difficult to identify. This may be caused by the lower intake manifold side gaskets and/or front cover gaskets allowing coolant to pass into the cylinders and/or the crankcase.

ACTION
Revised lower intake manifold side and front cover gaskets have been released for service. Refer to the following text and Application Chart for details.

WARRANTY STATUS
Eligible under the provisions of bumper to bumper warranty coverage and emissions warranty coverage.

Make sure you get your emissions system checked out thoroughly by a dealer or independent garage before the emissions warranty expires and before having the vehicle inspected by provincial emissions inspectors. In addition to ensuring you pass provincial tests, this precaution could save you up to $1,000 if both your catalytic converter and other emissions components are faulty.

"Goodwill" hunting: tracking secret warranties

Few vehicle owners know that secret warranties exist. Automakers are reluctant to make these free repair programs public because they feel it would weaken confidence in their product and increase their legal liability. The closest they come to an admission is sending a "goodwill policy," "product improvement program," or "special policy" technical service bulletin (TSB) to dealers or first owners of record. Consequently, the only motorists who find out about these policies are the original owners who haven't moved or leased their vehicles. The other motorists who get compensated for repairs are the ones who read *Lemon-Aid* each year, wave TSBs, and yell the loudest.

This year's *Lemon-Aid* guides shine a light on all of these secret warranties, including reprints of confidential TSBs and automaker memoranda that allow car owners to stand toe-to-toe with automakers and service managers. An up-to-date listing of TSBs for free repairs under secret warranties and other service programs can be found in Part Three under the heading "Secret Warranties/Service Tips/TSBs." Some may be less secret than others, as secret warranties go through the four stages enumerated below.

1st Stage—Service advisories are posted on an automaker's internal computer network. They offer troubleshooting tips and allow the dealer to bill the manufacturer for the repair. This info is never shared with the customer and doesn't appear on the ALLDATA or NHTSA database.

2nd Stage—If the defect grows in scope and a more involved solution is needed (for example, one requiring upgraded parts), automakers then draw up a technical service bulletin (TSB) and distribute it to dealers and U.S. and Canadian government agencies. The TSB is only issued after the manufacturer thinks it has a solution for the defect. TSBs issued by Chrysler, Ford, and GM will usually spell out clearly which base warranty will cover the repair (emissions warranty, bumper-to-bumper, etc.). Interestingly, Asian and European automakers are vague in describing their warranty obligations. Honda, for example, uses the term "goodwill" as a euphemism to describe its warranty extensions and Toyota advises dealers to carry out the free repairs only if the owner complains (of course, owners don't know a free repair program exists).

97-060   September 22, 1997

Applies To: 1994-97 Accord 4-door - All

Front Door Glass Comes Out of Run Channel

SYMPTOM

When operating a front window (power or manual), the rear edge of the glass comes out of the B-pillar run channel.

PROBABLE CAUSE

The window regulator is out of adjustment.

CORRECTIVE ACTION

Adjust the window regulator, the front channel, and the glass.

WARRANTY CLAIM INFORMATION

In warranty:

The normal warranty applies.
Failed part: P/N 72250-SV-A11, H/C 4272282
Defect Code: 030
Contention Code: B01
Skill level: Repair Technician

Out of warranty:

Any repair performed after warranty expiration may be eligible for goodwill consideration by the District Service Manager or your Zone Office. You must request consideration, and get a decision, before starting work.

3rd Stage—More and more customers hear through *Lemon-Aid*, ALL-DATA, friends, and relatives that some TSBs recognize that a common factory-related defect exists, and find that the base warranty is clearly inadequate to deal with the scope of the problem. Dealers and customers exert pressure for additional after-warranty assistance. This, in turn, results in a second TSB, sent only to dealers, extending the warranty coverage to correct the defect and usually leaving the amount of the customer's refund to the dealer's discretion. Ford calls this second TSB a Special Service Instruction and assumes the full cost of the adjustment, repair, or replacement of the defective part.

Now, customer dissatisfaction builds to a crescendo, since the dealers and automakers keep the extended guidelines to themselves and customers get widely divergent refunds. This only angers the owners more, brings in the media, and leads to a proliferation of Internet gripe sites and lawsuits (small claims and class actions).

4th Stage—Finally, the aggravation is too great and the automaker decides to mail out an owner notification letter (sent to first owners only, at their last known address) that clearly spells out what all owners will get and which vehicles are involved. A special bulletin or letter is also sent out to dealers to ensure they follow the guidelines 100 percent. Ford calls these Owner Notification Programs, GM calls them Special Policies, and Chrysler calls them Owner Satisfaction Notifications. No matter the euphemism, they are all an extension of the original warranty and apply to vehicles purchased new or used.

Remember, second owners and repairs done by independent garages are included in these secret warranty programs. Large, costly repairs, such as blown engines, burned transmissions, and peeling paint, are often covered. Even mundane little repairs, which can still cost you a hundred bucks or more, are frequently included in these programs. Take, for example, the elimination of foul, musty, or mildew odours emitted by your air conditioning unit. Despite what the dealer may say, it's covered by the base warranty provided by all automakers.

If you have a TSB but you're still refused compensation, keep in mind that secret warranties are an admission of manufacturing negligence. Try to compromise with a pro rata adjustment from the manufacturer. If polite negotiations fail, challenge the refusal in court on the grounds that you should not be penalized for failing to make a reimbursement claim under a secret warranty you never knew existed!

Here are a few examples of the latest, most comprehensive secret warranties that have come across my desk in the last several years.

Acura/Honda
1994–97 Acura CL and Honda Accord, Prelude, and Odyssey models equipped with 4-cylinder engines
Problem: Defective engine oil seals can slip, causing the engine to drain of oil and eventually seize. **Warranty coverage:** Although Honda maintains this isn't a safety recall (hmm, sudden engine seizure on the highway certainly sounds scary to me), the company will inspect and replace the seal and install a clip to ensure the seal cannot move. There are about 1.4 million vehicles involved in this worldwide program. Repairs had been delayed due to poor parts availability. This free repair was also confirmed by the *National Post*, December 1, 2000, in its "Driver's Edge" column.

1999 Odyssey
Problem: Canadians vacationing in the States may discover that U.S. brands of gasoline (California excluded) may cause the intake manifold

EGR port to clog, causing hard starts or no-starts, stalling, poor fuel economy, and overall poor engine performance. The malfunction indicator light (MIL) will also come on. **Warranty coverage:** No matter the mileage or number of previous owners, Honda will replace, free of charge, the rear intake manifold end plate and gasket, the intake manifold cover, and the PCV hose. Although the repair—installation of a special "Intake Manifold Kit"—should only take a half hour, Honda suggests you plan to leave your minivan at the dealer for at least a half day. All the details about this free correction are contained in TSB #00-009, published March 2, 2000.

Chrysler
1991–99 models with A604, 41TE, and 42LE automatic transmissions

Problem: Faulty automatic transmissions that shift erratically, gear down to "limp mode," are slow to shift in or out of Reverse, and self-destruct. This is an A604 (and its spin-offs) software and hardware problem that has bedevilled Chrysler owners for over a decade. Dozens of service bulletins address the problem and can be useful in small claims court. However, it's likely your filing won't go beyond the pre-trial mediation stage: Chrysler reps are loath to defend the cases in front of independent garage testimony. **Warranty coverage:** Without a court threat, Chrysler usually denies any problem or refund program exists. If you have the assistance of your dealer's service manager, expect an offer of 50 percent (about $1,500). File the case in small claims court and Chrysler will sweeten the offer considerably.

Chrysler/Jeep
1989–93 Cherokee and Wagoneer; 1990–93 Dynasty, New Yorker, Fifth Avenue, and Imperial; 1991–92 Eagle Premier; 1991–93 minivans

Problem: ABS brakes that fail or malfunction. **Warranty coverage:** Piggybacking a service campaign onto a recall, Chrysler extended the warranty to 10 years/160,000 km on a number of costly ABS components. Owners will also be reimbursed for previous ABS repairs—not applicable to calipers, pads/shoe linings, or other maintenance items. Two other ABS components—piston seals (excessive wear) and the pump motor (deterioration)—will be repaired free of charge at any time during the life of the vehicle.

Hi Phil. I thought I should let you know that Chrysler sent me a cheque to cover the full cost of the repair of my ABS brakes. I appreciate your book providing the copy of Safety Recall 685 as it sure makes things a whole lot easier when you have a document like that to refer to.

I have written a letter to the local dealer requesting that they cover the cost of the rental car. I did let them know that I would take them to small claims court if the reimbursement was not made. What really bothers me is that I had asked about service bulletins or free repairs when the van was brought in and was still charged the full cost of the repair. How many other people have been ripped off by this scam? The other thing I am currently wondering is, "Has my local dealer already been paid for the repair by Chrysler, and still collected the money from me?" If they have, it is a nice little scam they have going to collect double for the work they do.

Fred K.

1993–99 Concorde, Intrepid, New Yorker, LHS, Vision, and Grand Cherokee

Problem: AC evaporator failure or malfunction. **Warranty coverage:** 7 years/115,000 km. Chrysler is free to limit this program to the evaporator and to the vehicles listed above; after all, they are simply modifying their *expressed* warranty. But you are just as free to plead the *implied* warranty (in your letter to Chrysler and small claims filing). Argue that this extension sets a benchmark for the warranty repairs on the entire AC as to what Chrysler considers reasonable durability. A copy of this secret warranty can be found in the Introduction. Also, make the point that Chrysler is unfairly excluding other models using the same system with the same AC failures. (C'mon, what's applicable to a Concorde should be applicable to a Caravan, *n'est-ce pas?*)

Chrysler, Ford, and General Motors
All years, all models
Problem: Faulty paint jobs that cause paint to turn white and peel off horizontal panels. Ford and GM internal memos and service bulletins admit this is a factory defect. Out-of-court settlements proffered by all three automakers also confirm the 6-year benchmark, although Chrysler confirmation is anecdotal, not written. In *Frank v. GM*, the Saskatchewan small claims court set a 15-year benchmark for paint finishes, and three other Canadian small claims judgments have extended the benchmark to seven years, second owners, and pickups. **Warranty coverage:** Automakers will offer a free paint job or partial compensation up to 6 years/no mileage limitation. Thereafter, all three manufacturers offer 50–75 percent refunds on the small claims courthouse steps.

Nancy Frith, a Nova Scotia owner of a 1992 Dodge Shadow, was awarded $2,000 for the paint delamination/peeling of her car. CBC Television interviewed her and you can capture the 5-minute program at *cbc.ca/consumers/market/files/cars/paintpeel/index.html*.

Problem: Premature wearout of key front and rear brake components. **Warranty coverage:** Calipers and pads: Goodwill settlements confirm that brake calipers and pads that fail to last 2 years/40,000 km will be replaced for 50 percent of the repair cost; components not lasting 1 year/ 20,000 km will be replaced for free. Rotors: If they last less than 3 years/ 60,000 km, they will be replaced at half price; replacement is free up to

2 years/40,000 km. Interestingly, premature brake component wearout is quite common among all automobile manufacturers, although only Chrysler, Ford, and GM have standardized their policies for goodwill refunds.

Apparently, brake suppliers are using cheaper calipers, pads, and rotors that can't handle the heat generated by normal braking. Consequently, drivers find routine braking causes rotor warpage that produces excessive vibrations, shuddering, noise, and pulling to one side when braking.

Ford
1994-99 models equipped with automatic transmissions, particularly Taurus, Sable, and Windstar
Problem: Forward clutch piston, planetary gear, and clutch slave cylinder may fail prematurely. This problem is usually indicated by erratic shifting, delayed shifting, harsh engagement, and a tendency for the transmission to "hunt" for the proper gear. Barely noticeable at first, it will worsen progressively, until the transmission breaks down completely. **Warranty coverage:** Ford will repair or replace the transmission at no charge up to 7 years/160,000 km, no matter if the vehicle was bought new or used. The company's initial offer is about 50 percent of the estimated $3,000 repair cost. Vehicles that have exceeded the above limitations will receive pro-rated refunds.

Affected owners should still claim 100 percent refunds for 7 years/160,000 km, in conformity with Ford's engine ONP guidelines (1994–95 Taurus, Sable, and Windstar engine headgaskets). The transmission is simply the other end of the powertrain, and it's idiotic to maintain that the engine should last two years and 60,000 km longer than the automatic transmission, particularly since the original powertrain warranty doesn't differentiate between the two components.

1995-98 Windstar
Problem: Defective front coil springs may suddenly break, puncturing the front tire, leading to loss of steering control. **Warranty coverage:** Ford will replace the defective coil spring at no charge up to 10 years/unlimited mileage. The company won't replace the springs until they have broken—if you're alive to submit a claim. My suggestion: take a copy of the NHTSA's defect report (see below) and demand that the springs be changed before they fail, or you'll sue for their replacement in small claims court while holding the dealer and automaker responsible for any fatalities or injuries occurring in the interim.

NHTSA Campaign ID Number: 011007000

Defect Summary:

This is not a safety defect in accordance with the safety act. However, it is deemed a safety improvement campaign by the agency. Vehicle description: 1995-1998 Ford Windstar Minivans. The front coil springs could potentially fracture due to corrosion.

Consequence Summary:

Some tires have deflated due to contact with a broken spring.

Corrective Summary:

Ford is extending the warranty for front coil spring replacement to a total of 10 years of service from the warranty start date, with unlimited mileage. This coverage is automatically transferred to subsequent owners at no charge. If either front coil spring fractures during the coverage period noted above, the dealer will replace both springs at no charge to the owner.

All of these minivans should have been recalled, instead of being the object of a Ford special warranty extension subject to the whims and dictates of Ford management.

1996–97 Mustang, Cougar, and Thunderbird; 1997 F-Series trucks equipped with 3.8L or 4.2L engines

Problem: These vehicles may experience engine coolant leaks at the front cover gasket; this could cause severe engine damage from over-heating if not corrected. **Warranty coverage:** At no charge to the owner, the dealer will replace the engine front cover gasket with a redesigned gasket and—now get this—*replace the engine oil and filter!* This is a generous special warranty extension because: 1) it also covers lower intake side gaskets; 2) the free repair is still applicable even if there is a repeat failure; 3) there is no engine test required to get the new, more durable components installed; 4) costs for previous repairs will be paid in full; and 5) it includes vehicles purchased used and there is no mileage limitation. Although this program expired March 21, 2001, it has been extended on a case-by-case basis.

Owners whose cars already have been repaired should take their original receipt to a Ford or Lincoln-Mercury dealer. However, Ford has acknowledged that some of those consumers may have had their gaskets replaced with the older, troublesome gasket. That gasket could leak, too, and those consumers are eligible not only for the reimbursement but for a new repair, say Ford spokespeople.

The easiest way to tell if a new, improved gasket was used is to check the part number on the receipt or to call the dealer who did the work. An "early upgraded" gasket had this part number: F8ZZ-6020-AA. However, since the middle of 1999, an even newer design was used. Its part number is YF2Z-6020-AA. Ford engineers believe that the "early upgraded" gasket will be fine, but consumers who worry that it is not good enough are eligible for a second repair.

My only gripe about this warranty extension is that it leaves out the 1996–98 Windstar and Econoline E-150 and E-250, the 1998 Mustang, and 1998 F-Series trucks, which are all included in service bulletin #99-20-7, detailing the failure that Ford is correcting. If you are the owner of one of these excluded vehicles, send the dealer and Ford a claim letter. If refused compensation, subpoena Ford's bulletin and owner letter as proof that you should have been included.

Ford/Lincoln
1996–2001 Crown Victoria and Lincoln Town Car fleet vehicles
Problem: Intake manifolds may crack at the coolant crossover, resulting in engine coolant leakage. **Warranty coverage:** ONP #01M02 will pay for the intake manifold's replacement up to seven years, regardless of mileage.

1998–2000 Crown Victoria and Lincoln Town Car fleet vehicles
Problem: Rear suspension upper control arm brackets may crack and allow the bracket to separate from the frame. This will cause a clunking noise and cause the rear suspension to feel loose. **Warranty coverage:** ONP #00B60 will pay for the crack repair and the installation of a rein-forcement bracket until January 31, 2002. After that date, owners should seek pro rata compensation, using small claims court action as their final recourse.

General Motors
1991–96 S/T-series 4X4 Blazers and pickups; 1992–95 Astro/Safari minivans; 1993–96 full-sized vans equipped with three-sensor EBC4 ABS brakes
Problem: Complete or partial brake failure. **Warranty coverage:** GM ini-tially recalled 1.1 million 1991–96 S/T-series 4X4 Blazers and pickups equipped with EBC4 ABS to change a sensor switch. Additionally, GM has a "Special Policy" to reprogram, at no charge, the software control-ling the ABS system on 2.4 million 1994–96 S/T-series Blazers and pickups; 1992–95 Astro and Safari minivans; and 1993–96 full-sized vans. Access the NHTSA website for a copy of GM's "Special Policy."

1995–96 Cavalier/Sunfire and the 4X2 models of the 1996 Chevrolet S-10 and GMC Sonoma pickups with 2.2 L 4-cylinder engines
Problem: Engine head gasket failures that include overheating, loss of coolant, the smell of coolant, coolant leaks around the cylinder head, and white smoke from the exhaust. Sometimes the heater won't work or a film (from the coolant) will be deposited on the inside glass surfaces. If the coolant leaks inside the engine, it can cause severe engine damage from overheating. **Warranty coverage:** The 1995 and 1996 vehicles are

now covered for head gasket problems for seven years or 160,000 km, whichever comes first. Anyone who has paid for repairs at a dealership should contact the dealership to be reimbursed. Owners who did not have a GM dealership do the work aren't excluded from the refund program and should contact the toll-free customer assistance number in the owner's manual. Future repairs, however, must be done at a GM dealership. The program is not a recall, and owners should take their vehicles to a dealership only if it appears they have a problem.

Remember, if you have an engine head gasket failure on a GM vehicle or engine not included in the above-noted programs, don't despair. Simply use the same benchmarks for your own vehicle and threaten small claims action on those grounds.

1998 Cavalier/Sunfire
Problem: Excessive oil consumption. **Warranty coverage:** Customer Satisfaction Campaign will cover all the cost incurred to eliminate the problem. Service bulletin number: 98017; Date of bulletin: 08/98; NHTSA Item Number: SB615103.

1999 Cavalier/Sunfire
Problem: Defective throttle valve cable produces erratic engine performance. **Warranty coverage:** Customer Satisfaction Campaign will cover the cost of replacing the throttle valve cable. Service bulletin number: 99039; Date of bulletin: 07/99; NHTSA Item Number: SB606219.

2001 Alero
Problem: Transmission bearing failure. **Warranty coverage:** Customer Satisfaction Campaign for 4T40-E transaxle converter bearing failure inspection/replacement. Service bulletin number: 01031; Date of bulletin: 04/01; NHTSA Item Number: SB619400.

2001 DeVille
Problem: Engine crankshaft pulley failure. **Warranty coverage:** Customer Satisfaction Campaign allows for a rebuilt crankshaft or engine replacement. Service bulletin number: 01012; Date of bulletin: 02/01; NHTSA Item Number: SB619207.

Toyota
1988–96 compact pickups, T100 pickups, and 4Runner sport-utilities with 3.0L and 3.6L 6-cylinder engines
Problem: Defective head gaskets may cause loss of engine coolant, engine overheating, or destruction of the engine's short block. **Warranty coverage:** Toyota will replace the defective components at no charge up to 8 years/160,000 km (*Automotive News*, February 10, 1997). Although some repairs have been attempted, it's recommended that the entire short block be replaced and new head bolts installed. This has resulted in warranty claims as high as $6,000 (U.S.) among the 36,000 vehicles

repaired in the U.S. up to February 1997. Although Toyota doesn't mention it, Canadian jurisprudence, as well as similar warranty extensions set up by other automakers, leads one to assume that second owners and repairs done by independent garages are included in this program. Incidentally, there have been a lot of 1995–96 model head gasket failures reported to the U.S. National Highway Traffic Safety Administration (NHTSA); Toyota has extended this warranty's parameters to include 1996 models on a case-by-case basis.

Toyota/Lexus
1997–2001 Camry, Avalon, Celica, Sienna, and RX300
Problem: Engine oil sludge buildup requires a $4,500–$6,000 engine rebuild or an engine replacement. The problem can be spotted by performing this simple check: Remove the oil filler cap from the rocker cover and check for the presence of white sludge on the cap or in the lip. If there is sludge, this will indicate a presence of water in the oil or a damaged cylinder head gasket. The sludge problem is said to be caused by a reduction in the size of the coolant passages in the head gasket. This results in the cylinder heads running at an extremely hot temperature. It is literally frying the oil. Although Toyota tried to pin the blame on owners for not changing the oil frequently enough, Toyota whistle-blowers say it doesn't matter when you change the oil—you will get sludge. If you have very frequent changes (more than the manual recommends), then the sludge may not cause any problems for many more miles than folks who follow the owner's manual. The only solution is synthetic oil or another engine.

A Vancouver owner of a 2000 Sienna writes:

> Every six weeks I travel about 1,200 km on the highway at an average speed of 100 km/hr. The engine seems incredibly hot but the heat gauge stays in the middle. I am afraid the engine will catch fire. I must add a full quart of oil during my trip.
>
> I told Toyota Canada and they say it sounds like sludge and it will cost $300 to check the problem and most likely it will cost big bucks to fix because I missed a couple of oil changes. Well excuse me!
>
> My van is leased through Toyota where they are all high and mighty that it says in the manual that I must change the oil according to exact km. Well excuse me again! I have had many Japanese cars in my 34 years of driving and have never ever encountered such a problem and such a load of crap! The engine in the Sienna is mechanically flawed and Toyota needs to fix the problem.

Warranty coverage: A reconditioned engine up to 5 years/no limitation on mileage or prior ownership, if claim is received by February 28, 2003. See Toyota's "Engine Sludge Policy" guidelines, expressed at *www.remarketing.toyota.com/sludge.htm*. Toyota recognizes the sludge problem and sets the following guidelines for settling disputes arising from auction sales by Toyota and Lexus remarketing agencies:

> Effective June 18, 2001, the following arbitration rules will be the basis for any and all possible repurchases over Toyota Financial Services/ Lexus Financial Services Direct.
>
> TFS/LFS adheres to the arbitration rules of the auctions represented on TFS/LFS Direct, which are incorporated herein by reference, with the following exception(s): Buyer may arbitrate the following item on or before the close of business on the 14th day after purchase (day one begins the day of the sale) if not announced at the point of sale: engine sludge. In order to begin the arbitration process, the buyer must contact the auction's arbitration manager.
>
> Eligibility:
>
> Toyota: 5 model years and newer with no more than 60,000 miles [95,000 km].
>
> Lexus: 5 model years and newer with no more than 70,000 miles [110,000 km].

Tires

Firestone Affinity brand tires

Problem: Sudden blowout or tread separation, premature tread wear, and gradual loss of air. **Warranty coverage:** Consumers (particularly Honda Odyssey owners) report their tires have been replaced free of charge up to 3 years/60,000 km.

Firestone Affinity tires are reported to be splitting on their sidewalls.

Goodyear 16-inch load-range E tires used by DaimlerChrysler and Ford full-sized vans, 2¹/₂-ton or larger pickups, and commercial vehicles like school vans and large SUVs, including the Chevy Suburban (brand names include Wrangler AT, Wrangler HT, Workhorse, Kelly-Springfield Trailbuster, and Kelly-Springfield Power King); 15-inch load-range D tires sold under the Marathon name

Problem: Premature tread wear, bulges in the tires, and sudden tread separation. Problems are presently under investigation by NHTSA. **Warranty coverage:** According to the *Los Angeles Times*, Goodyear has received more than 3,000 claims about its light-truck tires fitted on vans, light trucks, sport-utility vehicles, and RVs since 1995. A majority of those claims have been quietly settled, with consumers receiving replacement tires and reimbursements if their vehicles were damaged. Goodyear also has been replacing its load-range D 15-inch tires, fitted mainly on recreational vehicles, after RV owners and manufacturers reported widespread Marathon brand tire failures. Some RV owners said it was only after they had experienced tread separation several times that they learned Goodyear would replace them for free. A class-action suit filed in Massachusetts accuses Goodyear of failing to warn consumers that its 15-inch Marathon tires are unsafe and unsuitable for campers.

Goodyear denies that it is conducting a silent recall. It says it is providing "customer satisfaction" replacements on a case-by-case basis. Interestingly, Goodyear's problems and PR campaign are quite similar to Firestone's early stonewalling of customer complaints. For example, the number of complaints received by Goodyear is nearly as high as the 3,700 complaints NHTSA has received about Firestone tires, and, while pledging "total disclosure," Goodyear is fighting desperately to keep the courts from disclosing the documents, previously kept secret.

How Long Should a Part or Repair Last?

Let's say you can't find a service bulletin that says your problem is factory related or covered by a special compensation program. Or a part lasts just a little longer than its guarantee, but not as long as is generally expected. Can you get a refund if the same problem reappears shortly after it has been repaired? The answer is yes, if you can prove the part failed prematurely.

Automakers, mechanics, and the courts have their own benchmarks as to what's a reasonable period of time or amount of mileage one should expect a part or adjustment to last. I've prepared the following table to show what most automakers consider is reasonable durability, as expressed by their original and "goodwill" warranties.

ACCESSORIES

Air conditioner	7 years
Cellular phone	5 years
Cruise control	5 years/ 100,000 km
Power antenna	5 years
Power doors, windows	5 years
Radio	5 years

BODY

Paint (peeling)	10–15 years
Rust (perforations)	7 years
Rust (surface)	5 years
Water/wind/air leaks	5 years

BRAKE SYSTEM

Brake drum	120,000 km
Brake drum linings	35,000 km
Brake rotor	60,000 km
Disc brake calipers	30,000 km
Disc brake pads	30,000 km
Master cylinder, rebuild	100,000 km
Wheel cylinder, rebuild	80,000 km

ENGINE AND DRIVETRAIN

Constant velocity joint	6 years/ 160,000 km
Differential	7 years/ 160,000 km
Engine (gas)	7 years/ 160,000 km
Radiator	4 years/ 80,000 km
Transfer case	7 years/ 150,000 km
Transmission (auto.)	7 years/ 150,000 km
Transmission (man.)	7 years/ 200,000 km
Transmission oil cooler	5 years/ 100,000 km

EXHAUST SYSTEM

Catalytic converter	5 years/ 100,000 km or more

Muffler	2 years/ 40,000 km
Tailpipe	3 years/ 60,000 km

IGNITION SYSTEM

Cable set	60,000 km
Electronic module	5 years/ 80,000 km
Retiming	20,000 km
Spark plugs	20,000 km
Tune-up	20,000 km

SAFETY COMPONENTS

Airbags	life of vehicle
ABS brakes	7 years/ 160,000 km
ABS computer	10 years/ 160,000 km
Seatbelts	life of vehicle

STEERING AND SUSPENSION

Alignment	1 year/ 20,000 km
Ball joints	80,000 km
Power steering	5 years/ 80,000 km
Shock absorber	2 years/ 40,000 km
Struts	5 years/ 80,000 km
Tires (radial)	5 years/ 80,000 km
Wheel bearing	3 years/ 60,000 km

VISIBILITY

Halogen/fog lights	3 years/ 60,000 km
Sealed beam	2 years/ 40,000 km
Windshield wiper motor	5 years/ 80,000 km

Much of the preceding guidelines were extrapolated from Chrysler and Ford payouts to thousands of dissatisfied customers over the past decade, in addition to Chrysler's original 7-year powertrain warranty applicable from 1991–95. Other sources for this chart were the Ford and GM transmission warranties outlined in their secret warranties; Ford, GM, and Toyota engine "goodwill" programs laid out in their internal service bulletins; and court judgments where judges have given their own guidelines as to what is reasonable durability, such as the 15-year paint finish benchmark set down in *Frank v. GM*.

Auto recalls are valid for 10 years and safety features generally have a lifetime warranty, with the exception of ABS, which is considered a maintenance item. Nevertheless, the Chrysler ten-year "free-service" program portion of its ABS recall announced six years ago can serve as a handy guide as to how long one can expect expensive brake components to last.

Airbags are a different matter. Those that are deployed in an accident—and the personal injury and interior damage their deployment will likely have caused—are covered by your accident insurance policy. However, if there is a sudden deployment for no apparent reason, the automaker and dealer should be held jointly responsible for all injuries and damages caused by the airbag. This will likely lead to a more generous settlement from the two parties and prevent your insurance premiums from being jacked up. Inadvertent deployment may occur after passing over a bump in the road, slamming the car door, or, in some Chrysler minivans, simply putting the key in the ignition. This happens more often than you might imagine, judging by the hundreds of recalls and thousands of complaints recorded on the U.S. National Highway Traffic Safety Administration's (NHTSA) website (*www.nhtsa.dot.gov/cars/problems/complain/index.cfm*).

Finally, the manufacturer's emissions warranty is the primary guideline showing the expected durability of high-tech electronic and mechanical pollution control components, like powertrain control modules (PCM) and catalytic converters. Look first at your owner's manual for an indication of which parts on your vehicle are covered. If you come up with few specifics, ask the auto manufacturer for a list of specific components covered by the emissions warranty. If you're stonewalled, ask your local MP to get the info from Transport Canada or Environment Canada, and invest in an ALLDATA service bulletin DVD, where your car's emissions parts will be outlined.

Recall repairs

Let the automaker know who and where you are. If you've moved or bought a used vehicle, it's smart to pay a visit to your local dealer and get a "report card" on which recalls, free service campaigns, and warranties apply to it. Simply give the service advisor your vehicle identification number (VIN)—found on the dash just below the windshield on the driver's side, or on your insurance card—and have the number run through the automaker's computer system ("Function 70" for Chrysler, "OASIS" for Ford, and "CRIS" for GM). Ask for a computer printout of the vehicle's history (have it faxed to you, if you're so equipped) and make sure you're listed in the automaker's computer as the new owner. This ensures that you'll receive notices of warranty extensions and emissions and safety recalls.

Still, don't expect to be welcomed with open arms when your vehicle develops a safety- or emissions-related problem that's not yet part of a recall campaign. Automakers and dealers generally take a restrictive view of what constitutes a safety or emissions defect and frequently charge for repairs that should be free under federal safety or emissions legislation. To counter this tendency, look at the following list of typical defects that are clearly safety related, and if you experience similar problems, insist that the automaker fix the problem at no expense to yourself, including a car rental:

- airbag malfunctions
- corrosion affecting safe operation
- disconnected or stuck accelerators
- electrical shorts
- faulty windshield wipers
- fuel leaks
- problems with original axles, drive shafts, seats, seat recliners, or defrosters
- seatbelt problems
- stalling or sudden acceleration
- sudden steering or brake loss
- suspension failures
- trailer coupling failures

When a safety recall is announced, automakers will pay the entire cost of fixing a vehicle's safety-related defect up to eight years. Recalls may be voluntary or ordered by the U.S. Department of Transportation. Canadian regulations have an added twist: Transport Canada can only order automakers to notify owners that their vehicles may be unsafe; it can't force them to correct the problem. Nevertheless, when Transport Canada makes a defect determination on its own, automakers generally comply with an owner notification letter and free repairs.

Voluntary safety recall campaigns, frequently called Special Service Campaigns or Safety Improvement Campaigns, are a real problem, though. The notification of owners isn't monitored by government; dealers and automakers routinely deny there's a recall, thereby dissuading most claimants; and the company's so-called fix, not authorized by any governing body, may not correct the hazard at all. Also, it may leave out many of the affected models or unreasonably exclude certain

owners. Take, as an example, Bridgestone/Firestone's voluntary replacement program that targeted 1.4 million tires found to be "hazardous" by
NHTSA. Bridgestone/Firestone replaced the tires free of charge in the
States, while denying Canadians the same privilege. The Windstar's hazardous front coil springs are another example: when they break, *then*
they get replaced.

Safety defect information

If you wish to report a safety defect or want recall info, you may access
Transport Canada's website at *apps.tc.gc.ca/roadsafety/recalls/recintro_e.htm*.
You can get recall information in French or English, as well as general
information relating to road safety and importing a vehicle into Canada.
Cybersurfers can now access the recall database for 1970–2001 model
vehicles but, unlike NHTSA's website, owner complaints aren't listed,
defect investigations aren't disclosed, and service bulletin summaries
aren't provided. You can also call Transport Canada at 1-800-333-0510
(toll-free within Canada) or 613-993-9851 (within the Ottawa region or
outside Canada) to get additional information. Be wary of promises to
call you back, though.

Unfortunately, there are some problems with Ottawa's database—and
attitude. First, when calling Transport Canada through the toll-free line,
Transport Canada bureaucrats insist that the dealer must already have
refused you the recall info before they will give it to you. You won't be
told if others have reported similar safety problems affecting your
vehicle. And more often than not, if you suspect your car has a safety
defect, you'll be asked to take it to the dealer for a safety exam (where
there's a good chance the problem will be covered up or you'll be blamed
for the malfunction).

If you're not happy with Ottawa's treatment of your recall inquiry, try
the U.S. government's NHTSA website. It's more complete than Transport
Canada's site. (NHTSA's database is updated daily and covers vehicles
built since 1952.) You can search the database for your vehicle or tires at
www.nhtsa.dot.gov/cars/problems/. You'll get immediate access to four
essential database categories applicable to your vehicle and model year:
the latest recalls, current and closed safety investigations, defects
reported by other owners, and a brief summary of technical service bulletins.

NHTSA's fax-back service provides the same info through a local line
that can be accessed from Canada—although long-distance charges will
apply. (Most calls take 5–10 minutes to complete.) The following local
numbers get you into the automatic response service quickly and can be
reached 24 hours a day: 202-366-0123 (202-366-7800 for the hearing
impaired).

Three Steps to a Settlement

Step 1: Informal negotiations

If your vehicle was misrepresented, has major defects, or wasn't properly repaired under warranty, the first thing you should do is give the seller (the dealer and automaker or a private party) a written summary (by registered mail or fax) of the outstanding problems and stipulate a time period in which they will need to be corrected or your money will be refunded. Keep a copy for yourself, along with all your repair records. Be sure to check all of the sales and warranty documents you were given to see if they conform to provincial laws. Any errors, omissions, or violations can be used to get a settlement with the dealer in lieu of making a formal complaint.

At the beginning, try to work things out informally and, in your attempt to reach a settlement, keep in mind the cardinal rule: ask only for what is fair and don't try to make anyone look bad.

- Listen. The really tough part of negotiating is listening. Listen to the automaker's representative or the dealership principal and try to understand their problem while thinking of a co-operative solution. This means frequently restating the other side's position so they realize you understand their offer.
- Line up evidence and allies. Be sure to line up your proof (like work orders, technical service bulletins, and independent garage reports) before making your claim.
- Be reasonable and give as well as take. Consumers are frequently given a "let's make a deal" spiel where the initial offer of 50 percent is often boosted to 75 percent compensation if the customer will agree—at that very moment—to pay 25 percent of the repair.
- Keep your demands reasonable but add a request for consequential damages (frustration, inconvenience, rental cars, missed work/vacation, etc.) and keep it as a throwaway claim to be used at a critical juncture in the talks.
- Know when to shut up.
- Don't set an unrealistic timetable.

Finally, when negotiating, speak in a calm, polite manner and try to avoid polarizing the issue. Talk about how "we can work together" on the problem. Let a compromise slowly emerge—don't come in with a hard-line set of demands. Don't demand the settlement offer in writing, but make sure that you're accompanied by a friend or relative who can confirm the offer in court if it isn't honoured. Be prepared to act upon the offer without delay so your hesitancy won't be blamed for its withdrawal.

Dealer/service manager

If you bought a used vehicle from a dealer who sells the same make new, you stand a good chance of getting free repairs, particularly if the vehicle is still under warranty, it's covered by a "goodwill" program, or if you intend to plead premature failure of a specific part based upon the parameters listed in the chart found on page 44.

Service managers have more power than you may have realized. They make the first determination of what work is covered under warranty or through post-warranty "goodwill" programs and are directly responsible to the dealer and manufacturer for that decision (dealers hate manufacturer audits that force them to pay back questionable warranty decisions). Service managers are paid to save the dealer and automaker money and to mollify irate clients—almost an impossible balancing act. Nevertheless, when a service manager agrees to extend warranty coverage, it's because you've raised solid issues that neither the dealer nor automaker can ignore. All the more reason to present your argument in a confident, forthright manner with your vehicle's service history and *Lemon-Aid*'s "How Long Should Parts/Repairs Last?" chart. Also bring as many technical service bulletins and owner complaint printouts as you can find, from websites like NHTSA's or *www.thecomplaintstation.com*.

Don't use your salesperson as a runner, since the sales staff are generally quite distant from the service staff and usually have less pull than you do. If the service manager can't or won't set things right, your next step is to convene a mini-summit with the service manager, the dealership principal, and the automaker's rep. By getting the automaker involved, you run less risk of having the dealer fob you off on the manufacturer and can often get an agreement where the seller and automaker pay two-thirds of the repair cost.

Independent dealers and dealers who sell a brand of used vehicle that they don't sell new give you less latitude. You have to make the case that the vehicle's defects were present at the time of purchase or should have been known to the seller, or that the vehicle doesn't conform to the representations made when it was purchased. Emphasize that you intend to use the courts if necessary to obtain a refund—most independent sellers would rather settle than risk a lawsuit with all the attendant publicity. An independent estimate of the vehicle's defects and cost of repairs is essential if you want to convince the seller that you're serious in your claim and stand a good chance of winning your case in court. Come prepared with an estimated cost of repairs to challenge the dealer who agrees to pay half the repair costs and then jacks up the costs 100 percent so that you wind up paying the whole shot.

Step 2: Sending a registered letter, fax, or email

This is the next step to take if your claim is refused. Send the dealer and manufacturer a polite registered letter or fax that asks for compensation for repairs that have been done or need to be done; insurance costs while the vehicle is being repaired; towing charges; supplementary transportation costs like taxis and rented cars; and damages for inconvenience.

Specify five days (but allow ten) for either party to respond. If no satisfactory offer is made, file suit in small claims court. Make the
manufacturer a party to the lawsuit, especially if the emissions warranty,
a secret warranty extension, a safety-recall campaign, or extensive chassis
rusting is involved.

**Used Car or Minivan Complaint Letter/Fax/Email
Without Prejudice**

Date: _____
Name: _____

Please be advised that I am dissatisfied with my used vehicle, a (state
model), for the following reasons:

1. _____
2. _____
3. _____
4. _____
5. _____

In compliance with the provincial consumer protection laws and the
"implied warranty" set down by the Supreme Court of Canada in
Donoghue v. Stevenson and *Longpré v. St-Jacques Automobile*,
I hereby request that these defects be repaired without charge.

This vehicle has not been reasonably durable and is, therefore, not as
represented to me.

Should you fail to repair these defects in a satisfactory manner and within
a reasonable period of time, I reserve the right to have the repairs done
elsewhere by an independent source and claim reimbursement in court,
without further delay. I also reserve my right to claim up to $1 million for
punitive damages, pursuant to the Supreme Court of Canada's February
22, 2002, ruling in *Whiten v. Pilot*.

I have dealt with your company because of its honesty, competence, and
sincere regard for its clients. I am sure that my case is the exception and
not the rule.

A positive response within the next five (5) days would be appreciated.

Sincerely,

(signed with telephone or fax number)

Secret Warranty Claim Letter/Fax/Email
Without Prejudice

Date: _____
Name: _____

Please be advised that I am dissatisfied with my vehicle, a _____,
bought from you on _____.
It has had the following recurring problems that I believe are factory-
related defects, as confirmed by internal service bulletins sent to dealers,
and are covered by your "goodwill" policies:

1. _____
2. _____
3. _____

If your "goodwill" program has ended, I ask that my claim be accepted
nevertheless, inasmuch as I was never informed of your policy while it
was in effect and should not be penalized for not knowing it existed.

I hereby formally put you on notice under federal and provincial
consumer protection statutes that your refusal to apply this extended
warranty coverage in my case would be an unfair warranty practice within
the purview of the above-cited laws.

Your actions also violate the "implied warranty" set down by the
Supreme Court of Canada (*Donoghue v. Stevenson* and *Longpre v. St.
Jacques Automobile*) and repeatedly reaffirmed by provincial consumer
protection laws (*Lowe v. Chrysler, Dufour v. Ford du Canada*, and *Frank v.
GM*).

I have enclosed several estimates (my bill) showing that this problem is
factory related and will (has) cost $_____ to correct. I would
appreciate your refunding me the estimated (paid) amount, failing which,
I reserve the right to have the repair done elsewhere and claim
reimbursement in court without further delay. I also reserve the right to
claim up to $1 million for punitive damages, pursuant to the Supreme
Court of Canada's February 22, 2002, ruling in *Whiten v. Pilot*.

A positive response within the next five (5) days would be appreciated.

Sincerely,

(signed with telephone or fax number)

Lowe, Dufour, and *Frank* are summarized in Part Two; *Whiten*, in Appendix I.

Step 3: Mediation and arbitration

If the formality of a courtroom puts you off or you're not sure that your claim is all that solid and don't want to pay legal costs to find out, consider using mediation or arbitration. These services are sponsored by the Better Business Bureau, Automobile Protection Association, Canadian Automobile Association, Canadian Automobile Manufacturers Vehicle Arbitration Program (if you bought your vehicle new—see their website at *camvap.ca*), small claims court (mediation is often a prerequisite to going to trial), and consumer mediation services set up by provincial and territorial governments.

Getting outside help

Don't lose your case due to poor preparation. Ask government or independent consumer protection agencies to evaluate how well you're prepared before going to your first hearing. Also, use the Internet to ferret out additional facts and gather support (*www.lemonaidcars.com* is a good place to start).

On-line services/Internet/websites

America Online and CompuServe are two on-line service providers with active consumer forums that use experts to answer consumer queries and to provide legal and technical advice. The Internet offers the same information using a worldwide database. If you or someone you know is able to create a website, you might consider using this site to attract attention to your plight and arm yourself for arbitration or court. You may wish to follow the example of some existing websites I've listed in Appendix I. A few of my favourites are Chrysler Paint Peeling, Neon Enthusiasts Page (engine head gaskets), and Ford Transmission Victims. I don't know why, but Ford seems to attract the most web-savvy complainers.

Classified ads

Use your local paper's classified section or the *Globe and Mail's* "National Personals" column to gather data from others who may have experienced a problem similar to your own. This alerts others to the potential problem, helps build a base for a class action or group meeting with the automaker, and puts pressure on the dealer or manufacturer to settle. Sometimes the paper's news desk will assign someone to cover your story after your ad is published.

Federal and provincial consumer affairs

The wind left the sails of the consumer movement over a decade ago, leaving provincial consumer affairs offices understaffed and unsupported by the government. This has created a passive mindset among many staffers, who are tired of getting their heads kicked in by businesses and budget-cutters.

Consumer affairs offices can still help with investigation, mediation, and some litigation. Strong and effective consumer protection legislation has been left standing in most of the provinces, and resourceful consumers can use these laws in conjunction with media coverage to prod provincial consumer affairs offices into action. Furthermore, provincial bureaucrats aren't as well shielded from criticism as their federal counterparts. A call to your MPP or MLA, or to their executive assistant, can often get things rolling.

Federal consumer protection is a government-created PR myth. Don't expect the staffers in the reorganized Office of Consumer Affairs to be very helpful—they've been de-fanged and de-gummed through budget cuts and a succession of ineffective ministers. Although the beefed-up Competition Act has some bite with regards to misleading advertising and a number of other illegal business practices, the federal government has downplayed the act's usefulness to consumer groups and individual consumers.

Nevertheless, when used creatively, the revised Competition Act can be a powerful tool for forcing a formal government investigation and prosecution, attracting media attention, and obtaining individual and collective compensation. The act costs little to use. Five years ago, the Ontario-based Consumer Action Group brought together six consumer complainants and successfully used the Competition Act to file a "six-citizen declaration" against a number of auto leasing companies that had allegedly misled the public by not disclosing various hidden fees. When word leaked out that the government was investigating auto leasing (it had no choice—the act requires a formal inquiry), the major automakers and dealer organizations started scrambling over themselves to find ways to disclose the extra charges without losing customers.

Safety and Performance Defects: Step-by-Step Resolution

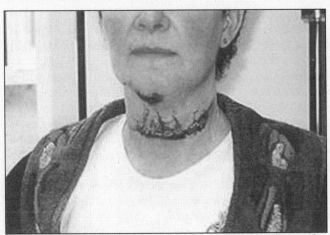

This woman had just negotiated a traffic circle on a busy, single-lane road when her airbag exploded. "I was doing about 60 km/h, no more. The road was straight and I hadn't hit anything."

Sudden acceleration, chronic stalling, and ABS and airbag failures

Incidents of sudden acceleration or chronic stalling are difficult to diagnose and are treated quite differently by federal safety agencies. Sudden acceleration is considered a safety-related problem—stalling isn't. Never mind that a vehicle's sudden loss of power on a busy highway puts everyone's life a risk. The same problem exists with engine and transmission powertrain failures, which are only occasionally considered to be safety related. ABS and airbag failures are universally considered to be life-threatening defects. If your vehicle manifests any of these conditions, here's what you need to do:

1. Get independent witnesses that the problem exists (mechanic or passengers). Notify the dealer/manufacturer by fax, email, or registered letter that you consider the problem to be a factory-induced, safety-related defect. Make sure you address your correspondence to the manufacturer's product liability or legal affairs department. At the dealership's service bay, make sure that every work order clearly states the problem as well as the number of previous attempts to fix it. (This should result in you having a few complaint letters and a handful of work orders, confirming that this is an ongoing deficiency.) If the dealer won't give you a copy of the work order because the work is a warranty claim, ask for a copy of the order number "in case your estate wishes to file a claim, pursuant to an accident." (This will get the service manager's attention.) Leaving this kind of "paper trail" is crucial for any claim you may have later on because it shows your fear and persistence, and clearly indicates that the dealer and manufacturer had ample time to correct the defect. In California, for example, the state's recently revamped Lemon Law requires that car owners clearly show they made two attempts to have a safety defect corrected (other states require three or four attempts) before the court will grant a refund, order the car taken back, or impose punitive damages.

2. Note on the work order that you expect the problem to be diagnosed and corrected under the emissions warranty or a "goodwill" program. It also wouldn't hurt to add the phrase on the work order or in your claim letters that any deaths, injuries, or damage caused by the defect will be the dealer's and manufacturer's responsibility since this work order (or letter, fax, or email) constitutes you putting them on "formal notice."

3. If the dealer does the necessary repairs at little or no cost to you, send a follow-up confirmation that you appreciate the assistance. Also, emphasize that you'll be back if the problem reappears, even if the warranty has expired, because the repair renews your warranty rights applicable to that defect. In other words, the warranty clock is set back to its original position. Understand that you won't likely get a copy of the repair bill, either, because dealers don't like to admit that there was a serious defect present. Keep in mind, however, that you can get your complete vehicle file from the dealer and manufacturer by issuing a subpoena

(cost: about $25), if the case goes to small-claims or a higher court. This request has produced many out-of-court settlements when the internal documents show extensive work was carried out to correct the problem.

4. If the problem persists, send a letter, fax, or email to the dealer and manufacturer saying so, look for ALLDATA service bulletins to confirm your vehicle's defects are factory related, and call Transport Canada or NHTSA or log onto NHTSA's website to report the failure. Also, contact the Montreal-based APA, the Toronto Automobile Consumer Coalition, or the Center for Auto Safety in Washington, D.C., for a lawyer referral and an information sheet covering the problem. For tire complaints, also log onto the Strategic Safety website (see Appendix I).

5. Now come two crucial questions: repair the defect now or later; use the dealer or an independent? Generally it's smart to use an independent garage if you know the dealer isn't pushing for free corrective repairs from the manufacturer; weeks or months have passed without any resolution of your claim; the dealer keeps repeating it's a maintenance item; and you know an independent mechanic who will give you a detailed work order showing the defect is factory related and not due to poor maintenance. Don't mention that a court case may ensue, since this will scare the dickens out of your only independent witness. An added bonus is that the repair charges will be about half of what a dealer would demand. Incidentally, if the automaker later denies warranty "goodwill" because you used an independent repairer, use the argument that the defect's safety implications required emergency repairs, carried out by whomever could see you first.

6. Dashboard-mounted warning lights usually come on prior to airbags suddenly deploying, ABS brakes failing, or engine glitches causing the vehicle to stall out. (Sudden acceleration usually occurs without warning.) Automakers consider these lights to be critical safety warnings and generally advise drivers to *immediately* have the vehicle serviced to correct the problem (advice found in the owner's manual) when any of the above lights come on. This bolsters the argument that your life was threatened, emergency repairs were required, and your request for another vehicle or a complete refund isn't out of line.

7. Sudden acceleration can have multiple causes, isn't easy to duplicate, and is often blamed on the driver mistaking the accelerator for the brakes or failing to perform proper maintenance. Yet NHTSA data shows that with the 1992–2000 Explorer, for example, a faulty cruise control or PCV valve and poorly mounted pedals are the most likely causes of the Explorer's sudden acceleration. So how do you satisfy the burden of proof, showing the problem exists and is the automaker's responsibility? Use the legal doctrine called "the balance of probabilities" by eliminating all of the possible dodges the dealer or manufacturer may trot out. Show that proper maintenance has been carried out, you're a safe driver, and the incident occurs frequently and without warning.

8. If any of the above defects causes an accident, the airbag fails to deploy, or you're injured by its deployment, ask your insurance company to

have the vehicle towed to a neutral location and clearly state that neither the dealer nor automaker should touch the vehicle until your
insurance company and Transport Canada have completed their investigation. Also, get as many witnesses as possible and immediately go to
the hospital for a check-up, even if you're feeling okay. You may be
injured and not know it because the adrenalin coursing through your
veins is masking your injuries. Plus, a hospital exam will easily confirm
that your injuries are accident related, which is essential in court or for
future settlement negotiations.

9. Peruse NHTSA's on-line accident database to find reports of other accidents caused by the same failure.
10. Don't let your insurance company settle the case if you're sure the acci-
    dent was caused by a mechanical failure. Even if an engineering
    analysis fails to directly implicate the manufacturer or dealer, you can
    always plead the aforementioned balance of probabilities. If the insur-
    ance company settles, your insurance premiums will probably be
    increased.

Defective tires
Tire companies are far easier to deal with than automobile manufacturers
because, under the legal doctrine of *res ipsa loquitor* (liability is shown by
the failure), tires aren't supposed to fail. It's for this reason that tire companies try to avoid liability by imputing blame to someone or something
else, like punctures, impact damage, overloading, over-inflating, or
under-inflating. If you have a premature tire failure, consider the 10
steps outlined previously, plus include the following:

1. Access NHTSA and Strategic Safety websites on the Internet (see
   Appendix I) or current data on which tires are failure prone and which
   companies are under investigation, conducting recalls, or carrying out
   "silent recalls."
2. Keep the tire. If the tiremaker says an analysis must be done, permit
   only a portion of the tire to be taken away.
3. Plead the balance of probabilities, using friends and family to refute the
   tire company's contention that you caused the failure.
4. Ask for damages that are adequate for the replacement of all the tires on
   your vehicle, including mounting costs.
5. Include in your damage claim any repairs needed to fix body damage
   caused by the tire's failure.

Paint and body defects
The following settlement advice applies mainly to paint defects, but you
can use these tips for any other vehicle defect that you believe is the
automaker's/dealer's responsibility. If you're not sure that the problem is
a factory-related deficiency or a maintenance item, have it checked out
by an independent garage or get a technical service bulletin summary for

your vehicle. The summary may include specific bulletins relating to the diagnosis, correction, and ordering of upgraded parts needed to fix your problem.

1. If you know your vehicle's paint problem is factory related, take your vehicle to the dealer and ask for a written, signed estimate. When you're handed the estimate, ask that the paint job be done for free under the manufacturer's "goodwill" program. (Ford's euphemism for this secret warranty is "Owner Notification Program" or "Owner Dialogue Program," GM's term is "Special Policy," and Chrysler simply calls it "Owner Satisfaction Notice" or "goodwill." Don't use the term "secret warranty" yet; you'll just make the dealer and automaker angry and evasive.)

2. Your request will probably be met with a refusal, an offer to repaint the vehicle for half the cost, or (if you're lucky) an agreement to repaint the vehicle free of charge. If you accept half-cost, make sure that it's based on the original estimate you have in hand, since some dealers jack up their estimates so that your 50 percent is really 100 percent of the true cost.

3. If the dealer/automaker has already refused your claim and the repair hasn't been done yet, get an additional estimate from an independent garage that shows the problem is factory related.

4. Again, if the repair has yet to be done, mail or fax a registered claim to the automaker (send a copy to the dealer), claiming the average of both estimates. If the repair has been done at your expense, mail or fax a registered claim with a copy of your bill. A sample letter/fax can be found on page 51.

5. If you don't receive a satisfactory response within a week, deposit a copy of the estimate or paid bill and claim letter/fax before the small claims court and await a trial date. This means that the automaker/dealer will have to appear, no lawyer is required, costs should be minimal (under $100), and a mediation hearing or trial will be scheduled in a few months, followed by a judgment a few weeks later (the time varies among different regions).

Things that you can do to help your case: collect photographs, maintenance work orders, previous work orders dealing with your problem, and technical service bulletins; and speak to an independent expert (the garage or body shop that did the estimate or repair is best, but you can also use a local teacher who teaches automotive repair).

Other situations

- If the vehicle has just been repainted but the dealer says that "goodwill" coverage was denied by the automaker, pay for the repair with a certified cheque and write "under protest" on the cheque. Remember, though, if the dealer does the repair, you won't have an independent expert who can affirm that the problem was factory related or that it was a result of premature wearout. Plus, the dealer can say that you or the environment caused the paint problem. In these cases, technical service bulletins can make or break your case.

- If the dealer/automaker offers a partial repair or refund, take it. Then sue for the rest. Remember, if a partial repair has been done under warranty, it counts as an admission of responsibility, no matter what "goodwill" euphemism is used. Also, the repaired component/body panel should be just as durable as if it were new. Hence, the clock starts ticking from the beginning until you reach the original warranty parameter—again, no matter what the dealer's repair warranty limit says.

- It's a lot easier to get the automaker to pay to replace a defective part than it is to be compensated for a missed day of work or a ruined vacation. Manufacturers hate to pay for consequential expenses, apart from towing bills, because they can't control the amount of the refund. Fortunately, Canadian courts have taken the position that all expenses (damages) flowing from a problem covered by a warranty or service bulletin are the manufacturer's/dealer's responsibility under negligence and product liability provisions found in provincial consumer protection statutes, common law jurisprudence, Quebec civil law, and federal consumer protection legislation. Nevertheless, don't risk a fair settlement for some outlandish claim of "emotional distress," "pain and suffering," etc. If you have invoices to prove actual consequential damages, then use them. If not, don't be greedy.

Very seldom do automakers contest these paint claims before small claims court, opting instead to settle once the court claim is bounced from their customer relations people to their legal affairs department. At that time, you'll probably be offered an out-of-court settlement for 50–75 percent of your claim.

Stand fast and make reference to the service bulletins you intend to subpoena in order to publicly contest in court the unfair nature of this "secret warranty" program. (Automaker lawyers cringe at the idea of trying to explain why consumers aren't made aware of these bulletins.) One hundred percent restitution will probably follow.

Three good examples of favourable paint judgments are *Shields v. General Motors of Canada, Bentley v. Dave Wheaton Pontiac Buick GMC Ltd and General Motors of Canada,* and, the most recent, *Maureen Frank v. General Motors of Canada Limited.*

Shields v. General Motors of Canada, No. 1398/96, Ontario Court (General Division), Oshawa Small Claims Court, 33 King Street West, Oshawa, Ontario L1H 1A1, July 24, 1997, Robert Zochodne, Deputy Judge. The owner of a 1991 Pontiac Grand Prix purchased the vehicle used with over 100,000 km on its odometer. Commencing in 1995, the paint began to bubble and then flake and eventually peel off. Deputy Judge Robert

Zochodne awarded the plaintiff $1,205.72 and struck down every one of GM's environmental/acid rain/UV rays arguments. Other important aspects of this 12-page judgment that GM did not appeal:

1. The judge admitted many of the technical service bulletins referred to in *Lemon-Aid* as proof of GM's negligence.
2. Although the vehicle had 156,000 km when the case went to court, GM still offered to pay 50 percent of the paint repairs if the plaintiff dropped his suit.
3. Deputy Judge Zochodne ruled that the failure to protect the paint from the damaging effects of UV rays is akin to engineering a car that won't start in cold weather. In essence, vehicles must be built to withstand the rigours of the environment.
4. Here's an interesting twist: the original warranty covered defects that were present at the time it was in effect. The judge, taking statements found in the GM technical service bulletins, ruled the UV problem was factory related, and therefore it existed during the warranty period and thereby represented a latent defect that appeared once the warranty expired.
5. The subsequent purchaser was not prevented from making the warranty claim, even though the warranty had long since expired from a time and mileage standpoint and he was the second owner.

Bentley v. Dave Wheaton Pontiac Buick GMC Ltd and General Motors of Canada, Victoria Registry No. 24779, British Columbia Small Claims Court, December 1, 1998, Judge Higinbotham. This small claims judgment builds upon the Ontario *Shields v. General Motors of Canada* decision and cites other jurisprudence as to how long paint should last on a house. If you're wondering why Ford and Chrysler haven't been hit by similar judgments, remember that they usually settle.

Maureen Frank v. General Motors of Canada Limited, No. SC#12 (2001), Saskatchewan Provincial Court, Saskatoon, Saskatchewan, October 17, 2001, Provincial Court Judge H. G. Dirauf.

On June 23, 1997, the Plaintiff bought a 1996 Chevrolet Corsica from a General Motors dealership. At the time the odometer showed 33,172 kilometres. The vehicle still had some factory warranty. The car had been a lease car and had no previous accidents.

During June of 2000, the Plaintiff noticed that some of the paint was peeling off from the car and she took it to a General Motors dealership in Saskatoon and to the General Motors dealership in North Battleford where she purchased the car. While there were some discussions with the GM dealership about the peeling paint, nothing came of it and the Plaintiff now brings this action claiming the cost of a new paint job.

During 1999, the Plaintiff was involved in a minor collision causing damage to the left rear door. This damage was repaired. During this repair some scratches to the left front door previously done by vandals were also repaired.

The Plaintiff's witness, Frank Nemeth, is a qualified auto body repairman with some 26 years of experience. He testified that the peeling paint was a factory defect and that it was necessary to completely strip the car and repaint it. He diagnosed the cause of the peeling paint as a separation of the primer surface or colour coat from the electrocoat primer. In his opinion no primer surfacer was applied at all. He testified that once the peeling starts, it will continue. He has seen this problem on General Motors vehicles. The defect is called delamination.

Mr Nemeth stated that a paint job should last at least 10 years. In my opinion most people in Saskatchewan grow up with cars and are familiar with cars. I think it is common knowledge that the original paint on cars normally lasts in excess of 15 years and that rust becomes a problem before the paint fails. In any event, paint peeling off, as it did on the Plaintiff's vehicle, is not common. I find that the paint on a new car put on by the factory should last at least 15 years.

General Motors acknowledge that the Plaintiff had a General Motors Warranty of 36 months or 60,000 kilometres, whichever comes first. The Plaintiff was not given a GM booklet at the time she bought the car. She knew of the 36 months but was unaware of the 60,000 kilometres. At the time the Plaintiff noticed the delamination, a service invoice D-2 shows that on June 18, 1999 the odometer showed 72,504 kilometres.

Invoice P-6 shows that on August 4, 2000, the odometer reading was 92,043 kilometres. It is therefore clear that in June 2000, when the Plaintiff noticed the delamination problem, her car had exceeded the 60,000 kilometres warranty limit. The warranty booklet was not placed into evidence and I do not have the benefit of the exact wording of the warranty. I do not know if the 60,000 kilometres limit applies to the whole car or only to the moving parts. On the evidence presented, I find the warranty coverage for the delamination has expired. However, the Consumer Protection Act also gives the Plaintiff a warranty that the paint is of acceptable quality and that it is durable for a reasonable period: Sections 48 (d), 48 (g), 50 (2).

It is clear from the evidence of Frank Nemeth (independent body shop manager) that the delamination is a factory defect. His evidence was not seriously challenged. I find that the factory paint should not suffer a delamination defect for at least 15 years and that this factory defect breached the warranty that the paint was of acceptable quality and was durable for a reasonable period of time.

I accept the testimony of Frank Nemeth that the whole car needs to be stripped and painted.

The Defendant did not call any witnesses. (I note section 51 (1) of the *Consumer Protection Act* with respect to the onus of proof).

Counsel for the defendant submitted that any award I should make should be reduced because of betterment. While betterment was discussed at trial, I am not persuaded that any award for damages should be reduced in this case. See *Scheeler v. C. M. Holdings Inc.* (1997) 183 Sask R (Q.B.) and *Nan v. Black Pine Manufacturing Ltd.* (1991) 5WWR172 (B.C.C.A.). I have reviewed *Pitch Snyder, Damages for Breach of Contract,* 2nd edition, pages 2-14.3 to 2-22 and read *Betterment Before Canadian Common Law Courts* by J. Berryman, (1993) 72 *Canadian Bar Review.*

It is clear that the onus to show and calculate any betterment is on the Defendant. He has not done so. In any event, I doubt that any betterment in this case would be significant.

The repair cost given by Mr. Nemeth of Superior Auto Body Ltd., Exhibit P-7 shows the repair cost (including minor dents) to be $3,679.90. I reduce the sum by $267.52 for the repair cost of the dents.

There will be judgment for the Plaintiff in the amount of $3,412.38 plus costs of $81.29.

Some of the important aspects of the *Frank* judgment are:

1. The judge accepted that the automaker was responsible, even though the car was bought used. The subsequent purchaser was not prevented from making the warranty claim, even though the warranty had long since expired from a time and mileage standpoint and she was the second owner.
2. The judge stressed that the provincial warranty can kick in anytime the automaker's warranty has expired or isn't applied.
3. By awarding full compensation to the plaintiff the judge didn't feel there was a significant "betterment" or improvement added to the car that would warrant reducing the amount of the award.
4. The judge decided that the paint delamination was a factory defect.
5. The judge also concluded that without this factory defect a paint job should last up to 15 years.
6. GM offered to pay $700 of the paint repairs if the plaintiff dropped the suit; the judge awarded five times that amount.
7. Maureen Frank won this case despite having to confront GM lawyer Ken Ready, a lawyer who has argued other paint cases for GM and Chrysler.

Going to Court

When to sue
If the seller you've been negotiating with agrees to make things right, give him or her a deadline and then have an independent garage check

the repairs. If no offer is made within 10 working days, file suit in court. Make the manufacturer a party to the lawsuit only if the original, unexpired warranty was transferred to you; your claim falls under the emissions warranty, a secret warranty extension, or a safety recall campaign; or there is extensive chassis rusting due to poor engineering.

Choosing the right court
You must decide what remedy to pursue; that is, whether you want a partial refund or a cancellation of the sale. To determine the refund amount, add the estimated cost of repairing existing mechanical defects to the cost of prior repairs. Don't exaggerate your losses or claim for repairs that are considered routine maintenance.

A suit for cancellation of sale involves practical problems. The court requires that the vehicle be "tendered" or taken back to the seller at the time the lawsuit is filed. This means you are without transportation for as long as the case continues, unless you purchase another vehicle in the interim. If you lose the case, you must then take back the old vehicle and pay storage fees. You could go from having no vehicle to having two, one of which is a clunker.

Generally, if the cost of repairs or the sales contract amount falls within the small claims court limit (discussed later), file the case there to keep costs to a minimum and get a speedy hearing. Small claims court judgments aren't easily appealed, lawyers aren't necessary, filing fees are minimal (about $125), and cases are usually heard within a few months.

> Mr. Edmonston, I emailed you earlier in the year seeking help on my small claims case against Ford. I'm happy to report that I won my case and received a $1,900 settlement check from Ford in the mail yesterday! As you may recall I have a 1991 Explorer that has a significant paint peel problem.
>
> I followed all the steps recommended by your web site—ultimately I ended up in small claims court. Ford had indicated in court documents that they were going to send a representative to the hearing, but nobody showed. The judge made a quick ruling in my favor and I was out the door. I didn't even get a chance to show the load of material I had brought to make my case.
>
> I'm spreading the word about your web site (and my victory) to all the paint peel victims I see! Thanks for all your help. Sincerely,
>
> Mark G.

If the damages exceed the small claims court limit and there's no way to reduce them, you'll have to go to a higher court—where costs quickly add up and delays of a few years or more are commonplace.

Small claims courts
There are small claims courts in most counties of every province, and you can make a claim in the county where the problem happened or

where the defendant lives and conducts business. The first step is to make sure that your claim doesn't exceed the dollar limit of the court. (The limits differ from province to province.) Then, you should go to the small claims court office and ask for a claim form. Instructions on how to fill it out accompany the form. Remember, you must identify the defendant correctly. It's a practice of some dishonest firms to change a company's name to escape liability; for example, it would be impossible to sue Joe's Garage (1999) if your contract is with Joe's Garage Inc. (1984).

At this point, it would be a smart idea to hire a lawyer or a paralegal for a brief walk-through of small claims procedures to ensure that you've prepared your case properly and that you know what objections will likely be raised by the other side. If you'd like a lawyer to do all the work for you, there are a number of inexpensive law firms around the country that are experienced in small claims litigation. In Toronto, some law offices charge a flat fee of $750 for the basic small claims lawsuit and trial.

Remember that you're entitled to bring to court any evidence relevant to your case, including written documents, such as a bill of sale or receipt, contract, or letter. If your car has developed severe rust problems, bring a photograph (signed and dated by the photographer) to court. You may also have witnesses testify in court. It's important to discuss a witness's testimony prior to the court date. If a witness can't attend the court date, he or she can write a report and sign it for representation in court. This situation usually applies to an expert witness, such as an independent mechanic who has evaluated your car's problems.

If you lose your case in spite of all your preparation and research, some small claims court statutes allow cases to be retried, at a nominal cost, in exceptional circumstances. If a new witness has come forward, additional evidence has been discovered, or key documents (that were previously not available) have become accessible, apply for a retrial. In Ontario, this little-known provision is Rule 18.4(1).B.

Key Court Decisions

The following Canadian and U.S. lawsuits and judgments cover typical problems that are likely to arise. Use them as leverage when negotiating a settlement or as a reference should your claim go to trial. Legal principles applying to Canadian and American law are similar; however, Quebec court decisions may be based on legal principles that don't apply outside that province.

Additional court judgments can be found in the legal reference section of your city's main public library or at a nearby university law library. Ask the librarian for help in choosing the legal phrases that best describe your claim.

Paint and Body Defects

When a new or used vehicle no longer falls within the limits of the warranty expressed by the manufacturer or dealer, it doesn't necessarily mean that the manufacturer can't be held liable for damages caused by defective design. As mentioned before, the manufacturer is always liable for the replacement or repair of defective parts if independent testimony can show that the part was incorrectly manufactured or designed. The existence of a secret warranty extension or technical service bulletins will usually help to prove that the part has a high failure rate. For example, in *Lowe v. Fairview Chrysler* (see page 71), technical service bulletins were instrumental in showing an Ontario small claims court judge that Chrysler had a history of automatic transmission failures since 1989!

In addition to replacing or repairing the part that failed, an automaker can also be held responsible for any damages arising from the part's failure. This means that loss of wages, supplementary transportation costs, and damages for personal inconvenience can be awarded.

Paint delamination/peeling

A defect that first appeared on Ford sport-utilities, vans, and pickups in the '80s, paint delamination occurs when the top coat of paint separates from the primer coat or turns a chalky colour, mostly along horizontal surfaces and often as a result of intense sunlight. When the paint peels, the entire vehicle must be repainted after a new primer resurfacer has been added. For some vehicles, the labour alone can run about 20 hours, at a cost of $75 an hour.

The same paint problem affects mostly 1986–97 Chrysler, Ford, and GM vehicles equally; however, each company has responded differently to owners' requests for compensation. To help you prepare the best arguments for negotiations or court, each automaker is profiled separately, with an analysis of the problem and website references, as well as references to lawsuits, judgments, or technical service bulletins that will help your claim.

Chrysler

Chrysler's paint deficiencies include paint delamination, cracking, and fading between the third and fifth year of ownership. Chrysler service bulletin number 23-11-90, "Base/Clearcoat Paint Damage," issued September 10, 1990, can serve as a guide for paint claims. It contains a number of illustrations relating to the kinds of paint problems that Chrysler will repair under its base warranty on all of its vehicles, and puts Chrysler on record as accepting so-called environmental paint damage. That bulletin and other helpful documents can be downloaded at *www.wam.umd.edu/~gluckman/Chrysler.*

A class action lawsuit filed in the state of Washington seeks damages for all American Chrysler owners who have owned or leased paint-delaminated 1986–97 models (see *peelingpaint.homestead.com/cause.html*).

The suit, *Schurk, Chanes, Jansen, and Ricker v. Chrysler*, No. 97-2-04113-9-SEA, was filed in the Superior Court of King County, Washington, on October 2, 1997. (You can contact Steve Berman or Clyde Platt with the Seattle, Washington, law firm of Hagens and Berman at 206-623-7292.)

The 29-page Statement of Claim uses many photos, technical service bulletins, and memos to show that Chrysler engaged in

> unlawful, unfair, and fraudulent business practices and unfair competition by treating different members of the class differently with respect to repairs it agrees to perform as "goodwill gestures," and by effecting partial repairs that do not address the true nature and extent of the delamination defect.

Ford

Faced with an estimated 13 percent failure rate of its painting process, Ford repainted its delaminated 1983–93 cars, minivans, vans, F-Series trucks, Explorers, Rangers, and Broncos free of charge for five years under a secret "Owner Dialogue Program." Ford whistleblowers say the company discontinued the program in January 1995 because it was proving to be too costly. Nevertheless, owners of 6- to 7-year-old cars who cry foul and threaten small claims action are still routinely given initial offers of 50 percent compensation, and eventually complete refunds if they press further.

In your negotiations with Ford, be sure to refer to Ford's admission of the delamination problem found in Ford's technical service bulletins (see the "Secret Warranties" section at *www.lemonaidcars.com*) and in the Washington Chrysler class action. Ford hasn't been a party to many lawsuits, as it prefers to settle before cases come to trial. You can get the latest information and internal documents relating to Ford's secret warranty for repainting by logging on to the following site set up by dissatisfied Ford owners: *www.ihs2000.com/~peel*.

General Motors

The technical service bulletin that GM put out several years ago (see the "Jurisprudence" section at *www.lemonaidcars.com*) guides dealers in determining whether paint delamination is a factory defect or is due to external causes like acid rain, stone chips, etc. Pay particular attention to GM's explanation of the cause of the delamination problem. In effect, the automaker admits that it didn't apply sufficient primer to protect the clearcoat from ultraviolet light. Also, look at the masking-tape test GM recommends in its "Problem Identification" section to diagnose clearcoat delamination; it's the same test used by Ford and Chrysler. Another helpful site for the GM paint delamination problem is *www.geocities.com/ihategm*.

Before settling your paint claim with GM or any other automaker, download the latest information from dissatisfied customers who've banded together and set up their own self-help websites. Follow the links at *www.lemonaidcars.com*.

Other paint/rust cases

Martin v. Honda Canada Inc., March 17, 1986, Ontario Small Claims Court (Scarborough), Judge Sigurdson. The original owner of a 1981 Honda Civic sought compensation for the premature "bubbling, pitting, cracking of the paint and rusting of the Civic after five years of owner-ship." Judge Sigurdson agreed and ordered Honda to pay the owner $1,163.95.

Thauberger v. Simon Fraser Sales and Mazda Motors, 3 B.C.L.R., 193. This Mazda owner sued for damages caused by the premature rusting of his 1977 Mazda GLC. The court awarded him $1,000. Thauberger had previously sued General Motors for a prematurely rusted Blazer truck and was also awarded $1,000 in the same court. Both judges ruled that the defects could not be excluded from the automaker's express warranty or from the implied warranty granted by ss. 20, 20(b) of the B.C. Sale of Goods Act.

Whittaker v. Ford Motor Company (1979), 24 O.R. (2d), 344. A new Ford developed serious corrosion problems in spite of having been rustproofed by the dealer. The court ruled that the dealer, not Ford, was liable for the damage for having sold the rustproofing product at the time of purchase. This is an important judgment to use when a rustproofer or paint protector goes out of business or refuses to pay a claim, since the decision holds the dealer jointly responsible.

See also:
- *Danson v. Chateau Ford* (1976) C.P., Quebec Small Claims Court, No. 32-00001898-757, Judge Lande
- *Doyle v. Vital Automotive Systems,* May 16, 1977, Ontario Small Claims Court (Toronto), Judge Turner
- *Lacroix v. Ford,* April 1980, Ontario Small Claims Court (Toronto), Judge Tierney
- *Marinovich v. Riverside Chrysler,* April 1, 1987, District Court of Ontario, No. 1030/85, Judge Stortini

Implied Warranty

Dufour v. Ford Canada Ltd., April 10, 2001, Quebec Small Claims Court (Hull), No. 550-32-008335-009, Justice P. Chevalier. Ford was forced to reimburse the cost of engine head gasket repairs carried out on a 1996 Windstar 3.8L engine—a vehicle not covered by the automaker's Owner Notification Program, which cut off assistance after the '95 model year. Use this as a guide for any complaint relating to premature engine failure and cite the judgment in your claim.

COUR DU QUÉBEC
Division petites créances

QUÉBEC
DISTRICT DE HULL

NO: 550-32-008335-009

Hull, le 10 avril 2001

SOUS LA PRESIDENCE DE:
L'HONORABLE PIERRE
CHEVALIER
Juge de la Cour du Québec

BASTIEN DUFOUR
Partie requérante,
-c.-
FORD DU CANADA LTÉE, 7800,
route Transcanadienne à Pointe-
Claire (Québec) H9H 1C6
Partie intimée

JUGEMENT

Les parties essentielles de la requête se lisent comme suit :

I am hereby claiming from Ford Canada expenses and collateral expenses incurred for the repair of the 3.8 litter engine of a Ford Windstar GL 1996, VIN 2FMDA5147TBA95586.

The said engine had to have the head gasket and thermostat replaced on 02 June 2000, after a total of 118,892 kms indicated on the vehicle odometer. This repair was deemed necessary by my hometown Ford dealership (Mont-Bleu Ford in Gatineau, Que.) after I observed inadequate performance of the interior heating system and abnormal engine coolant temperature indications, and after a leak down test performed by the Mont-Bleu Ford dealership.

I consider such a defect to be abnormal as components such as an engine should have a life expectancy of at least 160,000 kms of 7 years without major repairs such as head gasket repair or replacement.

2

I have enclosed a copy of my bill showing that this problem is factory related and has cost $1364.35 to correct; this amount includes the cost for the engine head gasket repair and appropriate provincial and federal sales taxes

L'ensemble de la preuve satisfait le Tribunal par prépondérance de preuve que la détérioration impliquée est survenue prématurément par rapport à un bien identique et que cette détérioration n'est pas due à un défaut d'entretien.

L'article 1729 C.c.Q. stipule qu'en cas de vente par un vendeur professionnel, l'existence d'un vice au moment de la vente est présumée, lorsque la détérioration du bien survient prématurément par rapport à des biens identiques. De plus, les intimés n'ont pas repoussé la présomption en établissant que le défaut serait dû à une mauvaise utilisation du bien par l'acheteur. Selon l'art. 1730, le fabricant est soumis à cette même garantie.

Vu les articles 1729 et 1730 du Code civile du Québec, le Tribunal fait droit à la réclamation et condamne la partie intimée à payer à la partie requérante la somme de 1 364,35 $ avec intérêts au taux légal de 5% depuis la requête, soit le 19 septembre 2000 et les frais de 72 $.

PIERRE CHEVALIER
Juge de la Cour du Québec

Fissel v. Ideal Auto Sales Ltd. (1991), 91 Sask. R. 266. Shortly after the vehicle was purchased, the car's motor seized and the dealer refused to replace it, even though the car was returned on several occasions. The court ruled that the dealer had breached the statutory warranties in s. 11 (4) and (7) of the Consumer Products Warranties Act. The purchasers were entitled to cancel the sale and recover the full purchase price.

Friskin v. Chevrolet Oldsmobile, 72 D.L.R. (3d), 289. A Manitoba used-car buyer asked that his contract be cancelled because of a chronic stalling problem. The garage owner did his best to correct it. Despite the seller's good intentions, the Manitoba Consumer Protection Act allowed for cancellation.

Graves v. C&R Motors Ltd., April 8, 1980, British Columbia County Court, Judge Skipp. The plaintiff bought a used car on the condition that certain deficiencies be remedied. They never were, and he was promised a refund, but it never arrived. The plaintiff brought suit, claiming that the dealer's deceptive activities violated the provincial Trade Practices Act. The court agreed, concluding that a deceptive act that occurs before, during, or after the transaction can lead to the cancellation of the contract.

Hachey v. Galbraith Equipment Company (1991), 33 M.V.R. (2d) 242. The plaintiff bought a used truck from the dealer to use in hauling gravel. Shortly thereafter, the steering failed. The plaintiff's suit was successful because expert testimony showed that the truck wasn't roadworthy. The dealer was found liable for damages for being in breach of the implied condition of fitness for the purpose for which the truck was purchased, as set out in s. 15 (a) of the New Brunswick Sale of Goods Act.

Henzel v. Brussels Motors (1973), 1 O.R., 339 (C.C.). The dealer sold this used car while brandishing a copy of the mechanical fitness certificate as proof that the car was in good shape. The plaintiff was awarded his money back because the court held the certificate to be a warranty that was breached by the car's subsequent defects.

Johnston v. Bodasing Corporation Limited, February 23, 1983, Ontario County Court (Bruce), No. 15/11/83, Judge McKay. The plaintiff bought a used 1979 Buick Riviera, for $8,500, that was represented as being "reliable." Two weeks after purchase, the motor self-destructed. Judge McKay awarded the plaintiff $2,318 as compensation to fix the Riviera's defects.

One feature of this particular decision is that the trial judge found the Sale of Goods Act applied, notwithstanding the fact that the vendor used a standard contract that said there were no warranties or representations. The judge also accepted the decision in *Kendal v. Lillico* (1969), 2 Appeal Cases, 31, which indicates that the Sale of Goods Act covers not only defects that the seller ought to have detected, but also latent defects that even his utmost skill and judgment could not have detected. This places a very heavy onus on the vendor and it should prove useful in actions of this type in other common-law provinces with laws similar to Ontario's Sale of Goods Act.

Kelly v. Mack Canada, 53 D.L.R. (4th), 476. Kelly bought two trucks from Mack Sales. The first, a used White Freightliner tractor and trailer, was purchased for $29,742. It cost him over $12,000 in repairs during the first five months, and another $9,000 was estimated for future engine repairs. Mack Sales convinced Kelly to trade in the old truck for a new Mack truck. Kelly did this, but shortly thereafter, the new truck had similar problems. Kelly sued for the return of all his money, arguing that the two transactions were really one.

The Ontario Court of Appeal agreed and awarded Kelly a complete refund. It stated, "There was such a congeries of defects that there had been a breach of the implied conditions set out in the Sale of Goods Act."

Although Mack Sales argued that the contract contained a clause excluding any implied warranties, the court determined that the breach was of such magnitude that the dealer could not rely upon that clause. The dealer then argued that since the client used the trucks, the depreciation of both should be taken into account in reducing the award. This was refused on the grounds that the plaintiff never had the product he bargained for and in no way did he profit from the transaction. The court also awarded Kelly compensation for loss of income while the trucks were being repaired, as well as the interest on all of the money tied up in both transactions from the time of purchase until final judgment.

Kravitz v. General Motors, January 1979, Supreme Court of Canada, I.R.C.S., No. 393. This owner of a new Oldsmobile was never able to have it properly repaired under warranty. When the warranty period was over, General Motors and the dealer refused to do further free work or to give him another vehicle. The presiding judge awarded the car owner damages and a refund of the purchase price. This Quebec precedent is based on articles 1522–1530 of the Quebec Civil Code (hidden defects), but it applies in common-law provinces as well. The Supreme Court ruled that both the dealer and the manufacturer can be held jointly or separately responsible and that the manufacturer's warranty does not negate the implied legal warranty of fitness.

Morrison v. Hillside Motors (1973) Ltd. (1981), 35 Nfld. & P.E.I.R. 361. A used car advertised to be in A-1 condition and carrying a 50/50 warranty developed a number of problems. The court decided that the purchaser should be partially compensated because of the ad's claim. In deciding how much compensation to award, the presiding judge considered the warranty's wording, the amount paid for the vehicle, the year of the vehicle, its average life, the type of defect that occurred, and how long the purchaser had use of the vehicle before its defects became evident. Although this judgment was rendered in Newfoundland, judges throughout Canada have used a similar approach for more than a decade.

Neilson v. Maclin Motors, 71 D.L.R. (3d), 744. The plaintiff bought a used truck on the strength of the seller's allegations that the motor had been rebuilt and that it had 210 hp. The engine failed. The judge awarded damages and cancelled the contract because the motor had not been rebuilt, it did not have 210 hp, and the transmission was defective.

Parent v. Le Grand Trianon and Ford Credit (1982), C.P., 194, Judge Bertrand Gagnon. Nineteen months after paying $3,300 for a used 1974 LTD, the plaintiff sued the Ford dealer for his money back because the car was prematurely rusted out. The dealer replied that rust was normal, there was no warranty, and the claim was too late. The court held that the garage was still responsible, for the following reasons:

- When purchased, the car had been repainted by the dealer to camouflage rust and perforations.
- During the 19 months, the plaintiff and the dealer continued to explore ways the rusting could be stopped.
- It wasn't until just before the lawsuit that the plaintiff found out how bad the rust was.

- Ford and its dealers admitted they knew that many of their 1970–74 cars had serious premature corrosion problems.

The plaintiff was awarded $1,500 for the cost of rust repairs.

"As is" clauses

Since 1907, Canadian courts have ruled that a seller can't exclude the implied warranty as to fitness by including such phrases as "there are no other warranties or guarantees, promises, or agreements than those contained herein" (*Sawyer-Massey Co. v. Thibault* (1907), 5 W.L.R. 241).

Adams v. J&D's Used Cars Ltd. (1983), 26 Sask. R. 40 (Q.B.). Shortly after purchase, the engine and transmission failed. The court ruled that the inclusion of "as is" in the sales contract had no legal effect. The implied warranty set out in Saskatchewan's Consumer Products Warranties Act was breached by the dealer. The sale was cancelled and all monies were refunded.

Repairs

Babcock v. Servacar (1970), 1 O.R., No. 125. A motorist took a car he was planning to buy to an Ottawa Esso Diagnostic Clinic to determine its condition. He did the recommended repairs, and then had serious problems with the car while on vacation. The judge ruled that the clinic would have to pay for the repairs and reimburse the diagnostic cost as well. The court held that the garage's advertising claims gave rise to a contractual warranty that promised to root out the car's defects before it was purchased.

Davies v. Alberta Motor Association, August 13, 1991, Alberta Provincial Court, Civil Division, No. P9090106097, Judge Moore. The plaintiff had a used 1985 Nissan Pulsar NX checked out by the AMA's Vehicle Inspection Service prior to buying it. The car passed with flying colours. A month later, the clutch was replaced and numerous electrical problems ensued. At that time, another garage discovered that the car had been involved in a major accident, had a bent frame and a leaking radiator, and was unsafe to drive. The court awarded the plaintiff $1,578.40 plus three years of interest. The judge held that the AMA set itself out as an expert and should have spotted the car's defects. The AMA's defence—that it was not responsible for errors—was thrown out. The court held that a disclaimer clause could not protect the association from a fundamental breach of contract.

Secret Warranties

It's common practice for manufacturers to secretly extend their warranties to cover components with a high failure rate. Customers who complain vigorously get extended warranty compensation in the form of "goodwill" adjustments.

François Chong v. Marine Drive Imported Cars Ltd. and Honda Canada Inc., May 17, 1994, British Columbia Provincial Small Claims Court, No. 92-06760, Judge C.L. Bagnall. Mr. Chong was the first owner of a 1983 Honda Accord with 134,000 km on the odometer. He had seven engine camshafts replaced—four under Honda "goodwill" programs, one where he paid part of the repairs, and one via a small claims court judgment. (Please note that the Honda no longer has serious engine problems.)

In his ruling, Judge Bagnall agreed with Chong and ordered Honda and the dealer to each pay half of the $835.81 repair bill, for the following reasons:

> The defendants assert that the warranty which was part of the contract for purchase of the car encompassed the entirety of their obligation to the claimant, and that it expired in February 1985. The replacements of the camshaft after that date were paid for wholly or in part by Honda as a "goodwill gesture." The time has come for these gestures to cease, according to the witness for Honda. As well, he pointed out to me that the most recent replacement of the camshaft was paid for by Honda and that, therefore, the work would not be covered by Honda's usual warranty of twelve months from date of repair. Mr. Wall, who testified for Honda, told me there was no question that this situation with Mr. Chong's engine was an unusual state of affairs. He said that a camshaft properly maintained can last anywhere from 24,000–500,000 km. He could not offer any suggestion as to why the car keeps having this problem.
>
> The claimant has convinced me that the problems he is having with rapid breakdown of camshafts in his car is due to a defect, which was present in the engine at the time that he purchased the car. The problem first arose during the warranty period and in my view has never been properly identified nor repaired.

Automatic transmission failures (Chrysler)

Lowe v. Fairview Chrysler-Dodge Limited and Chrysler Canada Limited, May 14, 1996, Ontario Court (General Division), Burlington Small Claims Court, No. 1224/95. The following judgment, in the plaintiff's favour, raises important legal principles relative to Chrysler:

- Technical dealer service bulletins are admissible in court to prove that a problem exists and certain parts should be checked out.
- If a problem is reported prior to a warranty's expiration, warranty coverage for the problematic component(s) is automatically carried over after the warranty ends.
- It's not up to the car owner to tell the dealer/automaker what the specific problem is.

- Repairs carried out by an independent garage can be refunded if the dealer/automaker unfairly refuses to apply the warranty.
- The dealer/automaker cannot dispute the cost of the independent repair if they fail to cross-examine the independent repairer.
- Auto owners can ask for and win compensation for their inconvenience, which in this judgment amounted to $150.

Court awards quickly add up. Although the plaintiff was given $1,985.94, with the addition of court costs and prejudgment interest, plus costs of inconvenience fixed at $150, the final award amounted to $2,266.04.

False Advertising

MacDonald v. Equilease Co. Ltd., January 18, 1979, Ontario Supreme Court, Judge O'Driscoll. The plaintiff leased a truck that was misrepresented as having an axle stronger than it really was. The court awarded the plaintiff damages for repairs and set aside the lease.

Seich v. Festival Ford Sales Ltd. (1978), 6 Alta. L.R. (2nd), No. 262. The plaintiff bought a used truck from the defendant after being assured that it had a new motor and transmission. It didn't, and the court awarded the plaintiff $6,400.

Damages (Punitive)

Punitive damages (also known as exemplary damages) allow the plaintiff to get compensation that exceeds his or her losses, as a deterrent to those who carry out dishonest or negligent practices. These kinds of judgments, common in the U.S., sometimes reach hundreds of millions of dollars.

Punitive damages are rarely awarded in Canadian courts and are almost never used against automakers. When they are given out, it's usually for sums less than $100,000. The most recent award, in *Prebushewski v. Dodge City Auto (1985) Ltd. and Chrysler Canada Ltd.* (2001 SKQB 537; Q.B. No. 1215) was for $25,000 and was handed down December 6, 2001, in Saskatoon, Saskatchewan. It followed testimony from Chrysler's expert witness that the company was aware of many cases where daytime running lights shorted and caused 1996 Ram pickups to catch fire. The plaintiff's truck had burned to the ground and Chrysler refused the owner's claim, in spite of its knowledge that fires were commonplace.

Angered by Chrysler's stonewalling, Justice Rothery rendered the following judgment:

> While the defendants called no evidence at the trial, the admissions of Eric Durance on behalf of Chrysler clearly show that not only did

Chrysler know about the problems of the defective daytime running light modules, it did not advise the plaintiff of this. It simply chose to ignore the plaintiff's requests for compensation and told her to seek recovery from her insurance company. Chrysler had replaced thousands of these modules since 1988. But it had also made a business decision to neither advise its customers of the problem nor to recall the vehicles to replace the modules. While the cost would have been about $250 to replace each module, there were at least one million customers. Chrysler was not prepared to spend $250 million even though it knew what the defective module might do.

Mr. Durance admits that there is no other explanation for the fire in the plaintiff's truck. There is no indication that the plaintiff did anything to the truck to cause the fire. Jim Wilkins, the proper officer for Dodge, admitted that Dodge has done nothing to find out why the truck burned. Mr. Wilkins admits that Dodge has done nothing to compensate the plaintiff.

Counsel for the defendants argues that this matter had to be resolved by litigation because the plaintiff and the defendants simply had a difference of opinion on whether the plaintiff should be compensated by the defendants. Had the defendants some dispute as to the cause of the fire, that may have been sufficient to prove that they had not wilfully violated this Part of the Act. They did not. They knew about the defective daytime running light module. They did nothing to replace the burned truck for the plaintiff. They offered the plaintiff no compensation for her loss. Counsels' position that the definition of the return of the purchase price is an arguable point is not sufficient to negate the defendants' violation of this Part of the Act. I find the violation of the defendants to be willful. Thus, I find that exemplary damages are appropriate on the facts of this case.

In this case, the quantum ought to be sufficiently high as to correct the defendants' behaviour. In particular, Chrysler's corporate policy to place profits ahead of the potential danger to its customer's safety and personal property must be punished. And when such corporate policy includes a refusal to comply with the provisions of the Act and a refusal to provide any relief to the plaintiff, I find an award of $25,000 for exemplary damages to be appropriate. I therefore order Chrysler and Dodge City to pay:

1. Damages in the sum of $41,969.83;
2. Exemplary damages in the sum of $25,000;
3. Party and party costs.

Vlchek v. Koshel (1988), 44 C.C.L.T. 314, B.C.S.C., No. B842974. The plaintiff was seriously injured when she was thrown from a Honda all-terrain cycle on which she had been riding as a passenger. The Court allowed for punitive damages because the manufacturer was well aware of the injuries likely to be caused by the cycle. Specifically, the Court ruled that there is no firm and inflexible principle of law stipulating that punitive or exemplary damages must be denied unless the defendant's acts are specifically directed against the plaintiff. The Court may apply punitive damages "where the defendant's conduct has been indiscriminate of focus, but reckless or malicious in its character. Intent to injure the plaintiff need not be present, so long as intent to do the injurious act can be shown."

See also:
- *Granek v. Reiter*, Ont. Ct. (Gen. Div.), No. 35/741.
- *Morrison v. Sharp*, Ont. Ct. (Gen. Div.), No. 43/548.
- *Schryvers v. Richport Ford Sales*, May 18, 1993, B.C.S.C., No. C917060, Judge Tysoe.
- *Varleg v. Angeloni*, B.C.S.C., No. 41/301.

Provincial business practices acts cover false, misleading, or deceptive representations, and allow for punitive damages should the unfair practice toward the consumer amount to an unconscionable representation. (See C.E.D. (3d) s. 76, pp. 140–45.) "Unconscionable" is defined as "where the consumer is not reasonably able to protect his or her interest because of physical infirmity, ignorance, illiteracy, or inability to understand the language of an agreement or similar factors."

- Exemplary damages are justified where compensatory damages are insufficient to deter and punish. See *Walker et al. v. CFTO Ltd. et al.* (1978), 59 O.R. (2nd), No. 104 (Ont. C.A.).
- Exemplary damages can be awarded in cases where the defendant's conduct was "cavalier." See *Ronald Elwyn Lister Ltd. et al. v. Dayton Tire Canada Ltd.* (1985), 52 O.R. (2nd), No. 89 (Ont. C.A.).
- The primary purpose of exemplary damages is to prevent the defendant and all others from doing similar wrongs. See *Fleming v. Spracklin* (1921).
- Disregard of the public's interest, lack of preventive measures, and a callous attitude all merit exemplary damages. See *Coughlin v. Kuntz* (1989), 2 C.C.L.T. (2nd) (B.C.C.A.).
- Punitive damages can be awarded for mental distress. See *Ribeiro v. Canadian Imperial Bank of Commerce* (1992), Ontario Reports 13 (3rd) and *Brown v. Waterloo Regional Board of Comissioners of Police* (1992), 37 O.R. (2nd).

PART THREE

Car and Minivan Ratings

3

It's *So* Hard to Forget the Pony and Stellar

"Hyundai will be showing up on consumer consideration lists in greater and greater numbers because each time they do a new product it's better than the one before. And not all manufacturers can make that claim. If you squint real hard, you can get a feel for what it was like when Honda cars first got their first serious buzz 25 years ago."

Autoextremist.com
Issue 128, December 12, 2001

Finding a Good Vehicle

A good used car or minivan must first meet your everyday driving needs as determined by taking it out—not merely for a spin, but for at least overnight—so you can drive it as you normally would. Secondly, the vehicle must be crashworthy and reasonably durable (at least 10 years), cost no more than $700 to $800 a year to maintain, and provide you with a fair resale value a few years down the road. Parts should be reasonably priced and easily available, and servicing shouldn't be given with a shrug or a snarl.

Definitions of Terms

Ratings
This edition makes use of owner complaints, confidential technical service bulletins (TSBs), and test-drives to expose serious factory-related defects, design deficiencies, or servicing glitches. It should be noted that customer complaints alone do not make a scientific sampling, and that's why they are used in conjunction with other sources of information. On the other hand, owner complaints combined with inside information found in TSBs are a good starting point to cut through the automakers' hyperbole and get a glimpse of reality. Since ratings can change dramatically from one year to the next, depending upon the manufacturers' warranty performance, you will want to keep abreast of these changes between editions by logging onto *www.lemonaidcars.com*.

Models are rated on a scale from Recommended to Not Recommended, with the most recent year's rating reflected by the number of stars beside the vehicle's name. *Recommended* vehicles are those that will give their owners relatively trouble-free service. This doesn't mean that only high-quality, luxury Japanese models get a Recommended rating. In fact, Ford

Escorts, Hyundai Elantras, and GM minivans get high marks because they are easy to find, fairly reliable, *and* reasonably priced—not the case with many overpriced Hondas and Toyotas.

Ford's post-'91 Escort/Tracer is a Recommended buy because it is both reliable and reasonably priced. Too bad it was dropped for 2001.

Vehicles that are given an *Above Average* or *Average* rating are good second choices if a Recommended vehicle isn't your first choice or is too expensive. A *Below Average* vehicle will likely be troublesome; however, a low price and reasonably priced servicing may make it an acceptable buy. Vehicles given a *Not Recommended* rating are best avoided, no matter how low the price. They may be attractively styled and loaded with convenience features (the Ford Windstar and Chrysler minivans, for example), but they're likely to suffer from a variety of durability and performance problems that will make them expensive and frustrating to own. Sometimes, however, a Not Recommended model will improve over several model years and garner a better rating (as the Ford Aerostar and GM Astro and Safari minivans have done).

Incidentally, for those owners who wonder how I can stop recommending model years I once recommended, let me be clear: as vehicles age, their ratings always change to reflect new information from owners, service bulletins, etc., relating to durability and the automaker's warranty performance. Unlike Enron and Nortel stock analysts, I warn shoppers of changes in subsequent editions of *Lemon-Aid* or in updates to my website, *www.lemonaidcars.com*. Additionally, throughout the year, I lobby automakers to compensate out-of-warranty owners through formal "goodwill" programs or on an individual case-by-case basis. This way, I help my readers to avoid a bad purchase and provide an additional means to get compensation if that purchase has already been made.

Some enterprising readers of *Lemon-Aid* use the ratings as a buying opportunity. Dave Ingram, a friend and well-known BC broadcaster, uses my Not Recommended list as a shopping guide for cheap vehicles: he buys them up at depressed prices and refurbishes them, using garages that offer lifetime warranties on major components that I rate as weak. He's done that with several used Cadillacs and Jeep Wagoneers and seems happy with the system. Personally, I don't think he would have done so well without the complicity of his independent garage contacts in North Vancouver, like Gerry Graca at Gerry's Auto Repairs and Sales (604-987-2515) and Dave Daye at Fountain Tire (604-985-9131), two experts who bail him out whenever he gets in a bit over his head.

Reliability data is compiled from a number of sources: confidential technical service bulletins; owner complaints sent to the author each year by *Lemon-Aid* readers; vehicle-owners' comments posted on the Internet; and survey reports and tests done by auto associations, consumer groups, and government organizations. Some auto columnists feel this isn't a scientific sampling, and they're quite right. Nevertheless, it seems to have been right on the mark over the past 30 years. Not all vehicles sold during the last decade are profiled; those that are newer to the market or relatively rare may receive only an abbreviated mention until sufficient owner or service bulletin information becomes available. Best and worst buys for each model category (e.g., "Small" or "Medium") are listed in a summary at the beginning of each rating section. Also, don't forget to look up the cheap alternative choices profiled in Appendix II.

Strengths and weaknesses
Every carmaker has quality shortcomings: with the Detroit Big Three it's engine head gaskets and automatic transmissions; South Korean vehicles have weak transmissions; and Japanese makes are noted for their electrical system, brake, door, and window glitches. Unlike other auto guides, *Lemon-Aid* pinpoints potential parts failures, explains why those parts fail, and advises you as to your chances of getting a repair refund. We also give parts numbers for upgraded parts (why replace poor-quality brake pads with the same ones, for example?) and offer troubleshooting tips direct from the automakers' bulletins, so your mechanic won't replace parts unrelated to your troubles before coming upon the defective component that is actually responsible. The "Secret Warranties/Service Tips/TSBs" and vehicle "Profile" tables show a vehicle's overall reliability and safety, providing details as to which specific model years pose the most risk. This helps an independent mechanic check out the likely trouble spots before you make your purchase.

Safety summary
Ongoing safety investigations, safety-related complaints, and safety probes make up this section. NHTSA complaints are summarized by model year, even though they aren't all safety related. The summary will help you spot a defect trend before a recall or bulletin is issued (like

Toyota engine sludge problems or Firestone tire failures on Honda Odysseys). Another advantage is that you can prove a part failure is wide-spread and factory related, and use that information for free "goodwill" repairs or in litigation involving accident damage, injuries, or death. NHTSA records indicate that ABS and airbag failures represent the most frequent complaints from car and van owners. Other common safety-related failures concern sudden acceleration, the vehicle rolling away with the transmission in Park, and minivan sliding doors not opening when they should or opening when they shouldn't.

If *Lemon-Aid* doesn't list a problem you have experienced, go to the NHTSA website's database at *www.nhtsa.dot.gov/cars/problems* for an update. Your vehicle may be currently under investigation or may have been recalled since this year's guide was published.

People Saving People
http://www.nhtsa.dot.gov

www.nhtsa.dot.gov
Office of Defects Investigation
Complaints Database

Call the Auto Safety Hotline toll free at (888) 327-4236 to report safety defects or to obtain information on cars, trucks, child seats, highway or traffic safety.

Report Date: January 22, 2001 08:42:57 AM

ODI ID: 737643

Make: CHEVROLET

Model: CORVETTE

Year: 1999

Date of Failure: Thursday, September 21, 2000

Incident: No

Fire: No

Number of Injuries: 0

Component: STEERING: WHEEL AND COLUMN

Summary: STEERING LOCKING UP, IS A REAL SCARY PROBLEM THAT APPEARS TO BE WIDE SPREAD. I AM GRATEFUL THAT IT ONLY WAS A QUICK LOCK UP.

ODI ID: 730883

Make: CHEVROLET

Model: CORVETTE

Year: 1999

Date of Failure: Friday, September 08, 2000

Incident: No

Fire: No

Number of Injuries: 0

Component: STEERING: WHEEL AND COLUMN

Summary: ON ATTEMPTING TO DRIVE CAR THE VEHICLE STARTED BUT THE STEERING WHEEL DID NOT UNLOCK LEAVING ME STRANDED.

ODI ID: 72995

Make: CHEVROLET

Model: CORVETTE

Year: 1999

Date of Failure: Thursday, August 31, 2000

Incident: No

Fire: No

Number of Injuries:

Component: STEERING: WHEEL AND COLUMN

Summary: YOU BETTER ISSUE A RECALL BECAUSE I'M PISSED ANY DAY YOU WAIT IS
             IMMORAL THERE ARE MORE THAN ENOUGH COMPLAINTS ANY OTHER RESPONSE
             IS BULLSHIT.

Steering wheel lockup is common, but these Corvettes have yet to be recalled.

Recalls aren't listed in this guide because there are so many and the info can be easily obtained from either NHTSA or Transport Canada by telephone or on the Internet at *apps.tc.gc.ca/roadsafety/recalls/recintro_e.htm*. Furthermore, most dealers willingly give out recall info when they run a "vehicle history" search through their computer, since they hope to snag the extra service.

Secret warranties/Service tips/TSBs

It's not enough to know which parts on your vehicle are likely to fail. You should also know which repairs will be done for free by the dealer and automaker, even though you aren't the original owner and the manufacturer's warranty has long since expired.

Welcome to the hidden world of secret warranties, found in confidential technical service bulletins or gleaned from owner feedback. Over the years, I've grown tired of having service managers deny that service bulletins exist to correct factory-related defects free of charge. That's why I pore over thousands of bulletins and summarize or print out the important ones for each model year, along with selected diagrams. These bulletins target defects related to safety, emissions, and performance that service managers would have you believe don't exist or are your responsibility. If you photocopy the exact service bulletin reproduced or summarized in *Lemon-Aid*, you'll have a better chance of getting the dealer or automaker to cover all or part of the repair cost. Bulletins taken from *Lemon-Aid* have also been instrumental in helping claimants win in small claims court mediation and trials (remember to have the bulletins validated by an independent mechanic).

Service bulletins cover repairs that may be eligible for warranty coverage in one or more of the following five categories:

- emissions warranty (5–8 years/80,000–130,000 km)
- safety component warranty (this covers seatbelts, ABS, and airbags, and usually lasts eight years—the lifetime of the vehicle)

- body warranty (paint: 6 years; rust perforations: 7 years)
- secret warranty (coverage varies)
- factory defect/implied legal warranty (depends on mileage, use, and repair cost)

Use these bulletins to get free repairs—even if the vehicle has changed hands several times—and to alert an independent mechanic about which defects to look for. They're also great tools for getting compensation from automakers and dealer service managers after the warranty has expired, since they prove that a failure is factory related and therefore not part of routine maintenance or an environmental anomaly (like bird droppings and acid rain).

Their diagnostic shortcuts and lists of upgraded parts make these bulletins invaluable in helping mechanics and do-it-yourselfers troubleshoot problems inexpensively and replace the right part the first time. Auto owners can also use the TSBs listed here to verify that a repair was diagnosed correctly, the right upgraded replacement part was used, and the labour costs were fair.

Getting your own bulletins

Summaries of service bulletins relating to 1982–2000 vehicles can be obtained for free from the ALLDATA or NHTSA websites (listed in Appendix I, "Helpful Internet Info Sites"). If you want individual bulletins for your car, they can be ordered from ALLDATA; $25 (U.S.) will get you a DVD or Internet download containing all the bulletins applicable to your vehicle (BMW, Acura, and Honda excepted).

Vehicle profile tables

These tables cover the various aspects of vehicle ownership at a glance. Included for each model year are the vehicle's original selling price (manufacturer's suggested retail price, or MSRP), the wholesale and retail price you can expect to pay, reliability ratings (specific defective parts are listed in the "Strengths and weaknesses" section), which model years have secret warranties or should be bought with an extended warranty, and details on crashworthiness.

Prices

Dealer profit margins on used cars vary considerably—giving lots of room to negotiate a fair price if you take the time to find out what the vehicle is really worth. Three prices are given for each model year: the vehicle's selling price when new as suggested by the manufacturer; its maximum used price (A), which is often the starting price with dealers, and its lowest used price (V), more commonly found with private sellers.

The original selling price (MSRP) is also given as a reality check for greedy sellers who inflate prices on some vehicles (mostly Japanese imports, minivans, and sport-utilities) in order to get back some of the money *they* overpaid in the first place. This is particularly true in the Prairie provinces and British Columbia.

Used prices are based on sales recorded as of April 2002. Prices are for the lowest-priced standard model that is in good condition with a maximum of 20,000 km for each calendar year. Be watchful for price differences reflecting each model's equipment upgrades, designated by a numerical or alphabetical abbreviation. For example, L, LX, and LXT usually mean more standard features are included. Numerical progression usually relates to engine size.

Prices reflect the auto markets in Quebec and Ontario, where the majority of used-vehicle transactions take place. Residents in eastern Canada should add 10 percent, and western Canadians should add 15–20 percent to the listed price. Why the higher cost? Less competition and inflated new-vehicle prices in these regions. Don't be too disheartened, though; some of what was overpaid will be recouped when you resell the vehicle down the road.

MERCURY 1999

Fact S.R.P.	Avg Whsl	Mod No	Description		Avg Retail
MYSTIQUE(Continued)					
21245	11325			2.5L-E V6	13325
SABLE					
24594	11350	50	4d Sdn GS	3.0L-E V6	13700
25295	11625	53	4d Sdn LS	3.0L-E V6	13975
25795	12025	58	4d Wgn LS	3.0L-E V6	14375

MERCURY 1998

Model Nos. are (6,7) Digits of VIN

Fact S.R.P.	Avg Whsl	Mod No	Description		Avg Retail
GRAND MARQUIS GS					
32895	13150	74	4d Sdn	4.6L-E V8	15850
GRAND MARQUIS LS					
34395	13650	75	4d Sdn	4.6L-E V8	16350
MYSTIQUE					
17795	7800	65	4d Base	2.0L-E 4	9600
18895	8050	65	4d Sdn GS	2.0L-E 4	10050
20895	8400			2.5L-E V6	10400
20495	8450	66	4d Sdn LS	2.0L-E 4	10450
21495	8800			2.5L-E V6	10800
SABLE					
24395	9125	50	4d Sdn GS	3.0L-E V6	11425
25095	9300	53	4d Sdn LS	3.0L-E V6	11600
25096	9600	58	4d Wgn LS	3.0L-E V6	11900

MERCURY 1997

Model Nos. are (6,7) Digits of VIN

Fact S.R.P.	Avg Whsl	Mod No	Description		Avg Retail
COUGAR XR-7					
24995	6675	62	2d Sdn	3.8L-E V6	10875
25595	8975			4.6L-E V8	11175
GRAND MARQUIS GS					
32195	10425	74	4d Sdn	4.6L-E V8	13075
GRAND MARQUIS LS					
33295	10725	75	4d Sdn	4.6L-E V8	13425
MYSTIQUE					
17795	6250	65	4d Base	2.0L-E 4	8150
18795	6550	65	4d Sdn GS	2.0L-E 4	8450
20795	6850			2.5L-E V6	8750
20395	6700	66	4d Sdn LS	2.0L-E 4	8600
22395	7000			2.5L-E V6	8900
SABLE GS					
23595	7050	50	4d Sdn	3.0L-E V6	9300
23596	7300	55	4d Wgn	3.0L-E V6	9550
SABLE LS					
26595	7900	53	4d Sdn	3.0L-E V6	10150
26596	8150	58	4d Wgn	3.0L-E V6	10400

MERCURY 1996

Model Nos. are (6,7) Digits of VIN

Fact S.R.P.	Avg Whsl	Mod No	Description		Avg Retail
COUGAR XR-7					
23495	6575	62	2d Sdn	3.8L-E V6	8675
24095	6825			4.6L-E V8	8925
GRAND MARQUIS GS					
30295	7425	74	4d Sdn	4.6L-E V8	10025
GRAND MARQUIS LS					
31395	7825	75	4d Sdn	4.6L-E V8	10425
MYSTIQUE					
17995	4775	65	4d Sdn GS	2.0L-E 4	6575
19595	5200	66	4d Sdn LS	2.0L-E 4	7000
SABLE GS					
22595	5600	50	4d Sdn	3.0L-E V6	7600
22596	5800	55	4d Wgn	3.0L-E V6	7800
SABLE LS					
25495	6125	53	4d Sdn	3.0L-E V6	8125
25496	6325	58	4d Wgn	3.0L-E V6	8325

MERCURY 1995

Model Nos. are (6,7) Digits of VIN

Fact S.R.P.	Avg Whsl	Mod No	Description		Avg Retail
COUGAR XR-7					
22095	5225	62	2d Sdn	3.8L-E V6	7225
22495	5475			4.6L-E V8	7475
GRAND MARQUIS GS					
26695	6875	74	4d Sdn	4.6L-E V8	9375
GRAND MARQUIS LS					
27795	7200	75	4d Sdn	4.6L-E V8	9700
MYSTIQUE					
17295	3850	65	4d Sdn GS	2.0L-E 4	5550
18655	4100			2.5L-E V6	5800
18995	4150	66	4d Sdn LS	2.0L-E 4	5850
20355	4400			2.5L-E V6	6100
SABLE GS					
21195	3975	50	4d Sdn	3.0L-E V6	5875
22079	4075			3.8L-E V6	5975
21196	4125	55	4d Wgn	3.0L-E V6	6025
22080	4225			3.8L-E V6	6125
SABLE LS					
24195	4500	53	4d Sdn	3.0L-E V6	6400
25079	4600			3.8L-E V6	6500
24196	4650	58	4d Wgn	3.0L-E V6	6550
25080	4750			3.8L-E V6	6650

The *Canadian Red Book* shows that Ford's Taurus and Sable lose over half their value after only three years of use.

Why are *Lemon-Aid*'s prices sometimes lower than the prices found in dealer guides (like the *Red Book*)? The answer is simple: dealer guides inflate their prices (much like homeowners in real estate transactions) so that you can bargain the price down and wind up convinced that you made a great deal.

I use newspaper classified ads from Quebec, Ontario, and B.C., as well as auction reports, for my used values. I then check these figures with the *Red Book* and *Black Book*. I don't start with the *Red Book*'s retail or wholesale figures (prices are inflated about 10 percent for wholesale-private sales and almost 20 percent for retail-dealer sales—compare the two and you'll see what I mean). I then project what the value will be by mid-model year, and that lowers my prices further. I'll almost always fall way under the *Red Book*'s value, but not far under the *Black Book*'s prices.

I print a top and bottom price to give the buyer some margin for negotiation, as well as to account for regional differences in prices, the sudden popularity of certain models or vehicle classes, and the generally depreciated value of used vehicles.

Most new cars depreciate 30–40 percent during the first two years of ownership, despite the fact that good-quality used cars are in high demand. On the other hand, some minivans and most vans, pickups, and sport-utilities lose barely 30 percent of their value, even after four years of ownership.

"I'll take 7 seats and an order of fries—to go!"

Since no evaluation method is foolproof, check dealer prices with local private classified ads and add the option values listed below to come up with a fairly representative offer. Don't forget to bargain down the price further if the odometer shows a cumulative reading of more than 20,000 km per calendar year. Inter-estingly, the value of anti-lock brakes in trade-ins has plummeted in the last few years as they became a standard feature on many entry-level vehicles.

It will be easier for you to match the lower used prices if you buy privately. Dealers rarely sell much below the maximum prices. They inflate their prices to cover the costs of reconditioning or paying future warranty claims and to make you feel better. If you can come within 5–10 percent of this guide's price, you'll have done well.

Value of Options by Model Year

Option	1994	1995	1996	1997	1998	1999	2000	2001
Air conditioning	$200	$300	$300	$400	$500	$600	$800	$900
AM/FM radio & CD player	100	100	100	150	175	200	300	500
Anti-lock brakes	0	50	100	125	150	175	300	300
Automatic transmission	150	200	250	275	300	400	500	700
Cruise control	0	50	50	75	100	125	225	300
Electric six-way seat	0	50	100	125	150	175	200	400
Leather upholstery	50	100	200	225	325	400	500	800
Level control (suspension)	0	50	75	100	125	150	250	350
Paint protector	0	0	0	0	0	0	0	0
Power antenna	0	0	0	0	0	75	75	75
Power door locks	0	50	100	125	150	175	200	250
Power windows	0	50	100	125	150	175	225	275
Rustproofing	0	0	0	0	25	25	50	50
Sunroof	0	50	50	75	125	150	300	500
T-top roof	150	200	300	400	500	700	1,000	1200
Tilt steering	0	50	50	75	75	100	175	250
Tinted windows	0	0	0	0	25	50	50	50
Tires (Firestone)	-100	-100	-100	-100	-100	-150	-150	-150
Traction control	50	100	125	150	175	275	400	500
Wire wheels/locks	50	75	100	125	150	175	275	350

In the table above, take note that some options—like paint protection, rustproofing, and tinted windows—have little worth on the resale market, though they may make your vehicle easier to sell.

Extended warranties and secret warranties

Usually, but not always, an extended warranty is advised for those model years that aren't rated Recommended. But don't buy too much warranty. For example, if the vehicle has a history of powertrain problems, only buy the cheaper powertrain warranty—not the bumper-to-bumper product. Also, only invest in enough extra warranty to get you through the critical fifth year of ownership. In shopping for an extended warranty, don't be surprised to discover that dealers have the market practically sewn up. You can bargain the price down by getting competing dealers to bid against each other, contacting them by fax or through their websites. Be wary of extended-warranty companies that aren't backed by the major automakers.

Model years that are eligible for free repairs under a secret warranty are listed in this section and further detailed in the "Secret Warranties/Service Tips/TSBs" section. A Y signifies that one or more secret warranties exist or that an extended warranty is needed. An N means that no secret warranty applies or that an extended warranty is unnecessary.

Reliability

The older a vehicle, the greater the chance that major components like the engine and transmission will fail as a result of high mileage and environmental wear and tear. Surprisingly, there's a host of other expensive-to-repair failures that are just as likely to occur in a new vehicle as in an older one. Air conditioning, electronic computer modules, electrical systems, and brakes are the most troublesome components, manifesting problems early in a vehicle's life. Other deficiencies that will appear early, due to sloppy manufacturing and a harsh environment, include failure-prone body hardware (trim, finish, locks, doors, and windows), water leaks, wind noise, and paint peeling/discoloration.

The following legend is used to show a vehicle's relative degree of overall reliability; the numbers lighten as the rating becomes more positive.

❶	❷	③	④	⑤
Unacceptable	Below Average	Average	Above Average	Excellent

Crash data

Front and side impact protection figures and rollover resistance ratings are taken from NHTSA's New Car Assessment Program. The Insurance Institute for Highway Safety (IIHS) supplies data on off-set crash and head restraint protection. The frontal collision test crashes a vehicle into a fixed barrier, head-on, at 57 km/h (35 mph), in order to evaluate the effects of the consequent forces exerted on the specially constructed dummies placed in the front seat. *Lemon-Aid* gives the crash score for the driver.

NHTSA shows a vehicle's level of crashworthiness by the likelihood, expressed as a percentage, of the belted occupants being seriously injured. The higher the number, the greater the protection:

NHTSA Front Collision Ratings

⑤ 10 percent or lower chance of serious injury
④ 11–20 percent chance of serious injury
③ 21–35 percent chance of serious injury
❷ 36–45 percent chance of serious injury
❶ 46 percent or greater chance of serious injury

Vehicles that are identical but carry different nameplates from the same manufacturer can be expected to perform similarly in these crash tests. On the other hand, sometimes the same vehicle will post dramatically different results when tested from one year to the next, even though the model has remained relatively unchanged. Safety experts admit that this happens occasionally and that consumers should look at the trend established over three or more model years.

NHTSA Side Collision Ratings

⑤   5 percent or lower chance of serious injury
④   6–10 percent chance of serious injury
③   11–20 percent chance of serious injury
❷   21–25 percent chance of serious injury
❶   26 percent or greater chance of serious injury

SMALL CARS

The proverbial "econobox," this size of car is for city dwellers who want economy at any price. Small cars offer excellent gas economy, easy manoeuvrability in urban areas, and a low retail price.

One of the more alarming characteristics of a small car's highway performance is its extreme vulnerability to strong lateral winds, which may make the car difficult to keep on course. Most of these cars can carry only two passengers in comfort—rear seating is limited—and there is insufficient luggage capacity. As well, engine and road noise are fairly excessive.

Crash safety may be compromised by the small size and light weight of these vehicles. Nevertheless, engineering measures that direct crash forces away from occupants and the addition of airbags have made many small cars safer in collisions than some larger cars.

SMALL CAR RATINGS

Recommended

Honda Civic, del Sol
 (1996–2001)
Hyundai Accent (2000–01)
Hyundai Elantra (2001)
Mazda 323, Protegé (1996–2001)
Nissan Sentra (1995–2001)

Subaru Forester (2001)
Suzuki Esteem (1996–2001)
Toyota Echo (2000–01)
Toyota Paseo (1994–99)
Toyota Tercel (1993–99)

Above Average

Ford Escort, ZX2 (1999–2001)
General Motors Saturn L-series
 (2000–01)
General Motors/Suzuki Firefly, Metro,
 Sprint/Swift (1998–2001)
Honda Civic, del Sol (1996–2001)
Hyundai Accent (1995–99)
Hyundai Elantra (1996–2000)
Mazda 323, Protegé (1991–95)

Nissan Sentra (1991–94)
Subaru Forester (1998–2000)
Subaru Impreza (1997–2001)
Subaru Legacy, Outback (1997–2001)
Toyota Corolla (1991–2001)
Toyota Paseo (1992–93)
Toyota Tercel (1991–92)
Volkswagen Cabrio, Golf,
 Jetta (1997–2001)

Average

Ford Escort, ZX2 (1996–98)
General Motors Cavalier, Sunfire
 (1996–99)
General Motors Saturn S-series
 (1997–2001)
General Motors/Suzuki Firefly, Metro,
 Sprint/Swift (1995–97)
Honda Civic, del Sol (1984–95)
Hyundai Elantra (1991–95)

Mazda 323, Protegé (1985–90)
Nissan Sentra (1988–90)
Subaru Impreza, Loyale
 (1994–96)
Subaru Legacy, Outback (1989–96)
Toyota Corolla (1985–90)
Toyota Tercel (1987–90)
Volkswagen Cabrio, Golf,
 Jetta (1994–96)

Below Average

DaimlerChrysler Neon (2000–01)
Ford Escort, ZX2 (1992–95)
Ford Focus (2001)
General Motors/Suzuki Firefly, Metro
  Sprint/Swift (1987–94)

Volkswagen Cabrio, Golf,
  Jetta (1993)

Not Recommended

DaimlerChrysler Neon (1995–99)
Ford Escort (1981–91)
Ford Focus (2000)
General Motors Cavalier, Sunfire
  (Sunbird) (1984–95)

General Motors Saturn S-series
  (1992–96)
Nissan Sentra (1983–87)
Volkswagen Cabrio, Golf,
  Jetta (1985–92)

Hatchbacks and wagons

As the auto market gradually evolves from one with a few distinct categories into a confusing array of overlapping styles and sizes, the difference between such categories as hatchbacks and wagons, wagons and SUVs, or SUVs and pickups becomes increasingly blurred. Nevertheless, small hatchbacks and wagons ("grocery getters") have remained popular and represent a niche market rediscovered by automakers for 2002. Here are a few choices of recommended used hatchbacks and wagons for the discerning used-car buyer. The number in parenthesis following the model indicates its estimated cargo capacity as expressed in cubic feet.

Acura Integra (16)
Chrysler Colt (12)
Chrysler LeBaron (18)
Chrysler Omni/Horizon (15)
Dodge Stealth (12)
Eagle Summit (12)
Eagle Talon (8)
Ford Escort (15–18)
Ford Festiva (12)
Ford Mustang (12)

Ford Probe (19)
General Motors Camaro/Firebird (12)
General Motors Corsica/Beretta (22)
General Motors Firefly
Geo Metro (10)
Geo Spectrum (17)
Honda Accord (19)
Honda Civic, CRX (12–13)
Hyundai Accent (16)
Hyundai Elantra (11)

A '99 Hyundai Elantra GL wagon sells for about $9,000 and will likely still have some of the original warranty left.

Mazda 323 (15–16)
Mazda 626 (21)
Mazda MX-3 (15)
Mazda MX-6 (19)
Mazda Protegé (17)
Subaru DL/GL (11)
Subaru Forester
Subaru Impreza
Subaru Legacy
Suzuki Esteem

Suzuki Swift (10)
Toyota Camry
Toyota Celica (13–15)
Toyota Supra (11)
Volvo S40/V40
Volvo V70
Volkswagen Golf/Jetta (18)
Volkswagen New Beetle (12)
Volkswagen Passat

South Korean cars made by Daewoo and Kia haven't been rated in this year's guide. This is because owner feedback and service bulletin information is insufficient to get a clear idea of the relative merits of these vehicles. Furthermore, with Daewoo's impending bankruptcy or purchase by GM still to be sorted out, *Lemon-Aid* will wait another year before rating these vehicles as used-car buys.

DaimlerChrysler

NEON   ★★

RATING: Below Average (2000–01); Not Recommended (1995–99). A low-quality econobox that eats engine head gaskets for breakfast and wallets for lunch. Log onto *www.neons.org* for updated reports from owners. The Highline and Sport versions are more feature-laden. **Maintenance/Repair costs:** Higher than average. **Parts:** Easily found and relatively inexpensive. However, Chrysler is particularly slow in distributing parts needed for safety recall campaigns; waits of several months are commonplace. **Best alternatives:** Other cars worth considering are the Ford Escort/Tracer (post-'91), Geo Metro, Honda Civic, Hyundai Accent, Mazda Protegé, Suzuki Esteem, and Toyota Corolla or Tercel.

Strengths and weaknesses: A small, noisy car with big quality problems, the Neon does offer a spacious interior and responsive steering and handling. Nevertheless, it uses an antiquated 3-speed automatic gearbox, a DOHC 150-hp powerplant that has to be pushed hard to do as well as the SOHC 132-hp engine, and a mushy base suspension.

Consumer Reports says that its member survey found that first-year (1995 model) Neons had nearly twice the problems of the average 1995 model car. As for reliability: when *Autoweek*, an American car enthusiast magazine, tested a '96 Neon Sport Coupe with only 16,566 miles (26,506 km) on the odometer, it concluded that "aliens" had invaded the test car.

A perusal of service bulletins and owner comments doesn't support the "aliens" theory, but it's evident that these cars have a plethora of serious factory-related defects. These deficiencies include a biodegradable 2.0L 4-cylinder engine and engine head gasket (covered by a 7-year/160,000 km secret warranty, confirmed by anecdotal feedback from successful claimants), an abrupt-shifting and unreliable automatic transmission, an air conditioning system that often requires expensive servicing, a multitude of electrical glitches, lots of interior noise and leaks, uneven fit and finish, and poor-quality trim items that break or fall off easily. The finish is not as good as on most other subcompacts; the thickness of the coat varies considerably and can chip easily. 2000 and 2001 model engine and transmission glitches are mostly caused by poorly calibrated computer modules (an emissions warranty item).

Except for the addition of a cast aluminum oil pan to reduce engine vibrations, redesigned wheel covers, improved sound system, and a centre console with armrest for 1997–98 models, the Neon remained basically unchanged until the '99 models got de-powered airbags. Year 2000 versions dropped the coupe and 150-hp 2.0L engine, and increased interior room and trunk space. The manual transmission and stereo were also upgraded, traction control offered, and redesigned doors reduced wind noise and water leaks. 2001s were carried over without any significant changes.

Safety summary: All models: 1995—Steering column fires. • 98 reports of "inappropriate" airbag deployment, causing 13 crashes and injuring 28 people. • Sudden steering loss. • Small horn buttons are hard to find in an emergency. • Headlight switch is a "hide and go seek" affair. • Axle shafts may suddenly fail, as the owner of a 1995 Neon discovered:

I was driving in traffic and the car just stopped. I couldn't move forward or backwards but the engine was still going. It turned out that the left front axle of the car had collapsed. I was just lucky that I wasn't driving on the highway when this occurred, because I would have been severely injured or killed. I had the car towed to the dealer, and they repaired the broken axle, but I just don't feel safe in the vehicle.

1995–96—Engine compartment fires. • Electrical short in dashboard. • Sudden acceleration. • ABS brake failures. • Inadvertent airbag deployment. • Failure of airbag to deploy. • Seatbelt failed to restrain driver. • Driver's seatbelt tightens uncomfortably. • Driver's side seatbelt pulled out from buckle during collision. • Premature front brake pad/rotor wearout. • Excessive wearout of brake rotors, apparently caused by premature pitting of the rotors due to bubbles created during the casting process. • Front brake caliper sticking. • Chronic engine head gasket failures. • Engine camshaft seal leaks oil • Engine motor mount and exhaust donut gasket failures. • Sticks in idle. • Chronic stalling. • Throttle system failures. • Faulty cruise control. • Chronic transmission failures. • Transmission suddenly downshifts to First gear when accelerating at 90 km/h. • Sudden steering loss. • Steering locks up every time it rains. • Trunk springs won't hold lid up. • Door hinge failures. • Premature wheel bearing and steering knuckle wear. • Chronic light and gauge failures. • Faulty Goodyear tires. • Fuel gauge failures. • Defective brake master cylinder. • Window rattles, goes off track, or shatters when door is closed. • AC condenser and compressor failures. • Water leaks in from dash on driver's side. • Poor door fit allows water to enter cabin. 1997— Circuit board behind dash caught fire. • Sudden acceleration. • Cruise control won't disengage when braking. • Chronic stalling. • Airbag failed to deploy. • Gas tank leaks fuel. • O-ring in the fuel rail leaks fuel. • Chronic sudden brake failures. • Noisy brakes. • Brake rotor failures. • Steering belt failures. • Sudden steering lockup after passing over speed bump. • Engine head gasket failures. • Window seal failures. • Fuel pump failures. • Seatbelt failed to restrain occupant. • Catalytic converter failure. • Hood fell, injuring driver's arm. 1998—Sudden acceleration. • Airbag failed to deploy. • Driver-side window exploded in warm weather. • Front right wheel bolt fell out, causing wheel to bend. • Trunk lid may fall. • Engine surging and stalling. • Engine loses speed rapidly when going uphill. • Excessive engine carbon buildup. • Timing belt broke, causing extensive engine damage. • Engine mounts broke and head gaskets leaked. • Erratic automatic transmission performance. • There is a partial steering hang-up when making a right turn. 1999—Ignition fire. • Automatic transmission suddenly self-destructed. • Vehicle suddenly "jumps" out of gear. • Airbags failed to deploy. • In rainy weather, vehicle makes loud noise, sometimes stalls, or loses steering power. • Engine mounts crack prematurely. • Defective ignition switch fuse causes sudden shutdown. 2000—Over 178 safety complaints as of January 2002 indicate that the 2000 refinements haven't improved overall reliability or safety. Main problem areas: airbag, automatic transmission, power steering, Goodyear tire, and brake failures; engine fires; premature brake rotor and pad wear, signalled by excessive vibrations and squealing when brakes are applied; steering lockups; stalling and stumbling; interior/exterior light dimming; seatbelts failing to retract; and an inoperative horn. **2001**—Brake failures, stalling and stumbling, and airbags failing to deploy are the most frequent problems reported. Other incidents include electrical shorts (lights and gauges), Eagle low-profile tire blowouts, engine damage caused by water ingested through the air intake system, loss of steering, weak trunk lid springs, and an annoying reflection in the front windshield.

Secret Warranties/Service Tips/TSBs

All models: 1995—Engine sags, hesitates, shudders, and surges. • Rough idle especially bad during cold start-up. • Oil leaks at the cam position sensor. • Buzzy manual and automatic gearshift lever, and erratic, harsh-shifting automatic transmission. • Noisy clutch pedal and wheel cover. • Rear suspension bottoms out. • Steering wheel shakes and accelerator pedal vibrates. • Premature front brake pad wear. • AC freeze-up, poor performance, and evaporator odours. • Inaccurate fuel gauge readings, instrument panel glare, and water leaks. • Water leaks into the passenger compartment on left-hand turns. • Flickering headlights. • Discharged battery. • Intermittent wiper operation. • Excessive engine noise in passenger compartment, exhaust noise/hiss, B-pillar wind noise, power-steering rattles, steering column and right engine-mount click, and chattering steering column tilt lever. • More noise: front seat rattle and front seatback squeak, hood prop-rod rattle, idle air control motor whistle, front brake moan, poorly fitted deck-lid rattle, and poor AM reception (static). • Tips on how to fix paint fogging and stained white bumpers are offered. **1995–97**—If water drips into the vehicle from the roof-rail weather-strip channel, install an anti-drip roof-rail retainer channel. **1995–99**—A new Multi-Layer Steel engine head gasket will provide superior sealing characteristics (see following bulletin).

Cylinder Head Gasket: Technical Service Bulletins

Multi-Layer Steel Head Gasket Installation Procedures
No.: 09-09-98   Group: Engine   Effective Date: Nov. 6, 1998
Subject: Multi-Layer Steel (MLS)
Head Gasket installation
Procedures
MODELS:

1995-1999	(JA)	Cirrus/Stratus/Breeze
1996-1999	(JX)	Sebring Convertible
1996-1999	(NS)	Town & Country/Caravan/Voyager
1995-1999	(PL)	Neon
1997-1999	(GS)	Chrysler Voyager (International Market)

NOTE:

THIS INFORMATION APPLIES TO MODELS WITH A 2.0L SOHC/DOHC OR 2.4L ENGINE

DISCUSSION:

A new Multi-Layer Steel (MLS) head gasket has been developed and is being implemented into production vehicles. Additionally, it has been approved for service applications.This new gasket will provide superior sealing characteristics, but will require extra care in its installation where a composite gasket was previously in place.

This improved head gasket replaces Chrysler's original failure-prone gasket.

• Oil leakage at the cam position sensor is often mistaken for an engine head gasket failure. • Paint delamination, peeling, or fading (see Part Two). **1996**—Cold-start hesitation, engine misfiring, and erratic idling. • Excessive engine vibration and exhaust noise. • Transmission slippage from Second to Third gear during light acceleration. • Speed control overshoots or undershoots. • Rear brake chirps or howls. • AC evaporator produces a high-pitched whistle. • Fuel tank won't fill or is slow to fill. • Interior window film buildup. • Water leaks at cowl cover seam. Water could enter the air cleaner housing, be ingested into the engine, and cause serious engine damage. To prevent this from occurring, the dealer will drill a hole in the housing and seal the cowl-to-head weather stripping. This 30-minute correction is free of charge under Chrysler Customer Satisfaction Notice #660. It's not a safety recall, so you may have a hard time getting Chrysler to acknowledge the problem. **1997**— Rear brake howl. • Front footwell creak/rattle. • Scratched door glass. • Improper AC compressor engagement. • Loss of power steering in heavy rain or when passing through puddles. • Poor radio reception. • Warning that premium fuel may cause stalling, long cold-start times, hesitation, and warm-up sags. • Front suspension popping/creaking noise. **1998**— AC compressor lockup at low mileage. • Sag, hesitation, harsh AC operation, and headlight flickers. • Steering wheel/column rattles and clunks. • Cold-start power-steering noise. • Front brake squeal, creep, or groan. • Paint fogging. • Warning that premium fuel may cause stalling, long cold-start times, hesitation, and warm-up sags. • Popping noise when passing over bumps or making turns. • Sunroof shade rattles in open position. • Vehicle overheats or radiator fan runs continuously. **1998–99**—A water leak in the left side of the trunk below the body exhauster and/or water pooled in the spare tire well is caused by a gap between the wheelhouse outer panel and the left body side aperture panel (see following bulletin):

Water Leak In Left Side of Trunk

NO: 23-55-98   GROUP: Body   DATE: Nov. 13, 1998
SUBJECT: Water Leak In Left Side of Trunk
MODELS:
1998-1999 (PL) Neon
SYMPTOM/CONDITION:
A water leak in the left side of the trunk below the body exhauster and/or water pooled in the spare tire well. This is caused by a gap between the wheel house outer panel and the left body side aperture panel where the fascia is bolted through the weld flanges.

This half-hour repair is covered under the base warranty.

1999—Oil leakage at cam position sensor (a recurring problem since 1995). • Low mileage AC lockup. • Smooth road steering wheel vibration. • Sunroof ratcheting noise. • Steering wheel clunk/rattle. • Water leak at left side of trunk (see above). **2000**—Erratic engine performance may be fixed by recalibrating the PCM. • Delayed automatic transmission engagement likely caused by a faulty front pump. • AC compressor locks up at low mileage. • Harsh AC engagement and clunk noise. • Measures to reduce steering wheel column clunks and rattles. • Front suspension creaking. • Front door water leaks. • Power steering moan. • Shake in steering wheel and/or seat at idle. • Poorly seated instrument panel top cover. • Instrument panel creaks. • Rear door glass won't roll down all the way. • High window cranking effort or slow power window operation. • Blower motor noise or vibration. • Front suspension snapping noise. • Deck-lid rattle and water/dust intrusion past the deck-lid seal. • Difficulty moving front seats forward. • Discoloured B-pillar appliqué. • Water enters the horn assembly. **2000–01**—Rough idle requires reprogramming the PCM. • Power-steering moan. • Remedy for AC honking. • Rattling wheel covers. **2001**—AC expansion valve noise. • Poor performance of AC and engine. • Engine hesitation. • Delamination may require the replacement of the accessory drive belt for the power-steering pump and AC compressor. • Excessive AC compressor or expansion valve noise. • Front seat rattling. • No-start problem in cold weather. • Rear window may not go all the way down.

Neon Profile

	1995	1996	1997	1998	1999	2000	2001
Cost Price ($)							
Base	11,866	12,835	14,750	15,350	15,215	17,995	18,375
Sport 4d	16,126	15,515	16,900	17,500	—	—	—
Used Values ($)							
Base ʌ	3,500	6,000	7,000	8,500	10,000	12,000	14,000
Base v	3,000	4,500	6,000	7,000	9,000	11,000	12,500

Sport 4d ▲	5,500	7,000	8,000	10,000	—	—	—
Sport 4d ▼	4,500	6,000	7,000	9,000	—	—	—
Extended Warranty	Y	Y	Y	Y	Y	Y	Y
Secret Warranty	Y	Y	Y	Y	Y	N	N
Reliability	❶	❶	❷	❷	❷	❷	❷
Crash Safety (F)	③	④	④	③	③	—	④
Side Impact	—	—	—	❷	❷	—	③
Off-set	❶	❶	❶	❶	❶	❷	❷
Rollover Resistance	—	—	—	—	—	—	④
Head Restraints (F)	❶	—	❶	—	❷	❶	④
Rear	—	—	—	—	—	—	③

Ford

ESCORT, ZX2

RATING: Above Average (1999–2001); Average (1996–98); Below Average (1992–95); Not Recommended (1981–91). The LX became the base Escort during the 1994 model year. Lots of upgraded 1999 Escorts are coming off lease now; they represent an exceptionally good buy. The Escort was joined by the 2000 Focus and replaced by the Focus for the 2001 model year. A smattering of 2001 Escorts were sold to fleets. **Maintenance/ Repair costs:** Higher than average on pre-1991s; below average for later models. Repairs can be done by independents or Ford or Mazda dealers. **Parts:** Expensive, but easily found. **Best alternatives:** The Geo Metro, Honda Civic, Hyundai Accent, Mazda Protegé, Suzuki Esteem, and Toyota Corolla or Tercel.

Strengths and weaknesses: These front-drive small cars are usually reasonably priced and economical to operate, and they provide a comfortable though busy ride and adequate front seating for two adults. However, they have a "Dr. Jekyll and Mr. Hyde" disposition, depending on which model year you buy. From 1982 through 1991, these subcompacts were dull performers with uninspiring interiors. Worse, they had a nasty reputation for being unreliable and expensive to repair.

Be wary of early Escorts; from 1987 until 1991, quality went steadily downhill. The 1.9L engine used from 1985 to 1990 gives respectable highway performance, but its failure rate is still much higher than average. The radiator and other cooling components, including the fan switch and motor, are failure prone. Carburetors and fuel-injection systems are temperamental. Ignition modules are often defective. Power-steering racks fail prematurely. Front and rear wheel alignment is difficult. Exhaust systems rust rapidly.

The 1991 model's changeover to mostly Mazda 323 components gave it a longer wheelbase, making for a more comfortable ride and a bit roomier interior. The 1.9L engine runs more smoothly, as well. The GT and Tracer LTS are equipped with Mazda's powerful 127-hp 1.8L, 4-cylinder engine, and their overall highway performance and fuel economy are far superior to what previous models offered. Wagon versions are particularly versatile and spacious. The front seats on the Tracer GS and LS are very comfortable, and the cargo area is especially spacious in the wagon. Rear seat room is a bit cramped on all other models.

Owner complaints relating to the 1991–95 model years concern primarily seatbelts and airbags, fuel tanks, coil spring and tie-rod failures; automatic transmission and engine (premature timing belt replacement around 90,000 km) breakdowns; and cooling system, brakes, electrical, air conditioning, fuel pump, and ignition-system failures. Quality control and reliability improved a bit with the 1996 model, but many of the earlier deficiencies remained until the arrival of the 1999 models.

The 1997 models are more attractively designed; ride and handle better; and feature improved comfort, a quieter interior, and more standard equipment. The car is four inches longer, mostly taken up by a larger trunk. Three-door, five-door, and GT models were dropped, and the ZX2—a revived, high-performance coupe—made its debut in late 1997 as a 1998 model. It's a peppier machine, with a less raucous engine, that sells in the U.S. for a $2,000 premium over the Escort. In Canada, it debuted for the 1999 model year. Year 2000 and 2001 models were carried over unchanged.

Safety summary: All models: 1995—Fuel tank leaks (regional recall). • Wiring harness fires. • Dead battery due to heat from engine. • Headlight lenses discolour with time. **1995–2000**—Almost 600 safety-related complaints were recorded for the 1995 Escort; '96 models have less than 200 incidents reported. The following problems return over many model years: no airbag deployment; inadvertent airbag deployment; airbag-induced injuries; electrical and engine wiring fires; brake failures, and premature rotor and pad replacement; snapped front and rear coil springs damage tire; sudden tie-rod failure leads to steering loss; automatic transmission slips, jumps out of gear, leaks, or fails early; unanticipated acceleration; seatbelt malfunctions; horn blows inadvertently, won't blow, or is hard to access; faulty door locks; and speedometer failures ($400 repair). **1996**—Many complaints that the fourth cylinder piston self-destructs, destroying engine. • Early steering assembly replacement. • Fuel line failures. • Doors stick shut. • Rear quarter panel water leaks. **1997**—Engine head gasket failures. • Chronic stalling caused by faulty fuse connection. • Check Engine light stays on constantly. • Heater core leak may cause a fire in the airbag assembly. • Crankshaft pulley failure results in steering loss. **1998**—ABS brake lockup. • Faulty fuel pump/pressure regulator,

CV joints, and wheel bearings. • Delayed shifts. • Steering lockup. • Defective engine mounts cause excessive vibration. • AC leaks onto front carpet, creating a musty odour. **1999**—Chronic surging and stalling. • Headlight socket melts. • Hood flew open. • ABS brake lockup. • Heater core leakage. • Faulty motor mounts cause excessive vibration. • Poor structural integrity (broken welds, distorted sheet metal, and extensive flexing throughout vehicle). • Suspension and alignment problems. • Poor defrosting. **2000**—Airbag deployed for no reason and caught on fire. • Chronic stalling. • Excessive vibration. • Transmission coolant line clamp came apart. • Delayed transmission engagement. • Power-steering loss due to snapped serpentine belt. • Sunroof shattered while vehicle was parked. • Windshield suddenly shattered. **2001**—Sudden steering loss. • Stalling while downshifting. • Engine overheating. • Long hesitation before accelerating. • All automatic transmission–equipped vehicles tend to pull to the left when accelerating and cruising at any speed. • Vehicle won't decelerate when foot is taken off the accelerator.

Secret Warranties/Service Tips/TSBs

All models: 1991–94—Under a recall and Service Program #94B55, Ford will install, at no charge, a fused jumper harness in the fuel pump electrical circuit. This will prevent short-circuit problems such as stalling, erratic instrument gauge readings, and extensive wiring damage, which are caused by water intrusion. **1993–99**—Paint delamination, peeling, or fading (see Part Two). **1994–98**—Tips on eliminating wind noise around doors are given in TSB #97-15-1. **1997–99**—PCV (positive crankcase ventilation) system may freeze, resulting in a serious oil leak through the dipstick tube (see following bulletin).

No.: 98-10-5   05/26/98
ENGINE - 2.0L SPI - PCV FREEZING AT COLD
AMBIENT TEMPERATURES - VEHICLES WITH
SOHC
LEAK - ENGINE OIL LEAK FROM OIL LEVEL
INDICATOR TUBE - PCV FREEZE - VEHICLES
BUILT WITH 2.0L SPI ENGINE
FORD:
1997-98 ESCORT
LINCOLN-MERCURY:
1997-98 TRACER
ISSUE

At cold ambient temperatures, the Positive Crankcase Ventilation (PCV) system may freeze causing the engine to unseat the dipstick and vent crankcase gasses through the dipstick tube. This may result in oil being discharged on some vehicles.

ACTION

Install PCV Service Kit (refer to Parts Block for correct service application) per this TSB.

WARRANTY STATUS: Eligible Under The Provisions Of Bumper To Bumper Warranty Coverage And Emissions Warranty Coverage

---

The above kit doesn't work any better than the original component; Ford says it's still working on a solution to the problem. Remember all losses caused by this defect are Ford's responsibility.

• A front brake grinding noise, pulling or drag, and uneven brake pad wear are all signs of corrosion affecting the caliper slide pins; Ford will correct the problem under its bumper-to-bumper warranty, says TSB #00-6-9. • Excessive vibration at idle may be corrected by replacing the motor mount. • Tips on silencing a variety of squeaks and rattles. • No restart in cold weather, the cooling fan won't shut off, or the battery going dead all signal the need to change the IRCM under the bumper-to-bumper warranty (see following bulletin).

No Restart In -20 F/Cooling Fan Stays On, Engine Off

Article No.: 98-13-8   07/06/98

NO START - AFTER SHORT DRIVE IN COLD AMBIENT TEMPERATURE (-29 DEGREES CELSIUS 9-20 DEGREES FAHRENHEIT))

BATTERY - DISCHARGED DUE TO COOLING FAN NOT TURNING OFF AFTER SHUTDOWN

COOLING FAN - DOES NOT TURN OFF AFTER SHUTDOWN

FORD:

1997-98 ESCORT

LINCOLN MERCURY:

1997-98 TRACER

ISSUE

A no restart may occur after a short drive in cold ambient temperature of -29°C (-20°F), or the cooling fan may not turn off with key out of the ignition on some vehicles. This may result in a discharged battery. These concerns may be due to water or ice accumulation in the Integrated Relay Control Module (IRCM).

ACTION

Replace the IRCM with a revised moisture resistant IRCM.

1998—An erratic transaxle shift may simply be caused by a pinched wire. • Erratic fuel gauge operation or slow fillups may be corrected by installing a slosh module fuel gauge kit. 1999—Tips on reducing noise, vibration, and harshness. 2000—Delayed transmission engagement; MIL light comes on. 2000–01—Exhaust system buzzing or rattling (a problem for almost a decade). • Fuel fill nozzle clicks off too soon when fueling up. • Positive crankcase ventilation (PCV) freezes up. • Inoperative CD player. • Tips on properly adjusting the transmission range sensor. •

Remedy for a burning oil smell. • Troubleshooting poor engine performance at idle and excessive gas consumption. • Remedies for an engine that won't start or shut down properly. • Engine oil leak at the oil pan, front cover, or the front and rear crankshaft oil seal. • Engine oil pan gasket and oil filter leaks. • Vehicle may not start in freezing weather, due to moisture freezing in the fuel pump relay. • Fuel delivery malfunctions. • Eliminating a high idle condition when starting or decelerating. • Improved parking brake cables and rear brake linings are available to reduce rear brake drag. • Light to moderate rear axle whine. • Squeak, creak from driver's area. • Possible causes of a thump or clunk coming from the suspension. • Improved rear shock absorbers are available to reduce suspension noise. • Front seat cushion sagging. • Cause and correction of vinyl dash abrasions and premature wear. • Diagnostic tips to eliminate wind noise around doors. • Revise hood seal to reduce wind whistle. • AC goes into defrost mode when vehicle goes uphill. Repeated heater core failures.

Escort, ZX2 Profile

	1994	1995	1996	1997	1998	1999	2000
Cost Price ($)							
Escort Base/LX	12,195	12,995	13,595	14,595	14,895	14,895	—
GT	13,995	14,295	15,295	—	—	—	—
ZX2	—	—	—	—	—	15,895	17,995
Used Values ($)							
Base/LX ʌ	3,500	4,500	5,500	6,500	8,000	9,000	—
Base/LX v	3,000	4,000	4,500	5,500	7,000	8,000	—
GT ʌ	4,000	5,000	6,500	—	—	—	—
GT v	3,500	4,000	5,500	—	—	—	—
ZX2 ʌ	—	—	—	—	—	10,000	12,500
ZX2 v	—	—	—	—	—	9,000	11,000
Extended Warranty	Y	Y	Y	Y	Y	Y	Y
Secret Warranty	Y	Y	Y	Y	Y	Y	N
Reliability	❷	❷	③	③	③	④	④
Crash Safety (F)	⑤	④	④	④	③	③	③
Side Impact	—	—	—	—	③	③	③
Off-set	—	—	—	③	③	③	③
Head Restraints	—	❶	—	❶	—	❶	—

Note: Ratings and prices are also applicable to the Mercury Tracer.

FOCUS   ★★

RATING: Below Average (2001); Not Recommended (2000). **Maintenance/Repair costs:** Predicted to be higher than average once warranty expires. **Parts:** Expensive and not yet easily found. **Best alternatives:** the Ford Escort, Geo Metro, GM Cavalier and Sunfire, Honda Civic (it's softer riding, quieter, and has a smoother-running engine), Hyundai Accent, Mazda Protegé, Suzuki Esteem, and Toyota Corolla, Echo, or Tercel.

Strengths and weaknesses: Hailed as Europe's 1999 Car of the Year, Ford's sleek 2000 Focus came to North America shortly thereafter as an uplevel, premium small car, positioning itself between the entry level four-door Escort and Contour. Two inches taller and almost seven inches longer than the Escort, and embodying Ford's "new edge" styling (read less aero, more creases), are three body styles: a two-door hatchback in sporty ZX3 trim; LX, SE, and upscale ZTS four-door sedans; and a four-door SE wagon. The Escort's base engine, a 110-hp 2.0L 4-cylinder, is carried over to the Focus LX and SE, while the 130-hp twin-cam 2.0L (also used on the Escort ZX2 coupe) is standard on the ZTS and ZX3 and optional on the SE. Either engine may be hooked to a manual or an optional 4-speed automatic transmission. Safety features include standard head/chest front airbags, optional side airbags, optional anti-lock brakes (standard only on the ZTS), and rear child safety seat anchors. 2001 versions debuted with few changes.

A disturbingly large number of glitches (brakes, body and moulding, transmission, fuel pump, power control module, and ignition switch) have been reported, yet few service bulletins offering remedies have been found. Overall reliability is predicted to be worse than average, particularly in view of the many powertrain problems, which include chronic stalling and hard starting. Other owner-reported problems: ignition switch failure (18 days for part arrival); seatback bar digs into driver's back (three-week wait for part); power window failure; excessive vibration when underway; excessive engine, brake, steering column, suspension, and wheel noise; trunk lid won't open; passenger-side carpet wet from AC; AC leaks coolant; driver's door won't open from the inside; fuel door lid broke in half; hood latch broke off when closing hood; right rear door moulding fell off; and poor-fitting interior panels. Engine malfunction light comes on for no apparent reason, and a fluttering noise comes from the PCV when the car is turned off.

Safety summary: In addition to an incredibly high number of safety-related recall campaigns, owner complaints confirm that the Focus suffers from serious quality deficiencies that may compromise safety. **All models: 2000–01**—Airbag deploys for no apparent reason or after vehicle hits a pothole. • Several complaints of second- and third-degree facial and hand burns arising from airbag deployment. • Airbag light remains on for no reason. • Sudden brake loss. • Differential fluid leaks on brake components (right side), causing brake loss. • Defective speed control causes sudden acceleration in spite of corrective recall. • Other sudden acceleration incidents ascribed to faulty power control module (PCM) and driver's shoe being caught under the plastic console. • Sudden acceleration in Reverse. • Chronic stalling, with loss of brakes and steering, believed to be caused by faulty fuel pump. • Collapse of tie-rod and axle, leading to loss of control. • Defective axle wheel bearing. • Sudden pull to the left when turning left. • Clutch pedal spring pops out, injuring driver. • Pedal fell on floorboard. • Transmission slippage and failure. • Inaccurate fuel gauge (sender and fuel pump replaced). • Windshield cracks for no reason. • AC condensation drips on accelerator pedal. • Exhaust fumes enter passenger compartment.

Secret Warranties/Service Tips/TSBs

All models: 2000—Under Special Service Instruction 00204, Ford will reprogram the powertrain computer module to correct poor engine performance on vehicles equipped with a manual transmission. • Vehicles equipped with a manual transmission will have their clutch master cylinder and pedal return spring replaced, free of charge, under ONP 00B59. • AC evaporator case/cowl leaks water into the interior (see following bulletin):

Evaporator Case/Cowl - Interior Water leaks

Article No. 01-9-2 05/14/01

^Water leak - water leak at front cowl area and/or from evaporator case area
^Climate control - water leak from evaporator case are and/or front cowl area

FORD:
2000-2001 Focus

ISSUE
Some vehicles may exhibit a water leak at the cowl or evaporator case area. This may be caused by water leaking from around the cowl grille seal to the windshield, the inlet housing seal to sheet metal sheet or the evaporator case seal to the lower dash panel.

ACTION
Repair the leaks to the body or cowl area or replace the evaporator case assembly.

• Whistling from the heater plenum. • AC fluttering noise. **2000–02**—Repeated heater core failure. **2001**—Shifter difficult to shift out of Park. • 2.0L Zetec engines may hesitate, surge, or idle roughly in cold weather. • Intermittent stall, hesitation, or lack of power. • Engine may produce higher-than-normal idle speed, or run roughly at idle. • Slight engine vibration at idle. • Troubleshooting the Check Engine light. • Eliminating a burning oil smell. • Rear brake squeal may be caused by the composition of the lining material. • Power-steering pump pulley may squeak or chirp upon start-up. • A squeaking may emanate from the door check strap area. • Ignition key may be difficult to turn in cylinder. • Seat seams may split.

Focus Profile

	2000	2001
Cost Price ($)		
LX	14,995	16,015
ZX3	16,697	16,690
Wagon SE	17,695	17,271
Used Values ($)		
LX ▲	11,000	13,000
LX ▼	10,000	12,000
ZX3 ▲	12,500	14,000
ZX3 ▼	11,000	13,000
Wagon SE ▲	13,000	14,500
Wagon SE ▼	11,500	13,500
Extended Warranty	Y	Y
Secret Warranty	Y	N
Reliability	❶	❷
Crash Safety (F)	⑤	⑤
Side Impact	③	④
Off-set	④	④
Head Restraints	③	④
Rollover Resistance	—	④

General Motors

CAVALIER, SUNFIRE (SUNBIRD) ★★★

RATING: Average (1996–2001); Not Recommended (1984–95). One of the better American small cars, which isn't saying much; repair bills will run you bankrupt if you get a pre-1996 model or if maintenance schedules aren't followed to the letter. Try to get a recent model with a 4-speed automatic transmission; it will be a bit more reliable, reduce engine noise, and make for more responsive performance. The base Sunbird became the LE in 1989, and then changed its name to the Sunfire in 1995. The Cavalier Z24 convertible was replaced by the LS in 1995. **Maintenance/Repair costs:** Average; repairs aren't dealer dependent; however, ABS troubleshooting is a real head-scratcher. **Parts:** Reasonably priced; often available for much less from independent suppliers. **Best alternatives:** The Ford Escort and Tracer, Geo Metro, GM Cavalier and Sunfire, Honda Civic, Hyundai Accent and Elantra, Mazda Protegé,

Nissan Sentra, Suzuki Esteem, and Toyota Corolla, Echo, or Tercel. Also take a look at the slightly more upscale Hyundai Tiburon.

Strengths and weaknesses: These twins are two of the lowest-priced cars to come equipped with standard ABS and dual airbags. They have exceptional styling (especially the coupe) and lots of interior room, with a nicely tuned suspension. The ride and handling have also improved markedly over the past three years, with power rack-and-pinion steering, a longer wheelbase, and a wider track. The Sunfire is identical to the Cavalier, except for its more rakish look. The Cavalier Z24 and Sunfire GT are performance versions of the compacts introduced four years ago. They use a more refined version of the Quad 4 2.4L DOHC 16-valve 4-cylinder powerplant.

Snappy road performance (with the right engine and transmission hookup), though, has been marred by abysmally poor reliability. The early 2.0L versions are lacklustre performers—overwhelmed by the demands of passing and merging. On top of that, major reliability weaknesses afflict many mechanical and body components prior to the 1997 model year, where engine, transmission, electronic module, and brake failures are particularly common. Specifically, owners report engine blocks crack, cylinder heads leak, and the turbocharged version frequently needs expensive repairs.

For 1990–94 versions, the Cavalier's base 2.2L 4-cylinder and optional 3.1L engines replaced the failure-prone 2.0L and 2.8L powerplants. Unfortunately, the newer engines also have a checkered reputation, highlighted by reports of chronic head gasket failures afflicting the 4-cylinder powerplant. Air conditioning and hood latch failures, seatbelt defects, and a plethora of body deficiencies are also commonplace. Door bottoms and wheel housings are particularly vulnerable to rust perforation. Premature paint peeling and cracking, discoloration, and surface rust have been regular problems through 1997.

Since 1996, these vehicles have become more reliable and durable. Nevertheless, owners are still plagued by faulty brakes, airbags that continue to malfunction and injure occupants, chronic stalling, and transmission and fuel pump failures. The Getrag manual gearbox isn't very reliable nor is it easily repaired, and faulty computer modules, fuel injection, and cooling systems cause stalling and a shaky idle. The power steering may lead or pull, and the steering rack tends to deteriorate quickly, usually requiring replacement some time shortly after 80,000 km. The front MacPherson struts also wear out rapidly, as do the rear shock absorbers. Many owners complain of rapid front brake wear and warped brake discs after a year or so. One owner reported the following brake repairs to NHTSA:

Front brake rotors are warping and had to be turned at 1,600 miles [2,560 km] and 1,800 miles [2,880 km]. They then were replaced at

2,800 miles [4,480 km]. They would cause the vehicle to jump when braking.

Fit and finish quality is variable, often leading to poor paint application, inside and outside body panel gaps, and lots of exposed screw heads. Most body hardware is fragile.

The 1995 model is wider and taller. Although its wheelbase is a bit longer, the body is about two inches shorter. Nevertheless, occupants get two additional inches of rear leg room in the coupe and about an inch and a half more in the sedan. The station wagon was dropped, but a wagon and convertible were added. Standard dual airbags and ABS, a stiffer structure, and an improved suspension were all part of the '95 redesign. In subsequent years, the '96 LS sedan and convertible got standard traction control, and the Z24 picked up a new dual-camshaft 2.2L engine. 1997 models were carried over with minor styling changes for the Z24 and a new Rally Sport coupe. For 1998, the base engine actually lost five horses. The 1999 2.4L twin-cam engine received a number of refinements to enhance reliability and fuel economy, in addition to longer-lasting front brake linings. Year 2000 models have a slightly restyled front and rear end, an improved storage area, standard AC and Pass Lock security system, upgraded ABS, and a smoother-shifting 5-speed manual transmission. 2001 versions returned unchanged.

Safety summary: All models: 1995—Steering locks up. • Faulty cruise control. • Windshield wipers fail in cold weather. • **1995–96**—ABS brake failure. • Airbags fail to deploy or deploy accidentally. • Inoperative horn. • Transmission slips out of Park. • Sudden acceleration, stalling. • Passenger-side seatbacks won't stay upright. **1996**—NHTSA has received 96 complaints of inadvertent airbag deployment, which include 10 crashes and injuries to 53 people. • Engine gaskets leak oil. **1997**— Engine fires. • Inadvertent airbag deployment. • Airbag failed to deploy. • During a collision, driver sustained serious leg injuries when the seat pushed her lower body under the instrument panel. • Sudden acceleration. • Chronic stalling and hesitation, particularly when it rains. • Premature engine cylinder failure; leaks oil. • Premature oil pump failure. • Faulty fuel pump relay provokes stalling. • Failure of the engine mounts and ignition switch. • Cruise control failure. • Restart after stalling causes engine to race. • Sudden loss of power. • Steering wheel locked up. • Transmission failures. • Noisy rear end due to faulty suspension struts. • Faulty master cylinder and modulator assembly led to brake failure. • Frequent front brake rotor warpage, premature pad wear, and excessive vibrations when braking. • ABS brake failure. • Horn failed. • Cracked water pump. • Dashboard cracking, rattling, and popping. • Defective instrument panel control module. • Low beam switch failure. • Inoperative lighting due to rotted-out wiring harness. • Door hinges don't hold door open. • Door came ajar while driving. •

Windshield wiper failure. • When turned off, windshield wiper stops in the field of vision. • Lug nuts are easily broken when changing tire. **1998**—Fire in the trunk area. • Odour of burning wires when driving. • Sudden acceleration. • Chronic stalling at idle or highway speeds, when turning, or whenever the AC or defroster is engaged. • Brakes continue to be a common safety complaint. Owners report complete brake failure and lockup, extended stopping distances, ABS that self-activates, premature rotor warpage and pad wear, and a grinding and knocking noise when braking. • Other reports target airbags that go off when they shouldn't and don't deploy when they should. • Airbag-induced burns and fractures are common. • Loose or broken engine mounts. • Chronic engine overheating. • Many reports of automatic transmission failures, slippage, and failure to hold in Park. • Steering wheel locks up after a cold start. • Steering shaft sheared off when turning. • Inaccurate fuel gauge. • One Saskatchewan *Lemon-Aid* reader reports that the rear bumper will crack extensively in cold weather if hit only slightly. • Windshield glare from the dash. • Driver seat lever interferes with entry/exit. **1999–2000**—The trunk lid remains open at such a low angle that it's easy to hit your head. **2001**—Fire caused by shorted wire in the back seat area. • Chronic stalling (fuel pump suspected) and hard starting. • Vehicle loses power due to a vacuum leak. • Gears slip and grind when shifting automatic transmission. • Steering loss; steering column creaking. • Noisy steering gear box. • Brake pulsation caused by brake rotor warping. • Reports of windshield and sunroof suddenly shattering. • Windshield constantly fogs up. **Cavalier: 1999–2000**—Engine fires. • Leaking fuel tank. Plastic fuel tank is easily punctured. • Right wheel axle twisted off vehicle. • Chronic hesitation, stalling, and surging. • Sudden acceleration. • Clutch will not disengage, causing sudden acceleration. • Faulty ABS. • Brake failure due to leaking master cylinder fluid. • ABS locked up, causing vehicle to go into a skid. • Airbags failed to deploy. • Seatbelt failed to retract. • Transmission wouldn't go into Reverse, transmission failed to engage upon start-up, automatic transmission locks up in Second gear, and vehicle rolled away even though parked with parking brake engaged. • When vehicle is in Drive with foot on the brake, it lurches forward, stalls, and produces a crashing sound. • During highway driving, the vehicle suddenly accelerated without steering control. • Rear leaf spring U-bolts broke, causing entire rear end to drop. • Front right side of the vehicle collapsed due to wheel bolts shearing off, causing the wheel to detach completely. • Springs are too weak, causing poor stability and control. • Floor mat impedes clutch pedal travel. • Sudden brake cable breakage while driving, brake grinding noise, and early warping of the front and rear brakes. • When stopping, vehicle makes a thumping noise. • When driving with door locked, it came ajar. • Hood flew up while driving. • Misaligned driver's door. • Windshield water leaks. • Check Engine light came on due to loose fuel cap. **Sunfire: 1999–2000**—Chronic stalling and brake failures. • Brake master cylinder leaks. • When brakes are applied, all the interior lights go out. • Dash warning light indicating time to upshift comes on at the wrong time. • Sudden transmission failure. • Fuel tank leakage. • AC fumes enter the interior at idle. • Airbags failed to fully inflate. • Horn only works intermittently. • Annoying squeak from both doors.

Secret Warranties/Service Tips/TSBs

All models: 1985–2000—Snow may intrude into the rear brake drum assembly and interfere with braking (see following bulletin):

Snow Intrusion Into Rear Drum Brake Assemblies

Bulletin No.: 00-05-24-001 Date: April, 2000

MODELS:

1985-87	Buick Somerset
1985-89	Buick Skyhawk
1985-98	Buick Skylark
1985-88	Cadillac Cimarron
1985-2000	Chevrolet Cavalier
1985-88	Oldsmobile Firenza
1985-91	Oldsmobile Cutlass Calais
1992-98	Oldsmobile Achieva
1985-94	Pontiac Grand Am
1995-2000	Pontiac Sunfire

CONDITION:

Some customers may comment that after operating their vehicle in snow and then parking the vehicle for an extended period, the rear brakes appear to remain applied.

CAUSE:

On rare occasions, light powdery snow may enter one or both or the vehicle's rear drum brake assemblies. If the vehicle is parked prior to the snow melt (water) being expelled, this may result in the rear brake shoe(s) adhering/freezing to the brake drum(s). Normally, the brake shoe(s) will break free of the drum upon placing the vehicle in gear. However, cases have been noted where vehicle movement has been restricted until the brake assemblies have had an opportunity to thaw.

CORRECTION:

Replace existing rear brake backing plates with new backing plates, P/N 18015841. Refer to the Drum Brake sub-section in the Service Manual for replacement procedures.

1992–97—Excessive timing chain noise is likely due to lack of maintenance; inspect the timing chain around 100,000 km to make sure the front oil passage plug isn't blocked by debris. **1993–94**—Excessive engine vibrations at idle or a clunk upon acceleration are most likely due to a defective engine mount. **1993–2002**—GM has a new kit that it says will eliminate AC odours. • A rotten-egg odour coming from the exhaust is probably caused by a malfunctioning catalytic converter; this repair is covered by GM's emissions warranty. • Paint delamination, peeling, or fading (see Part Two). **1994**—A squeaking noise heard when going over bumps, accelerating, or shifting can be stopped by replacing the exhaust manifold pipe seal. • Water leaks into the front footwell are discussed in depth in a December 1993 TSB. **1994–97**—An engine knock, rattle, or tap noise can be silenced by installing new pistons or rod assemblies. **1995–97**—Axle seal leakage may be caused by a pinched transaxle vent hose. • Delayed automatic transmission engagement after a cold soak signals the need to install a revised forward clutch housing assembly. • Rear brakes that heat up or drag may need the brake lamp switch adjusted or new parking brake cables. • Repair tips are offered for scuffed interior quarter-trim panels on convertibles. • A sticking deck lid may need an upgraded lid release cable. • A dome light that won't shut off probably has a corroded doorjamb switch. • The left-hand mirror may not adjust if the lever has become disengaged. • A popping noise originating from the engine compartment may mean that the torque strut-mount attaching bolts are loose. • Rear shock noise can be silenced by installing upgraded upper shock mounts. • Troubleshooting tips on silencing rear shock noise and rear seatback rattles and squeaks are available. • Door rattles when the window is lowered may be silenced by replacing the door glass downstop or front guides. **1995–98**—A bulge in the front bucket seatback requires additional bracing to correct. • Install a drain path in convertibles to prevent water from collecting in the rear footwell area. **1995–99**—A faulty rear lid (trunk) latch may only need a new cable. **1995–2000**—Instrument panel squeak or rattle, scratched right front door trim panel, or right-side end of instrument panel contacting door trim panel can be fixed by removing the instrument panel assembly and realigning the tie bar. This two-hour repair will be covered under GM's base warranty or through its "goodwill" policy. • GM will install upgraded rear brake backing plates to prevent snow intrusion freezing the brake shoes to the drums. **1996–97**—Coolant odour or leakage may occur at the joint where the radiator outlet pipe is connected to the coolant pump cover or at the joint between the cooling system air-bleed pipe and the coolant outlet. • Coolant loss, leakage, coolant lamp on, or coolant odour can be corrected by installing a new thermostat gasket. **1997**—A Low Engine Coolant light may come on to signal that the cooling system surge tank is defective. **1998**—A delayed, slow, or no Second-to-Third-gear upshift may require a new transmission case cover or assembly. • A 2.2L cold engine hesitation, sag, or stall may be corrected by recalibrating the power control module (PCM). **1999–2000**—No Third and Fourth gear may require a new direct clutch piston assembly (see following bulletin).

No Third and Fourth Gear

File in Section: 07 - Transmission/Transaxle
Bulletin No.: 99-07-30-031   Date: December, 1999

TECHNICAL

Subject:

No Third and Fourth Gear (Replace Direct Clutch Piston Assembly)

Models:

1999	Oldsmobile Cutlass
1999-2000	Oldsmobile Alero
1999-2000	Pontiac Grand Am, Sunfire

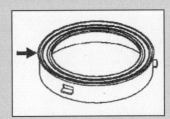

2000—Premature connecting rod failure if engine run at high rpms at low mileage. • Rough engine idle, misfire, Check Engine light all due to poorly calibrated computer module. • Possibility of engine coolant leaks caused by the upper radiator hose rubbing against the battery tray. • Automatic transmission may not go into Third or Fourth gear. • Mismachined sealing surface on forward clutch housing (4T40-E transmission). • Grinding or growling from transmission when in Park on an incline. • Vehicles equipped with a 2.2L engine may produce an annoying engine or transmission whine. • Door rattles. • Driver-side manual mirror doesn't adjust when the adjusting lever is moved. **2000–01**—Inaccurate fuel gauge readings can be corrected for free by installing a new fuel tank sender sensor kit under Customer Satisfaction Campaign #00101 (see following bulletin).

Fuel Gauge - Inaccurate/Erratic readings

Bulletin No.: 01-06-04-008 Date: February, 2001
Inaccurate or Erratic Fuel Gauge Reading
(Install New Fuel Tank Sender Sensor)

Models:

2000-01	Chevrolet Cavalier, Malibu
2000-01	Oldsmobile Alero
2000-01	Pontiac Grand Am, Sunfire
2000-01	Toyota Cavalier

Condition

Some customers may comment about inaccurate or erratic fuel gauge readings. A typical comment might be that it appears from the gauge reading that there is fuel available, yet the tank is nearly empty.

Cause

This condition may be the result of the corrosive effect of certain fuel blends on the contact surfaces of the fuel tank sender sensor.

Correction

Important: Dealers within the provinces of British Columbia, Quebec, New Brunswick and the State of Maine, should refer to Customer Satisfaction Campaign 00101, dated January 2001.

Part Number	Description
88950891	Fuel Tank Sender Sensor Kit

Warranty Information

Labor Operation	Description	Labor Time
L1197	Sensor, Fuel Level (Tank Unit) - Replace	1.2 hrs.

For vehicles repaired under warranty, use table as shown.

Dealers will do this repair free of charge under the base warranty.

Cavalier, Sunfire, and 2WD Chevrolet S-10 and GMC Sonoma pickups with 2.2L 4-cylinder engines: 1995–96—Engine head gasket failures that include overheating, loss of coolant, coolant odour, coolant leaks, around the cylinder head, and white smoke from the exhaust. Sometimes the heater won't work, or a film (from the coolant) will be deposited on the inside glass surfaces. If the coolant leaks inside the engine, it can cause severe engine damage from overheating. These vehicles are covered for head gasket problems for seven years or 100,000 miles (160,000 km), whichever comes first. Remember, if you have an engine head gasket failure on a GM vehicle or engine not included in the above-noted programs, don't despair. Simply use the same benchmarks for your own vehicle and threaten small claims action on those grounds.

Cavalier, Sunfire (Sunbird) Profile

	1994	1995	1996	1997	1998	1999	2000	2001
Cost Price ($)								
Cavalier	10,998	12,245	13,030	14,390	14,765	15,365	15,915	16,905
Z24	17,298	16,895	17,643	19,000	19,295	20,035	20,515	21,165
Z24 Conv./LS	20,298	22,185	22,925	24,285	25,880	26,450	27,200	—
Sunbird/LE	11,498	—	—	—	—	—	—	—
Sunfire	—	12,945	13,380	15,340	15,960	16,135	16,165	14,765
Used Values ($)								
Cavalier ʌ	3,500	4,500	5,500	7,000	8,000	9,000	10,500	12,000
Cavalier v	3,000	3,500	4,500	5,500	6,500	8,000	9,500	11,000
Z24 ʌ	5,000	6,000	7,000	8,500	10,000	12,500	14,500	16,000
Z24 v	4,000	5,000	5,500	7,000	8,000	11,000	13,000	15,000
Z24 Conv. /LS ʌ	6,500	7,500	9,500	11,000	13,000	16,000	18,000	—
Z24 Conv. /LS v	5,000	6,000	8,000	9,000	11,500	14,000	16,000	—
Sunbird/LE ʌ	3,000	—	—	—	—	—	—	—
Sunbird/LE v	2,500	—	—	—	—	—	—	—

Sunfire A	—	4,500	6,000	7,000	8,000	9,500	10,000	10,500
Sunfire V	—	3,500	4,500	5,500	6,500	8,000	8,500	9,000
Extended Warranty	Y	Y	Y	Y	Y	Y	Y	Y
Secret Warranty	Y	Y	Y	Y	Y	Y	Y	Y
Reliability	❶	❶	❶	③	③	③	③	③
Crash Safety (F)								
Cavalier 2d	—	—	—	—	③	③	③	③
Cavalier 4d	④	④	③	③	④	④	④	④
Side Impact								
Cavalier 2d	—	—	—	—	❶	❶	❶	❶
Cavalier 4d	—	—	—	—	❶	❶	❶	❶
Off-set	—	❷	❷	❷	❷	❷	❷	❷
Head Restraints	—	❷	—	❷	—	❷	—	❷
Rollover Resistance	—	—	—	—	—	—	—	④

Note: NHTSA says the Sunbird and Sunfire safety ratings should be identical to the Cavalier's score.

SATURN S-SERIES, L-SERIES   ★★★☆

RATING: *S-series:* Average (1997–2001); Not Recommended (1992–96). *L-series:* Above Average (2000–01). The fewer complaints registered against the L-series may mean better quality control or insufficient owner feedback. Nevertheless, Japanese and South Korean competitors have been proven to offer far better quality. Even GM's less pretentious models, like the Cavalier and Sunfire or the miniscule Metro and Firefly, offer better quality and value for your money. Don't go anywhere near a used Saturn unless you're armed to the teeth with a comprehensive extended warranty or have thoroughly perused this Saturn owners' forum: *www.pedsweb.com/saturn/.* As bizarre as it may appear, the Saturn division has a better reputation than the car it sells. **Maintenance/ Repair costs:** Average; repairs aren't dealer dependent, unless you're seeking some Saturn "goodwill" refunds. **Parts:** Higher-than-average cost, but not hard to find through independent suppliers. **Best alternatives:** The Honda Civic LX, Hyundai Elantra, and Toyota Corolla perform well and offer better quality.

Strengths and weaknesses: The entry-level S-series is far from high-tech and has remained virtually unchanged, except for the addition of a larger L-series for the 2000 model year, a minor face-lift, and a bit more leg room (phased in since it was launched in 1991). The base model provides a comfortable driving position, adequate instrumentation and controls, unobstructed visibility, good braking, dent-resistant body panels, and better-than-average crashworthiness scores. But, balancing these advantages, buyers have to contend with excessive engine noise, limited rear

seat room, optional ABS and traction control, the coupe's third-door
window that doesn't roll down, and serious factory-related deficiences.

L-series

In an attempt to save money by adapting a European car to the American
market, Saturn brought out the LS sedan and LW wagon, derivatives of
GM's Opel Vectra. Some major differences, however, include a length-
ened body, a standard ignition theft-deterrent system, a re-engineered
chassis to give a more comfortable ride, and the use of a home-grown
137-hp 2.2L 4-banger constructed with aluminum components
(remember the Vega?). Other components lifted directly from the
European parts bin are the Opel's 3.0L V6 engine, a manual transmission
from Saab, and German-made braking systems.

The more-expensive L-series models provide a more comfortable
driving position and a roomy interior with a full range of convenience
features, instruments, and controls. The V6 powertrain matchup, firm
ride, impressive high-speed stability, and impressive braking all point to
the L-series' European heritage. Additionally, there's better soundproofing and lots of storage areas, including a large, accessible trunk.

On the other hand, the interior isn't as refined as what you would
find in a Toyota or Honda, rear visibility is limited, the steering feels
heavy at low speeds and too light at higher speeds, audio controls seem
too small, and wagons give a jarring ride over bumps.

Saturns have exhibited a plethora of serious body and mechanical problems, which GM has masked by generously applying its base warranty to
original buyers. Second owners aren't treated as well, however, and
owners of used Saturns (taken in by all the "different car company"
hype) frequently complain that they had to pay dearly for GM's powertrain and body mistakes. Servicing quality has been spotty, too, and will
likely become more problematic as GM takes the division off life-support
in an effort to produce its first profitable year.

If the company can't make a profit, what's so great about Saturn? Its
advertising agency.

The loud, coarse, standard single-cam engine gives barely adequate
acceleration times with the manual transmission. This time is increased
with the 4-speed automatic gearbox, which robs the engine of what little
power it produces. Other generic problems affecting all model years are
stalling and hard starting. One Ontario owner of a 1994 Saturn plagued
with chronic stalling problems had this to say:

> After stalling in rush hour traffic, car was towed as hazard lights failed
> after ten minutes; unable to restart. Car was then towed. Cause indi-
> cated: bad fuel tank, pump, battery, ECM and ignition module.
> Replaced probe, module, pump, tank, valve, module, and battery.

After stalling a dozen or so times on my way to work and almost getting into an accident with a bus, I told the Customer Service in Toronto that they could come get the car from my work as I was not driving it home.

Technical service bulletins and owner complaints indicate that a variety of major quality problems are likely to crop up. These include self-destructing engines; chronically malfunctioning automatic transmissions; failure-prone brakes, ignition, fuel, and electrical systems; electrical short circuits; alternator and AC compressor failures; a host of body defects, led by paint delamination, rattles, wind and water leaks; and failure-prone Firestone tires (mostly the Affinity brand).

I bought your 2002 *Lemon-Aid* book last week and would like to bring something to your attention. You mention on page 82 about blow-outs with Affinity tires. Our 1997 SL2 Saturn had a blow-out at 100 km/h on the TransCanada this past summer about 115 km west of Sault Ste. Marie.... I contacted Transport Canada who advised me to keep the tire in case something becomes of this in the future. It ripped open on the side. Nothing is wrong with the tread. The car had 55,000 kilometres on it at the time.

Would I buy another car with Firestone tires? Absolutely not!

R.C.
Ontario

Safety summary: All models/years: Owners say horn isn't well positioned for emergency use and isn't sensitive enough. **All models: 1995**—Reports of stuck accelerators. • Plastic fuel line leaks fuel. • Airbag failed to deploy. • Seatbelt failed to restrain driver in collision. • Gear lever slips out of gear and is hard to put into Reverse. • Manual transmission jumps out of Third and Fifth gear. • Brake rotor warpage and failures. • Steering wheel shakes uncontrollably at 65 km/h. • Sudden head gasket failure caused other engine components to self-destruct. • Prematurely worn engine timing chain. • AC fan knob broke in half. • Windshield wiper nut fell out, causing the wiper to fail. **1996**—Airbag failed to deploy. • Rack-and-pinion steering gear failure. • Frequent brake failures. • Firestone tire blowouts. • Inadequate defrosting. • Engine suddenly accelerates to 3500 rpm at idle or when driving. • Engine suddenly stalls and can't be restarted. • Car slips out of Fifth gear. **1997**—Steering wheel came apart while car was being driven. • Several complaints of total loss of steering control. • Engine suddenly loses power while cruising on the highway. • In a rear-end collision, driver's seatback broke, causing serious injuries. **L-series: 2000–01**—Transmission can't be shifted into a forward gear. • Location of power seat button allows it to be accidently activated, causing seat to suddenly recline. • Power door locks short out. • Electrical short causes all lights and gauges to suddenly come on. • Faulty evaporator surge solenoids. • Seatbelt won't lock up at sudden stops. **SC1: 2000–01**—When applying brakes, there's excessive noise coming from the rear end. • Fuel sloshing sound when fuel tank is half full. **SC2: 2000–01**—Seatbelt tightens on any sudden movement, however slight. • The small, recessed horn buttons make it hard to find and activate the horn without looking down. **SL: 2000–01**—Steering wheel came apart while driving. • Total loss of steering when the retaining clip was omitted during assembly. **SL1: 2000–01**—Windshield wipers fail to adequately clean the windshield. • Defrosting system doesn't work properly, causing moisture damage and poor visibility. **SL2: 2000–01**—Sudden acceleration. • Complete brake failure. • Turn signal indicator sticks in the resume position. • Seatbelts are hard to engage. • When driving at night, one sees multiple lights when looking through the rear view mirror at the vehicle in back, as well as the reflection of the defroster lights. • During rainy weather, rear windshield view is distorted or wavy. **SW2: 2000–01**—Automatic transmission slippage caused collision. • Film collects on interior of windshield.

Secret Warranties/Service Tips/TSBs

All models: 1991–94—Rough running or surging after a cold start may signal the need to clean carbon or fuel deposits from the engine's intake valves. • The many causes of hard-to-crank windows are covered in TSB #94-T-19. • Inoperative electric door locks may have been shorted by water contamination. The design and positioning of the relay for the power door lock allows this to occur. • Whistling noises are also treated in two different bulletins published in June and October 1994. **1991–95**—Erratic cruise control operation can be corrected by replacing the cruise control module assembly. • If the engine stalls within five minutes of starting or when coming to a stop, or is difficult to restart, the oil viscosity or engine's hydraulic lifters may be at fault. • Engine squealing after a cold start can be corrected by installing an upgraded belt idler pulley assembly. **1991–97**—Engines that run hot or have coolant mixed in the engine oil probably have a defective engine cylinder—a factory-related goof, according to a GM service bulletin. As a partial response to angry Saturn owners, GM has set up a "goodwill" warranty to pay for head gasket repairs for 6 years/160,000 km on all 1994–96 models. Owners of model years not covered will get their refunds from small claims court.

Saturn Corporation
100 Saturn Parkway
PO Box 1000
Spring Hill, TN 37174-1500

June, 1999

SΛTURN

Dear Saturn Owner,

We are writing to let you know of a Special Policy relating to 1994 through 1996 Saturn vehicles equipped with 1.9L Single Over Head Cam (SOHC) engines.

Certain Saturn Vehicles equipped with 1.9L SOHC engines may develop a crack internal to the cylinder head. Early evidence of this would be abnormal discoloration within the coolant reservoir, and/or the engine may run hot.

As a result, this Special Policy provides cylinder head coverage for a period of six years from the date the vehicle was originally placed in service, or 100,000 miles, whichever comes first. The policy covers both the original owner, and any subsequent owners for the six-year/100,000 mile duration. Please keep this letter with your other important glovebox literature for further reference.

If your vehicle should develop a cylinder head crack within six-years/ 100,000 miles, whichever comes first, Saturn will repair your vehicle at no charge. A Saturn Retailer must perform repairs qualifying for this special coverage, and the time needed to replace a cylinder head is approximately ten (10) hours. Due to scheduling and processing time, your Retailer may need to keep your vehicle overnight.

You will be eligible for reimbursement if you have already paid for some or all of the cost to have the cylinder head replaced, and your vehicle was within the six-year/100,000 mile parameter at the time of repair.

Saturn Corporation
99P01

This letter sets the latest benchmark as to how long GM feels its engine head gaskets should last. Bring it to court with you, if polite negotiations fail.

• If your Saturn runs out of fuel while the fuel gauge reads one-quarter full, it's likely you have a plugged EVAP canister vent, which should be repaired free of charge under the emissions warranty (1996–97 models). • Excessive front brake noise or pulsation requires the installation of upgraded brake pads, according to TSB #96-T-40A. **1991–98**—Excessive rear brake noise or pulsation requires the installation of upgraded rear brake pads, according to TSB #855001. • Water leaks into the front footwell and at the front upper door frame are treated in depth in TSB

#481503R. **1993–97**—Troubleshooting tips are available for diagnosing delayed or harsh automatic transmission shifting into Reverse. **1993–2001**—A rotten-egg odour coming from the exhaust is likely the result of a malfunctioning catalytic converter, which you can have replaced free of charge under GM's emissions warranty (1996 and later models). • Paint delamination, peeling, or fading (see Part Two). **1994**—A Saturn equipped with a manual transmission may have the transaxle stuck in gear due to a defective shift control housing. • Excessive vibration at 77–87 km/h may be corrected by installing a powertrain damper kit. **1994–95**—Excessive engine knocking can be corrected by changing the clearance between the piston pin and connecting rod bushing. **1994–98**—Loss of airflow from the AC vents is likely due to the evaporator freezing; re-adjust the compressor. **1995–97**—Electrical accessories may lose power after the car is started or while it's on the road. GM blames the problem on a defective ignition lock cylinder. **1996–97**—If your security alarm won't work properly or your dome light won't go out, GM suggests you change the doorjamb switches. • Water leaks into the headliner on cars equipped with a sunroof require new drain hoses or better sealing. **1996–98**—A knock or rattle heard from the front of the vehicle when decelerating may be caused by a wiring harness short circuit. If the same noise is heard at all times, you may need to replace the clutch disc and the clutch cover. • A no-start condition accompanied by electrical malfunctions may be caused by a shorted instrument panel wire harness (see following bulletin).

Eng No Crnk, MIL/ABS Lght On, Prk Imp/Fuel Gge/Spkr inop

BULLETIN NO.: 98-T-22   ISSUE DATE: July, 1998
GROUP/SEQ. NO.: Electricl-03   CORPORATION NO.: 887202
SUBJECT: Engine will not Crank, MIL and ABS Light On, Park Lamps Inoperative, Fuel Gauge Inoperative, and/or Radio Speaker Inoperative (Repair Wire Harness)
MODELS AFFECTED:
1996-1998 Saturns equipped with MP2/MP3 manual transaxles
CONDITION:
The customer may comment that on occasion, one of more of the following conditions may have occurred:
• Engine will not crank
• Malfunction indicator lamp (MIL)(SERVICE ENGINE SOON lamp) on with or without inoperative fuel gauge
• Anti-Lock brake system (ABS) light on
• Park lamps inoperative
• One or more of the radio speakers inoperative
CAUSE
The cause of the above conditions may be the Instrument Panel wire harness coming into contact with the clutch pedal pivot bolt/clip causing a short ground.

1996–99—A noisy window regulator may need a new counter-balance spring. • Water leaks into the rear luggage compartment area need the body seam sealer gaps plugged. **1997–98**—A leaking automatic transaxle case assembly should be replaced with an upgraded assembly. **1998**— Dozens of bulletins target a plethora of rattles, whistles, pops, clicks, knocking, and grinding noises. • Sunroof, footwell, and trunk water leaks are also common problems addressed in a variety of service bulletins. • Excessive vehicle vibration. • Noisy window regulator. • Premature corrosion near door weather strip. • Loss of AC vent airflow. • Reducing AC odours. • Power-steering pump drive shaft seal leak. • Intermittent no-start. • Transaxle whine in Second gear. • Rear brake noise and pulsation countermeasures. **1999**—Harsh shifting. • Excessive exhaust system noise. • Steering column popping. • Rattle, pop, or clicking noise from front of vehicle. • AC noise (hissing). • Clunking noise in front side door when windows are operated. • Troubleshooting chronic short circuits. • Water leak onto headliner and/or left footwell area and rear luggage compartment. • Excessive vibration at cruising speed. **2000**—In a March 2000 Customer Satisfaction Campaign letter (No: 00-C-09) sent to dealers, GM admits that the Saturn 2.2L 4-cylinder engines "were produced with internal engine components that may fail prematurely. The most likely symptom you may experience is an engine miss accompanied by an engine noise." GM says it will replace the engine at no charge with no mileage or time limitations, in addition to providing a loaner vehicle or paying rental costs. **2000–01**—Delayed, harsh engagement into Reverse or Drive, erratic shifting between First and Second gear, or no Second or Third gears. • AC odours upon start-up; AC sizzling or hissing type noise heard when the AC has been used. • Service Engine light comes on for no reason. • Front door outside handle may come in contact with the front door outer panel. • Steering column popping noise during low-speed turns; steering wheel shake or vibration at highway speeds (see following bulletin).

Steering Wheel - Shake or Vibration

Bulletin No.: 99-T-55A   Issue Date: September, 2000
Group/Seq. No.: Chassis-05   Corporation No.: 99-00-91-002A
Subject: Steering Wheel Shake or Vibration at Highway Speeds (Balance Tire/Wheel Assemblies, Replace Front Lower Control Arm Rear Bushings, and Replace Tires if Necessary). Due to updated lower control arm rear bushings being available, this bulletin has been revised and supersedes bulletin 99-T-55, which should be discarded.

Models Affected:
2000-2001 Saturn L-Series vehicles
Condition:
Some customers may comment regarding a steering wheel shake or vibration felt when driving vehicle at highway speeds. This condition is most noticeable on smooth road surfaces at vehicle speeds above 65 mph (105 km/h). ➤

Cause:

Vehicle sensitivity to out-of-balance tire/wheel assemblies or excessive force variation within the tire/wheel assembly.

Correction:

Balance all four tire/wheel assemblies and evaluate. (Regardless of VIN.)
Replace front lower control arm rear bushings.
(On vehicles built before and including VIN YY697118.)
It may also be necessary to replace two or four tires with qualified tires. (Regardless of VIN.)

Procedure:

Balance, Rotate, and/or, Replace Tires.

Take note: this problem may involve replacing all four tires, *at Saturn's expense*, during the warranty period.

• Dome lamp, sunroof or headliner rattling. • Muffler assembly rattling or clunk noise. • Defective sunroof sunshade fabric. • Inoperative power windows and sunroof. • Rear compartment side carpet falls down at deck-lid hinge area. • Intermittent operation or difficulty in programming remote keyless entry transmitter. **1996–2001 S-series sedans and 1997–2001 S-series coupes equipped with sunroofs**—Water leaks onto headliner are likely caused by a faulty sunroof or plugged drain hole grommets. **2000–01 L-series**—No Third and Fourth gear (replace direct clutch piston assembly). • Steering wheel shake or vibration at highway speeds. • Service Engine light and engine coolant temperature gauge needle in the red zone.• Noisy cooling fan operation. • Front doors relock after being unlocked with key. • Rattle from behind the right-hand side of the instrument panel. • Wind whistle from the front door glass area and from the outside rear-view mirror. • Door glass may bind and distort outer window run channel weather strips. • Headliner sagging.

Saturn S-series, L-series Profile

	1994	1995	1996	1997	1998	1999	2000	2001
Cost Price ($)								
SL	11,595	12,395	12,998	13,948	14,188	13,488	13,588	14,358
SC	13,895	14,795	15,348	16,028	16,418	16,618	16,743	16,763
LS/L100	—	—	—	—	—	—	19,255	20,065
LW/LW200	—	—	—	—	—	—	24,400	25,235
Used Values ($)								
SL ⋀	3,500	4,000	5,000	6,000	7,000	8,000	10,000	11,500
SL ⋁	3,000	3,500	4,500	5,000	6,000	7,000	9,000	10,000
SC ⋀	5,000	6,500	7,000	8,000	10,000	11,000	12,500	13,500
SC ⋁	4,000	5,000	6,000	7,000	8,500	9,500	11,000	12,500
LS/L100 ⋀	—	—	—	—	—	—	14,000	16,500
LS/L100 ⋁	—	—	—	—	—	—	12,500	15,000
LW/LW200 ⋀	—	—	—	—	—	—	18,000	20,500
LW/LW200 ⋁	—	—	—	—	—	—	16,000	18,500

Extended Warranty	Y	Y	Y	Y	Y	Y	Y	Y
Secret Warranty	Y	Y	Y	N	N	N	N	N
Reliability	❷	❷	❷	③	③	③	④	④
Crash Safety (F)	④	④	④	④	⑤	⑤	—	—
L-series	—	—	—	—	—	—	—	④
Side Impact	—	—	—	③	③	③	—	—
L-series	—	—	—	—	—	—	—	❷
Off-set	—	③	③	③	③	③	③	③
L-series	—	—	—	—	—	—	③	③
Head Restraints	—	❶	❶	❶	❶	❶	❶	❶
Rollover Resistance	—	—	—	—	—	—	—	④

Note: Poor head restraint rating includes both S- and L-series.

General Motors/Suzuki

FIREFLY, METRO, SPRINT/SWIFT ★★★★

RATING: Above Average (1998–2001); Average (1995–97); Below Average (1987–94). Stay away from AC-equipped versions, unless you want to invest in an AC repair facility. Look at the redesigned 1998 version for better quality, a new body style, standard dual airbags, and a peppier 4-cylinder engine. Convertibles pack plenty of fun and performance into a reasonably priced subcompact body. The Suzuki Swift carried on alone after the 2000 model year. **Maintenance/Repair costs:** Average. **Parts:** Expensive; sometimes drivetrain and body components are back-ordered several weeks. **Best alternatives:** The Honda Civic LX, Hyundai Accent, Suzuki Esteem, and Toyota Tercel perform well and offer better quality.

Strengths and weaknesses: Cheap to buy and run, providing better-than-average quality control and crashworthiness, these tiny, 3- and 4-cylinder front-drive hatchbacks offer good performance and impressive economy for urban dwellers. In fact, these little squirts should be considered primarily city vehicles due to their small size, small tires, low ground clearance, and average high-speed handling. Interior garnishing is decent but plain, and there's plenty of room for two passengers, with four fitting in without too much discomfort. The turbocharged convertible model is an excellent choice for high-performance thrills in an easy-to-handle ragtop.

On the downside, owners will face an anemic, noisy engine that makes these cars the antithesis of "swift"; a harsh, choppy ride; lots of interior noise; a spartan interior; poorly performing original equipment tires; and inadequate braking.

Mechanically speaking, the GM/Suzuki partnership has kept factory-related defects to a minimum, particularly following the '95 model's redesign. Trouble spots on pre-'95 models: excessive oil consumption; automatic transmission and differential failures around 80,000 km; electrical system shorts; a faulty AC and cooling system (fogging of the side windows and windshield due to inadequate heat distribution is a common complaint); premature brake, clutch, and exhaust system wearout; and minor fuel-supply malfunctions. Body construction is the pits on these models.

The cars were redesigned for the 1995 model year and were built with more care. Additionally, they gained more horsepower, standard dual front airbags, improved road feel, a more comfortable ride, quieter operation, and more cabin space. The '98 models underwent another revamping and replaced the Geo moniker with Chevrolet. The engine got nine additional horses, de-powered airbags (important for short drivers) became a standard feature, the front and rear end were re-styled, and radios and interior fabrics were upgraded. Since then, these econoboxes haven't had any important upgrades.

Remaining problems on the 1995–2001 models have been premature front brake wear; electrical system and AC malfunctions; and subpar body assembly, highlighted by paint peeling and discoloration, early rusting, and poorly fitted body panels, leading to rattles and air and water leaks.

Safety summary: All models/years: Side window defogging is slow and sometimes inadequate. • Driver's window continually pops out of its mount. • A Maritimes couple reported that their '91 Firefly suddenly careened out of control after the "control" bar broke. **All models: 1999—**Airbags failed to deploy. • Airbags deployed at very low collision speed. • Loose fuel hose caused fuel leak. • Cracked engine head gasket. • Premature wearout of front brake pads. • Defective suspension strut and mount caused premature tire wear, vibration, and pulling. Tires aren't very durable. • Inaccurate speedometer; dealer says it can't be repaired. • Key is hard to insert into doors, often jams. • Sealant seeps out of windshield, windows, and doors. **2000—**Sudden, unintended acceleration accompanied by brake failure. • Loss of steering control. • Excessive vibration/shimmying when underway. • Chronic stalling when shifting from Park to Drive or when the AC is engaged. • Airbag warning light stays lit.

Secret Warranties/Service Tips/TSBs

All models: 1993–99—Troubleshooting tips on correcting condensation in exterior lights. • Paint delamination, peeling, or fading (see Part Two). **1993–2000—**GM has a special kit that will reduce AC odours. Its installation falls under the base warranty. **1994–98**—GM outlines which conditions require new or refaced brake rotors. **1997–2000**—Reasons why speedometer gives inaccurate readings. **1998–2000**—Outside rear mirror housing turns chalky/dull. **1999–2000**—Engine overheating and/or loss of coolant may be due to a faulty radiator filler neck or cap.

Firefly, Metro, Sprint/Swift Profile

	1994	1995	1996	1997	1998	1999	2000	2001
Cost Price ($)								
Firefly	9,145	10,395	10,995	11,495	11,680	10,690	11,410	—
Metro	8,995	10,395	10,995	11,495	11,680	10,690	11,410	—
Swift	8,995	10,495	10,995	10,995	11,495	11,595	11,595	11,595
Used Values ($)								
Firefly ⋀	3,000	3,500	4,000	5,000	6,000	6,500	7,500	—
Firefly ⋁	2,000	3,500	3,500	4,000	4,500	5,000	6,500	—
Metro ⋀	3,000	3,500	4,000	5,000	6,000	6,500	7,500	—
Metro ⋁	2,000	3,500	3,500	4,000	4,500	5,000	6,500	—
Swift ⋀	3,000	3,500	4,000	5,000	6,000	7,000	7,500	8,500
Swift ⋁	2,500	3,000	3,500	4,500	5,000	5,500	7,000	7,500
Extended Warranty	N	N	N	N	N	N	N	N
Secret Warranty	Y	Y	Y	Y	Y	N	N	N
Reliability	➋	➋	③	④	④	④	④	④
Crash Safety (F)	③	③	④	④	—	—	—	—
Head Restraints	—	➊	—	—	—	—	—	—

Honda

CIVIC, DEL SOL   ★★★★

RATING: Above Average (1996–2001); Average (1984–95). A high resale value prices these cars beyond many buyers' budgets; if you want to get a good buy at a fair price, the 1996–98 models are your best bet. These small cars have been downgraded due to the increasing number of safety- and performance-related defects reported by owners of recent models. Defects include airbags that fail to deploy or deploy with such force that they cause severe injuries, ABS brake failures and constant rotor and pad maintenance, sudden acceleration, original equipment tire failures, and considerable instability on wet roads. **Maintenance/Repair costs:** Average. Repairs can be carried out by independent garages, but the 16-valve engine's complexity means that dealer servicing is a must. To avoid costly engine repairs, owners must check the engine timing belt every 3 years/ 60,000 km and replace it every 100,000 km ($300). **Parts:** Parts are a bit more expensive than most other cars in this class; airbag control modules and body panels for 2001 models may be back-ordered for weeks. **Best alternatives:** GM's Firefly or Metro, the Hyundai Accent or Elantra, Mazda Protegé, Nissan Sentra, Suzuki Esteem, and Toyota Echo or Corolla. The CRX's '93 del Sol replacement was a cheapened spin-off that carried over the CRX's disadvantages, without the high-performance thrills. Si models are Honda's factory hot rods (the Acura 1.6 EL is an Si clone), which provide lots of high-performance thrills, without the bills. Equipped with four-wheel disc brakes, the Si's mediocre braking and its lack of low-end torque are the car's main performance flaws.

Strengths and weaknesses: The quintessential econobox, Civics have distinguished themselves by providing sports-car acceleration and handling with excellent fuel economy and quality control that is far better than what American, European, or Asian automakers can deliver. Other advantages: a roomy, practical trunk; smooth-shifting automatic transmission; a comfortable ride; good front and rear visibility; high-quality construction; bulletproof reliability; and simple, inexpensive maintenance.

Some Civic disadvantages: the Si's suspension may be too firm for some, and its spoiler may block rear visibility. It's hard to modulate the throttle without having the car surge or lurch. The base engine loses its pep when the Overdrive gear on the automatic transmission engages in city driving, and the VTEC variant is noisy. Seats lack sufficient padding, rear access is difficult, rear seat room is limited to two adults, there's lots of engine and road noise, and an unusually large number of safety-related complaints include airbag malfunctions, sudden acceleration, and complete brake failure.

1984–91 Civics suffer from failing camshafts, crankshafts, and head gaskets, as well as prematurely worn piston rings. The 12-valve engine is prone to valve problems and is costly to repair. Early fuel-injection units were also problematic until the system was redesigned in 1988. Manual transmission shifter bushings need frequent replacement, and the automatic version needs careful attention once the 5-year/150,000 km point has been reached.

What are minor body faults with recent models turn into major rust problems with older Civics, where simple surface rust rapidly turns into perforations. The underbody is also prone to corrosion, which leads to severe structural damage that compromises safety. The fuel tank, front suspension, and steering components, along with body attachment points, should be examined carefully in any Civic more than a decade old. All hatchbacks let in too much wind and road noise due to poor sound insulation. Owners complain of water leaking into the engine compartment and trunk area, where suspension component mountings are weakened by corrosion and trunk wheelwells perforate quickly.

The 1988 redesign improved handling and increased interior room, but engine head gasket failures on non-VTEC engines became a problem through 1999, although the following bulletin only includes 1988–95 models:

Head Gasket Leaks.

97-047   November 10, 1997

Applies To: 1988 - 95 Civic - All, except VTEC
Head Gasket Leaks
(Supercedes 97-047, dated September 29, 1997)

PROBLEM

The head gasket leaks oil externally or allows coolant into the combustion chambers.

CORRECTIVE ACTION

Install the new style cylinder head gasket and the new head bolts in the Cylinder Gasket Kit listed under PARTS INFORMATION. Use the cylinder head bolt torque sequence described in this bulletin.

Out of warranty:

Any repair performed after warranty expiration may be eligible for goodwill consideration by the District Service Manager or your Zone Office. You must request consideration, and get a decision, before starting work.

The repair is free, if the client squawks.

On 1988–91 models, there isn't a great deal of torque with the 1.6L engine below 3500 rpm, and serious powertrain, brake, electrical-system and body problems—present since the car's debut—continue to appear. The front brakes continue to wear out quickly and are often noisy when applied, causing excessive steering wheel vibration. Premature constant velocity joint and boot wear on all cars is another problem area that needs careful inspection before purchasing. The rack-and-pinion steering assembly often needs replacement around the 5-year mark.

The 1992 Civic redesign axed the wagon, added standard driver-side airbags, and offered upgraded engines to some models. As for performance and other features: EX and Si acceleration is smooth and sprightly, but CX and VX acceleration is painfully slow. The four-door models ride extremely well, and all models exhibit nimble handling and good road holding under dry conditions. Unfortunately, the hatchback offers little rear-seat room, insufficient cargo space, and allows too much engine noise to intrude into the interior.

These models continued to be both more rugged and more reliable than the competition, yet they too have their faults. As an addendum to the safety problems mentioned earlier, owners report engine head gasket and crankshaft failures, transmission slippage, frequent and expensive brake repairs (rotor warpage, pad replacement, and defective master cylinder), AC failures, chronic water leaks, and early exhaust system rust-out.

1993 models returned practically unchanged, except for an optional passenger-side airbag offered with the EX. The same airbag was added as a standard feature on all '94 models, in addition to 14-inch tires for the LX and greater availability of optional ABS. The '95 models remained unchanged.

The '96 model changes added standard dual airbags and ABS for EX sedans, additional length and soundproofing, and upgraded engines throughout the model lineup. Outward visibility is much improved through thinner roof pillars and a larger rear window. Cargo capacity was also expanded with split-folding rear seatbacks. 1997–98 models saw larger wheels, a slight restyling, and manual seat-height adjusters, while the '99 model year was highlighted by the mid-year debut of the upgraded Si, revised front and rear styling, and an improved instrument panel.

Year 2000 models returned unchanged, but the 2001 Civic got more interior room, a horsepower boost, and styling similar to a small Accord. The hatchback was dropped, however.

Quality control on the 1996 through 2001 models is still better than the competition; however, decade-old safety and performance problems continue to appear year after year with increasing severity. Owners complain of a constantly lit Check Engine light; faulty engine computer module and oxygen sensor; early replacement of the crankshaft pulley and timing belt; fuel system, transmission, and electrical failures; expensive front brake maintenance caused by warped rotors and prematurely worn pads; AC malfunctions; clogged AC drain, pooling water on front passenger floor area; a clunky suspension; windshield air leaks and noise; hard-to-access horn buttons; windows that fall off their tracks; side mirrors that vibrate excessively; headlights that can't be focused properly and are prone to water leaks; gas-tank fumes that leak into the interior; and (are you ready for this?) premature rusting, uneven paint application, and *paint delamination*. Here's what this owner of a 2001 Civic discovered:

> Paint is developing crows feet in four separate places...body shop said it was due to bird droppings or sap. I believe this to be impossible and believe it to be a defect in the paint. Blemishes and loss of gloss continue to develop in the paint.

Safety summary: All models: 1995–99—Spoiler restricts rear visibility, and large rear-view mirror restricts forward visibility for tall drivers. • Civic owners report numerous safety defects that include airbags that fail to deploy, deploy inadvertently, or deploy with such force they cause severe injuries. • Ball joints on these vehicles don't have a castilated nut to secure the ball in position; the nut can back off, and the ball pulls out of the steering arm. • Other safety-related complaints: dangerous instability on wet roads, sudden acceleration or stalling, faulty cruise control,

ABS brake failures and constant rotor and pad replacement, defective automatic transmission, transmission that suddenly jumps into Reverse, original equipment tire failures, hood and trunk lids that come crashing down, inoperative door locks, cracked windshields, and headlights and interior lights that suddenly go out. **2000**—Airbags failed to deploy. • Accelerator pedal sticks; cables mounted too tight. • Accelerator cable got hung up in the cruise control, causing the vehicle to suddenly accelerate. • While driving, vehicle suddenly accelerated due to the throttle sticking open, and brakes couldn't stop the car. • Car suddenly accelerated when passing another vehicle. • Gas pedal keeps sticking, while driving at a low speed. • Transmission popped out of gear and brake pedal went right to the floor, without any braking effect. • Brakes locked up and vehicle pulled to the left when coming to an emergency stop. • Sudden steering loss while driving. • Excessive vibration due to engine main bearing failure. • Transmission sometimes fails to change gear. • Vehicle suddenly went into Reverse although shift lever was put into Drive. • While stopped at a light on a hill, vehicle suddenly shifted into Reverse. • Another driver had the same thing happen, except this time the transmission shifted into Neutral. • Transmission was stuck in Reverse. • Faulty power door lock makes it impossible to open door from the inside or outside. • Dome light won't work when doors are open. • Taillights don't work when the headlights and dash lights are on. • Rear-view mirror is poorly located and is non-adjustable, creating a large forward blind spot for tall drivers. • Sheet metal fatigue on both front fenders. • Faulty hood support rod causes the hood to come crashing down. • Exterior rear-view mirror becomes loose, despite dealer efforts to tighten it. **2001**—Car caught on fire near where the oxygen sensor wires are located. • Child became entangled in rear-seat shoulder belt; had to be cut free. • Airbag failed to deploy. • Car hesitates or stalls when decelerating. • Vehicle surged forward when put into Reverse and engaged Reverse when put into Drive (transmission solenoid suspected cause). • Transmission may suddenly pop out of Second gear while underway or refuse to shift into Third or Fourth gear. • Transmission leaks. • Vehicle rolls back when stopped on an incline. • Sudden brake failure (master cylinder replaced). • When brakes are applied first thing in the morning, they don't "grab," resulting in extended stopping distance. • Leaking front strut causes poor handling and front-end noise. • Incorrect fuel gauge and speedometer readings. • Airbag warning light is constantly lit (heating coil or core is suspected). • Loose door latches. • Interior lights dim when AC is engaged. • Rear-view mirror blocks forward vision of tall drivers. • Ignition buzzes at first attempt to start the car; engine catches on the second try. • Water leaks into trunk through taillights, onto driver's side carpet through door or firewall, or wets front passenger-side carpet (AC condensate suspected).

Secret Warranties/Service Tips/TSBs

Most Honda TSBs allow for special warranty consideration on a "good-will" basis even after the warranty has expired or the car has changed hands. Referring to this euphemism will increase your chances of getting some kind of refund for repairs that are obviously related to a factory defect. **All models: 1988–2000**—A rear suspension clunk can be silenced by replacing the rear trailing arm bushing.

Rear Suspension - Clunk Noise

00-006   March 28, 2000
Applies To: 1988-00 Civic - ALL

Clunk From Rear Suspension
Symptom:
A clunk from the rear suspension when going over rough or bumpy roads.
Probable Cause:
Broken rear trailing arm bushing(s).
Corrective Action:
Replace the rear trailing arm bushing(s).
Warranty Claim Information:

OP#	Description	FRT	Template ID
419104	Replace right bushing	0.9	00-006A
419103	Replace left bushing	0.9	00-006B
419102	Replace both bushings	1.8	00-006C

In warranty: The normal warranty applies.
Failed Part: P/N 52385-SR3-000
                    H/C 4098299
Defect Code: 042
Contention Code: B07
Skill Level: Repair Technician

Out of warranty: Any repair performed after warranty expiration may be eligible for goodwill consideration by the District Service Manager or your Zone office. You must request consideration, and get a decision, before starting work.

Don't expect any "goodwill" assistance beyond 5 years/100,000 km.

1992–97—An abnormally long crank time before the car starts may be caused by a leaking check valve inside the fuel pump. • Water leaking into the footwell from under the corner of the dash can be stopped by applying sealer to the seam where the side panel joins the bulkhead. **1994–97**—If the AC doesn't blow cold air, you may need to replace both the evaporator and the receiver/dryer. • When operating a manual or power-assisted front window, the rear edge of the glass comes out of the channel. **1995–97**—A wind whistle at the top of the windshield can be silenced by applying additional sealer. **1996–97**—In a settlement with the

U.S. Environmental Protection Agency, Honda paid fines totalling $17.1 million and extended its emissions warranty on 1.6 million 1995–97 models to 14 years or 150,000 miles (240,000 km). This means that costly engine components and exhaust system parts like catalytic converters will be replaced free of charge, as long as the 14-year/ 150,000 mile limit hasn't been exceeded. Additionally, the automaker will provide a full engine check and emissions-related repairs at 50,000 to 75,000 miles (80,000–120,000 km) and will give free tune-ups at 75,000 to 150,000 miles (120,000–240,000 km). It is estimated the free checkups, repairs, and tune-ups will cost Honda over $250 million. The story of the settlement was first reported on page 6 of the June 15, 1998, edition of *Automotive News*. Canadian owners may wish to use this settlement as leverage for free repairs in Canada, or use the full terms of the settlement when visiting the States. One thing is certain: neither Transport Canada nor Environment Canada are sufficiently enthused to render any assistance. **1996–98**—Windows that bind or fall out of their run channels need new run channels. • A poorly performing AC may need a new condenser fan motor and shroud. • An exhaust rattle or buzz can be silenced by replacing the heat shield or exhaust pipe. **1996–2000**—Harsh shifts (see following bulletin).

A/T - Harsh Shifts/MIL ON

00-012   June 20, 2000

Applies To:
1996-00 Civic - See VEHICLES AFFECTED
1997-99 CR-V - See VEHICLES AFFECTED
Harsh Shifting Automatic Transmission
(Supersedes 00-012, dated April 4, 2000)

Symptom:
The transmission shifts harshly, or it may stay in first gear. The MIL may be on with DTC P0730 or P0715 stored.

Probable Cause:
Contamination of the linear solenoid and its associated passages inside the transmission.

Corrective Action:
Flush the transmission with Genuine Honda ATF, then replace the linear solenoid.

This repair takes about an hour and may be covered by "goodwill" if the base warranty has expired.

1996–2001—Oil pressure switch Product Update Campaign (secret warranty). Another free fix if the dealer is on your side. **1998–2000**—Rear shelf rattling or buzzing. **1999–2000**—Coolant may leak from the reservoir cap outlet. • Popping noise or vibration from driver's footrest. **2000**—Steering pull or drifting. • Whistling or howling noise coming from the top middle of the windshield at highway speeds. • Moon roof seal sticks up or leaks. • Key is difficult to remove from the ignition switch; rear door lock tab is hard to open. • Warped wheel covers. 2001—Product Update Campaign for the inspection or replacement of the engine control module/PCM.

Product Update: Civic Powertrain Control Module

January 2001

Dear Civic Owner:
We have sent this letter to notify you of a potential problem with your 2001 Civic, and to inform you of what you need to do to have it repaired.

What is the problem?
The Powertrain Control Module (PCM), the computer that controls the engine, could possibly be damaged by a power surge in your car's electrical system. If this happens, the Malfunction Indicator Lamp (MIL) may come on. Additional symptoms could be flashing shift indicator lights, inability to shift out of Park, and/or an erractic engine idle.

What should you do?
Call your Honda dealer at your earliest opportunity and make an appointment to have your car repaired. The dealer will replace the PCM with an updated module. *This repair will be done free of charge.*

This campaign applies only to DX and LX models and takes about an hour to perform.

• Delayed upshift after a cold start. • Stiff manual transmission shifter; pops out of gear. • Rear main seal leak troubleshooting tips. • Separation of the lower control arm ball joints. • Noisy or stiff steering; fluid leakage. • Troubleshooting tips for front-brake groan or squeal. • Engine vibration and under-hood rattling; rattling when passing over rough roads; headliner may rattle from hitting the frame. • Creaking sound heard coming from the right side of the dash when passing over rough terrain. • Front suspension noise. • Clutch pedal squeaks or clicks when pressed. • Erratic fuel gauge readings, especially when parked on an incline; fuel gauge won't read full. • Sticking speedometer and tachometer needles. • Windshield cracking at the lower corners. • Damaged or cracked foglight lens. • Audio Update Campaign (secret warranty). • AC condensate drips onto passenger-side carpet. • Water leaks into trunk. • Loose or deformed upper windshield mouldings. • Driver's seat rocks back and forth. • Seatbelt slow to retract. • Centre vent may be hard to adjust. • Uneven glove box fit.

Civic, del Sol Profile

	1994	1995	1996	1997	1998	1999	2000	2001
Cost Price ($)								
Civic	10,595	11,495	12,995	13,495	14,000	14,200	14,200	18,900
Si	16,595	17,495	17,895	17,995	18,300	18,800	18,800	18,802
del Sol	18,595	20,295	20,495	20,995	—	—	—	—
Used Values ($)								
Civic ▲	4,500	6,000	6,500	8,000	9,500	10,500	12,000	16,500
Civic ▼	3,500	4,500	5,500	7,000	8,000	9,000	10,500	15,000
Si ▲	6,500	7,000	9,000	10,500	12,500	14,000	16,000	17,500
Si ▼	5,000	5,500	7,500	9,000	11,000	12,500	14,500	16,000
del Sol ▲	7,000	8,500	10,000	12,500	—	—	—	—
del Sol ▼	5,500	7,000	8,500	11,000	—	—	—	—
Extended Warranty	N	N	N	N	N	N	N	N
Secret Warranty	Y	Y	Y	Y	Y	Y	Y	Y
Reliability	③	③	③	③	③	④	④	④
Crash Safety (F)	③	③	—	④	④	④	④	⑤
4d	③	③	④	④	④	④	④	⑤
Side Impact	—	—	—	—	③	❷	❷	⑤
4d	—	—	—	③	③	③	③	④
Off-set	—	—	③	③	③	③	③	④
Head Restraints	—	❷	—	❷	—	❷	—	❷
4d	—	—	—	—	—	—	—	④
del Sol	—	—	—	④	—	—	—	—
Rollover Resistance	—	—	—	—	—	—	—	④

Hyundai

ACCENT ★★★★★

RATING: Recommended (2000–01); Above Average (1995–99). Think of it as a more refined Metro/Sprint from South Korea with lots of standard features. **Maintenance/Repair costs:** Average. The timing chain should be replaced every 100,000 km. **Parts:** Reasonably priced and easily found. **Best alternatives:** GM's Firefly or Metro, the Honda Civic (a decade-old Honda CRX in good condition would be a master stroke), Hyundai Elantra, Mazda Protegé, Nissan Sentra, Suzuki Esteem, and Toyota Echo or Corolla.

Strengths and weaknesses: Launched as a '95 model, the early Accents were basically Excels that had been substantially upgraded to provide decent performance and reliability at a phenomenally low price. Of course, with its small 4-cylinder engine, it's no tire-burner, but it will do nicely for urban commuting and grocery-getting.

Until the redesigned 2000 models arrived, the Accent hadn't changed much over the years. 1996 models got height-adjustable seatbelts and a 105-hp GT hatchback; '97 models saw the debut of a GS hatchback and a GL sedan; '98s got new engine mounts to cut down vibration, in addition to re-styled front and rear ends; and base '99 models were given standard power steering and longer warranties. Year 2000 models got a smoother-shifting automatic transmission; stiffer, better-performing suspension; a stronger and quieter-running engine; and a more comfortable driving position with good visibility. A 1.6L engine replaced the 1.5L, giving the 2001 models 16 additional horses.

Problem areas include the engine cooling system and cylinder head gaskets (engine overheating), engine sputters, a Check Engine light that constantly comes on, and chronic automatic transmission failures. Owners also frequently complain of excessive front-end vibration; wheel bearings, fuel system, and electrical component failures; premature front brake wear; and excessive noise when braking.

Safety summary: All models/years: Horn controls may be hard to find in an emergency. • Rear head restraints appear to be too low to protect occupants. • Rear seatbelt configuration complicates the installation of a child safety seat (pre-2001 models). **All models: 1995–97**—NHTSA believes airbags may deploy with too much force; seven children have been killed. **1998–99**—Airbags failed to deploy, or deploy inadvertently. • Complete brake failure. • Sudden transmission failure. • Headlights flicker when turning and high beam is inadequate. • Engine control monitor melted. • Fuel gauge failures. **2000**—Fire erupted in the dashboard area. • Accelerator sticks. • Hood flew up and smashed through the windshield. • Left and right axles broke while vehicle was underway. • Transmission sticks between First and Second gear and pops out of Fifth gear. • No shifting, due to a failure of the control shaft assembly. • Premature transmission clutch replacement. • In snowy, icy, or wet road conditions, there's an unpredictable loss of rpms and powertrain response, making for difficult handling and control. • Headlight failures caused by defective relay switch. • Windshield wipers fail, due to the wiper linkage disconnecting from the wiper motor. • Seatbelts tighten uncomfortably. **2001**—Gas pooled underneath the rear seat. • Airbags fail to deploy. • Steering shook so badly that driver lost control of vehicle. • Transmission jumps from Drive to Neutral. • Gearshift jumps out of Reverse. • Seatbelts unlatch during impact; passenger seatbelt tightens uncomfortably. • Windshield and rear window suddenly shattered. • Early ignition coil replacement.

Secret Warranties/Service Tips/TSBs

All models/years: Tips on troubleshooting excessive brake noise. •
Apparent slow acceleration upon cold starts is dismissed as normal. • A
new AC "refresher" will control AC odours. **All models: 1995–98**—Harsh
shifting may be fixed by installing an upgraded transaxle control module
(TCM). • Clutch drag may be caused by a restriction in the hydraulic line
from grease used during the assembly of the clutch master assembly.
1995–2001—In the following bulletin, Hyundai says a faulty transaxle
oil temperature sensor could be the cause of poor automatic transmission performance on Accent, Elantra, Tiburon, and Sonata models.

A/T - MIL ON DTCs P0712/P0713 Set

Group: Transaxle   Number: 00-40-10   Date: August, 2000   Model: All
Subject: Automatic Transaxle Oil Temperature Sensor Diagnosis

Description:
An automatic transaxle oil temperature sensor with an OPEN circuit may result in the following
symptoms:
^ Harsh P-R or P-D engagement
^ No 4th gear engagement (1996-2000 Elantra & Tiburon1, 1995-2001 Accent)
^ 2nd Gear Hold (1999-2001 Sonata)
^ Damper clutch not engaged
^ MIL illuminated
^ Diagnostic Trouble Code: P0713 - Fluid temperature sensor - open circuit
An automatic transaxle oil temperature sensor with a SHORT circuit may result in the following
symptoms:
^ 2-3 shift flare (Accent, Elantra, Tiburon)
^ MIL illuminated
^ Diagnostic Trouble Code: P0712 - Fluid temperature sensor - short circuit

1996–2001—The following TSB, published in April 2001, says many
automatic transmission breakdowns can be traced to faulty transaxle
solenoids.

A/T - Erratic Shifts/Slipping/MIL ON/DTCs Set

Group: Transaxle   Number: 00-40-011   Date: April, 2001
Model: 1996-00 Elantra, 1997-01 Tiburon, 1996-01 Accent

Description:
Incorrect operation of the transaxle solenoids for the 1996-00 Elantra, 1997-01 Tiburon and the
1996-01 Accent may result in the following symptoms:
^ Erratic shift or slipping
^ Transaxle held in 3rd gear Fail-Safe
^ Diagnostic Trouble Codes - P0740, P0742, P0743, P0745, P0747, P0748, P0750, P0752, P0753, P0755,
  P0757, P0758, P0760, P0765 (see DTC information).
^ MIL illuminated

This bulletin shows Hyundai's transmission problems are factory related and affect many models
and model years. Don't let the service manager convince you the failure is your responsibility.

2000–01—Hyundai has a free kit that will free up stiff manual transmission shifting.

Accent Profile

	1995	1996	1997	1998	1999	2000	2001
Cost Price ($)							
L	9,295	10,495	10,995	11,295	11,565	11,565	11,995
GL 4d	10,995	12,195	12,695	12,995	12,995	13,245	13,595
Used Values ($)							
L ▲	3,000	3,500	5,000	6,000	7,500	8,500	9,500
L ▼	2,500	3,000	4,000	5,000	6,000	7,000	8,500
GL 4d ▲	3,500	4,000	6,000	7,000	8,000	9,500	10,500
GL 4d ▼	3,000	3,500	5,000	5,500	6,500	8,000	9,000
Extended Warranty	Y	Y	Y	Y	N	N	N
Secret Warranty	N	N	N	N	N	N	N
Reliability	③	③	④	④	⑤	⑤	⑤
Crash Safety (F)	—	③	③	③	—	—	—
Head Restraints	❶	—	❶	—	❶	—	③
Rollover Resistance	—	—	—	—	—	—	④

Note: An extended transmission warranty is suggested for models no longer under warranty.

ELANTRA ★★★★★

RATING: Recommended (2001); Above Average (1996–2000); Average (1991–95). Try to find a '98 with an unexpired comprehensive 5-year/100,000 km base warranty. There's a $1,000–$3,500 difference between the high-end and entry-level models. Frequent automatic transmission failures require an extended powertrain warranty. **Maintenance/Repair costs:** Average. Dealer servicing has been substandard in the past. Hyundai says that the timing chain should be replaced every 100,000 km. **Parts:** Reasonably priced and easily found. **Best alternatives:** GM's Firefly or Metro, the Honda Civic, Hyundai's Accent, Mazda Protegé, Nissan Sentra, Suzuki Esteem or Swift, and the Toyota Echo, Tercel, or Corolla.

Strengths and weaknesses: This conservatively styled "high-end" sedan is only marginally larger than the Excel, but its overall reliability is much better. It's a credible alternative to the Toyota Corolla, Nissan Sentra, and Saturn, and the redesigned 1996–97 versions actually narrow the handling and performance gap with the Honda Civic. The 16-valve 1.6L 4-cylinder is smooth, efficient, and adequate when mated to the 5-speed manual transmission. It's not very quiet, however. The smooth ride causes excessive body lean when cornering, but overall handling is fairly good, due mainly to the Elantra's longer wheelbase and more sophisticated suspension.

The 4-speed automatic transmission robs the base engine of at least 10 horses. Brakes are adequate, though sometimes difficult to modulate. Conservative styling makes the Elantra look a bit like an underfed Accord, but there's plenty of room for four average-sized occupants. Tall drivers might find the driver's seat rearward travel insufficient, which makes head room a bit too tight.

1996 through 2000 Elantras are the better buy for budget shoppers due to their reasonable cost, additional interior room, improved performance and handling, and quieter-running engine. Still, passing power with the automatic gearbox is perpetually unimpressive, and the trunk's narrow opening makes for difficult loading. The best of the lot, however, are the revamped 2001 versions, which offer additional horsepower, a larger interior, and enhanced performance features.

Hyundai owners report few serious defects; however, transmission failures are commonplace and have been the object of numerous service bulletins (see the Accent "Secret Warranties/Service Tips/TSBs") and recalls. Airbag failures are another frequent complaint. Other problem areas: body deficiencies (fit, finish, and assembly), paint cracking, engine misfire and oil leaks, hard starting, and warped brake rotors.

Safety summary: All models: 1998–99—Airbags failed to deploy. • Faulty speed sensor. • Passenger shoulder belt locks up and traps occupant. • Cracked transmission case. • Low beam headlights give poor illumination. • Poorly designed jack. **1999**—Defective relay switch causes engine to shut down. • Faulty mass airflow sensor causes chronic stalling. • Sudden brake loss. • Warped front brake rotors and master cylinder failure. • Erratic transmission shifting (recalled). • Cracked transmission case. • High-pitched automatic transmission whine. • AC makes a grinding noise. • Defective heater fan and motor assembly. • Passenger seatbelt retracts and locks so that passengers are unable to move. • Trunk lid doesn't close properly. • Loose driver's seat. • Defective door handle. • Paint/clearcoat cracking. **2000**—Airbags failed to deploy. • Chronic stalling with cruise control engaged and brakes applied. • Faulty transmission/ignition harness. • Frequent transmission failures; automatic transmission slips, or transmission goes into low gear periodically and gets stuck there. • Automatic transmission shifts erratically between Second and Third gear. • Vehicle rolled forward even though emergency brake was applied. • Clutch slave cylinder failure. • Transmission produces clunking and whining noises. • Brakes not very efficient; brake master cylinder failure. • Vehicle pulls left continuously. • Sudden steering failure. • Loose steering. • Low beam doesn't light up driver's view—instead, the light reflects outward to the left or right. • AC circulates bad air. • Tire jack is too small and weak. • Defective side moulding.

2001—Airbags failed to deploy. • Driver-side airbag deployed for no reason. • Sudden, unintended acceleration. • Check Engine light remains lit. • Child had to be cut from rear centre seatbelt. • Seatbelt failed to lock up in a collision. • Brakes randomly engage by themselves and over-heat/pulsate. • Rear doors freeze shut in cold weather.

Secret Warranties/Service Tips/TSBs

All models/years: Hyundai has a new brake pad kit (#58101-28A00) that the company says will eliminate squeaks and squeals during light brake application. Hyundai also suggests that you replace the oil pump assembly if the engine rpm increases as the automatic transmission engages abruptly during a cold start. • A harsh downshift when decelerating may require a free transmission replacement, says bulletin #98-40-001. • Bulletin #98-50-001 provides information regarding some brake noises and appropriate services for each condition. **All models: 1995**—The exhaust system releases a rotten-egg odour. • Rear suspension squeaking noises. • An inaccurate fuel gauge. • Trunk water leaks and troubleshooting tips for locating and plugging other interior water leaks. **1996**—A cold exhaust system buzz can be silenced by installing a sub-muffler resonator. • Improved shifting into all gears can be accomplished by installing an upgraded transaxle control module (TCM). **1996–97**—Automatic transmission won't engage Overdrive. • Clutch pedal squeaking. • Tapping noise coming from the passenger-side dash panel/engine compartment area. • Exhaust system buzz. • Improved shifting into all gears. • Improved shifting into Reverse. • Clutch drag. **1996–98**—DOHC engine timing chain noise repair. **1996–99**—Transmission oil leakage likely caused by a defective oil pump housing seal.

A/T - Fluid Leak Behind Torque Converter

Number: 00-40-005   Date: May, 2000

Model:

1996-99 Elantra
1997-99 Tiburon

Description:

Some 1996-99 Elantra and 1997-99 Tiburon transaxles produced prior to 05/15/99 may experience an oil leak in the bellhousing behind the torque converter. If this occurs, the oil leak will be observed at the drain hole on the lower surface of the transaxle.

An oil leak at this location on a vehicle with less than 15,000 miles in service may be due to case porosity.

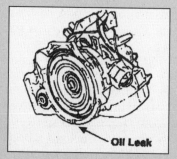

Oil Leak

Service Information:

Model	Repair
1996-99 Elantra or 1997-99 Tiburon with more than 15,000 miles since installation of the Transaxle	Replace the oil pump seal, P/N 43119-28001
1996-99 Elantra or 1997-99 Tiburon with less than 15,000 miles since installation of the Transaxle	1. Remove the transaxle and install a remanufactured transaxle. 2. Write on the Core Return Checklist and ATM Diagnosis Worksheet: "Oil leak at bellhousing."

Elantra Profile

	1994	1995	1996	1997	1998	1999	2000	2001
Cost Price ($)								
GL	11,795	12,295	13,495	13,995	14,295	14,595	14,875	14,875
GLS/VE	13,695	14,195	16,745	17,245	17,545	17,695	17,475	17,075
Used Values ($)								
GL ▲	3,500	4,000	4,500	6,000	7,500	9,000	10,500	12,000
GL ▼	3,000	3,500	4,000	4,500	6,000	7,500	9,000	10,000
GLS/VE	4,500	5,500	6,500	8,000	10,000	11,500	12,500	13,500
GLS/VE ▼	4,000	5,000	6,000	6,500	8,500	10,000	11,000	12,000
Extended Warranty	Y	N	N	N	N	N	N	N
Secret Warranty	N	Y	Y	Y	Y	Y	Y	Y
Reliability	③	③	③	④	④	④	④	⑤
Crash Safety (F)	❶	④	④	③	③	③	—	④
Side Impact	—	—	—	—	③	—	—	⑤
Off-set	—	—	③	③	③	③	③	—
Head Restraints	—	❷	—	❶	—	③	—	④

Mazda

323, PROTEGÉ ★★★★★

RATING: Recommended (1996–2001); Above Average (1991–95); Average (1985–90). If you can't find a reasonably priced 323 or Protegé, look for a Ford Escort or Tracer instead—they're basically Mazdas disguised as Fords. The redesigned 1995–96 Protegé offers fresh styling, a larger wheelbase, standard dual airbags, and a new 4-banger. Along with the 1997–98 versions—which were mostly carried over unchanged, with a slightly restyled grille and headlights and interior refinements—they are good used-car buys. Plus, they should be plentiful at bargain prices as they come off their two- and three-year leases. The best buy of all,

though, is the totally revamped 1999 model. Be wary of Firestone tires.
Maintenance/Repair costs: Higher than average. Repairs are dealer
dependent. To avoid costly engine repairs, check the engine timing belt
every 2 years/40,000 km and replace it every 96,000 km ($300). **Parts:**
Expensive, but easily found. **Best alternatives:** GM's Firefly or Metro, the
Honda Civic, Hyundai's Accent or Elantra, Nissan Sentra, Suzuki Esteem
or Swift, and the Toyota Echo or Corolla.

Strengths and weaknesses: These Mazdas are peppy performers with a
manual transmission hooked to the base engine. The automatic gearbox,
however, produces lethargic acceleration that makes highway passing a
bit chancy. Handling and fuel economy are fairly good for a car design
this old. However, overall durability is not as good as that of more recent
Mazda designs, beginning with the 1991 Mazda 323 and Protegé, both of
which were also sold as Ford Escorts. Catalytic converters plug up easily,
and other pollution-control components have been troublesome.
Automatic transmission defects, air conditioner breakdowns, and engine
oil leaks are also commonplace. Oil leaks in the power-steering pump
may also be a problem.

The fuel-injected 1.6L engine is a better performer than the 1.5L,
but you also get excessive engine and exhaust noise. Stay away from
the 3-speed automatic transmission. The car's small engine can't handle
the extra burden without cutting fuel economy and performance. Both
models are surprisingly roomy, but the Protegé's trunk is small for a
sedan.

The 1985–90 models aren't very reliable at all. Owners report hard
starting in cold weather, in addition to automatic transmission problems
and electrical system failures. The engine camshaft assembly and belt
pulley often need replacing around 120,000 km. Clutch failure and
exhaust system rust-out are also common. Other areas of concern are
constant velocity joint failures, and rack-and-pinion steering wearout.
The front brakes wear quickly due to poor-quality brake pads and seizure
of the calipers in their housings. Check for disc scoring on the front
brakes. Stay away from models equipped with a turbocharger—few
mechanics want to bother repairing it or hunting for parts.

The 1991–95 models are a bit more reliable and reasonably priced;
however, the redesigned 1995–98 versions are *la crème de la crème* for
buyers on a limited budget looking for a reliable small car. Powered by a
standard, fuel-efficient, 1.5L engine mated to a manual 5-speed transmission, the 1995 Protegé became one of the most responsive and roomiest
small cars around. Smart buyers will want to buy a '96 version, or later,
to avoid some of the first-year redesign glitches. Subsequent model years
were carried over unchanged until the reworked '99s arrived. That year
Mazda re-styled the interior and exterior and introduced a more powerful engine lineup. Year 2000 premium models received front-seat side
airbags and an improved ABS system. The following year's models were
carried over virtually unchanged.

Although 1995–2001 Protegés are far more reliable than most American-made small cars, their automatic transmissions are the pits. Owners report that fuel system and electrical problems return year after year, and the front brakes (excessive noise, vibration, rotor warping, and premature pad wear) are a continual annoyance. Other generic deficiencies: weak rear defrosting; chronic engine stalling; noisy suspension; AC failures; and body defects, including wind and water leaks into the interior.

Safety summary: All models: 1995–99—Airbags failed to deploy. • Cracked fuel line caused fire. • Sudden tire tread separation (Firestone). • Chronic stalling. • Excessive brake fade. • Harsh transmission shifts. • Metal rods in driver's seat could cause severe back injuries in a rear-end collision. • Driver's seatbelt buckle wouldn't unlatch. • Brake pedal pad is too narrow and should be coated with non-skid material. • Severe static electricity shock when exiting vehicle. **1999–2000**—No airbag deployment. • Delayed braking. • Erratic, noisy automatic transmission performance; early replacement. • Check Engine light activation is your first warning sign that automatic transmission is faulty. • Car rolled backward and hit a tree, despite being parked with brakes applied. • Vehicle constantly pulls to the right. • Passenger unable to disengage seatbelt. • Bucket seat seatbacks contain metal support bars that are extremely uncomfortable. • Poor headlight illumination. • Loud windshield whistling. • Seat lever underneath seat catches shoe laces. **2001**—No airbag deployment. • Loss of brakes. • Gear shift lever jumped from Drive to Neutral while vehicle was underway. • High revs. • Transmission makes a ticking sound. • Defective steering column coupling. Broken rear axle causes severe pulling to one side. • Windows take a long time to defrost. • AC produces foul-smelling fumes. • Poor headlight illumination.

Secret Warranties/Service Tips/TSBs

All models: 1995–98—Poor engine performance may require a new intake valve. • Excessive vibration in gear or at idle may mean the engine mount material has hardened or cracked. • Erratic shifting may signal that the valve body harness is defective. • If the gear selector lever is hard to operate, it's likely that the lower manual shaft in the transfer case has excessive rust. • An inoperative AC may have a corroded pressure switch terminal assembly (see following bulletin).

A/C Inop., P/S Pressure Sw. Terminal Assembly Corroded

Bulletin No. 001/00   Issued 02/07/00   Section: 07

Revised

Applicable Model/s

1995-98 Protegé
1996-97 Miata

Subject

A/C INOPERATIVE - P/S PRESSURE SWITCH TERMINAL ASSEMBLY CORRODED

DESCRIPTION

Some vehicles may exhibit the air
conditioning (NC) system inoperative with
the Malfunction Indicator lamp (MIL) ON.
This may be due to the Power Steering
Pressure (PSP) switch terminal assembly
becoming corroded causing the
Powertrain Control Module (PCM) to open
the A/C relay circuit and set Diagnostic
Trouble Code (DTC) P0550. A modified
PSP switch terminal assembly is available
to resolve this concern. Customers having
this concern should have their vehicle
repaired using the following procedure.

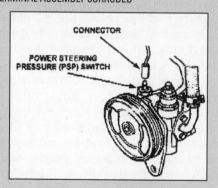

1996–98—A noisy driveshaft can be silenced by installing a countermeasure dynamic damper. • If the door mirror cracks in freezing
temperatures, install an upgraded mirror. 1997–98—A 1–2 upshift shock
at light throttle may require the replacement of the large and small accumulator spring with a single spring. • If the brake warning light is
constantly lit, even though the brakes check out okay, it's likely the
speedometer assembly transistor has been damaged. • A thumping noise
from the rear suspension can be corrected by installing a modified
adjusting sheet. 1999—No shift from Second to Third gear. • Manual
transmission jerking or hesitation. • Inoperative wiper motor. • Weather
strip comes off rear doors. • Door key may jam in locks. • Excessive
exhaust resonance noise. • Engine rattling. • Clutch squealing. • Off-
centre steering wheel. 2000—Excessive exhaust resonance noise.
2000–01—Clutch squealing. • Inoperative wiper motor. • Off-centre
steering wheel.

323, Protegé Profile

	1994	1995	1996	1997	1998	1999	2000	2001
Cost Price ($)								
323	9,965	—	—	—	—	—	—	—
Protegé	13,265	13,370	13,895	14,685	14,675	14,970	15,095	17,610

Used Values ($)								
323 ⋀	3,500	—	—	—	—	—	—	—
323 ⋁	2,500	—	—	—	—	—	—	—
Protegé ⋀	4,500	5,000	6,000	7,500	9,000	10,500	12,000	15,500
Protegé ⋁	3,500	4,500	5,000	6,000	8,000	9,000	10,500	14,000
Extended Warranty	N	N	N	N	N	N	N	N
Secret Warranty	N	N	N	N	N	N	N	N
Reliability	④	④	④	④	④	④	⑤	⑤
Crash Safety (F)	—	—	—	③	③	—	④	⑤
Side Impact	—	—	—	—	—	—	③	③
Off-set	—	③	③	③	③	③	③	③
Head Restraints (F)	—	❶	—	❶	—	❷	❷	③
Rear	—	—	—	—	—	—	—	❷

Nissan

SENTRA ★★★★★

RATING: Recommended (1995–2001); Above Average (1991–94); Average (1988–90); Not Recommended (1983–87). The redesigned 1995 version offers fresh styling, a longer wheelbase, a peppier powerplant, standard dual airbags, and side door beams. **Maintenance/Repair costs:** Higher than average on early models, but anybody can repair these cars. **Parts:** Reasonably priced and easily obtainable. **Best alternatives:** A GM Firefly or Metro, Honda Civic, Hyundai Elantra, Mazda Protegé, Suzuki Esteem or Swift, and Toyota Echo or Corolla.

Strengths and weaknesses: Late-model Sentras aren't expensive to buy; they're generally reliable, relatively easy and inexpensive to repair; and they give good fuel economy. On the other hand, ride and handling are mediocre and build quality is spotty at best. Until 1991, mechanical and body components suffered from poor quality control, making these cars quite unreliable and sometimes expensive to repair. Clutches and exhaust systems were particularly problematic. The 1.6L engine is much more reliable, but even with it the oil pressure switch may develop a leak that can lead to sudden oil loss and serious engine damage. Quality improved considerably with the 1991 version, yet the vehicle's base price rose only marginally, making these later model years bargain buys for consumers looking for a reliable "beater."

1991–94 Sentras are a bit peppier and handle better. Some owner-reported problems: faulty fuel tanks, leaking manual and automatic transmissions, a persistent rotten-egg smell, and noisy engine timing chains and front brakes. With the exception of electronic component failures, repairs are relatively simple to perform.

Redesigned for the 1995 model year, Sentra sedans were much improved, larger, and better-performing vehicles. 1997 models got additional soundproofing; the '98s got new front and rear ends and added a new SE sedan, equipped with a 140-hp engine; and the '99s benefited from a slightly re-styled front end. The 2000 Sentra underwent a major redesign, offering more powerful engines, a better ride, and enhanced handling. It's well worth the $1000–$2,000 increase from the '99 version and is basically identical to the costlier 2001 version.

Most 1995–2001 owner complaints concern stalling and hard starting; engine rattles; electrical glitches; premature brake wear and excessive brake noise; automatic transmission whine; AC solenoid failures and AC that blows hot air or freezes up; and accessories that malfunction. Owners have also had to contend with recurrent clutch, clutch switch, suspension strut, wheel bearing, and catalytic converter failures. Crank position sensor malfunction may prevent vehicle from being started. Body assembly is also targeted with some complaints of loose windshield mouldings, poor body fits, paint defects, and air and water leaks into the interior through the trunk and doors.

Safety summary: All models/years: Brake and accelerator pedals set too close together. • Airbags fail to deploy, or deploy inadvertently. • Steering lockup. • Chronic stalling. • Sudden acceleration. • Premature tire wear. • Horn blows on its own. **All models: 1995**—Rusted-out gooseneck and line going to the fuel tank. • Premature failure of the airbag module. **1996**—Airbag deployment caused severe injuries. • Airbag ruptured. • Premature automatic transmission failures. • Dash light suddenly goes out, or blinks intermittently like a strobe light. • Rusty rear coil springs broke in two. • Hubcaps frequently fall off. **1997**—Driver shut off the engine, shut the door, and both airbags deployed. • Sudden failure of the brake lights, headlights, and dash lights. **1998–99**—ABS failures. • Defective brake master cylinder. • Excessive stopping distance. • Sticking throttle. • Ignition key breaks off in the ignition. • Faulty power door locks. • Vehicle leaks when it rains. • Windshield wiper washer leaks, and washer produces acrid fumes that enter the cabin. • Front seats jam when moved back. **1999**—Loss of braking; extended braking distance. • Fuel filler flap fell into fuel filler tube. **2000**—Steering lockup. • Suspension attachment bolts broke off. **2001**—Brakes easily lock up at all speeds. • Warped brake rotors.

Secret Warranties/Service Tips/TSBs

All models: 1995—AC compressor leaks or noise. • Excessive brake noise. • C-pillar finisher lifting. • Faulty fuel gauge. • Self-activating horn. • Poor driveability—Code 45. • Power door locks self-activate during periods of high heat or humidity. • Power windows won't roll up unless ignition key is cycled. • Front window misalignment. • Front window won't go completely down. **1995–96**—An engine that cranks but won't start may need TSB #96-032 for the correct repair. • An engine malfunction light that is constantly lit may be fixed by installing a new rear heated oxygen sensor under the emissions warranty. • An automatic transmission that won't shift out of Park may need a countermeasure interlock cable. • TSB #NTB96-001 gives lots of troubleshooting tips on finding and correcting various squeaks and rattles. • Nissan has a special kit to improve brake pedal feel, according to TSB #NTB96-041. **1995–99**—Harsh shifts and low power with the automatic transmission may be due to reduced movement of the A/T throttle wire cable inside the cable housing. • A self-activating horn can be fixed by replacing the horn springs and spring insulators. **1996**—An AC refrigerant leak may require an upgraded valve core. **1997–99**—Harsh shifts and low power with the automatic transmission. • Horn self-activates. • More tips on silencing squeaks and rattles. • Diagnosing causes of brake judder and steering wheel shimmy. • Extended-life pads for the front brakes. • Curing sulfur odour. • Slow retraction of the front seat belt. **1999–2001**—Hard starting in cold weather or at high altitude. • Engine pings with light to moderate acceleration. • Exhaust manifold heat shield rattle. • Automatic transmission won't upshift. • Tips to improve downshifting (modified downshift spring). • Brake pedal slowly drops to floor (master cylinder check). • Vehicle wanders or pulls to one side. • Horn activates randomly. • Noisy, vibrating speedometer. • Water condensation from AC. • Rotten-egg exhaust odour. Anti-theft system prevents starting. **2000**—Vehicle lacks power; transmission sticks in Third gear. • Slow fuel fill; pump nozzle clicks off continually. • Erratic AC vent flow. • Front suspension squeak, rattling. • Windshield hum or whistle.

Sentra Profile

	1994	1995	1996	1997	1998	1999	2000	2001
Cost Price ($)								
Sentra	10,990	12,290	13,448	13,698	14,498	15,398	15,398	15,298
Used Values ($)								
Sentra ∧	3,500	4,500	5,500	6,500	8,000	9,500	11,000	12,500
Sentra ∨	3,000	3,500	4,500	5,000	7,000	8,500	10,000	11,500
Extended Warranty	N	N	N	N	N	N	N	N
Secret Warranty	N	N	N	N	N	N	N	N
Reliability	❷	③	④	④	④	⑤	⑤	⑤
Crash Safety (F)	④	④	—	④	③	—	—	④
Side Impact	—	—	—	—	③	—	—	—
Off-set	—	—	—	—	③	③	③	③
Head Restraints	—	❶	—	❷	❷	❷	❷	❷

Subaru

IMPREZA, FORESTER, LOYALE   ★★★★☆

RATING: *Impreza:* Above Average (1997–2001). *Forester:* Recommended (2001); Above Average (1998–2000); Average (1994–96). 1994 was the 4X4 Loyale wagon's last model year. **Maintenance/Repair costs:** Higher than average. Mediocre, expensive servicing is hard to overcome because independent garages can't service key AWD components. Only buy a Subaru if you must have AWD and you're confident you can get dependable service from your local Subaru dealer. **Parts:** Expensive and hard to find. Emissions components are often back-ordered for months, but cheap aftermarket components can be found outside the dealer network. **Best alternatives:** If you don't need the AWD capability, you're wasting your money. Here are some front-drives worth considering: a GM Firefly or Metro, the Honda Civic, Hyundai Elantra, Mazda Protegé, Nissan Sentra, Suzuki Esteem or Swift, and Toyota Echo or Corolla. Some recommended small vehicles with 4X4 capability that are set on a car, not a truck, frame (providing more carlike handling), include the Ford Escape/Mazda Tribute, Honda CR-V, and Toyota RAV4.

Strengths and weaknesses: These well-equipped small cars have one of the most refined and reliable AWD drivetrains you'll find. They provide excellent handling without any torque steer, good braking, lots of storage space with the wagons, nice control layout, and better-than-average quality control.

On the other hand, Subaru makes you pay dearly for the AWD capability, small doors and entryways restrict rear access, the coupe's narrow rear window and large rear pillars hinder rear visibility, heat and air distribution is inadequate, and front and rear seat leg room may be insufficient for tall drivers.

The full-time 4X4 Impreza is essentially a shorter Legacy with additional convenience features. It comes as a four-door sedan, a wagon, and an Outback Sport wagon, all powered by a 135-hp 2.2L or a 165-hp 2.5L 4-cylinder engine. The 2.5L performs much better with the Impreza and Forester than with the Legacy Outback. It is smooth and powerful, with lots of low-end torque for serious off-road use. The automatic transmission shifts smoothly. The manual transmission's "hill holder" clutch prevents the car from rolling backward when starting out.

These Subarus hurtle through corners effortlessly with a flat, solid stance and plenty of grip. Tight cornering at highway speeds is done with minimal body lean and no loss of control, and steering is precise and predictable.

The 1995 entry-level Imprezas got a coupe and an Outback model, though AWD was optional. The 1996 models were a mix of front-drives and all-wheel drives, along with a new sport model, a new Outback wagon (for light off-roading), and larger engines. The 1997s got additional power and torque, a re-styled front end, and a new Outback Sport wagon. The 1998 Imprezas got a revised dash and door panels. Brighton was dropped and the high-end 2.5 RS was added. The 1999s got stronger engines, more torque, and upgraded transmissions, while the 2000 and 2001 models returned relatively unchanged.

Forester
Another Subaru spin-off, the Forester is a cross between a wagon and a sport-utility. Based on the shorter Impreza, the Forester uses the Legacy Outback's 2.5L 165-hp engine coupled to a 5-speed manual transmission or an optional 4-speed automatic. Its road manners are more subdued, and its engine provides more power and torque for off-roading. Launched as a 1998 model, the 1999 model Forester got a quieter, torquier engine, a smoother-shifting transmission, and a more solid body. The 2000 models got standard cruise control (L) and limited-slip differential (S), but the 2001s returned unchanged.

All post-'95 Subarus are noted for better-than-average quality control and above-average-quality mechanical components. Powertrain components should be durable, and there are few mechanical problems that take these Subarus out of service. However, servicing quality is spotty, and there's a history of premature clutch failures and some body panel and trim fit and finish deficiencies. Owners also report poor engine idling; frequent cold-weather stalling; manual transmission malfunctions; rear wheel bearing failures; excessive vibration caused by the alloy wheels; premature exhaust system rust-out and early brake wear; minor electrical short circuits; catalytic converter failures; water leaks and condensation problems from the top of the windshield or sunroof; windshield scratches too easily; and paint peeling. In addition to the paint peeling from delamination, owners report that Subaru paint chips much too easily. Says the Alberta owner of a 2001 Impreza,

I have a chipping 2001 Subaru Impreza Outback Sport and have been trying to get the dealership to deal with it. The care is now one year old and has over 50 rock chips on the hood alone. I barely touched the car when putting in the gas and the point fell off. I spent the extra money on paint protection when I got the car and I am afraid of what might be left after I pay this car off. We use the car for skiing so it does see a little gravel (it's Alberta!) and I bought it because it was backed by the Ski Association.

Safety summary: All models: 1994–2001—Airbags are a serious problem with all Subarus: either they fail to deploy in an accident, or they deploy inadvertently while parked, when turning, if the underside of the car scrapes the road, or if the car drives over a dip in the road, hits a pothole, is stuck in a ditch, or is being washed—or the key is simply put into the ignition. • Two other common problems are the premature replacement of brake sensors, pads, and rotors and wheel hubcaps that constantly fall off due to their poor design. • Front shoulder belts are uncomfortable and rear seatbelts are hard to buckle up. **1996**—Short seatback and absence of head restraint could cause severe neck injuries in a collision. • Sudden acceleration. • When the vehicle is being driven, transmission may suddenly jump out of Drive into Neutral. • Inadvertent airbag deployment. • Seatbelt failed to retract in an accident. • Floor carpet prevented brake pedal application. • Complete engine failure at 18,000 km. • Chronic stalling. • Computer sensor control unit failure. • Intermittent brake loss. • Excessive shaking at highway speeds. • Windshield wiper bolt failure. • Left turn signal fails intermittently. • AC seizure. • O-ring failure causes AC to leak freon. • Bridgestone tires frequently blow out. • Keyless entry failed due to pinched wire in driver's door. • New-design headlights give poor illumination. **1997**—Airbags deployed in an accident and a brown liquid burned driver's arms. • Airbags failed to deploy and seatbelts failed to tighten in accident. • ABS brakes aren't effective and take a long distance to stop vehicle. • Sudden engine shutdown on the highway and won't restart. • Sudden acceleration. • Cruise control failed to disengage when brakes were applied. • Ignitor failed, allowing unburned fuel to flow into catalytic converter. • AC blew fumes into interior, causing driver to black out. • Stalling caused by ignitor failure. • Complete engine failure due to defective valves and pistons. • Sudden loss of steering. • Transmission surges when cold, or shifts into Neutral at low speed or when descending a small hill. • Transmission failures. • Frequent electronic control unit failures. • Rear seatbelts are too long to properly secure child safety seat, and the locking mechanism doesn't lock properly. • Brake and engine lights continually on. • Three alternators replaced by one owner. • Shorted hazard switch drained battery. • Alternator belt snapped, causing battery and brake warning lights to come on and making car hard to steer. • Alternators frequently quit while vehicle is under power. • Hubcaps fall off. • Brake lights often fail. • Headlights are mistakenly turned off when turn signal lever is engaged. **1998**—Oil leak from oil filter seam caused fire. • Front strut assembly failure. • Cruise control failed to disengage when brakes were applied. • Excessive shaking at highway speeds. • Seatback collapsed when vehicle was rear-ended. • Subaru told car owner that tendency to pull to the right was a design feature. • Tire blowouts. • Sudden brake loss after linings, calipers, and master cylinder had been replaced. **1999**—Sudden acceleration. • Chronic cold engine hesitation, stalling. • Engine failure due to cracked #2 piston. • When accelerating or decelerating, vehicle will begin to jerk due to excessive play in the front axle. • Wheel bearing failures. • Transmission plug fell out. • Tire blowout; air slowly escapes. • Front bumper skirt catches on parking blocks, resulting in bumper twisting and being ripped off. • The centre rear seatbelt's poor design prohibits the installation of many child safety seats. **2000–01**—Driver burned from airbag deployment. • Clunking noise when brakes are applied. • **Forester: 2001–02**—Brake and accelerator pedals are too close together. • In a collision, airbags failed to deploy and seatbelt didn't restrain occupant. • In a similar incident, shoulder belt allowed driver's head to hit the windshield. • Sudden, unintended acceleration. • Headlights don't illuminate the edge of the road and are either too bright on High or too dim on Low.

Secret Warranties/Service Tips/TSBs

All models/years: Troubleshooting tips on a sticking anti-lock brake relay are offered. This problem is characterized by a lit ABS warning light or the ABS motor continuing to run/buzz when the ignition is turned off. • Diagnostic and repair tips are offered on transfer clutch binding and/or bucking on turns. • A rotten-egg smell could be caused by a defective catalytic converter. It will be replaced, after a bit of arguing, free of charge, up to five years under the emissions warranty. **All models: 1997–99**—Excessive driveline vibration is covered in TSB #05-33-98R. Subaru's fix requires modifying the differential. **2000–01**—Likely reasons why the automatic transmission light comes on. **Forester: 2000–01**—Front oxygen air/fuel sensor cracking.

Impreza, Forester, Loyale Profile

	1994	1995	1996	1997	1998	1999	2000	2001
Cost Price ($)								
Forester	—	—	—	—	26,695	26,695	26,895	28,395
Base/Brighton	14,395	17,995	17,995	16,991	16,240	17,795	—	—
Sedan 4X4	16,695	19,695	17,995	21,395	21,395	21,995	21,995	22,196
Loyale	14,995	—	—	—	—	—	—	—
Used Values ($)								
Forester ⋏	—	—	—	—	15,000	18,000	20,500	23,000
Forester ⋎	—	—	—	—	13,000	16,000	19,000	21,000
Base/Brighton ⋏	4,000	5,500	7,000	8,000	9,500	11,000	—	—
Base/Brighton ⋎	3,000	5,000	6,000	6,500	8,000	9,500	—	—
Sedan 4X4 ⋏	5,000	6,500	8,000	10,000	12,000	14,000	16,000	18,500
Sedan 4X4 ⋎	4,000	6,000	6,500	9,000	11,000	13,000	14,500	17,000
Loyale ⋏	3,000	—	—	—	—	—	—	—
Loyale ⋎	2,500	—	—	—	—	—	—	—
Extended Warranty	Y	Y	Y	Y	Y	Y	Y	Y
Secret Warranty	N	N	N	N	N	N	N	N
Reliability	③	③	③	④	④	④	④	⑤
Crash Safety (F)								
Forester	—	—	—	—	—	④	④	④
Side Impact	—	—	—	③	③	—	⑤	⑤
Off-set (Forester)	—	—	—	—	—	④	④	④
Head Restraints								
Impreza (F)	—	❷	—	❷	—	—	—	❷

Impreza (Rear)	—	—	—	❶	—	—	—	—
Forester (F)	—	—	—	—	—	❷	—	③
Forester (Rear)	—	—	—	—	—	❶	—	❷
Rollover Resistance								
Forester	—	—	—	—	—	—	—	③

Note: Budget an extra $500 or more for an extended powertrain warranty to protect you from premature and repeated clutch failures.

LEGACY, OUTBACK   ★★★★

RATING: Above Average (1997–2001); Average for AWD (1991–96); Average for front-drives (1989–96). A competent, full-time 4X4 performer for drivers who want to move up in size, comfort, and features. Available as a four-door sedan or five-door wagon, the Legacy is cleanly and conventionally styled, with even a hint of the Acura Legend in the rear end. The AWD is what this car is all about. It handles difficult terrain without the fuel penalty or clumsiness of many truck-based SUVs. **Maintenance/Repair costs:** Higher than average. Repairs are dealer dependent. **Parts:** Parts aren't easily found and can be costly. **Best alternatives:** The Honda CR-V, Hyundai Santa Fe, Suzuki Grand Vitara, and Toyota RAV4.

Strengths and weaknesses: Costing a bit more than the Impreza, these Subarus are well appointed, provide a comfortable ride with acceptable handling, and have lots of cargo room. On the downside, owners report problematic automatic transmission performance when hooked to the base engine; the 2.5L is a sluggish performer, due undoubtedly to the car's heft; excessive engine noise; mediocre handling on base models; excessive 4-cylinder engine noise; power window and lock switches aren't easily accessible; there's a tight fit for the middle rear-seat passenger; cramped back seat; limited rear head room for tall passengers; trunk hinges can damage cargo and cut into storage space; seatbelts may be too short for large occupants; and servicing is very dealer-dependent.

The Outback is a marketing coup that stretches the definition of sport-utility by simply customizing the AWD Legacy to give it more of an outdoorsy flair. American Motors tried the same marketing approach with the Eagle in the '70s and failed miserably, due to poor quality control, lousy marketing, and a passive public whose concept of off-road thrills was watching James Dean at the drive-in.

First launched in 1989 as front-drives, these compacts are a bit slow off the mark. The 5-speed is a bit notchy, and the automatic gearbox is slow to downshift, has difficulty staying in Overdrive, and is failure prone. Early Legacys are noisy, fuel-thirsty cars with bland styling that masks their solid, dependable AWD performance. Actually, the availability of a proven 4X4 powertrain in a compact family sedan and wagon makes these cars appealing for special use. In spite of their reputation for dependability, though, Subarus are not trouble-free—engine, clutch, turbo, and driveline defects are common on the early models through to the 1998 versions.

The redesigned 1995–98 models have sleeker styling, additional interior room (though leg room is still at a premium), a bit more horsepower with the base engine, and a new 2.5L 4-cylinder driving the 1996 AWD GT and LSi. The Outback, a Legacy/Madison Avenue spin-off, was transformed into a sport-utility wagon with a taller roof. Even with the improvements noted above, acceleration is still only passable (if you don't mind the loud engine), but highway handling and ride are remarkably good.

Subaru's overall product lineup for 1997 marked a return to the company's 4X4 roots, with the repackaging of its Legacy and Impreza 4X4 lineup as Outbacks. A Legacy 2.5L GT all-wheel-drive sporting sedan, or wagon variant, also joined the group that year. In addition to these redesignated models—and the squeezing out of a bit more horsepower from its limited range of engines—Subaru continued to tap the sport-utility craze by offering a greater variety of AWD vehicles.

1998 models were carried over practically unchanged, while the '99s were given an upgraded 2.2L engine. 2000s are longer, carry a new 2.5L engine, and offer a manual or automatic transmission. Two new Outback wagons, featuring a more powerful 3.0L engine, joined the lineup late in the 2001 model year.

The 2.5L engine is a competent performer only with a manual gearbox. The 4-cylinder engine is noisy and rough-running. It's tuned more for low-end torque than for speedy acceleration. The 6-cylinder is adequate, but doesn't feel like it has much in reserve. The automatic transmission shifts into too high a gear to adequately exploit the engine's power and is reluctant to downshift into the proper gear. Manual transmission's shift linkage isn't suitable for rapid gear changes.

Base models don't handle well. They bounce around on uneven pavement, the rear end tends to swing out during high-speed cornering, and there's too much body lean in turns at lesser speeds. Higher-end models handle well, though there's some excessive lean when cornering. The GT's firmer suspension exhibits above-average handling.

Legacys and Outbacks have had more than their share of reliability problems over the years. Powertrain defects can sideline the car for days. Engine and transmission problems keep showing up. One owner of a '98 Legacy Outback has replaced his engine twice, at 800 km and 4,000 km. There are several reports of the transmission jumping out of gear when using First gear to slow down or to descend a steep grade. Through 1999, automatic transmission (front seals, especially) and clutch breakdowns are the most common complaints. Despite some improvements, the transmission sometimes downshifts abruptly while descending a long grade or travelling on snow-packed highways. Front brakes require frequent attention, and the Check Engine and ABS warning lights come on constantly for no reason. Shock absorbers, constant velocity joints, and catalytic converters often wear out prematurely. Other problems that appear over most model years include chronic electrical and fuel system malfunctions; surging and stalling in cold weather; starter and ignition relay failures; and snow packed inside the wheelwells, binding steering. Premature exhaust system rust-out is common, and early Subarus' underbody and chassis components should be examined very carefully for corrosion damage.

Safety summary: All models/years: Many reports of ABS brake failure and premature wearout of brake components. **All models: 1996—**Car suddenly fishtails out of control when making a lane change. • Electrical system fire. • Cruise control won't disengage. • Premature tire failures (Bridgestone). • Hood flew up while driving. • Engine replaced at 18,000 km. • AC condenser and alternator failures. • Sudden electrical shutdown. • Chronic hesitation, high-speed miss, and stalling. • Fuse blew out five times, causing stall. • Faulty gas gauge. • Low rear bench seat and no head restraints. • Sudden acceleration. • When the vehicle is being driven, transmission may suddenly jump out of Drive into Neutral. • Inadvertent airbag deployment. • Floor carpet prevented brake pedal application. • Complete engine failure at 18,000 km. • Chronic stalling. • Computer sensor control unit failure. • Excessive shaking at highway speeds. • Windshield wiper bolt failure. • Alternator failures while driving. • Left turn signal fails intermittently. • Climate control button sticks. • AC seizure. • O-ring failure causes AC to leak freon. • Bridgestone tires frequently blow out. • Keyless entry failed due to pinched wire in driver's door. • New-design headlights give poor illumination. **1997—**Sudden acceleration. • Cruise control failed to disengage when brakes were applied. • Ignitor failed, allowing unburned fuel to flow into catalytic converter. • AC blew fumes into interior, causing driver to black out. • Stalling caused by ignitor failure. • Complete engine failure due to defective valves and pistons. • Sudden loss of steering. • Transmission surges when cold, or shifts into Neutral at low speed or when descending a small hill. • Transmission failures. • Frequent electronic control unit failures. • Rear seatbelts are too long to properly secure child safety seat, and the locking mechanism doesn't lock properly. • Brake and engine lights continually on. • Three alternators replaced by one owner. • Shorted hazard switch drained battery. • Alternator belt snapped, causing battery and brake warning lights to come on and making car hard to steer. • Alternators frequently quit while vehicle is under power. **1998—**Oil leak from oil filter seam caused fire. • Sudden brake loss after linings, calipers, and master cylinder had been replaced. • Cruise control failed to disengage when brakes were applied. • Excessive shaking at highway speeds. • Seatback collapsed when vehicle was rear-ended. • Subaru told car owner that tendency to pull to the right was a design feature. **1999—**Sudden acceleration. •

Chronic cold engine hesitation, stalling. • Engine failure due to cracked #2 piston. • When accelerating or decelerating, vehicle will begin to jerk due to excessive play in the front axle. • Tire blowout; air slowly escapes. • Front bumper skirt catches on parking blocks, resulting in bumper twisting and being ripped off. • The centre rear seatbelt's poor design prohibits the installation of many child safety seats. 2000–01—Ignitor failure allowed unburned gasoline to flow into catalytic converter and resulted in chronic stalling. • Sudden, unintended acceleration in forward gear and in Reverse. • Vehicle suddenly veers to the right when accelerating or braking. • Cruise control failed to disengage when brake pedal was depressed. • Fuel sloshes in fuel tank due to the absence of baffles. • During a collision, airbags deployed but failed to inflate. • The suspension's design causes severe pulling to one side. • Excessive steering and vehicle vibration when passing over uneven pavement. • Steering lockup while driving. • Knocking and clunking noise heard when turning. • Vehicle's rear end bounces about when passing over bumps. • Engine failure due to a cracked #2 piston. • Frequent surging from a stop. • Hard to shift from Park to Reverse. • Cracked seatbelt buckle. • Seatbelts are too short for large occupants. • Rear centre seatbelt prevents the secure attachment of child safety seats. • Misadjusted door strikers make for hard closing/opening. • Snowstorm ice builds up in the wheelwell, making turning difficult. • Sudden tire blowout.

Secret Warranties/Service Tips/TSBs

All models/years: Troubleshooting tips on a sticking anti-lock brake relay are offered. This problem is characterized by a lit ABS warning light or the ABS motor continuing to run/buzz when the ignition is turned off. • Diagnostic and repair tips are offered on transfer clutch binding and/or bucking on turns. • A rotten-egg smell could be caused by a defective catalytic converter. It will be replaced, after a bit of arguing, free of charge, up to five years under the emissions warranty. **All models: 1995**—Tips are provided on silencing excessive front strut noise and engine oil pump leaks. **1995–96**—If the antenna won't fully retract, Subaru suggests cleaning the antenna mast and replacing the dress nut. **1997–99**—Excessive driveline vibration is covered in TSB #05-33-98R. Subaru's fix requires modifying the differential. **2000–01**—Loose bolts on the front seatbelt retractor. • Inlet heater hose leaks engine coolant. • Probable causes for the automatic transmission temperature light flashing. **Legacy: 1997–99**—Troubleshooting body driveline vibration.

Legacy, Outback Profile

	1994	1995	1996	1997	1998	1999	2000	2001
Cost Price ($)								
Legacy	19,995	17,995	23,195	—	—	—	—	—
Legacy 4X4	22,695	24,695	19,495	19,995	19,995	20,495	23,595	24,295

Used Values ($)								
Legacy ▲	4,500	6,000	8,500	—	—	—	—	—
Legacy ▼	3,500	4,500	7,000	—	—	—	—	—
Legacy 4X4 ▲	5,500	8,000	9,500	11,000	12,500	15,000	17,500	19,500
Legacy 4X4 ▼	4,000	6,000	8,000	9,500	10,000	12,500	16,000	18,000
Extended Warranty	Y	Y	Y	Y	Y	Y	Y	Y
Secret Warranty	N	N	N	N	N	N	N	N
Reliability	③	③	③	④	④	④	⑤	⑤
Crash Safety (F)								
Legacy 4d	④	④	④	④	④	④	—	④
Side Impact	—	—	—	—	③	③	—	④
Off-set	—	③	③	③	③	③	⑤	⑤
Head Restraints	—	❷	❷	❷	❷	❷	❷	③

Note: Consider an extended powertrain warranty to protect you from premature and repeated clutch and transmission failures.

Suzuki

ESTEEM ★★★★★

RATING: Recommended (1996–2001). Getting the most horsepower bang for your buck means shopping for a Sport model or looking over the upgraded year 2000 versions. Wagons are especially versatile and reasonably priced for the equipment provided. Both the base GL and upscale GLX come loaded with standard features that cost extra on other models. The GL, for example, comes with power steering, rear window defroster, remote trunk and fuel-filler door releases, tinted glass, and a fold-down rear seat (great for getting extra cargo space). GLX shoppers can look forward to standard ABS, power windows and power door locks, and a host of other interior refinements. **Maintenance/Repair costs:** Average. **Parts:** Average cost, and parts are easily found. **Best alternatives:** The GM Firefly or Metro, Honda Civic, Hyundai Accent or Elantra, Mazda Protegé, Nissan Sentra, and Toyota Echo, Tercel, or Corolla.

Strengths and weaknesses: The Esteem, Suzuki's largest car, is a small four-door sedan that is a step up from the Swift (see General Motors/Suzuki). Smaller than the Honda Civic and Chrysler Neon, it has a fairly spacious interior, offering rear accommodation (for two full-sized adults) that is comparable to or better than most cars in its class. It stands out with its European-styled body and large array of such standard features as air conditioning, a fold-down back seat, and remote trunk and fuel-door releases. The roomy cabin has lots of front and rear head room and leg room for four adults. Cargo space is fairly good with the sedan; exceptional with the wagon's rear seats folded.

The small 95-hp engine delivers respectable acceleration and overall performance is acceptable, thanks to the Esteem's four-wheel independent suspension, which gives just the right balance between a comfortable ride and no-surprise handling. For a bit more power, look for a '96 or later Sport variant that carries a 125-hp powerplant.

A wagon version joined the lineup for the 1998 model year, and the '99s received new front-end styling, 14-inch wheels, and an upgraded sound system. More power was given to the year 2000 models with the introduction of a standard 122-hp 1.8L engine. 2001 models were carried over without any significant changes.

Some of the drawbacks to owning one of these econoboxes: small tires compromise handling, and power steering doesn't transmit much road feedback. The Esteem's automatic transmission also may shift harshly and vibrate excessively between gear changes. Braking is mediocre for a car this light.

The Esteem has been on the market for only a short time, but early reports indicate a high level of quality and dependability. In this respect, it competes well with rivals like the Chevrolet Cavalier, Ford Escort, and Honda Civic. Problems reported by owners: premature front brake wear, noisy front brakes, occasional electrical short circuits, wind and water intrusion into the passenger compartment, and fragile body panels and trim items.

Safety summary: All models: 1996—Airbag failed to deploy. • ABS failure. • Engine crankshaft pulley broke while driving. • Transmission failure. **1997**—Sudden brake failure. • Seatbelts failed to secure occupants in a collision. • Sudden, total electrical shutdown.• Plastic outside door handles break easily. • Horn doesn't work. **1998**—Airbag failed to deploy. • Seatbelt failed to lock up in a collision. • Vehicle is unstable at high speed. • Door handle failures. **1999**—Engine oil leak sprays oil throughout the engine compartment. • Stuck accelerator. • Loss of power when accelerating. • Stuck accelerator pedal. • Chronic stalling. • Transmission and brake failures. • Brakes continue to squeal even after installing new rotors and pads. **2000**—No airbag deployment. • Sudden acceleration from a stop. • Automatic transmission bangs into gear. • Gear shift lever fell from Drive to Neutral and is hard to move. • Excessive steering wheel vibration and noise. • Windshield seal vibrates and cracks in cold weather. **2001**—Brake failure. • Complete electrical failure fixed temporarily by lifting the hood and jiggling the master control fuse.

Secret Warranties/Service Tips/TSBs

All models: 1996–97—Uneven wear of the front disc brake pads can be corrected by modifying the upper bushing tolerance, says TSB #TS 5-03-04126. **1998–99**—Remote entry battery failure due to defective fob diode.

Esteem Profile

	1996	1997	1998	1999	2000	2001
Cost Price ($)						
GL	13,495	13,495	13,895	13,995	15,495	15,695
GLX	14,495	15,495	16,895	17,195	18,491	18,795
Used Values ($)						
GL ⋀	4,500	6,500	7,500	9,000	11,000	12,500
GL ⋁	4,000	5,000	6,000	7,500	9,500	11,000
GLX ⋀	6,000	7,500	9,000	10,500	13,500	15,000
GLX ⋁	5,500	5,500	7,500	9,000	12,000	14,000
Extended Warranty	N	N	N	N	N	N
Secret Warranty	N	N	N	N	N	N
Reliability	④	④	④	④	⑤	⑤
Head Restraints	—	—	—	❷	—	❷

Note: The Esteem hasn't been crash-tested yet.

Toyota

COROLLA   ★★★★

RATING: Above Average (1991–2001); Average (1985–90). Be wary of serious safety deficiencies that include airbag malfunctions, airbag-induced injuries, seatbelt failures, and poorly designed headlights that misdirect the light beam. Since the 1997 model was "de-contented" (less soundproofing, fewer standard features, etc.), there has been a noticeable reduction in quality control. The 1995–96 models combine the best array of standard features, quality control, and "reasonable" (for a Toyota) used prices. 1998–99 models are good second choices with their horse-power-enhanced engine. **Maintenance/Repair costs:** Lower than average, and repairs can be done anywhere. ECP extended warranty performance is unimpressive. **Parts:** Reasonably priced and easily found. **Best alternatives:** The Ford Escort or Tracer, GM Firefly or Metro, Hyundai Accent or Elantra, Mazda Protegé, Nissan Sentra, Suzuki Esteem, and Toyota Echo.

Strengths and weaknesses: A step up from the Tercel/Echo, the Corolla has long been Toyota's standard bearer in the compact sedan class. Over the years, however, the car has grown in size, price, and refinement to the point where it can now be considered a small family sedan. All Corollas ride on a front-drive platform with independent suspension on all wheels.

Corollas are economical, dependable little cars, but age can take its toll, especially in Eastern Canada, where rust snacks on their little bodies. 1985–87 versions may carry the Toyota name and appear to be bargains at first glance, but they're likely to have serious rusting problems and need costly brake, steering, and suspension work. Stay away from the 1.8L diesel version; it lacks performance and parts aren't easy to find. 4X4 versions are also risky. Wiper pivot assemblies may seize due to corrosion. Front shocks on rear-drive models wear out more quickly than average. Exhaust parts aren't very durable.

Post-1987 models are much improved. The two-door models provide sporty performance and good fuel economy, especially when equipped with the 16-valve engine. The engines and drivetrains are exceptionally reliable. Front-drive sedans and five-door hatchbacks offer more room than their rear-drive counterparts. The base engine, however, lacks power and is especially deficient in low-end torque, making for agonizingly slow merging and passing on the highway. Owners report problems with premature front suspension strut and brake wear; brake vibration; faulty defrosting that allows the windows to fog up in winter; and rusting of body seams, especially door bottoms, side mirror mounts, trunk and hatchback lids, and wheel openings.

The 1990–94 Corolla's problems are limited to harsh automatic shifting, early front brake pad and strut/shock wearout, AC high-pressure tube leaks ($650), electrical glitches, ignition problems, windshield wiper linkage failures ($300), motor, and some interior squeaks and rattles. They do, however, still require regular valve adjustments to prevent serious engine problems. Less of a problem with later models, rusting is usually confined to the undercarriage and other areas where the mouldings attach to sheet metal.

1995–99 models have chronic seatbelt retractor glitches and airbag malfunctions (the warning light comes on constantly). Additionally, owners report powertrain, brake, and electrical problems; poor rear windshield defrosting; vibration, squeaks, and rattles afflicting the brakes, steering, and suspension; and body trim imperfections that include water leaking through the doors.

The 2000–01 models have fewer deficiencies reported by owners, partly because they're still under warranty and haven't been on the market that long. Nevertheless, owners report that fenders are easily dented, the windshield and windshield frame may suddenly crack, engine may leak oil, and the seatbelt shoulder strap is mounted too high, cutting across the driver's neck.

Here's a summary of recent Corolla model changes: 1995s returned with a de-powered 1.8L engine that was a bit torquier, but had ten horses less than the '94. New front and rear ends and an upgraded manual transmission highlight the '96 model changes. '97s got a new CE version and the DX wagon got axed. '98 models went through a major redesign that included a new engine, sheet metal, and optional front passenger side-impact airbags. '99s didn't have any significant changes, and the year 2000 model got five additional horses. 2001 models were given a slight facelift and saw the addition of a new sport-oriented variant called the Corolla S. The VE was dropped and the formerly mid-level CE replaced it, carrying less standard features. The LE dropped to the CE's former level and was also "de-contented," losing its standard AC and power windows, locks, and mirrors.

Safety summary: All models: 1995—Fires originating in the defrost relay switch, starter, and battery storage area (not part of recall). • Steering wheel came off in driver's hands when making a left turn. • Dozens of reports that the airbag failed to deploy or deployed for no reason. • Many reports of injuries (one death) caused by airbag deployment. • Several reports of faulty seatbelt retractors. • Gearshift lever is easily knocked out of gear when car is underway. • Faulty door locks. **1996**—Fires originating in the fuel tank, dash, and engine compartment areas. • Airbag failed to deploy or deployed for no reason. • Brake failures and high maintenance costs. • Driver headrest too wide for adequate rear visibility. • Seatbelt failures and malfunctioning retractors. • Hood flew up while vehicle was underway. • Inoperative door locks. **1997**—Fires reportedly caused by faulty seatbelt wiring. • Brake failures. • Sudden acceleration. • Inadvertent airbag deployment (when the ignition is turned on) and no deployment during collisions. • Steering column grinding. • Interior water leaks. • Malfunctioning door locks. • Windshield wipers suddenly quit. • Poor visibility due to film on windshield interior and lack of an adequate rear defroster. • Frequent reports that the seatbelt retractors won't release or retract. • Researchers are looking into 20 incidents where the turn signal failed after the hazard warning light activated. **1998**—Airbag failures still lead the list of owner-reported problems recorded in the NHTSA database; however, '98 models also have a high incidence of airbag warning lights that stay lit when no fault can be found. • Other recurring problems are engine compartment fires, gas fumes in the interior, brake and power-steering failures, and excessive steering column noise. • Excessive drifting and high-speed instability, due to lack of a stabilizer bar. • Sudden acceleration. • Premature control arm failure. • Seatbelt released in accident. • Rear wheel broke at the axle. • Random honking. **1998–2000**—Airbag failed to deploy in a collision. • Brakes lock up. • Vehicle continues to wander and sway at moderate speed; side winds increase the vehicle's instability. • Gear shift dropped from Drive to Neutral while driving. • Floor mat jams the accelerator. • Engine stalls after refuelling. • Front strut assembly failure. • Inadequate headlight illumination; one side will be aimed too high, other side, too low. **1999**—Airbags failed to deploy. • Inadvertent airbag deployment. • Engine compartment fire. • Loss of braking ability. • Defective tires (Firestone). • Sudden acceleration. • Cruise control self-activates. • Automatic transmission locked up while driving. • Vehicle went out of control after rear control arm failure. • At cruising speed, vehicle tends to wander all over the road. • Windshield shattered when door was closed. • Poor headlight design causes blind spot and poor visibility. • Defective engine camshaft gets inadequate oil lubrication and loses compression. • Rear seatbelts aren't compatible with many child safety seats. • Muffler scrapes the ground with three occupants in the rear seat. **2001**—Airbags failed to deploy. • Sudden acceleration. • Stuck accelerator pedal. • Headlight illumination problem continues; high beam shoots skyward and is especially hazardous in rain or fog. • Rear driver-side axle sheared in half; vehicle rolled over. • Excessive front brake pad wear; premature failure of the brake proportioning valve and rear brake shoes. • Hole in the oil pan. • Failure of all four Goodyear Integrity tires. • Inside trunk release handle doesn't glow as advertised.

Secret Warranties/Service Tips/TSBs

All models/years: Improved disc brake pad kits are described in TSB #BR94-004. • Brake pulsation/vibration, another generic Toyota problem, is fully addressed in TSB #BR94-002, "Cause and Repair of Vibration and Pulsation." • Complaints of steering column noise may require the replacement of the steering column assembly, a repair covered under Toyota's base warranty. • AM static noise on all vehicles with power antennas usually means the antenna is poorly grounded. • Toyota has developed special procedures for eliminating AC odours and excessive wind noise. These problems are covered in TSB #AC00297 and #BO00397, respectively. **All models: 1990–2001**—Toyota has developed a special grease to eliminate clicking when the vehicle goes into Drive or Reverse. **1993–96**—Toyota has upgraded the hazard switch to improve turn signal performance in cold climates. **1993–97**—Inoperative front passenger-side power window switch may be caused by lubricant from the wire harness contaminating the window switch contacts. **1995–96**—To enhance the performance of the rear door glass, Toyota has upgraded the mounting channel rubber insert and offers it as a service part. **1996**—An axle hub squeaking noise can be fixed by installing an oil seal kit. • A fuel door that's hard to operate in cold weather should be replaced with one containing an upgraded inlet gasket. **1997**—Cutting sulfur odours from exhaust. **1998**—Tips on reducing excessive engine V-belt noise. • Delayed upshift to Overdrive with cruise control engaged can be fixed by changing the cruise control ECU logic. • Water leakage into the rear cab can be plugged by installing an improved C-pillar moulding clip. • If the rear door glass malfunctions when temperatures dive, install an upgraded mounting channel insert bar. • Toyota will replace the airbag computer under a service campaign. **1998–99**—A front suspension squeaking noise can be silenced by replacing the steering rack end shaft under the base warranty, but only if customer requests the repair. **1998–2000**—In an attempt to reduce brake vibration complaints, Toyota will install a new front disc brake pad kit, says TSB #BR002-00, issued March 10, 2000. This fix is covered by Toyota's base warranty, but the customer must request the service (it also might help if you show the service manager the following bulletin).

Front Brake Vibration

Bulletin: BR002-00   Group: Brakes   Date: March 10, 2000

Introduction

A new Front Disc Brake Pad kit is available and a procedure has been developed for applying Disc Brake Grease to the brake cylinder mountings, brake pads, and pad support plates to reduce the possibility of front brake vibration under certain operating conditions.

Applicable Vehicles

1998-2000 model year Corolla

Parts Information

Previous Part Number	Current Part Number	Part Name
04465-12520	04465-02050	Pad Kit, Front Disc Brake
04945-02020	Same	Shim Kit (if needed*)
08887-80409	Same	Grease, Disc Brake Shim
04947-02020	Same	Fitting kit, Front Disc Brake (if needed**)

* Visually inspect shims for heat discolouration. If discoloured, replace the shims.
* Visually inspect pad support plates for damage. If damaged, replace the pad support plates.

OPCODE	DESCRIPTION	TIME	OPN	T1	T2
473025	Grind Front Discs and Replace Pads, Shims (if needed), and Apply Grease to Front Disc Brake	1.3	43512-12550	21	99
Combo A	Cylinder Mountings, Brake Pads, and Pad Support Plates for Vibration (both sides).	0.8			

Warranty Information

Applicable Warranty*:

This repair is covered under the Toyota Basic Warranty. This warranty is in effect for 36 months or 36,000 miles, whichever occurs first, from the vehicle's in-service date.

* Warranty application is limited to correction of a problem based upon a customer's specific complaint.

Brake pulsation has been a recurring Toyota problem, affecting its entire model lineup over the past decade. Many "goodwill" programs cover its diagnosis and correction.

1999—A single-cylinder misfire that causes a rough idle or the activation of the malfunction indicator light (MIL) will be fixed under Toyota's base warranty.

Corolla Profile

	1994	1995	1996	1997	1998	1999	2000	2001
Cost Price ($)								
Base	14,798	15,628	13,508	13,968	14,928	15,090	15,625	15,625
Used Values ($)								
Base Λ	5,000	6,000	7,500	8,500	9,500	10,500	12,000	14,000
Base V	4,000	5,000	6,000	7,000	8,500	9,500	10,500	13,000
Extended Warranty	N	N	N	N	N	N	N	N
Secret Warranty	N	N	N	Y	Y	Y	Y	Y
Reliability	③	③	③	③	③	③	③	③
Crash Safety (F)	④	④	④	④	④	—	④	④
Side Impact	—	—	—	③	③	—	④	④
Off-set	—	—	—	—	③	③	③	③
Head Restraints	—	❷	—	❶	③	③	—	❷
Rollover Resistance	—	—	—	—	—	—	—	④

ECHO   ★★★★★

RATING: Recommended (2000–01). An incredibly practical small car, if you can get by the tall, function-over-form styling. **Parts:** Should be easily obtainable from the Tercel parts bin. Body panels may be back-ordered. **Maintenance/Repair costs:** Too early to tell. **Best alternatives:** A Ford Escort or Tracer, GM Firefly or Metro, Honda Civic, Hyundai Accent, Mazda Protegé, Nissan Sentra, and Suzuki Swift or Esteem.

Strengths and weaknesses: Toyota scrapped its stripped-down Tercel in favour of the year 2000 Echo, an entry-level five-passenger model that uses some of the same engine technology as the Lexus to give great fuel economy without sacrificing performance.

Both two- and four-door models are available, and the car costs substantially less than the Corolla. Echo offers about the same amount of passenger space as the Corolla, thanks to a high roof and low floor height.

Cockpit controls and instrumentation are particularly user-friendly, located high on the dash and more toward the centre of the vehicle, rather than directly in front of the driver, where many gauges and controls are hidden by the steering column.

The Echo is powered by an all-new, 108-hp 1.5L DOHC 4-cylinder engine featuring Variable Valve Timing cylinder head technology. It's the same design used in the Lexus to combine power and fuel economy in a low-emissions vehicle. Normally, an engine this small would provide wimpy accelration for most cars, but, thanks to the Echo's light weight, acceleration is more than adequate with a manual gearbox and acceptable with the automatic.

Standard safety features: five three-point seatbelts (front seatbelts have pretensioners and force limiters), two front airbags (side airbags are not available), four height-adjustable head restraints, rear child seat tether anchors, and rear child door locks.

The Echo has more usable power than the Tercel and provides excellent fuel economy and lots of interior space. There's plenty of passenger room, along with an incredible array of storage areas, including a huge trunk and standard 60/40 split-folding rear seats. All models are reasonably well equipped with good-quality materials, well-designed instrument and controls, comfortable seating, easy rear access, and excellent fore and aft visibility. It's quite nimble when cornering, very stable on the highway, and surprisingly quiet for an economy car.

What's there not to like? Try the tall profile and light weight, which make the Echo vulnerable to side-wind buffeting; base tires that provide poor wet traction; excessive torque steer that makes for sudden pulling to one side when accelerating; and the narrow body width, which limits rear bench seating to two adults.

Safety summary: All models: 2001—Toyota should reposition the Overdrive switch; the right thigh may bump against it. • At 100 km/h, the engine jumps to higher rpms and causes a bit of a surprise. • Vehicle drifted off the highway at 110 km/h.

Secret Warranties/Service Tips/TSBs

All models: 2000—Toyota has a Special Service Campaign (secret warranty) that allows for the free replacement of the brake booster and front brake pads on vehicles equipped with an automatic transmission. Confirmation of this campaign can be found in Toyota Service Bulletin Number: TC01027; Bulletin Sequence Number: 625; published: 10/01; and recorded in the NHTSA database as Item Number: SB625616. • MIL light may indicate a single-cylinder misfire (modify the ECM). • Probable causes for interior squeaks and rattles. • Wheel covers may click or squeak. • Excessive wind noise. • Fuel gauge and speedometer malfunctions. • Brake clicking countermeasures. • Defective airflow rotary control knob.

Echo Profile

	2000	2001
Cost Price ($)		
Base	13,835	13,980
Used Values ($)		
Base ▲	10,500	12,000
Base ▼	9,500	10,500
Extended Warranty	N	N
Secret Warranty	N	N

Reliability	⑤	⑤
Crash Safety (F)	—	④
Side Impact	—	③
Head Restraints	—	⑤
Rollover Resistance	—	④

PASEO   ★★★★★

RATING: Recommended (1994–99); Above Average (1992–93). 1999 was the Paseo's last model year. **Maintenance/Repair costs:** Lower than average. Repairs can be done anywhere. **Parts:** Reasonably priced and easily found. **Best alternatives:** The GM Metro, Honda Civic, Hyundai Accent, Mazda Protegé, Nissan Sentra, Suzuki Esteem, and Toyota Echo.

Strengths and weaknesses: This baby Tercel's main advantages are a peppy 1.5L 4-cylinder engine, a smooth 5-speed manual transmission, good handling, a supple ride, great fuel economy, and above-average reliability. On the other hand, this light little sportster is quite vulnerable to side winds; there's lots of body lean in turns; there's plenty of engine, exhaust, and road noise; front head room and leg room are limited; and there is very little rear seat space.

Safety summary: All models: 1996–97—No airbag deployment, and one report of an engine compartment fire of unknown origin.

Secret Warranties/Service Tips/TSBs

All models/years: TSB #B0003-97 recommends the use of a new wind noise repair kit. • TSB #AC002-97 gives lots of troubleshooting tips on eliminating AC odours. • AM radio static is likely caused by a damaged power antenna or by poor grounding due to corrosion. **All models: 1996**—Toyota has developed an upgraded thermostat to improve heater performance. **1997**—Fujitsu radios may not eject/accept CDs.

Paseo Profile

	1992	1993	1994	1995	1996	1997	1998	1999
Cost Price ($)								
Base	13,338	14,398	14,698	16,878	17,215	17,608	15,998	16,150
Used Values ($)								
Base Λ	3,500	4,000	5,000	6,500	8,000	9,500	10,500	12,000
Base V	3,000	3,500	4,500	5,000	6,500	8,000	9,000	10,500
Extended Warranty	N	N	N	N	N	N	N	N
Secret Warranty	N	N	N	N	N	N	N	N
Reliability	④	④	④	⑤	⑤	⑤	⑤	⑤
Crash Safety (F)	③	③	—	—	—	④	—	—
Head Restraints	—	—	—	❶	—	❷	—	—

TERCEL   ★ ★ ★ ★ ★

RATING: Recommended (1993–99); Above Average (1991–92); Average (1987–90). **Maintenance/Repair costs:** Inexpensive. Repairs can be done anywhere. **Parts:** Reasonably priced and easily obtainable. **Best alternatives:** A GM Firefly or Metro, Honda Civic, Hyundai Accent, or Elantra, Mazda Protegé, Nissan Sentra, Suzuki Esteem, and Toyota Echo or Corolla.

Strengths and weaknesses: Don't buy a Toyota on reputation alone, because many early models (1985–90) can have serious braking, electrical, and rusting problems, and may be overpriced to boot. Also, stay away from the troublesome 4X4 versions made from 1984 to 1987.

All Tercels should be checked for door panel and underbody rust damage. 1987–90 Tercels are prone to rust around the rear wheels and side mirror mounts, and along the bottoms of doors, hatches, and rear quarter panels. Early models suffer from extensive corrosion of rear suspension components.

1991–94 Tercels are pretty reliable, but they're not perfect. They were the first to be fuel-injected, which makes for livelier and smoother acceleration, and the interior space feels much larger than it is. Owners report faulty clutch-sleeve cylinders, hard shifting with the automatic transmission, premature brake and suspension component wearout, brake pulsation, defective CD players, leaking radiators, windshield whistling, and myriad squeaks and rattles.

Redesigned 1995–99 Tercels offer a bit more horsepower, standard dual airbags, side-door beams, aero styling, and a redesigned interior. They continue, however, to have brake, electrical system, suspension, and body/accessories problems.

Safety summary: Interestingly, there are far fewer safety-related Tercel and Paseo complaints recorded over the years than those listed for the Corolla, Camry, or Sienna. **All models: 1995**—Most common problems in the NHTSA database: airbag failing to deploy, seatbelt lockup, and windshield seal leaks. • Other problems include brake failure, inadequate defrosting, stalling, vehicle jumping out of gear, and engine failure due to defective oil indicator. **1996**—No airbag deployment. • Fuel line explosion. • Fire caused by an overheated heater fan motor. • Brake failure. • Inadequate defrosting. • Light rear end makes car unstable at higher speeds. **1997**—No airbag deployment. • Seatbelt and brake failures. • Front ball joints snapped while car was underway. **1998**—No airbag deployment. • Seatbelt malfunctions. • Inoperative AC. • Excessive engine noise.

Secret Warranties/Service Tips/TSBs

All models/years: TSB #B0003-97 recommends the use of a new wind noise repair kit. • Interior squeaks and rattles can be fixed with Toyota's kit (#08231-00801). • TSB #AC002-97 gives lots of troubleshooting tips on eliminating AC odours. • Older Toyotas with stalling problems should have the engine checked for excessive carbon buildup on the valves before any other repairs are done. • Improved disc brake pad kits are described in TSB #BR94-004. • Brake pulsation/vibration, another generic Toyota problem, is fully addressed in TSB #BR94-002, "Cause and Repair of Vibration and Pulsation." • A damaged power antenna or poor grounding due to corrosion are the most likely causes of AM radio static. **All models: 1994**—A whistling noise coming from the windshield requires a urethane sealant applied at key points. • A steering column that's noisy or has excessive free play may need an upgraded steering main-shaft bushing. **1995**—Troubleshooting windshield-moulding wind noise is covered in TSB #BO95-005. **1995–96**—Toyota has developed an upgraded thermostat to improve heater performance. • The company will also make available a longer passenger-side seatbelt. **1997**—Fujitsu radios may not eject/accept CDs. **1998**—Diagnostic tips for eliminating vehicle vibration. Countermeasures for reducing sulfur odour from exhaust emissions. • Front door belt-moulding wind noise.

Tercel Profile

	1992	1993	1994	1995	1996	1997	1998	1999
Cost Price ($)								
Base	8,798	9,098	9,618	10,998	11,948	12,498	12,498	12,625
Used Values ($)								
Base ⋏	2,500	3,000	3,500	4,000	5,000	6,000	7,000	8,500
Base ⋎	2,000	2,500	3,000	3,500	4,500	5,000	6,000	7,000
Extended Warranty	N	N	N	N	N	N	N	N
Secret Warranty	N	N	N	N	N	Y	Y	Y
Reliability	③	③	③	④	⑤	⑤	⑤	⑤
Crash Safety (F)	❷	❷	④	④	③	④	—	—
Side Impact	—	—	—	—	—	③	③	—
Head Restraints	—	❷	—	❶	—	❶	—	—

Volkswagen

CABRIO, GOLF, JETTA   ★★★★

RATING: Above Average (1997–2001); Average (1994–96); Below Average (1993); Not Recommended (1985–92). These small imports age particularly badly, and VW is not very generous with "goodwill" repairs. A Jetta is a Golf with a trunk; a Cabrio is a Golf without a roof. There was no 1994 model Cabrio. Interestingly, the early convertibles (Cabriolets) are real bargains, inasmuch as they depreciate steeply after their first five years on the market. **Maintenance/Repair costs:** Higher than average. Repairs are dealer dependent. **Parts:** Expensive, but generally available from independent suppliers. Recall campaign parts may be back-ordered for months. **Best alternatives:** The GM Cavalier or Sunfire, Honda Civic, Hyundai Elantra or Tiburon, Mazda Protegé, Nissan Sentra, and Toyota Corolla.

Strengths and weaknesses: On the positive side, these small Europeans are fun to drive and provide great fuel economy. The 1.8L gasoline engine is very peppy, and the diesel engines are very reliable and good all-around performers. Both engines are easily started in cold weather. But here's the rub: Golfs and Jettas, like the failure-prone Rabbit they replaced, age badly. What you save in fuel, you lose in the car's high retail price, which is carried over into the used-car market; and the ever-mounting maintenance costs as the vehicle gains years and mileage will easily wear you down.

Reliability is impressive—for the first three years. Then the brake components and fuel and electrical systems start to self-destruct as your wallet gets lighter. Exhaust system components aren't very durable, body hardware and dashboard controls are fragile, and the paint often discolours and is easily chipped.

Although the 1990–93 models are a tad improved, Volkswagen still has terrible quality problems. Owners report electrical short circuits; heater/defroster resistor and motor failures; leaking transmission and stub axle seals; and defective valve-pan gaskets, head gaskets, timing belts, steering assemblies, suspension components, alternator pulleys, and brake and electrical systems. Body problems are legion, with air and water leaks; faulty catalytic converters; inoperative locks and latches; poor-quality body construction and paint; and cheap, easily broken accessories and trim items.

The redesigned 1994–96 models are a bit safer and more reliable. Nevertheless, problems disclosed in service bulletins for these model years include poor driveability, water leaks, trim defects, and premature rear tire wear. Owners report the following: electric door locks that take a long time to lock; paint that is easily nicked, chipped, and marked; a variety of trim defects; premature rear tire wear; and poor-quality seat cushions.

Factory defects on 1990–96 Golfs and Jettas are so numerous they make these models very risky buys. Problems include automatic transmission, engine, suspension component, and catalytic converter failures; electrical short circuits; AC malfunctions; and fragile trim items. Body assembly and paint are second-class, leading to rattles and air leaks as the vehicles age.

For 1997, Golfs and Jettas equipped with the 116-hp 4-cylinder engine got a redesigned cylinder head that cuts engine noise. The Golf GTI VR6 rides lower, thanks to new shocks, springs, and anti-roll bars. The Cabrio Highline received standard AC, 14-inch alloy wheels, halogen driving lights, and leather upholstery. The base convertible lost its standard ABS and a few other goodies in an unsuccessful attempt to keep a lid on price. 1998 and 1999 models were returned relatively unchanged, except for side airbags and rear disc brakes; however, the 1999 Jetta debuted with junior-Passat features (adopted the following year by the Golf and GTI).

Jettas provide slightly more comfort and better road performance than their Golf hatchback counterparts. The 1.6L 4-cylinder found on early Jettas was surprisingly peppy, and the diesel engine is very economical, although quite slow to accelerate. Diesels have a better overall reliability record than gasoline models and are popular as taxis. Jettas are far more reliable than Rabbits, but they, too, suffer from rapid body deterioration and some mechanical problems after their fourth year in service. For example, on post-1988 Jettas, starters often burn out because they are vulnerable to engine heat; as well, sunroofs leak, door locks jam, window cranks break, and windows bind. Owners also report engine head gasket leaks and water-pump and heater-core breakdowns. It's axiomatic that all diesels are slow to accelerate, but VW's Fourth gear can't handle highway speeds above 90 km/h. Engine noise is deafening when shifting down from Fourth gear.

All 1996–99 models are much more reliable, but, nevertheless, owners still report chronic automatic transmission, brake, and electrical system problems, in addition to subpar body construction and paint, leaky sunroofs, malfunctioning gauges and accessories, fragile locks and latches, bumpers that become brittle and crack as the temperature falls, and defective security systems.

Owners of 2000–01 models report the following problems: airbags failed to deploy in an accident; airbag light stays on for no apparent reason; cracked oil pan; engine burns oil; chronic stalling in traffic; hard starting; noisy brakes; sudden headlight failure; poor headlight illumination; faulty power window regulators; broken centre armrest; glovebox hinge and handle breakage; discoloured side mirror.

Safety summary: All models: 1995—Alternator harness failure. **1995–98**—The NHTSA database shows the following problems are reported repeatedly: fires; airbags that fail to deploy or cause severe injuries when they go off; airbag light stays on for no apparent reason; transmission and wheel-bearing failures; transmission pops out of gear; electrical malfunctions leading to chronic stalling; self-activating alarms; lights going out; erratic cruise control operation; brake, tire, and AC failures; inadequate defrosting; AC mould and mildew smell; and poor-quality body components. • Also, doors may open suddenly; locks jam shut, fall out, or freeze; power window motors and regulators self-destruct; hood suddenly flies up; cigarette lighter pops out of holder while lit; the seat heater may burn a hole in the driver's seat; and battery acid can leak onto the power-steering reservoir and cause sudden steering loss. **1996**—Rear wheel and axle may separate. • Door mouldings fall off. **1997**—Fire caused by faulty driver-seat wiring. • Battery exploded. **1998**—Engine damaged after water was ingested through the air intake system. • Transmission locked into Third gear. • ABS brake failures. • Head restraints suddenly drop down. • Michelin tire failure. • Noisy brakes. • Inaccurate fuel gauge. • Faulty factory alarm. **1999**—Plastic fuel line fails in cold weather. • Engine burns oil. • Vehicle may suddenly spin out of control. • Chronic stalling in traffic with engine warning light lit. • Headlight failure; no low beam. • Window fell into door, due to defective window regulator. **2000**—No airbag deployment. • Airbag warning light stays lit; will cost $700 to fix. • Sudden acceleration. • Cracked axle. • Early replacement of the rear brake pads. • Dashboard causes excessive windshield glare. • Glovebox door hinge snapped. • Window regulator failure; power windows inoperable. **2001**—Airbag light stays lit. • Timing chain exploded. • Frequent stalling due to defective airflow sensor. • Premature constant velocity joint replacement.

Secret Warranties/Service Tips/TSBs

All models: 1996–97—A shifter that's hard to move side-to-side or won't go into Reverse may signal that the selector shaft is binding in the selector shaft housing bearing. **1997**—Erratic electrical functions may be caused by a loose ground at one of two grounding studs located under the battery tray. • If the transmission pops out of gear, check for a hairline crack on the selector shaft shift detent sleeve. • Buzzing noise from right-side air outlet may be caused by loose outlet mounting screws. **1998–99**—Noisy, vibrating blower motor. • Defective instrument cluster. • Radio volume control malfunction. **1999**—Humming noise from front of vehicle when turning may be caused by the differential spider gear. **2000**—Automatic transmission may go into limp mode without malfunction indicator light (MIL) activated. **2000–01**—Troubleshooting prematurely worn rear brake pads (see following bulletin).

Rear Brake Pads - Prematurely Worn

Group: 46   Number: 00-01   Date: Nov. 27, 2000
Subject: Rear Brake Pads, Worn Prematurely

Model(s):

Golf, Jetta, New Beetle - 2000, 2001

Condition

While inspecting front and rear brake pads, the rear brake pads appear to be prematurely worn.

May be caused by combination of a customer who frequently applies his/her brakes with heavy pressure and a softer brake pad composition (for noise elimination).

Service

When inspecting a customer's brake system:
If rear brake pads appear to be prematurely worn:
- Inspect front brake pads.
If front pads are original (factory) pads and are still good:
- Install new rear brake pads Part No. 1J0 698 451 on vehicle, see appropriate Repair Manual CD-ROM, Group 46 - Rear Wheel Brakes "Disc brakes, servicing."

Note:

For Part No: 1J0 698 451 (used on 1999 m.y vehicles), the brake pad composition is harder and while it is more durable, may in some applications (depending on the customer's driving/braking habits) be noisier.

For Part No: 1J0 698 451 B (used on 2000 m.y vehicles), the brake pad composition is softer, therefore may be less durable (depending on the customer's driving/braking habits), and may in some application (depending on the customer's driving/braking habits) be quieter.

Part Indentifier:	4638
Labor Operation:	46382050 40 TU

When procedure applies to vehicles within the first 12 months or 12,000 miles/20,000 km, (whichever occurs first) of the Limited New Vehicle Warranty period, use the table.

Note:

For vehicles which have exceeded 12 months or 12,000 miles/20,000 km (whichever occurs first) of the Limited New Vehicle Warranty period, contact your OTS.

Volkswagen says that this repair is eligible for after-warranty "goodwill" assistance. Make your service manager aware of this important fact.

2001—Leaking intake hoses. • Inoperative secondary air pump (blown fuse). • Troubleshooting "defective control module" indication. • Leaking transmission pan gasket.

Cabrio, Golf, Jetta Profile

	1994	1995	1996	1997	1998	1999	2000	2001
Cost Price ($)								
Cabrio	—	26,495	26,495	25,230	25,300	25,300	25,300	28,530
Golf	12,600	12,995	14,325	14,690	16,765	15,610	18,950	19,040
Jetta	15,370	18,995	17,650	18,050	18,620	18,620	21,170	21,280
Used Values ($)								
Cabrio Λ	—	12,000	13,500	15,000	17,500	19,500	21,500	26,000
Cabrio V	—	10,000	12,000	13,000	15,000	17,000	19,000	24,000

Golf Λ	5,000	6,500	7,500	8,500	11,000	11,500	14,500	16,000
Golf V	4,000	5,000	5,500	6,500	9,500	10,000	12,500	14,000
Jetta Λ	6,500	8,000	9,000	10,500	12,500	13,500	16,000	17,500
Jetta V	5,500	6,500	7,500	9,000	10,500	11,500	14,5,00	15,500
Extended Warranty	Y	Y	Y	Y	Y	Y	Y	Y
Secret Warranty	N	N	N	N	N	N	N	N
Reliability	❷	❷	❷	❷	③	③	④	④
Crash Safety (F)								
Golf	—	—	—	③	③	—	—	⑤
Jetta	—	—	③	③	③	—	—	⑤
Side Impact (Jetta)	—	—	—	—	③	③	—	④
Off-set	❷	❷	❷	❷	❷	③	③	④
Head Restraints (F)	—	❷	—	❷	—	❷	—	❷
Rear	—	—	—	—	—	❶	—	—
Rollover Resistance	—	—	—	—	—	—	—	④

MEDIUM CARS

Medium-sized cars, often referred to as "family" cars, are a trade-off between size and fuel economy, offering more room and comfort but a bit less fuel economy (9.5–11.5L/100 km) than a small car. These cars are popular because they combine the advantages of smaller cars with those of larger vehicles. As a result of their versatility, as well as both upsizing and downsizing throughout the years, these vehicles shade into both the small and large car niches. The trunk is usually large enough to meet average baggage requirements, and the interior is spacious enough to meet the needs of the average family (seating four people in comfort and five in a pinch). These cars are best for combined city and highway driving, with the top three choices traditionally dominated by Japanese automakers: the Honda Accord, Mazda 626, and Toyota Camry. VW's Passat has just recently taken top honours in *Consumer Reports'* annual listing of Best Buys; however, its high resale value is a real budget buster.

✘ RISKY BUY

How the mighty have fallen. Ford's Taurus and Sable have gone from being sales leaders (like the redesigned 2000 Taurus above) to industry losers as their safety and reliability problems become known and Ford cuts off their after-warranty assistance life-support.

Ford's Taurus and Sable are in a sales death spiral following persistent owner complaints of drivetrain deficiencies and generally poor quality control. Chrysler's Breeze, Cirrus, and Stratus have improved in quality over the past several years and generally offer the most interior space and competitive used prices. GM is the best of the Detroit Big Three. Its models may be bland, but quality control is better than both Ford and Chrysler. Plus, there are more models from which to choose.

MEDIUM CAR RATINGS

Recommended

Acura 1.6, 1.7L EL (1997–2001)
Honda Accord (2000–01)

Mazda 626 (1999–2001)
Toyota Camry (1994–96)

Above Average

Acura CL-Series (1998–99)
Acura Integra (1990–2001)
General Motors Bonneville, Cutlass,
  Cutlass Supreme, Delta 88, Grand
  Prix, LeSabre, Regal (1984–87)
Honda Accord (1990–99)

Hyundai Sonata (1999–2001)
Mazda 626, MX-6 (1996–98)
Nissan Altima (1998–2001)
Toyota Camry, Solara (1988–93,
  1997–2001)
Volkswagen Passat (1998–2001)

Average

Acura CL-Series (1997)
Acura Integra (1986–89)
General Motors Bonneville, Cutlass,
  Cutlass Supreme, Delta 88, Grand
  Prix, Intrigue, LeSabre, Lumina,
  Malibu, Monte Carlo, Regal
  (1997–2001)
General Motors Century (1998–2001)

General Motors Grand Am (1999–2001)
Honda Accord (1985–89)
Hyundai Sonata (1995–98)
Mazda 626, MX-6 (1994–95)
Nissan Altima (1993–97)
Toyota Camry (1985–87)
Volkswagen New Beetle (1998–2001)
Volkswagen Passat (1995–97)

Below Average

DaimlerChrysler Breeze, Cirrus,
  Stratus (1995–2000)
Ford Sable, Taurus (2000–01)

General Motors Century (1997)
General Motors Achieva, Grand Am,
  Skylark (1995–98)

Not Recommended

Ford Contour, Mystique (1995–99)
Ford Sable, Taurus (1986–99)
General Motors Achieva (Calais),
  Grand Am, Skylark (1985–94)
General Motors Bonneville, Cutlass,
  Cutlass Supreme, Delta 88, Grand
  Prix, Intrigue, LeSabre, Lumina,
  Malibu, Monte Carlo, Regal
  (1988–96)

General Motors Century, Ciera
  (1982–96)
Hyundai Sonata (1986–93)
Mazda 626, MX-6 (1985–93)
Volkswagen Passat (1989–93)

Acura

1.6, 1.7L EL   ★★★★★

RATING: Recommended (1997–2001). The Honda equivalent for the revised 2001 1.7L EL is the Civic EX Sedan. The 2001 EL Premium commanded a $2,000 premium over the base version. **Maintenance/Repair costs:** Average. Repairs aren't dealer dependent. **Parts:** Average parts cost, thanks to the use of generic Honda Si parts sold through independent suppliers. **Best alternatives:** The Honda Civic EX or Si; Hyundai Elantra wagon, Sonata, or Tiburon; Mazda 626 or Protegé, Nissan Sentra or Stanza, and Toyota Camry or Corolla.

Strengths and weaknesses: The first Japanese automobile built exclusively in and for the Canadian market, the EL is essentially an all-dressed Civic sedan, sold under the Acura moniker. It came about as an answer to Canadian Acura dealer pleadings for a more affordable Acura. Since its '97 model launch, the car has been immensely popular—and hard to find on the used-car market.

Based on the top-line Civic Si, the EL comes with a peppy 127-hp VTEC 1.6L 4-banger that's both reliable and economical to run. Add to this the Civic's chassis and upgraded suspension components and you have outstanding performance, as good as or better than that of the Civic Si. Some of the 1.6 EL's weak points: a narrow interior, with seats and seatbacks not to everyone's liking; emergency braking that's only average; head restraints rated "poor" by IIHS; and excessive engine noise intruding into the passenger compartment despite upgraded soundproofing.

Style-wise, the EL still looks like a Civic—large, square headlights; upgraded cloth and plastic; and standard features that include a standard AM/FM cassette four-speaker audio system, dual vanity mirrors, tilt steering wheel, and cruise control. In 1997, $20,000 got you the upscale sport version with a CD player, Acura's Acoustic Feedback Audio system, and air conditioning. For 2,000 additional loonies, the Premium version offered both the cassette and CD players, power sunroof, and leather-covered seats.

In just over four years on the market, the EL has done quite well, even though it hasn't changed much. The 1.7L 2001 model is an all-new incarnation (as is the 2001 Civic) that is roomier, better-equipped, and more fuel efficient, even though horsepower remains the same. And, unfortunately for bargain hunters, the EL's value holds up extremely well, with first-year '97 models still worth about 65 percent of their original selling price.

No safety complaints have been reported, and the few owner complaints recorded have mostly concerned wind noise, easily dented body panels, malfunctioning accessories (AC, audio system, electrical components, etc.), and fragile trim items. Some minor turn-offs with the 2001 model: car loses power when the AC is activated; there are no stereo controls on the steering wheel; and the driver's seat armrest can interfere with the gearshift lever.

Secret Warranties/Service Tips/TSBs

All models/years: Most Honda/Acura TSBs allow for special warranty consideration on a "goodwill" basis even after the warranty has expired or the car has changed hands. Referring to this euphemism will increase your chances of getting some kind of refund for repairs that are obviously related to a factory defect. Keep in mind that many Honda bulletins often apply to Acuras, as well. So, check out the Civic and Accord's TSBs and safety complaints before assuming a particular Acura problem is your responsibility. • Acura says it will replace any seatbelt's tongue stopper button for the life of the vehicle.

1.6 EL Profile

	1997	1998	1999	2000	2001
Cost Price ($)					
1.6 EL	17,800	18,800	19,800	20,005	21,500
Used Values ($)					
1.6 EL ▲	11,000	12,500	14,500	16,500	18,500
1.6 EL ▼	9,000	11,000	13,000	15,000	17,000
Extended Warranty	N	N	N	N	N
Secret Warranty	N	N	N	N	N
Reliability	[5]	[5]	[5]	[5]	[5]

Note: These vehicles have not been crash-tested.

CL-SERIES ★★★★

RATING: Above Average (1998–99); Average (1997). Overpriced and hard to find; be wary of the first-year models. You may have to be astute in negotiating a fair price, particularly in rural areas; there's an unusually high $2,000 margin between the high (dealer) and low (private) values. Most vehicles show a $1,000–1,500 difference. **Maintenance/Repair costs:** Lower than average. Repairs can be done practically anywhere. **Parts:** Cost is a bit higher than average, but they're not hard to find. **Best alternatives:** BMW 318, Honda Accord, Lexus SC 300, Nissan Maxima, and Toyota Camry.

Strengths and weaknesses: The only difference between the 2.2L CL and the 3.0L CL is the 3.0L CL's larger engine, different wheels, and larger exhaust tip. The 2.2L CL's engine was upgraded to 2.3L on the 1998 models.

These cars are stylish, front-drive, five-passenger luxury coupes that are American designed and built. They have a flowing, slanted back end and no apparent trunk lock (a standard remote keyless entry system opens the trunk from the outside and a lever opens it from the inside). And while other Japanese automakers are taking content out of their vehicles, Acura has put content into the CL, making it one of the most feature-laden cars in its class.

Sure, we all know that the coupe's mechanicals and platform aren't that different from the Accord's, but when you add up all of its standard bells and whistles, you get a fully loaded medium-sized car that costs thousands of dollars less than such competing luxury coupes as the BMW 318 and the Lexus SC 300. Consider this array of standard features: power windows, power mirrors, power moon roof, six-way power driver's seat, remote keyless entry system, ABS, leather-wrapped steering wheel, simulated wood trim, automatic climate control, dual airbags, tilt steering wheel, cruise control, and CD player and AM/FM stereo with six speakers.

Although no one would consider the CL a high-performance car, it gets plenty of power from its quiet and smooth-running 3.0L 24-valve SOHC Variable Valve Timing and Lift Electronic Control (VTEC) V6, as well as from the Accord's 2.2L, single overhead cam 4-cylinder VTEC engine (upgraded to a 2.3L on the '98 models). The latter engine's 145 horses take the CL from 0 to 100 km in a respectable nine seconds, but the engine works hard and is noisy. Handling is better than average, thanks to the Accord's upgraded suspension, variable assisted steering, and 16-inch wheels, which are one inch larger than the Accord's (I told you there was a lot of Accord in the CL). Confirming that fact, the 2000 coupe is set on the Accord's platform.

Now that I've whetted your appetite with all that's right about these little Acuras, let's look at some of the problems reported with the 1997–99 models. This is not a car for seating passengers in the rear. Backseat room is insufficient, unless the front seats are pushed all the way forward. And the rear windows don't roll down all the way. Furthermore, owners have become so incensed at what they perceive as Acura's arrogant stonewalling of customer complaints that one owner, Michael Hos, set up his own Acura Lemon website to air Acura gripes and put pressure on the company. He got his money back after a few months and took down his website as part of the bargain. Nevertheless, for other helpful automotive websites, see Appendix I.

Some of the common defects reported on the Hos website: faulty transmission control unit; transmission downshift problems; chronic brake rotor pulsation and other brake problems, leading to resurfacing of brake rotors and replacement of brake pads, rotors, calipers, and springs; repeated front-end realignments; door and wind noise leading to replacement of door; and a sunroof that won't stop at closed position, requiring replacement of sunroof switch and controller.

Consider the following two repair programs: Honda's 14-year EPA-mandated free tune-ups, and engine emission component repairs applicable to all 1996–97 Acuras, except for the Type R models, and the replacement of defective oil seals on 4-cylinder-equipped 1994–97 models. The latter repair will probably entail paying a pro-rated charge.

Safety summary: All models: 1997—Complete brake failure; vehicle hit a wall. • Frequent brake rotor replacement. • Chronic hesitation and stalling. • When accelerating, vehicle will appear to stall, and then suddenly accelerate. • Inadvertent airbag deployment. • Passenger front seatbelt locks up and won't retract. • Leaky oil pan seals. • Premature catalytic converter failure. • Subframe out of alignment, causing vehicle to pull to one side. • Complete automatic transmission failure, or transmission locks in Fourth gear. • Main computer failure. **1998**—When driving on a flat surface at 45 km/h, or 1500 rpm, vehicle will jerk and pull for about 30 seconds. • Transmission seals failed. • Chronic electrical shorts.• Premature shock failure. • Sudden power steering loss. • Excessive steering play due to faulty steering column coupling. • Vehicle will sometimes accelerate when slowing for a stop. **1999**—Transmission failure; inoperative gear shift due to water on the horn.

Secret Warranties/Service Tips/TSBs

All models/years: Most Honda/Acura TSBs allow for special warranty consideration on a "goodwill" basis even after the warranty has expired or the car has changed hands. Referring to this euphemism will increase your chances of getting some kind of refund for repairs that are obviously related to a factory defect. • Acura says it will replace any seatbelt's tongue stopper button for the life of the vehicle. **All models: 1997**—Under a Product Update Campaign (secret warranty), Acura will re-route the hood cable so it doesn't cause a coolant leak from rubbing against the radiator. • Remedy for front seat that won't slide forward or backward. • Freeing up seatback adjustment lever • Silencing a dash pop or creak. • Fix for incorrect fuel gauge and speedometer readings. • Correction for brake fluid leaking from the ABS modulator. • Fix for wind noise from front side windows. **1997–98**—Power seat noise. • Power windows don't work. • Window rattling. **1998–99**—Steering wheel remote audio switches may not work properly. **2.2L: 1997**—Front balancer shaft oil seal may back out of the oil pump housing, resulting in the oil rapidly pumping out of the engine without warning. **1999**—Coolant leak from the engine block. **3.0L: 1997–99**—A Product Update Campaign calls for the re-routing of the PCV hose to prevent the intake manifold EGR port from clogging. This is especially applicable to vehicles using fuel sold in the United States. • V6 engine oil leaks. **1998–99**—Troubleshooting the inadvertent activation of the MIL (malfunction indicator light).

CL-Series Profile

	1997	1998	1999
Cost Price ($)			
2.2L/2.3L CL	27,800	30,000	30,900
3.0L CL	30,650	34,000	35,000
Used Values ($)			
2.2L/2.3L CL ʌ	14,500	18,000	21,500
2.2L/2.3L CL v	12,000	16,000	19,000
3.0L CL ʌ	15,500	19,500	22,500
3.0L CL v	13,000	17,000	21,000
Extended Warranty	N	N	N
Secret Warranty	Y	Y	N
Reliability	④	⑤	⑤
Head Restraints	—	—	❶

Note: These vehicles have not been crash-tested.

INTEGRA   ★★★★

RATING: Above Average (1990–2001); Average (1986–89). These cars are noted for a stiff price for the Acura cachet and limited passenger room. Interestingly, there's little price difference between a used entry-level and high-end model, despite a $4,000 premium when new. **Maintenance/ Repair costs:** Lower than average. Repairs can be done practically anywhere. **Parts:** Cost is a bit higher than average, but they can be bought from cheaper independent Honda suppliers. **Best alternatives:** The Honda Accord; Mazda 626; Hyundai Elantra wagon, Sonata, or Tiburon; Nissan Altima; and Toyota Camry.

Strengths and weaknesses: A Honda spin-off, early Integras (1986–89) came with lots of standard equipment and are a pleasure to drive, especially when equipped with a manual transmission. The 4-speed automatic saps the base engine's power considerably. Engine and tire noise are intrusive at highway speeds. The car corners well and is more agile than later 1990–93 models. Its hard ride can be reduced a bit by changing the shocks and adding wide tires. The front seats are very comfortable, but they're set a bit low, and the side wheelwells leave little room for your feet. Rear-seat room is very limited, especially on the three-door version.

Since its 1994 redesign, the Integra has changed little over the years. '98 models got a slight front-end restyling; the RS version was dropped for 1999; the 2000 model year saw the return of the Type R and the addition of an upgraded 4-speed automatic transmission to the general lineup. 2001 models return practically unchanged, except for an emergency trunk release. The sedan will be dropped at the end of the model year (the 2002 model will be a three-door hatchback).

Overall, assembly and component quality are good but not exceptional, as you can see from the "Secret Warranties/Service Tips/TSBs" list. To avoid costly engine repairs, check the engine timing belt every 4 years/ 80,000 km.

For model years 1990–93, the high-revving 1.7L powerplant growls when pushed and lacks guts (read, torque) in the lower gears. The 1.8L engine runs more smoothly but delivers the same maximum horsepower as the 1.7L it replaced, until the '94 model year, when it gained 10 extra horses. Surprisingly, overall performance has been toned down and is seriously compromised by the 4-speed automatic gearbox. Interior design is more user-friendly, with the front seating roomier than in previous years, but reduced rear seating is still best left to small children.

Mechanical reliability is impressive, but that's the case with most Hondas, which sell for far less, and many mechanical components are so complex that self-service can pretty well be ruled out. The Integra's front brakes may require more attention than those of other Hondas. Surprisingly, what Integras give you in mechanical reliability, they take away in poor quality control on body components and accessories. Water leaks, excessive wind noise, low-quality trim items, and plastic panels that deform easily are all commonplace. Owners also report severe steering shimmy, excessive brake noise, premature front brake pad wearout, and radio malfunctions.

In the 1994 model year, the Integra was dramatically re-styled with a more aerodynamic profile, and a few more horses were wrung out of the venerable 1.8L 4-banger through variable valve timing. The 1994–98 models also offer a smoother ride than previous versions. On the other hand, the powerful VTEC engine requires lots of shifting, and interior room is still problematic. Overall, there are too few improvements to justify the high prices that late-model Integras command.

Owners report that some automatic transmission defects, steering wheel shimmy, fit and finish deficiencies, and malfunctioning accessories continue to be problematic on later models. Premature front brake wear is also an ongoing concern. Squeaks and rattles frequently crop up in the door panels and hatches, and the sedan's frameless windows often have sealing problems.

Safety summary: All models/years: No airbag deployment or inadvertent deployment, sudden acceleration, automatic transmission defects, poor headlight illumination, and chronic brake failures are common to all model years. **All models: 1995—**Fire erupted in the sunroof. • Another fire started in the engine compartment on the passenger side. • Airbag deployed after the undercarriage scraped the driveway. • Brake pedal goes to floorboard without effect. • ABS malfunctions; brake lockup. • Early rear brake pad wear results in brake lockup. • Automatic transmission jolts into gear or shifts erratically. • Vehicle rolled away when parked on hill with parking brake applied. • Condensation in the headlight assembly causes poor lighting and headlight failure. • Hatchback failure. • Passenger seat falls straight back when reclined. • Early disintegration of the catalytic converter shield. **1996**—Engine wiring fire. • Prematurely warped rotors are the cause of excessive vibration and pulling. • Power-steering pump failure. • Clutch spring failure. • Vehicle surges forward, as if cruise control suddenly engaged at a higher speed; brakes failed. • Gas pedal jams open. **1997**—Key can be removed from ignition without putting transmission in Park. • Moon roof motor failure. • Passenger seatbelt releases inadvertently. • Ignition interlock failed. **1998**—Sudden steering lockup. • Battery leak could have caused fire by burning hole in charcoal canister. • Driver's seatbelt won't loosen. • Horn failure. • Sunroof malfunctions. • Window motor inoperative. • Windshield wipers suddenly stopped working; resumed operation when car was restarted. **1999**—Front windshield distorts vision. • Check Engine light comes on constantly. **2000**—Small horn buttons are difficult to activate in an emergency. • Check Engine light stays on. • Seatbelts fail to release when unbuckled. • Steering wheel obstructs view of speedometer.

Secret Warranties/Service Tips/TSBs

All models/years: Most Honda/Acura TSBs allow for special warranty consideration on a "goodwill" basis even after the warranty has expired or the car has changed hands. • Vehicle cranks but won't start. • Severe and persistent steering wheel shimmy is likely due to an imbalanced wheel/tire/hub/rotor assembly. • Check Engine light constantly lit. • Headlight fogging. • Debris in blower motor (install protective screen). • Window guide channel comes loose. Front brake squeal countermeasures. • Reducing rattles from the rear shelf area. • Noisy power steering. **All models: 1990–97**—Rear trailing arm bushing noise can be corrected by installing plastic shims. **1992–99**—A defective seatbelt tongue stopper will be replaced free of charge with no ownership, time, or mileage limitations. **1994–95**—Rattling from a partially open window may be caused by excess clearance between the window guide pin and the centre sash guide or by the glass run channel having come out of the centre channel. These are also likely causes of moon roof chattering or shuddering. **1994–97**—Rear seatback rattles mean the latch needs to be readjusted. • Exhaust system buzzing can have two sources: the flexible joint connections may have insufficient spring tension or the inner exhaust pipe is vibrating against the outer pipe. **1996–97**—A squeaking steering wheel heard when turning signals the need to grease the pinion shaft and grommet. • In a settlement with the U.S. Environmental Protection Agency, Honda agreed that costly engine components and exhaust system parts, like catalytic converters, will be replaced free of charge, as long as the 14-year/150,000 mile (240,000 km) limit hasn't been exceeded. Canadian owners may wish to use this settlement as leverage for free repairs in Canada, or use the full-terms of the settlement when visiting the States. One thing is certain: neither Transport Canada nor Environment Canada are sufficiently enthused to render any assistance.

Integra Profile

	1994	1995	1996	1997	1998	1999	2000	2001
Cost Price ($)								
LS/SE	22,095	23,095	23,245	23,800	23,800	21,800	22,000	22,500
RS	17,655	18,595	18,795	19,500	21,000	—	—	—
Used Values ($)								
LS/SE ▲	6,000	9,000	10,500	12,500	14,500	15,500	17,500	19,500
LS/SE ▼	5,000	7,000	9,000	11,000	12,500	13,000	15,500	18,000
RS ▲	7,000	8,000	10,500	12,500	14,500	—	—	—
RS ▼	5,500	6,500	8,500	10,500	12,500	—	—	—
Extended Warranty	N	N	N	N	N	N	N	N
Secret Warranty	Y	Y	Y	Y	Y	Y	N	N
Reliability	④	④	④	④	④	⑤	⑤	⑤
Crash Safety	—	—	④	—	—	—	—	—
Head Restraints (F)	—	❷	—	③	—	③	—	③
Rear	—	—	—	—	—	❷	—	—
Rollover Resistance	—	④	—	—	—	—	—	—

DaimlerChrysler

BREEZE, CIRRUS, STRATUS ★★

RATING: Below Average (1995–2000). Stay away from any model carrying the anemic and failure-prone 4-cylinder engine. Fewer mechanical and safety problems than found on the Ford competition; nevertheless, be prepared to experience a number of nasty safety-related failures such as blown engine head gaskets, airbags that don't deploy, sudden acceleration, a jerky automatic transmission that suddenly drops out of gear, and loss of braking. **Maintenance/Repair costs:** Higher than average, but repairs aren't dealer dependent. **Parts:** Higher-than-average cost (independent suppliers sell for much less), but they are not hard to find. Recall parts, though, tend to dribble in; a month's wait isn't unusual (as has been the case with the transaxle oil cooler hose campaign for 2001 models). Don't even think about buying any one of these cars without a three- to five-year supplementary warranty. **Best alternatives:** The Acura Integra, Hyundai Elantra wagon or Sonata, Mazda 626, Nissan Altima or Stanza, and Toyota Camry.

Strengths and weaknesses: Roomy and stylish, well appointed, comfortable, and smooth, the Chrysler Cirrus and Dodge Stratus are mid-sized sedan replacements for the LeBaron. The Breeze, launched as a 1996 model, is essentially a "de-contented" version of the more expensive Cirrus.

For 2001, the Avenger coupe and sedan were dropped and the Stratus and the Cirrus coupe, sedan, and convertible fell under the Sebring moniker. The Plymouth Breeze was also discontinued. Other improvements for the renamed models: a smoother ride and the addition of a 2.7L engine.

Most components have been used for some time on other Chrysler models, particularly the Neon subcompact and the Avenger and Sebring sports coupes. Power is supplied by one of four engines: a 2.0L 4-cylinder engine (shared with the Neon), a 2.4L 4-banger, or the recommended 2.5L and 2.7L V6. Carrying Chrysler's "cab-forward" design a step further up the evolutionary ladder, these cars have short rear decks, low noses, and massive sloping grilles. A wheelbase that's two inches longer than the Ford Taurus makes these cars comfortable for five occupants, with wide door openings and plenty of trunk space.

Judged by their styling and roominess alone, these cars would appear to be great buys. But they aren't.

They are, in fact high-risk buys from both a performance and a quality control standpoint. Problems reported by owners include the following: chronic automatic transmission failures; early and frequent engine head gasket failures, through 1998 models (no doubt part of the Neon engine legacy), and erratic engine operation; ABS malfunctions and sudden brake loss; paint delamination; electrical short circuits; weak headlights; underperforming AC; water leaks into the trunk area and interior; easy-to-break trim items; lots of squeaks and rattles; and head restraints that are set too far back. Incidentally, in 1999 the manual seat height adjuster was dropped, making it difficult for short drivers to distance themselves safely from the airbag deployment. Additionally, this complicates both forward and rearward visibility, which is already seriously compromised by the cars' styling.

Safety summary: All models: 1995–96—Frequent reports of engine fires. • Chronic engine oil leaks and oil galley plug failures. • Repeated engine head gasket failures, some resulting in engine compartment fires. • Timing belt failure after recall correction. • Chronic stalling or loss of engine power blamed on timing belt tensioner and pulley failure. • Engine sometimes loses power, then quickly accelerates. At other times, while at highway speeds, vehicle won't slow down when foot is taken off the gas pedal; instead, it speeds up. • Engine warning light often alight for no reason. • Reports of sudden acceleration in Drive and Reverse. • Owner claims that sudden acceleration is caused by a design flaw in cable to throttle body. • Airbags often fail to deploy. • Frequent

ABS failures and prematurely worn rotors, calipers, and pads. • Rear brake failures also reported. • Faulty master cylinders are the cause of some early brake failures. • Floormat can catch the steering shaft clamp and jam the steering column assembly, causing the steering to lock up. • While driving off the highway at 100 km/h, steering tie-rod came apart, resulting in complete steering loss. • Steering components worn out prematurely. • Main computer failed seven times. • Oxygen sensor prone to early failure and fluid leakage. • Alternator burned out. • Child was able to take parked vehicle out of gear without applying brake. • Vehicle jumped out of Third gear. • Defective electrical switch causes transmission to stick in Second gear. • Sudden transmission lockup. • Transmission won't engage or upshift to Third or Fourth gear. • Leaking transmission front pump seal. • Prematurely worn strut links and wheel bearings. • Heat is unevenly distributed, causing front and rear passengers to be cold. • Heater failures. • Defogger doesn't adequately defrost windshield. • AC fails to cool interior unless vehicle is travelling at high speed. • AC failures. • Dash reflection into windshield hampers view. • Inadequate headlight illumination. • Windshield wipers don't run fast enough to clear windshield in a heavy downpour. • Rear brake lights and brake switch failure. • Sloping hood design creates poor visibility for parking. • Fuel tank gauge indicates empty when tank is half full. • Trunk lid closes on its own; this gave one owner a mild concussion. • Plastic on seatbelt clinch bar is self-destructing. • Seatbacks collapsed when vehicle was rear-ended. • Seat frame and anchor broke as driver sat down. • Power window motor failures. • Door locks work intermittently. • Binding door hinges make for difficult closing. • Door handle design pinches fingers. • Key sticks in the ignition when vehicle is shut off. • Weak front speakers prevent radio balance. **1997**—Engine compartment fire ignited while car was parked in garage. • Reports of sudden acceleration in Drive and Reverse. • Chronic stalling at highway speeds. • Vehicle rolled away while parked with shifter in Park position and keys pulled from ignition. • Shifter came off in hand when shifting. • Airbags fail to deploy. • Floormat can catch the steering shaft clamp and jam the steering column assembly, causing the steering to lock up. • Frequent engine head gasket failures. • When the head gasket blew, one driver believes it overheated the transmission, causing it to lock up. • It's common for the engine timing belt idler pulley to fail and damage the timing belt. • Sudden brake and power-steering loss. • Brake pads and rotors fail prematurely. • Noisy brakes. • AC emits odour and white flakes through ventilation system, causing headaches, burning sensation, and congestion. • Noise coming from the high-pressure power-steering line. • Missing part causes seatbelt to twist. • Seat buckle design is too short, causing difficulty in latching. • Driver-side shoulder belt failed to restrain driver in a collision. • Starter short caused fuse to blow. • Fuel sender for dash gauge often defective. • Inoperative power door lock motor. **1997–98**—NHTSA is looking into complaints of steering shaft binding.

1998—Airbag exploded rather than inflated. • Airbags fail to deploy. • Frequent complaints of ABS failures; ABS brakes failed five times on one owner despite dealer attempts to correct the problem. • There is excessive brake noise whenever brakes are applied. • Floormat jammed the steering column assembly, causing the steering to lock up. • Automatic transmission (floor console design) throw from Drive to Reverse to Park is too long, resulting in consumer thinking vehicle is in Park when it's really in Reverse. • Floor shift indicator on the dash doesn't give a true reading of which gear is engaged. • Gearshift lever can be moved into Drive without putting foot on brakes to engage the transmission/brake interlock system. • High trunk lid makes it impossible to see directly behind the vehicle. **1999**—Several trunk fires reported from a too-intense trunk-mounted light bulb. • Airbags failed to deploy in a collision. • Airbag deployed inadvertently, knocking driver out and causing an accident. • Sudden acceleration; stuck throttle. • Stalling upon acceleration and when foot is taken off of the gas pedal. • Steering locks up when making left-hand turns. • Automatic transmission has a short lifespan; sensors are the first to go. • Transmission lever can be shifted into Drive without first depressing brake pedal. • Cracked axle. • Dash reflects onto front windshield. • Many incidents reported of sudden brake failure without any prior warning. • While driving, brake vacuum hose separated, causing complete brake failure. • Chronic brake rotor warpage around 5,000 miles [8,000 kilometres], resulting in severe brake vibrations, noise, and extended stopping distance. • Engine fumes invade the cabin, causing driver drowsiness. • Frequent electrical shorts cause gauges, wipers, and windows to function erratically. • Engine, ABS, and airbag warning light often come on for no reason. • Seatbelts fail to tighten. **2000**—Electrical system fire. • Brake lockup; no airbag deployment in resulting collision. • Low-speed gear whine. • Automatic transmission has a hard 3–2 shift. • Transmission drops out of gear at 75 km/h. • Brake system failures due to loss of vacuum. • Warped brake drums and rotors; very noisy braking. • Wheel lug nuts loosen on their own. • Gas pedal sticks. • Excessive rear window fogging. • Windshield wiper doesn't clear snow adequately from driver-side windshield. • Excessive dashboard reflection onto windshield. • Driver's door jams due to faulty door panel. • Seatbelts too tight. • Chronic dead battery. • Hot trunk light will burn items stored in trunk. • Space-saver spare tire is only good for a few miles and at slow speeds. **2001**—No airbag deployment. • Chronic engine surging, especially when the AC is activated. • Engine surges when putting vehicle into Reverse. • Engine continues to stall after refuelling, despite recall campaign fix. • Engine stalls out when foot is taken off the accelerator. • Transmission jerks into gear or suddenly drops out of gear. • Complete brake failure. • Brake fluid level keeps dropping. • Brake and gas pedal are set too close together. • Suspension is dangerously loose at high speeds. • Back windows suddenly exploded while vehicle was parked. • 2001 Stratus coupe's driver's seat doesn't face full-front; it's disorienting to be sitting at an angle to the steering wheel and dash.

Secret Warranties/Service Tips

All models/years: Anecdotal reports confirm Chrysler has a 7-year/ 160,000 km secret warranty covering engine head gasket failures. • Chrysler will replace AC evaporators up to 7 years/115,000 km. **All models: 1995–96**—Water leaks into the passenger compartment from behind the door trim panel. Correct the leakage by installing new door panel clips, door watershields, and additional tape to seal the watershield (see following bulletin).

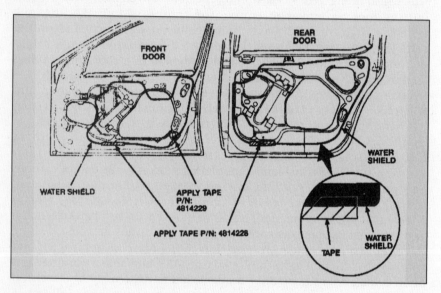

• Front brake lining wears prematurely (see TSB #05-01-96). **1995–97**— Troubleshooting tips are available to correct poor AC performance. • A powertrain "bump" when the AC engages is normal, according to Chrysler. • Transmission shudder could be caused by using the wrong transmission fluid. **1995–98**—Repair procedure for the evaporator failure (see following bulletin).

NO: 24-04-98   GROUP: Air Conditioning DATE: Apr. 17, 1998
SUBJECT: A/C Systems Performance

MODELS:

1995-1998 (JA) Breeze/Cirrus/Stratus
1996-1998 (JX) Sebring Convertible

SYMPTOM/CONDITION:

A/C performance complaints and/or A/C compressor failure (seized) in high ambient temperatures (90°+F). This condition is aggravated by start and stop city driving and/or extended periods of idling with the A/C running.

DIAGNOSIS:

If the vehicle operated in high ambient temperatures or A/C compressor has failed (seized) or system passes the Performance Test Procedure as described on page 24-5 of the Breeze/Cirrus/Stratus Service Manual (Publication No. 81-270-8121) perform the Repair Procedure.

PARTS REQUIRED:

1	05011395AA	Kit, A/C Condenser Contains: A/C Condenser Foam Seals, Radiator to Condenser Label, Refrigerant Charge Level
1	04796282AB	Kit, Retaining Strap Transmission Cooler
5	06502625	Retainer, Fascia
AR(1)	04886129AA	SP-15 PAG Oil
AR(1)	04883308	Air Seal, Radiator Right Side
AR(1)	04883308	Air Seal, Radiator Left Side

POLICY: Reimbursable within the provisions of the warranty.

1995–99—Chrysler will replace faulty 4-cylinder engine head gaskets free of charge. • Paint delamination, peeling, and fading (see Part Two). **1995–2000**—A steering wheel rattle or clunk can be silenced by replacing the steering gear under warranty.

Steering Wheel/Steering Column - Clunking or Rattle

NUMBER: 19-02-99 Rev. A   DATE: Oct. 22,1999

OVERVIEW: This bulletin involves resetting the steering column preload.

MODELS:

1995-**2000**	(JA) Breeze/Cirrus/Stratus
1996-**2000**	(JX) Sebring Convertible
1995-2000	(PL) Neon

SYMPTOM/CONDITION:

Steering wheel/column clunking or rattle is more frequent while hitting bumps or on hard turns.

DIAGNOSIS:

Inspect steering wheel/column for any rattle or clunking noise. If symptoms exist perform the Repair Procedure.

PARTS REQUIRED:

1	05015627AA	Bolt, Steering Gear Coupler Retaining, PL
1	**06506112AA	Bolt, Steering Gear Coupler Retaining, JA/JX**
1	**06036212AA	Clip, Steering Gear Coupler Retaining, JA/JX**

POLICY: Reimbursable within the provisions of the warranty.

This 20-minute repair also applies to the Neon and the Sebring convertible.

1997—A low-frequency rumble heard while at highway cruising speed can be silenced by replacing the front hub bearing assemblies. **1997–98**—Excessive cold crank time, start die-out, or weak run-up may be corrected by replacing the powertrain control module (PCM) under warranty, according to TSB #18-18-98. **1998–99**—Poor AC performance or compressor failure will be repaired under warranty or under "goodwill." **1999**—A metallic noise heard from the rear doors can be silenced by modifying the window regulator channel. **1999–2000**—No-starts and stalling may be caused by a malfunctioning sentry key immobilizer system. • Windshield washer nozzle plugging.

Breeze, Cirrus, Stratus Profile

	1995	1996	1997	1998	1999	2000
Cost Price ($)						
Breeze	—	18,200	18,865	19,505	21,090	—
Cirrus	22,115	23,235	24,125	—	22,180	22,365
LXi	24,555	25,695	26,465	26,465	24,840	25,050
Stratus	17,895	18,200	18,865	19,505	21,090	—
V6	19,750	20,100	24,060	24,475	25,025	—
Used Values ($)						
Breeze ▲	—	6,500	8,000	10,000	12,500	—
Breeze ▼	—	4,500	6,000	8,000	10,500	—
Cirrus ▲	5,500	7,000	8,500	—	13,000	14,000
Cirrus ▼	4,000	5,000	6,500	—	11,000	12,000
LXi ▲	6,000	7,000	9,000	12,500	14,000	16,000
LXi ▼	4,000	5,000	7,000	11,000	12,000	14,000
Stratus ▲	5,000	6,500	8,000	10,000	12,500	—
Stratus ▼	3,500	5,000	6,000	8,000	10,500	—
V6 ▲	5,500	7,000	8,500	11,500	13,000	—
V6 ▼	4,000	5,000	7,000	9,500	11,000	—
Extended Warranty	Y	Y	Y	Y	Y	Y
Secret Warranty	Y	Y	Y	Y	Y	N
Reliability	❷	❷	❷	❷	❷	③
Crash Safety	③	③	③	③	③	⑤
Side Impact	—	—	③	③	③	③
Off-set	❶	❶	❶	❶	❶	❶
Head Restraints						
Avenger	❶	—	❷	—	❷	—
Stratus (F)	❶	—	❶	—	❷	—
Stratus (Rear)	—	—	—	—	❶	—

Note: Crash ratings are applicable to all models.

Ford

CONTOUR, MYSTIQUE ★

RATING: Not Recommended (1995–99). One of the most failure-prone, hazardous vehicles you can buy—industry insiders call the Mystique the "Mistake." The only reason this car is an even worse buy than the Taurus and Sable is that it has been taken off the market—drying up a miniscule parts supply and driving up part prices (one owner told of paying $700 for an alternator). For the latest owner reports and money-saving tips, look at the Contour website at *www.contour.org/FAQ.* Although discontinued in Canada, the Contour continued to be sold in the States through the 2001 model year. **Maintenance/Repair costs:** Higher than average. Most repairs are dealer dependent. **Parts:** Higher-than-average cost, and body parts are sometimes hard to find. **Best alternatives:** The Ford Escort wagon, Honda Accord, Hyundai Elantra wagon or Sonata, Nissan Altima or Stanza, and Toyota Camry. Mazda's 626 is a particularly worthwhile alternative to the Contour and Mystique—it's a more stylish, reasonably priced, highway-proven sedan with a better reliability record.

Strengths and weaknesses: These front-drive, mid-sized twin sedans (the Contour has a more angular nose and a different dashboard) are based on the European-designed Mondeo. They are set on a wheelbase slightly larger than that of the Taurus and come with a choice of two engines and transmissions: a base 16-valve 125-hp, 2.0L 4-cylinder or an optional 24-valve 170-hp, 2.5L V6. Either engine may be hooked to a standard 5-speed transaxle or an optional 4-speed automatic.

The main advantages of the Contour and Mystique are exceptional handling and a powerful, limited-maintenance V6 engine. Their drawbacks are a plethora of safety-related defects; an inadequate parts supply; cramped rear seating; a wimpy, noisy 4-banger; and atrocious quality control that is highlighted by powertrain failures, electrical system shorts, poor body assembly, and ineffective, noisy brakes that are costly to maintain.

Owners report chronic steering and transmission failures, frequent computer module failures, and a long wait for parts—even those parts needed to carry out safety-related recall campaigns. One owner had the following to say:

My '95 Mystique ran fine for six months, but has been in the dealer repair shop—still not fixed—for three weeks now. First the "overlock" froze, so you couldn't shift out of Park—even with a foot on the brake. The dealer said an "electrical short circuit kept making a module fail." They told me the part was part of a recall that had not yet been announced. No sooner had they fixed that when the Overdrive on-off button on the automatic gearshift stopped working. That's still not fixed after 11 working days. First the dealer claimed they couldn't "locate the cause." They sent the car out to a transmission expert who found another "failed module." The current problem is that the replacement part is "much in demand," and they're "trying to locate one."

Safety summary: All models: 1995–1996—NHTSA has opened an official probe into front-suspension coil spring failures and engine cooling fan fires on the 1995 Contour, and headlight switch failures on 1996 models. **1995–99**—Many reports of engine fires, fuel tank leaks, fuel and oil odours permeating the interior, difficulty in filling the fuel tank, and inaccurate fuel readings. • Malfunctioning airbags that go off when they shouldn't or don't go off when they should. • Reports of serious injuries caused by airbag deployment. • Airbag light stays on for no reason. • Chronic stalling at idle or after attained cruising speed. • Complete electrical shutdown. • Lights come on or shut off unexpectedly, as the following owner discovered:

I recently rented a 1999 Contour and drove it across country between dusk and dark. When I stopped to refuel, the overhead dome light turned on, and would not shut off. I drove to the next rest area and took out the owners manual, which was of no help. While I was alone in the rest area, with the car lit up like a spotlight (I am a female), a strange man approached my car from behind with what I assume were bad intentions.

I then drove to 7 gas stations before I found one with an attendant. He also had no idea how to turn off the dome light. I then had to choose between spending the night in a rental car in a parking lot near the interstate or driving home with a lit dome light and close to zero visibility.

As my life insurance is paid up, I chose option (B) and drove home.

The government should require carmakers to supply all interior lights with an on-off switch, or supply large sledgehammers to Contour/Mystique owners.

• Seatback often collapses for no reason or after a rear fender-bender. • Brakes often fail, make a grinding noise when applied, and often need replacing (warped rotors and prematurely worn pads). This repair doesn't ensure the brakes will work properly, or that other safety-related failings won't occur:

Brakes failed and replaced during the first month I had my '99 Contour. After that repair, I had an accident due to lack of braking ability. During the collision, there was no deployment of the airbag and the seatbelt came loose.

• Frequent engine and transmission failures. • Transmission will not hold vehicle in Park. • Check Engine light stays lit for no reason.

Secret Warranties/Service Tips/TSBs

All models/years: 1995–97—Air that blows out the defroster ducts only may signal that the defrost actuator door linkage has become disconnected from the crank. • Transaxle fluid seepage can be corrected by servicing with a remote vent kit or by replacing the main control cover. • Parking brakes that stick or bind need a parking brake cable service kit. • Front-end accessory drivebelt slippage can be corrected by installing an upgraded FEAD belt, steel idler pulley, and splash shield kit. **1995–98**— Stall and/or exhaust sulfur smell requires a revised power control module. • Stall, hooting, or moosing noise from engine compartment can be fixed by replacing the air intake duct, idle air resonator, and idle air hose with a revised duct and resonator assembly (#F6RZ-9B659-CA). **1995–99**—Upgraded front brake pads have been put into service to silence front brake groaning (see following bulletin).

Groaning Noise from Front Brakes During City Driving

Article No. 99-8-9   05/03/99

FORD:

1995-1999 Contour

LINCOLN-MERCURY:

1995-1999 Mystique
1999 Cougar

ISSUE

A "groaning" noise from the front brakes during city driving may occur on some vehicles. This may be caused by the damping rate of the front brake pads.

ACTION

Replace the front brake pads with revised brake pads.

WARRANTY STATUS

Eligible Under the Provisions of Bumper to Bumper Warranty Coverage

OPERATION	DESCRIPTION	TIME
990809A	Replace Front Brake Pads	0.5 Hr.

• Tips for fixing windshield water leaks. • Paint delamination, peeling, and fading (see Part Two). **1995–2000**—Repeat failure of the heater core. • Automatic transmission fluid leakage. **1997–99**—Fuel pump whine heard through the speakers. **1998**—Harsh automatic shifting is likely caused by a miscalibrated PCM (powertrain control module). • Frequent shut-off when fueling can be fixed by installing a new flapper baffle in the fuel-filler pipe. • Inaccurate fuel gauge readings may be corrected by installing either a new fuel tank or a fuel pump. **1998–99**—Water may leak through the door into the interior. **1998–2000**—Eliminate spark knock by recalibrating the PCM. • Interior dome lamp may remain lit. • Ford suggests the catalytic converter be changed to prevent a rotten-egg exhaust smell (see following bulletin).

Exhaust - Sulfur Odors After Hard Driving

Article No.: 00-25-2   12/11/2000

EXHAUST - SULFUR ODOR FOLLOWING AGGRESSIVE DRIVING - 2.5L VEHICLES - CONTOUR/MYSTIQUE AND COUGAR WITH AUTOMATIC TRANSAXLE BUILT FROM 5/7/99 - COUGAR WITH MANUAL TRANSAXLE BUILT FROM 5/24/99 ONLY

FORD:

1998-2000 CONTOUR

MERCURY:

1998-2000 MYSTIQUE
1999-2000 COUGAR

This TSB is being republished in its entirety to update the vehicle models covered.

ISSUE

An objectionable exhaust, sulfur, or rotten egg odor following aggressive driving, such as full-throttle acceleration, may occur on some vehicles. This may be caused by excessive sulfur in the fuel reacting with the normal chemical reactions which take place in the catalytic converter.

ACTION

Replace the catalytic converter with a revised catalytic converter.

NOTE: SINCE EXHAUST ODOR VARIES WITH THE LEVEL OF SULFUR CONTENT IN THE FUEL, IT MAY ALSO BE APPROPRIATE TO ADVISE THE CUSTOMER TO CHANGE FUEL BRAND (NOT THE OCTANE RATING) TO ACHIEVE MAXIMUM SATISFACTION.

Part Number:	Part Name:
YS8Z-5E212-AA	Catalytic Converter
W520103-S309	Nut (5 Required)
XS8Z-9450-AA	Inlet Gasket
F5RZ-5E241-A	Outlet Gasket

This is an emissions warranty repair; don't pay a dime.

1999—Automatic transmission won't shift into any forward gear. • "Fluttering" heard from the heater area. 1999–2000—Engine hesitation upon start-up requires the recalibration of the PCM (an emissions warranty item). • Owner Notification Program 01B78 provides for the free repair or replacement of warped instrument panel covers. Depending on the degree of warpage, the cover will be repaired or replaced for free until August 31, 2002, regardless of mileage.

Contour, Mystique Profile

	1995	1996	1997	1998	1999
Cost Price ($)					
GL/LX	15,470	15,980	16,020	17,305	17,595
SE	18,355	18,865	19,350	19,475	19,695

Used Values ($)					
GL/LX ▲	4,500	5,500	7,000	9,000	10,500
GL/LX ▼	3,500	4,000	6,000	7,000	9,000
SE ▲	5,500	6,500	8,500	10,000	12,000
SE ▼	4,000	5,000	7,000	8,000	10,000
Extended Warranty	Y	Y	Y	Y	Y
Secret Warranty	Y	Y	Y	Y	Y
Reliability	❶	❶	❶	❶	❶
Crash Safety	⑤	⑤	⑤	⑤	—
Side Impact	—	—	③	③	③
Off-set	❷	❷	❷	❷	❷
Head Restraints (F)	❶	—	❷	—	❷
Rear	—	—	❶	—	❶

SABLE, TAURUS ★★

RATING: Below Average (2000–01); Not Recommended (1986–99). The worst of a bad lot; these cars are bargain-priced because their owners can't wait to get rid of them. An extended bumper-to-bumper warranty is a prerequisite for anyone seriously thinking of buying a Sable or Taurus. Of course, this extra protection will wipe out any savings realized from a low selling price. The high-performance Taurus SHO (Super High Output) has fewer engine breakdowns (it's Yamaha-sourced); however, it shares most of the other generic safety- and performance-related defects that have long plagued these family sedans and wagons. Supposedly improved through a redesign, the recent models continue to generate a large volume of safety- and performance-related failures. 1999 was the last model year for Sable and the Mercury brand in Canada; they're still sold in the States, however. **Maintenance/Repair costs:** Much higher than average, but repairs aren't dealer dependent. Shopping at engine, transmission, brake, and muffler shops offering lifetime warranties can prevent some repeat repair costs. **Parts:** Average cost (independent suppliers sell for much less) and very easy to find, except for the discontinued SHO and parts like fuel pumps and electrical components, needed to correct chronic stalling and electrical shorts. **Best alternatives:** The Honda Accord, Hyundai Elantra wagon or Sonata, Mazda 626, Nissan Sentra or Stanza, and Toyota Camry. A good alternative to the SHO would be a Ford Mustang GT or Probe GT, or the Probe's twin, the Mazda MX-6.

Strengths and weaknesses: Although they lack pickup with the standard 4-cylinder engine, these mid-sized sedans and wagons are competent family cars, offering lots of interior room, nice handling, a good crash rating, and many convenience features. The best powertrain combination for all driving conditions is the 3.0L V6 hooked to a 4-speed for the family sedan, and the Yamaha powerplant harnessed to a manual gearbox on the high performance SHO.

These cars are aging badly. To see just how badly, take a look at the "Dead Ford," "Ford Taurus, Sable Automatic Transmission Victims," and NHTSA website links listed in Appendix I. Chronic 3.8L engine head gasket and automatic transmission failures; a plethora of hazardous airbag, fuel system, brake, suspension, and steering defects; and chronic paint/rust problems are the main reasons their rating is so low this year. Plus, owners are reporting that engine and transmission repairs don't last: some owners are routinely putting in new 3.8L engines or transmissions every year.

I've recommended these cars in the past because Ford's "goodwill" programs usually compensated owners for most of the above-noted failures once the warranty had expired. Unfortunately, these refund programs have dried up and owners are now frequently faced with $3,000 engine or automatic transmission repair bills, in addition to thousands of dollars in repairs for defective fuel systems, brakes, suspension and steering assemblies.

And the situation isn't likely to improve, judging by Ford's rejection of more and more consumer complaints on the grounds that repairs were done by independent agencies, the vehicle was bought used, or is no longer under the original warranty. Furthermore, some key consumer allies at Ford, like Ford Canada President Bobbie Gaunt, have retired, leaving consumers to fend for themselves before a corporation that values stonewalling over integrity.

SHO

The Taurus SHO sedan, debuting in 1989, carries a Yamaha 24-valve 3.0L V6 with 220 horsepower; a stiff, performance-oriented suspension; and 5-speed manual transmission. As of 1993, a 4-speed automatic transmission became available. In mid-1996, a redesigned SHO debuted with a standard Yamaha 32-valve V8. Unfortunately, the manual transmission was dropped at that time, a move that turned off most die-hard performance enthusiasts. The SHO is an impressive high-performance car that is apparently better built than regular-production Sable and Taurus versions. Unfortunately, the SHO has its own unique engine problems and also uses Ford's failure-prone automatic transmission. Both problems were well-detailed in the following recent email sent to me by Cold Lake, Alberta, resident and '97 SHO owner David S.:

> The 3.4 L V8 engine found in 1996–1999 Ford Taurus SHO's seems to be failing at a high rate, mostly with camshaft failures. The information on this can be found at *www.v8sho.com* which details fairly well the problem. The repair costs for this failure are astronomical.... Mr. Edmonston, I have to tell you my good news(?). I had to get the automatic transmission replaced (147,000 km), but using the name from

your website I sent an email just to see what would happen. After a few days, I was contacted by a Mr. Chris Samadh and he offered to pay half of the cost of the transmission pretty much immediately. He did go thru the spiel that I should have taken it to a Ford dealer, we don't usually do this, etc., but I received my cheque for $1231.00 a couple of days ago.

As an aside, there was a reference number on the cheque stub that kind of resembles an 'internal' recall number 2003M0925233. Anyway I have included Mr Samadh's email address for you. He was very helpful and easy to get along with, and thank you for the information and keep up the good work.

Is the SHO a good buy? The answer is yes, but only if you're willing to spend big bucks for your performance thrills and have had the power-train thoroughly checked out. SHOs do hold their value well, but they're hard to find (1999 was the last model year) in good shape.

Automatic transmission failures

Since 1991, Ford's automatic transmissions have been failure-prone, function erratically, and are slow to shift—an annoying drawback if you need to rock the car out of a snowbank, and fairly dangerous if you need to pull out onto a busy roadway. These problems are caused principally by a cracked aluminum forward clutch piston, although dozens of other causes, including major hardware and software components, have been linked to the above failures. Breakdowns usually occur after three years of use, around the 80,000–120,000 km mark, and can cost $3,000–$3,500 to repair at the dealer, or half that much at an independent garage.

Ford Admits Transmission Defect! (1986–95)

Article No.: 94-24-7   11/28/94

TRANSAXLE - AXOD, ACOD-E, AX4S - FORWARD/REVERSE ENGAGEMENT CONCERN - REVISED FORWARD CLUTCH PISTON

FORD:

1986-95 TAURUS
1993-95 TAURUS SHO

LINCOLN-MERCURY:

1986-95 SABLE
1988-94 CONTINENTAL

LIGHT TRUCK:

1995 WINDSTAR

ISSUE

The forward clutch piston may crack on its diameter, seal groove or apply wall (bottom of piston). This condition could allow internal clutch leakage resulting in engagement concerns. ➤

STEEL CLUTCH PISTON PART APPLICATIONS

F4DZ-7A262-A	F4DZ-7A262-B
3.0L Taurus	
3.0L Sable	
3.8L Taurus	
3.8L Sable	
3.8L Continental	
3.8L Windstar	3.2L Taurus SHO

Use this and subsequent technical service bulletins as arguing points with Ford service managers, or as support for a small claims filing. Get Ford or your own independent expert to confirm the bulletin's text in court, so it's not thrown out as hearsay.

Transmission Failures Continue (1994–98)

Article No.: 98-3-7   02/16/98

TRANSAXLE - AX4N - INTERMITTENT NEUTRAL CONDITION - NO FORWARD OR REVERSE MOVEMENT - VEHICLES BUILT THROUGH 2/1/98

FORD:

1994-98 TAURUS

LINCOLN-MERCURY

1994-98 SABLE
1995-98 CONTINENTAL

ISSUE:

Some vehicles may experience an intermittent Neutral condition after driving and coming to a stop. This may be caused by the bonded seal on the forward clutch piston intermittently not sealing during the 3-2 downshift.

ACTION:

Replace the forward clutch piston with a revised Forward Clutch Piston (F8DZ-7A262-AB). Refer to the following Service Procedure for details.

PART NUMBER	PART NAME
F5ZJ153-AA	Seal and Gasket Kit
F8DZ-7A262-AB	Forward Clutch Piston
F8DZ-7B164-AC	Forward Clutch Plates - Friction (4)
F2DZ-7B442-A	Forward Clutch Plates - Steel (4)

Apparently, the move to a steel piston didn't make Ford's transmissions more reliable or durable, as the above bulletin clearly demonstrates. Hence, my ratings downgrade Ford's latest models.

3.8L engine failures

Ford's other major powertrain problem is the 3.8L engine's chronic head gasket failures. Symptoms include engine overheating; poor engine performance; and a thin film deposited on the inside of the windshield, thus cutting down night driving visibility. Repairs range from $700 to $1,000, depending upon what other damage has occurred from overheating. Left untreated, the failure can "cook" your engine, requiring $3,000–$4,000 in repairs. And, even if treated in time, this defect can cause failures in emissions components (oxygen sensors and various computer modules) and other hardware malfunctions that can lead to other, expensive repairs.

There have been hundreds of cases reported to me of head gasket failures after three to five years or 60,000–100,000 km of use. Although these engine repairs are covered by Ford's 00M09 "goodwill" engine warranty up to seven years or 160,000 km, many Sable, Taurus, and Windstar owners have had their claims rejected because their vehicles fell outside of the 1994–95 limit set out in the above warranty extension. This makes no sense whatsoever, especially since Ford's own bulletin (see following) traces the problem back to the 1988 models and through to 1996.

3.8L V6 Engines Blow Their Tops (1988–96)

Article No.: 98-4-9   03/02/98
COOLING SYSTEM - OVERHEATING AND/OR LOSS OF COOLANT - 3.8L VEHICLES
FORD:
1988-96 TAURUS
LINCOLN-MERCURY
1988-94 CONTINENTAL
1988-95 SABLE
LIGHT TRUCK
1996 WINDSTAR
ISSUE:
Coolant may leak from the head gaskets and/or the vehicle may overheat. There may also be concerns of reduced heater output due to low coolant levels. This may be caused by insufficient sealing of the head gaskets.
ACTION:
Replace the head gaskets and head bolts. The revised head gaskets and bolts provide improved sealing copability and higher clamping force between the cylinder head and block. Refer to the following Service Procedure for details.

PART NUMBER   PART NAME
F5PZ-6051-AA   Head Gasket and Bolt Kit (One Side)

WARRANTY STATUS:
Eligible Under the Provisions of Bumper to Bumper Warranty Coverage

Interestingly, the above head gasket failures have also been reported with 3.8L V6 engines equipping Ford's Mustang through 1998.

Paint delamination
Over the past decade, there have been frequent complaints of paint delamination, peeling, and premature rusting affecting 1986–97 Taurus and Sables. Ford is the target of multiple class action paint lawsuits and is settling most small claims court cases, although more class actions may still be imminent.

A paint-delaminated Ford Taurus. Chrysler, Ford, and GM will repaint their vehicles for free, if threatened with a small claims lawsuit.

Other problems

The 4-cylinder engine is a dog that no amount of servicing can change. It's slow, noisy, prone to stalling and surging, and actually consumes more gas than the V6.

The 3.0L 6-cylinder is noted for engine head bolt failures and piston scuffing, and is characterized by hard starting, stalling, excessive engine noise, and poor fuel economy. Transmission cooler lines leak and often lead to the unnecessary repair or replacement of the transmission—note the advice given to this vacationing owner of a 1993 Taurus:

> While in Florida a month ago the local Ford dealer plugged a tester in our car and announced that our problem with the transmission could only be fixed by a new one—at an estimated $2,800 US. Another garage checked the colour of the transmission fluid and came to the same conclusion...a new transmission, but the estimate was lover, about $1,800 US. They added oil which temporarily fixed the problem. On our long drive home, towing a boat, we kept the fluid level topped up.
>
> On arrival, we visited our local CTC station in Port Hope, and discovered that a transmission cooling line had been leaking. The two mechanics who listened while I described the problem, immediately guessed what it would likely be. It turns out they have seen a lot these rusted lines on Fords. The fix cost $150, because the radiator had to be removed to get at the line. in fairness to the mechanics in Florida, perhaps this rusting problem is limited to climates where salt is used on roads.

Other things to look out for: blown heater hoses, malfunctioning fuel gauge sending units, and brakes that need constant attention—in front, they're noisy, pulsate excessively, tend to wear out prematurely, require a great deal of pedal effort, and are hard to modulate. Master cylinders need replacing around 100,000 km.

1988–95 models continue to have defective ignition modules, oxygen sensors, and fuel pumps, which cause rough running, chronic stalling, hard starting, and electrical system short circuits. Other problem areas include the following: biodegradable tie-rods, ball joints, coil springs, and motor mounts; an automatic transmission that is slow to downshift, hunts for Overdrive, and gives jerky performance; air conditioners that are failure prone and can cost up to $1,000 to fix; malfunctioning heaters that are slow to warm up and don't direct enough heat to the floor (particularly on the passenger side); a defective heater core that costs big bills to replace (buy from an independent supplier); and noisy, prematurely worn rack-and-pinion steering assemblies. Front suspension components also wear out quickly.

Electrical components, like windshield wipers, fuel pumps, and the rear defroster, interfere with radio reception. The automatic antenna often sticks, electric windows short-circuit, power door locks fail, and the electronic dash gives inaccurate readings. Owners report that electrical short circuits—which illuminate the Check Engine light and cause flickering lights and engine surging—are frequently misdiagnosed. Customers end up paying for the unnecessary replacement of the alternator, voltage regulator, or battery, in addition to unnecessary tune-ups. The speedometer is noisy and often inaccurate in cold weather.

Body/trim items are fragile on all cars (did somebody mention door handles?). Paint adherence is particularly poor on plastic components, weld joints, and the underside—even with mudguards. Owners also report that water leaks into the trunk through the taillight assembly and that 1986–95 versions produce an annoying sound of fuel sloshing when accelerating or stopping.

1996 models were radically redesigned with a totally new, more rounded styling that turned off as many buyers as it turned on. Other changes included upgraded engines, new electronic controls for the LX, and a revamped, oval dash panel. Other improvements: better handling and ride quality, more effective soundproofing, and some transmission refinements (beginning with the 1997 models, but ineffective from a reliability standpoint). Despite these changes, owners still report serious safety-related deficiencies (see "Safety summary") and other performance-related problems, like the non-upgraded engines being noisy, slow, and hard to start; the automatic transmission shifting erratically or not at all; engine gaskets still failing; front-end failures including the outer tie-rods, ball joints, and stabilizer bar links; and power windows that fail one after the other and cost $300–$500 each to repair. Plus, there's an assortment of rattles, buzzes, whines, and moans to keep you company on long drives. The most annoying? The incessant snapping and creaking of the plastic in the centre console and dash from the plastic sections binding against each other when the body flexes, especially if the sun has been shining on it.

2000 models went through another redesign that included a slight re-styling, a more comfortable ride, a more powerful and quieter powertrain, upgraded airbags, adjustable pedals, seatbelt pretensioners, and improved child safety seat anchors. Despite these pluses, overall reliability continues to go downhill. Fuel system failures result in surging, stalling, and a gasoline smell that invades the interior; electrical shorts cause the vehicle to suddenly shut down and not start; malfunctioning ABS, airbag, and Check Engine lights stay lit; powertrain and body components have a short lifespan; and owners have found that the re-styled head restraints block rear and side visibilty. 2001 models returned relatively unchanged.

Getting compensation

Canadian owners tell me that they still have to threaten small claims court action to get Ford Canada to accept repairs done by independent garages, repeat failures, or failures that occur in the 100,000–160,000 km ("no man's land") range, where warranty decisions are particularly inconsistent.

As always, I'll continue monitoring Ford's customer assistance activities throughout the year, and invite readers to use *www.lemonaidcars.com* for the latest updates and Appendix I, "Helpful Internet Info Sites," to link up with websites specifically oriented toward Ford transmission, head gasket, and warranty servicing deficiencies.

In the meantime, anyone seeking assistance should call Ford's toll-free number, 1-800-565-3673 (FORD). I have been assured each owner will have his or her claim reviewed fairly. I hope this will be the case; however, keep in mind what one Ford customer assistance whistleblower whispered in my ear:

> The company has taken a harder line in reviewing customer claims. *The only thing that gets our attention is if a small claims lawsuit is threatened or has been filed.* These are kicked upstairs to Legal Affairs and are settled right away.

Safety summary: All models/years: Tie-rod may collapse suddenly. Although the 1992 models were recalled to fix this defect, many other model years are affected and haven't been recalled. The son of a West Coast Taurus owner relates this incident:

> The right inner tie-rod, a piece of the suspension critical to the steering and thus safety of my 1992 Taurus, broke while my father was attempting to make a right turn from a stop sign. The car lost all steering control and the front wheels were seized. Fortunately, the car was barely moving, and no collision occurred.... I hope you can inform all Taurus and Sable owners of the inherent dangers lurking in their steering system.

• Front coil springs may fracture due to excessive corrosion. Ford has replaced many coils for free under a secret warranty. Interestingly, Ford's Windstars have the same problem and benefit from a 10-year extended warranty. Use that as your Taurus coil benchmark, as this Whitby, Ontario, engineer should do:

> I have a 1995 Mercury Sable that has developed two broken coil springs, on front right and rear left wheel. The fracture surfaces on the front spring show no fatigue bands and are compatible with intergranular stress corrosion or hydriding, both indicating a manufacturing defect. Microscopic examination would be required to confirm the cause of failure.
>
> This car has seen only light duty service, is low mileage, and has always been garaged. I feel this is a significant safety issue. The failures have given no warning signs, and only the front one was detected during routine maintenance. The front spring has broken in two places, leaving a broken spring end only 1/4 inch from the tire. I cannot easily see what is stopping it going right into the tire and suspect it would have worked its way in over the course of a few more miles. I am also concerned that a local independent mechanic says he has seen several spring failures on the Taurus/Sable, but that the local dealer's Service rep has not. I note from the Lemon-Aid web site that Transport Canada is investigating spring failures on this vehicle type.

• These vehicles eat brake rotors, calipers, and pads every 5,000 miles (8,000 km). • Brakes produce a grinding, growling noise in addition to an acrid smell. **All models: 1995**—Sudden windshield shattering. • AC failures. • Headlight failures. **1995–96**—Fuel pump failures. • Airbag fails to deploy or is accidentally deployed. • Transmission slips out of Park. • Engine compartment fires. • Defective door locks. **1995–97**—Sudden acceleration. • Stalling. • ABS failures. **1996**—Chronic stalling. • Cruise control won't slow vehicle on slopes. • Left front wheel may separate from car. • Loss of steering when it rains. • Loss of power steering. • Frequent engine head gasket failures. • Transmission fails or shifts erratically. • Dash reflects into the windshield. • Faulty door lock switch. • Defective heating/defrosting system causes excessive windshield fogging. **1997**—Transmission jumps from Park to Reverse. • Sudden steering loss. • Wheels fly off. • Engine head gasket and automatic transmission failures. **1998**—Accelerator and brake pedals are too close to each other. • Vehicle won't slow when accelerator pedal is released. • Faulty cruise control won't slow vehicle down. • Automatic transmission malfunctions. • Chronic brake failures. • Defective rotor and wiring assembly caused ABS failure. • Loss of steering when steering belt pulley and pump failed. • Defective rack-and-pinion steering spring yoke. • Sudden steering lockup. • Trunk lid fell on owner's head, due to defective torsion bar. • Trunk light burned garment in the trunk. • Faulty headlights.

• Headlights don't give enough light to the sides. • Daytime running lights flicker due to defective module. • Dashboard reflects in the windshield, causing reduced visibility. • Heater system failed. • Driver's seatbelt won't retract or lock into position. • Hatchback window suddenly exploded while vehicle was parked. **1999**—Engine fires. • No airbag deployment and inadvertent air deployment. • Frequent complaints of sudden acceleration or high idle when taking the foot off the gas pedal, at a standstill, or when shifting into Reverse, slowly accelerating, or applying the brakes. • Reports of accelerator sticking. • Many reports of no-starts or sudden stalling caused by fuel pump failure. • Defective power-steering pump causes sudden steering lockup. • ABS brakes locked up when applied and vehicle suddenly accelerated. • Many reports of brake pedal having been pushed to the floor with no braking effect. One '99 Taurus owner recounts the following tragic experience in his NHTSA complaint:

> Sudden brake loss, cruise control wouldn't disengage, brakes to floor, emergency brake pulled to no effect, death of four.

Every element of this owner's story is repeated throughout the NHTSA database from reports of other Taurus and Sable owners. • Cruise control fails to disengage when vehicle is going downhill. • Frequent automatic transmission failures that include: slipping, hesitation, lurching into gear, failure to engage First gear, and a defective fluid pump destroying the catalytic converter. • Transmission in Park position allowed vehicle to roll downhill. • Transmission may leak fluid onto the exhaust manifold. • Steering wheel and brakes vibrate excessively when braking. • Front passenger's seatbelt won't retract or lock into position. • Seatbelt broke. • Seatbelts fail to retract in a collision. • In the morning and evening, the light tan dashboard reflects upon the windshield, causing reduced visibility. • Rear defroster/defogger works poorly. • Rear windshield exploded when defroster/defogger activated. • In another incident, rear windshield exploded while vehicle was underway. • Headlights dim when brakes are applied. • Trunk light bulb burned part of luggage. • Electrical system shorts lead to the erratic operation of power door locks (they unlock while vehicle is underway) and windows. • AC discharges a foul odour that causes eyes to water and burn. • Fuel tank leaks. • Vehicle will stall out when fuel gauge shows the tank is one-quarter full. In fact, the gauge is so inaccurate that it will vary its reading by a half a tank depending upon whether you are going uphill or downhill. **2000**—Almost 300 safety failures have been recorded (50 complaints would be normal) for the first year of the Taurus' latest redesign. Most of the problems are similar to those reported for previous years: evidence that Ford doesn't want to spend the money or squeeze its suppliers to install better quality components. No airbag deployment and inadvertent activation; gas fumes in the interior (driver found it exceeded CO_2

monitor limits and caused drowsiness and headaches); constantly lit warning lights; complete electrical failure; and sudden acceleration, surging, and stalling, accompanied by brake failure, continue to be the most frequent complaints:

> I released the brake after stopping at a stop sign, and turned the wheel to the right, the vehicle suddenly accelerated to what seemed about 100 km/h in about ten seconds. The vehicle went towards the right and struck a curb, and the brakes did not appear to work. Once the vehicle came to a rest, the engine then shut off, the windshield broke, and the drivers side door wouldn't open.
>
> I suffered minor injuries.

Whatever you do, don't ignore the Check Engine light. In another recorded incident, the car didn't run away, stall, or lose its brakes; it simply exploded:

> At startup the intake manifold exploded, resulting in total destruction. Shrapnel was imbedded in the insulation cover on the hood and found throughout the engine compartment. The windshield washer module on the right side was blown off and found approximately five feet from the car.
>
> This vehicle has been in for service for hard starting and fuel system Check Engine light for the past year.

2001—Less than a hundred incidents reported so far; complaints echo those from previous years. • When coming to a stop, vehicle continues to accelerate because foot presses brake and gas pedal at the same time. • Car accelerated while backing up. • Airbag warning light comes on for no reason. • Inadvertent airbag deployment. • Sudden brake failure. • Strong fuel odour seeps into the interior. • Power steering suddenly failed. • Warped rotors. • Rear-view mirror too low on windshield; blocks view to the right. Dash reflects onto windshield. • Early automatic transmission replacement. • Transmission clunks and jerks into gear. • Driver-side seatbelt tightens by itself while driving. • Left rear wheel came off in transit; lost control of car.

Secret Warranties/Service Tips/TSBs

All models/years: A cracked forward clutch piston may cause Forward/Reverse problems. Install the improved clutch piston and ask Ford to cover part of the cost inasmuch as their bulletins confirm it's a design defect. • Repeated heater core leaks. • A rotten-egg odour coming from the exhaust probably means that you have a faulty catalytic converter; replacement may be covered under the emissions warranty. • A buzz or rattle from the exhaust system may be caused by a loose heat shield catalyst. • A sloshing noise from the fuel tank when accelerating or stopping requires the installation of an upgraded tank. • Paint delamination, fading, and peeling (see Part Two). **All models: 1993–94**—An inoperative AC blower probably needs an improved cold engine lockout switch and hose assembly. **1993–97**—If the front end accessory drive belt (FEAD) slips during wet conditions, it can cause a reduction in steering power assist. **1994–98**—No Fourth gear may signal the need to install an upgraded forward clutch control valve retaining clip. **1994–99**—Service tips to silence wind noise around doors. **1995–98**—No-starts may be caused by a defective fuel pump. **1995–99**—Tips for sealing windshield water leaks and reducing noise, vibration, and harshness while driving. **1995–2000**—A harsh 3–2 downshift/shudder when accelerating or turning may have a simple cause: air entering the fluid filter pickup area due to a slightly low ATF fluid level. **1996–97**—An acceleration or deceleration clunk is likely caused by the rear lower subframe isolators allowing movement between the mounts and the subframe. • A front suspension clunk may signal premature sway bar wear. • Harsh automatic 1–2 shifting may be caused by a malfunctioning electronic pressure control or the main control valves sticking in the valve body (see following bulletin).

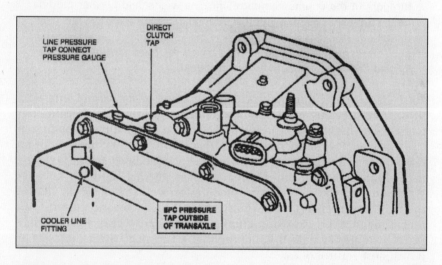

1996–98—Troubleshooting tips for a torque converter clutch that won't engage. • Hard starts or long cranks may be caused by a miscalibrated PCM, a faulty IAC, or a malfunctioning fuel pump. • Install a power-steering service kit to silence steering moan. • A rattle heard when accelerating may be corrected by replacing the exhaust pipe flex coupling. • Water leaking onto the passenger floor area is likely caused by insufficient sealing of the cabin air filter to the cowl inlet. **1996–99**—Frequent no-starts, long cranks, or a dead battery may be caused by excessive current drain or water entry in the ABS module connector. **1996–2001**—Inoperative power windows may need a new motor and lubrication of the glass run weather stripping (see following bulletin).

Power Windows - Stick/Do Not Operate

Article No. 00-26-3   12/25/00

Ford:

1996-2001 Taurus

Mercury:

1996-2001 Sable

ISSUE

Some vehicles may exhibit a power window that will not operate downward because it's stuck/bound to the weatherstrip header. This may be due to infrequent use and environmental contaminants on the weatherstrip seal.

ACTION

Check window motor operation and lubricate the weatherstrip.

Part Number:	Part Name:
F5AZ-19553-AA	Silicone Spray
F8DZ-5423395-AA	Window Motor - RH
F8DZ-5423394-AA	Window Motor - LH

WARRANTY STATUS

Eligible Under the Provisions of Bumper to Bumper Warranty Coverage.

Take note that Ford says the base warranty will cover this failure. If the warranty has expired, ask for a partial refund, since window motors should last at least 5 years/100,000 km.

1997—Stalling or surging of 3.0L engines when shifting may signal the need to reprogram the power control module (PCM). **1997–98**—Lack of AC temperature control may be corrected by replacing the blend air door actuator. **1999**—Owner Notification Program regarding transmission rear lube tube and bracket replacement. • Engine buzz or rattle. • Slight vibration upon acceleration. • Lack of engine braking. • Excessive spark knock with the 3.0L engine. • Engine oil pan leaks. • No Reverse engagement is likely caused by the Reverse clutch lip seals shearing or tearing during Reverse engagement in cold weather. • No 3–4 shifts; 3–4 shift shuddering. • Outer tie-rod squeaks or pops. • Excessive steering noise on vehicles equipped with the 3.0L engine. • Inoperative speed control and blower motor. • Self-activating front wipers need an upgraded multifunction switch (covered under warranty or "goodwill"). • Hard to turn ignition key. • Wagons display a false "door ajar" warning. • Intermittent loss of instrument panel illumination. • Separation between the layers of the instrument panel. • Premature deterioration of the front seat trim. • Power window binding. • Inaccurate fuel tank gauge; fuel tank causes gas pump to shut off prematurely. **2000**—Engine pan oil leaks. • Automatic transmission may operate erratically. • A hissing sound may be heard coming from the intake manifold. • A growling or scraping sound may be heard during acceleration. **2000–01**—3.0L engines may exhibit a rough start or poor idle, excessive spark knock, or backfire on startup. • 3–4 shift shudder. • The exhaust pipe contacts the rear control arm, resulting in rear end buzzing, groaning, and rattling. • Fuel smell permeates the interior (see following bulletin).

Intake Manifold Gaskets - Fuel Smell to the Interior

Article No. 01-4-3   03/05/01

Ford

2000-2001 Taurus
2001 Escape

Mercury

2000-2001 Sable

This article applies to 2000-2001 Taurus/Sable vehicles with 3.0L 4V Duratec engine built through 4/1/2001 and 2001 Escape vehicles with 3.0L 4V Duratec engine built through 6/1/2001 only.

Issue

Some vehicles may exhibit a fuel odor noticed through the vents inside the vehicle. The odor may be noticed upon initial startup after "Hot Soak." This condition produces a fuel odor only and does not involve visible fuel or include the presence of a combustible mixture. This may be caused by the lower intake manifold gaskets.

Action

If fuel odor condition is verified and no fuel leaks or mechanical problems are found, replace the lower intake gaskets with revised gaskets.

Part Number:	Part Name:
YF1Z-9439-AC	Gasket Set - Lower Intake Manifold

2001—Side airbag light may remain lit. • Rough idle; Check Engine light remains lit. • Automatic transmission fluid leakage from the main control cover area. • Blower motor may overheat. • Sticking/binding ignition key lock cylinder.

Sable, Taurus Profile

	1994	1995	1996	1997	1998	1999	2000	2001
Cost Price ($)								
Sable GS	20,995	21,195	22,595	23,595	24,395	24,595	—	—
LS Wagon	24,196	24,195	25,496	26,596	25,096	25,795	—	—
Taurus GL	19,295	20,695	22,195	23,195	—	—	—	—
Taurus LX	23,495	23,895	25,095	26,195	23,295	23,495	24,495	24,250
GL/SE Wagon	19,296	20,636	22,196	23,196	23,995	24,695	26,495	26,555
SHO	30,095	31,095	32,430	32,695	37,795	37,995	—	—
Used Values ($)								
Sable GS Λ	3,500	5,000	6,000	8,000	10,000	12,500	—	—
Sable GS V	3,000	3,500	5,000	6,500	8,000	10,500	—	—
LS Wagon Λ	4,000	5,500	6,500	9,000	11,000	13,000	—	—
LS Wagon V	3,500	4,000	5,500	7,000	9,000	11,000	—	—
Taurus GL Λ	3,000	3,500	5,000	7,000	—	—	—	—
Taurus GL V	2,500	3,000	4,000	5,000	—	—	—	—

Taurus LX ▲	3,500	5,500	7,000	9,000	10,000	12,500	15,000	17,500
Taurus LX ▼	3,000	3,800	5,000	7,000	8,000	10,500	13,000	15,500
GL/SE Wagon ▲	4,000	5,000	6,500	8,500	10,500	13,000	16,000	18,500
GL/SE Wagon ▼	3,500	4,000	5,500	6,500	8,500	11,000	14,000	16,500
SHO ▲	5,000	6,500	9,000	12,000	15,500	20,000	—	—
SHO ▼	4,500	5,000	7,000	10,000	13,300	17,500	—	—
Extended Warranty	Y	Y	Y	Y	Y	Y	Y	Y
Secret Warranty	Y	Y	Y	Y	Y	Y	Y	Y
Reliability	❶	❶	❶	❶	❶	❶	❶	❷
Crash Safety	④	④	④	④	④	⑤	—	⑤
Side Impact	—	—	—	③	③	③	—	③
Off-set	⑤	⑤	⑤	⑤	⑤	⑤	⑤	⑤
Head Restraints (F)	—	❶	❶	❶	—	❶	❷	④
Rear	—	—	—	—	—	—	—	③
Rollover Resistance	—	—	—	—	—	—	—	④

General Motors

ACHIEVA (CALAIS), GRAND AM, SKYLARK ★★★

RATING: Average (1999–2001); Below Average (1995–98); Not Recommended (1985–94). Only the Grand Am survived through the 1999 model year. The 1992 Achieva replaced the Calais; except for styling, this Achieva is practically identical to the others. **Maintenance/Repair costs:** Higher than average. Repairs aren't dealer dependent. **Parts:** Higher-than-average cost, but they can be bought for much less from independent suppliers. **Best alternatives:** The Acura Integra; Honda Accord; Hyundai Elantra wagon, Sonata, or Tiburon; Mazda 626; Nissan Altima; and Toyota Camry.

Strengths and weaknesses: These cars come with a standard 150-hp Quad SOHC engine, a 5-speed transaxle, and ABS. The basic front-drive platform continues to be a refined version of the Sunfire (Sunbird) and Cavalier J-body. They are too cramped to be family sedans (rear entry/exit can be difficult), too sedate for sporty coupe status, and too ordinary for inclusion in the luxury car ranks.

In their basic form, these cars are unreliable, unspectacular, and provide barely adequate performance. An upgraded 3.1L V6 powerplant gives you only five more horses than the base 4-banger and frequently requires intake manifold gasket repairs covered by a 6-year/100,000 km secret warranty. There's been a lot of hype about the Quad 4 16-valve engine, available with all models, but little of this translates into benefits for the average driver. A multi-valve motor produces more power than a standard engine, but always at higher rpms and with a fuel penalty and excess engine noise.

These cars ride and handle fairly well but share chassis components with the failure-prone J-bodies. This explains why engine, transmission, brake, and electronic problems are similar. Fortunately, manual transmissions are much more reliable and are also the better choice for fuel economy. Water leaks and body squeaks and rattles are so abundant that GM has published a six-page troubleshooting TSB that pinpoints the noises and lists fixes.

1996 Skylarks were re-styled and given standard AC, dual airbags and three-point seatbelts. Additionally, a new twin-cam engine replaced the 2.3L Quad 4. '97s were unchanged and dropped later that year. Grand Ams were given similar improvements to the Skylark. '98 models received depowered airbags, though. The '99 Grand Am was given more standard equipment and had their interior re-styled. Year 2000 models got some engine and interior upgrades, while the following year's models were given a better sound system and upgraded wheels.

The 2.5L 4-cylinder engine doesn't provide much power and has a poor reliability record. Avoid the Quad 4 and 3.0L V6 engines with SFI (sequential fuel injection) because of their frequent breakdowns and difficult servicing. Poor engine cooling and fuel system malfunctions are common; diagnosis and repair are more complicated than average, however. The engine computer on V6 models has a high failure rate, and the oil pressure switch often malfunctions. The electrical system is plagued by gremlins that cause gauges and controls to go haywire and result in the car shutting down on the highway. Seals and pumps in the power-steering rack deteriorate rapidly. Front brake discs, rotors, and pads need replacing every 5,000 miles (8,000 km). Locks and headlights self-activate.

Among body deficiencies, owners note that windshield mouldings fall off, water leaks into the trunk and through the doors, door panels often need replacing, the sun visor fails to stay in place, seat cushions aren't durable, and paint defects are quite common.

Safety summary: All models: 1995—Fire ignited in the engine compartment while vehicle was on the road. • Sudden acceleration due to weak pedal return spring. • Chronic stalling. • Airbag failed to deploy. • Malfunctioning airbag causes horn to suddenly go off. • Driver's seatbelt failed to restrain driver. • Frequent brake failures and extended stopping distance. • Power-steering fluid leak due to high pressure hose chafing by the two fuel-injector tabs. • Brake caliper seizure damages pads and rotors. • Transmission jumps out of gear. • Shoulder belt rides across driver's neck. • Driver-side door handle popped out. • Erratic fuel gauge operation. • Headlights suddenly shut off. • Passenger seat not anchored securely. **1996**—Inadvertent airbag deployment. • Airbag failed to deploy. • Sudden acceleration and stalling. • When putting car in Reverse, it suddenly accelerated forward. • Left wheel came off after the stud that holds the wheel unbolted from the wheel. • Oxygen sensor failures cause Check Engine light to come on. • Frequent brake failures. • Excessive brake noise. • Defective master cylinder, drums, pads, and rotors. • Engine, transmission, and AC failures. • Seatbelt sticks into driver's side or will not fasten properly. • Insufficient insulation under steering column allows draft to come in under left lower dash area. • Headlight failure. • Water leaks into the trunk. • Cracking around the outside edge of all tires. • Passenger-side power door lock and window lock do not work properly. **1997**—Many reports of vehicle first losing power and then suddenly accelerating. • Accelerator cable snapped, causing pedal to go to the floor. • While vehicle was being driven, the hood suddenly flipped backward, hitting the windshield. • Windshield reflection obstructs vision. • Premature brake replacements. • Seatbelt improperly fitted. • Design flaw allows wheels to rub against front fender. • Mirrors aren't adjustable enough to see other vehicles, and seatbacks are too high for some drivers to see over. • Driver-side bucket seat isn't anchored properly; rocks from side to side. • Intermittent windshield wiper failures. • Headlights sometimes cut out. **1998–99**—Vehicle caught fire while parked. • Airbag failed to deploy, or deployed inadvertently. • Premature brake pad wearout and warped rotors every 3,000–5,000 miles (4,800–8,000 km). • Sudden acceleration. • Cruise control is either inoperative or fails to disengage. • Chronic hesitation and stall-out, accompanied by dash lights and other electrics going haywire. • Enhanced traction system engages when not needed. • Complete electrical system shutdown while underway. • Rainwater leaks through the dash panel into the fuse box. • Wheel lug nuts sheared off, causing wheel to fall away. • Severe brake, steering, and body vibrations; vehicle intermittently violently jerks to one side. • Sudden steering loss; steering pump failure. • Fuel pressure regulator leaks fumes into the interior. • Sunroof exploded when side window was opened while vehicle was underway. • Windows run off their channels and shatter. • Power window motors often need replacing. • Windshield washer fluid freezes due to poor tubing design. • Headrests obstruct rear visibility. • Locks and headlights self-activate. • Headlights give inadequate illuminate on turns. • Faulty fuel level sensor gives a false Empty reading. • Seatbelts tend to twist when retracting. **2000**—Although there aren't an unusually large number of complaints recorded, the same problems keep appearing. They include airbag malfunctions; frequent brake light burnout; poor braking or the complete loss of braking; overheated, warped brake rotors and excessive vibration when braking; chronic stalling; the trunk lid opening on its own while the vehicle is underway; and water leaks through the doors and sunroof. The sunroof leaks result in the electrical system shorting out and the vehicle shutting down. **2001**—Very few complaints reported so far; however, airbag malfunctions, stalling, brake rotor warpage, and sunroof leaks appear, once again. Other problems: fire ignited at the right rear of vehicle; fuel tank is easily punctured; and rear axle bent or broken, leading to loss of control.

Secret Warranties/Service Tips/TSBs

All models: 1990–2000—Countermeasures for water collecting in the taillights. **1991–95**—Front brake linings can be made to last longer by replacing the front brake pads with a new 8100 lining compound (#18022600). **1992–97**—Inoperative power door locks may need an upgraded external bumper on the actuator arm. **1993–98**—A front suspension/engine squawk may be reduced by applying ultra-high molecular tape to the area producing the noise. **1993–99**—A rotten-egg odour coming from the exhaust may be the result of a malfunctioning catalytic converter—possibly covered by the emissions warranty. Stand your ground if GM or the dealer claims you must pay. • Tips on removing AC odours. • Paint delamination, peeling, or fading (see Part Two). **1993–2002**—GM has a special kit to keep AC odours at bay. **1994**—Gear whine with the 4T60E automatic transaxle can be stopped by replacing the final drive and updating the PCM calibration. • Insufficient AC cooling may be due to a leak at the low-charge primary-port seal. • Loss of Drive or erratic shifts may be caused by an intermittent short to ground on the A or B shift solenoid or an electrical short circuit in the transaxle. • A front-end clunking noise when driving over rough roads may require the repositioning of the diagonal radiator support braces. **1995–97**—Intermittent loss of Drive at highway speeds may require the replacement of the control valve body assembly. • Engine popping noises can be silenced by tightening the torque strut mount bolts. **1995–98**—A steering squeak or squawk may be reduced by installing a rack and pinion service kit. **1996–98**—Install a seatbelt webbing stop button if the seatbelt latch slides to the anchor sleeve. • Passenger compartment water leaks can be plugged by applying silicone sealer to the top vent grille assembly. **1997**—No-starts may be due to an improperly routed and pinched wire from the generator to the wiring harness. • Excessive oil consumption in the 2.5L engine may be caused by one or more damaged intake valve guides. • Hard starting and engine pinging can be fixed by the installation of a new PROM module (#16121217), says TSB #88-6E-11. **1997–98**—Hard starting or a weak or dead battery may signal the need to repair the B+ stud and/or starter wiring. **1999–2000**—No Third or Fourth gear may signal a defective direct clutch piston. • Upgraded pads and rotors will fix brake pulsation/vibration • A wet front or rear carpet may mean the front door water deflectors need to be replaced. • Simply changing the radiator cap may cure your hot-running engine. **Grand Am: 1999**—Hesitation or lack of power when accelerating on vehicles equipped with the 3.4L engine may simply require reprogramming the power control module (PCM). • Paint chipping from the Grand Am SE's rocker panel and lower quarter panel can be prevented by installing upgraded driver- and passenger-side rocker mouldings. **1999–2001**—A front-end clunk or rattle can be silenced by replacing the brake pedal assembly under warranty. **2000**—If the vehicle stalls, hesitates or won't start, you may need to replace the modular fuel sender strainer. **2000–01**—If the Check Engine light comes on, it may mean the fuel-sender-to-tank O-ring is defective. • Install a fuel tank sender kit under warranty if the fuel gauge gives inaccurate readings. • TSB #01-06-01-005 allows for free 3.1L engine piston replacement to cure an engine ticking noise. **Skylark: 1995–98**—Intermittent Neutral/loss of Drive at highway speeds can be fixed by replacing the control valve body assembly.

Achieva (Calais), Grand Am, Skylark Profile

	1994	1995	1996	1997	1998	1999	2000	2001
Cost Price ($)								
Achieva S	16,698	18,485	19,925	20,735	21,200	—	—	—
Grand Am	15,798	17,365	18,000	19,035	19,610	21,795	20,625	20,915
Skylark	16,398	19,035	20,035	21,220	22,965	—	—	—
Used Values ($)								
Achieva S ʌ	3,500	4,500	6,000	7,500	9,000	—	—	—
Achieva S v	3,000	3,500	5,000	6,000	7,500	—	—	—
Grand Am ʌ	4,500	5,500	7,000	8,000	10,000	12,000	14,000	15,500
Grand Am v	3,500	4,500	6,000	6,500	8,000	10,000	12,000	14,000
Skylark ʌ	4,000	5,000	6,500	8,000	10,000	—	—	—
Skylark v	3,500	4,000	5,000	6,500	8,000	—	—	—
Extended Warranty	Y	Y	Y	Y	Y	N	N	N
Secret Warranty	Y	Y	Y	Y	Y	Y	Y	Y
Reliability	❷	❷	❷	③	③	④	④	④
Crash Safety								
Achieva 2d	④	④	—	④	—	—	—	—
Achieva 4d	—	④	④	⑤	—	—	—	—
Grand Am 2d	④	④	—	④	—	—	—	④
Grand Am 4d	—	—	④	⑤	—	④	④	④
Skylark 2d	④	④	—	④	—	—	—	—
Skylark 4d	—	—	④	⑤	—	—	—	—
Side Impact								
Achieva 4d	—	—	—	❶	❶	—	—	—
Grand Am 2d	—	—	—	—	—	—	—	❶
Grand Am 4d	—	—	—	❶	❶	③	③	③
Skylark 4d	—	—	—	❶	❶	—	—	—
Off-set	—	—	—	—	—	❶	❶	❶
Head Restraints	—	❶	—	❶	—	❷	—	③
Rollover Resistance	—	—	—	—	—	—	—	④

BONNEVILLE, CUTLASS, CUTLASS SUPREME, DELTA 88, GRAND PRIX, INTRIGUE, LESABRE, LUMINA, MALIBU, MONTE CARLO, REGAL   ★★★

RATING: Average (1997–2001); Not Recommended for front-drives (1988–96); Above Average for rear-drives (1984–87). Although these GM models are generally classed as medium-sized cars, some of them move in and out of the large car class as well. Overall, the Intrigue, Malibu, Monte Carlo, and Grand Prix provide the best quality at the highest depreciation rate (for used-car bargain hunters). **Maintenance/Repair costs:** Higher than average, but repairs aren't dealer dependent. **Parts:** Higher-than-average cost (independent suppliers sell for much less), but not hard to find. Nevertheless, don't even think about buying one of the front-drives without a three- to five-year supplementary warranty. **Best alternatives:** The Acura Integra; GM Cavalier or Sunfire; Honda Accord; Hyundai Elantra wagon, Sonata, or Tiburon; Mazda 626; Nissan Altima; and Toyota Camry.

Strengths and weaknesses: Body assembly on all models is notoriously poor and is no doubt one of the main reasons why GM has lost so much market share over the past decade. Premature paint peeling and rusting, water and dust leaks into the trunk, squeaks and rattles, and wind and road noise are all too common. Accessories are also plagued by problems, with defective radios, power antennas, door locks, cruise control, and alarm systems leading the pack. Premature automatic transmission failures and excessive noise when shifting have been endemic up to the 1998 model year. Since then, the company's powertrain problems have been less frequent. Engine intake manifold gaskets, though, have a high failure rate and are covered by a 6-year/100,000 km secret warranty.

Rear-drives
The rear-drives are competent and comfortable cars, but they definitely point to a time when handling wasn't a priority and fuel economy was unimportant. Their overall reliability is pretty good, though not exceptional, repairs are easy to perform, defects aren't hard to troubleshoot, and cheaper independent garages can service them quite easily. Older models equipped with diesel engines or with the turbocharged gas V6 should be approached with extreme caution. These cars have a higher-than-average incidence of repairs and parts can be hard to find. Late-'90s diesel engines, used mostly on trucks, are considerably improved over the bastardized versions of the '80s and early '90s.

Original-equipment shock absorbers and springs aren't durable, and electrical malfunctions increase proportionally with extra equipment. The AC module and condenser and wheel bearings (incredibly expensive) also have short life spans. The 4-speed automatic transmission isn't very durable and begins failing by hunting for the right gear and then noisily jerking into gear. Surface rust caused by poor paint quality and application is common. The rear edge of trunk lids, roof areas above doors, and the windshield and windshield posts rust through easily.

Front-drives

The front-drives are a different breed of car: less reliable and more expensive to repair, with a considerable number of mechanical and electrical deficiencies directly related to their front-drive configuration. Nevertheless, acceleration is adequate, fuel economy is good, and they're better at handling than their rear-drive cousins—except in emergencies, when their brakes lock up or fail and directional stability is compromised. The front-drives' many design and manufacturing weaknesses make for unimpressive high-speed performance, mediocre interior comfort, a poor reliability record, and expensive maintenance costs. That's why most fleets and police agencies use rear-drives when they can get them. They've seen the rear-drives' safety and operating cost advantages. Interestingly, Chrysler, Ford, and GM have announced a return to rear-drive full-sized cars by 2005.

Front-drives aren't driver-friendly cars. Many models have a dash that's replete with confusing push-buttons and gauges that are washed out in sunlight or reflect annoyingly upon the windshield. At other times, there are retro touches, like the Intrigue's dash-mounted ignition, that simply seem out of place. The keyless entry system often fails, the radio's memory is frequently forgetful, and the fuel light comes on when the tank is just below the "1/2" fuel-level mark. The electronic climate control frequently malfunctions and owners report that warm air doesn't reach the driver-side heating vents. Servicing, especially for the electronic engine controls, is complicated and expensive, forcing many owners to drive around with their Service Engine, airbag, and ABS warning lights constantly lit.

Other major problem areas found over the past decade: engine head gasket leaks; plastic intake manifold cracking; automatic transmission failures and clunking; leaking and malfunctioning AC systems (due mainly to defective AC modules); faulty electronic modules; rack-and-pinion steering failure; weak shocks; excessive front brake pad wear; warping rotors; seizure of the rear brake calipers; rear brake/wheel lockup; myriad electrical failures, requiring replacement of the computer module; leaking oil pan; and suspension struts.

The base 2.3L and 2.5L engines found on pre-'95 models provide insufficient power. The more powerful 3.1L V6 is peppier, but it's seriously hampered by the 4-speed automatic transaxle. The high-performance 3.4L V6, available since 1991, gives out plenty of power, but only at high engine speeds. Other deficiencies: the instruments and steering column shake when the car is travelling over uneven road surfaces; and lots of road and wind noise comes through the side windows, thanks to the inadequately soundproofed chassis. Seating isn't very comfortable due to the lack of support caused by low-density foam, knees-in-your-face low seating, and the ramrod-straight rear backrest. The ride is acceptable with a light load, but when fully loaded, the car's back end sags and the ride deteriorates. Owners report that 3.8L engines won't continue running after a cold start, the exhaust system booms, 3T40 automatic transmissions may have faulty Reverse gears, and the instrument panel may pop or creak.

Intrigue

Strikingly similar to the Alero, the Oldsmobile Intrigue is GM's replacement for the Cutlass Supreme and represents the most refined iteration of the W-body shared by the Century, Grand Prix, Lumina, and Regal. It's more luxurious than the Lumina and performs as well as the Accord, Camry, and Maxima. Its rigid chassis has fewer shakes and rattles than are found on GM's other models, and its 3.8L engine provides lots of low-end grunt but lacks the top-end power that makes the Japanese competition so much fun to toss around. '99 versions got a torquier 3.5L V6 coupled to standard traction control. This engine's a bit more refined, but it's still not smooth, and the automatic transmission still struggles to get past its first two gears. Year 2000 models returned unchanged, while the 2001 Intrigue was given a couple of new colours and an upgraded air filtration system.

1995–2001 Lumina and Monte Carlo

The redesigned Lumina and Monte Carlo are popular two- and four-door versions of Chevy's "large" mid-sized cars, featuring standard dual airbags, ABS, and 160-hp V6 power. The Monte Carlo was formerly sold as the Lumina Z34. Powertrain enhancements have increased horsepower and fuel efficiency. Each car has been given a slightly different appearance and a distinct "personality." A 3.1L V6 is the standard engine, a standard 3.4L 210-hp V6 powers the coupe and is optional with the LS Lumina, and a 3.8L V6 equips the more upscale versions. In 1996, the 3.4L got a slight horsepower boost, and all-disc braking was adopted on the Monte Carlo Z34 and upscale versions of the LS. For 1997, a better performing transmission, mated to the 3.4L engine, gives smoother shifts. The '98 and '99 models got few changes, except for the addition of the 3.8L V6 to the Monte Carlo Z34 and Lumina LTZ. The year 2000 Lumina's standard 3.1L engine got a bit more torque and a small horsepower boost, in addition to more standard equipment. Sold only in the States, this was its last year before it was replaced by the Impala. But the Monte Carlo soldiered on, having been reworked and brought out on the Impala platform for 2000. It was carried over unchanged for the 2001 model year.

Except for the automatic transmission upgrade, owners report that newer versions still have some of the same shortcomings seen on earlier front-drive models. For example, in spite of some noise reduction progress, body construction is still below par, with loose door panel mouldings, poorly fitted door fabric, and misaligned panels. Other common problems: fuel pump whistling, frequent stalling, vague steering, premature paint peeling on the hood and trunk, heavy accumulation of hard-to-remove brake dust inside the honeycomb-design wheels, and front tires that scrape the fenders when the wheel is turned. Despite its own recent redesign, the 3.1L engine isn't entirely problem-free. Faulty intake manifold gaskets, electronic fuel-injection systems, and engine controls have created many problems for GM owners. The 4-speed automatic transmission still has some bugs. The front brakes wear quickly, as do the MacPherson struts and shock absorbers. Steering assemblies tend to fail prematurely. The electrical system is temperamental. The sunroof motor is failure prone. Owners report water leaks from the front windshield. Front-end squeaks may require the replacement of the exhaust manifold pipe springs with dampers.

Cutlass and Malibu

These two front-drive, medium-sized sedans are slotted in between the Cavalier and Lumina in both size and price. This niche was once filled by the long-gone and failure-prone Corsica, Beretta, Tempest, Celebrity, and Ciera. The Malibu and Cutlass are boringly styled cars that use a more rigid body structure to cut down on noise and improve handling. Standard mechanicals include a 2.4L twin-cam 4-cylinder engine or an optional 3.1L V6. There's plenty of passenger and luggage space. Although head room is tight, the Malibu can carry three rear passengers and gives much more leg room than either the Cavalier or Lumina.

Other points to consider: the base 4-cylinder is loud, handling isn't on par with the Japanese competition, there's lots of body lean in turns, outside mirrors are too small, there's no traction control, and the ignition switch is mounted on the dash (a throwback to your dad's Oldsmobile).

In addition to the generic front-drive problems listed previously, owners also report the following: early failure of the 3.1L intake manifold gasket; fuel-injector deposits cause chronic stalling, poor idling, or hard starts; excessive vibration occurs at any speed; transmission doesn't lock when the key is in the accessory position; steering is very loose; backfires caused by defective computer modules; premature suspension strut failures (vehicle bottoms out with four or more passengers aboard); excessive AC noise; and the high-beam light switch fails intermittently.

Safety summary: All models: 1995–1997—Airbag failed to deploy. • Seating design forces driver to sit too close to airbag mechanism in the steering column. • Chronic stalling. • Throttle sticks. • Frequent cruise control failures. • Inadequate braking. • ABS brake failures are common. • Emergency brake doesn't work properly; it won't remain locked. • Ventilation system emitted fumes that made occupants ill. • Frequent AC compressor failures. • Seatbelt didn't restrain passenger sufficiently in an accident. • Inoperative rear seat buckles. • Rear seatbelts are too short to secure a child seat or large person. • Plastic part of buckle came off when trying to buckle up. • Rear seatbelt design forces user to sit on buckles; they are too close to the seat and difficult to fasten. • Turn signal lever won't return to neutral position. • Excessive wind noise comes in around the door openings. • Many reports that door locks continually engage and disengage while driving. • Power window motor failure. • Outside rear-view mirrors positioned too far back for a clear view. • Dash reflection in windshield cuts visibility. • Windshield wipers operate erratically. • Water collects in the headlight lenses, causing them to fog or malfunction. • Headlights often dim for no apparent reason. • Brake lights and taillights aren't very durable. **1998**—Airbags failed to deploy. • Sudden acceleration; faulty fuel pressure regulator suspected. • Power seat puts occupant too close to airbag. • Headrest can't be raised high enough for someone over six feet tall. • Engine hesitates when accelerating. • Many reports of vehicle suddenly stalling in traffic. • Ignition coil failure also causes engine to stall and backfire. • Flexible hose line from fuel pump rests against sharp metal edge of the heat shield. • Trunk popped open while driving. • Excessive wind noise enters the interior. **1998–99**—Automatic transmission and electrical system failures. **2000–01**—Airbag malfunctions. • Sudden electrical shutdown. • Chronic stalling. • Exhaust/gas fumes in the interior. • Automatic transmission failure. • Hard, noisy shifting. • Excessive vehicle vibration while underway. • Front control arm breakage. • Horn is hard to access. • Blurred windshield and annoying dash reflection onto the windshield. • Tires mounted on aluminum wheels tend to leak air. • Vehicle wanders or floats on the highway. • Heater gives out insufficient heat. • Automatic trunk flys up and falls down on one's head. • Headlight switch overheats. **Bonneville: 2000–01**—Battery located in the back of the rear seat went bad, causing sulfuric acid fumes to escape into the passenger compartment, making passengers ill. • Weak spring design allowed trunk lid to fall on person's head, causing injury. • Automatic trunk lid flies up and then comes down on driver's head. **LeSabre: 2000–01**—Under-hood fire erupted as driver was parking car. • When the fuel tank is full, fuel leaks from the top. • False airbag deployment injured driver. • Airbag deployment when key inserted into the ignition. • Airbag failed to deploy in an accident. • Sudden, unintended acceleration. • Many complaints of sudden stalling while driving on the highway. • Car stalled because fuel lines leaked. • Cruise control cable disconnects from cruise control module, jamming the accelerator cable to full throttle. • Accelerator cable popped out of its bracket, causing vehicle to go to full throttle. • Brake pedal went all the way to the floor due to missing brake shaft retainer clip. • When applying brakes, pedal becomes very hard, resulting in extended stopping distance. • Sudden steering loss. • Excessive highway wander. • Shoulder belt crosses at driver's neck. • Hard-to-read speedometer. •

Difficulty seeing dashboard controls due to dash-top design. • A reflection in the windshield coming from the dashboard obstructs view. • ABS and service light come on for no reason. • Engine head gasket failure. • Intermittent windshield wiper failure. • Horn is hard to operate, unless driver balled her hand into a fist and pounded on it. • Water leaks into interior through the dash. • Headlight design creates a shadow, impeding visibility. **Monte Carlo: 1995–2001**—Under-hood fires. • Airbag deployment caused driver's shirt to catch on fire. • Side airbag flap material falls off, leaving a large hole. • Side airbag falls out of its mounting. • Extremely poor wet traction. • Chronic stalling. • Frequent loss of braking and premature rotor warpage and pad wearout. • Although GM TSB asks dealers to re-weld the subframe engine cradle, owners say the fix isn't effective. • Early fuel pump and water pump failures. •Vehicle rolls downhill when parked on an incline. • Dash gauges go haywire from chronic electrical shorts. • Check Engine, ABS, and airbag lights stay lit despite dealers' best troubleshooting attempts. • Shoulder belt crosses at neck and seatbelts don't retract properly. • Horn is hard to access.

Secret Warranties/Service Tips/TSBs

Keep in mind that some of the following service bulletins may apply to more than one model and to subsequent model years. **All models: 1988–96**—Frequent reports of wind noise affecting the 1990–96 Cutlass, Grand Prix, and Regal and the 1988–94 Lumina have led to the publication of TSB #53-15-16, which outlines the causes of and remedies for persistent wind noise. **1991–97**—Bulletin #83-20-06 outlines procedures for fixing prematurely rusted door bottoms. **1992–94**—A front-end engine knock troubleshooting chart is found in TSB #306001. • Water leaking from the doors into the passenger compartment has a number of causes and remedies, according to TSB #431003. **1993–94**—Knocking from the accessory drive belt tensioner requires an upgraded replacement. • Owners who complain of automatic transmission low-speed miss, hesitation, chuggle, or skip may find relief with an improved MEMCAL module. **1993–99**—Odours can be eliminated by using a coil coating kit. • A rotten-egg odour coming from the exhaust is probably caused by a malfunctioning catalytic converter (covered by the emissions warranty). • Paint delamination, peeling, or fading (see Part Two). **1994–98**—A cold engine tick or rattle heard shortly after start-up may be fixed by replacing the piston/pin assembly. • A front suspension scrunch or pop may be silenced by merely installing a jounce washer. **1995–96**—Diagnosis and repair for wind noise around front and rear doors. **1995–97**—Intermittent Neutral/loss of Drive at highway speeds can be fixed by replacing the control valve body assembly. **1995–2001**—Troubleshooting engine oil pan leaks. **1996**—Second-gear starts; poor 1–3 shifting. • Steering column noise. • Air conditioning odours and diagnosis of AC noises. • Whistle noise from HVAC. • Diagnosis and correction of fluttering, popping, ticking, and clunking noises. • Popping

noise from the front of the vehicle when turning. **1997**—AC flutter or
moan. • Cold-start rattle. • Engine cranks but will not run. • Engine oil
leak at oil pan sealing flange and rear of engine near flywheel cover. •
Engine oil level indicates over-full. • Excessive vibration of elec-
trochromic mirror. • High beams are intermittent. • Inoperative power
door locks. • Intermittent Neutral/loss of Drive at highway speeds. •
Instrument panel buzzes and rattles when the brakes are applied. •
Popping or thump noise from the left rear of vehicle is normal,
according to GM. • Transmission gear whine at 40–70 km/h. **1997–98**—A
rough-running engine may be fixed by merely changing the plug wires.
1997–99—A low-speed steering shudder or vibration may be corrected
by replacing the steering pressure and return lines with revised "tuned"
hoses. • Front disc pads have been upgraded to reduce brake squeal. • A
shaking sensation at cruising speed may be fixed by replacing the transmission mount. **1997–2000**—Front disc brake pulsation will be corrected
by installing upgraded pads and rotors, says TSB #00-05-23-002 (see bulletin below). **1998**—A wet right rear floor signals the need to reseal the
stationary glass area. • Engine runs rough. • Power-steering shudder and
vibration. • Front suspension scrunch/pop. • Reducing AC odours. •
Inaccurate speedometer. **1998–99**—Power-steering shudder/vibration
may be fixed by replacing the pressure pipe/hose assembly. **1999–2000**—
No Third and Fourth gear may mean the direct clutch piston assembly
needs to be replaced. • An engine that runs hot, overheats, or loses
coolant may only need an upgraded radiator cap (check this before
authorizing any expensive repairs). **2000–01**—TSB #01-06-01-005 allows
for free 3.1L engine piston replacement to cure an engine ticking noise. •
Reduced AC performance; AC makes a tick-tock noise. • Eliminating an
air vent whistling noise or a steering vibration, shudder, or moan.
2001—Remedies for delayed automatic transmission shifts. **Cutlass and
Malibu: 1997–99**—Front disc brake pulsation will be corrected by
installing upgraded pads and rotors, says TSB #00-05-23-002. Another
bulletin outlines under what conditions repair will be done for free (see
following bulletin).

Bulletin No.: 00-05-22-002 February, 2000
Brake Rotor Warranty Service Procedure

Models:

1995-2000 Passenger Cars and Light Duty Trucks

The following are examples of pulsation conditions and reimbursement recommendations:

1. If a customer noticed the condition after 4800-11300 kilometers (300-7000 miles) and it gradually
   got worse, normally the repair would be covered. The customer may tolerate the condition until
   it becomes apparent.
2. If a customer indicated that they had wheel service, ask who performed the service.
   Then:
   If a dealer performed the service, consider paying for the repair and then strongly reinforce the
   use of torque sticks at that dealer. Two common size torque sticks cover 90% of all GM products.
   Each technician needs to use torque sticks properly every time the wheel nuts are tightened.

> If the customer had the wheel service done outside of our dealer network, normally GM would not offer any assistance.
>
> Customer assistance concerning brake pulsation and brake wear should always take into account the individual circumstances on a case by case basis. The recommendations previously should only be used a s a general guide. REMEMBER THAT CUSTOMER SATISFACTION IS CRITICAL TO GM AND THAT OFTEN IT IS IN GM'S BEST INTEREST TO SATISFY AND EDUCATE THE CUSTOMER CONCERNING FUTURE BRAKE SERVICE.

GM's guidelines for free brake vibration/pulsation repairs can be extrapolated to other models, as well.

Bonneville, Cutlass, Cutlass Supreme, Delta 88, Grand Prix, Intrigue, LeSabre, Lumina, Malibu, Monte Carlo, Regal Profile

	1994	1995	1996	1997	1998	1999	2000	2001
Cost Price ($)								
Bonneville	25,298	28,175	29,440	31,175	33,255	29,000	30,740	32,065
Cutlass Supreme	21,398	24,310	25,285	26,355	—	—	—	—
Delta 88 LSS	25,598	28,320	30,190	32,185	32,950	32,515	—	—
Grand Prix	22,098	24,555	23,940	26,305	26,035	27,489	28,050	28,110
Intrigue	—	—	—	—	27,998	27,994	28,365	28,450
LeSabre	25,498	28,235	29,560	32,370	33,100	28,845	30,465	32,120
Lumina	19,898	20,730	21,455	22,340	22,980	23,074	—	—
Malibu	—	—	—	19,995	20,595	20,895	22,050	22,495
Monte Carlo	—	22,578	23,625	24,275	24,895	24,715	26,090	26,165
Regal	21,898	20,060	25,035	27,795	28,410	27,695	29,120	28,895
Used Values ($)								
Bonneville Λ	5,500	7,000	9,500	11,000	14,500	17,500	19,500	23,000
Bonneville V	4,000	5,500	7,000	9,000	12,000	15,000	17,000	21,000
Cutlass Supreme Λ	4,500	6,000	8,000	10,000	—	—	—	—
Cutlass Supreme V	3,500	5,000	6,000	8,000	—	—	—	—
Delta 88 LSS Λ	5,500	7,500	9,500	12,500	15,000	18,000	—	—
Delta 88 LSS V	4,500	6,000	7,500	10,000	13,000	16,000	—	—
Grand Prix Λ	4,000	7,000	8,000	10,500	12,000	13,000	18,500	21,000
Grand Prix V	3,500	5,000	6,500	9,000	10,500	10,500	16,500	18,500
Intrigue Λ	—	—	—	—	13,000	15,500	17,500	20,500
Intrigue V	—	—	—	—	11,500	13,000	15,500	18,000
LeSabre Λ	6,000	8,000	9,000	12,000	15,000	17,500	19,500	23,000
LeSabre V	5,000	6,000	7,000	9,500	12,000	15,000	17,000	21,000
Lumina Λ	4,500	5,500	6,500	8,000	10,500	12,500	—	—
Lumina V	4,000	4,500	5,500	6,000	8,000	10,000	—	—
Malibu Λ	—	—	—	8,000	9,500	11,500	13,500	15,500
Malibu V	—	—	—	6,000	8,000	10,000	11,500	14,000
Monte Carlo Λ	—	6,500	7,500	10,500	12,500	15,000	17,000	19,500
Monte Carlo V	—	5,500	6,000	9,000	11,000	13,000	15,000	18,000
Regal Λ	5,500	7,000	8,000	11,000	13,000	16,000	18,500	21,000
Regal V	4,500	5,000	6,000	9,000	11,000	14,000	16,000	19,000

Extended Warranty	Y	Y	Y	Y	Y	Y	N	N
Secret Warranty	Y	Y	Y	Y	Y	Y	Y	N
Reliability	❶	❷	❷	③	③	③	③	③
Crash Safety								
Bonneville 4d	⑤	⑤	⑤	⑤	⑤	—	—	④
Cutlass 4d	—	—	—	—	—	④	④	—
Cutlass Supreme 2d	—	—	④	—	—	—	—	—
Cutlass Supreme 4d	④	—	—	—	—	—	—	—
Delta 88 4d	—	—	④	—	—	—	—	—
Grand Prix 2d	④	④	—	—	—	—	—	—
Grand Prix 4d	—	—	—	④	—	—	—	④
Intrigue	—	—	—	—	④	④	④	—
LeSabre 4d	—	—	—	④	④	④	—	—
Lumina 4d	④	—	⑤	⑤	④	④	—	④
Malibu	—	—	—	④	④	④	—	④
Monte Carlo	—	④	④	④	—	—	—	⑤
Regal 2d	—	—	④	—	—	—	—	—
Regal 4d	④	—	—	—	—	④	—	④
Side Impact								
Intrigue	—	—	—	—	—	—	—	③
Lumina	—	⑤	⑤	⑤	⑤	⑤	—	⑤
Malibu	—	—	—	❶	❶	❶	—	❷
Monte Carlo	—	④	④	④	—	—	—	③
Regal 4d	—	—	—	—	③	③	③	③
Off-set								
Bonneville 4d	—	—	—	—	—	—	⑤	⑤
Cutlass 4d	—	—	—	③	③	③	—	—
Grand Prix 4d	—	—	—	③	③	③	③	③
Intrigue	—	—	—	—	③	③	③	③
LeSabre 4d	—	—	—	—	—	—	⑤	⑤
Lumina 4d	—	⑤	⑤	⑤	⑤	⑤	⑤	⑤
Malibu (F)	—	—	—	❷	—	❷	—	❷
Malibu (Rear)	—	—	—	—	—	❶	—	❶
Regal 4d	—	—	—	③	③	③	③	③
Head restraints								
Intrigue	—	—	—	—	—	❶	—	❶
LeSabre 4d	—	❶	—	❶	—	—	④	④
Lumina	—	❶	—	❶	—	❶	—	—
Malibu (F)	—	—	—	❷	—	❷	—	❷
Malibu (Rear)	—	—	—	—	—	❶	—	❶
Monte Carlo	—	—	—	❶	❶	❶	—	—
Regal 4d	—	❶	—	—	—	❶	—	❶
Rollover Resistance								
Lumina 4d	—	—	—	—	—	—	—	④
Monte Carlo	—	—	—	—	—	—	—	④

CENTURY, CIERA

RATING: Average (1998–2001); Below Average (1997); Not Recommended (1982–96). In the early years, the same failure-prone components were used year after year. The 1996 Century isn't in the same league as the revised 1997 version, which adopted the W platform used by the Chevrolet Lumina, Pontiac Grand Prix, and 1998 Oldsmobile Intrigue. A 1996 Ciera is cheaper, but you won't have the important mechanical and body upgrades offered by its 1998 replacement, the '98 Oldsmobile Cutlass. The new Cutlass is an upgraded mid-sized sedan similar to the new Malibu (be careful not to confuse the new Cutlass with the Cutlass Supreme, a 10-year-old model that was replaced by the Intrigue, which is equipped like the Century). **Maintenance/Repair costs:** Higher than average, but repairs aren't dealer dependent. **Parts:** Higher-than-average cost (independent suppliers sell for much less), but not hard to find. Nevertheless, don't even think about buying one of these front-drives without a three- to five-year comprehensive warranty. **Best alternatives:** The Acura Integra; GM Cavalier or Sunfire (Sunbird); Honda Accord; Hyundai Elantra wagon, Sonata, or Tiburon; Mazda 626 or Protegé; Nissan Sentra or Stanza; and Toyota Camry.

Strengths and weaknesses: The A-body line, long a mainstay in GM's family sedan market, has disappeared. This is good news, because these cars are outclassed by the competition and are in desperate need of high-quality components and fresher styling. Overall quality has improved somewhat since the introduction of these cars in 1982, but with the arrival of better quality Japanese imports, these derivatives of the X-bodies aren't really in the running.

Nevertheless, these cars were consistently popular with fleet buyers and car rental agencies because they were useful as comfortable family sedans and wagons. Handling and other aspects of road performance varied considerably depending on the suspension and powertrain chosen.

1988–96 models are particularly unreliable. The 2.5L 4-cylinder engine suffers from engine-block cracking and a host of other serious defects. The 2.8L V6 engine hasn't been durable either; it suffers from premature camshaft wear and leaky gaskets and seals, especially the intake manifold gasket. The 3-speed automatic transmission is weak and the 4-speed automatic frequently malfunctions. Temperamental and expensive-to-replace fuel systems (including the in-tank fuel pump) afflict all models/years, causing chronic stalling, hard starting, and poor fuel economy (use the emissions warranty as leverage to get compensation). Fuel system diagnosis and repair for the 3.0L V6 are difficult, and the electronic controls are often defective. Air conditioners frequently malfunction and the cooling system is prone to leaks.

Prematurely worn power-steering assemblies are particularly common-place. Brakes are weak and need frequent attention due to premature wear and dangerously rapid corrosion; front brake rotors warp easily; excessive pulsation is common; and rear brake drums often lock up, particularly when damp. Shock absorbers and springs wear out quickly. Rear wheel alignment should be checked often. Electric door locks frequently malfunction. Water leaks onto carpeting. Premature and extensive surface rust—due to poor paint application, delamination, and defective materials—is common for all years. Far more disturbing are scattered reports of severe undercarriage/suspension rusting, possibly making the vehicles unsafe to drive—and costing lots of money to correct, as the owner of a 1990 Century relates:

> Recently I was doing an oil change on my car and I noticed a small divot in the engine cradle (or sub frame). I poked at it and put my finger right through it! I discovered that the cradle was rotted on both sides near the idler arm. The car is only 8 years old and has only 112,000 km on it. I have had it into two collision repair places and they both said they have never seen a rotted engine cradle. One man has been in the business 25 years!

The 1997 Century received a complete make-over that includes the following: a spunkier 160-hp 3.1L V6 engine; gobs of room and trunk space (rivaling that of the Taurus, Concorde, Accord, and Camry); sleeker styling; a much quieter interior; and an upgraded, standard ABS system that produces minimal pedal pulsation. Engine noise was also reduced, although insufficient firewall insulation means a considerable amount of noise still gets into the interior. Other new features include upgraded door seals, steering-wheel-mounted radio controls, and additional heating ducts for rear passengers. '98 models come with reduced-force airbags; '99 versions offer a revised ABS system, better traction control, and an enhanced suspension to reduce body roll. Year 2000 models were given a small horespower boost, and the 2001s returned unchanged.

On the downside, the post-'96 Century's speed-dependent power steering is too light and vague, and its suspension and handling are more tuned to comfort than performance. Engine intake manifolds have a short lifespan (covered by a 6-year/100,000 km warranty). The Century's front air deflector shield has also been the object of many complaints. Its low placement causes the shield to hit the roadway whenever passing over a small dip or bump. Furthermore, the bumper pulls off when passing over parking blocks.

Overall reliability has improved considerably over the past five years. Although fit and finish are still subpar, particulary when compared with the Japanese competition, powertrain dependability is pretty good.

Safety summary: All models: 1996—Vehicle suddenly accelerated on its own. • Cruise control speed increases upon descending a hill. • Sudden brake loss. • Chronic stalling. • Oxygen sensor failures believed to be cause of stalling problems. • Steering radius is too large, and steering response is sluggish. • Dash reflection in windshield causes poor visibility. • Cannot read clock in daylight. • Airbag assembly on steering wheel blocks view of instrument panel. • Back windows often shatter. • Frequent battery failures. • Fuel pump failures. • Transmission failures. • Gearshift lever fell off in driver's hand. • Front door power motors failed. **1997**—Sudden brake loss. • Car moved forward when put into Reverse. • Battery exploded twice. • Poor design of magnetic variable steering results in difficult handling, with vehicle swaying at 60 km/h, and struts contributing to instability. • Sway bar links failure. • Horn buttons difficult to access and depress due to their small size; must take eyes off the road. • Fuel tank warning system activates prematurely. • Dash reflection in windshield causes poor visibility. • Poor headlight design makes for poor visibility, as well. • Defroster system button breaks easily. • Windshield wipers fail frequently. • Defective airbag cover. • Power door lock failures. • Driver's seatbelt won't fully retract. **1998**—Airbags failed to deploy. • Idle surge after releasing brake due to faulty oxygen sensor. • Leaking lower intake manifold. • Engine oil pan leakage. • Chronic stalling. • Transmission shifts erratically. • Transmission hard to put into Reverse; faulty gearshift lever. • Sudden loss of electrical power. • Climate control switch failures. • Dash reflection on windshield causes poor visibility. • Excessive brake vibrations. • Headlights provide poor visibility. • Headlight switch failure. • Windshield wiper arm failures. • Water leaks into trunk. • Drivers report that the head restraints don't stay up. • Horn buttons hard to access in an emergency because of the airbag located directly under the horn and the radio control on the steering wheel. • Horn blows on its own when car is not running. **1999**—Airbags failed to deploy in a collision. • Engine fire upon startup. • Chronic engine hesitation when accelerating or changing gears. • Vehicle suddenly accelerated when brakes were applied. • Sudden, unintended acceleration once car was underway. • Cruise control failed to disengage. • Premature transmission failure: won't go into Reverse; shift lever hangs up; Drive gear won't hold vehicle when stopped on an incline. • Seatbelt trapped child around waist; had to be cut free. • Dash and seatcover reflect upon the windshield. • Front right window suddenly exploded. • Horn isn't loud enough, and "sweet" spot to sound horn is hard to locate. • Headlights are too dim and have a narrow beam. • Front seat headrests won't stay in the raised position. • Tire jack won't hold vehicle's weight. **2000**—Sudden, unintended acceleration. • Engine replaced twice. • Transmission has a tendency to shift often, whether it's necessary or not. • Engine produces a metallic noise. • If vehicle is driven with the windows down, there is a loud, shaking noise and the vehicle vibrates violently. • Steering wheel heats up when the radio and headlights are on. • Horn is hard to access. • Driver's seat leans to the side. • Large head restraints block vision. • Low beams don't illuminate the highway adequately; the light spreads only to the side end of the front fender, resulting in poor visibility. • Air scoop/spoiler hits or scrapes the ground. • If vehicle is parked on uneven ground, the doors stick due to body flexing. • Driver-side window suddenly exploded, as from decompression, while underway. • Wipers can't be aligned. 2001—Brakes failed. • Airbags failed to deploy. • Dash continues to reflect onto windshield. • Horn is hard to access. • Headlights don't illuminate the roadway sufficiently. • Transmission won't hold vehicle parked on an incline. • Cannot drive car with rear windows down due to the air pressure hurting eardrum.

Secret Warranties/Service Tips/TSBs

All models: 1992–97—Troubleshooting a grinding or growling noise that occurs when vehicle is parked on an incline. **1993–99**—A rotten-egg odour coming from the exhaust is probably the result of a malfunctioning catalytic converter; replacement cost may be covered by the emissions warranty. • Eliminate AC odours by installing an evaporator cooling coil coating kit. • Paint delamination, peeling, or fading (see Part Two). **1993–2002**—GM has an AC odour kit that keeps odours out of the AC system. **1994–95**—TSB #43-81-29 troubleshoots cruise controls that fail to engage. **1995–97**—Intermittent Neutral/loss of Drive at highway speeds can be fixed by replacing the control valve body assembly. **1997**—Rear brake clicking or squealing may be caused by a maladjusted parking brake cable. • Insufficient heater performance on the passenger-side floor area can be fixed by installing a new I/P insulator panel and bracket. **2001**—Delayed automatic transmission shifting (see following bulletin).

A/T - 4T65E, Delayed Shifts/Flares/Extended Shifts

Bulletin No.: 01-07-30-014   Date: April, 2001
Technical
Subject:
4T65-E Transmission Delayed Shifts, Slips, Flares or Extended Shifts During Cold Operation (Replace Shift Solenoid Valve Assembly)
Models:

2001 Buick Century, LeSabre, Park Avenue, Regal
2001 Chevrolet Impala, Lumina, Monte Carlo, Venture
2001 Oldsmobile Aurora, Intrigue, Silhouette
2001 Pontiac Aztek, Bonneville, Grand Prix, Montana
with 4T65-E Automatic Transmission (RPOs MN3, MN7, M76, M15)

Condition:

Some owners may comment on one of several delayed shifts, slips, flares or exteneded shifts during cold operation. These symptoms can affect the 1-2 shift only. The transmission won't shift out of 1st gear until the temperature is high enough to unstick the solenoid. This condition can last up to several shift patterns. These symptoms can return after the vehicle sits, usually 6 hours or more.

Century: 1994–98—A cold engine tick or rattle heard shortly after start-up may be fixed by replacing the piston/pin assembly. 1997–99—A low-speed steering shudder or vibration may be corrected by replacing the steering pressure and return lines with revised "tuned" hoses. • Front disc pads have been upgraded to reduce brake squeal. • A shaking sensation at cruising speed may be fixed by replacing the transmission mount. • TSB #00-03-06-001 gives a comprehensive listing of common front-end noises and what's needed to silence them. • Install a new steering wheel inflatable restraint module to make it easier to sound the horn. • Installing an upgraded low level fuel sensor will fix a fluctuating fuel gauge. 1997–2001—Binding automatic transmission shift lever (see following bulletin).

A/T - Difficult Shift Lever Operation

Bulletin No.: 01-07-30-017 Date: April, 2001
Technical
Subject: Transmission Shift Lever is Difficult to Move
(Replace Shift Lever)
Models:
1997-2001 Buick Century
Condition:
Some owners may comment that the transmission range selector lever is difficult to move/shift.
Cause:
The original shift lever may not impart enough mechanical advantage on the shift linkage to provide low enough effort when shifting gears.

1998—A wet right rear floor signals the need to reseal the stationary glass area. 1998–99—Poor AM reception on vehicles with a windshield-mounted antenna may be improved by installing an in-line antenna jumper. 1999–2000—Simply changing the radiator cap may cure your hot-running engine and prevent coolant loss. 2000–01—GM's TSB says the best way to eliminate an engine ticking noise is to replace the engine's pistons (covered by a secret warranty, of course).

Century, Ciera Profile

	1994	1995	1996	1997	1998	1999	2000	2001
Cost Price ($)								
Century	20,398	23,080	23,820	24,545	25,215	25,199	25,570	25,200
Ciera S/SL	20,598	22,960	23,625	—	—	—	—	—
Used Values ($)								
Century ʌ	5,500	7,000	8,500	10,500	12,500	14,500	17,000	19,500
Century v	4,500	5,000	6,500	8,500	10,000	13,000	15,000	17,500
Ciera S/SL ʌ	4,000	6,000	7,500	—	—	—	—	—
Ciera S/SL v	3,500	4,500	6,000	—	—	—	—	—

Extended Warranty	Y	Y	Y	Y	N	N	N	N
Secret Warranty	Y	Y	Y	Y	Y	Y	Y	Y
Reliability	❷	❷	❷	❷	③	③	③	③
Crash Safety								
Century 4d	④	④	④	④	④	—	—	④
Ciera	—	④	—	—	—	—	—	—
Side Impact (Century 4d)	—	—	—	—	—	—	③	③
Off-set	—	—	—	③	③	③	③	③
Head Restraints (F)	—	❶	—	❶	—	❶	—	❷
Rear	—	—	—	—	—	—	—	❶

Honda

ACCORD   ★★★★★

RATING: Recommended (2000–01); Above Average (1990–99); Average (1985–89). With the 16-valve 4-cylinder engine or V6, the Accord is one of the most versatile compacts you can find. It offers something for everyone, and its high resale value means there's no way you can lose money buying one. Unfortunately, the car has racked up an unusually large number of safety- and performance-related complaints. They include reports of sudden acceleration and stalling, brake failures, and airbag malfunctions that cause the devices to go off when they shouldn't and not deploy when they should. Also be wary of Honda's servicing and sales practices; they're not of the same caliber as Honda's products. **Maintenance/Repair costs:** Lower than average. Repairs aren't dealer dependent. **Parts:** Higher-than-average cost, but they can easily be found for much less from independent suppliers. **Best alternatives:** The Acura Integra; Hyundai Elantra wagon, Sonata, or Tiburon; Mazda 626; Nissan Altima; and Toyota Camry.

Strengths and weaknesses: The Accord doesn't really excel in any particular area; it's just very, very good at everything. It's smooth, quiet, mannerly, and competent, with outstanding fit and finish, inside and out. Every time Honda redesigned the line, it not only caught up with the latest advances, but went slightly ahead. Strong points are comfort, fit and finish, ergonomics, impressive assembly quality, reliability, and driveability. Some of its weak points: insufficient torque with the base engine makes for constant highway downshifting; the automatic transmission tends to shift harshly and slowly; rear passenger room is tight; and the aforementioned safety-related complaints reported to NHTSA.

Despite all the foregoing praise, this hasn't always been a great car. During the '80s, Accords were beset with severe premature rusting, frequent engine camshaft and crankshaft failures, and severe front brake problems. Engines leaked or burned oil and blew their cylinder head gaskets easily, and carbureted models suffered from driveability problems through 1986.

If left untreated, rust perforations develop unusually quickly. Especially vulnerable spots are front fender seams; door bottoms; and areas surrounding side-view mirrors, door handles, rocker panels, wheel openings, windshield posts, front cowls, and trunk and hatchback lids.

1990–93 models got more room (stepping up to the mid-sized car niche) and additional power through a new and quieter 2.2L 4-cylinder engine. Nevertheless, rear seating space remains inadequate, the added weight saps the car's performance, and the automatic transmission shifts harshly at times. Owners report prematurely worn automatic transmissions, constant velocity joints, and power-steering assemblies. Poor quality control in the choice of body trim and assembly leads to numerous air and water leaks.

Redesigned again for the 1994 model year, the Accord continues to add interior room and other refinements. However, the addition of the V6 powerplant in the 1995 model year gives the Accord plenty of power in reserve without the high rpms. The automatic transmission still works poorly with the 4-banger, producing acceleration times that are far from impressive, and owners still complain of excessive road noise and tire whine. Nevertheless, no significant reliability problems have been reported with that redesign. 1996 models were slightly re-styled, the trunk opening was enlarged, and a rear-seat pass-through feature increased cargo space. Although the '97s were carried over unchanged, the '98 Accord was substantially reworked. Notable changes: no more wagon version, more powerful 6- and 8-cylinder engines, a more refined suspension and automatic transaxle, upgraded ABS, additional interior space, and more glass. The '99s were mostly carried over unchanged, except for standard ABS on the LX. Side airbags are standard with all V6-equipped 2000 models, and the all-dressed SE was introduced later that model year. 2001 models got a re-styled exterior, upgraded airbags, and improved soundproofing.

Confidential technical service bulletins show that the 1994–97 models are susceptible to AC malfunctions, engine oil leaks, Check Engine light coming on for no reason, transmission glitches, power-steering pump leaks, windows falling off their channels, and numerous air and water leaks. Usually, these problems are simple to repair and Honda customer relations staff are helpful; however, Honda staffers and dealers are reluctant to admit their mistakes and may be getting a bit too arrogant in their dealings with the public. Witness the company's failure to publicly disclose its 1994–97 engine oil leak problems over the past seven years and its delay in setting up a free repair program until the end of 2000. Honda has also asked that ALLDATA no longer share Honda service bulletin information with owners. Yet these service bulletins help owners and independent garages to quickly zero in on a problem without wasting time and money. One *Lemon-Aid* reader wrote the following:

> We returned the car to the dealer several times (at least six) to have the doors adjusted to reduce wind noise affecting my 1994 Accord LX sedan. They were finally able to reduce the noise a small amount. A letter written to Honda explaining our dissatisfaction with the car resulted in a response letter with very definite "screw you" overtones.

In another email posting that reinforces owner comments I've received over the past few years, a 2000 Accord owner had praise for his car but felt that Honda's sales practices and servicing were subpar:

> I have been buying new Honda Accords since 1987 and the car just keeps getting better but the service and dealer ethics just keep getting worse.
>
> When I bought my latest 2000 Accord the dealer wouldn't budge from the MRSP but threw in a "free" cruise to make the deal.... I have been trying to collect on this free cruise for a year, but the only way to retrieve your money is to buy a cruise at an inflated price.
>
> As part of the deal, I also ordered the Keyless Accessory feature that the salesman showed me in the Honda brochure. Several months after numerous complaints the dealer finally admitted they had farmed this work out to a one-man shop who installed a $100.00 system even though I was charged the Honda accessory price. In reviewing my service bills, I actually discovered that they had doctored the documentation to pretend it was a Honda System. All they have done for me is to have this piece of junk replaced 3 times; who knows what my wiring harness looks like by now.
>
> The regular warranty service has also been a rip-off, being charged at least 3 times what the work was actually worth. I have since discovered that I can apparently get the work done at an independent garage at a fraction of the price (what would we do without the internet?).
>
> I have written 3 letters to Honda Canada complaining about the dealer with only one response that basically said that they don't care how their dealers carry on their business as long as they sell cars, have a nice day but quit bothering us.
>
> The lesson to be learned in all of this for both Honda and potential Honda customers is that just because Honda is a great car don't expect the service to match the product. In fact, the service can be quite lousy because the cars sell themselves regardless of what the dealer does or doesn't do.

Bulletins and owner complaints relating to the reworked 1998–2000 models show a surprisingly large number of factory-related powertrain and body defects, undoubtedly due to the Accord's redesign. Some of those deficiencies, affecting both safety and performance: chronic lurching, hesitation, and stalling while on the highway, accompanied by the Check Engine light coming on; hard starting; frequent transmission failures; poor tracking that allows vehicle to wander; defective rear-computerized motor mounts; electrical shorts; coolant and brake master cylinder leakage; ABS and AC failures; poor radio reception.

Body and accessory problems for these same model years include a plethora of squeaks, creaks, groans, and rattles; wind noise; water leaks; fuel gauge defects; paint chipping, bubbling and peeling on hood, trunk, and roof (Honda blames it on bird droppings); leaky sunroof; windshield with vertical lines of distortion; driver-side mirror that shakes excessively; faulty fuel sending unit makes for inaccurate fuel readings (when full, indicates three-fourths full); speedometer off by 10 percent.

2001 models have generated fewer complaints, partly because they haven't been on the market that long; nevertheless, owners report that sudden, unintended acceleration remains a serious problem and can occur at any time, as the owner of this 2001 Accord relates:

While taking the car through a car wash, vehicle accelerated and ran into two other cars and through a fence.

Other performance-related problems include automatic transmission breakdowns, expensive and frequent servicing of the brake rotors and pads, and electrical glitches.

Safety summary: All models: 1995—Rear seatbelt buckle has insufficient slack, preventing buckle from latching. • Airbag warning light stays on. • Excessive windshield glare. • AC failure. • Headlight failure. • Cruise control malfunctions. • Premature front/rear brake wear. **1995–96**—Faulty power windows. • Brake failures/lockup. • Airbag failed to deploy or deployed accidentally. • Injury from airbag. • Sudden acceleration, stalling. • Passenger-side seatbacks won't stay upright. **1996**—Front passenger seatbelt locks up. • The door lock design gives a boost to thieves. • The Check Engine light is always on. • The defroster could be faulty. • Faulty power door locks. • The steering column separates from the shaft. **1997**—Airbags failed to deploy. • Inadvertent airbag deployment. • Fire caused by faulty wiring harness. • Sudden acceleration while braking. • Cruise control doesn't accelerate properly and won't downshift the transmission. • Transmission shifted into Reverse and vehicle moved forward. • ABS brakes lock up. • Sudden brake failure. • Location of the oil filter allows oil to leak onto the exhaust system and catalytic converter. • Faulty brake master cylinder. • All four front brake pads cracked right down the centre. • Power-steering fluid leakage. • Oil plug fell off into the oil pan and sprayed oil everywhere. • Left side seatbelt fails to retract. • Seatbelt tightened and locked up; occupant had to cut belt. • Seatbelt continually ratchets tighter. • When sun visor is opened, it blocks driver's vision due to its large size. • Check Engine light stays on continually. • Defroster fails to defrost side windows, and actually causes them to fog up. • Power windows fail to operate properly in cold weather. • Door continually out of adjustment. **1998**—Sudden acceleration while vehicle stopped in traffic. • Sudden acceleration occurred when vehicle hit from the rear. • Chronic stalling. • ABS brake light comes on continually. • Gas and brake pedals are too close together and often get pressed at the same time. • Airbag failed to deploy. • Frequent brake failures. • Sudden brake lockup. • Brake master cylinder failures. • Floormat bunches under the brake pedal. • Engine oil leakage. • Power-steering fluid leakage, causing sudden loss of steering control. • Vehicle rolled back when parked. • Automatic transmission gears disengage and make a loud noise when engaging. • Transmission fails to engage at slow speeds. • Transmission fails to fully lock up in Overdrive. • Transmission hunts for the right gear. • Clutch pedal failure. • Automatic transmission parking mechanism failure. • Due to design of dashboard lights, it's hard to read odometer, digital clock, and radio indicator. • Can't see high beam indicator light in the daytime. • Light tan dash reflects too much sunlight into the eyes. • Instrument panel lights are too bright at night and can't be dimmed enough. • To activate horn, driver must remove hand from steering wheel. • Fuel gauge shows two-thirds full when the gas tank is full, or indicates an empty tank with warning light on while five gallons (23 litres) remain in the tank. • Poor seatbelt design allows for belt to wrap around the release lever and get stuck, or causes seatback to suddenly recline. • Seatbelts get trapped underneath the seatback electric switch. • Seatbelts ratchet too tight, trapping occupants. • Rear passenger-side door won't unlock. • Sunroofs and headliners often need replacing. **1999–2000**—Airbags failed to deploy. • Over-sensitive airbag sensors caused airbags to deploy when bumper touched curb while parking. • Airbag deployment caused extensive neck and head injuries. • Sudden acceleration. • Gas and brake pedals placed too close together; foot easily slips off brake pedal. • Sudden brake loss. • Emergency brakes failed to hold on hill, allowing car to roll into lake. • Brake master cylinder leakage. • Driver's seatback suddenly fell back. • Steering knuckle broke while driving. • Bolt that holds the lower control arm assembly broke away from the frame, causing wheel to come out of fender. • Many complaints of chronic lurching, hesitation, and stalling while on the highway, accompanied by Check Engine light coming on (dealers can't duplicate the problem). • Sudden tire tread failures (Michelin MXV4). • Engine sputters at half throttle. • Hard starting. • Frequent transmission failures. • Vehicle doesn't track well; wanders all over the road. • Engine mount makes a clunking sound. • Defective rear-computerized motor mounts on '98 and '99 models. • Exhaust pipe runs under oil pan plug, causing dripped oil to burn off exhaust. • Seatbelts fail to retract or continually tighten up, choking occupant. • Right front passenger window exploded while driving. •

Windshield has vertical lines of distortion. • Driver-side mirror shakes excessively. **2001**—Excessive front end vibration and wandering over the highway. • Automatic transmission leaks and jerks into gear. • Airbag failed to deploy or deployed for no reason. • Rear stabilizer bar links broke. • Vehicle rolls back when stopped on an incline. • Complete brake loss. Check Engine and airbag lights remain lit. • Incorrect fuel gauge readings. • The front windshield has a UV protective coating that gives the windshield a wavy appearance.

Secret Warranties/Service Tips/TSBs

All models/years: Steering wheel shimmy is a frequent problem, and is taken care of in TSB #94-025. **All models: 1994–97**—Poor radio reception may be caused by a corroded coaxial connector. • If the AC doesn't blow cold air, consider replacing both the evaporator and the receiver/dryer. • Oil seepage from the engine block requires sealing and the installation of a new exhaust manifold bracket. • Acura CL and Honda Accord, Prelude, and Odyssey models equipped with 4-cylinder engines may have defective engine oil seals that can slip, causing the engine to drain of oil and eventually seize. Although Honda maintains this isn't a safety recall (hmm, sudden engine seizure on the highway, sounds scary to me), the company will, at no charge, inspect and replace the seal and install a clip to ensure the seal cannot move. • Power-steering pump fluid leakage requires a new O-ring. **1995**—TSB #95-017 shows which rear brake pads produce less noise and which ones last the longest. • Noise from the front passenger's footwell, exhaust system, and shoulder belt anchors. • Rear shelf buzz. • The dash panel and clutch pedal may creak. • Heater control indicators may not light. • A whistling or howling noise coming from the top of the windshield can be silenced by applying sealant under the upper windshield moulding. • Honda has developed an exhaust buzz silencing kit. **1995–96**—A creaking noise coming from the instrument panel can be silenced through a variety of measures outlined in a series of Honda bulletins. • Screeching noise when lowering the driver's window. • Seatbelt is slow to retract. **1996–97**—In a settlement with the U.S. Environmental Protection Agency, Honda paid fines totaling $17.1 million and extended its emissions warranty on 1.6 million 1995–97 models to 14 years/150,000 miles (240,000 km). See the Honda Civic rating for full details (page 125). **1997**—AC won't blow cold air. • Oil seepage from the engine block. • Torque converter won't lock up. • Fifth gear grinds during upshift. • Leak from the power-steering pump. • Rear wheel bearing noise. • Static when adjusting the radio volume. • Front door glass comes out of run channel. • Cracking paint on passenger-side airbag cover. • Missing alloy wheel center cap. **1998**—Trunk spoiler damages paint. • Creak from the rear shelf area, headliner, windshield, and rear window. • Front ABS wheel sensor harness rubs against wheel. • Rattle from rear stabilizer bar. • If the brake system indicator stays on, install an improved master cylinder reservoir cap float. • A flickering ceiling light may be caused by a poor ground contact in the switch. • An inaccurate fuel gauge must be replaced with an upgraded unit. • Tips on eliminating wind noise from the top of the front windshield and a creaking noise from the rear shelf, headliner and windshield area. • Coolant leakage from the radiator drain plug may require the replacement of the drain plug/O-ring assembly. • Rear door water leaks may be plugged simply by removing excess weather stripping. **1998–99**—A clutch pedal squeak or groan is likely due to insufficient lubrication of the piston cup seal. **1998–2000**—Manual transmission bangs in Reverse. • Warped, deformed windshield moulding. **1998–2001**—Tips on silencing a moon roof squeak (eligible for "goodwill" consideration). **1999**—Wrinkled rear door sash trim. • Glove box door rattles, wheels clicking, and clutch pedal and rear wheel bearing noise. • Loose AC, heater, temperature and fan control knobs. • Inaccurate fuel gauge. **1999–2000**—Automatic transmission vibration at low speeds requires an upgraded torque converter covered by the base warranty or by a "goodwill" program.

A/T - Vibration While Driving at Low Speeds

00-038   April 25, 2000

Applies To:

1999 Accord V6- 4-door from VIN 1HGCG1...XA050000 thru 1HGCG1...XA068508
                 2-door from VIN 1HGCG2...XA026000 thru 1HGCG2...XA033528
2000 Accord V6- 4-door from VIN 1HGCG1...YA000001 thru 1HGCG1...YA028000
                 2-door from VIN 1HGCG2...YA000001 thru 1HGCG2...YA006000

Vibration While Driving At Low Speeds

SYMPTOM

A shudder or judder when driving at speeds between 20 and 40 mph. This vibration is most noticeable when the torque converter lock-up clutch is in the partial lock-up mode.

PROBABLE CAUSE

Irregularities in the torque converter face prevent the lock-up clutch from smoothly engaging.

CORRECTIVE ACTION

Replace the torque converter.
Out of warranty: Any repair performed after warranty expiration may be eligible for goodwill consideration by the District Service Manager or our Zone Office. You must request consideration, and get a decision, before starting work.

Take note that Honda covers this five-hour repair under its "goodwill" policy even if your warranty has expired.

2000—Engine hard starts. • Coolant leaks from the water passage near the EGR valve. • PCM computer module needs to be recalibrated under warranty to prevent MIL (malfunction indicator light) from coming on for no reason. **2001**—Windshield hum or whine.

Accord Profile

	1994	1995	1996	1997	1998	1999	2000	2001
Cost Price ($)								
LX	18,695	19,795	20,295	20,995	23,800	23,800	23,000	22,800
EXi/EX	21,495	22,595	22,995	23,495	26,800	26,801	31,300	30,800
Used Values ($)								
LX Λ	6,500	8,000	9,500	11,500	14,000	16,000	18,500	20,000
LX V	5,000	6,000	8,000	10,000	12,000	14,000	17,000	18,000
EXi/EX Λ	7,500	9,000	11,000	13,000	16,000	18,500	24,000	27,000
EXi/EX V	6,000	7,500	9,500	11,000	14,000	16,500	22,000	25,000
Extended Warranty	N	N	N	N	N	N	N	N
Secret Warranty	Y	Y	Y	Y	Y	Y	Y	Y
Reliability	④	④	④	④	④	④	④	⑤
Crash Safety (2d)	—	—	—	④	④	④	—	⑤
4d	④	④	④	④	④	④	—	⑤
Side Impact (2d)	—	—	—	—	—	③	—	④
4d	—	—	—	❷	④	④	—	④
Off-set	③	③	③	③	③	③	③	③
Head Restraints (F)	—	❶	—	❷	③	③	—	③
Rear	—	—	—	❶	❷	❷	—	❷
Rollover Resistance	—	—	—	—	—	—	—	⑤

Hyundai

SONATA ★★★★

RATING: Above Average (1999–2001); Average (1995–98); Not Recommended (1986–93). The 1994 model year was skipped. These cars haven't registered one-tenth the number of safety complaints as the higher-rated Honda Accord. For maximum savings, I suggest you buy a 1996–99 version, with some of the original warranty left, plan to keep it at least five years to shake off the depreciation, and put some of the savings on the purchase price into a comprehensive supplementary warranty to protect yourself when the warranty ends. (I exclude the '95 version because it was the first year of its redesign.) **Maintenance/Repair costs:** Higher than average. Repairs aren't dealer dependent. **Parts:** Higher-than-average cost, and often back-ordered. **Best alternatives:** The Acura Integra, GM Cavalier or Sunfire, Honda Accord, Hyundai Elantra wagon or Tiburon, Mazda 626, Nissan Altima, and Toyota Camry.

Strengths and weaknesses: This mid-sized front-drive sedan was built under Mitsubishi licensing, but its overall reliability isn't anywhere near as good as what you'll find with Mitsubishi's cars and trucks sold in Canada under the Chrysler and Eagle monikers. Acceleration is impressive with the manual gearbox, but only passable with the automatic. Handling and performance are also fairly good, although emergency handling isn't confidence inspiring, particularly due to the imprecise steering and excessive lean when cornering. As with other Hyundai models, the automatic transmission performs erratically, the engine is noisy, and reliability is a problem—it's way below average for the 1989–93 models; the 1995–98 models are moderately improved (remember, Hyundai skipped the 1994s).

Redesigned for the 1995 model year, the car got additional interior room, more horsepower, and an upgraded automatic transmission. Nevertheless, acceleration with the automatic is still below average with the 4-banger, and the automatic gearbox downshifts slowly. (The manual transmission is still more reliable and fuel efficient.) 1996 model Sonatas came with more standard features, like air conditioning, power steering, a split-folding rear seatback, liquid-filled engine mounts, and additional sound deadening to make for a more comfortable ride. The 1997–98 versions returned virtually unchanged, but the '99 version arrived with a redesigned body and suspension, side airbags, two new engines, and a huge price increase that's not reflected in its resale value. Year 2000 models took on standard side airbags and larger wheels, while the following year's models got a new grille and additional standard features.

Throughout the Sonata's history, Hyundai technical service bulletins are replete with references to automatic transmissions that exhibit what Hyundai describes as "shift shock," as well as delayed shifting. In addition to the tranny problems, owners of pre-1995 models report poor engine performance (hard starting, poor idling, stalling); the engine runs hot, and when you're stopped at a traffic light, it shakes like a boiling kettle; #3 spark plug often needs replacing or cleaning; rough engine rattle; high oil consumption (one litre every two to three months); excessive front brake pulsation and premature wear; steering defects (when the steering wheel is turned to either extreme, it makes a sound like metal cracking); cruise control malfunctions and electrical short circuits; battery life of only 18 months; malfunctioning lights; radio failures; falling interior roof liner; faulty hood locks; rotten-egg smell coming from the catalytic converter; broken muffler; faulty resonator; defective exhaust pipe; poor door and window sealing (water leaking into the interior when the car is washed); and premature paint peeling and rusting.

The 1995–2001 Sonatas have elicited very few quality-control and safety complaints and represent the better buys in this group, following the '95 model's redesign. However, automatic transmissions, brakes, airbags, steering, and fuel- and electrical-system components still top the list of parts most vulnerable to premature failure or malfunctioning. Airbag and Check Engine lights are constantly lit, and fit and finish continue to be only average.

Safety summary: All models/years: Emergency handling leaves a lot to be desired. **All models: 1996**—Tire fell off car. • Battery blew up while car was idling. • Airbag light is continuously lit. • Brake malfunctions. • Chronic stalling, particularly when AC is engaged. • Frequent engine valve cover gasket failures. • Poor-quality spark plugs cause sluggish acceleration. • Check Engine light is lit continuously. • Frequent automatic transmission failures. • Water leaks from the front of the car. **1997**—Airbags fail to deploy. • Frequent engine failures. • Transmission gearshift will not stay in place. • Power window switch failed. **1998**—Frequent inadvertent airbag deployment. • Sudden transmission failure while driving. **1999**—Complete brake failure. • Airbag failed to deploy. • Airbag warning light comes on for no reason. • Sudden alternator failure causes entire vehicle to shut down. • Hyundai doesn't offer a seatbelt extension for large occupants. **2000**—Seatbelt extensions for large passengers weren't available. • Driver-side airbag deployed when driver slammed the door. • Airbag light stays lit, and corrective parts are on national back-order. • Sudden brake loss; brakes don't hold in a panic situation. • Warped front brake rotors produce excessive steering shimmy. • Stalls when in low gear or when decelerating (recall campaign didn't remedy the problem). • Power-steering leaks and early replacement. • Window often comes off its track. • Power window caught child's head and neck. • Headlights dim when AC engages. **2001**—Hood flew up and shattered windshield. • Engine sleeves can come loose, causing pistons to smash spark plugs. • Engine bucks and hesitates before rpms suddenly increase and car takes off. • Frequent stalling upon deceleration. • Faulty crankshaft position sensor is blamed for the poor engine performance. • Automatic transmission may suddenly shift into Neutral, or the shift lever sometimes pops out of gear.

Secret Warranties/Service Tips/TSBs

All models/years: Troubleshooting tips for delayed engagement of the automatic transmission. • Harsh shifting when coming to a stop or upon initial acceleration is likely caused by an improperly adjusted accelerator pedal switch TCU. • A faulty air exhaust plug could cause harsh shifting into Second and Fourth gears on vehicles with automatic transmission. • Brake pedal pulsation can be corrected by installing upgraded front discs and pads. • Troubleshooting tips for reducing brake noise. **All models: 1989–98**—Revised measures to reduce AC odours. **1992–95**—Difficult-to-engage Reverse gear needs an upgraded part. **1995–98**—Harsh shifting might be fixed by installing an upgraded transaxle control module (TCM) under a "goodwill" warranty. • If wind noise makes a "kazoo" sound, try installing an additional drip rail moulding. **1995–99**—Tips are offered on getting the automatic transmission to shift properly. **1999**—Shudder or vibration during acceleration can be eliminated by correcting a sticking inboard CV-tripod joint assembly. • A humping/knocking noise heard from the left front side of the vehicle on hard right turns may be caused by the left rear corner of the transaxle mounting bracket base touching the body. • Tips on silencing front wheel bearing noise. 1999–2000—No-starts, hard starting, or erratic idling may all be caused by a canister purge valve that's stuck open. Correcting hard manual shifting into First or Second gear and shudder on acceleration (CV joints). 1999–2001—Correcting erratic shifts. • Key sticks in ignition cylinder. • Silencing gear whine. 2000—Rear suspension produces a metallic rubbing noise. 2000–01—Correcting droning or rumbling brake noise at freeway speeds.

Sonata Profile

	1993	1995	1996	1997	1998	1999	2000	2001
Cost Price ($)								
Base	13,495	15,595	16,595	16,995	17,495	19,495	19,995	20,495
Used Values ($)								
Base ⋏	3,000	4,500	5,500	7,500	9,000	12,000	14,000	15,500
Base ⋏	2,500	3,500	4,500	6,000	7,000	10,000	12,000	14,000
Extended Warranty	Y	Y	Y	Y	Y	Y	N	N
Secret Warranty	N	N	Y	Y	Y	Y	Y	Y
Reliability	❷	❷	③	③	③	③	④	④
Crash Safety	—	③	③	③	③	—	—	—
Side Impact	—	—	—	❶	❶	—	—	④
Off-set	—	❶	❶	❶	❶	③	③	③
Head restraints	—	❶	❶	❶	—	③	—	③

Mazda

626, MX-6   ★★★★★

RATING: Recommended (1999–2001); Above Average (1996–98); Average (1994–95); Not Recommended (1985–93). An extended powertrain warranty is recommended as protection against automatic transmission breakdowns. 1997 was the last model year for the MX-6 and the Probe, its Ford twin. Make sure the car fits your size: tall drivers should be wary of the low headrests, which can be hazardous in a collision, and short drivers will want to ensure they can see adequately without getting dangerously close to the airbag housing. All other drivers are warned that the airbags often go off for no reason. **Maintenance/Repair costs:** Higher than average. Repairs aren't dealer dependent. Mazda suggests changing the engine timing chain after 100,000 km. **Parts:** Easily found, but sometimes costly. Although Mazda has promised to cut prices, you should still compare prices with independent suppliers. **Best alternatives:**

The Acura Integra; GM Cavalier or Sunfire; Honda Accord; Hyundai Elantra wagon, Sonata, or Tiburon; Nissan Altima; and Toyota Camry.

Strengths and weaknesses: Although far from being high-performance vehicles, these cars ride and handle fairly well and still manage to accommodate four people in comfort. The 1988–92 versions incorporated a third-generation redesign that added a bit more horsepower to the 4-banger. Apart from that improvement, these cars are still easy riding, fairly responsive, and not hard on gas. On the downside, the automatic transmission downshifts roughly, the power steering is imprecise, and the car leans a lot in turns.

Four-wheel steering was part of the sedan's equipment in 1988, and it was added exclusively to the MX-6 a year later. Wise buyers should pass over this option and look instead for anti-lock brakes and airbags on 1992 LG and GT versions. The manual transmission is a better choice because the automatic robs the engine of much-needed horsepower, as is the case with most cars this size. A passenger-side airbag was added to all '94 models.

A mid-sport and mid-compact hybrid, the MX-6 is a coupe version of the 626. It has a more sophisticated suspension, more horsepower, and better steering response than its sedan alter ego. The 1993 model gained a base 2.5L 165-hp V6 powerplant. Overall reliability and durability are on par with the 626.

1995–97 models offer improved performance, handling, and overall reliability, plus reasonable fuel economy. Owners still complain, though, of subpar body construction, electrical system and cruise control glitches, dim headlights, brakes and AC compressors that wear out prematurely, and automatic transmissions that shift poorly and are prone to premature failure. The Check Engine light comes on and goes off repeatedly due to oil spilling into the air flow sensor or the intake manifold gasket leaking. Expect jerky downshifts when the 4-cylinder is at full throttle. Shocks and struts (MacPherson) aren't very durable and are expensive to replace (especially when the model is equipped with the electronic adjustment feature).

Body problems include windshield mouldings that flake and fall off; door and hatch locks that often freeze up; the right side of the dash is often loose; the interior door panel pulls away; interior colours fade; headliner rattles; and the metal surrounding the rear wheelwells is prone to rust perforation, as are hood, trunk, and door seams. The paint seems particularly prone to chipping. The underbody and suspension components on cars older than five years should be examined carefully for corrosion damage. The exhaust system rarely lasts more than two years, and wheel bearings fail repeatedly within the same period.

1998 models underwent a major redesign, making them the better buy on the used-car market today. Some of the '98's best new features were attractive Millenia-type styling, a longer wheelbase and larger cabin, a reinforced body to keep creaks and rattles to a minimum, and more powerful engines. Unfortunately, the 1998–2001 models still have malfunctioning automatic transmissions, engine head gasket failures, fuel system glitches that cause sudden acceleration and stalling, faulty airbags, and electrical shorts that result in the Check Engine light staying lit.

'99 models were carried over unchanged, except for a larger selection of standard accessories. They are Recommended buys because they don't have as many of the redesign glitches found with the previous year's version. Re-styled year 2000 models were substantially improved with enhanced handling, steering, and interior appointments. The following year's models got few changes, except for an improved sound system, an emergency trunk release, and user-friendly child safety seat anchors.

Safety summary: All models/years: Interestingly, these vehicles have registered far fewer complaints than their Asian, European, or American counterparts. • Head restraints are too low. One Canadian neurologist wrote *Lemon-Aid* that the 626's head restraints are set too low and cannot extend to a safe level; he says there is an additional two inches required for a six-foot-tall occupant. When informed of his assessment, the dealer replied that Mazda "cannot help you with your problem." The doctor maintains his '97 Mazda 626 (and other model years) cannot be safely operated by a driver over five feet, ten inches in height. He concludes, "As a result of my occupation, I see many motor vehicle accident neck injuries and have a keen interest in making my new vehicle, and those of others, safe." **All models: 1995–96**—Inadvertent airbag deployments. **1997**—Airbags continue to deploy for no reason, injuring occupants (recall announced). • Several incidents where the steering failed without warning. • Frequent transmission failures. • Premature tire wear. • Brake failures and extended stopping distance. • Chronic electrical shorts. • Exhaust fumes enter into the interior. • Horn button hard to locate in an emergency. • Poor braking on wet roadways. • Headrest too low for tall drivers. Vehicle started on its own, then fire erupted. • Hesitation or stalling while driving. **1998**—Sudden, unintended acceleration. • Many incidents continue to be reported where airbags deployed for no reason. • Airbags failed to deploy in a collision. • Front axle pulled out of the transmission. • Steering rack gear broke in two without prior warning. • Sudden automatic transmission downshifts. • Frequent transmission failures. • Many reports of tire tread separation. • Poor braking leads to extended stopping distance. • Driver's seat is so low that it must be brought dangerously close to the airbag housing for maximum visibility. **1999**—Left lower strut bolts loose, bent, and broken, causing the driver-side wheel to fall. • Premature tire wear. • When AC engages, engine hesitates and causes car to jerk. • Automatic transmission shift shock. • Transmission fails upon deceleration, it downshifts harshly, O/D light flashes, and then engine compartment starts to fill with transmission fluid. • Headlights dim intermittently. • Excessive vibration at low speeds. • Seatbelts won't properly secure a child safety seat. **2000**— Inadvertent airbag deployment. • Cylinder head failures at the #2 cylinder. • 4-cylinder engine stumbles badly in cold weather. • Automatic transmission jerks during 2–1 shift, lurches into gear due to sudden high revs, and sometimes won't go into gear. • Cracked passenger-side rear axle. • Check Engine light stays on. **2001**—Airbags failed to deploy. • Automatic transmission jerks into gear. • Seatbelts fail to retract.

Secret Warranties/Service Tips/TSBs

All models/years: Non-turbo models that idle roughly after a warm restart could have fuel vaporizing in the distribution pipe (TSB #023/87R). • Excessive rear brake squealing can be reduced with improved brake pads (TSB #015/89-11). • Excessive vibrations felt in the brake pedal, steering wheel, floor, or seat when applying the brakes can be fixed by installing a redesigned brake assembly. • TSB #50901898 gives tips for eliminating wind noise around doors. **All models: 1993–97**—Engine camshaft noise may be corrected with a new friction gear spring and lock nut. **1995**— Camshaft friction gear noises. • Door side moulding detaches in cold weather. • Expansion valve whistling noise. • Heater and AC unit noise after long storage. • Loose, rattling sunroof and outer door handles. • Creak/rattle noise from passenger-side wiper. • Steering wheel slightly off-centre. **1995–96**—A 3–4 shift hunt is probably caused by failure in the 3–4 shift solenoid hydraulic circuit. • Front strut squeaks on turns could be caused by interference between the upper seat spring and the strut dust cover, or between the dust cover and the rubber bump stopper. **1996–97**—Unwanted 4–3 downshifts or intermittent shifting into Overdrive is covered in bulletin #015/98. **1997**—Camshaft friction noise. **1997–98**—Wind noise around doors. • Inoperative speedometer. • Steering wheel slightly off centre. • Brake pulsation repair. • Dead battery troubleshooting. • Tips on fixing faulty sunroofs, a seatbelt warning buzzer that sounds for no reason, rough automatic transmission shifts, excessive idle vibration, rear brake squeal, coolant leaks, and hard-to-close trunk lid. **1998–2000**—Tips on silencing a rear end tapping noise, and preventing AC odours. **2000**—Troubleshooting an MIL light that won't go off.

626, MX-6 Profile

	1994	1995	1996	1997	1998	1999	2000	2001
Cost Price ($)								
626	18,725	19,365	19,995	19,995	20,140	20,140	23,175	23,470
MX-6	20,695	21,835	22,780	23,325	—	—	—	—
Used Values ($)								
626 ▲	4,000	5,000	6,500	9,000	12,000	13,500	16,500	19,000
626 ▼	3,000	4,000	5,500	8,000	9,500	11,000	15,000	17,000

MX-6 Λ	5,500	7,000	8,000	10,000	—	—	—	—
MX-6 V	4,000	6,000	7,000	8,500	—	—	—	—
Extended Warranty	Y	Y	Y	Y	Y	Y	Y	Y
Secret Warranty	N	N	N	N	N	N	N	N
Reliability	❷	❷	③	④	④	④	④	④
Crash Safety (626 4d)	④	④	④	—	④	④	④	④
Side Impact (626 4d)	—	—	❷	③	③	③	③	③
Off-set	—	—	—	—	③	③	④	④
Head Restraints	—	❶	—	❶	—	❶	—	❶

Nissan

ALTIMA   ★★★★

RATING: Above Average (1998–2001); Average (1993–97). The 4-cylinder engine barely provides the necessary versatility needed to match the competition. Although the SE gives the sportiest performance, the less expensive GXE is the better deal from a price/quality standpoint. You will need an extended powertrain warranty to protect you from automatic transmission failures. **Maintenance/Repair costs:** Higher than average. Repairs are dealer dependent. **Parts:** Owners complain of parts shortages, and parts may be more expensive than those for most other cars in this class. **Best alternatives:** The Acura Integra; GM Cavalier or Sunfire; Honda Accord; Hyundai Elantra wagon, Sonata, or Tiburon; Mazda 626; and Toyota Camry.

Strengths and weaknesses: The Altima's wheelbase is a couple of inches longer than the Stanza's, and the car is touted by Nissan as a mid-size, even though its interior dimensions put it in the compact league. The small cabin seats only four, and rear-seat access is difficult to master due to the slanted roof pillars, inward-curving door frames, and narrow clearance.

The base engine gives average acceleration and fuel economy. Manoeuvrability is good around town. There are no reliability problems reported with the 16-valve powerplant, although the automatic transmission's performance has been problematic through the '96 model year. The manual transaxle is a better choice for all years from a reliability and fuel-economy standpoint. The uncluttered under-hood layout makes servicing easy. Body assembly is only so-so, with more than the average number of squeaks and rattles.

With its noisy and rough engine performance, this car cries out for a V6 like the one used in the Maxima. The 4-banger has insufficient top-end torque and gets buzzier the more it's pushed. In order to get the automatic to downshift for passing, for example, you have to practically stomp on the accelerator. The 5-speed manual transmission is sloppy. The Altima's sporty handling is way overrated; there's excessive body roll and front-end plow in hard cornering, tires squeal at moderate speeds, and steering isn't as precise or responsive as befits a car with performance pretensions. In spite of the car's independent suspension, it gives a busy, uncomfortable ride that's punishing over bumps. Lots of engine, road, and tire noise.

Redesigned '98 and '99 models came with depowered airbags and a more powerful powertrain setup. Year 2000 models were slightly re-styled and given comfort and convenience upgrades, along with some minor engine and suspension enhancements. 2001s returned relatively unchanged.

Prior to the 1998 models' redesign, Altimas had a fairly good reliability reputation; only problem areas then were prematurely worn, noisy front brakes, fuel system malfunctions, transmission and electrical system failures, and body glitches. '99 and later models have generated very few complaints, but owners still report sudden acceleration and stalling, front brakes locking up or failing completely, failure of the airbags to deploy, transmission breakdowns, and poor body fit and finish, notably water leaks (trunk, mainly) and body squeaks and rattles.

Safety summary: All models: 1995–97—Fire ignited in the engine compartment while vehicle was parked. • Fire started by fuse box in passenger compartment. • Sudden acceleration. • Frequent reports that the airbag failed to deploy. • Poor braking performance. • Poor design causes electronic control unit failure. • Defective automatic transmission solenoid. • Windshield wiper fails periodically. • Water leaks into trunk area, causing premature rusting. • Automatic door lock failure. • Seat and shoulder belts lock up and don't retract. **1998**—Stalling when accelerating. • Rear seats won't lock upright. • Windows rattle excessively. • Wheel cover failure. **1999**—Several incidents where engine or electrical fires ignited while vehicle was parked. • Sudden acceleration. • Vehicle unstable on wet roadway. • Airbags failed to deploy. • Airbag light comes on for no reason. • Gearshift lever sticks in Park. • Transaxle snapped in half, taking suspension and steering knuckle with it. • Sudden tire separation; tires gradually lose air (Continental-General). • Premature tire wear (Firestone). • Chronic brake problems. • Exhaust fumes (rotten-egg smell) enters into the interior. • Driver's seat moves forward when braking. **2000**—Exhaust fumes enter vehicle. • Dashboard burst into flames while vehicle was underway. • Vehicle continues to accelerate when slowing down to a stop, or when put into Reverse. • Chronic stalling. • Automatic transmission won't stay in gear. • The rear wheel well inner fender has sharp, jagged edges. • Firestone Affinity tire blowout. • All windows have a film on them that makes it difficult to see at night or during rainy weather. • Windshield cracks frequently. **2001**—

Sudden, unintended acceleration. • Engine will suddenly shut down. •
Engine motor mount failure. • Airbags failed to deploy. • Automatic
transmission makes a grinding or clunking noise when shifting. •
Defective sway bar bushing. • Wheel fell off, causing vehicle to slam into
a wall.

Secret Warranties/Service Tips/TSBs

All models/years: Diagnostic and correction tips for brake vibration and
steering wheel shimmy. • TSB #NTB99-028 outlines the procedures necessary to fix slow-to-retract seatbelts. • TSB #NTB00-037a covers possible
causes of the vehicle pulling to the side. **All models: 1993–96**—No-starts
or hard starts may be caused by an automatic transmission control cable
that's too short; TSB #96-032 gives additional diagnostic tips. • If the
transmission won't shift into Reverse, it may mean the Reverse clutch
drum, snap ring, and two dish rings need replacing. • A worn differential
pinion shaft may require an upgraded transmission differential case. •
Rear brake squeal can be reduced by installing improved rear brake shoes.
• TSB #NTB96-046 gives lots of useful tips for troubleshooting squeaks
and rattles. **1995**—An AC refrigerant leak at the charge port may be corrected by replacing the Schrader valve. **1995–96**—If the MIL light stays
lit, it may mean the rear heated oxygen sensor needs replacing.
1998–2000—Troubleshooting a rattling in the engine compartment. •
Tips for eliminating brake vibration and shudder. **1999–2000**—A sunroof
that jams when opening rearward requires a readjustment of the sunroof
links. This half-hour repair is covered by Nissan's base warranty. •
Guidelines as to what constitutes suspension strut leakage qualifying for
warranty coverage are found in TSB #NTB99-001. • Remedies for a noisy
automatic transmission. • Fixing a sunroof that jams.

Altima Profile

	1994	1995	1996	1997	1998	1999	2000	2001
Cost Price ($)								
XE	17,690	18,990	20,598	20,798	19,398	19,898	19,998	19,998
GXE	19,990	21,690	23,298	23,498	21,398	21,998	22,698	22,698
Used Values ($)								
XE ▲	5,500	7,000	8,000	9,500	12,000	13,500	15,000	16,500
XE ▼	4,500	5,000	6,000	8,000	10,000	12,000	13,000	15,000
GXE ▲	6,000	7,500	8,500	10,500	12,500	14,500	16,000	18,000
GXE ▼	5,000	6,500	7,500	8,000	10,500	12,500	14,000	16,500
Extended Warranty	Y	Y	Y	Y	Y	Y	Y	Y
Secret Warranty	N	N	N	N	N	N	N	N
Reliability	④	④	④	④	④	④	④	④
Crash Safety	④	—	④	④	③	③	—	④
Side Impact	—	—	—	—	③	③	③	③
Off-set	—	—	—	—	—	—	③	③
Head Restraints	—	③	—	❷	—	❷	❶	❶

Toyota

CAMRY, SOLARA

RATING: Above Average (1997–2001); Recommended (1994–96); Above Average (1988–93); Average (1985–87). 1996 was the wagon's last model year. The Solara, a two-door Camry clone, is outrageously overpriced. For the past five years, Camrys have elicited an unusually high number of safety complaints that are carried over from one model year to the next. The complaints include V6 engine failures from sludge buildup; severe wandering at highway speeds; sudden acceleration; engine compartment fires; brake failures; poor headlight illumination; and transmission interlock failures, which allow a parked vehicle to roll away. **Maintenance/ Repair costs:** Higher than average, but repairs aren't dealer dependent. **Parts:** Parts can be more expensive than for most other cars in this class, making it worth your while to shop at independent suppliers. Parts availability is excellent. **Best alternatives:** The Acura Integra; Honda Accord; Hyundai Elantra wagon, Sonata, or Tiburon; Mazda 626; and Nissan Altima.

Strengths and weaknesses: Safety complaints aside, the Camry is an excellent family-car buy because of its spacious, comfortable interior; good fuel economy; and impressive reliability and durability. Just make sure you change the oil more frequently than Toyota suggests for its V6 engine (see engine sludge comments below).

1988–93 models have few problems, although they're far from perfect. Main areas of concern are failure-prone cylinder head gaskets; suspension and electrical system failures; defective starter drive and ring gear; leaking low-pressure and high-pressure power-steering lines; outer CV boots that split, causing grease to leak; premature brake wear; and some paint peeling and rusting. Mufflers last only two years on earlier models, and sunroofs are rattle prone.

Persistent problems with all Toyota vehicles are premature brake wear, and excessive noise and vibrations. Stung by consumer criticism that these problems haven't been fixed for over a decade and that owners are charged for useless repairs, Toyota published a "Brake Repair" service bulletin (POL94-18) in October 1994, which defines those repairs that will be done under warranty. Toyota states that premature brake wear and noise will be fixed under warranty for the first 12 months/15,000 miles (240,000 km), and that vibrations will be attended to, under warranty, up to 3 years/50,000 miles (80,000 km). Canadians should use these parameters as their guide in requesting "goodwill" repairs.

Front suspension bushings wear out quickly, leading to clunking and squeaking noises when going over bumps or when stopping quickly.

There's also the so-called Camry chop (exceptionally rough rides when passing over uneven roadways) reported by owners of 1992–94 models. Cruise control fails frequently on all years. Owners of the 1992 Camry have reported that a chronic drone noise, along with a vibration felt from the floor and the gas pedal, occurs mostly when the automatic transmission changes from Second to Third gear at 1800–2000 rpm. Incidentally, manual transmissions are exceptionally reliable and fuel-efficient.

1994–99 Camrys are still fairly reliable, but they too have their short-comings. Owners report premature brake failures; faulty window regulators; smelly ACs; and myriad rattles, clunks, and groans that seem to come from everywhere. There is also an annoying surging and shuddering when decelerating, which appears to be more common with the 1995–96 models. It seems as though it's a sticking throttle position sensor, but mechanics say that the problem is intrinsic to the way the engine/transmission computer module is calibrated. Other deficiencies reported by owners: brake vibrations, premature brake pad wear, AC malfunctions, and defective automatic transmissions that slip out of gear when parked. 1994–99 model body problems include excessive wind noise coming from the front windshield, back doors, and sunroof. Trim items rust and fall off, door handles pull away, and mufflers have a short life span. No reports of rust perforation problems, but weak spots are door bottoms, rear wheel openings, and trunk and hatchback edges. There are complaints concerning premature rusting on cars painted white. Toyota generally corrects these rust/paint deficiencies for free.

The totally redesigned 1997 Camry is taller, longer, wider, more powerful, and cheaper, in both a literal and a figurative sense. Gone are the coupe and station wagon variants. The wheelbase was extended by two inches, giving backseat passengers more room. Other changes: it's powered by a base 2.2L 133-hp 16-valve 4-cylinder engine (taken from the Celica) and an optional 3.0L 24-valve V6 that unleashes 194 horses. Either engine will be mated to a 5-speed manual or an electronically controlled 4-speed automatic. ABS and traction control are standard on all V6-equipped Camrys, rear seats have shoulder belts for the middle passenger, low beam lights are brighter, and optional heated mirrors are available, as well as more cup holders, a sunglasses holder, and an additional power port in the centre console.

"De-contenting" hit Toyota's 1997 lineup hard, resulting in many changes that cheapened the Camry and precipitated a huge increase in owner complaints over problems that never appeared on Toyota vehicles before. One of the worst problems first showing up in 1997, and continuing through the year 2000 models, is engine sludge buildup, leading to engine failures that may cost as much as $7,000 to correct (see full report in the Sienna minivan section or go to *www.minivanreview.com/ MiniVans*). Toyota has also admitted to engine head gasket leaks for the first time (see "Secret Warranties/Service Tips/TSBs"), although, unlike the sludge problem, overall reliability doesn't appear to have been affected.

Other changes you'll note on post-'96 models are less expensive S-rated tires on models with 4-cylinder engines, cheaper heating/ventilation system components, no more assist handles for front occupants, no more chrome trim around the windshield, one door seal instead of three (greater chance for wind and water leaks), fewer airbag sensors, an LCD odometer, a distributorless ignition with the 4-cylinder, and a windshield-embedded antenna. Owners report the 1997 models have limited rear visibility (due to the side pillars and high trunk lid), less steering "feel," and more squeaks and rattles than previous versions.

Quality problems continue to plague the more recent models. Specifically, owners report that the vehicle often hesitates or stalls, when accelerating; front power windows often run off their channel; the steering wheel vibrates excessively; brake components (calipers, rotors, pads, master cylinder and the ABS valve) often fail within the first year or 20,000 km; warning lights constantly come on; charcoal canister failure; suspension "bottoms out" when carrying four adults; struts leak and are noisy; and moon-roof leaks are commonplace.

The '98 models returned unchanged, except for optional side airbags and an improved anti-theft system. '99 models changed little, apart from adjustable front headrests, new upholstery, a revised accessory list, and the addition of a new coupe, called the Solara. Year 2000 models were slightly re-styled, given larger tires, and a small horsepower boost (4-cylinders only). The following year's models remained unchanged.

Solara

Introduced in the summer of 1998 as a '99 model, the Solara is essentially a longer, lower, bare-bones, two-door coupe or convertible Camry with a sportier powertrain and suspension and a more stylish exterior. But don't let this put you off. Most new Toyota model offerings, like the Sienna, Avalon, and RAV4, are Camry derivatives. Year 2000 models returned unchanged except for the addition of a convertible version and three additional horses; 2001s were carried over without any significant improvements.

Relatively rare on the used-car market, a base model Solara will cost you $3,000–$4,000 more than an entry-level Camry sedan. And if you get one with the Sienna and Lexus ES 300's V6 powerplant, you're looking at a couple thousand dollars more.

You have a choice of either a 4- or 6-cylinder powerplant. Unfortunately, vehicles equipped with a V6 also came with a gimmicky rear spoiler and a head room-robbing moon roof. The stiff body structure and suspension, as well as tight steering, make for easy sports car-like handling, with lots of road feel and few surprises.

Safety summary: All models/years: Owners report that the Dunlop D60 A2 tire is a poor wet-weather performer and the Firestone original equipment tires fail prematurely. **All models: 1995**—Injury from airbag.

• Premature front/rear brake wear. • Defective, poorly performing (when wet) Goodyear Invicta tires. • Windshield reflects dashboard image. **1995–96**—Brake failure. • Noisy, vibrating brakes. • Premature front and rear brake wear. • Excessive engine noise. • Transmission lever can slip from Drive to Neutral. • Airbag fails to deploy or is accidentally deployed. • Sudden acceleration, stalling. • Passenger-side seatbacks won't stay upright. • Passenger seatbelts over-retract. • Defective radio antenna. • Taillight and turn signal bulbs frequently burn out. • **1996**— Vehicle wanders over road. • Door bottom/undercarriage rusting. • Airbag warning light and Check Engine light always on. • Windshield film buildup. • Window water leaks. • Rocking driver and passenger seats. • Steering system leaks. **1997**—Engine compartment fire following ABS brake failure. • Airbags failed to deploy. • Violent deployment of airbag during an accident caused death. • Sudden acceleration when brakes were applied. • Tendency for car to wander all over the roadway. • Steering wheel suddenly locked up, causing an accident. • Many reports of transmission interlock system failures. • Many other reports, probably related to the interlock system, that vehicle was put in Park and keys taken out of ignition, and car then proceeded to roll away. • Century infant seat won't fit in the centre of rear seat. • Seatbelts continually ratchet tighter; rear seatbelt was strangling child, who had to be cut free. • Plastic part fell behind the dash and lodged behind the brake pedal arm, causing an accident. • Frequent brake failures. • Premature brake pad and caliper wear or failure. • Loud grinding brake noise when braking. • Excessive noise coming from underneath the car at highway speeds. • Vehicle sits too low, has minimal ground clearance. • Driver's knee can hit the steering wheel adjuster lever, making steering wheel go up and down. On several occasions, steering wheel suddenly tilted all the way up while on the highway. • Very poor headlight illumination; headlight safety cap cover design cuts visibility severely and there's a blind spot on the driver-side headlights. • Low beam lights aren't bright enough. • Dash indicator lights are too small and low in intensity. • Inoperative rear window defroster. • Driver's seatback rocks back and forth. • Power door lock relay failure. • Car locks and unlocks on its own. • Fuel door doesn't open fully when lever is pulled. • Rear windshield exploded while car was parked overnight. **1998**—Several reports of engine fires. • Vehicle stalled, oil light came on, and fire ignited in engine compartment. • Sudden acceleration. • Many reports that airbags failed to deploy. • Frequent complaints that vehicle wanders at highway speeds and is difficult to control in a crosswind. • Overly soft suspension allows the chassis to scrape the roadway when passing over a small bump. • Frequent ABS brake failures. • Excessive brake noise and extended stopping distances. • Transmission gearshift lever went from Neutral to Drive without pressing button. • Airbag service indicator light stays on. • Engine malfunction light stays on. • Inadequate night illumination from headlights: low beam halogen headlights don't carry very far, dark spot cast from left headlight results in poor visibility, and metal deflector inside the concealed headlights blocks out all light beyond 10 metres. • Electrical system failure; running lights won't shut off. • Lock design allows for occupants to be temporarily locked in vehicle if someone gets out before them and locks the doors. • Power door locks fail intermittently. • Front restraints lock up when vehicle is parked on an incline. • Sun visors are too small to block the sun, and they cut visibility. • Back windshield shattered. • Fumes from inside the vehicle fog up the windshield. • Gas tank makes sloshing noise when brakes are applied. • General Tire wears excessively on the inside tread. • Frequent complaints of moon-roof leaks, which may cause electrical short. • Doors have to be slammed shut. **1999**—Incredible as it may seem, the Camry continues to have serious safety-related defects that aren't much different than what's been recorded for previous model years. They include, in order of frequency: sudden unintended acceleration; airbags not deploying during a collision; inadvertent airbag deployment, injuring occupants; complete brake failure or extended stopping distances caused by poor braking; sudden acceleration; chronic engine hesitation when accelerating or stalling; engine, airbag, and ABS warning light come on constantly; premature tire wear or blowout (Cooper and General tires); optically distorted windshield; and the transmission won't hold when stopped on a hill. **2000–01**—Safety-related incidents return unabated. • Under-hood fire (left side) while vehicle was parked overnight. • Fire ignited from underneath vehicle while driving. • Airbags failed to deploy. • Inadvertent airbag deployment. • Faulty cruise control caused vehicle to suddenly accelerate. • Sudden acceleration without braking effect. • Excessive grinding noise and long stopping distances associated with ABS braking. • Brake pedal went to floor but no braking effect. • ABS brakes suddenly locked up when coming to a gradual stop. • Defective rear brake drum. • Vehicle tends to drift to the right at highway speeds. • Excessive steering wheel vibrations at speeds over 100 km/h. • Entire vehicle shakes excessively when cruising. • Vehicle's weight is poorly distributed, causing the front end to lift up when the vehicle's speed exceeds 90 km/h. • Suspension bottoms out too easily, damaging the undercarriage. • Too-compliant shock absorbers make for a rough ride over uneven terrain. • Rear suspension noise at low speeds. • Automatic transmission slippage. • With engine running and transmission in Park position, car rolled down a hill. Two small girls inside of car jumped out, but one was run over. • Car rolled backward after it was put into Park and ignition key was removed. • Vehicle parked overnight had its rear window suddenly blow out. • Windshield distortion is a strain on the eyes. • Floor-mounted gear shift indicator is hard to read. • Seatbelts are too tight on either side and tighten up uncomfortably with the slightest movement. • Shoulder belt twists and won't lie straight. • Leaking suspension struts and strut rod failure. • Trunk lid may suddenly collapse. • Faulty driver's window track. • Driver-side door latch sticks. • Sulfuric acid odour enters the interior. • Fuel tank makes a sloshing noise when three-quarters full. • Clunking noise heard from rear of vehicle when gas tank is half full. • Tire jack collapsed while changing tire.

Secret Warranties/Service Tips/TSBs

All models/years: To reduce front brake squeaks on ABS-equipped vehicles, ask the dealer to install new, upgraded rotors (#43517-32020). • Owner feedback over the last decade plus dealer service managers who wish to remain anonymous tell me that Toyota has a secret warranty that will pay for replacing front disc brake components that wear out before 2 years/40,000 km. If you're denied this coverage, threaten small claims court action. • Toyota has a special kit to reduce AC odours. **All models: 1990–2000**—Measures to eliminate front brake clicking. **1993–96**—Suspension squeaks and groans are addressed in TSB #SU95-003. **1995**—Moon-roof panel wind noise. • Improved power window regulator. • Rear brake squeak. • Rear suspension noise. • Use upgraded brake pad material to eliminate brake groaning, says TSB #BR002-96. **1996–97**—A charcoal canister humming noise can be silenced by installing an upgraded vacuum hose. **1997**—Head gasket leaks are covered by a special Toyota program that is applied only if the customer complains. • If the driver's seat rocks, Toyota has an upgraded assembly that will secure the seat. • Difficulties with moon-roof operation. • Exterior rear-view mirror improvement. • Steering rack housing bushing noise. • Front shoulder belt anchor buzzes. • Front suspension groans. • Suspension rattle and popping. • Tailpipe contact with heat shield. • Headliner buzzes or rattles. • Moon-roof rattles. • Manual front seat movement/noise. • Power front seat chattering. • Radio volume control too sensitive. • Rubbing noise from door trim. • Seatcover loose at lower rear corners. • Seat movement field fix procedure. • Armrest bum improvement. • CD player won't accept/eject CDs. • Fuel door operation improvement. • Wind noise repair kit. **1997–98**—A front suspension groan can be fixed by replacing the front spring bumper. • Steering rack bushing noise (see following bulletin).

STEERING

ST004-98   August 21, 1998
STEERING RACK HOUSING BUSHING NOISE
Models:
'97 & '98 Camry

➤

Introduction

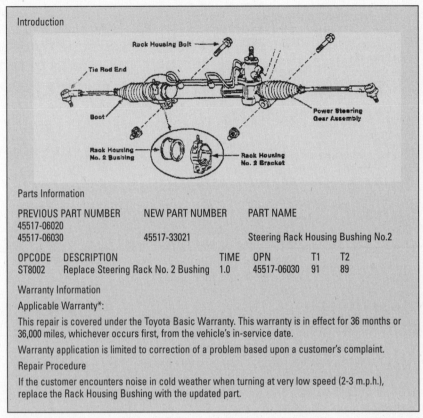

Parts Information

PREVIOUS PART NUMBER	NEW PART NUMBER	PART NAME
45517-06020		
45517-06030	45517-33021	Steering Rack Housing Bushing No.2

OPCODE	DESCRIPTION	TIME	OPN	T1	T2
ST8002	Replace Steering Rack No. 2 Bushing	1.0	45517-06030	91	89

Warranty Information

Applicable Warranty*:

This repair is covered under the Toyota Basic Warranty. This warranty is in effect for 36 months or 36,000 miles, whichever occurs first, from the vehicle's in-service date.

Warranty application is limited to correction of a problem based upon a customer's complaint.

Repair Procedure

If the customer encounters noise in cold weather when turning at very low speed (2-3 m.p.h.), replace the Rack Housing Bushing with the updated part.

Toyota won't give you the upgraded steering component unless you ask for it.

1997–99—Fuel door operation improvement. • Tips on reducing steering noise. • New front brake pad kits will reduce brake grinding or groaning, says bulletin #BR001-99. • To enhance headlight performance, the alignment process has been modified. 1997–2000—Silencing steering rack end noise. 1997–2001—Engine oil sludge will be corrected for free up to February 28, 2003. • Trunk leaks will be fixed under Toyota's base warranty. 1998–99—Door glass that runs off its channel is a common factory-related problem that Toyota admits is covered under its base warranty. Here's the catch: the dealer isn't authorized to upgrade the channel (a half-hour procedure) unless the customer asks for the service. 1999–2000—Seat movement, or no movement of seat adjustment. 2000–01—Wheel bearing dust deflector ticking noise. 2001—Troubleshooting a false MIL warning.

Camry, Solara Profile

	1994	1995	1996	1997	1998	1999	2000	2001
Cost Price ($)								
Base Coupe	19,238	19,998	20,488	—	—	—	—	—
Base Sedan	20,138	20,638	21,138	21,178	21,348	21,680	22,180	24,565
LE	24,918	24,718	25,458	25,268	26,508	27,070	27,225	27,695
Wagon V6	29,708	31,278	32,178	—	—	—	—	—
Base Solara	—	—	—	—	—	26,245	26,665	27,580
V6	—	—	—	—	—	29,815	30,270	30,650
Used Values ($)								
Base Coupe Λ	7,000	9,000	10,000	—	—	—	—	—
Base Coupe V	5,500	7,000	8,000	—	—	—	—	—
Base Sedan Λ	7,500	9,000	10,000	12,000	13,500	15,500	17,500	20,000
Base Sedan V	6,500	7,000	8,000	10,000	11,500	13,000	15,500	18,000
LE Λ	8,000	9,500	11,000	13,000	15,500	18,500	21,000	24,000
LE V	7,000	8,000	9,000	11,000	14,000	17,000	19,500	22,000
Wagon V6 Λ	8,000	9,500	11,000	—	—	—	—	—
Wagon V6 V	7,500	8,500	9,500	—	—	—	—	—
Base Solara Λ	—	—	—	—	—	18,000	21,000	24,000
Base Solara V	—	—	—	—	—	16,000	19,000	22,000
V6 Λ	—	—	—	—	—	20,000	23,000	26,000
V6 V	—	—	—	—	—	18,000	21,000	24,000
Extended Warranty	N	N	N	N	N	N	N	N
Secret Warranty	N	N	Y	Y	Y	Y	Y	Y
Reliability	⑤	⑤	⑤	④	④	④	④	④
Crash Safety	④	④	④	④	④	④	—	④
Solara	—	—	—	—	—	③	—	—
Side Impact	—	—	—	③	③	④	③	④
Solara	—	—	—	—	—	③	③	③
Off-set	③	③	③	⑤	⑤	⑤	⑤	⑤
Head Restraints	—	❷	—	③	—	③	—	❷
Solara	—	—	—	—	—	③	—	③
Rollover Resistance	—	—	—	—	—	—	—	⑤

Volkswagen

NEW BEETLE ★★★

RATING: Average (1998–2001). The New Beetle is an expensive trip
down memory lane carried along on a Golf/Jetta platform. Personally, I
don't think it's worth it—with or without its speed-activated spoiler

and dash-mounted bud vase. Another negative is the large number of safety-related complaints registered by NHTSA involving electrical fires, chronic stalling, and transmission failures. **Maintenance/Repair costs:** Average, but only a VW dealer can repair these cars. **Parts:** Easily found, since they're taken mostly from the Golf parts bin. Body parts are harder to find. **Best alternatives:** The Acura Integra; GM Cavalier or Sunfire; Honda Accord; Hyundai Elantra wagon, Sonata, or Tiburon; Mazda 626; Nissan Sentra or Altima; Toyota Camry; and VW Cabrio, Golf, or Passat.

Strengths and weaknesses: The New Beetle was a hands-down marketing and public relations winner when the model was re-introduced last year after being absent since 1979. By the end of March 1998, over 56,000 were sold, and sales for '99 versions are tracking first-year sales.

Why so much emotion for an ugly German import that never had a functioning heater, was declared "Small on Safety" by Ralph Nader and his Center for Auto Safety, and carried a puny 48-hp engine? The simple answer is that it was cheap and represented the first car most of us could afford as we went through school, got our first job, and dreamed of...getting a better car. Time has taken the edge off of the memories of the hardship the Beetle made us endure—like having to scrape the inside windshield with our nails as our breath froze—and left us with the cozy feeling that the car wasn't that bad after all.

But it was.

Now VW has resurrected the Beetle and produced a competent front-engine, front-drive, compact car—set on the chassis and running gear of the Golf hatchback—that's much safer than its predecessor, but oddly enough is still afflicted by many of the same deficiencies we learned to hate with the original.

Again, without the turbocharger, the 115-hp base engine is underwhelming when you get it up to cruising speed (the 90-hp turbodiesel isn't much better), there's still not much room for rear passengers, engine noise is disconcerting, radio buttons and power accessory switches located on the door panels aren't user-friendly, front visibility is hindered by the car's quirky design, and storage capacity is at a premium.

On the other hand, the powerful, optional 1.8L turbocharged engine makes this Beetle an impressive performer; the heater works fine; steering, handling, and braking are quite good; and the interior is not as spartan or tacky as it once was.

In its four years on the market, the Beetle has changed little: '99s got a 150-hp turbocharged 4-cylinder engine, year 2000 versions were given improved theft protection, and the 2001 models received larger exterior mirrors and a trunk safety release.

In a nutshell, here are the New Beetle's strong points: standard side airbags; easy handling; sure-footed, comfortable, though firm, ride; impressive braking; comfortable and supportive front seats with plenty of head room and leg room; cargo area can be expanded by folding down the rear seats; and top-quality mechanical components and workmanship.

On the minus side: serious safety defects have been reported by owners (see NHTSA data below), powertrain performance is unimpressive, and body construction is second-rate. Specific owner gripes: the base engine runs out of steam around 100 km/h; diesel engines lack pep and produce lots of noise and vibration; faulty O2 sensor causes the Check Engine light to come on; frequent ECM (electronic control module) failures; delayed shifts from Park to Drive, or failure to shift into Fourth gear; car is easily buffeted by crosswinds; optional high-mounted side mirrors, large head restraints, and large front roof pillars obstruct front and rear visibility; limited rear leg and head room; difficult rear entry/exit; excessive engine and brake noise; awkward-to-access radio buttons and door panel-mounted power switches; skimpy interior storage and trunk space; interior vent louvre loosens and breaks; hatchback rattles and sometimes fails to open; AC disengages when decelerating; low-slung chassis causes extensive undercarriage damage when going over a curb; and engine cover often gets pulled back and scrapes on the ground.

Safety summary: All models: 1998—Driver's head restraint sits too high and can't be lowered, seriously restricting rear visibility. • Oil pan hole leaked oil and caused vehicle to stall. • Sudden loss of power while driving at 100 km/h, forcing driver to reset computer by restarting the vehicle. • While driving at any speed, vehicle goes into emergency mode and suddenly slows down to about 20 km/h. • Instrument cluster failure. • Vehicle was smoking under the hood because a faulty hose leaked oil onto the engine. • While stopped at a traffic light, vehicle just exploded into flames and was a total loss. **1999**—Vehicle caught fire on inside of ignition switch box. • Another fire reportedly ignited in the wiring harness behind the dashboard. • Brake and accelerator pedals are too close together. • Sudden, unintended acceleration, and steering locked up. • Cruise control wouldn't disengage when brakes were applied. • Airbags failed to deploy. • Airbag warning light often comes on for no reason. • Sudden tread separation on the low-profile sporty tires. • When brakes are applied in a panic stop, one of the rear wheels will lock up along with one of the front wheels, causing vehicle to go into a spin. • Chronic hesitation and stalling on the highway (one fatality reported). • Vehicle won't start when facing down on a slope. • Frequent automatic transmission breakdowns. • Clutch failure causes vehicle to stall. • Left-side driveshaft cracked twice. • Driver's seat broke in a collision, causing severe injuries. • Driver-side seat came off its track and fell into back seat. • Tire jack fails to hold vehicle. • Cracked battery leaked acid onto power-steering fluid reservoir. • Vehicle shakes and shudders when driven with the sunroof fully open. • Headrest cannot be adjusted down to permit driver to see through rear and side windows; it's also quite uncomfortable for short drivers. 2000–01—Many complaints of prolonged hesitation when accelerating. • Steering suddenly locked up. • Low-mounted fuel tank is easily punctured. • Mass airflow sensor and secondary air injection pump motor failures. • Back glass suddenly shattered. • Windows fall into door channel due to defective regulators. • Hard to keep rear window free of rain, snow, or dew. • Windshield distortions impede vision. • Airbags failed to deploy. • Airbag warning light stays lit constantly. • Rear seatbelted passengers hit their heads on the unpadded side pillars.

Secret Warranties/Service Tips/TSBs

All models: 1998–99—An erratic-shifting automatic transaxle is likely caused by an improper throttle angle setting. VW will correct the problem under its base warranty. • Troubleshooting tips on silencing instrument panel, front door lock/latch, and door speaker squeaks or rattles. • Possible causes and fix for wind noise or whistle coming from the instrument panel. • Diagnosing humming noise from front of vehicle when cornering. • No adjustment of air flow from centre air outlets. • Throttle pedal and shifter lever vibration or knocking vibration. • AM radio static. **1998–2001**—Troubleshooting a noisy blower motor. • Malfunctioning instrument cluster. • Hood emblem chrome peeling off. **1999–2000**—Poor AM radio reception. **2000–01**—Prematurely worn rear brake pads. **2001**—Inoperative secondary oil pump.

New Beetle Profile

	1998	1999	2000	2001
Cost Price ($)				
Base	19,940	21,500	21,950	21,950
Used Values ($)				
Base ⋀	13,500	15,500	17,000	19,000
Base ⋁	11,500	13,500	15,000	17,500
Extended Warranty	Y	Y	Y	Y
Secret Warranty	N	N	N	N
Reliability	③	③	④	④
Crash Safety	—	④	④	④
Side Impact	—	⑤	⑤	⑤
Off-set	④	④	④	④
Head Restraints (F)	④	④	—	④
Rear	③	③	—	—

PASSAT   ★★★★

RATING: Above Average (1998–2001); Average (1995–97); Not Recommended (1989–93). There was no 1994 model. Don't buy any

Passat without a comprehensive extended warranty. The Audi spin-off 1998 Passats are just now coming off their three-year leases. Post-'98 models stick you with a high cost price due to their slow depreciation. **Maintenance/Repair costs:** Much higher than average. Most major repairs are dealer dependent. **Parts:** Parts and service are more expensive than average; long waits for parts are commonplace. **Best alternatives:** The Acura Integra; Honda Civic or Accord; Hyundai Elantra wagon, Sonata, or Tiburon; Mazda 626 or Protegé; Nissan Sentra or Stanza; and Toyota Camry or Corolla.

Strengths and weaknesses: This front-drive compact sedan and wagon uses a standard 2.0L engine and other mechanical parts borrowed from the Golf, Jetta, and Corrado. However, a 2.8L V6 became the standard powerplant beginning with the '99 wagon. Its long wheelbase and squat appearance give the Passat a massive, solid feeling, while its styling makes it look sleek and clean. As with most European imports, it comes fairly well appointed.

As far as overall performance goes, the Passat is no slouch. The multi-valve 4-cylinder engine is adequate, and its handling is superior to that of most of the competition. The 2.8L V6 provides lots of power when revved and is the engine that works best with an automatic transmission.

The redesigned 1995 version came with standard dual airbags, a re-styled interior, rear headrests, a softened suspension, and a much-improved crashworthiness rating. The 1998 Passat, however, is practically an entirely different car, based upon the Audi A4 and A6, and offers much better performance.

Passats are infamous for transmission malfunctions and fuel system glitches that are hard to diagnose and costly to repair. Even when they're operating as they should, the Passat's manual and automatic gearboxes leave a lot to be desired. For example, the 5-speed manual transmission gear ranges are too far apart: there's an enormous gap between Third and Fourth gear, and the 4-speed automatic shifts poorly with the 4-banger. Also, owners report that the transmission won't shift from lower gears, as well as problems with clutch slave cylinder leaks, front brakes (master cylinder replacements, brake booster failure, rotor warpage, premature wear, and excessive noise), MacPherson struts, and fuel and electrical systems as the car ages. Owners mention defective tie-rod and constant velocity joint seals that allow debris to enter into system, effectively causing premature wearout of internal components; engines often leak oil; early replacement of the power steering assembly; and fuel and computer module problems that lead to hard starts and chronic stalling.

On the body side, there's a helicopter-type wind noise when cruising with the windows or sunroof open; a persistent water leak from the pollen filter; interior trim and controls are fragile; door speakers are frequently replaced; fuel gauge malfunctions, indicating fuel in tank when it's empty; windshields may be optically distorted; rear-view passenger-side mirrors are too small and cause several blind spots.

Owners report that VW dealer servicing is the pits. Cars have to be brought in constantly to fix the same problem, recall campaign repairs are often slow because parts aren't available, and warranty coverage is spotty because VW headquarters doesn't empower or pay dealers sufficiently to take the initiative. Competent servicing and parts are particularly hard to find away from the larger cities, and many of the above-mentioned deficiencies can cost you an arm and a leg to repair.

Safety summary: All models: 1996—Many complaints that transmission slips out of Third gear into Neutral. • Vehicle suddenly accelerated forward as lever was put into Reverse. • Intermittent stalling due to electronic control module failure. • Check Engine light constantly goes on and off. • Engine-valve cover gasket failures. • Plastic shroud on top of engine rubs against the fuel line. • Leaking windshield and door seals. • Premature wheel-bearing failure on the driver's side. • Door lock failure allows door to open while under power, or makes doors difficult to open. • Instrument cluster wiring harness failures. • Repeated trunk-switch failures. • Chronic trunk water leaks. • Premature brake pad wearout. • All dash gauges suddenly stop working. **1997**—When manual transmission lever is put into Reverse, it often goes into First gear instead. • Sudden steering-wheel lockup. • Cooling fan control module failure. • Rear window defroster power button works only when held in the On position. • Door handle failures. • Frequent window regulator failures. **1998**—Engine head gasket leaks. • Erratic transmission performance. • Gas tank can't be filled without the pump shutting off repeatedly. • AC recirculation switch failure. • Serious blind spots caused by the small size and narrow view of the three mirrors. • Front seats move back and forth when braking or accelerating. • Total electrical-system failure. **1999**—Electrical fire. • Airbags failed to deploy. • Airbag light comes on for no reason. • Sudden, unintended acceleration. • Cruise control doesn't disengage, or engages on its own. • Accelerator pedal fails to return after full throttle. • Chronic stalling on the highway. • Early transmission clutch failure. • Clutch depressed to the floor and gear stayed engaged. • Front suspension's lower right arm failure due to a faulty bushing. • Front left wheel came off when making a turn. • Premature failures of the Michelin MXV4 tire; when rear tires blow out, they wreck havoc on vehicle's undercarriage (wheelwell and well lining), in some cases, causing the fuel tank to leak. • Other complaints of ruptured fuel tanks. • Oil line ruptured while driving. • Missing power steering cap caused fluid to leak out. • Driver's seat has excessive fore and aft movement. • Windshield cracked while vehicle was parked in direct sunlight.

Secret Warranties/Service Tips/TSBs

All models/years: Vehicles that won't move into any forward gear could have broken retaining lugs for selector plugs of B2/K1, which causes the selector valve to partially protrude or fall out of the valve body. **All**

models: 1990–95—On Passats equipped with an automatic transmission, an engine that won't start could have a loose contact in the ECM power supply relay. 1992–94—Poor 2.8L engine performance or a rough idle could be due to a misrouted EVAP vacuum hose or an improperly routed positive crankcase ventilation hose, which will cause a vacuum leak. 1995—Poor fuel-system performance. • Engine won't start. • Drifting, pulling to one side. • Instrument cluster loss of memory. 1995–96—Troubleshooting tips are offered on automatic transmission fluid seepage. 1995–99—An erratic-shifting automatic transmission may be due to an improper throttle angle setting. 1996–97—If the transmission pops out of gear, check for a hairline crack on the selector shaft shift detent sleeve. • Transmission fluid seepage. • Shifter is hard to move or won't go into Reverse. • Knocking/vibrating shift lever. • Vehicle will not move into any forward gear. • Malfunctioning CD player. 1998–99—Tips on fixing a door speaker rattle or vibration. • VW says a delayed upshift after a cold start is normal and a wait of 40 seconds isn't too long (typical of German logic: "Our cars are perfect, our customers aren't."). 1998–2000—Defective fresh air control lever light affects operation of heating/AC system. 1998–2001—Malfunctioning radio volume control and instrument cluster. 1999—Engine cranks, but won't start. • Malfunctioning windshield wipers. • Engine misfire. • 1999–2000—Poor AM radio reception. 2000–01—Airbag warning light remains lit. 2001—Noisy sunroof.

Passat Profile

	1993	1995	1996	1997	1998	1999	2000	2001
Cost Price ($)								
Base	21,525	25,870	27,230	28,620	28,450	29,100	29,100	29,500
Used Values ($)								
Base ∧	4,500	8,000	9,000	11,500	16,000	19,000	21,000	24,000
Base ∨	3,500	6,500	7,000	9,500	14,000	17,000	19,000	22,000
Extended Warranty	Y	Y	Y	Y	Y	Y	Y	Y
Secret Warranty	N	N	N	N	N	N	N	N
Reliability	③	④	④	④	④	④	⑤	⑤
Crash Safety	❷	④	④	④	—	—	⑤	⑤
Side Impact	—	—	—	—	—	—	④	④
Off-set	—	❶	❶	❶	⑤	⑤	⑤	⑤
Head restraints (F)	—	❶	—	❶	❷	❷	—	❷
Rear	—	—	—	—	❶	❶	—	—

LARGE CARS/WAGONS

These are the cars you're most likely to see in your rear-view mirror with their red and blue lights flashing. Quintessential highway cruisers for travelling salespeople, law enforcement agencies, large families, and retirees, the full-sized American car is an icon of a time long passed. No longer able to compete with high fuel costs and more versatile minivans and small sport-utilities, most of these "land yachts" have been axed or are being phased out, as is the case with Ford's Crown Victoria and Grand Marquis. Only Chrysler is still in the game with its spacious and attractively styled Concorde, Intrepid, and 300M sedans.

The term "large car" is relative. It once designated vehicles that had a wheelbase of more than 114 inches and that weighed about 3,200 lb. (1,450 kg). But now that the automakers have shortened most of the wheelbases of their large cars, reduced their weight, and switched to front-drives, traditional definitions of "large" may no longer be accurate indicators of a car's size. Some large cars, like GM's Caprice and Roadmaster, bucked this trend, however, and remained long and heavy.

Owners once had to pay a premium for these behemoths, which usually came fully loaded with performance and convenience features, but they were happy to do so because these vehicles offer considerable comfort and stability at high speeds. They also depreciate relatively quickly, making them great used-car bargains, can seat six adults comfortably, and are ideal for motoring vacations. Repairs are a snap and can be done almost anywhere, and there's a large reservoir of reasonably priced replacement parts sold through independent agencies.

The downside?

Highway performance and handling is smooth and competent, but not precise or exciting; the interior is comfortable, but not as versatile as a minivan or SUV; and you don't get as commanding a view of the road as in other, taller vehicles.

And you'll have to reconcile yourself to the notion that you actually *enjoy* driving your father's old car.

LARGE CAR/WAGON RATINGS

Recommended
Ford Crown Victoria, Grand Marquis (1997–2001)

Above Average
Ford Cougar, Thunderbird (1995–97)
Ford Crown Victoria, Grand Marquis (1994–96)

General Motors Caprice, Impala SS, Roadmaster (1995–96)

Chrysler's full-sized sedans, like the 2000 LHS above, have more sizzle than substance. Quality problems mar what is otherwise an attractive buy.

Average

DaimlerChrysler 300M, Intrepid (2000–01)

DaimlerChrysler Concorde, Intrepid (1999–2001)

Ford Crown Victoria, Grand Marquis (1984–93)

General Motors Caprice, Impala SS, Roadmaster (1994)

Below Average

DaimlerChrysler 300M, LHS (1999)

Ford Cougar, Thunderbird (1985–94, 1999–2001)

Not Recommended

DaimlerChrysler Concorde, Intrepid, LHS, New Yorker, Vision (1993–98)

General Motors Caprice, Impala SS, Roadmaster (1982–93)

Station wagons (full-sized)

If passenger and cargo space and carlike handling are what you want, a large station wagon may not be the answer—a used minivan, van, light truck, or compact wagon can fill the same need for less cost and will probably still be around a decade from now. Popular (though troublesome) wagons—like the Caprice and Roadmaster (both axed in 1996)—in which you could cram a Little League team are an endangered species, losing out to the van and minivan craze.

Some disadvantages of large station wagons: difficulty in keeping the interior heated in winter, atrocious gas consumption, sloppy handling, and poor rear visibility. Exterior road noise is also a frequent problem, since the vehicle's interior has a tendency to amplify normal road noise. Rear hatches and rear brake supporting plates tend to be rust prone.

DaimlerChrysler

300M, CONCORDE, INTREPID, LHS, NEW YORKER, VISION ★★★

RATING: Average (1999–2001); Not Recommended (1993–98). *Revised LHS and 300M:* Average (2000–01); Below Average (1999). Stay away from the discontinued pre-1999 LHS, New Yorker, and Vision. Parts are rare and mechanics cringe when these hard-to-service low-quality cars arrive in their service bay. Whichever vehicle you're considering buying, before paying a cent, make sure you get an extended warranty and take a test drive at night to assess the efficacy of the headlights and the clarity of the windshield. Only vehicles that carry an extended powertrain and body warranty are worthy of any consideration. These cars have elicited fewer safety-related complaints than the competition (think GM and Ford). Nevertheless, they have chronic problems with unintended acceleration that have carried over year after year. The 2000–01 models have elicited fewer safety-related complaints than expected, however. **Maintenance/Repair costs:** Higher than average, but most repairs aren't dealer dependent. **Parts:** Higher-than-average cost (independent suppliers sell for much less), but not hard to find (if cars are still in production). **Best alternatives:** A GM Bonneville, Caprice, LeSabre, or Roadmaster or Ford's early Cougar and T-Bird, Crown Victoria, or Mercury Grand Marquis.

Strengths and weaknesses: These full-sized cars share the same chassis and offer most of the same standard and optional features. They provide loads of passenger space and many standard features that usually sell as options, such as four-wheel disc brakes and an independent rear suspension. The Concorde is marketed to the more conservative buyer, while the Intrepid, the more popular model, is the entry-level version. Since their 1998 redesign, base models are equipped with a 2.7L V6 aluminum engine that delivers 200 hp. Higher line variants get a more powerful 3.2L V6 225-hp powerplant, or a 242-hp 3.5L V6. Earlier models carried a 3.3L 153-hp 6-banger, but 70 percent of buyers chose the 3.5L for its extra horses. Both engines provide plenty of low-end torque and acceleration, but this advantage is lost somewhat when traversing hilly terrain: the smaller V6 powerplant strains to keep up. These are more reliable vehicles, with better handling and steering response, than the Sable and Taurus or GM mid-sized front-drives, and the independent suspension maximizes control, reduces body roll, and provides lots of suspension travel so that you don't get bumped around too much on rough roads.

With all these positives, why aren't these cars recommended? Simple: they can be as unsafe as they are unreliable. Read the following owners' experiences, which are both scary and typical:

The headlights on my 1998 Intrepid will turn on and off intermittently while driving, or will turn on by themselves without the key in the ignition. Dealer had vehicle three times and couldn't duplicate the problem.

Traveling on the freeway at 100 km/h, my 1999 Chrysler 300M's rear windshield was sucked out and flew to the side of the road. I had no prior problems with the windshield. Entire rear windshield and casing flew off.

My 2000 Concorde accelerated on its own. I had to hit a tree to stop the car. The airbags did not deploy upon impact. Tires continued spinning after impact, until I turned off the ignition.

Owner reports confirm that there are chronic problems with leaking 3.3L engine head gaskets and noisy lifters that wear out prematurely around 60,000 km. Water pumps often self-destruct and take the engine timing chain along with them (a $1,200 repair). Engine surging and unintended acceleration is also a frequent refrain, affecting all model years.

The 4-speed LE42 automatic transmission is a spin-off from Chrysler's failure-prone A604 version—and owner reports show it to be just as unreliable. Owners tell of chronic glitches in the computerized transmission's shift timing and other computer malfunctions, which result in early replacement and driveability problems (stalling, hard starts, and surging).

Body problems abound, with lots of interior noise; uneven fit and finish; poor-quality trim items that break or fall off easily; exposed screw heads; faulty door hinges that make the doors rattle prone and hard to open; distorted, poorly mounted windshields; windows that come off their tracks or are misaligned and poorly sealed; power window motor failures; and steering wheel noise when the car is turning.

AC failures are commonplace and costly to repair. The problem has become so prevalent that Chrysler has a little-known warranty extension that will pay for the replacement of the evaporator up to seven years. Chrysler has tried to limit compensation to a limited number of models, but the company can't escape its 7-year benchmark or arbitrarily exclude owners of other vehicles made by the company (see page 2).

In deciding which cars offer the most for your used-car dollar, remember that the Concorde and Intrepid were completely redesigned for the 1998 model year, so the following year's 1999 versions will not only carry over the refinements but also escape many of the factory glitches found in newly designed models. '99s also were given suspension improvements, for a smoother ride.

300M and LHS

These two models represent the near-luxury and sport clones of the Chrysler Concorde. Although they use the same front-drive platform as the Concorde, their bodies are shorter and they're styled differently. In fact, the 300M is the shortest of Chrysler's mid-sized sedans. Both cars are powered by a 253-hp 3.5L V6 and mated to Chrysler's AutoStick semi-automatic transmission. Year 2000 models have an improved rear suspension for a more comfortable ride and a brake/transmission inter-lock safety feature.

Although mechanical and body deficiencies generally mirror those of the Concorde and Intrepid, 300M and LHS owners report the following problems: a rough-running engine and transmission, excessive road and wind noise, only five-passenger capacity, no side airbags, mediocre fit and finish, and questionable reliability. The 300M has limited rear leg room, a narrow rear windshield reduces rear visibility, and it carries a smaller trunk with a smaller opening than the LHS. Owner-reported problems include glitches in the computerized transmission's shift timing, which cause driveability problems (stalling, hard starts, and surging). Amazingly, the 4-speed LE42 automatic transmission—a spin-off from Chrysler's failure-prone A604—appears to be just as problem-plagued as its predecessor, with reports of driveline shudder during 3–4 shifts and frequent transmission defaults into Second gear (limp-in mode). Other owner-reported defects include premature brake wear and brake malfunctions, electrical problems, and sloppy body con-struction. For example, owners complain of water and air leaks into the interior, uneven fit and finish, poor-quality trim items that break or easily fall off, exposed screw heads, faulty door hinges that make the doors rattle prone and hard to open, windows that come off their tracks or are misaligned, and power window motor failures.

Safety summary: All models/years: Engine surging and sudden, unin-tended acceleration. • No airbag deployment in a collision. • Gas fumes enter the interior. • Windshields are often distorted and may fall out while vehicle is underway. • A high rear windowsill obstructs rear visi-bility. • Headlights may be too dim for safe motoring and cut out completely or come on by themselves. Defrosting is also inadequate, allowing ice and moisture to collect at the base of the windshield. Chrysler has a fix for these two problems that requires the installation of a new headlight lens and small foam pads into the defroster outlet ducts. • Both ABS and non-ABS brakes perform poorly, resulting in excessively long stopping distances or the complete loss of braking ability. • The overhead digital panel is distracting and forces you to take your eyes from the road. • The emergency brake pedal catches pant cuffs and shoelaces as you enter or exit the vehicle. **All models: 1994–97**—NHTSA is looking into reports that the front suspension may collapse, causing the driver to lose control of the vehicle. This government agency knows of 26 complaints and 105 warranty claims for 1994 models and another 49 complaints covering 1995–97 years that used an upgraded suspension. Broken welds or cracks where the lower control arm attaches to the front cradle may be the cause of the failures. **1996**—Many reports that while the vehicle is being driven at 100 km/h, there's a sudden loss of power, the engine shuts down, power steering and brakes become inoperative, and the Check Engine light comes on. • High-pressure fuel lines between the two cylinder heads leak gas onto the engine. • When shifting into Reverse from Park, automatic transmission acts as if it's in Neutral, and the engine races when the accelerator is pressed. • Brake rotors rust prematurely and warp easily, and pads have to be changed every 15,000 km. • Vehicle shakes violently when ABS brakes are applied. • Dashboard reflection in the windshield hampers visibility. • Horn buttons difficult to access in emergency situations. • Stuck right rear door lock won't allow door to open. • Door hinges don't hold door open securely, causing injury to occupants when door closes unexpectedly. • Frequent water pump, AC, and battery failures. **1997**—Fire ignited in trunk. • Fuel line hoses disconnected from the engine, spilling fuel into the engine area. • Vehicle decelerates while driving. • Premature wearout of front brake pads and rotors (rotors warp or become rust-pitted). • Excessive brake noise. • Several reports that Goodyear Eagle tires tend to hydroplane. • Steering linkage failure causes vehicle to wander all over the roadway. • Power-steering failure—extremely hard to turn. • Many reports of sudden transmission failures, many due to cracked transmission casings. • Transmission fluid leakage caused by defective transmission casing bolt. • Seat backrest failure. • Frequent windshield replacements due to distortion—particularly annoying at night when combined with poor headlight illumination. • Intermittent turn signal operation. • Flawed interior door panels. • Frequent instrument panel malfunctions: lights, gauges, AC all go out at once. • Cigarette lighter shoots out so hard it shoots under driver's seat—while red-hot. **1998**—Reports of sudden acceleration when shifting into Reverse. • When transmission relay fails, it causes a harsh downshift to Second gear while at highway speeds. • Rear brakes improperly adjusted by Chrysler result in overloaded front brakes and warped front brake rotors. **1999**—Vehicle suddenly accelerated when shifted into Reverse at a car wash. • The bolt that holds the fan and engine pulley came loose, resulting in complete loss of steering ability. • Brakes continually lock up, grind when applied, and result in extended stopping distance. • With cruise control engaged, brakes will suddenly lock up. • Chronic automatic transmission failures (the speed sensor often fails, causing the engine warning light to come on). • Vehicle will suddenly shudder or lurch violently while underway at cruising speed. • The #4 engine cylinder failed, causing vehicle to lose power. • Check Engine light comes on constantly. • Fuel smell invades the interior. • Shifter pin to interlock cable broke off, causing the ignition key to be removable while vehicle is in gear. • Glove box can't be locked. • Frequent failure of the power window motors. **2000–01**—Transmission won't shift to reverse and engine stalls. • Side seatbelts don't retract. • Front and rear windshields distort view; there may be an annoying reflection on the inside of the windshield, particularly evident on vehicles with beige interiors. **300M: 1999**—Airbags suddenly deployed for no reason when changing lanes. • Transmission jumped from Park to Reverse with engine running. • Driver's son took shifter out of Park without key in ignition, and vehicle rolled down hill. • Premature wearout of brake rotors. • Vehicle constantly shakes and shimmies; wobbles and bobbles on the highway. • Early wearout of original equipment Goodyear tires.

Secret Warranties/Service Tips/TSBs

All models/years: A rotten-egg odour coming from the exhaust is probably caused by a malfunctioning catalytic converter; this is covered by Chrysler's original warranty *and* the emissions warranty. Don't take "no" for an answer. The same advice goes for all the squeaks and rattles and the water and wind leaks that afflict these vehicles. Don't let Chrysler or the dealer pawn these problems off as maintenance items. They're all factory related and should be covered for at least five years. **All models: 1993–98**—Delayed transaxle engagement can be corrected through upgraded hardware and software components. **1993–99**—Troubleshooting tips for trunk water and dust leaks. • Paint delamination, peeling, or fading (see Part Two). **1993–2000**—If the vehicle leads or pulls at highway speeds, TSB #02-16-99 suggests a whole series of countermeasures, including replacing the engine mounts, if necessary. Chrysler will apply the base warranty to this repair. • Loose or noisy steering may be corrected by servicing the inner tie-rod bushings or simply replacing the tie-rod. • Harsh, erratic, or delayed transmission shifts can be corrected by replacing the throttle position sensor (TPS) with a revised part. **1994–95**—The intermittent or total loss of air conditioning may be corrected by installing a revised AC pressure transducer. **1995–99**—More troubleshooting tips are offered on diagnosing and fixing trunk water leaks. **1995–97**—If the AC suction line fails, replace it and install a revised right-side engine ground strap; the original ground strap probably caused the failure. **1996–97**—If you hear a metallic popping noise coming from the front of the vehicle when you accelerate from a stop, install two new upper and two new lower cradle mounting isolators. • Rear drum brake ticking can be silenced by burnishing the rear brakes. **1998**—Tips on correcting inadvertent door lock operation. **1998–99**—A rough idle or poor driveability may require the testing and replacing of the EGR valve and power control module (PCM). • An engine hiss noise can be silenced by replacing the throttle body assembly. • Delayed shifts and other transmission malfunctions affecting a broad range of models are addressed in TSB #21-03-98. This is proof positive that Chrysler's transmission woes are far from over. • Troubleshooting tips for no hot air or lack of cold air. • Poor heater performance may mean the PCM should simply be reprogrammed. • Window sticks in the up position. • Countermeasures for correcting excessive road noise and a variety of squeaks, rattles, and squawks. •

Troubleshooting tips for correcting water leaks on top and/or under floor carpets. • Poor AM radio reception can be fixed by installing a new electronic back light module. **1998–2000**—Poor AC performance can be fixed by first carrying out Customer Satisfaction Recall #857 and then reprogramming the power control module. • Repair procedures are outlined for reattaching the rear door trim panel. • Guidelines for silencing wind noise emanating from the sunroof and the area in front of the B-pillars. • Front suspension strut squeaking can be stopped by installing a revised front strut striker cap. **2000–01**—Front strut noise. • Front suspension or steering gear rattle. • Vehicle leads or pulls. • Speaker screw contacts door seal.

300M, Concorde, Intrepid, LHS, New Yorker, Vision Profile

	1994	1995	1996	1997	1998	1999	2000	2001
Cost Price ($)								
300M	—	—	—	—	—	39,150	39,675	40,900
Concorde	22,590	24,420	26,005	26,815	26,915	27,635	28,115	28,485
Intrepid	19,170	21,010	22,980	24,055	24,395	25,060	25,520	25,910
LHS	35,020	37,625	38,420	40,500	40,500	41,150	41,370	41,655
New Yorker	29,990	32,080	34,490	—	—	—	—	—
Vision	21,485	22,910	23,770	24,775	—	—	—	—
Used Values ($)								
300M ▲	—	—	—	—	—	20,500	25,000	28,000
300M ▼	—	—	—	—	—	18,000	22,000	26,000
Concorde ▲	5,500	6,500	8,000	10,000	13,000	15,500	18,500	20,500
Concorde ▼	4,500	5,000	6,000	8,000	11,000	14,000	16,000	18,500
Intrepid ▲	4,500	5,500	6,500	8,000	10,000	11,500	16,500	18,500
Intrepid ▼	4,000	4,500	5,000	6,500	8,500	9,000	15,000	17,000
LHS ▲	6,500	8,000	10,000	14,000	26,000	21,000	25,500	29,000
LHS ▼	6,000	6,000	8,000	11,000	15,000	18,000	23,000	27,000
New Yorker ▲	6,000	7,500	9,000	—	—	—	—	—
New Yorker ▼	5,500	6,000	7,000	—	—	—	—	—
Vision ▲	4,500	5,500	7,000	8,500	—	—	—	—
Vision ▼	4,000	5,000	5,500	7,000	—	—	—	—
Extended Warranty	Y	Y	Y	Y	Y	Y	Y	Y
Secret Warranty	Y	Y	Y	Y	Y	Y	Y	Y
Reliability	①	①	②	②	②	③	③	③
Crash Safety	④	④	④	④	—	④	④	④
Side Impact	④	④	④	④	—	④	④	④
Off-set	—	—	—	—	—	—	②	③
LHS/300M	—	—	—	—	—	①	①	③
Head Restraints (F)	—	①	—	①	—	③	—	①
Rear	—	—	—	—	—	②	—	—
300M	—	—	—	—	—	②	—	②
Intrepid	—	①	—	①	—	—	②	④
LHS	—	①	—	①	—	②	—	③

| New Yorker | — | ❶ | — | — | — | — | — | — |
| Vision | — | ❶ | — | ❶ | — | — | — | — |

Note: All these vehicles are practically identical and should have similar crashworthiness scores, even though not every model was tested each year.

Ford

COUGAR, THUNDERBIRD   ★★

RATING: Below Average (1999–2001); Above Average (1995–97); Below Average (1985–94). Just about when Ford was getting its act together with the T-Bird and Cougar, it took both off the market and returned a year later with a poor-quality, unreliable Contour *cum* Cougar that's frankly an embarrassment, considering the millions invested and advertising hype we've endured. The Cougar's history is pretty much irrelevant now because it has no future. Ford has just announced the car will be dropped in the 2003 model year. For readers wondering how the Cougar could go from a below-average rating to above average, and then fall again to below average, remember that we are reviewing distinctly different vehicles. The early rear-drives improved over the years; however, the 1999 front-drive iteration carries all of the deficiencies of Ford's front-drives, coupled to the Contour and Mystique's own sub-set of problems. Plus, as a first-year vehicle, the Cougar's quality control suffered even more (see "Safety summary" and "Secret Warranties/Service Tips/TSBs"). Get rid of the original equipment Firestone Firehawk tires; they're too risky. **Maintenance/Repair costs:** About average, and most repairs aren't dealer dependent. **Parts:** Moderately priced (independent suppliers sell for much less), and not hard to find for rear-drives. Front-drive parts, however, are more expensive and not as easily found. And they will likely become rarer, with both the Contour and Cougar taken off the market. Despite the fact that 1997 was the last model year for both rear-drive models, their parts have remained plentiful. **Best alternatives:** A GM Bonneville, Caprice, LeSabre, or Roadmaster or Ford's early Cougar and T-Bird, Crown Victoria, or Mercury Grand Marquis.

Strengths and weaknesses: These are no-surprise, average-performing, two-door, rear-drive, luxury cars that have changed little over the years. Nevertheless, they offer more comfort and performance and greater reliability than GM rear-drives and most of the Big Three-produced front-drives. Handling and ride are far from perfect, though, with considerable body lean and rear-end instability when taking curves at moderate speeds.

Overall reliability of these models has been average, as long as you stay away from the turbocharged 4-cylinder engine and watch out for 3.8L V6 engine head gasket failures and automatic transmission glitches.

True, these cars offer lots of power, but excessive noise and expensive repairs are the price you pay when they're pushed too hard. Front suspension components wear out quickly, as do power-steering rack seals. Owners of recent models have complained of ignition module defects, electrical system bugs, premature front brake repairs, steering pump hoses that burst repeatedly (one owner of a 1994 Cougar wrote that he replaced the hose twice in the same year), erratic transmission performance, early AC failures, defective engine intake manifolds, excessive vibrations when driving, numerous squeaks and rattles, faulty heater fans, and failure-prone power window regulators.

1999–2001 Cougar

Essentially a Contour spin-off, this Cougar's main attributes are its attractive styling and pleasant handling. On the other hand, owners have to accept so-so acceleration with the base models, problematic transmission performance, a four-seater with a narrow, claustrophobic interior, limited rear-seat room, obstructed rear visibility, an ugly and superfluous trunklid spoiler, and excessive interior noise.

The front-drive Cougar, re-styled as a hatchback, is equipped with a 16-valve, 125-hp 2.0L inline-four and a 24-valve, 170-hp 2.5L V6, later replaced with an upgraded 200-hp powerplant and optional ABS and side airbags. It shares the Contour's chassis (with an inch added), base 4-banger, and V6, but its suspension and steering are much tighter.

Emergency handling is acceptable, but not in the same league as Japanese sedans. The firm suspension and quick, responsive steering make the Cougar both nimble and stable when cornering under speed, especially with the optional Sport Group's rear disc brakes and larger wheels (you'll have to put up with a harder, noisier ride, though). The car is also quite peppy around town, with a good amount of low-end torque. Braking is also quite good, with little fading after successive stops.

Acceleration is only so-so with the base 4-cylinder or V6 engine and they both run roughly; the 4-banger is not as refined or fun to push as the Japanese competition. The 170-hp V6 lacks passing or merging power; 0–100 km/h takes about 10 seconds. The automatic transmission tends to "hunt" the proper gear when going over hilly terrain, and there's no way to lock out Overdrive in Fourth gear. The 5-speed hooked to the V6 also shifts roughly. The base suspension doesn't absorb bumps very well and the optional Sports Group tires produce a busy, jostling ride on any surface that's less than perfect. Steering is also a bit heavy in city traffic.

Owner-reported problems include automatic transmission failures accompanied by slipping, humming, and clanking noises; electrical glitches; engine increases rpms when shifting; chronic stalling, rough running, and hard starts; premature front and rear brake wear and a low grinding noise or squeak heard when the brakes are applied; trunk, sunroof, door, and side window jamming; a sun visor that keeps falling down; door latch failures; doors that lock and unlock themselves; faulty driver-side door weather stripping that produces excessive wind noise; and water leakage into the interior.

Safety summary: All models: 1996—Vehicle caught fire after being parked for 13 hours. • Airbags failed to deploy. • Airbag indicator light comes on for no reason. • Right rear wheel came off. • During inclement weather, design of engine allows water to saturate the air filter, causing engine to die out. • PCM chip defect causes engine to cut out and the Check Engine light to come on. • Malfunctioning crankshaft and oxygen sensors may cause chronic stalling and no-starts. • Cracked intake manifold allows coolant leakage. • Frequent motor mount failures. • Transmissions are noisy, won't shift properly, and frequently won't shift at all. • Excessive driveshaft vibrations. • Power steering works poorly at low speeds and sometimes cuts out completely when cruising on the highway. • Heater and AC compressor failures. • Defective AC fan switch. • Frequent reports of sudden brake failures, front brake rotor warpage, and noisy brakes. • Brake pedal sinks below the accelerator pedal level, causing driver to depress the accelerator. • Hood struts are too weak to keep hood in open position. • Crooked steering wheel replaced. • Power window regulator failures. • Electric door locks are failure prone. • Doors fit poorly. • Headlights require constant adjustment and don't provide as much illumination as with other model years. • Seatbelt doesn't release properly. • Defective sunroof guides, and the gasket barely lasts two years. • Sun visor hits driver in the head when it's adjusted. • Speedometer and gauges work erratically. **1997**—Sudden acceleration while stopped at a traffic light. • Left vehicle in Park with engine running and it suddenly lurched into Reverse. • Car suddenly pulled to the left when braking, and steering locked up. • Excessive vibrations while cruising that increase in intensity when braking. • Premature front brake wear. • Headrests can't be raised high enough to protect the head. • Seat won't latch. • Brake caliper moves in its bracket.• Transmission fluid leakage. • Water leaks onto passenger-side floor due to missing wiring harness plug. • Dash reflection on the windshield obstructs visibility. • Dealer can't correct windshield washer spray to prevent it from spraying the rear window. • Multiple Firestone tire failures. **1998**—Airbag failed to deploy. • Tire sidewall failure. • Engine increases rpms when shifting. • Sudden stalling with locked-up steering. • Engine and airbag service lights stay on for no apparent reason. • Key won't work in the ignition. • Hard to find a child safety seat that fits in the rear. • The silly, nonfunctional rear spoiler is distracting and cuts rearward vision. **1999**—Inadvertent airbag deployment. • Driver's airbag deployed after collision and seatbelt failed to lock up. • Sticking throttle causes sudden, unintended acceleration. • Cruise control wouldn't disengage. • Chronic hesitation or stalling (electrical shorts or a faulty fuel pump, fuel regulator, intake gaskets, or IAC solenoid are the prime suspects). • No-start due to faulty ignition or starter. • Transmission failures. • While driving at 110 km/h, transmission downshifted on its own. • Sudden brake failure (locked up). • Total brake failure when ABS brake master cylinder "exploded." • Brake pads, calipers, and rotors need replacing after only 20,000 miles (32,000 km). • Power steering fails and dash lights go out when car is driven through a rain puddle. This may be caused by the serpentine belt getting wet. • Plastic fuel tank is prone to early disintegration, contributing to stalling; vehicle bought back by Ford. • Gas tank seal swells and breaks, spilling fuel. • Fuel tank wiring harness melted. • Brake lights don't come on when brakes are applied. • Electrical failures tend to blow out the fuel pump. • On another occasion, dash lights suddenly came on, engine died, and brakes and steering ability were gone. • Steering failures due to a broken suspension strut or the tie-rod bolt shearing off. • Wheel may crack, causing a tire blowout. • Frequent reports of tire tread separation at the sidewalls or prematurely wearing out (Firestone Firehawk). • Lugnut wrench doesn't work. • Trunk won't open or close, and remote release is useless. • Horn is hard to activate. • Inadequate rear windshield defogger. **2000–01—** Broken stabilizer bar bracket allowed wheel to drop under car. • Intermittent brake failure. • Automatic transmission hesitates, as it "hunts" for the correct gear and then shifts with a jerk. • Faulty seal causes fuel tank leakage. • Fuel smell in the interior comes in through the vents; fuel also leaked onto the ground. • Horn is hard to activate. • Engine hangs in higher rpms when foot is taken off the gas pedal and clutch is depressed. • Chronic stalling. • Lights flicker and loss of all electrical power. • Headlight failures. • Airbag and engine warning lights stay lit. • Cupholder spills drinks on right hand turns at speeds higher than 35 km/h (upgraded console/cupholder installed in mid-2000). • Tire sidewall failure. • Key won't work in the ignition. • Hard to find a child safety seat that fits in the rear. • The silly, non-functional rear spoiler is distracting and cuts rearward vision.

Secret Warranties/Service Tips/TSBs

All models/years: Ford's "goodwill" warranty extensions cover engine and transmission breakdowns up to about seven years. There's nothing like a small claims court action to "focus" Ford's attention (pun intended). The same advice applies if you notice a rotten-egg odour coming from the exhaust. **All models: 1985–97—**A buzz or rattle from the exhaust system may be caused by a loose heat shield catalyst. **1989–97—**Water dripping from the floor ducts when the AC is working requires a relocated evaporator core. **1992–95—**A corroded solenoid may be the cause of starter failures. **1993–97—**Roughness when braking from 105 km/h is likely caused by a distorted rear brake drum. • Paint delamination, peeling, or fading (see Part Two). **1993–2000**—Brake vibration diagnosis and correction. **1994**—Automatic transmissions with delayed or no forward engagement, or a higher engine rpm than expected when coming to a stop, are covered in TSB #94-26-9. • A no-crank condition in cold weather may be due to water freezing in the starter solenoid. • Hesitation or stumble in vehicles equipped with a 3.8L engine may be fixed by installing an upgraded PCM that allows for low-grade fuel. **1994–97**—An erratic or prolonged 1–2 shift can be cured by replacing the cast aluminum piston with a one-piece stamped steel piston that has bonded lip seals, and by replacing the top accumulator spring. • A simple solution for correcting a transmission shudder or vibration in Third or Fourth gear may be to simply change the transmission fluid or recalibrate the PCM. **1995–97**—Tips on sealing windshield water leaks and reducing noise, vibration, and harshness while driving. **1998–2000**—Engine knock. • An exhaust sulfur odour evident just after highway cruising may signal the need to replace the catalytic converter under the emissions warranty. • **1999**—Three bulletins target automatic transmission failures, suggesting that either the Overdrive/Reverse ring gear be replaced or an upgraded transaxle assembly be installed. • Front brake groaning during city driving can be silenced by installing revised brake pads under warranty, says TSB #99-8-9. **1999–2000**—Engine hesitation and a rough idle may be corrected by reprogramming the power control module. • Transmission won't shift into any forward gear. • Automatic transmission fluid leaks. • Water leaks and wind noise troubleshooting tips. • Exterior lights flicker in cold weather. • Engine won't start with the wiper switch on. **1999–2001**—Rear brakes moan or groan. • Brake warning light stays lit. **1999–2002**—Repeated failure of the heater core. **2000**—Airbag light remains lit. • Low coolant lamp on for no apparent reason. • Automatic transmission fluid leakage. • Water leak or wind noise at the upper corner of the B-pillar.

Cougar, Thunderbird Profile

	1993	1994	1995	1996	1997	1999	2000	2001
Cost Price ($)								
Cougar	19,650	21,395	22,095	23,495	24,995	19,995	20,595	23,655
T-Bird	19,695	21,895	22,995	23,595	25,095	—	—	—
T-Bird SC	26,500	27,395	28,697	—	—	—	—	—
Used Values ($)								
Cougar ⋀	4,500	5,000	6,000	8,000	10,000	13,500	15,000	18,500
Cougar ⋁	4,000	4,500	4,500	6,000	8,000	11,500	13,000	17,000
T-Bird ⋀	4,500	5,000	6,000	7,500	10,000	—	—	—
T-Bird ⋁	4,000	4,500	5,000	6,000	8,000	—	—	—
T-Bird SC ⋀	5,500	6,000	7,000	—	—	—	—	—
T-Bird SC ⋁	5,000	5,500	6,000	—	—	—	—	—

Extended Warranty	Y	Y	Y	Y	Y	Y	Y	Y
Secret Warranty	N	Y	Y	Y	Y	Y	Y	Y
Reliability	❷	❷	❷	③	④	❷	③	③
Crash Safety	—	⑤	⑤	⑤	⑤	—	—	—
Side Impact	—	—	—	—	③	—	—	③
Head Restraints	—	—	❶	—	❶	—	—	—
Cougar (F)	—	—	❶	—	❶	❷	—	❷
Cougar (Rear)	—	—	—	—	—	❶	—	—

CROWN VICTORIA, GRAND MARQUIS   ★★★★★

RATING: Recommended (1997–2001); Above Average (1994–96); Average (1984–93). Overall, these cars aren't as reliable as Japanese luxury vehicles, but they're the best of the domestic crop when it comes to price, power, performance, and overall comfort. Don't waste your money buying a 1998 or 1999 version if you can find a low-mileage 1996. It'll cost much less and give you most of the same features. Only the Marquis was continued into the 2001 model year in Canada; both models are still sold in the States. The Marquis is a slightly more luxurious version that costs more but gives little of consequence for the extra expense. Make sure you check out the headlight illumination. **Maintenance/Repair costs:** Average, but some electronic repairs can be carried out only by Ford dealers. **Parts:** Higher-than-average cost (independent suppliers sell for much less), but they're not hard to find. **Best alternatives:** A Buick LeSabre, an early Ford Thunderbird or Cougar, or GM Caprice and Roadmaster.

Strengths and weaknesses: These cars are especially suited to people who need lots of room, oodles of convenience features, and the safety blanket provided by road-hugging, gas-guzzling weight. Handling is mediocre, but it's about average for cars this size. Both the 4.6L and 5.0L V8s provide adequate though sometimes sluggish power, with most of their torque found in the lower gear ranges.

Over the years, these cars haven't changed much. For example, the '95s were re-styled and given standard heated outside mirrors and a new interior treatment; '96s dropped the towing package and added a new gas cap and steering wheel; the '97s got improved steering and rear air suspension (a horror to diagnose and repair); minor power steering and suspension improvements were added to the '98 models; '99s got standard ABS and a new stereo system; year 2000 models were given an emergency trunk release, user-friendly child safety seat anchorages, and an improved handling package for quicker acceleration; and the 2001s were carried over in the States with a small horsepower boost, minor interior improvements, adjustable pedals, seatbelt pretensioners, and improved airbag systems.

On the downside, there are a number of factory-related problems that reappear year after year. They include failure-prone fuel pump, sender, fuel filter, and fuel hose assemblies; ignition module and fuel cut-off switch malfunctions that cause hard starting and frequent stalling; brakes (rotors, calipers, and pads), shock absorbers, and springs that wear out more quickly than they should; and chronic front suspension noise when passing over small bumps. Inadequate inner fender protection allows road salt to completely cover engine wiring, brake master cylinder, and suspension components; frequent inspection and cleaning is required. Hubcaps frequently fall off. Finally, there is such a high number of safety-related complaints concerning brake and fuel lines, suspension, and steering components that an undercarriage inspection is a prerequisite to buying models three years or older.

Safety summary: All models/years: Fuel line and electrical fires. • Sudden, unintended acceleration. • Airbags that fail to deploy. • ABS brake failures. **All models: 1992–2001**—Rear-end impact may puncture fuel tank; two TSB repairs already carried out. **1996**—Engine surges without warning or shuts down when brakes are applied. • Cruise control won't disengage when brakes are applied. • Oil pan/gasket leaks. • Many reports that the left frame bracket broke at weld, causing vehicle to pull sharply to the right when brakes were applied. • Reports of ball joint and lower control arm failures say that the vehicle's front wheel assembly is also affected. • Police department inspectors report their vehicles have shown excessive play in the Pitman arms. • Brake lines are routed too close to the body and chafe excessively. • Brake pedal went to the floor due to failure of the stop switch and clip-on pedal. • Frequent replacement of front brake components. • Steering locks up, will not return, or is so loose it won't steer vehicle. • Cracked intake manifolds cause loss of coolant (see "Secret Warranties/Service Tips/TSBs"). • Frequent catalytic converter failures. • Inoperative rear window defroster. • Seatbelt buckle doesn't stay latched. • Seatbelts failed to restrain occupants during a collision. **1997**—Sudden acceleration due to a design flaw of the throttle linkage and bracket. • Floormats can shift under the gas or brake pedals, causing them to jam. • Vehicle left in Park position with engine on slipped into Reverse. • Collapsed body mounts allow undercarriage to rub flat spots on steel brake lines, causing brake failure. • Steering wheel lockup while driving. • Front suspension ball joint failure after having recall campaign correction done. • Lower passenger-side control arm fell off when vehicle was in First gear. • Sharp door edges have injured three people. • Engine intake manifold failures that cause anti-freeze to leak into the engine compartment (see "Secret Warranties/Service Tips/TSBs"). **1998**—NHTSA investigators are looking into reports that the inertia fuel shutoff switch operates when it shouldn't, stalling the vehicle. • Sudden loss of power; stalling. • Traction control engages for no reason, causing loss of power and control. •

Steering too sensitive when changing lanes, making it easy to lose control. • Dome light switch is poorly designed; it can only be activated by the driver due to its location. • Loss of lighting caused by sudden electrical system failure. • Rubber hose leading from the fuel tank is easily hit when going over a bump or pothole. **1999**—Sudden stalling while underway (fuel inertia cutoff switch self-activates when vehicle hits a pothole or goes over a small bump). • Steering shaft failure when turning. • Cracked rear trailing arm assembly frames. • Transmission jumps from Park into gear. • Premature brake rotor warpage and pad wearout causes excessive brake noise (grinding), vibration, and extended stopping distance. • Sticking front calipers cause vehicle to veer to the right or left. • Premature wear of the lower control arm. • Headlights aren't bright enough. • Loose rear outer door handles. • Driver's seat misalignment places steering wheel and gas/brake pedals too far to the right. **2000**—Oversensitive steering causes vehicle to wander. • Power window failures in cold weather. • Headlights short out intermittently. **2001**— ABS failure leading to brake lockup or loss of braking ability. • When driving in rainy weather, water gets into the engine compartment, causing the water pump to throw the fan belt and leading to loss of control of the vehicle.

Secret Warranties/Service Tips/TSBs

All models: 1985–2002—Repeated heater core failure. **1990–2001**— Correcting a radio whine or buzz in the speakers. **1993–99**—An exhaust buzz or rattle may mean you have a loose catalyst or muffler heat shield. • Paint delamination, peeling, or fading (see Part Two). **1994–99**—Tips on preventing wind noise around the doors. **1995–97**—ABS brakes that activate on their own or produce a grinding, pulsing, fluttering effect on the brake pedal probably need upgraded wiring connectors at the ABS sensors. **1995–99**—Tips on reducing noise, vibration, and harshness, as well as plugging windshield water leaks. **1996–97**—Spark knock during acceleration can be silenced by replacing the sensor and reprogramming the power control module (PCM). **1996–98**—A steering vibration or buzzing when making right turns can be silenced by replacing the power-steering pressure hose. **1997–98**—Lack of AC temperature control may require a new air door actuator. **1997–99**—Delayed upshifts may require a new 2–3 accumulator along with a revised piston. • A rough idle or exhaust system resonance can be fixed by installing an exhaust system mass damper. **1998–99**—A pull or drift when braking in rainy weather can be corrected by installing upgraded front brake linings that are less sensitive to water, says TSB #98-13-4. • A poorly performing AC that also makes a thumping noise may need a new suction accumulator and suction hose assembly. **1998–2000**—Ford Special Service Campaign 00B60 (January 31, 2002) allowed for the free installation of control arm reinforcing brackets or new control arms, regardless of mileage. Ask for a partial refund. **1998–2001**—A Ford special service campaign will replace the engine mounts free of charge on vehicles in fleet service. •

In a separate campaign, the automaker has extended the intake manifold warranty to seven years, without any mileage limitation. This campaign is in response to complaints of coolant leakage leading to engine overheating. **1999–2001**—Correcting a 2–1 shift clunk noise. **2000–01**—Trouble-shooting a ticking noise in First gear.

Crown Victoria, Grand Marquis Profile

	1994	1995	1996	1997	1998	1999	2000	2001
Cost Price ($)								
Crown S/LTD	22,495	24,695	27,195	29,895	30,995	31,895	32,095	—
Grand Marquis GS	23,795	26,695	30,295	32,195	32,895	33,695	31,195	34,125
Used Values ($)								
Crown S/LTD ▲	5,500	7,500	8,500	11,000	14,000	16,500	19,000	—
Crown S/LTD ▼	5,000	6,000	7,000	9,500	12,000	14,000	17,000	—
Grand Marquis GS ▲	6,000	8,500	9,000	12,000	15,000	17,000	20,000	23,500
Grand Marquis GS ▼	5,500	6,500	7,500	10,000	12,500	15,000	18,000	21,000
Extended Warranty	Y	Y	Y	Y	N	N	N	N
Secret Warranty	Y	Y	Y	Y	Y	Y	Y	Y
Reliability	③	④	④	④	④	④	⑤	⑤
Crash Safety	③	③	④	⑤	⑤	⑤	⑤	⑤
Side Impact	—	—	—	—	④	④	④	⑤
Head Restraints	—	❶	—	❶	—	❶	—	❶
Rollover Resistance	—	—	—	—	—	—	—	⑤

General Motors

CAPRICE, IMPALA SS, ROADMASTER ★★★★

RATING: Above Average (1995–96); Average (1994); Not Recommended (1982–93). This group of cars ceased production in 1996. **Maintenance/Repair costs:** Maintenance is inexpensive and easy to perform, and repairs can be done by any corner garage. **Parts:** Average parts costs can be cut further by shopping at independent suppliers, who are generally well stocked. **Best alternatives:** An early Ford Thunderbird or Cougar, Crown Victoria or Mercury Grand Marquis, and GM Bonneville or LeSabre.

Strengths and weaknesses: These cars are large, comfortable, and easy to maintain. The trunk is spacious. Overall handling is acceptable, but expect a queasy ride from the too-soft suspension. Gas mileage is particularly poor. Despite the many generic deficiencies inherent in these rear-drives, they still score higher than GM's front-drives for overall reliability and durability. The Impala SS is basically a Caprice with a 260-hp Corvette engine and high-performance suspension.

On 1988–91 models, engine problems include crankshaft and head gasket failures, cracked cylinder heads, injection pump malfunctions, and oil leaks. Engine knocking is another common problem on early models that's hard to correct inexpensively, due to the various possible causes that have to be eliminated. Early V8s, in particular, suffer from premature camshaft wear, and the 350-cubic-inch V8s often fall prey to premature valve guide wear caused by a faulty EGR valve. Cars equipped with the 5.7L diesel V8 should be approached with caution; they aren't very durable and cost an arm and a leg to troubleshoot and repair. The 4-speed automatic transmission was troublesome until 1991, with burnt-out clutches and malfunctioning torque converters being the most common failures.

The 1991–96 models have elicited few engine and transmission complaints, although they have shown the following deficiencies: chronic AC and ignition glitches; prematurely worn brakes (lots of corrosion damage), steering, and suspension components, especially shock absorbers and rear springs; serious electrical problems; and poor-quality body and trim items.

Body assembly is not impressive, but paint quality and durability is fairly good, considering the delamination one usually finds with GM's other models. Wagons often have excessive rust around cargo-area side windows and wheelwells, and hubcaps on later models tend to fly off.

Safety summary: All models: 1996: Child was able to shift gear into Neutral, jumped out of car, and was run over. • Airbags failed to deploy. • Airbag light stays lit for no apparent reason. • Gas pedal sticks on initial application. • ABS brakes lock up. • Transmission torque converter/ engine flywheel breakage. • Broken torque converter bolts. • Steering box loosens up despite new bolts. • Steering lockup. • Sometimes vehicle fishtails uncontrollably while at moderate speed. • Front coil spring failure. • Premature tire wear caused by faulty suspension components that can't be fixed by repeated alignments. • Fuel pump failure caused by wiring harness short.

Secret Warranties/Service Tips/TSBs

All models/years: A rotten-egg odour coming from the exhaust is usually the result of a malfunctioning catalytic converter. **All models: 1993–96**—Paint delamination, peeling, or fading (see Part Two). **1994**— Excessive oil consumption is likely due to delaminated intake manifold gaskets. Install an upgraded intake manifold gasket kit. • GM campaign 94C15 will adjust, at no charge, a misadjusted automatic transmission shift linkage that could, if left alone, burn out the Low/Reverse clutch. **1994–96**—Excessive engine noise can be silenced by installing an upgraded valve stem oil seal. • A chuggle or surge condition in vehicles

with a with 5.7L engine will require a reflash calibration. **Roadmaster:**
1994—Excessive oil consumption is likely due to delaminated intake
manifold gaskets. Install an upgraded intake manifold gasket kit. • Poor
AC performance can be improved by replacing the temperature control
cable. • Delayed automatic transmission shift engagement is a common
problem addressed in TSB #47-71-20A. **1995–96**—Delayed automatic
transmission shift engagement may require the replacement of the pump
cover assembly.

Caprice, Impala SS, Roadmaster Profile

	1990	1991	1992	1993	1994	1995	1996
Cost Price ($)							
Caprice	20,128	19,698	20,298	20,806	22,500	25,455	28,345
Caprice wagon	21,347	20,398	21,598	22,138	24,985	29,120	30,980
Impala SS	—	—	—	—	—	29,005	30,675
Roadmaster	—	—	25,398	26,298	29,798	32,930	34,230
Used Values ($)							
Caprice ʌ	3,500	4,000	5,000	6,000	7,500	8,500	9,500
Caprice v	3,000	3,500	4,500	5,000	6,500	7,000	8,000
Caprice wagon ʌ	4,500	5,000	6,000	7,000	8,000	9,000	10,500
Caprice wagon v	4,000	4,500	5,000	6,000	7,000	8,000	9,000
Impala SS ʌ	—	—	—	—	—	11,500	14,500
Impala SS v	—	—	—	—	—	10,000	12,500
Roadmaster ʌ	—	—	5,000	6,000	7,500	8,500	10,000
Roadmaster v	—	—	4,500	5,000	6,500	7,500	8,500
Extended Warranty	N	N	N	N	N	N	N
Secret Warranty	N	Y	Y	Y	Y	Y	Y
Reliability	❷	❷	❷	❷	③	③	③
Crash Safety	—	④	④	④	④	④	④
Head Restraints	—	—	—	—	—	❶	—

LUXURY CARS

Beware of luxury lemons

Used luxury cars can be great buys, if you know how to separate symbol from substance and are smart enough to know that most of the high-end models don't give you much more than their lower-priced entry-level versions. For example, the Lexus ES 300 is a Toyota Camry with a higher sticker price; the Audi A4 isn't much different from the Volkswagen Passat; Lincoln's Continental uses mostly Ford Taurus and Sable powertrains; and the Acura 3.2TL, Infiniti I35 (formerly called the I30), and Jaguar X-Type are fully loaded, high-tuned versions of the Honda Accord, the Nissan Maxima, and the European Ford Mondeo, respectively.

Both high- and low-end models project a flashy cachet; come loaded with high-tech safety, performance, and comfort features; and can be bought, after three years or so, for half of what they sold for new. Furthermore, if you can get servicing and parts from independent garages, you'll save even more. On the downside, there *are* overpriced luxury lemons out there (like the Continental and the Cadillac Allanté and Catera, for example) that aren't built anymore and are known to be unreliable, with hard-to-service engines and transmissions and servicing costs that rival Neiman Marcus.

Take Mercedes-Benz, for example. The company has always been seen as an icon of innovative engineering and quality control, yet a $5-million study conducted over five years by the Massachusetts Institute of Technology says the company makes lousy cars. The MIT study concluded over a decade ago that Mercedes built poor-quality vehicles and then attempted to fix its mistakes at the end of the assembly line. As one reviewer of *The Machine that Changed the World*, by James P. Womack, Daniel T. Jones, and Daniel Roos (HarperCollins, November 1991), wrote,

> This study of the world automotive industry by a group of MIT academics reaches the radical conclusion that the much vaunted Mercedes technicians are actually a throwback to the pre-industrial age, while Toyota is far ahead in costs and quality by building the automobiles correctly the first time.

Readers of my *Lemon-Aid SUVs, Vans, and Trucks 2002* know from the internal service bulletins I quote extensively that Mercedes' M-Class sport-utilities have been plagued by serious factory defects (running the gamut from powertrain failures to the dye on red leather seatcovers rubbing off on clothing). However, a confidential January 2002 quality survey leaked to the press confirms that Mercedes' quality problems now affect its entire vehicle lineup. The survey, commissioned by European automakers from TUV, a German auto-inspection and research association, ranked Mercedes twelfth in quality control, just behind GM's much-maligned Opel. A few weeks earlier, J.D. Power & Associates released a study of 156,000 car owners that showed five-year-old Mercedes vehicles had a higher-than-average number of problems. Power subsequently lowered the company's rating for quality control to "fair" from "good."

Industry insiders believe Mercedes' quality problems are symptomatic of a malaise affecting many luxury car builders: rushing too many new models into production (Mercedes has gone from four model lines to nine since 1997) and building cheaper, smaller, bare-bones knock-offs of popular models.

Mercedes' CLK320: would you spend big bucks on cars rated only "fair" for overall quality?

American luxury cars are still seen by most consumers as overweight and unreliable land yachts. And do remember this: spending more on a luxury car doesn't always mean you'll get a safer vehicle, as thousands of Cadillac owners with airbags exploding whenever the carpet gets wet will confirm. See "Safety summary" for more sorry facts about General Motors and Ford safety-related failures. Traditionally, the luxury-car niche has been dominated by American and German automakers. During the past decade, however, buyers have gravitated towards Japanese models. This shift in buyer preference has forced Chrysler out of the market, made Ford drop its problem-plagued Lincoln Continental, and has GM reconsidering a return to rear-drive Cadillacs.

OK, so you're well advised to choose a Japanese model, but doesn't that mean you'll have to dig deep in your wallet, wiping out most of your expected savings? Not necessarily. You don't always have to spend a lot to get true luxury and ironclad reliability. Smart buyers can target the fully equipped Toyota Camry or Avalon, Honda Accord, Nissan Maxima, and Mazda 929, all of which offer similar equipment, reliability, and performance to Lexus, Infiniti, and Acura models, but for much, much less.

Forget the overpriced Lexus and get a Toyota Camry or Avalon (shown above) instead.

It's sad but true. There aren't any American luxury cars that can match an equivalent Japanese model for overall reliability, durability, and value. And this isn't because Japanese products are that well made; far from it, as anyone who's purchased a quirky Saab 9000 or a transmission-challenged Lexus will attest. No, it's simply because GM, Ford, and Chrysler's vehicles are so poorly made that they make everyone else look better. A fact that's reflected in the head-spinningly high depreciation rates and plummeting market share seen with most large-*cum*-luxury cars put out by the Big Three. GM's rear-drive Cadillac DeVille and Ford's rear-drive Crown Victoria, Grand Marquis, and Lincoln Town Car come closest to meeting the imports in overall reliability and durability, yet they still come nowhere near the quality level of many *entry-level* imports. Examples of lousy American luxury cars abound: the Chrysler front-drive New Yorker and LHS are unremarkable and are plagued by serious powertrain reliability problems, and most GM Cadillacs have been characterized by innovative, albeit unreliable, technology like variable-cylinder engines (the 4-6-8 engine), cobbled-together diesel powerplants, and poorly engineered, high-maintenance, low-quality front-drive components. Only Ford, with its aforementioned luxury rear-drives, has presented any credible competition, and now, with the dropping of the Lincoln Town Car and the Crown Victoria being reserved solely for fleet sales, it's just a matter of time before Ford is taken out of the running.

What does this foretell for the future of used luxury cars? Firstly, prices will plummet as a souring economy takes its toll. Plus, a flood of off-lease cars will further cut into prices and give buyers a wider choice. Finally, we'll likely see the renaissance of rear-drives, with Cadillac and Ford leading the parade.

LUXURY CAR RATINGS

Recommended

Acura TL (1999–2001)
Audi A4, A6 (100), A8, TT Coupe
  (2000–01)
BMW 5 Series (1992–2001)
BMW M Series (1997–2001)
BMW Z3 (1996–2001)

Lexus ES 300, GS 300, LS 400,
  SC 400 (1996–2001)
Mercedes-Benz 300 series,
  400 series, 500 series,
  E-Class (1993–2001)

Above Average

Acura RL (1996–2001)
Acura TL (1996–98)
Audi A4, A6 (100), A8, S6
  (1996–99)
BMW 3 Series (1995–2001)
Ford/Lincoln Mark VII, Mark VIII
  (1995–98)
General Motors Cadillac Brougham,
  Fleetwood rear-drive (1993–96)
General Motors Cadillac DeVille
  (2000–01)
Infiniti I30, J30, Q45 (1995–2001)

Lexus ES 300, GS 300, LS 400,
  SC 400 (1990–95)
Mazda Millenia (1995–2001)
Mercedes-Benz 300 series,
  400 series, 500 series,
  E-Class (1992)
Mercedes-Benz C-Class
  (1995–2001)
Nissan Maxima (1989–2001)
Toyota Avalon (1995–2001)
Volvo 850, C70, S40, S70, V40,
  V70 (1993–2001)
Volvo 900 series (1989–96)

Average

BMW 3 Series (1994)
BMW 5 Series (1985–91)
Ford/Lincoln LS (2000–01)
Ford/Lincoln Mark VII, Mark VIII
  (1994)
Ford/Lincoln Town Car (1995–2001)
General Motors 98 Regency, Park
  Avenue (1997–2001)
General Motors Aurora (1995–2001)
General Motors Cadillac Brougham,
  Fleetwood rear-drive (1984–92)

General Motors Cadillac Concours,
  DeVille, Fleetwood front-drive
  (1995–99)
General Motors Riviera (1995–99)
Infiniti J30, Q45 (1991–94)
Mercedes-Benz C-Class (1994)
Nissan Maxima (1986–88)
Saab 9-3, 9-5 (1999–2001)
Volvo 900 series, S80, S90, V90
  (1997–2001)

Below Average

BMW 3 Series (1984–93)
Ford/Lincoln Continental (1988–2001)
Ford/Lincoln Mark VII, Mark VIII
  (1986–93)
General Motors 98 Regency, Park
Avenue (1991–96)

General Motors Cadillac Catera,
  Eldorado, Seville (1992–2001)
General Motors Concours, DeVille,
  Fleetwood front-drive (1985–94)
Mercedes-Benz 300 series, 400 series,
  500 series, E-Class (1985–91)
Saab 900, 9000 (1995–98)

Not Recommended

Audi 90, A6 (100), S6 (1984–95)
General Motors 98 Regency, Park
 Avenue (1985–90)
General Motors Cadillac Eldorado,
 Seville (1986–91)

General Motors Riviera (1986–93)
Infiniti G20 (1994–2001)
Saab 900, 9000 (1985–94)

Acura

RL ★★★★

RATING: Above Average (1996–2001). Basically a fully loaded, longer, wider, and heavier TL, equipped with a larger engine that produces less horsepower than its smaller brother. Resale value is high on all Acura models. **Maintenance/Repair costs:** Average, and most repairs are dealer dependent. **Parts:** Most mechanical and electronic components are easily found and moderately priced. Some reports that recall repairs are often delayed because corrected parts aren't available (transmission/transfer case, for example). Body parts may be hard to come by and can be expensive. **Best alternatives:** Consider the departed Acura Legend, BMW's 5 Series, Infiniti's I30/I35, and the Lexus GS 300/400. You may want to take a look at the TL sedan: it's not as expensive, and is a better performer, though passenger room is more limited.

Strengths and weaknesses: Good, though not impressive, acceleration that's smooth and quiet in all gear ranges; exceptional steering and handling; comfortable ride; loaded with goodies; top-quality body and mechanical components. On the other hand, the steering can be numb, and manual and automatic transmissions are sometimes problematic.

The 3.5 RL is Honda's—oh, I mean, Acura's—flagship sedan. It's loaded with innovative high-tech safety and convenience features one would expect to find in a luxury car. These include heated front seats, front and rear climate controls, a rear-seat trunk pass-through, Xenon headlights (get used to oncoming drivers flashing you their headlights), "smart" side airbags, ABS, traction control, and an anti-skid system.

The 3.5L 210-hp V6 mated to a 4-speed automatic transmission provides good acceleration that's a bit slower and more fuel-thirsty than the TL, partly due to the RL's extra pounds. The car handles nicely, with a less firm ride than the TL, although steering response doesn't feel as crisp. Interior accommodations for four occupants are excellent up front and in the rear, due to the RL's use of a larger platform than the TL.

'98s got a sportier suspension, standard alloy wheels, and three-point rear-centre safety belts; '99s received standard side airbags, high-intensity discharge headlights, larger brakes, and a retuned suspension; year 2000 models were given a Vehicle Stability Assist system and upgraded side airbags. 2001s were carried over relatively unchanged.

Owner-reported problems: a mis-shifting manual transmission, noisy transmission engagement, frequent stalling, malfunctioning accessories, electrical shorts, and premature brake wear.

Safety summary: All models/years: It's interesting to note that the RL has had remarkably few complaints registered by NHTSA. **All models: 1996**—Airbags failed to deploy in a collision. **1998**—Premature wearout of the front and rear brake pads around 15,000 miles (240,000 kilometres). **1999**—ABS failed to respond, resulting in rear-end collision. **2000**—Vehicle suddenly stalls when decelerating or cruising on the highway; transmission replaced, but problem returned. • Premature transmission replacements. **2001**—Transmission shifts poorly when accelerating or decelerating; vehicle stalls at slower speeds. • 6-speed manual transmission mis-shifts when going from Third to Fourth gear; it engages Second gear instead, causing extensive engine damage. • In cold weather, Second gear is hard to engage and produces a grinding noise. • Sometimes transmission pops out of Second gear. • Cracked front wheel-well liners.

Secret Warranties/Service Tips/TSBs

All models/years: Like Honda's, most of Acura's TSBs allow for special warranty consideration on a "goodwill" basis, even after the warranty has expired or the car has changed hands. Referring to this euphemism will increase your chances of getting some kind of refund for repairs that are obviously factory defects. • Seatbelts that fail to function properly during normal use will be replaced for free under the company's lifetime seatbelt warranty. • Diagnostic procedures and correction for off-centre steering wheels. **All models: 1996**—Rapid rear brake pad wear can be corrected by installing upgraded pads. • Moon-roof wind noise can be corrected by replacing the visor clips and mounting hardware. • If the driver's seatback piping wears out prematurely, Acura suggests it be replaced. **1996–97**—Details of Acura's 14-year free engine repairs/ tuneups agreement with the United States' EPA. • Front window wind noise can be reduced by aligning the glass and sash. • Window noise during operation can be silenced by replacing the glass stabilizers and sashes, as well as the glass, if it's scratched. • Drivers who find the footrest is positioned too far away may obtain a replacement footrest from Acura. **1996–98**—A growling or whining coming from the rear wheels can be fixed by replacing the hub bearing unit. • Brake squeal during light application can be fixed by replacing the front pads (eligible for "goodwill"). **1996–2000**—Moon-roof rattles can be silenced by replacing the moon-roof glass. **1999**—A navigation system that locks up or resets can be corrected by rewriting the unit's software; a remanufactured unit may also be considered. **1999–2000**—A squeaking, creaking driver's seat is addressed in TSB #00-010. **2000**—Troubleshooting noisy automatic transmissions. • Moon-roof rattles. • Driver's seat noise. • Steering wheel clunk. **2000–01**—Stability Assist may activate too soon. • Engine starts and dies when ignition is released. • Intermittent electrical shorts.

RL Profile

	1996	1997	1998	1999	2000	2001
Cost Price ($)						
Base	52,300	54,600	55,000	52,000	52,000	53,000
Used Values ($)						
Base ʌ	15,500	19,000	24,000	30,000	36,000	41,000
Base v	13,500	17,000	21,000	27,000	34,000	39,000
Extended Warranty	N	N	N	N	N	N
Secret Warranty	N	N	N	N	N	N
Reliability	④	④	⑤	⑤	⑤	⑤
Crash Safety	—	—	—	④	④	④
Head Restraints	—	❷	❶	—	❷	❶

TL   ★★★★★

RATING: Recommended (1999–2001); Above Average (1996–98). Resale value is high on all Acura models. **Maintenance/Repair costs:** Average cost, but many repairs are dealer dependent. **Parts:** Higher-than-average cost (some independent suppliers sell for much less under the Honda name), but not hard to find. **Best alternatives:** Consider the Acura Integra, Audi A4, BMW's redesigned 3 series, Infiniti's redesigned I30/I35, the Mazda Millenia, and the Lexus ES 300. You may want to take a look at Acura's CL coupe: it's not as expensive, and is as close as you can get to the Accord with lots of standard bells and whistles thrown in.

Strengths and weaknesses: The TL has impressive acceleration, handles well, rides comfortably, and is well put-together, with quality mechanical and body components. However, the suspension may be too firm for some, and the vehicle has uncomfortable rear seating, excessive road noise, and problematic navigation system controls.

Filling the void left by the discontinued Vigor, the TL combines luxury and performance in a nicely styled front-drive five-passenger sedan that uses the same chassis as the Accord and CL coupe. Base models will likely carry an adequate, though unimpressive, 2.5L inline 5-cylinder engine. Performance enthusiasts will opt for versions equipped with the more refined 3.2L 225/260-hp V6 mated to a 4-speed automatic transmission. It provides impressive acceleration (0–100 km/h in just over 8 seconds) in a smooth and quiet manner, without any fuel penalty. Handling is exceptional with the firm suspension, but can be a bit tricky when pushed. Bumps are a bit jarring and the ride is somewhat busier than other cars in this class, but this is a small price to pay for the car's high-speed performance.

'98 TLs came with a bit more standard equipment than previous years; '99s dropped the 2.5L engine and upgraded practically everything else; year 2000 models got enhanced performance features that include a better-performing 5-speed transmission and free-flowing intake manifold. Standard side airbags and depowered frontal airbags were also new that year. The car was upgraded in the spring of 2001.

Interior accommodations are better than average up front, but rear occupants may discover that leg room is a bit tight and the seat cushions lack sufficient thigh support. The cockpit layout is very user-friendly, due in part to the easy-to-read gauges and accessible controls (far-away climate controls are the only exception). Standard safety features include ABS, traction control, childproof door locks, three-point seatbelts, and a transmission/brake interlock.

The only areas that have proven troublesome in the past have been engine surging and stalling, malfunctioning airbags and accessories, electrical shorts, premature brake wear, and poor body fits. Owners point out that the window regulator may need replacing, the ignition switch buzzes, the trunk lock jams, and the rear bumper is often loose.

Safety summary: All models/years: Horn is difficult to locate in emergency situations. • Airbags fail to deploy in a collision. • Sudden, unintended acceleration. **All models: 1996**—Both airbags suddenly deployed for no reason while vehicle was underway. • Driveline whines upon acceleration. • Rear brake failure; brakes are frequently in need of repair. • Prematurely worn rear brake pads. • Passenger-side window suddenly shattered. **1997**—Chronic stalling as vehicle decelerates. • Steering column fire. • Complete brake loss. • Check Engine light comes on often. **1999**—Airbags deployed in a collision and severely burned driver's hands. • Seatbelt failed to retract in a collision, allowing driver to hit windshield. • Transmission fails to downshift or upshift. • Front rotors warp within 10,000 miles (160,000 kilometres). • Door locks operate erratically. • Wiper blades leak graphite, smearing windshield. • Instrument panel is washed out in sunlight, making odometer practically invisible. **2000**—Brake pedal feels spongy, and it's easy to confuse brake and gas pedals. **2001**—Automatic transmission failures that leave the engine revving high (like when passing), but the car doesn't accelerate (it actually slows down).

Secret Warranties/Service Tips/TSBs

All models/years: Like Honda's, most of Acura's TSBs allow for special warranty consideration on a "goodwill" basis, even after the warranty has expired or the car has changed hands. Referring to this euphemism will increase your chances of getting some kind of refund for repairs that are obviously factory defects. • Seatbelts that fail to function properly during normal use will be replaced for free under the company's lifetime seatbelt warranty. • Diagnostic procedures and correction for off-centre steering wheels. **All models: 1996**—Rapid rear brake pad wear can be corrected by installing upgraded pads. • Moon-roof wind noise can be corrected by replacing the visor clips and mounting hardware. • If the driver's seatback piping wears out prematurely, Acura suggests it be replaced. **1996–97**—Details of Acura's 14-year free engine repairs/tuneups agreement with the the United States' EPA. • Front window wind noise can be reduced by aligning the glass and sash. • Window noise during operation can be silenced by replacing the glass stabilizers and sashes, as well as the glass, if it's scratched. • Drivers who find the footrest is positioned too far away may obtain a replacement footrest from Acura. **1996–98**—A growling or whining coming from the rear wheels can be fixed by replacing the hub bearing unit. • Brake squeal during light application can be fixed by replacing the front pads (eligible for "goodwill"). **1999**—A navigation system that locks up or resets can be corrected by rewriting the unit's software; a remanufactured unit may also be considered. **1999–2000**—A squeaking, creaking driver's seat is addressed in TSB #00-014. • A wrinkled rear door sash trim will be covered under a "goodwill" policy, even if correction was done by an independent bodyshop. • Tips on replacing a leaking torque converter. • Troubleshooting moon-roof creaks. **2000**—Excessive cranking when restarting. • Faulty front and rear water passage gaskets at the cylinder head can cause a coolant leak next to the EGR valve. • Radiator/condenser fan runs continuously, discharging battery. • Vehicle clunks when going over bumps. **2000–01**—MIL (malfunction indicator light) and airbag warning light may stay lit for no apparent reason. • V6 engine oil leaks. • Speed sensor plug may be missing. • Panic alarm activates inadvertently. • Brake pedal pulsation. • Windshield wiper smearing and streaking. **2001**—A booming sound may be heard when the moon roof is opened while the car is underway. • Moon-roof squeaks. • Climate control changes intermittently.

TL Profile

	1996	1997	1998	1999	2000	2001
Cost Price ($)						
Base	34,900	36,600	37,000	35,001	35,000	36,000
Used Values ($)						
Base ⅄	12,000	14,500	18,000	23,000	27,500	31,000
Base V	10,000	13,500	15,500	21,000	25,000	29,000
Extended Warranty	N	N	N	N	N	N
Secret Warranty	N	N	N	N	N	N

Reliability	④	④	④	⑤	⑤	⑤
Crash Safety	④	④	④	—	—	④
Side Impact	—	—	—	—	—	⑤
Head Restraints	—	❶	—	❶	—	❶

Audi

90, A4, A6 (100), A8, S6, TT COUPE   ★★★★★

RATING: Recommended (2000–01); Above Average (1996–99); Not Recommended (1984–95). Wet-weather braking can be atrocious. **Maintenance/Repair costs:** Higher than average, and almost all repairs have to be done by an Audi dealer. Long delays for recall repairs. **Parts:** Way-higher-than-average cost, and independent suppliers have a hard time finding parts. Don't even think about buying one of these front-drives without a 3- to 5-year supplementary warranty backed by Audi. **Best alternatives:** Other vehicles worth taking a look at: the Acura Integra, TL and RL; BMW 3 Series; Infiniti I30/I35; and Lexus ES300. TT Coupe shoppers may also want to look at the BMW Z3 Series, Honda S2000, and Mazda Miata.

Strengths and weaknesses: These cars are attractively styled and comfortable to drive, handle well, and provide a spacious interior. Yet the pre-1993 models, including the old 90 and 100, have a worse-than-average reliability record and are plagued by mechanical and electrical components that don't stand up to the rigors of driving in cold climates. Look for the better-built and more recent A4 and A6 models. The dealer body isn't strong enough to adequately service all of these vehicles when things go wrong, so owners of older models are generally left to independent garages to serve their needs. Airbags became a standard feature during the 1994 model year.

The 1996 and later models are the pick of the Audi litter (when all-wheel-drive became an optional feature on all entry-level models). The A6, the reincarnation of the 100 series, is packed with standard features, and is a comfortable, spacious, front-drive or all-wheel-drive luxury sedan that comes with dual airbags and ABS. It uses the same V6 power-plant as the A4, its smaller sibling, but has 47 additional horses. Unfortunately, the engine is no match for the car's size (0–100 km/h in 13 seconds), and steering and handling is decidedly trucklike. The A8, the first luxury car with an all-aluminum body, competes with the BMW 7 Series and the Mercedes S-Class. Equipped with a WHO 174-hp 2.8L V6 or a 300-hp V8, the A8 is an above-average buy. Its only drawbacks: it comes with a high price, steering is a bit imprecise for an Audi, and its aluminum body can only be repaired by an Audi dealer.

The S6 is a solid performer with its turbocharged 227-hp 2.2L 5-cylinder engine. Its reliability is better than average and its sports performance leaves the A6 in the dust. The S6 is equipped with sports suspension, a turbocharger, and four-wheel drive.

Audi renamed the 1997 A4 V6 sedan the 2.8 and introduced an entry-level A4 1.8T. An improved 190-hp DOHC V6 also debuted that year. '98s saw the addition of the A4 2.8 V6 wagon equipped with a 5-speed Tiptronic transmission; '99s were joined by an A4 1.8 wagon, and the base 1.8 model received additional insulation. For 2000, a high-performance S4 joined the A4 lineup, and A4 2.8s were given a power-assisted front passenger's seat. The S4 is a limited-production, high-performance spin-off that carries a 227-hp turbocharged rendition of the old 5-cylinder powerplant. 2001 models saw the base 1.8L engine get 20 extra horses; an all-new 2001 S4 sedan and Avant, featuring a 250-hp 2.7L twin-turbocharged V6, also joined the lineup.

The '99 A6 was carried over with minor changes; year 2000 models were joined by two performance sedans and side curtain airbags (standard on the 4.2); and the 2001 2.7T and the 4.2 A6 models got Audi's electronic stabilization program, which prevents fishtailing and enhances traction control. A new all-road version, featuring all-wheel drive, the 2.7L engine, and adjustable air suspension, arrived later that year.

These alphabetically named cars are conservatively styled, often slow off the mark (in spite of the V6 addition when hooked to an automatic), and plagued by electrical glitches. The 4-speed automatic shifts erratically (delayed and abrupt engagement), and the 2.8L V6 engine needs full throttle for adequate performance. Handling is acceptable, but the ride is a bit firm and the car still exhibits considerable body roll, brake dive, and acceleration squat when pushed. Handling is on a par with the BMW 3 Series, and acceleration times beat out those of the Mercedes. The AWD is extended to entry-level models at a time when most automakers are dropping the option on passenger cars.

Overall quality control has improved markedly since 1996, Nevertheless, 1996–99 models have an inordinate number of safety- and performance-related defects reported by owners. Brake failures in rainy weather, fuel system malfunctions leading to surging and stalling, electrical shorts, early lower control arm replacement, distorted windshields, and body glitches head the list of things likely to go wrong. Furthermore, servicing is still spotty due to the small number of dealers in Canada and the fact that these cars are extremely dealer-dependent.

90

Launched in 1988, these entry-level Audis share the same wheelbase and front-drive or 4X4 components. Equipped with an efficient but wimpy 4-cylinder (dropped in 1991) or the more powerful 2.3L 5-cylinder engine, four-wheel disc brakes, and galvanized body panels, these small sedans are leagues ahead of Audi's mid-1980s vehicles. The 1991 models are clearly a better choice; they use an improved 4-speed automatic transmission hooked up to a more powerful engine. 1992 was basically a carry-over year in which unsold 1991 models were recycled. Audi's first convertible, the Cabriolet, first appeared in 1994. It's essentially a 90 model set on a shorter wheelbase with a standard automatic transmission. The 90 was redesigned in 1995 (replacing both the 80 and the old 90) as the Sport 90, a stylish sporty version that was more show than go—it was dropped shortly thereafter. Common problems include AC, electrical system, and brake malfunctions.

TT Coupe

The TT Coupe is a sporty front-drive hatchback with 2+2 seating, set on the same platform used by the A4, Golf, Jetta, and New Beetle. A two-seat convertible version, the Roadster, was launched in the spring of 2000. The base 180-hp 1.8L engine (lifted from the A4) is coupled to a manual 5-speed, while the optional engine uses a 6-speed manual transaxle. Shorter and more firmly sprung than the A4, the TT's engines are turbocharged, though only the optional engine comes with standard all-wheel drive.

More beautifully styled and better handling than the Prowler, the TT comes with lots of high-tech standard features that include four-wheel disc brakes, airbags everywhere, traction control (front-drive models), a power top (Quattro), a heated-glass rear window, and a power-retractable glass windbreak between the roll bars (convertible). An alarm system employs a pulse radar system to catch prying hands invading the cockpit area.

Problem areas reported by owners: premature transmission failures and grinding of the Second gear synchronizers (see the websites *www.audi-tt.org* and *www.vwvortex.com*), excessive brake noise, electrical shorts causing dash gauges and instruments to fail, premature wheel bearing failure, and steering wheel clunks.

Safety summary: All models/years: Extremely poor wet braking on later models, caused by water contaminating the brake rotor and disc; braking delay is almost two seconds. • Chronic stalling. • Many cases of distorted windshields. **A4: 1997**—Sudden acceleration. • Ignition switch failure causes many electrical systems to malfunction. • Premature clutch failure. • Battery exploded. **1998**—Stuck gas pedal. • Premature transmission failure; car pops out of gear. • Front and rear brake rotor and pad failed. • Premature upper and lower control arm failures (50 complaints found on *www.audiworld.com* website). • Sunroof opens by itself. **1999**—Sudden, unintended acceleration when backing up. • Vehicle will roll away even though parking brake is engaged. • Brakes suddenly locked up. • Engine loses power when shifting. • Door locks don't work. • Airbag failures. • Headlights burn out prematurely and don't provide sufficient illumination. • Booming noise heard if the sunroof or any window is open when car is underway. **2001**—Brakes fail to stop vehicle. • Headlights blind oncoming drivers. • Hood latch broke, allowing hood to smash into windshield. **A6 sedan: 1998–99**—During refuelling, gasoline spits back violently from the filler pipe. **TT Coupe: 2000**—Engine compartment howling or moaning heard when accelerating. • Periodic grinding of the Second gear synchronizers is a common failure, said to affect many Audi and VW models. • Parking brake failure. • Engine exploded following a computer malfunction. • Electrical short causes vehicle to lose power. • Fuel gauge shows full, even though fuel is low. **2001**—Defective fuel gauge gives false reading (A6 models recalled for the same defect). • All windshields have some kind of visual distortion (anything viewed, especially straight lines, is distorted). Audi has a secret warranty to replace the windshields for free, regardless of mileage. • Sudden clutch failure (Audi paid half the replacement cost). • Central computer failure causes door locks to jam, trapping occupants. • Sudden windshield wiper failure.

Secret Warranties/Service Tips/TSBs

All models/years: Defective catalytic converters that cause a rotten-egg smell may be replaced free of charge under the emissions warranty. **A4, A6, S6: 1995–97**—Delayed 1–2 shift on cold-start warm-ups is a normal condition resulting from the emissions control settings, according to Audi. **A4, A6: 1998–2000**—Diagnostic and repair procedures for disc brake squeal, an engine that will crank but not start, and engine misfires. **1999**—AC doesn't provide enough cooling. • Tips to silence rear window creaking or popping. **A4: 1996–99**—Audi will install upgraded front brakes on a case-by-case basis to "fix" problems related to premature corrosion (*Automotive News*, February 8, 1999). **1997**—Turbocharger failure. • Rear axle knocking, creaking noise. • Tips on installing transmission sound-deadening shields. • Troubleshooting vehicles producing a whining, whirring noise when they're underway. **A6: 2000**—Automatic transmission goes into limp mode and won't shift.

90, A4, A6 (100), A8, S6, TT Coupe Profile

	1994	1995	1996	1997	1998	1999	2000	2001
Cost Price ($)								
Sport 90	35,250	38,750	—	—	—	—	—	—
A4	—	—	36,250	31,600	32,700	32,700	32,990	33,785
A6 (100)	48,250	47,480	48,904	49,270	48,800	48,880	49,170	49,835
A8	—	—	—	89,850	90,540	90,540	86,250	86,500
S6	—	59,900	61,400	63,550	—	—	—	—
TT	—	—	—	—	—	—	49,500	50,400
Used Values ($)								
Sport 90 ▲	8500	10,500	—	—	—	—	—	—
Sport 90 ▼	7,000	9,000	—	—	—	—	—	—

A4 ▲	—	—	12,000	15,000	18,500	22,000	25,000	28,000
A4 ▼	—	—	10,000	13,000	16,500	19,500	23,000	25,000
A6 (100)▲	10,500	13,000	15,500	20,000	26,000	33,000	38,500	43,000
A6 (100)▼	8,500	11,000	14,000	18,000	23,500	30,000	36,000	41,000
A8 ▲	—	—	—	30,000	40,000	50,000	61,000	69,000
A8 ▼	—	—	—	27,000	37,000	47,000	58,000	66,000
S6 ▲	—	15,000	18,500	23,000	—	—	—	—
S6 ▼	—	12,500	16,000	20,000	—	—	—	—
TT ▲	—	—	—	—	—	—	39,500	44,500
TT ▼	—	—	—	—	—	—	37,000	42,500
Extended Warranty	Y	Y	Y	Y	Y	Y	Y	Y
Secret Warranty	N	N	N	N	Y	Y	Y	Y
Reliability	❶	❶	❷	❷	③	④	④	④
Crash Safety								
A4	—	—	④	④	—	—	—	—
A6 (100)	—	—	⑤	⑤	⑤		—	—
A8	—	—	—	—	⑤	⑤	⑤	⑤
TT	—	—	—	—	—	—	—	—
Side Impact (TT)	—	—	—	—	—	—	—	⑤
Off-set (A6)	—	—	—	—	③	③	③	③
Head Restraints								
A4 (F)	—	—	—	❶	—	③	—	④
A4 (Rear)	—	—	—	—	—	—	—	③
A6	—	❶	—	❶	—	③	—	⑤
A8	—	—	—	❶	—	❷	—	③
TT	—	—	—	—	—	—	—	④

BMW

3 SERIES, 5 SERIES, M SERIES, Z3 ★★★★☆

RATING: *3 Series:* Above Average (1995–2001); Average (1994); Below Average (1984–93). *5 Series:* Recommended (1992–2001; there was no 1996 version); Average (1985–91). *M Series:* Recommended (1997–2001). *Z3:* Recommended (1996–2001). These cars come with a reputation that far exceeds what they actually deliver. Don't take my word for it; look at the BMW website at *www.bmwlemon.com.* Pre-'94 prices drop dramatically, making these years the bargain buys of the group. **Maintenance/Repair costs:** Higher than average, but many repairs can be done by independents who specialize in BMW repairs. Unfortunately, the specialists are concentrated around large urban areas. **Parts:** Higher-than-average cost, and they're often back-ordered. **Best alternatives:** Acura Integra, TL, and RL; Infiniti I30 or I35; Lexus ES 300; and Mercedes E-Class.

Strengths and weaknesses: The 3 Series vehicles exhibit great 6-cylinder performance with the manual gearbox, and ride and handling are commendable. The 318's small engine is seriously compromised, however, by an automatic transmission. The 325e is more pleasant to drive and delivers lots of low-end torque. Through 1998, rear passenger and cargo room is limited. After a redesign of the '99 models, passenger and cargo space was increased.

1991 and later models provide peppy 4-cylinder acceleration only with high revs and a manual transmission. Keep in mind that city driving requires lots of manual gear shifting characterized by an abrupt clutch. If you must have an automatic, look for a used model with the 6-cylinder engine. The larger 1.9L 4-cylinder that went into the mid-'96 models doesn't boost performance appreciably.

Although the 1997 models came with traction control, it is not very effective in giving these vehicles acceptable wet pavement traction. A problem since the early '90s, the rear end tends to slip sideways when the roadway is wet (much like Ford's rear-drive Mustang).

1998 3 Series models were given a 2.5L inline 6-cylinder, which had been standard on 1992–95 models, and standard side airbags. '99 models were revamped with a better-performing 2.5L base engine and 2.8L 6-banger, and a more refined transmission and chassis. Nevertheless, handling is still tricky on wet roads, despite the ASC+T traction control; rear seat access is problematic; rear passenger space is limited; and styling is the essence of bland. Year 2000 models comprise a redesigned lineup of coupes, convertibles, and wagons; the hatchback is gone. 2001s received an engine upgrade, larger brakes and wheels, and optional 4X4 capability.

5 Series

There is no problem with rear seat or cargo room with the 5 Series Bimmer. Handling and ride are superb, although these weighty upscale models do strain when going over hilly terrain if they have the automatic gearbox.

5 Series owners report numerous electrical and fuel glitches, faulty turn signal indicators, starter failures, self-activating emergency flashers, rotten-egg odours from the exhaust, and excessive steering wheel or brake vibration.

Overall reliability was very poor with early Bimmers, but has improved of late. Nevertheless, whenever a problem does arise, repair costs are particularly high due to the small number of dealers, the relative scarcity of parts, and the acquiescence of affluent owners.

Interestingly, BMW owners are very Internet conversant. A quick tour of the more popular websites listed in *Lemon-Aid* will give you plenty of information relating to the mechanical and body failures most likely to affect the vehicle you may buy.

Electrical and fuel system, automatic transmission, and front brake failures are the primary weak spots of 1984–93 models. Chronic engine surging at idle and a rotten-egg smell from the exhaust are also commonplace. Door seams, rocker panels, rear-wheel openings, and fender seams are particularly prone to rust. Check the muffler bracket for premature wear, and weather seals and door adjustments for leaks.

'94 and later models still have reliability problems affecting the automatic and manual transmissions, brakes, and fuel and electrical systems. Additionally, owners report that premature brake wear causes excessive vibration and noise when the brakes are applied. Some reports of water leaks through the doors.

Year 2000 and 2001 models are plagued by cooling fan malfunctions, leading to engine overheating and fires; airbag malfunctions; a manual transmission that's hard to shift into Second gear, pops out of gear, and grinds when shifting; automatic transmission screeches when shifting; steering degradation when braking at slow speeds; and front door water leaks.

M Series

Launched in 1997 as a four-door model, the M3 is a high-performance coupe equipped with a potent 240-hp 3.0L engine, a manual shifter, firmer suspension, and 17-inch tires. 1999 and 2000 cars were redesignated the M Series. The 2000 M5 is mostly a renamed 540i sports sedan. 2001 M Series models received a new 315-hp inline six, Dynamic Stability Control, and a tighter suspension (watch those kidneys), while the M3 returned for the 2001 model year in a convertible and coupe format, equipped with a high-performance 333-hp engine.

Z3

BMW's Z3 1.9L roadster arrived on the scene for the 1996 model year (an optional 2.8L engine was added in 1997, along with standard traction control). '98s got standard rollover bars and upgraded sport seats. '99 models received standard side airbags (318Ti excepted) and were joined by a new 2.8 Coupe. A 2.5L inline six replaced the 1.9L 4-cylinder engine. 2000 models got a slight re-styling and standard Dynamic Stability Control; 2001 roadsters and coupes adopted a 3.0L powerplant (instead of the 2.8L), and bigger brakes and wheels were added. Also, the 2.5L engine was tweaked to unleash 14 additional horses.

Safety summary: All models/years: Sudden acceleration. • Airbag malfunctions include bag deploying inadvertently, failing to go off in an accident, and a constantly lit warning light. • Transmission pops out of gear. **318: 1995**—During an accident, the driver-side seatbelt and airbags failed to operate as they should. • Other reports of airbags not deploying. • Sudden steering lockup. • AC expansion valve failures. • Noisy exhaust manifold. • Erratic automatic transmission shifting: hesitation and jerky shifts. • Transmission slips when accelerating, causing vehicle to stall. • Clutch pressure plate failures. • Electrical system malfunctions. **1996**— Sunroof motor shorts out. • AC failures. **1997**—Fire erupted near battery terminal. • Vehicle loses power and then surges. • Gas and brake pedals are too close together. **1998**—Finger was cut off when caught in the power window. • Glass came out of door channel. • Headlights provide poor illumination of the roadway. • Severe suspension hop when passing over small bumps. • Car's rear end slides out during turns. • Incorrect fuel gauge readings. **1999**—Front plastic grill piece fell off car and damaged the windshield. • Automatic transmission failures. • Seatbelt doesn't retract as it should. • Horn sounds when vehicle is put in Reverse. • Headlights come on and off intermittently. • Several incidents of fire erupting when high beams were activated. • Heated seats get too hot. **2000**—Poor wet braking. • Faulty steering damper and control arms. • Seatbelt warning light stays on. • Seatbelt doesn't retract properly. **2001**—Fire ignited due to defective fan assembly. • Defective cooling fan causes engine to overheat; seen as a widespread problem on the bulletin board at *www.roadfly.org/bmw*. • Premature replacement of the control arms. • Defective gas pedal assembly causes jerky acceleration. BMW will replace it on a case-by-case basis. **M3: 1998**—Brake failure. • Airbags failed to deploy. • Chronic horn failures. • Rear-view mirror blocks a substantial portion of the field of vision. • Inadvertent deployment of side airbags. **1999**—ABS failure. **2001**—Rear end clunking, leading to failure of the driveshaft attachment at the differential (confirmed by other complaints on *www.roadfly.org/bmw* website). **Z3: 1998**—Defective rear stabilizer bar. • Automatic transmission jumps out of gear. • Intermittent headlight and instrument cluster failures. • Rear-view mirror creates a huge blind spot. **1999**—Seatbelts don't spool out or retract as they should. **2000**—Computer keeps engine at high revs when throttle is released. • Passenger-side seatbelt jams. **2000–01**—Faulty speedometer. **2001**—Engine stalls when decelerating. • Interior and exterior lights dim when AC engages.

Secret Warranties/Service Tips/TSBs

All models/years: Rear sway bar links may come off the sway bar. • Front brake squeal. • Steering wheel buzz. • Door brake doesn't hold. • Driver's seat is loose. **All models: 1996–99**—Frequent crankshaft position sensor failures result in chronic Check Engine light illumination. This can be corrected by changing the sensor and installing an adapter harness under warranty or under a BMW "goodwill" policy. **3 Series: 1992–95**—Automatic transmission may be slow to shift after sitting overnight because fluid has drained out of the torque converter. **1996**— Transmission shuddering requires the installation of a modified transmission control module. **1996–97**—Delayed gear engagement or adapter case leak requires the installation of a new transmission seal kit (#21-41-422-762). **1998**—A no-start condition may signal that the oil level sensor is faulty. • A "clunk" heard during downshifts, when releasing the accelerator pedal, or when shifting into Reverse is likely caused by excessive axial clearance between the transmission output shaft and the output shaft. • Inoperative sunroof. **1998–2000**—Hard shifts or no shifts can be corrected by exchanging the valve body. **1999**—Tips for improving AM radio reception. • An inoperative cruise control may need a new brake light switch (strange but true). **1999–2000**—Guidelines for plugging manual transmission oil drain plug leaks. **5 Series: 1996**—Oil level sensor may give an incorrect reading. **1997**—Airbag light stays lit for no reason. **1998**—A no-start condition may signal that the oil level sensor is faulty. **525i, 535i: 1993–94**—Emergency flashers may self-activate. • Tips on fixing starter motor failures. **525i: 1990–94**—Brake light switch may fail. **525iT: 1992–94**—Brake light switch may fail.

3 Series, M Series, Z3 Profile

	1994	1995	1996	1997	1998	1999	2000	2001
Cost Price ($)								
318ti	—	24,900	25,900	26,900	27,800	27,800	—	—
318i 4d	26,900	28,900	30,900	32,300	33,300	34,301	—	—
Convertible	—	40,900	42,900	43,900	44,900	45,900	—	—
320i 4d	—	34,900	—	—	—	—	—	33,900
325i, 328i	38,200	41,900	43,900	46,900	47,900	50,902	44,900	37,950
Convertible	52,900	53,900	55,300	57,900	58,900	58,900	—	52,500
323 Coupe	—	—	—	—	39,900	—	—	—
M3 2d	—	—	—	61,900	62,900	62,900	62,900	69,800
Z3 1.9L/2.3L	—	—	38,900	40,500	41,500	43,900	45,901	46,900
Z3 2.8L	—	—	—	49,900	51,900	52,900	54,900	55,900
Used Values ($)								
318ti Λ	—	10,500	12,000	14,000	16,500	20,000	—	—
318ti V	—	8,500	10,000	12,000	14,000	18,000	—	—
318i 4d Λ	10,000	12,500	14,500	17,000	20,500	23,500	—	—
318i 4d V	8,500	10,000	12,500	15,000	18,000	21,000	—	—
Convertible Λ	—	16,000	20,000	23,000	26,500	31,400	—	—
Convertible V	—	14,000	18,000	21,000	24,000	29,500	—	—
320i 4d Λ	—	12,500	—	—	—	—	—	27,500
320i 4d V	—	11,000	—	—	—	—	—	25,000
323 Coupe Λ	—	—	—	—	22,500	—	—	—
323 Coupe V	—	—	—	—	20,000	—	—	—
325i, 328i Λ	12,500	14,000	17,500	19,500	24,500	31,000	36,000	32,000
325i, 328i V	11,000	12,400	15,000	17,000	22,000	28,500	34,000	29,500
Convertible Λ	16,000	21,000	25,000	29,500	35,000	41,000	—	44,500
Convertible V	14,000	19,000	23,000	27,000	32,000	39,000	—	42,500
M3 2d Λ	—	—	—	26,500	33,000	43,000	49,000	58,000
M3 2d V	—	—	—	24,000	30,500	41,000	46,000	56,000

Z3 1.9L/2.3L A	—	—	20,000	26,000	26,000	33,000	35,000	40,000
Z3 1.9L/2.3L V	—	—	17,500	23,000	24,000	30,000	32,500	37,000
Z3 2.8L A	—	—	—	22,500	31,000	30,000	42,000	48,000
Z3 2.8L V	—	—	—	20,000	29,000	27,000	39,000	45,000
Extended Warranty	N	N	N	N	N	N	N	N
Secret Warranty	N	N	Y	Y	Y	Y	N	N
Reliability	③	③	③	③	③	④	④	④
Crash Safety								
325i 4d	—	④	—	—	—	—	—	—
328i	—	—	④	④	—	—	—	—
Off-set	—	—	—	—	—	—	⑤	⑤
Head Restraints	—	❷	—	❶	—	❷	③	③
Rear	—	❶	—	—	—	❶	—	—

5 Series Profile

	1994	1995	1996	1997	1998	1999	2000	2001
Cost Price ($)								
525i, 528i	49,750	52,900	—	54,900	56,200	57,200	55,500	54,700
Used Values ($)								
525i, 528i A	16,000	22,000	—	30,000	35,000	36,000	42,000	45,000
525i, 528i V	13,500	18,500	—	27,500	31,000	33,000	39,000	42,000
Extended Warranty	Y	N	N	N	N	N	N	N
Secret Warranty	N	N	N	N	N	Y	Y	Y
Reliability	③	④	⑤	⑤	⑤	⑤	⑤	⑤
Off-set	—	—	—	⑤	⑤	⑤	⑤	⑤
Head Restraints (F)	—	③	—	③	—	③	—	⑤
Rear	—	—	—	❷	—	—	—	—

Note: The 5 Series hasn't been crash-tested by NHTSA.

Ford/Lincoln

CONTINENTAL, LS, MARK VII, MARK VIII, TOWN CAR ★★☆

RATING: *Continental:* Below Average (1988–2001). *LS:* Average (2000–01). *Mark VII, Mark VIII:* Above Average (1995–98); Average (1994); Below Average (1986–93). *Town Car:* Average (1995–2001); Below Average (1988–94); redesigned for 1998. Although early Continentals are dirt-cheap, their low quality make them risky buys. Now that Ford has decided to drop the Continental in 2003, servicing problems will likely increase as well. The rear-drive Town Car and LS are the best choice for quality and performance, but you are still taking a substantial risk. **Maintenance/Repair costs:** Higher than average, and they must be done by a Ford or Lincoln dealer. **Parts:** Higher-than-average cost, but not hard to find (except for electronic components and body panels). **Best alternatives;** Acura Integra, TL, and RL; Cadillac DeVille; Infiniti I30 or I35, Lexus ES 300; and Mercedes E-Class.

Strengths and weaknesses: These large luxury cruisers are proof that quality isn't proportional to the money you spend. Several designer series offer all the luxury options anyone could wish for, but the two ingredients most owners would expect to find—high quality and consistent reliability—are sadly lacking, especially with the front-drive versions. All models, however, have poor-quality automatic transmissions, electrical systems, brakes, body hardware, and fit and finish. NHTSA-recorded safety complaints also target more front-drives than rear-drive Lincolns, with engine, transmission, airbag, and brake failures cropping up repeatedly over the years—and increasing in severity and frequency.

A totally redesigned and re-styled Continental, equipped with a V8 DOHC, was launched for the '95 model year. '99s were given standard side airbags and an upgraded audio system; 2000s got improved child safety seat anchors; and the 2001s were carried over relatively unchanged.

'95 Town Cars were given a slight re-styling and steering improvements; '96 models received an engine upgrade and upgraded climate controls; more steering refinement for the '97s; '98s were totally redesigned, riding faster, lower and stiffer; standard side airbags were added to the '99s; year 2000 models got improved child seat anchorages; and the 2001 Town Car received added horsepower, adjustable pedals, and seatbelt pre-tensioners.

Continental (front-drive)
When the Continental went front-drive in 1988, what was a mediocre luxury car became a luxury lemon with serious safety-related deficiencies. The frequency and cost of repairs increased considerably, and parts became more complex, complicating easy diagnosis and repair. The automatic transmission tends to self-destruct, particularly on 1988–2000 models; engine head gaskets blow (see Part Two); electrical components are unreliable, with intermittent loss of all electrical power; stopping performance is compromised by premature brake wear and wheel lockup; and body hardware continues to be an embarrassment. The redesigned 1995 Continental featured a new V8 powerplant, more aerodynamic styling, and fibreglass panels. However, engine, transmission, electrical system, and brake problems actually worsened.

These cars don't offer the kind of trouble-free driving one would normally expect in a luxury vehicle selling for over $40,000. The automatic levelling air-spring suspension system makes for a stiff ride (especially on early models), while still allowing the Continental to "porpoise" due to its heavy front end. The Continental's anemic V6 powertrain is poorly suited to a car of this heft. The engine hesitates in cold weather and the automatic transmission shifts roughly.

Mechanical defects include frequent engine flywheel and transmission forward clutch piston replacements; failure-prone ABS, electrical, suspension, and steering systems; and glitch-ridden electronic modules, causing hard starts and sudden stalling. The mass of electrical gadgets increases the likelihood of problems as the cars age. For example, automatic headlight doors fail frequently, and the electronic antenna and power windows often won't go up or down. The computerized dashboard is particularly failure prone.

Other reliability complaints concern transmission fluid leakage due to misplaced bolts, rough upshifting caused by a defective valve body, and air conditioning and heating that sometimes work in reverse order.

Town Car

The rear-drive Town Car is the best of a bad lot. It's only saving grace is that, thanks to its rear-drive configuration, it's relatively inexpensive to repair and parts aren't hard to find. Nevertheless, the Town Car's still afflicted by many generic problems that reappear year-after-year. Some of the more common problems are safety-related defects; engine head gaskets warped because a plastic part in the intake manifold has failed; transmission, AC, and electrical glitches; biodegradable tie-rod ends; and body hardware deficiencies.

Incidentally, Ford will pay for intake manifold failures long after the warranty has expired—if you are a fleet customer (taxi, limousine, and law enforcement). Others are routinely denied after-warranty assistance. Unfair? You bet. Stupid? Absolutely!

One owner of a '97 Lincoln afflicted by this malady had this to say:

> Ford has extended a no-charge coverage for this part for 7 years and no mileage limitation, and it's automatically extended to subsequent owners. This should be extended to all owners of vehicles equipped with this defective part. Ford customer service has rejected [my] claim when contacted by telephone. They have not replied to two requests [sent] by mail.

LS

Lincoln's latest iteration, the LS rear-drive sedan comes with a high-performance 200-hp variant of the Taurus 3.0L V6, mated to an optional manual or a standard automatic gearbox. Also available: a 250-hp 3.9L V8, based on that of the Jaguar XK8 coupe, coupled to a semi-automatic transmission. Both engines are identical, but the Lincoln produces 30 less horses than the Jag equivalent. There is very little difference between the 2000 and 2001 models, except that the 2001 carries standard traction control.

The LS offers a lot for a reasonable base price. The V6 version is priced in the range of the BMW 3 Series, Lexus ES 300, and Mercedes C-Class, while delivering standard equipment and interior space that rivals the 5 Series, GS, and E-Class.

Lincoln's return to rear-drive has opened up a Pandora's box of power-train, AC, electrical system, and body glitches. Owners report jerky transmission shifting, excessive drivetrain and body noise and vibrations, inconsistent braking response, and erratic AC performance.

Safety summary: All models/years: Sudden, unintended acceleration; gas pedal sticks. • Loss of braking. • Inadvertent deployment of airbags or airbags don't deploy when they should. • Sudden loss of electrical power. • Severe pull and vibration when braking. • Brake failures due to premature wear of rear drums and rotor warpage. • Steering control degrades or locks up when passing through puddles. • Annoying reflections onto the front windshield. • Horn is hard to activate. • Mirrors vibrate excessively and don't adjust easily. **All models: 1996**—While parked, vehicle suddenly jumped out of Park and rolled forward and hit another car. • Several reports that the front suspension collapsed. • Front strut failures. • Clock spring broke, causing loss of steering. • Steering wheel jams intermittently. • Transmission jumped out of gear while driving. • Power seats malfunction. **1997**—Blown engine head gaskets. • Engine suddenly stalls in traffic. • Vehicle often won't start; starter whirrs, but won't crank. • Premature failure of the tie-rod ends. • Several incidents of steering failure; cracked steering gear. • Gasoline smell permeates interior. • Broken rear side door handle disables the door. • Rear-view mirror distortions. • Leaks oil onto the dash. • Speedometer is difficult to read in daylight and gas gauge is often in error. • Frequent complaints that Michelin XW4 and Green X tires split open. • Horn suddenly blows on its own. **1998**—Cracked high-pressure plastic line on top of engine caused fuel to spew out and catch fire. • Several complaints that engine coolant leaks and bubbles up onto the engine compartment, risking a fire. • Premature engine timing chain failure. • Gas pedal set higher than brake pedal, causing unintended acceleration. • Cruise control speeds up when vehicle goes downhill. • Frequent stalling and no-starts likely caused by a sensor failure. • Sudden steering failure. • Right front wheel assembly came off as vehicle came to a stop. • Power-steering pump fails periodically. • Front suspension failed as vehicle came to a stop. • Interior lights fail, smoke. • Many complaints that the interior ventilation system leaks exhaust fumes. • Rain leaks through right rear door. **1999**—Brake line ruptured. • Headlights fail to adequately light side of the road. • Visual image speedometer can't be seen by colour-blind drivers. **2000**—Warning lights come on constantly and car's central computer module often malfunctions. • Airbag deployed without warning. • Brakes don't work well; require extended stopping distance. • Side-view mirror can't be adjusted properly due to a design defect. **2001**—Car suddenly accelerated while in Reverse; brake/transmission interlock not connected. • Driver's foot can be snared by two console cables when going from gas pedal to the brakes. • Instrument panel washes out in bright sunlight. **Continental: 1995**—While parked, vehicle rolled backward and then suddenly accelerated forward. • Frequent reports of seatbelts failing to retract during an accident. • Defective inner tie-rod and strut causes severe steering shake. • Inadequate defogging leaves two small circles to see through. • Rear deck stereo hump obstructs rear visibility. **LS: 2000–01**—Sudden acceleration in forward or Reverse gear. • Airbag deployment for no reason. • Airbag failed to deploy. • Lurching, hesitating automatic transmission shifting. • Brakes fail during the first five minutes after a cold start. • Brake pedal becomes hard and resists application or turns mushy and goes to the floor. • Warning lights come on for no reason. • Defective steering causes violent swerving from side to side. • Automatic door locks engage by themselves, locking out driver. **Town Car: 1996**—Vehicle fires reportedly ignited in the engine compartment wiring. • Frequent reports of sudden acceleration. • Many reports of sudden acceleration while in Reverse, leading to the replacement of the speed control servo and servo cable. • Frequent complaints of chronic stalling. • Airbag packing gets hard in cold weather, leaving horn inoperative. • Trunk lid flew open on highway. • Many incidents where seatbelts either are too short for adults, won't retract, or ratchet tighter while being worn. • Two front seatbacks collapsed rearward when vehicle was rear-ended. • Excessive noise when braking. • Wind noise comes in through windshield. **1997**—Intake manifold failures caused by faulty plastic part. Fleet vehicles get special after-warranty assistance, but regular customers are left to slowly twist in the wind (see Part Two, "Secret Warranties"). • Shock absorbers fell off vehicle. • Repeated air spring failures. • Poorly designed sunroof switch is easily broken. • Rear suspension design leads to poor directional control. • Headlights fail when high or low beams are activated. • Water leaks through the windshield wiper motor assembly. **1998**—Traction control engages at the wrong time, making driver lose control of the vehicle. • Fuel may spit out of filler pipe when refuelling. • Easy to get foot stuck on accelerator pedal due to placement of partition. • Fuse panel location interferes with applying the brake pedal. • Rear-view mirror creates a large blind spot. • Passenger-side door won't open close to curb, due to car's low stance. **1999**—Loss of all electrical power while cruising on the highway. • Chronic stalling. • Head restraints won't lock into position. **2000**—Vehicle suddenly accelerates when cruise control is engaged and brakes are applied. The following NHTSA report is rather typical of other similar complaints:

Driver was going 75 mph [120 km/h] with cruise control set. When approaching a curve, driver applied the brakes to slow down, and as brake pedal was pressed, vehicle speeded up. Driver was coached from Limousine service on a 2-way radio how to control vehicle. Driver turned off cruise control switch and vehicle returned to normal.

• Inadvertent airbag deployment. • Frequent brake failures (brake pedal will fade and not hold). • Horn is hard to activate. • Vehicle pulls hard to one side when braking. • Defrost vents reflect onto the windshield. • Faulty trunk light bulb ignited clothing in trunk. • Power windows fail intermittently.

Secret Warranties/Service Tips/TSBs

All models: 1985–2002—Repeated heater core leaks. **1993–99**—Paint delamination, peeling, or fading (see Part Two). **Continental: 1984–94**—A hum from the air suspension system can be corrected by replacing the compressor isolators with upgraded parts. **1994–99**—Tips on plugging door, window, and moon-roof wind noise. **1995–97**—An acceleration or deceleration clunk is likely caused by the rear lower subframe isolators allowing movement between the mounts and the subframe. • A front suspension clunk may signal excessive sway bar wear. **1995–98**—No Fourth gear may mean you have a defective forward clutch control valve retaining clip. • Condensation buildup on the inside of windows may be stopped by installing an upgraded pressure cycling switch. • An intermittent shifting into Neutral or loss of forward or Reverse gear is likely caused by a defective forward clutch piston (a problem that has haunted Ford and Lincoln for over 12 years). • Front brake groaning, moaning, or squealing can be silenced by installing upgraded brake pads under the bumper-to-bumper warranty. **1995–99**—Troubleshooting tips for silencing a creak or pop while turning or braking and wind noise coming from the side doors. **1996–98**—No-starts may be due to fuel pump wire chafing. **1997–98**—Lack of AC temperature control. **1998**—Inaccurate fuel gauge readings. **1998–99**—Steering wheel vibration/moaning can be fixed by installing a longer power steering hose. **1999**—No Reverse engagement with the automatic transmission may be caused by torn Reverse clutch lip seals. Ford will cover the repair under a special "goodwill" policy (see Part Two). **1999–2000**—Hesitation when accelerating can be fixed by reprogramming the PCM. • Guidelines for diagnosing and preventing front brake vibration. **LS: 2000–01**—Frequent bulletin references to automatic transmission defects producing: delayed engagement (PCM module seen as likely culprit), driveline vibration and buzz/clunk/drone, and fluid leakage. • Trunk may suddenly open. • Inaccurate ambient temperature display. • Inoperative AC dual zone heater. • ABS, airbag, and service engine lights come on for no apparent reason. • Noisy front power windows. • Steering wheel "nibble," hum, or boom noise. • 3.9L oil leak from the bellhousing area. • Poor braking on

V6-equipped models. • V6 engine noise on acceleration and highway drone noise. • Hard starts or no-starts. • Instrument panel squeaks and rattles. **Mark VII, Mark VIII: 1985–99**—An exhaust buzz or rattle may be caused by a loose heat shield catalyst. **1986–94**—The in-tank fuel pump is the likely cause of radio static. Install an electronic noise RFI filter (#F1PZ-18B925-A). **1993–94**—A squeak or chirp coming from the blower motor can be stopped by installing an upgraded blower motor. • Automatic transmissions with delayed or no forward engagement, or a higher engine rpm than expected when coming to a stop, are covered in TSB #94-26-9. **Town Car: 1992–2001**—Rear-end impact may puncture fuel tank; two TSB repairs already carried out.

Continental Profile

	1994	1995	1996	1997	1998	1999	2000	2001
Cost Price ($)								
Continental Ex.	40,295	50,995	51,896	49,995	51,995	52,795	52,895	51,920
Used Values ($)								
Continental Ex. ʌ	7,500	9,000	11,000	14,500	19,500	25,000	31,500	37,000
Continental Ex. v	6,000	7,500	9,000	12,000	17,000	22,500	29,000	34,500
Extended Warranty	Y	Y	Y	Y	Y	Y	Y	Y
Secret Warranty	Y	Y	Y	Y	Y	Y	Y	Y
Reliability	❶	❷	❷	❷	❷	❷	❷	③
Crash Safety	③	—	—	—	—	—	—	—
Off-set	—	③	③	③	③	③	③	③
Head Restraints	—	❶	—	❶	—	❶	—	❷

LS Profile

	2000	2001
Cost Price ($)		
LS	40,595	40,870
Used Values ($)		
LS ʌ	28,000	31,000
LS v	26,000	29,000
Extended Warranty	N	N
Secret Warranty	N	N
Reliability	③	④
Crash Safety	⑤	⑤
Side Impact	—	④
Off-set	⑤	⑤
Head Restraints	❶	❷
Rollover Resistance	—	⑤

Mark VII, Mark VIII Profile

	1991	1992	1993	1994	1995	1996	1997	1998
Cost Price ($)								
Mark VII, VIII	38,895	41,010	43,968	47,995	50,996	51,895	53,695	56,595
Used Values ($								
Mark VII, VIII ▲	5,000	6,000	7,000	8,000	10,500	12,000	16,500	21,500
Mark VII, VIII ▼	4,000	5,000	6,000	7,000	8,000	9,500	14,000	18,000
Extended Warranty	Y	Y	Y	Y	Y	Y	Y	Y
Secret Warranty	N	N	Y	Y	Y	Y	Y	Y
Reliability	❷	❷	❷	❷	❷	③	③	③
Head Restraints	—	—	—	—	❶	—	❶	—

Note: The Mark series hasn't been crash-tested by NHTSA.

Town Car Profile

	1994	1995	1996	1997	1998	1999	2000	2001
Cost Price ($)								
Town Car	40,495	44,495	44,895	45,895	52,795	51,195	51,495	50,700
Used Values ($)								
Town Car ▲	7,500	9,500	11,500	15,000	21,000	26,500	32,000	37,000
Town Car ▼	6,000	7,500	9,000	13,000	18,500	24,000	30,000	35,000
Extended Warranty	N	N	N	N	N	N	N	N
Secret Warranty	Y	Y	Y	Y	Y	Y	Y	Y
Reliability	③	④	④	④	④	④	④	④
Crash Safety	⑤	⑤	④	④	—	—	④	⑤
Side Impact	—	—	—	—	—	④	④	④
Head Restraints	—	❶	—	❶	—	❶	—	❶

General Motors

98 REGENCY, PARK AVENUE ★★★

RATING: Average (1997–2001); Below Average (1991–96); Not Recommended (1985–90). **Maintenance/Repair costs:** Higher than average, but repairs aren't dealer dependent. **Parts:** Higher-than-average cost (independent suppliers sell for much less), but not hard to find. Nevertheless, don't even think about buying one of these front-drives without a 3- to 5-year extended warranty backed by the automaker. **Best alternatives:** Acura Integra, TL, and RL; Cadillac DeVille; Infiniti I30 or I35; Lexus ES 300; Mercedes E-Class; Nissan Maxima; and Toyota Avalon.

Strengths and weaknesses: These attractive, luxurious cars are billed as six-seaters, but only four passengers can ride in comfort. Although the 1991–96 Park Avenue and 98 Regency were improved over the years, they compiled one of the worst repair histories among large cars. Main problem areas are the engine, automatic transmission, fuel system, steering, brakes, electrical system (including defective PROM and MEMCAL modules), starter and alternator, and badly assembled, poor-quality body hardware. The 3.0L V6 engine is inadequate for cars this heavy, and the 3.8L has been a big quality disappointment. Stay away from the failure-prone diesel engine. Under-hood servicing is complicated. Other problems: automatic transmission and engine computer malfunctions are common, the fuel-injection system is temperamental, window mechanisms are poorly designed, the power-steering assembly is failure prone, there are frequent electrical failures, front brake pads and rotors require frequent replacement, and shock absorbers leak or go soft very quickly. Extensive surface corrosion has been a problem because of poor and often incomplete paint application at the factory.

Like the LeSabre, the 1997 Park Avenue and Ultra (its fully dressed version) were redesigned to include a reworked powertrain, a stiffer body, improved interior amenities, upgraded four-wheel disc brakes, and an upgraded ventilation system. The following model year adopted de-powered airbags. '99 models were carried over without any significant changes. StabiliTrak stability control was added to the year 2000 model, and the 2001s got only minor improvements of doubtful utility (like the Ultrasonic Rear Park Assist system).

Aficionados of full-sized luxury sedans love the flush glass, wrap-around windshield and bumpers, and clean body lines that lend the latest makeover an aerodynamic and pleasing appearance. But these cars are more than just pretty packages; they provide lots of room, luxury, style, and (dare I say) performance. Plenty of power is available with the 205-hp 3.8L V6 engine and the Aurora's 240-hp supercharged powerplant. It does 0–100 km/h in under 9 seconds (impressive, considering the heft of these vehicles), and improves low- and mid-range throttle response. Power is transmitted to the front wheels through an electronically controlled transmission that features "free-wheeling" clutches designed to eliminate abrupt gear changes. Both the Park Avenue and Ultra use a stretched version of the more rigid Riviera and Aurora platform.

The revised 1998–2001 Park Avenue models have generated fewer owner complaints, although the main problem areas continue to be powertrain malfunctions; airbag, fuel system, engine and transmission failures; AC not performing properly; and poor fit and finish leading to leaks, squeaks, rattles, moans, and whines.

Safety summary: All models: 1998—Chronic stalling and loss of electrical power, particularly when braking. • Vehicle also suddenly accelerates when braking. • With cruise control engaged, vehicle picks up speed when going downhill. • Faulty fuel sending unit; fuel gauge failure. • Cracked engine head gasket. • Transmission failures. • Brakes or steering fail in rainy weather. • ABS failure may be caused by defective computer module. • Steering failure caused by broken serpentine belt. • Premature failure of brake rotors, pads, and calipers. • Goodyear tire tread separation. • Faulty air level ride filled up rear shocks so rear end sticks up high in the air. • Seatbelts jam in the retractor; fail to extend or retract. • Door locks don't work properly. • Windshield dash glare. **1999**—Sudden acceleration after vehicle jumped from Park into Drive. • Frequent stalling; Check Engine light comes on. • Loss of steering due to premature steering pump failure. • Brake rotor overheating and warpage creates excessive vibration and pulling to one side when brakes are applied. • Transmission jerks when going from Reverse to Drive. • Airbag light comes on for no reason. • Shoulder belt twists in retractor. • Premature failure of Goodyear tires. • Keys won't lock or unlock the doors. • Battery often goes dead. **2000**—Airbags deploy when they shouldn't and fail to deploy when they should. • Steering may suddenly lock up. • Excessive steering wheel vibrations numb hands. • Horn is hard to activate, especially, in cold weather. • Front seat lapbelts may be too short; GM will give owners a free extension if they sign a waiver of liability. • Windshield wipers suddenly quit working. **2001**—Sudden acceleration while backing up. • Windshield wiper malfunctions. • Driver's seatbelt locks up. **98 Regency: 1994–95**—Headlight switch may not work. **1995**—Current leakage in models with Twilight Sentinel can cause loss of headlights and parking lights, or the lights may suddenly come on while the car is parked. **1996**—Damaged capacitor could cause confusing electronic warnings to be displayed. • Backfire upon start-up can damage the intake manifold and cause hard starting or a fire. **Park Avenue: 1997**—Centre seatbelt anchor bolts were improperly installed. • Brake/traction control module could cause ABS to lose its effectiveness and make for longer stopping distances.

Secret Warranties/Service Tips/TSBs

All models/years: The THM 44C-T4 automatic transaxles on front-drive models equipped with V6 engines are particularly failure prone: their pinched or kinked vacuum lines result in low oil pressure. **All models: 1993–2002**—AC odours can be reduced by applying a cooling coil coating or installing a special kit. • A rotten-egg odour coming from the exhaust is probably caused by a malfunctioning catalytic converter and may be covered under GM's emissions warranty. • Paint delamination, peeling, or fading (see Part Two). **1995–96**—Wind noise around front and rear doors; diagnosis and repair. **1995–97**—Transmission gear whine means the final drive assembly may have to be replaced. **1995–98**—A noise, growl, or vibration from the front when making a right turn or when accelerating may signal the need to replace or reposition the rear transaxle mount. **1995–2001**—Engine oil pan leaks. **1997–99**—Excessive brake noise can be reduced by installing upgraded pads and rotors. **1997–2001**—Troubleshooting steering vibration, shudder, or moan. **1998**—Spark plug electrode erosion is the likely cause of engine knock, a rough-running engine, or lack of power. • A fuel gauge that gives inaccurate readings probably needs a new fuel level sensor. • Rattling from the rear may mean the fuel tank strap is loose or defective. **1998–99**—Low power, stalling, or stumbling when accelerating can be cured by re-calibrating the PCM. **1998–2000**—A hard-to-shift gear shift lever may need a new cable assembly. **1999–2000**—An engine that runs hot, overheats, or loses coolant may simply need a new radiator cap. • Transmission whine in Park or Neutral may be silenced with a new drive sprocket support bearing. • Slips, harsh upshift or garage shifts, and launch shudders have a variety of causes and corrections, says TSB #00-07-30-002. • Diagnostic procedures for an engine that runs hot, overheats, or loses coolant are outlined in TSB #00-06-02-001. **1999–2001**—Tips on correcting excessive engine vibration and silencing generator whine, hum, and moan. **2000–01**—Inoperative power sunroof. **2001**—Delayed and extended shifts, slippage in cold weather.

98 Regency, Park Avenue Profile

	1994	1995	1996	1997	1998	1999	2000	2001
Cost Price ($)								
Park Avenue	33,798	37,115	38,150	40,865	41,850	41,060	42,075	43,000
98 Regency	34,498	35,525	36,610	—	—	—	—	—
Used Values ($)								
Park Avenue ▲	7,000	8,500	9,500	13,500	16,500	21,000	26,000	30,000
Park Avenue ▼	5,500	6,500	8,000	11,000	14,000	18,500	24,000	28,000
98 Regency ▲	7,000	8,500	9,500	—	—	—	—	—
98 Regency ▼	6,000	7,000	8,000	—	—	—	—	—
Extended Warranty	Y	Y	Y	Y	Y	Y	Y	Y
Secret Warranty	Y	Y	Y	Y	Y	Y	Y	Y
Reliability	❷	❷	❷	❷	③	③	④	④
Crash Safety	—	—	—	—	—	—	—	④
Side Impact	—	—	—	—	—	—	—	④
Off-set	—	—	—	⑤	⑤	⑤	⑤	⑤
Head Restraints								
Park Avenue	—	❶	—	❶	—	❶	—	❶
'98 Regency	❶	—	—	—	—	—	—	—

AURORA, RIVIERA ★★★

RATING: *Aurora:* Average (1995–2001); There was no year 2000 model. Now that GM is phasing out its Oldsmobile division, Aurora resale values are likely to suffer. *Riviera:* Average (1995–99); Not Recommended

(1986–93). GM skipped the 1994 model year and introduced an all-new 1995 version. **Maintenance/Repair costs:** Higher than average, but repairs aren't dealer dependent. **Parts:** Higher-than-average cost (independent suppliers sell for much less), but not hard to find. GM's phaseout won't affect availability or costs, since these vehicles use the same generic parts found on many other GM products. **Best alternatives:** Acura Integra, TL, and RL; Cadillac DeVille, Fleetwood, or Brougham; Ford Crown Victoria or Mercury Grand Marquis; Mercedes E-Class; Nissan Maxima; and Toyota Avalon.

Strengths and weaknesses: Although the redesigned 1988–93 cars got performance, handling, and ride upgrades, they kept the same low level of quality control, with multiple design and manufacturing defects, including serious fuel injection, engine computer, and electrical system problems that haven't been solved to this day. One particularly poor design was the complex Graphic Control Center, which used an oversensitive video screen and small push buttons. It's both distracting and expensive to repair. The automatic transmission is notoriously failure prone, and brakes wear out prematurely and perform poorly. Surface rust and poor paint quality are the most common body complaints on all years. Shock absorbers wear out quickly, and the diesel engine seldom runs properly.

The 1995 Riviera was totally redesigned with standard dual airbags, ABS, a 3.8L V6, and a supercharged variant. These upgrades were carried over for the '96 model. However, the '97s got additional standard features and a smoother-shifting automatic transmission. The supercharged engine became a standard feature on the '98s, and traction control became standard a year later, just before the Riviera was discontinued.

Overall, 1995–99 models offer many more luxury features but continue the checkered repair history. As with many of its front-drives during the latter half of the '90s, GM improved quality somewhat, but there are still many generic deficiencies affecting the automatic transmission (torque converter constantly engages and disengages), engine, fuel and electrical systems, computer modules, AC compressor, brakes (rotor warpage and premature pad replacement), steering, suspension, and fit and finish. Trunk wheelwell leaks are common. Because of their problematic brakes, these cars usually have a pronounced low-speed shudder/vibration and severe pull that intensifies when passing over uneven terrain or when braking.

Aurora
This front-drive Olds luxury sedan is aimed at the Acura, Infiniti, and Lexus crowd. It uses the same basic design as the Riviera but doesn't share the same major mechanical features or popular styling. Because it's a relatively new entry into the Oldsmobile line, GM took more care in the selection of mechanical, electronic, and body components. This has

made the Aurora more reliable and glitch-free than GM's other vehicles, which continue to be hobbled with poor-quality components and subpar fit and finish. Too bad that this progress is for naught, as Aurora folds along with the entire Oldsmobile line.

The Aurora's main advantages are its sporty handling and unusual aero-styling. In contrast to the Riviera, the Aurora seats five only and uses a 4.0L V8 derived from the Cadillac 4.6L V8 Northstar engine. Acceleration is underwhelming (this is a heavy car) but adequate for highway touring. Road and wind noise is omnipresent, and the rear trunk's small opening compromises the large trunk's ability to handle odd-sized objects.

1995–99 Auroras have similar quality failings to those of the Riviera listed above, except they're not as extensive and generally become less common with the 2000 and 2001 models. Nevertheless, owners of the 2000–01 model years report engine coolant leaks, chronic electrical and fuel supply glitches, brake failures and high maintenance costs, water leaks through the front corner moulding, and harsh Reverse engagement.

Safety summary: Aurora: 1995–2001—Chronic stalling. • Horn is hard to access and operates erratically. • Headlights short out or come on inadvertently. **1996**—Chronic stalling believed to be caused by faulty fuel pump wiring. • Fuel smell seeps into interior; fuel leaks at the fuel rail. • Car loses power steering on slow turns or when driving in the rain. • Defective headlight switch wouldn't turn lights off: $580 (U.S.) to repair. • Northstar engine aluminum block cracked. **1996–97**—Sudden acceleration may be due to defective cruise control. **1997**—Accelerator pedal jams. • Airbags may be hazardous to short occupants. • Head restraints won't hold factory settings. • When battery died, occupants had to break window to get out. **1999**—Water is sucked up into engine when passing over puddles. • Power steering loses power at low speeds. • Lost all electrical power, including interior and exterior lights. • Exhaust fumes enter interior. **2001**—Total brake failure. • Will not go into First gear when cupholder is extended. • Electrical shorts cause complete electrical shutdown or erratically operating interior and exterior lights and gauges. • Reflection of the defrost grate is very distracting to short drivers. • Head restraints block rear vision. • Windshield wipers fail intermittently. **Riviera: 1998**—Engine mount failure. • Brakes don't stop vehicle; frequent rotor replacement. • Horn won't blow at times.

Secret Warranties/Service Tips/TSBs

All models: 1993–99—AC odours can be reduced by applying a cooling coil coating. • A rotten-egg odour coming from the exhaust is likely the result of a malfunctioning catalytic converter, covered by GM's emissions warranty up to five years. • Paint delamination, peeling, or fading (see Part Two). **1995–96**—Intermittent Neutral/loss of Drive at highway speeds can be fixed by replacing the control valve body assembly.

1995–98—A noise, growl, or vibration from the front when making a right turn or when accelerating may signal the need to replace or reposition the rear transaxle mount. **1995–99**—Floor pan corrosion perforation in the battery compartment can be corrected for free, under the base warranty, by installing a GM repair kit. **1997–99**—Excessive front brake noise can be reduced by installing upgraded pads and rotors. • A faulty rivet in the catalytic converter heat shield may cause a popping noise heard in the passenger compartment. **1998**—A fuel gauge that gives inaccurate readings probably needs a new fuel level sensor. • Rattling from the rear may mean the fuel tank strap is loose or defective. **1998–99**—A clunk, rattle, or metal-to-metal noise coming from the front of the vehicle can be silenced by installing anti-slip/friction material between the engine frame and the stabilizer shaft insulator. **1999**—Curing front strut squeaks. **Aurora: 1995–99**—A cold engine knock or ticking may be caused by excessive carbon deposits in the engine. • A steering shudder at idle or during parking may be fixed by installing an anti-shudder power-steering outlet hose assembly. **1996–99**—GM has an enhanced crankshaft rear seal to use for complaints related to leaking or poor sealing. **1997–98**—Excessive front brake noise can be reduced by installing upgraded pads and rotors. **1998**—Harsh or delayed gear shifts may require the installation of an enhanced garage shift package. • Accessory drive noise may be caused by a misaligned accessory drive pulley. • Delayed or no engine braking in D3 may require the replacement of the forward and coast latch piston assemblies. **1998–99**—Diagnostic and repair tips for a faulty cruise control and speedometer. • Front-end clunks and rattles can be silenced by a judicious use of anti-friction materials. **1999–2000**—Overheating or coolant loss may be corrected by simply replacing the radiator cap and polishing the radiator filler neck. **2000–01**—If there's a sudden loss of power when accelerating, the transmission fluid pressure switch may be defective. **2001**—Cooler fitting coolant leaks. • Delayed Reverse engagement.

Aurora Profile

	1995	1996	1997	1998	1999	2001
Cost Price ($)						
Aurora	43,020	43,695	46,045	47,250	46,190	39,590
Used Values ($)						
Aurora ⋀	9,000	10,500	14,500	18,500	23,000	29,000
Aurora ⋁	7,000	8,000	12,000	16,000	21,000	26,000
Extended Warranty	Y	Y	Y	N	N	N
Secret Warranty	Y	Y	Y	Y	Y	N
Reliability	③	③	③	③	③	④
Crash Safety	③	③	③	③	③	④
Side Impact	—	—	—	—	—	③
Off-set	—	—	—	—	—	⑤
Head Restraints	❶	—	❶	—	❶	⑤

Riviera Profile

	1993	1995	1996	1997	1998	1999
Cost Price ($)						
Riviera	30,790	39,525	40,700	42,415	44,950	44,125
Used Values ($)						
Riviera ʌ	5,000	8,500	10,000	13,000	18,000	22,000
Riviera ᴠ	4,000	6,500	8,000	11,000	15,500	19,000
Extended Warranty	Y	Y	Y	Y	N	N
Secret Warranty	N	N	Y	Y	Y	Y
Reliability	②	③	③	③	③	③
Head Restraints	—	❶	—	❶	—	❶

Note: These vehicles haven't been crash-tested.

CADILLAC BROUGHAM, FLEETWOOD (RWD) ★★★★

RATING: Above Average (1993–96); Average (1984–92). A smart choice for retirees, these cars are on par with the Ford Crown Victoria and Grand Marquis when it comes to comfort and reliability. The '94 and later models feature the most performance for your money. **Maintenance/Repair costs:** Average, and repairs aren't dealer dependent. **Parts:** Reasonably priced (independent suppliers sell for much less) and not hard to find, despite the fact that these rear-drives were dropped in '96. **Best alternatives:** Acura Integra, TL, and RL; Cadillac DeVille; a fully loaded Ford Crown Victoria or Mercury Grand Marquis; and the Mercedes E-Class.

Strengths and weaknesses: The quintessential land yacht, these cars emphasize comfort over handling with their powerful engines and large chassis. Nevertheless, with their spacious interior and many convenience features, these large cars are ideal for vacationing and light trailer pulling.

'92 models got standard traction control; dual airbags and a goofy digital dash were added to the '93s; a new transmission and engine (from the Corvette) improved the '94s' performance; '95s came back unchanged; and the '96s got an upgraded sound system and improved centre storage armrest.

The most serious problem areas are the fuel-injection system, which frequently malfunctions and costs an arm and a leg to repair; engine head gasket failures; automatic transmissions that shift erratically; a weak suspension; computer module glitches; brakes that constantly need rotor and pad replacement; poor body assembly; and paint defects. From a reliability/durability standpoint, the rear-drives are much better made than their front-drive counterparts.

GM technical service bulletins show that these vehicles also have noisy power-steering units and cooling fans, the AC bi-level mode produces extreme temperature differences, the instrument panel squeaks and rattles, there are rear quarter-panel gaps and rusting at the rear side-door window moulding, and water leaks into the passenger side of the front compartment.

Safety summary: All models: 1995—Dashboard reflects into windshield. • Vehicle accelerated while braking. • Frequent stalling. • Trunk lid opened while driving. • Brakes require extended stopping distances. **1996**—Airbags failed to deploy. • Seatbelts didn't restrain driver and passenger during a collision. • Chronic stalling due to fuel sending unit failure. • Transmission pounds when shifting gears. • Water pump leakage on the serpentine belt may cause steering to lock up. • Power-steering hose and pump failure. • Brakes often lock up when applied. • Excessive brake noise caused by the premature wearout of brake rotor and drum. • AC cooling switch and high-pressure hose failures. • Instrument cluster hard to read in daylight. • Power door locks and trunk lock frequently fail to operate properly. • Loose windshield moulding. • Defective keyless entry module.

Secret Warranties/Service Tips/TSBs

All models: 1993–96—Paint delamination, peeling, or fading (see Part Two). **1995**—The engine cranks but won't start, no fuel pressure, or extended crank time after cold soak. • Lack of power. • Engine oil leak at the rear main seal or T-joint. • Low oil pressure, loss of oil pressure, or lack of power. • AC odour. • Grinding or scraping noise in Park or Neutral. • A cold-start rattle with the 4T60E automatic transmission. • Front brake vibration and/or pedal pulsation. • A rubbing noise when the front wheels are turned all the way. • Door window scraping noise or sticking, rattling noise from front of vehicle, and excessive radio static. • A clicking noise from under the dash or hood. • A front seat clicking noise. • Erroneous fuel gauge readings, a low voltage reading, or dim lights at idle, and frequent blown fuse or battery drain. • Malfunctioning remote keyless entry. • Wet or smelly carpet from water leaks. • Poor paint application and rust spots. **1996**—3–2 part throttle downshift flare. • Engine noise (install new valve stem oil seal). • Transmission chuggle/surge. • Transmission fluid leak from pump body (replace bushing). • Crunch/pop noise in steering system. • AC odours. • Radio frequency interference diagnosis.

Cadillac Brougham, Fleetwood (RWD) Profile

	1990	1991	1992	1993	1994	1995	1996
Cost Price ($)							
Brougham, Fleetwood (RWD)	39,816	37,298	37,488	39,988	41,798	46,830	46,965

Used Values ($)

Brougham, Fleetwood (RWD) Ʌ	4,500	6,000	7,000	8,500	9,000	10,500	12,000
Brougham, Fleetwood (RWD) V	4,000	5,000	5,500	7,500	7,500	8,000	9,500
Extended Warranty	Y	Y	Y	Y	Y	N	N
Secret Warranty	Y	Y	Y	Y	Y	Y	Y
Reliability	③	③	③	③	③	④	④
Head Restraints	—	—	—	—	—	—	❷

Note: The Brougham and Fleetwood (RWD) haven't been crash-tested.

CADILLAC CATERA, ELDORADO, SEVILLE   ★★

RATING: Below Average (1992–2001); Not Recommended (1986–91). The Catera has been discontinued. **Maintenance/Repair costs:** Higher than average, but repairs aren't dealer dependent. Long delays for recall repairs. **Parts:** Higher-than-average cost (independent suppliers sell for much less), but not hard to find. Don't buy one of the front-drives without a 3- to 5-year supplementary warranty. **Best alternatives:** Acura Integra, TL, and RL; Cadillac DeVille, Brougham, or Fleetwood; Ford Crown Victoria or Mercury Grand Marquis; and the Mercedes E-Class.

Strengths and weaknesses: The early Cadillacs are luxury embarrassments, and later models barely pass muster. Even though most use the same mechanical components with the same deficiencies as the Riviera and Toronado models, they're far more failure prone, due to the complexity of their different luxury features and hard-to-find Catera parts.

Catera
Assembled in Germany and based on the Opel Omega, the rear-drive, mid-sized Catera comes with a 200-hp V6 engine, 4-speed automatic transmission, 16-inch alloy wheels, four-wheel disc brakes, a limited-slip differential, traction control, and standard dual front airbags. The conservatively styled Catera (the uninspired styling has Lumina written all over it) was designed to compete with the BMW 328i, Lexus ES 300, and Mercedes-Benz C280. GM hoped not to drive away its more traditional "empty-nesters" (I guess that's a polite term for "old folks"), while luring more baby boomers to its higher-performance variations. '98 versions got de-powered airbags, while the '99s adopted even more complex electronics and emissions systems to meet federal fuel economy and emissions standards. Year 2000 models received slight interior, front, and rear-end styling changes, standard side airbags, improved throttle control, and a retuned suspension. 2001s were carried over unchanged.

The Catera has received good press reviews for its quiet, spacious, and comfortable interior; responsive handling; fine-tuned suspension; and almost nonexistent lean or body roll when cornering. On the downside,

though, the steering system lacks balance and allows the vehicle to
wander; the controls aren't easy to figure out, some gauges are hard to
read, and the driver's rear view is hindered by the large rear head
restraints and narrow back windshield. Furthermore, owners report
chronic stalling and hard starts, possibly due to a malfunctioning idle
control valve; the transmission "hunts" for the right gear; constant
warning light illuminations; poor AM radio reception (requiring an additional amplifier); and loose interior panels. Body fit and finish isn't
impressive: body panels are often misaligned, and door locks freeze shut.
Two other performance problems reported by owners: when you pass
over a large expansion joint, the floorpan vibrates annoyingly; if you
drive over a bump when turning, the steering wheel kicks back in your
hands.

A few other points you may wish to consider: GM dealers are notoriously bad when it comes to understanding and repairing European-
transplanted cars (just ask any Saab owner). As well, low-volume cars
generally don't have an adequate supply of replacement parts in the
pipeline until they've been on the market for a while. Add in the Catera's
European connection and the fact it has just been dropped by GM, and
you'd best be ready to endure long service waits and high parts costs for
those repairs not covered under warranty.

Finally, the fact that Cateras are European-built doesn't necessarily
mean that these Cadillacs will be reliable. In fact, just the opposite is
more likely. Based on the past performance of Big Three European
imports, it's a safe bet that these cars will be less reliable and more troublesome than the competition. GM first learned that lesson with the
British-built, failure-prone Vauxhall Firenza it unleashed on an unsus-
pecting Canadian public in the '70s. A few years later, it settled out of
court on several class actions that I piloted, and paid a $20,000 fine to
the federal government for misleading advertising. (On a nationally
advertised road trip across Canada, GM said the cars excelled. Truth is,
they were a mess. They required a team of engineers just to get started.)

Eldorado and Seville
From 1992 on, the Eldorado's styling became more distinctive, even
though the vehicle shares most powertrain and chassis components with
the Seville. Although the base 4.9L V8 provides brisk acceleration, the
32-valve Northstar V8, first found on the 1993 Touring Coupe, gives you
almost 100 more horses, with great handling and a comfortable ride.
Overall, the Touring Coupe or Sport Coupe will give you the best powertrain, handling, and braking features. Of course, you'll have to contend
with poor fuel economy, rear visibility that's obstructed by the huge side
pillars (a Seville problem, as well), confusing and inconvenient climate
controls, and a particularly complex engine compartment.

Sitting on the same platform as the Eldorado, the Seville has
European-style allure with a more rounded body than the Eldorado.

Apart from that, since its redesign in 1992 its engine, handling, and braking upgrades have followed the Eldorado's improvements in lockstep fashion.

Whether you buy a used Eldorado or Seville, keep in mind that the improved versions came out with the 1995 models, which carried on unchanged until their redesign for 1998. So, if you must buy one of these models, remember that the only distinguishing feature between them is styling, not performance. In fact, between the 1998 and 2001 models, the only real change was the Eldorado's Northstar engine tweaking for year 2000 models.

These cars have generic deficiencies that fall into common categories: poorly calibrated and failure-prone engines, transmissions, and fuel and ignition systems; a multiplicity of electrical short circuits; and sloppy body assembly using poor-quality components. Specifically, engines and fuel systems often produce intermittent stalling, rough idling, hesitation, and no-starts; the Overdrive automatic is prone to premature failure; oil pumps fail frequently; front brakes and shock absorbers wear out quickly; often, paint is poorly applied, fades, or peels away prematurely; fragile body hardware breaks easily (front bumper cracks are commonplace); and there are large gaps between sheet-metal panels and doors that are poorly hung and not entirely square. Other body problems include cracking of front outside door handles, door rattles (Eldorado), poor bumper fit, loose sun visor mounting, rear taillight condensation, fading and discolouring appliqué mouldings (Seville), interior window fogging, "creaking" body mounts, water leaking into trunk from licence plate holder (Eldorado), noisy roof panels and seatback lumbar motors, and a creaking noise at the front-door upper hinge area.

Safety summary: Catera: 1997—Engine coolant leaks. • Airbag malfunctions. • Tie-rod failure. • Loss of steering and hydroplaning when driving through puddles. • Front windshield moulding flew off. **1997–2001**—Chronic stalling. • Frequent wheel alignments. • Defective brake rotors cause excessive vibration and pull. • Premature tire wear. • Vehicle wanders and pulls to one side. • Door locks don't work and key sticks in the ignition. • Windshield wipers are inadequate in heavy rain. **1998**—Engine head gasket failures. **1999**—Accelerator can be floored and vehicle will only creep forward. • Head restraints block vision. • Loss of steering. • Excessive vehicle wandering. • Door latch sticks in the closed position. **2000**—Chronic stalling. • Hesitant shifting. • Defective ignition switch. **2001**—Gas pedal sticks. **Eldorado, Seville: 1986–2001**—A plethora of electrical short circuits, front axle, ABS brake, and steering failures. • Sudden, unintended acceleration. • Airbag malfunctions (deploying for no reason and injuring occupants). • Brake rotors and pads always need changing. • Excessive vibration at all speeds. • Poor headlight illumination. **Seville: 1999**—Front control arm snapped. • Tie-rod end came apart. • Loss of power steering when driving in the rain. •

Front and rear lights collect water. **2000**—Seatbelt retractors don't work properly. • Excessive drifting at any speed. • Brake caliper locked up. **2001**—While driving, passenger-side wheel collapsed due to a missing suspension bolt. • Steering column rubbing noise is heard when making a right turn.

Secret Warranties/Service Tips/TSBs

All models: 1993–99—A cold engine knock or ticking may be caused by excessive carbon deposits in the engine. • AC odours can be reduced by applying a cooling coil coating. • Defective catalytic converters that cause a rotten-egg smell in the interior may be replaced free of charge under the emissions warranty. • Paint delamination, peeling, or fading (see Part Two). **1994**—Condensation dripping from the heater duct requires the installation of a watertight dam in the HVAC case. • An inoperative cruise control or brake/transmission interlock may signal a misadjusted stop-light switch assembly. • A binding parking brake may need a new park-brake vacuum release switch. **1996–97**—A torque converter clutch buzz or moan requires the installation of an upgraded case cover assembly spacer plate and the upper control valve body. **1997**—Excessive front brake noise can be cured by installing upgraded front brake pads. **1997–98**—Excessive brake noise can be reduced by installing upgraded pads and rotors. **1998**—Harsh or delayed gear shifts may require the installation of an enhanced garage shift package. • Accessory drive noise may be caused by a misaligned accessory drive pulley. • Delayed or no engine braking in D3 may require the replacement of the forward and coast latch piston assemblies. **1998–99**—Diagnostic and repair tips for a faulty cruise control and speedometer. • Front-end clunks and rattles can be silenced by a judicious use of anti-friction materials. **1998–2001**—Inoperative heated seat. **1999–2000**—An engine that runs hot, overheats, or loses coolant may simply need a new radiator cap. **2000–01**—If there's a sudden loss of power when accelerating, the transmission fluid pressure switch may be defective. **2001**—Intermittent inoperative instrument panel (requires replacement of the I/P cluster assembly). • Cooler fitting coolant leaks. • Delayed Reverse engagement. **All models with 4.9L engines: 1991–95**—GM will install a new computer chip that reduces stalling. **Catera: 1997**—Brake squealing can be silenced by installing redesigned calipers. • Oil leakage from the engine timing cover can be corrected by installing a new oil pump gasket.

Cadillac Catera, Eldorado, Seville Profile

	1994	1995	1996	1997	1998	1999	2000	2001
Cost Price ($)								
Catera	—	—	—	42,690	43,250	42,310	42,635	42,485
Eldorado	46,498	50,430	50,745	52,015	53,000	52,660	53,455	56,600
Seville	49,998	55,315	55,635	57,000	59,900	59,195	60,195	58,710

Used Values ($)								
Catera ▲	—	—	—	13,000	17,500	21,500	26,500	30,000
Catera ▼	—	—	—	11,000	15,000	19,000	24,000	27,000
Eldorado ▲	7,500	10,500	12,500	17,000	22,500	27,500	33,500	41,000
Eldorado ▼	6,000	8,000	10,000	14,500	19,500	25,000	31,000	38,000
Seville ▲	9,000	11,500	13,500	18,000	24,000	30,000	37,500	43,500
Seville ▼	7,000	9,000	11,000	16,000	22,000	28,000	35,000	41,000
Extended Warranty	Y	Y	Y	Y	Y	Y	N	N
Secret Warranty	Y	Y	Y	Y	Y	Y	Y	Y
Reliability	❷	❷	❷	❷	③	③	③	④
Off-set								
Catera	—	—	—	⑤	⑤	⑤	⑤	⑤
Seville	❶	❶	❶	❶	—	—	⑤	⑤
Head Restraints								
Catera	—	—	—	③	—	❷	—	③
Eldorado	—	❶	—	❶	—	❶	—	❶
Seville	—	❶	—	❶	—	—	❶	❶

Note: Reliability figures apply to the Eldorado and Seville only; Catera reliability information is given in the text.

CADILLAC CONCOURS, DEVILLE, FLEETWOOD (FWD) ★★★★

RATING: Above Average (2000–01); Average (1995–99); Below Average (1985–94). Interestingly, a new Concours sold at a $10,000 premium over the DeVille, yet the difference narrowed to about $2,000 as the vehicles aged. There are two major safety problems affecting 1995–99 models: inadvertent side and front airbag deployment, and chronic stalling in traffic. Ask dealer to shut off the airbags until GM fixes your vehicle. **Maintenance/Repair costs:** Higher than average, and most repairs must be done by a dealer. Long delay for recall repairs. **Parts:** Higher-than-average cost (independent suppliers sell for much less), but not hard to find. All of these front-drives require a 3- to 5-year supplementary warranty. **Best alternatives:** Acura Integra, TL, and RL; Infiniti I30 or I35; Lexus ES 300; and Mercedes E-Class.

Strengths and weaknesses: Although they have better handling and are almost as comfortable as older, traditional Caddies, the early models of these luxury coupes and sedans aren't worth considering because of their dismal reliability and overly complex servicing. Redesigned 1995–99 versions have posted fewer complaints; however, they are still far below the industry norm for quality and reliability. As with the Eldorado and Seville, you get the best array of handling, braking, and performance features with the 1996 and later versions. They do ride more quietly and comfortably, but fuel economy is still poor, the dash controls and gauges are confusing and not easily accessible, and the rear view is obstructed by the high trunk lid and large side pillars.

'96 DeVilles were given the Northstar V8 and an upgraded automatic transmission and suspension. The Concourse received 25 additional horses along with improved steering and suspension. '97s were substantially reworked and given new styling, side airbags, and an upgraded interior. '98s got de-powered airbags. '99s returned mostly unchanged; year 2000 models received a number of high-tech improvements, including refinements to the V8 engine, Night Vision, Rear Parking Assist, and StabiliTrak traction control.

The 4.3L V6, 4.1L V8, and 4.5L V8 engines and 4-speed automatic transmission suffer from a variety of terminal maladies, including oil leaks, premature wear, poor fuel economy, and excessive noise. The electrical system and related components are temperamental. The suspension goes soft quickly, and the front brakes often wear out after only 18 months/20,000 km. Problems with the digital fuel-injection and engine control systems are very difficult to diagnose and repair. Poor body assembly is characterized by premature paint peeling and rusting, excessive wind noise in the interior, and fragile trim items.

Safety summary: Concours, DeVille: 1995–96—A short circuit caused by wet carpets could cause the airbags to suddenly deploy. **DeVille: 1998**—Inadvertent side airbag deployment. • Wheel flew off car after wheel studs failed. • Vehicle suddenly accelerated, killing one person and injuring others. • Accelerator sticking. • Cruise control self-activates. • Chronic stalling while underway. • Can't read speedometer in daylight. • Many complaints of front and rear brake rotor warpage and premature pad and caliper failure. • Sudden loss of power steering. • Vehicle tends to wander all over the road. • Leaking engine oil coolant. • Windshield washer fluid doesn't pump high enough. • Gas tank sensor failure causes inaccurate fuel readings. • Tire failure (Vogue). • Exterior mirrors are too small, and when vehicle is in Reverse, rear-view mirror automatically tilts down. • Interior lights frequently malfunction. • Chronic battery failure. **1999**—Airbags explode when vehicle is started, idles, accelerates, or is parked. Several occupants have been injured. NHTSA looked into a flood of complaints of inadvertent side airbag deployment on 1998 and 1999 models and forced GM to recall these cars. Problem is, GM says it won't have the parts to correct the defect before April 2001. Drivers are demanding that dealers disconnect the system until it is corrected. • Incidents where front and side airbags failed to deploy in a collision. • Engine overheating, loose head bolts, and excessive oil consumption. • Stalling when coasting or coming to a stop. • Vehicle rolls backward when in gear. • Fuel tank leaks fuel. • Premature warpage of the front and rear brake rotors. • Failure-prone ignition and electronic control module. • Tire flew off while vehicle was underway. • Factory-equipped jack inadequate to support vehicle. • Instrument panel lighting hard to read in daylight. • Power door locks operate erratically. • Windshield wipers won't come on unless turned on High. • Driver's seat-belt constantly tightens up. **2000**—Sudden, unintended acceleration and chronic stalling. • Steering locked up. • Automatic transmission jolts when shifting. • Airbags deploy inadvertently. • A shroud may impede accessing brake pedal. • Frequent crankshaft sensor failure. • Digital instrument panel can't be read in daylight. • Sun visor blocks out over-hanging traffic lights. • Horn is hard to access. **2001**—Transmission doesn't shift all the way into Drive; pops out of gear and allows vehicle to roll down an incline. • Brake pedal goes to the floor without braking. • Rear suspension make the DeVille unstable. • Steering wheel emits a grinding sound. • Side mirror creates a huge blind spot.

Secret Warranties/Service Tips/TSBs

All models/years: Defective catalytic converters that cause a rotten-egg smell in the interior may be replaced free of charge under the emissions warranty. • Paint delamination, peeling, or fading (see Part Two). **All models: 1994**—Condensation dripping from the heater duct requires the installation of a watertight dam in the HVAC case. • An inoperative cruise control or brake/transmission interlock may signal a misadjusted stop-light switch assembly. • TSB #476003 goes into great detail about how to troubleshoot the various engine oil leaks afflicting 1994 models. • Doors that won't stay open on slight grades require upgraded door springs. • Noisy fuel pumps can be silenced only by installing an upgraded fuel pump under warranty. • TSB #476506 gives lots of tips on fixing 4.6L engines that run roughly, miss, surge, or hesitate. • Poor heat distribution (driver's feet get cold) can be fixed by replacing the floor outlet assembly. • Rear compartment water leaks are addressed in TSB #311510. **1998**—Harsh or delayed gear shifts may require the installation of an enhanced garage shift package. • Delayed or no engine braking in D3 may require the replacement of the forward and coast latch-piston assemblies. **2001**—Intermittent inoperative instrument panel (requires replacement of the I/P cluster assembly). • Cooler fitting coolant leaks. • Delayed Reverse engagement. **All models with 5.7L engines: 1994–96**—A chuggle or surge condition will require a reflash calibration. • Excessive engine noise can be silenced by installing an upgraded valve-stem oil seal. **1995**—Intermittent Neutral/loss of Drive at highway speeds can be fixed by replacing the control valve body assembly. **1996–97**—A torque converter clutch buzz or moan requires the installation of an upgraded case-cover assembly spacer plate and the upper control valve body. **1997–98**—Excessive front brake noise can be reduced by installing upgraded pads and rotors. **1998–99**—Diagnostic and repair tips for a faulty cruise control and speedometer. • Front end clunks and rattles can be silenced by a judicious use of anti-friction materials. **1999–2000**—An engine that runs hot, overheats, or loses coolant may simply need a new radiator cap.

Cadillac Concours, DeVille, Fleetwood (FWD) Profile

	1994	1995	1996	1997	1998	1999	2000	2001
Cost Price ($)								
Concours	49,498	53,690	54,340	56,985	58,600	57,490	—	—
DeVille	41,998	46,635	48,125	49,400	50,495	49,710	51,995	51,895
Fleetwood (FWD)	41,798	46,830	46,965	—	—	—	—	—
Used Values ($)								
Concours Λ	10,000	13,500	12,500	18,000	24,000	29,500	—	—
Concours V	8,000	11,500	10,500	15,000	21,000	27,000	—	—
DeVille Λ	7,500	10,000	11,500	16,500	22,000	27,000	32,500	38,000
DeVille V	6,500	8,000	9,000	14,000	19,000	24,000	30,000	35,000
Fleetwood (FWD) Λ	8,000	10,500	12,000	—	—	—	—	—
Fleetwood (FWD) V	7,000	8,000	10,000	—	—	—	—	—
Extended Warranty	Y	Y	Y	Y	Y	Y	Y	Y
Secret Warranty	N	N	Y	Y	Y	Y	Y	Y
Reliability	❷	❷	❷	③	③	③	③	④
Crash Safety								
Concours	④	—	③	—	—	—	—	—
DeVille	④	—	③	④	④	④	③	③
Side Impact (DeVille)	—	—	—	④	④	④	④	④
Head Restraints (F)	—	❶	—	❶	—	❷	—	❷
Rear	—	—	—	—	—	—	—	❶

Infiniti

G20, I30, J30, Q45

RATING: †*G20:* Not Recommended (1994–2001). *I30, J30, and Q45:*
Above Average (1995–2001); Average (1991–94). The 1997–99 Q45s
were "de-contented" by Infiniti, meaning they sold for less because
they were made more cheaply, came with fewer standard features, and
were equipped with a smaller, less powerful engine. Unlike Toyotas that
went through the same cost-cutting, these vehicles have had surprisingly
few safety-related defects reported to the federal government.
Maintenance/Repair costs: Higher than average, and repairs must be
done by either an Infiniti or a Nissan dealer. **Parts:** Higher-than-average
cost, but not hard to find (except for body panels). **Best alternatives:**
The fully equipped Honda Accord, Mazda Millenia and 929, Nissan
Maxima, or Toyota Camry and Avalon are better buys from a price/quality
standpoint, but they don't have the same luxury cachet. Also consider the
Acura Integra, Legend, TL, and RL or the Mercedes E-Class.

Strengths and weaknesses: With its emphasis on sporty handling (diluted somewhat with the '97 and later model years), the Infiniti series takes the opposite tack from the Lexus, which puts the accent on comfort and luxury. Still, the Infiniti comes fully equipped and offers owners the prestige of driving a comfortable, reliable, and nicely styled luxury car.

G20

The least expensive Infiniti, the 1994–96 G20 is a front-drive luxury sports sedan that uses a base 2.0L 140-hp 16-valve, twin-cam, 4-cylinder powerplant to accelerate smoothly, albeit noisily, through all gear ranges. Dual airbags came on line midway through the 1993 model year, and ABS is standard. Towing capacity is 1,000 lbs. Cruise control is a bit erratic, particularly when traversing hilly terrain. Unlike the engine, the automatic transmission is silent, and power is reduced automatically when shifting. Steering is precise and responsive on the highway. However, the rear end tends to swing out sharply following abrupt steering changes. Early Infiniti G20s rode a bit too firmly, which led to the suspension being softened on the 1994 model. Now drivers say that the suspension tends to bounce and jiggle occupants whenever the car goes over uneven pavement or the load is increased.

Overall, however, the Infiniti G20s aren't as refined as their entry-level Lexus counterparts in interior space, drivetrain, or convenience features. Owners have complained that the engine's lack of low-speed torque means that it has to work hard above 4000 rpm—while protesting noisily—to produce brisk engine response in the higher gear ranges. The automatic transmission shifts roughly, particularly when passing (a problem corrected in the 1994 models); the power steering needs more assist during parking manoeuvres; and the dealer-installed fog lights cost an exorbitant $500 to replace. Poorly thought-out control layout is best exemplified by the hard-to-reach heat/vent controls, an armrest-mounted trunk and filler release that's inconvenient to operate, and centre console–mounted power window switches that are difficult to find while driving. Tall drivers will find the leg room insufficient. The trunk is spacious, but its small opening is limited by the angle of the rear window.

Owner complaints target failure-prone brake rotors, prematurely worn brake pads, and excessive noise when braking.

Returning after a three-year hiatus, the '99 G20 wasn't worth the wait. It's basically a package of unfulfilled expectations with its wimpy 2.0L 140-hp engine, firm ride, and ordinary styling. On the positive side, the car does handle well. Year 2000 models got a bit more horsepower and an upgraded transmission; 2001s returned unchanged.

J30, I30

Resembling the 929 Serenia, the rear-drive, four-door J30 and its high-performance variant, the I30, are sized and priced midway between the

G20 and the top-of-the-line Q45. The J30 uses a modified version of the Nissan 300ZX's 3.0L 210-hp V6 engine. Although the vehicle is replete with important safety features and it accelerates and handles well, its engine is noisy, passenger and cargo room have been sacrificed to styling, and fuel economy is underwhelming.

The J30 comes with a standard airbag (or dual airbags, depending on the model year), ABS, and traction control. It's changed very little over the years, meaning that there's no reason to choose a more recent model over a much cheaper older version.

Quality problems include airbag malfunctions (inadvertent deployment and failure to deploy), cracked exhaust manifold, leaking fuel injection system, and excessive vibration when accelerating.

The I30 is a sport sedan spin-off of the Nissan Maxima with additional sound-deadening material and a plusher interior. The car has a roomy interior, but its ride is unimpressive and handling is compromised by excessive body lean when cornering. Engine and road noise is omnipresent. The redesigned year 2000 model adds rear seat room and reduces body lean considerably.

Like the J30 and Maxima, the I30 comes loaded with standard safety, performance, and comfort features, notably a 190-hp 3.0L V6 engine with dual camshafts and anti-lock brakes. 1996–99 models changed little, except for front side airbags and new headlights and taillights added to the '98s and heated seats given to the '99s.

The year 2000 I30 represents the best value from a price/performance perspective. It was entirely revamped with more conservative styling, 37 more horses, and a larger cabin. Head restraints were also upgraded, suspension improved, larger wheels were added, and high-intensity headlights adopted. 2001 models returned mostly unchanged.

Q45

Faster and glitzier than other cars in its category, this luxury sedan provides performance, while its chief rival, the Lexus ES400, provides luxury and quiet. Up to the '96 model, the Q45 used a 32-valve 278-hp 4.5L V8 tire-burner not frequently found on a Japanese luxury compact. It accelerates faster than the Lexus, going 0–100 km/h in 7.1 seconds without a hint of noise or abrupt shifting. Unlike the base engine of the G20, though, the Q45's engine supplies plenty of upper-range torque as well. The suspension was softened in 1994, but the car still rides much more firmly than its Lexus counterpart. The four-wheel steering is precise, but the standard limited-slip differential is no help in preventing the car's rear end from sliding out on slippery roads, due mainly to the original equipment "sport" tires, designed mainly for 190 km/h autobahn cruising. There's not much foot room for passengers, and cargo room is disappointing. Fuel economy is nonexistent. ABS is standard, but a passenger-side airbag wasn't available before 1994. A redesigned 1994 version got a re-styled front end, a chrome grille, and an updated instrument panel.

Three years later, the car was again made over with the addition of a downsized 4.1L V8 set on a smaller platform, effectively changing the character of the car from a sporty performer to a highway cruiser. Other changes in the ensuing model years were minor: front seatbelt pretensioners for the '98s, and minor interior and exterior re-styling of the 1999 models. The next major redesign was applied to the 2002 models.

Owners report excessive wind noise around the A-pillars, sunroof wind leaks, tire thumping noise, cellular telephone echoing, faulty CD players, and a popping sound from the radio. Owners of 1999 Q45s report that the paint scratches and flakes off so easily that it has to be constantly touched up.

Technical service bulletins list the following defects affecting the 1994–96 models: AC not blowing cold, front brake pad noise, low or rough idle, doors locking/unlocking themselves, and windshield cracking. You may also be interested in reviewing other helpful bulletins that contain troubleshooting tips for AC compressor leaks and noise, brake clunking noises and pedal pulsation, booming/drone noise and vibration, cold-weather hard starts, rough idle, suspension noise, Code 45 driveability alerts, and brake shudder and steering-wheel shimmy.

Bulletins for the 1997 model don't cover much that's new, concerning themselves principally with clunking noises and pedal pulsation, cold-weather starting tips, hard starting, and rough idle and suspension noise diagnostic tips. 1998 bulletins contain no useful tips, and the 1999–2001 TSBs are integrated into the "Secret Warranties/Service Tips/TSBs" section.

Safety summary: G20: 1995—Driver seriously injured by airbag deployment when vehicle was pushed into a wall at low speed. • Faulty cruise control wouldn't disengage, brakes failed, and collision ensued. • Defective fuel filler tube or fuel vent tube. • Frequent stalling. • Large sun visor blocks driver's view of stoplights. • Passenger-side power windows operate erratically. • Defective speaker amplifier. • Centre console handle broke. **1996**—Violent deployment of airbag during collision resulted in permanent eye damage. • Brakes were applied to disengage cruise control and vehicle suddenly accelerated. • Noisy brakes; dealer cannot fix the problem. • Oil pressure switch failure. **1999**—Carbon monoxide poisoning. • When car is put into Reverse, driver's seat reclines, without warning. **2001**—Foul odour emitted by AC. • Brake failure. • Brake rotors glaze over and need turning. • Airbags failed to deploy. **J30: 1995**—Airbag failed to deploy. • Airbags deployed during low-speed (11 km/h) fender-bender, causing extensive injuries to occupants. • Rear end swings out when accelerating. • Fuel injector system leaks fuel. • Excessive vibrations when accelerating make vehicle difficult to steer. • Driver's seatbelt won't retract. **1996**—Cracked exhaust manifold. • Door locks lock and unlock on their own. **1997**—Sudden acceleration. Leaking fuel injectors. **I30: 1996**—Sudden, unintended acceleration. • Sunroof blew off vehicle. **1997**—Brakes failed. • Vehicle wouldn't decelerate. • Chronic stalling. **1998**—Airbag malfunctions. • Side window blew out. • Brake failure. **1999**—When using the turn signal, it's easy to turn off the headlights. • Airbag light stays on continuously. • Water seeps inside the vehicle from beneath. **2000**—Sudden, unintended acceleration. • Transmission jerks when shifting. • Premature wear of brake rotors. • Sunlight washes out gauges. • Headlight aimed too low. **2001**—Rear suspension failed. • Sudden, unintended acceleration. • Cruise control wouldn't disengage when brakes were applied. **Q45: 1995**—Sudden acceleration when coming to a stop. • Gas and brake pedals are set too close together. • Failure of driver's power seat adjuster motor. • Hood flew up while driving along the highway at about 100 km/h. **1996**—Airbag indicator flashes due to ECM failure. • Premature failure of the shock absorber and power window. **1997**— Owner alleges that vehicle design causes the vehicle to hydroplane where other cars wouldn't. • Airbag warning light comes on for no reason. • When car is put into Reverse, driver's seat reclines, without warning. • Severe front end vibration continued after tires were replaced. **1998**— Airbag failed to deploy. • Accelerator pedal stuck while vehicle was stopped. **2000**—Excessive vibration starts at 100 km/h.

Secret Warranties/Service Tips/TSBs

All models/years: Troubleshooting tips to correct hard starts. • Vehicles with sunroofs may have wind noise coming from the sunroof area because of a small pinhole in the body sealer at the rear C-pillar. • Windshield cracking. • Erratic operation of the power antenna requires that the antenna rod be replaced. • Slow retraction of the front seatbelt can be fixed by wiping off any residue found on the seatbelt D-ring. **G20: 1999**—Excessive blower noise can be reduced by installing a new cover. • Coolant leakage may be caused by a defective intake manifold expansion plug. • Replace the window glass run rubber if window makes a popping sound when opened. **1999–2000**—Countermeasures for front end clunks when turning or braking. **1999–2001**—Power seat won't move or makes a grinding noise. • Shock absorbers that clunk will be replaced under warranty. **2000**—Engine lacks power; stuck in Third gear. • Correcting a brake judder. • Cloudy, scratched instrument cluster lens. • Parcel shelf rattle or buzz. • Low idle or dies when put into gear. • Preventing a rotten-egg smell emitted by the exhaust. **I30: 1996–1998**—If either one of the front power seats won't move, check for a broken power seat drive cable. **1996–2000**—Excessive blower noise can be reduced by installing a new cover. **2000–01**—Transmission slippage. **Q45: 1994–96**—Doors that intermittently lock by themselves require the installation of countermeasure front door lock actuators (TSB #NTB96-027). **1997–99**—A lumbar support mechanism that's inoperative should be replaced with an upgraded support mechanism. • If either one of the front power seats won't move, check for a broken power seat drive cable. • Excessive blower noise can be reduced by installing a new cover. • TSB #ITB98-062 gives an exhaustive listing for a variety of squeak and rattle repairs. **1997–2000**—TSB #ITB00-010 gives a detailed list of brake judder countermeasures. **1998–99**—An automatic transmission that produces a "double thump" noise when coming to a stop likely needs a new transmission control module (TCM).

G20, I30, J30, Q45 Profile

	1994	1995	1996	1997	1998	1999	2000	2001
Cost Price ($)								
G20	26,440	29,540	31,440	—	—	29,950	29,950	29,900
I30	—	—	40,600	41,000	41,350	41,950	39,700	39,900
J30	45,000	48,100	51,600	52,600	—	—	—	—
Q45	72,000	75,450	72,000	65,000	66,500	71,000	71,000	70,000
Used Values ($)								
G20 ⋀	7,500	8,000	10,500	—	—	17,000	20,000	23,000
G20 ⋁	6,000	7,000	8,000	—	—	15,000	18,000	21,000
I30 ⋀	—	—	12,000	15,000	19,500	25,000	30,000	33,000
I30 ⋁	—	—	10,000	13,000	16,500	22,000	27,000	32,500
J30 ⋀	9,000	10,500	13,000	16,000	—	—	—	—
J30 ⋁	7,000	8,000	12,500	14,000	—	—	—	—
Q45 ⋀	9,500	11,000	12,000	17,000	23,000	31,000	40,000	50,000
Q45 ⋁	8,000	8,500	9,000	15,000	19,500	28,000	37,000	46,000
Extended Warranty	N	N	N	N	N	N	N	N
Secret Warranty	N	N	N	N	N	N	N	N
Reliability	❷	④	④	⑤	④	④	⑤	⑤
Crash Safety								
I30	—	—	—	—	④	—	④	④
J30	④	④	④	—	—	—	—	—
Side Impact (I30)	—	—	—	—	④	—	④	④
Off-set								
I30/I35	—	❶	❶	③	③	③	③	③
J30	—	—	—	—	—	—	③	③
Q45	—	—	—	❷	❷	❷	❷	❷
Head Restraints								
G20	—	❶	—	—	—	❷	—	❶
I30	—	—	—	❷	—	❷	⑤	⑤
J30	—	❶	—	❶	—	—	—	—
Q45	—	❶	—	❶	—	❶	⑤	⑤

Lexus

ES 300, GS 300, LS 400, SC 400   ★★★★★

RATING: Recommended (1996–2001); Above Average (1990–95). More reliable and better built than the Infiniti, but more costly, too. The 1996 and 1998 models were the first to incorporate important safety, perform-ance, and styling improvements. **Maintenance/Repair costs:** Higher than average, and repairs must be done by either a Lexus or a Toyota dealer. **Parts:** Higher-than-average cost, but not hard to find (except for body panels). **Best alternatives:** A fully equipped Legend, Honda Accord, Nissan Maxima, or Toyota Camry will provide airbags, comparable highway performance, and reliability at far less initial cost, but you don't get the Lexus *cachet*. If you do pay top dollar for a used Lexus, its slow rate of depreciation virtually guarantees that you'll get much of your money back.

Strengths and weaknesses: These are benchmark cars known for their bulletproof reliability and impressive performance. Sports cars, they're not. But if you're looking for your father's Oldsmobile (if your dad was Japanese), these luxury cars fill the bill. Like the Acuras and Infinitis, Lexus models all suffer from some automatic transmission, front-brake, electrical, body, trim, and accessory deficiencies that are confirmed by confidential technical service bulletins.

ES 300

Resembling an LS 400 dressed in sporty attire, the entry-level ES 300 was launched in 1992 to fill the gap between the discontinued ES 250 and the LS 400. In fact, the ES 300 has many of the attributes of the LS 400 sedan for much less money. A five-passenger sedan based on the Camry, it comes equipped with a standard 3.0L 24-valve engine that produces 181–210 horses, coupled to either a 5-speed manual or a 4-speed elec-tronically controlled automatic transmission. Unlike the Infinitis, the ES 300 accelerates smoothly and quietly, while averaging about 14L/100 km in mixed driving. The suspension is soft and steady. Passenger and cargo room are plentiful, with lots of leg and head room (except on sunroof-equipped versions).

ABS is standard, but a second airbag became available only on the 1994 model, which also introduced a new 3.0L 6-cylinder that boosted horsepower a bit. 1995 and 1996 models were carried over unchanged, but the '97 ES 300 was completely revamped, offering a re-styled interior and exterior, increased interior dimensions, and additional horsepower. '98s got de-powered airbags, along with side airbags and an upgraded anti-theft system. The 3.0L V6 got another small horsepower boost for

the 1999 model year. Year 2000 models were given re-styled front ends
and taillights, in addition to improved child safety seat anchors; 2001s
returned practically unchanged, except for further upgraded child safety
seat anchors and an emergency trunk release.

Surprisingly, for a vehicle this well made, government-reported safety-
related defects are legion. Airbag-induced injuries, sudden acceleration,
ABS and Goodyear tire failures, excessive vibration when underway, interior window fogging, and AC toxic emanations are only a few of the ES
300 complaints that are carried over many years and have been reported
with other Lexus models.

GS 300

The rear-drive GS 300 is a step up from the front-drive ES 300 and just a
rung below Lexus's top-of-the-line LS 400. It carries the same V6 engine
as the ES 300, except it has 20 more horses. This produces sparkling performance at higher speeds, though the car is disappointingly sluggish
from a start. Fuel economy is sacrificed for performance, however, and
the base suspension and tires pass noisily over small bumps and ruts.
Visibility is also less than impressive, with large rear pillars and a narrow
rear window restricting the view. There's not much usable trunk space,
either, and the liftover is unreasonably high.

This sports sedan, first launched as a 1993 model carrying standard
dual airbags and ABS, didn't change much until the 1996 model year,
when it got a light rear-end re-styling and a 5-speed automatic transmission. The car was totally reworked, however, for the '98 model year,
when it was once again re-styled and given an overhead-cam V8. '99s
returned unchanged; year 2000 models were given a new brake assist
system and more user-friendly child safety seat anchors. 2001s were substantially upgraded with a 300-hp 4.3L V8, upgraded transmission
controls, standard side curtain airbags, smart airbags, an emergency
trunk release, and a host of other convenience features.

Owner complaints have centred upon brake failures, electrical and
fuel system malfunctions resulting in unintended sudden acceleration
and hesitation, electrical shutdown, wheel bearings, excessive front end
vibration, and fragile wheel rims.

LS 400, LS 430

The Lexus flagship, the LS 400 rear-drive outclasses all other luxury
sedans in reliability, styling, and function. The base engine is a 242- to
290-hp 4.0L V8 that provides smooth, impressive acceleration and superior highway passing ability at all speeds. Its transmission is smooth and
efficient. The suspension gives an easy ride, without body roll or front-
end plow during emergency stops, thereby delivering a major comfort
advantage over other luxury compacts. There's an absence of engine and
wind noise.

ABS and dual airbags are standard. A passenger airbag, alloy wheels,
larger tires and brakes, interior upgrades and revised exterior styling

characterized the '93 models. Two years later, the '95 version got increased interior and exterior dimensions, a more powerful engine, and a better-performing drivetrain for quicker acceleration. Side airbags were added to the '97s. '98 models got a whole slew of improvements that included a four-cam V8 with continuously variable valve timing, a new 5-speed automatic transmission, Vehicle Skid Control (VSC), and a host of interior upgrades. There were no significant changes to the 1999 and 2000 LS 400, but the year 2001 version was totally redesigned. In addition to a sleeker body, it comes with a 4.3L V8, an upgraded suspension, and a more spacious, reworked interior. Additional safety and comfort features have also been added.

Owners have complained that the brakes don't inspire confidence, owing to their mushy feel and average performance. Furthermore, there's limited rear foot room under the front seats, and the rear middle passenger has to sit on the transmission hump. This car is a gas-guzzler that thirsts for premium fuel.

Owner complaints deal mainly with sudden, unintended acceleration; stalling due to a faulty throttle sensor; traction control causes vehicle to swerve (usually to the left) unexpectedly; failure of the Vehicle Skid Control to activate; main computer failures; spongy brakes; electrical glitches; and door locks that stick shut, trapping occupants.

SC 300, SC 400

These two coupes are practically identical, except for their engines and luxury features. The cheaper SC 300 gives you the same high-performance 6-cylinder engine used by the GS 300 and Toyota Supra, while the SC 400 uses the 4.0L V8 engine found in the LS 400. You're likely to find fewer luxury features with the SC 300 because they were sold as options. Nevertheless, look for an SC with traction control for additional safety during poor driving conditions. On the downside, V8 fuel consumption is horrendous, rear seating is cramped, and trunk space is unimpressive. Also, invest in a good anti-theft device, or your Lexus relationship will be over almost before it begins.

1993 models added a passenger airbag; '95s were slightly re-styled; and the '96 400 series was given the LS 400's V8. The '98 model year SC 400 got a 4.0L, four-cam aluminum V8 engine, while the SC 300 continued to use the previous year's inline six, but ditched its 5-speed manual transmission. Other upgrades: variable valve timing, a more refined 5-speed automatic transmission, a new anti-theft system, and de-powered airbags. American-sold '99s got larger brakes, and year 2000 models were left unchanged.

Safety summary: ES 300: 1995—Airbags failed to deploy. • Both front seatbelts failed to lock during a collision. • Seatbelt failed to restrain passenger during collision. • Goodyear Eagle tire blowout. • Premature failure of the electronic control unit. • Transmission leaks. • Brake pedal design makes it difficult for someone with a shoe larger than men's size 9 to use the brakes. • Excessive noise when braking. • Faulty windshield mouldings cause excessive wind noise. **1996**—Fire in the engine compartment. • Frequent reports that the airbag failed to deploy. • Weak seatback collapsed rearward in a collision. • Entire vehicle shimmies. • Sudden steering failure when turning. **1997**—Vehicle left in Park rolled backward and hit another car. Same thing occurred with a vehicle parked in a garage, but this time cause was isolated to a failure of the shift lock actuator fuse. • Owner says airbags are a hazard for short people. • Also, floor pedals are located too high and are too far apart for short people. • Middle rear shoulder belt locks up, making it very difficult to get occupant out; owner had to cut the belt. • Instrument cluster lights aren't bright enough for night driving. • AC assembly panel failure. **1998**—Vehicle accelerated as brakes were applied. • Premature front brake pad wearout. • Seat adjustment motor failure. **1999**—Rear seatbelts don't hold a child safety seat firmly. • Rodents have easy access to the car's innards. Says one owner of a '99 Lexus parked in a rural township:

> The only recommendations from Lexus is to "get moth balls, get a cat, get an exterminator".... My mechanic has a Camry that's parked in the same neighbourhood, within a closed garage, underneath a car cover. Five cats and liberal dousing of rat poison forces him to periodically clean out the mess, which includes dead rodents and snakes. Lexus won't acknowledge nor rectify a situation that's inconvenient, expensive, and hazardous. Vision may be more than impaired due to no air control to the front windshield as mouse excrement and nest crap gets sucked into the sophisticated air filtration system.

• Vehicle suddenly swerves from one lane to another. • Excessive oil consumption, blue smoke comes from the tailpipe, PCV valve is clogged up, and head gasket has failed (all symptomatic of Toyota's "oil sludge" problem, covered in the Sienna section). **2000**—Sudden, unintended acceleration when in Reverse. • Engine stalls or won't accelerate in traffic. • Vehicle suddenly downshifts from Fourth to First in heavy traffic; jerky shifting. • Rolls backward when transmission is in Drive. • Swerves left on a straight road. • Fails to start, intermittently. • Premature front brake wear. • Rear-view mirror doesn't move, resulting in poor visibility. **2001**—Engine fire erupted from what investigator said was fuel leaking from a rubber hose that had disconnected from the fuel filter. • Car suddenly accelerated as driver slowed coming to a stop sign, and again, when pulling into a parking space. • Traction control engages much too easily when merging into traffic. • Vehicle started up and began moving down the street in Reverse, despite the fact that there was no key in the ignition cylinder and vehicle was left in Park. • Vehicle hesitates when applying accelerator after decelerating; computer replacement is said to be on national back-order. **GS 300: 1998**—Vehicle surges or suddenly accelerates. • After yaw sensor replacement, as per recall, yaw sensor failure caused an accident. • Rear brake caliper plate for brake pads fell off after brake pins dislodged. • Poor low-beam illumination. • Trunk lid falls down unexpectedly. **1999**—Sudden, unintended acceleration and unexpected delayed acceleration. • Complete brake failure. • Excessive vibration at highway speeds.

Secret Warranties/Service Tips/TSBs

All models: 1990–2000—Eliminating brake clicking when changing direction of travel (requires a special grease recommended by Toyota/Lexus). **ES 300: 1996–99**—A knocking noise from under the floor in the rear of the car can be fixed by following the field fix outlined in TSB #SU005-96. **1997–99**—New front brake pads have been developed to reduce brake grind and groan. Toyota will install them at a reduced price under its "goodwill" policy. **1997–2000**—Front suspension noise may be silenced by installing an upgraded suspension support, says TSB #SU002-99. **1997–2001**—Turn signal flashes erratically. **1999**—Excessive engine noise when idling at normal operating temperature. • If the vehicle shudders during a 2–3 shift, try changing the transaxle valve body under warranty, before moving on to other repairs. • Rear suspension squeaks and groans. • Front brake groaning and grinding. • New, improved brake pads will reduce rear brake squeaks. • Tips on troubleshooting a false MIL alert. **1999–2001**— Information on correcting automatic transmission fluid leaks. **2000–01**—Procedures for obtaining a free seatbelt extender. **GS 300: 1998–2000**—Front window wind noise. • Noisy seatbelt retractor. **1998–2001**—Glove box rattling. **LS 400, LS 430: 1998–99**—An upgraded blower motor that is better at maintaining blower speed will be installed under warranty. **1999–2000**—Countermeasures to reduce steering noise and improve smoothness. **2000**—Moon-roof water leaks. **2001**—Moon-roof rattle and rear corner air leak. • Intrument panel rattling. • Rear seat and luggage compartment creaking. • False illumination of the MIL (malfunction indicator light).

ES 300, GS 300, LS 400, SC 400 Profile

	1994	1995	1996	1997	1998	1999	2000	2001
Cost Price ($)								
ES 300	41,300	44,700	45,600	42,960	43,820	44,235	43,995	44,000
GS 300	57,800	66,100	71,400	71,400	58,900	59,220	59,420	60,700
LS 400/430	71,100	75,900	78,700	78,700	78,300	78,690	78,950	80,000
SC 400	64,600	74,600	80,800	82,100	84,000	—	—	—
Used Values ($)								
ES 300 ⋏	10,000	13,500	16,000	19,500	23,000	26,000	31,000	35,000
ES 300 ⋎	8,500	12,000	14,000	18,000	20,000	24,000	29,000	33,000
GS 300 ⋏	13,000	15,000	17,000	22,000	27,000	33,000	40,000	46,000
GS 300 ⋎	12,000	13,500	15,000	20,000	25,000	31,000	38,000	44,000

LS 400/430 Λ	16,500	19,500	22,500	30,000	36,000	46,000	54,000	62,000
LS 400/430 V	15,500	17,000	20,000	27,000	34,000	43,000	51,000	59,000
SC 400 Λ	19,000	20,500	23,500	31,000	38,000	—	—	—
SC 400 V	17,000	18,000	21,000	28,000	35,000	—	—	—
Extended Warranty	N	N	N	N	N	N	N	N
Secret Warranty	N	N	N	N	N	N	N	N
Reliability	④	④	④	④	⑤	⑤	⑤	⑤
Crash Safety								
ES 300	—	—	⑤	—	④	④	—	—
GS 300	③	③	③	③	—	—	—	—
Side Impact (ES 300)	—	—	—	—	⑤	⑤	—	⑤
Off-set								
GS	—	—	—	—	—	⑤	⑤	⑤
LS	—	⑤	⑤	⑤	⑤	⑤	⑤	⑤
Head Restraints								
ES 300	—	❷	—	③	—	③	—	③
GS 300	—	❶	—	—	—	③	—	⑤
LS 400/430	—	❷	—	❷	—	③	—	⑤
SC 400	—	❶	—	—	—	❶	—	—

Mazda

MILLENIA   ★★★★

RATING: Above Average (1995–2001). Lots of power and sophisticated mechanicals make this luxury tourer a winner. Unusually rapid depreciation for a luxury Japanese car means there are plenty of bargains out there—just make sure the engine and transmission are functioning properly. **Maintenance/Repair costs:** Higher than average, and repairs must be done by a Mazda dealer. **Parts:** Higher-than-average cost, despite Mazda's recent pledge to lower prices. Parts are easily found, except for the Miller-Cycle 6-cylinder engine. **Best alternatives:** From a performance standpoint, the Toyota Camry V6 with its less complicated powertrain outruns the Millenia. Other choices: Acura Integra, TL, and RL; Infiniti I30 or I35; Lexus ES 300; Mercedes-Benz E-Class; Nissan Maxima; and Toyota Avalon.

Strengths and weaknesses: Smaller than the Mazda 929, the front-drive Millenia carries the same 2.5L 170-hp V6 used by the 626. An optional 2.3L Miller-Cycle "S" 6-cylinder engine, although smaller than the base powerplant, still manages to pump out 210 horses. Both engines use a standard 4-speed automatic transmission that shifts a bit harshly when pushed. As with all luxury cars, the Millenia comes with a wide array of standard features that would normally cost thousands of dollars more. Although billed as a five-passenger car, the middle occupant in the rear seat is cramped and has to sit on a hump. The '99 models have slightly re-styled front and rear ends, and the re-styled 2001 version received substantial handling improvements through a more rigid body, the addition of a new rear stabilizer bar, and a larger front stabilizer bar. It was also given larger brakes, a revised ABS system, standard side airbags, and an upgraded interior.

Assembly and component quality are fairly high; however, there have been some reports of Miller-Cycle engine failures and front brake, AC, fuel system, and electrical glitches. Among the powertrain problems, owners cite transmission failures and defective engine head gaskets with the base 2.5L powerplant. Paint delamination has also been a common complaint on 1995–96 models.

Safety summary: All models: 1995—Many complaints that vehicle surges when shifted into Reverse. • Inadvertent airbag deployment; failure to deploy. • Steering wheel back is open, allowing objects to jam the steering mechanism. • Driver's automatic seatbelt came loose when vehicle was rear-ended. • While vehicle was being driven on the highway, engine locked up due to leakage from the oil pan. • ABS brake failures. • Many reports of cracked engine valve cover gaskets, which allowed oil to leak onto the wiring and spark plugs. • Because the engine intake valve is set so low, whenever it comes in contact with water, the car stalls. • Premature AC and CV joint failures. • Sudden electrical system failure. • Defroster doesn't do an adequate job in cold weather; it collects water or quits altogether. • When AC is on, the headlights go dim. • Low-beam lights are inadequate for night driving. • Battery connections become loose, making it impossible to unlock or start vehicle. • When driver turned the ignition switch, the battery cable popped off; this caused the automatic door locks to become inoperative, trapping occupants. • Trunk won't open with inside latch release. • The location of the cup holder allows drinks to be spilled into the shifter mechanism, causing the shifter to lock up. • Cup holder doesn't always release. • Seatbelt buckle on passenger's side fell completely apart in driver's hand. • Aluminum alloy wheel cracked. **1996**—Airbag failed to deploy. • Transmission failures. • Intermittent starting problems. • Loose dashboard and interior trim. • It's easy to hit your head on the low trunk lid and latch. **1997**—Traction control system failure. **1998**—Fuel smell permeates the interior. • Car wouldn't accelerate. • Vehicle stalls in traffic, particularly when it rains. • Automatic transmission shifts erratically and jerks upon acceleration. • Brake pedal goes to floor and brakes don't react. **1999**—Hood popped open while driving. • Front airbag failed to deploy in a collision. • Emergency brake doesn't hold. • Spongy brakes result in extended stopping distances. • Front bumper cracked; dealer

says it's a common defect with the 626, as well. • Engine surges forward
and hesitates. 2000—Hard starts and stalling. 2001—Sudden acceleration. • Passenger airbag failed to deploy.

Secret Warranties/Service Tips/TSBs

All models/years: Troubleshooting tips for plugging wind noise around
doors. • Excessive brake pulsation. All models: 1995–96—A creaking or
knocking noise from the rear of the vehicle is likely caused by loose diagonal braces behind the rear seat. 1995–98—Rough shifting or erratic
automatic transmission performance may indicate a fluid leak at the oil
pan and transfer case. • A stuck tach needle must be reset manually.
1997–98—Inaccurate fuel gauge readings can be fixed by changing the
sender and instrument cluster. 1998–99—An exhaust system rattling can
be cured by replacing the pre-silencer. • Guidelines for correcting wind
noise around doors and removing musty AC odours. • If the steering
wheel is slightly off centre, Mazda suggests repositioning the tie-rod
ends. 1998–2001—If the Low Fuel light constantly comes on, or only a
small amount of fuel can be pumped into the fuel tank, Mazda will
install, under warranty, modified components to allow a complete fillup.
2000—Rear suspension creak or squeak. 2000–01—Transmission
whining and ringing. • False MIL light illumination. 2001—A drive belt
rubbing or squealing may be heard when the car is put into gear with the
AC engaged.

Millenia Profile

	1995	1996	1997	1998	1999	2000	2001
Cost Price ($)							
Base	38,055	42,035	42,900	38,660	36,535	39,595	41,450
Used Values ($)							
Base ▲	9,500	10,500	13,500	16,500	19,500	25,000	28,000
Base ▼	7,500	9,000	12,000	14,000	17,000	23,000	26,500
Extended Warranty	N	N	N	N	N	N	N
Secret Warranty	N	N	N	N	N	Y	Y
Reliability	③	④	④	④	④	⑤	⑤
Crash Safety	④	④	④	—	—	—	—
Side Impact	—	—	—	—	—	—	④
Off-set	③	③	③	③	③	③	③
Head Restraints (F)	❶	—	③	—	❶	—	❷
Rear	—	—	❷	—	—	—	—

Mercedes-Benz

300 SERIES, 400 SERIES, 500 SERIES, E-CLASS
★★★★★

RATING: Recommended (1993–2001); Above Average (1992); Below Average (1985–91). The 1994 and later models are referred to as the E-Class, with the entry-level model a 300 series diesel. Interestingly, with the increase in diesel fuel prices, early diesel versions are now depreciating just as rapidly as gasoline-powered models. **Maintenance/Repair costs:** Higher than average, and repairs must be done by a Mercedes dealer. **Parts:** Higher-than-average cost and limited availability. **Best alternatives:** Acura Integra, TL, and RL; Cadillac DeVille; Ford Crown Victoria or Mercury Grand Marquis; Infiniti I30 or I35; Lexus ES 300; Mazda Millenia; and Toyota Avalon.

Strengths and weaknesses: These cars are ideal mid-sized family sedans. They're reliable, depreciate slowly, and provide all the interior space that the pre-1994 190 series and C-Class leave out. Their only shortcomings are a high resale value that discourages bargain hunters and a weak dealer network that limits parts distribution and drives up parts costs. The 300 series offers a traction control system that prevents wheel spin upon acceleration—somewhat like ABS in reverse.

Another interesting feature is a 24-valve 220-hp high-performance version of the inline 6-cylinder engine that powers the 300 series. All this has its price, though. If, ironically, you'd like to drive one of these cars but are of an economical frame of mind, choose the 260E—it offers everything the 300 does, but for much less. The 300CE is a coupe version, appealing to a sportier crowd, while the 300TE is the station wagon variant.

'97 models received a new 5-speed automatic transmission, and the E420 got a V8 engine. The following year saw the addition of a station wagon and all-wheel drive. The 300D added a turbocharger for extra power; the E320 came with a new 3.2L V6. Other additions to the '98s: a BabySmart child protection system, Brake Assist, and an electronic Smart Key feature. '99s offered a new side impact head protection feature. The 300 diesel model was dropped from the year 2000 lineup, but a new all-wheel-drive E430 with standard side airbags was added. All models got new wheels, Touch Shift (an automanual device), and Electronic Stability. 2001s now come with one-touch opening sunroofs.

Quality control has traditionally been better than average with the 300 and higher series; however, owners still point out recurring problems with the fuel and electrical systems, causing lights, instruments, and gauges to shut off and the trunk lid to open when the engine is shut down. Other common problems: engine won't shut off; stalling and engine surging; engine problems caused by a stretched timing chain; computer module failures (for both engine and transmission); erratically performing and noisy transmission; leaking transmission transfer case; noisy power steering; front window noise; ignition key is difficult to remove; a clicking noise is heard from the front door lock trim; and the speedometer jumps when braking.

Safety summary: 300 series: 1994—Sudden acceleration caused accident and injuries. • Defective ABS brakes; brakes locked up and caused driver to lose control of vehicle. • Emergency brake cable failed twice. • Vehicle rolls backward when stopped on a hill. • Driver's seatbelt failed. • Accelerator pedal is too hard to press, causing fatigue in driver's leg. • Frequent power door lock and automatic antenna failures. • Front panels were cracked and loose. • Rear axle and fuel pump failures. **1995**—Sudden acceleration caused an accident. • Brake rotor and caliper failure. • Headlights cast dark shadows. • Windshield wipers fail to keep glass clean. • Automatic transmission slips or shifts erratically, as if hunting for the right gear. **1996**—Check Engine light flashes on and off at will. • AC fan starts and stops intermittently. • Door rattles. • Failure-prone headlight bulbs. **1997**—Airbag deployed for no reason. • Airbags failed to deploy in a collision. • Brakes locked up, causing extended stopping distance. • Premature failure of the automatic transmission, AC compressor, and hatch door release. • Single windshield wiper doesn't clear windshield adequately. • Instrument gauge cluster doesn't light gauges sufficiently. • Double-pane windows, rear windshield, and rear-view mirrors blur images. **1998**—Sudden, unintended acceleration while on the highway. • Airbag failed to deploy in a collision. • While parking, steering went out and car caught on fire. • Total loss of braking; pedal went to floor. • Premature failure of the automatic transmission, tie-rod, belt tensioner, fuel pump, fuel level sensor, oxygen sensor, windows, power-assisted sunroof, electric seats, turn signal switch, and brake lights. • Excessive wind noise emanating from the windows and sunroof. • Blue-tinted headlamps cause glare and are too bright. • Power seat suddenly moved back and reclined while vehicle was in traffic. • Bumper cracks from minor impacts. **1999**—Sudden acceleration when turning or decelerating to exit the freeway. • Engine fuel line leakage. • Sunroof electrical fire. • Fuel pump failures. • Inaccurate fuel gauge says tank is full, but almost five more gallons (23L) can be pumped. • Sudden stalling while underway, especially when going over a bump in the road. • Excessive vibration when decelerating. • Transmission leaks oil, disengages, and then suddenly locks up. • ABS suddenly activated, throwing vehicle to side of the road. • Self-activating door locks. • Severe window hazing in rainy weather. **2000**—Panic stops may produce a brake pedal stiffness and loss of braking ability. • Premature brake booster failure. • Poor acceleration said to be caused by fuel injection control module. •

Fuel gauge gives false low readings. • Horn blows on its own, and warning lights are constantly lit. 2001—Side airbags deploy inadvertently. The following owner of a 2001 300E recounts his surprise at the time:

> While driving down the highway, my passenger side curtain and rear side door airbags deployed for no reason at all…. It scared the hell out of me and nearly caused me to crash the car. This is a real hazard that must be investigated.

• Water enters the automatic transmission control module, preventing the transmission from changing gears. • Vehicle hesitates when accelerating with gas pedal halfway depressed, then it lurches forward. A control unit is said to be at fault.

Secret Warranties/Service Tips/TSBs

All models/years: Engine surges at full load. • Vacuum pump oil supply modified through the introduction of a second bore in oil spray nozzle. This helps reduce complaints that engine won't shut off. • Troubleshooting an engine ticking or noise. • Free seatbelt extensions are available. **All models: 1986–98**—Fuel pump relay failures. **1997**—Engine fails to start due to faulty DAS system. **1998**—Engine rattle countermeasures. **2000**—A special service campaign will replace, free of charge, side airbags that may deploy if the vehicle is left in the sun during warm months.

300 series, 400 series, 500 series, E-Class Profile

	1994	1995	1996	1997	1998	1999	2000	2001
Cost Price ($)								
300E	55,995	—	—	—	—	—	—	—
300ED	55,995	55,995	58,500	59,950	59,950	59,950	—	—
320E 4d	58,895	60,950	64,750	65,900	66,450	66,750	67,150	67,900
420E, 430	71,000	72,950	101,900	73,300	73,950	70,500	74,750	75,750
500E, 500S	108,000	124,900	132,500	132,950	117,900	122,900	112,851	114,650
Used Values ($)								
300E ʌ	16,500	—	—	—	—	—	—	—
300E v	14,000	—	—	—	—	—	—	—
300ED ʌ	16,000	18,500	22,000	27,000	34,000	39,000	—	—
300ED v	14,000	16,000	20,000	25,000	31,000	37,000	—	—
320E 4d ʌ	16,500	19,000	23,500	28,000	37,000	45,000	52,000	59,000
320E 4d v	14,500	16,500	21,000	26,000	35,000	42,000	50,000	56,000
420E, 430 ʌ	26,000	30,000	30,000	31,000	41,000	48,000	57,000	64,000
420E, 430 v	24,000	28,000	28,000	29,000	38,000	45,000	54,000	60,000
500E, 500S ʌ	33,000	34,000	37,000	40,000	54,000	67,000	75,000	90,000
500E, 500S v	31,000	32,000	35,000	37,000	51,000	62,000	71,000	85,000

Extended Warranty	N	N	N	N	N	N	N	N
Secret Warranty	N	N	N	N	N	N	N	N
Reliability	③	③	④	④	④	④	⑤	⑤
Off-set	—	—	—	③	③	③	⑤	⑤
Head Restraints (4d)	—	—	—	—	—	—	—	⑤
Wagon	—	—	—	—	—	—	—	③

Note: The above model years haven't been crash-tested by NHTSA.

C-CLASS ★★★★

RATING: Above Average (1995–2001); Average (1994). Although these cars beat out the Detroit Big Three in reliability and comfort, they've had a free ride by an automotive press that has ignored their quality and safety shortcomings when compared with the Asian competition. Keep in mind that you'll have to keep your car much longer to amortize its higher cost. **Maintenance/Repair costs:** Higher than average, and most repairs must be done by a Mercedes dealer if you don't live in an area where independent shops have sprung up. **Parts:** Higher-than-average cost. Parts are highly dealer dependent and relatively expensive. **Best alternatives:** Acura Integra, TL, and RL; BMW 3 Series; Infiniti I30 or I35; Lexus ES 300; and Toyota Avalon.

Strengths and weaknesses: Replacing the failure-prone 190-series, the 1994 C-Class gained interior room and two new engines: a base 147-hp 2.2L and a 194-hp 2.8L 6-cylinder—a real powerhouse in this small car, when coupled to the manual 5-speed transmission. The 4-speed automatic is a big disappointment—it requires a lot of throttle effort to downshift and prefers to start out in Second gear. The 1994 versions add much-needed horsepower, but lack the manual 5-speed transmission that would set those extra horses free. Rear seat room is limited, and a lot of road noise intrudes into the passenger compartment.

The 1997 C-Class replaced the standard 2.2L engine with the more robust 2.3L (C230) and revised headlamps. Bigger changes were in store for the following year's models: a new 2.8L engine (C280), BabySmart car seats, brake assist, and side airbags. 1999 models got the SLK's 2.3L supercharged engine, replacing the C230's normally aspirated powerplant, a better-performing drivetrain, and standard leather upholstery. All year 2000 models were given a Touch Shift auto-manual transmission, stability control, and Tele-Aid, a communications system for calling for assistance. 2001s were completely revamped, gaining two new engines, additional safety features, and more aerodynamic styling.

Keep in mind that owner surveys give the entry-level C-Class cars a *just* better-than-average rating, while the 300 and higher series have always scored way above average in owner satisfaction. The 1994 model

C-Class is the better buy from a quality and reliability standpoint; nevertheless, owners report frequent problems with sudden, unintended acceleration; drivetrain noise and vibration; and slipping or soft shifts. Brakes, AC, and the electrical system are also failure prone.

Safety summary: All models: 1994—Vehicle suddenly accelerated forward in garage. • Another report that, while coming to a stop at an intersection, vehicle will accelerate when foot is on the brake. • Airbag failed to deploy. • Upon braking, ABS pedal went to the floor, resulting in extended stopping distance. • Extreme pressure is needed to push horn button. • Cruise control failure. • Premature rear wheel bearing failure. • Windshield wiper is inadequate; poor visibility. **1995**—Check Engine light remains on for no apparent reason. • Frequent stalling due to defective idle-speed control unit. • Missing left rear wheelwell inside panel allows tire to spray debris into area. **1996**—Airbags failed to deploy. • Airbag light stays on for no apparent reason. • After parking the vehicle and turning off the ignition, the vehicle lurches forward or rocks backward. • In another incident, vehicle was put in Park on an incline and keys were removed; vehicle rolled backward down the hill. • Brakes are noisy when applied and don't brake well. • While car is being driven, engine light comes on for no apparent reason. • Complete electrical system failure. • Windshield washer fluid sensor failure. **1997**—While in Reverse, vehicle suddenly accelerated backward. **1998**—Airbag warning light came on and then airbag suddenly exploded. • Transmission fluid leakage. • Faulty gas gauge sensor. • Rear suspension bouncing makes it difficult to maintain directional control. • Noisy heat shield. • Inoperative windshield wipers. • Car is very vulnerable to side wind buffeting. • Window failures. **1999**—Vehicle suddenly accelerated and brakes couldn't stop it. • Brakes failed on incline. **2000**—Sudden acceleration when pulling into a parking space. • Automatic transmission slips when the vehicle is cold, sticks in gear, and shifts abruptly. **2001**—Unintended acceleration, as vehicle appears to stall and then takes off; fuel pump replaced but problem remains. • Vehicle suddenly stopped by the highway as engine self-destructed.

Secret Warranties/Service Tips/TSBs

All models/years: Excessive engine valve train noise may be caused by a stretched timing chain. After 48,000 km, the camshaft and timing chain drive should be checked carefully, especially if excessive noise is heard. • Water in the oxygen sensor connector in the front passenger wheelwell. • Ignition key difficult to remove. • Clicking from the front door lock trim. **All models: 1999**—Hesitation after a cold start and rough 1–2 and 2–3 shift during warmup. **1999–2000**—If the brake pedal is hard to apply, replace the brake booster and crankcase vent hoses. **2001**—Troubleshooting hard starts and poor engine performance.

C-Class Profile

	1994	1995	1996	1997	1998	1999	2000	2001
Cost Price ($)								
220C	34,350	34,995	35,995	—	—	—	—	—
230C	—	—	—	36,950	37,550	37,950	38,450	—
C240	—	—	—	—	—	—	—	37,450
280C	47,650	48,750	49,995	50,995	49,950	49,950	49,950	—
Used Values ($)								
220C A	9,500	12,500	15,000	—	—	—	—	—
220C V	8,000	10,000	13,000	—	—	—	—	—
230C A	—	—	—	18,000	22,000	25,000	29,000	—
230C V	—	—	—	15,500	19,000	23,000	26,000	—
C240 A	—	—	—	—	—	—	—	33,000
C240 V	—	—	—	—	—	—	—	31,000
280C A	13,000	16,000	19,000	23,000	30,000	35,000	40,000	—
280C V	11,000	14,000	17,000	21,000	27,000	33,000	37,000	—
Extended Warranty	Y	Y	Y	Y	Y	Y	Y	Y
Secret Warranty	N	N	N	N	N	N	N	N
Reliability	③	③	③	④	④	④	④	④
Crash Safety								
(C220, C230)	④	④	④	④	④	—	—	—
Side Impact								
(C230)	—	—	—	—	③	③	③	—
Off-set	—	—	—	—	—	—	—	⑤
Head Restraints (F)	—	❷	—	❷	—	③	—	⑤
Rear	—	—	—	—	—	❷	—	—

Nissan

MAXIMA ★★★★

RATING: Above Average (1989–2001); Average (1986–88). The redesigned 1995–99 version offers a peppier engine, more rounded styling, and a bit longer wheelbase; it apparently, has fewer factory-related problems, as well. **Maintenance/Repair costs:** Higher than average, but repairs can be done practically anywhere. **Parts:** Higher-than-average cost, but easy to find. **Best alternatives:** Acura Integra, TL and RL, Infiniti I30/I35, Lexus ES300, Mazda Millenia, and Toyota Avalon.

Strengths and weaknesses: These front-drive sedans are very well equipped and nicely finished, but cramped for their size. Although the trunk is spacious, only five passengers can travel in a pinch (in the literal sense). The 6-cylinder, 190-hp engine, borrowed from the 300ZX in 1992, offers sparkling performance; the fuel injectors, however, are problematic. '93 models got standard driver-side airbags, and the Maxima remained unchanged until the 1995 model's redesign and a second redesign of the year 2000 version.

Early Maximas are less expensive to buy, but more costly to maintain—for example, the exhaust manifold, a component that commonly fails, will set you back $300–$500 to replace on 1993–96 models. Owners report that the '95 Maxima's suspension was cheapened, to the detriment of both the ride and the handling.

Minor electrical and front suspension problems afflict early Maximas. Brakes and engine timing belts need frequent attention in all years. Newer models have a weak automatic transmission and the ignition system can malfunction. There have also been reports of "cooked" transmissions. This is due to a poorly designed transmission cooler. Mechanics say that this breakdown can be avoided by installing an externally mounted transmission cooler with a filter and replacing the transmission filter cooler at every oil change.

Owners report that the V6-equipped Maxima is sometimes hard to start in cold weather, due to the engine's tendency to flood easily. The cruise control unit is another problematic component. When it's engaged at moderate speeds, it hesitates or "drifts" to a lower speed, acting as if the fuel line were clogged. It operates correctly only at much higher speeds than needed. Incidentally, owners say that a new fuel filter will *not* correct the problem. Additionally, though warped manifolds were once routinely replaced under a "goodwill" warranty, Nissan now makes the customer pay. The warpage causes a manifold bolt to break off, thereby causing a huge exhaust leak. Most fuel-injector malfunctions are caused by carbon clogging up the injectors; there are additives you can try that might reduce this buildup. There have also been internal problems with the coil windings on the fuel-injectors. Your best bet is to replace the entire set.

Nissan has had problems with weak window regulators for some time. If the window is frozen, don't open it. The rubber weather stripping around the window is also a problem. It cuts easily and causes the window to go off track, which in turn causes stress on the weak regulators. Driver-side window breakage is common and can cost up to $300 to repair. Costly aluminum wheels corrode quickly and are easily damaged by road hazards. There have been a few reports of surface rust and paint problems. Pre-1990 Maximas suffer from rust perforation on the sunroof, door bottoms, rear wheelwells, front edge of the hood, and bumper supports. The underbody should also be checked carefully for corrosion damage. Premature wearout of the muffler is a frequent problem; it's often covered by Nissan's "goodwill" warranty, wherein the company and dealer will contribute 50 percent of the replacement cost.

1995–99

The redesigned '95 Maximas have a longer wheelbase (adding to interior room), a new 3.0L engine, and more rounded styling. They compete well with fully equipped Camrys, entry-level Infinitis, and Lexus models. Nevertheless, tall passengers will find the interior a bit cramped, and the automatic transmission is often slow to downshift and isn't always smooth. '97 models got a new front end re-styling, and optional side airbags were offered with the '98s; however, the '99s were the first Maximas to get optional traction control.

Quality control and overall reliability are apparently much better with these more recent iterations. Nevertheless, owners still report a variety of safety-related deficiencies, in addition to brake, electrical system, fuel system, and body glitches.

2000–01

The 2000 version was redesigned to offer more power, interior space (particularly for rear-seat passengers), and safety/convenience features; 2001s were carried over relatively unchanged, except for an Anniversary edition equipped with a 227-hp 3.0L V6, taken from the Infiniti I30.

Redesign glitches abound and include difficulty controlling the engine speed with the gas pedal; engine popping and knocking when accelerating; stalling when braking or decelerating; transmission malfunctions; premature front brake pad wear and rotor warpage; a choppy, jarring suspension; and excessive front end vibrations. Faulty ignition coils and inadequate headlight illumination continue to be major problems.

Safety summary: All models: 1996—Fire ignited from shorted wires under the passenger-side seat. • Airbag failed to deploy. • ABS failures. • Vehicle constantly pulls to the right. • Engine warning light flashes for no apparent reason. • Sudden loss of power, resulting in inoperative brakes and steering. • Chronic stalling. • Power steering failure. • Erratic transmission performance. • Hard to shift transmission out of Park. • Key can be taken out of ignition while vehicle isn't in Park. • Power door locks failed. • Defective AC expansion valve. • Several reports of headlight explosions. **1997**—Door latch won't engage in cold weather. • Front wheel suddenly locked up while driving. • Power steering leaks fluid. • Trunk lid opened while driving. • Pedal went to the floor when brakes were applied, resulting in extended stopping distance. **1998**—Vehicle intermittently accelerates while braking. • Hazy, milky pattern on glass exterior causes poor visibility. • Frequent windshield wiper failures. **1999**—Airbags failed to deploy. • Throttle "shock" and transmission hesitation. • Frequent ignition coil failures. • Rotten-egg odour enters the cabin area. • Vehicle pulls constantly to the left. • Cruise control resume feature doesn't work. • Power door locks cycle from lock to unlock.

2000—ABS brake failure. • Transmission may not shift. • Airbag failed to deploy. • Early replacement of the catalytic converter (alerted by Check Engine light) and #6 ignition coil. • Poor headlight illumination. • A chlorine-type smell permeates the interior. 2001—Engine compartment fire. • Steering lockup, loss of brakes, and failure of the airbag to deploy.

Secret Warranties/Service Tips/TSBs

All models/years: Defective catalytic converters that cause a rotten-egg smell may be replaced free of charge under Nissan's emissions warranty; the same principle applies to EVAP canister charcoal leakage. • TSB #P195-006 looks at the many causes and remedies for excessive brake noise. • Troubleshooting MIL light alerts. **All models: 1995–96**—Timing chain rattling noise can be silenced by replacing the timing chain tensioner and slack guide. • Brake squeak or squeal can be corrected by installing front and rear brake kits. **1995–98**—An inoperative power seat may require a new drive cable. **1995–99**—Blower motor noise can be cured by installing a new blower motor cover. • A front brake groan when stopping is addressed in TSB #99-032. • A rear brake groan or hum can be fixed by readjusting the parking brake cable. • If the rear brakes squeak or squeal when cold, replace the rear brake pads with upgraded ones. • Guidelines for correcting steering pull or drift. • Tips on eliminating a foul odour emanating from the sunroof sunshade. **1996–99**—Diagnostic tips for fixing a front seatbelt that's slow to retract. **1998–99**—An on-off transmission throttle shock can be attenuated by installing an upgraded ECM. **1999**—Guidelines for correcting rocker panel creaking or popping. **2000**—Low idle or stalling in gear. • Excessive brake vibration countermeasures. • Right front strut noise. • Rear bumper scratched by trunk lid. • Tips on silencing interior squeaks and rattles and front brake groan. **2000–01**—Automatic transmission gear slippage.

Maxima Profile

	1994	1995	1996	1997	1998	1999	2000	2001
Cost Price ($)								
Base	25,690	25,990	27,998	27,998	27,998	28,598	28,598	29,000
Used Values ($)								
Base ⋀	6,500	9,000	11,500	13,500	15,500	18,500	21,000	24,000
Base ⋁	5,000	7,500	9,500	11,500	14,000	17,000	19,000	22,000
Extended Warranty	N	N	N	N	N	N	N	N
Secret Warranty	N	N	N	N	N	N	N	N
Reliability	④	④	④	④	⑤	⑤	⑤	⑤
Crash Safety	③	③	④	④	④	④	—	④
Side Impact	—	—	—	④	④	④	—	④
Off-set	—	❶	❶	③	③	③	③	③
Head Restraints (F)	—	❷	—	❷	❷	③	③	⑤
Rear	—	—	—	—	—	❷	—	—

Saab

900, 9000, 9-3, 9-5   ★★★

RATING: Average (1999–2001); Below Average (1995–98); Not
Recommended (1985–94). Interestingly, the upscale 9000 series isn't as
crashworthy as the cheaper 900 versions, nor is it more reliable,
exhibiting similar generic deficiencies to its entry-level brother. Be wary
of the aluminum wheels; they're easily damaged and costly to replace.
Maintenance/Repair costs: Higher than average, and repairs must be
done by a GM or Saab dealer. **Parts:** Higher-than-average cost and limited
availability outside major urban areas. **Best alternatives:** Acura Integra,
TL, and RL; BMW 3 Series; Infiniti I30 or I35; Lexus ES 300; Mazda
Millenia; Nissan Maxima; and Toyota Avalon.

Strengths and weaknesses: These Swedish-built luxury cars combine
excellent handling and great interior ergonomics (one of the few imports
with the EPA's "large car" label), but without all the bells and whistles
found in domestic luxury breeds. Convenience items like a fuse box in
the glove box, a toolbox in the hatchback, and easy-to-replace bulbs add
to your comfort.

Unfortunately, Saabs aren't Volvos, and they don't live up to the
Swedish reputation for exceptional reliability. Quirky in design, servicing
is barely adequate and will probably get much worse in the future, now
that GM dealers are responsible for servicing.

Generally, the 900 and 9000 series have similar deficiencies affecting
the engine, cooling (biodegradable water pumps) and electrical systems,
brakes, automatic transmission (clutch O-rings), and body hardware
(alloy wheels are easily bent).

Short circuits are legion and run the gamut from minor annoyances to
fire hazards (see "Safety summary"). Electrical glitches in the traction
control system's relay module give a false reading that the tires are spinning, which shuts the engine down. Ignition switches can easily be
bumped and shut the vehicle down.

Turbos produce much stronger acceleration and better handling than
other 9000s without compromising their overall reliability. Nevertheless,
they should be approached with caution because owner abuse or poor
maintenance can quickly lead to turbocharger deterioration. Air conditioners and exhaust-system parts have a short life span, and leaky seals
and gaskets are common. Rust perforations tend to develop along door
bottoms and the rocker panels. The underbody, especially the floor,
should be inspected for corrosion damage on older models.

Over the years, Saab's 900 and 9000 have changed little. The '93 9000
got a 256-hp version of the inline 4-cylinder, while the 900 received

more standard features. A year later, the 900 was revamped, getting a new V6 and an upgraded optional automatic transmission, while the 9000 offered, for the first time, standard dual airbags. The following year, the '95 9000 got a new turbocharger and a V6 powerplant coupled with an automatic transmission. In 1996, 900 models got engine upgrades and standard seat lumbar support.

Major changes were incorporated into the 1999 model year. The entry-level 900 was renamed the 9-3 and given suspension, steering, and interior upgrades, in addition to a high-performance 200-hp 2.0L engine and a more responsive drivetrain. 1999 9000 models were re-designated the 9-5, limited to sedans, and equipped with either a turbocharged 4-cylinder or V6. Base models in 2000 received re-styled alloy wheels, SEs got increased horsepower and performance upgrades, and the 9-3 Viggen was given more horsepower, along with a new five-door and convertible version. The 9-3 convertible was dropped for the 2001 model year, and the 9-5 got a horsepower boost in addition to new telematics and turbo gauges.

Safety summary: 900: 1996—Under-hood fire ignited as vehicle was idling with transmission lever in the Park position. • Several reports that when shifting from Reverse to Drive, vehicle suddenly accelerated forward without braking or steering control. • Airbags failed to deploy, and the warning light comes on for no apparent reason • Fuel-filter failures caused fuel leak. • Car drifts to the right while driving. • Defective exhaust check valve lifters. • Transmission failures and excessive vibrations. • Repeated gear shifting problems cause the shifter bushings and motor-mount housing to be prematurely worn. • Sundry electrical system shorts and failures affecting the stereo and CD player, anti-theft system, and battery. • Frequent trunk latch release, door handle, and passenger seat adjuster failures. • Glass headlight cover is often broken. • Left side-view mirror can't be adjusted properly to see blind spots to left rear of vehicle. **1997**—Faulty power seat. • Aluminum wheels are easily bent. **1998**—Airbag deployed inadvertently. • Car can start in gear. • Alloy wheels are easily bent. • Power seat fails to respond to commands. **1999**—Airbag failed to deploy. • Cruise control fails to disengage when brakes are applied. • Early automatic transmission and suspension failure. • Vehicle tends to wander on the highway. Shock absorber failure. • Wheel rims are easily bent. • Door lock won't unlock from the inside. **2000**—There is no safety device preventing the car from starting in gear. • Airbag failed to deploy. **9-3: 2001**—While underway, ignition switch was bumped and vehicle shut down. • Ignition switch failure. **9-5: 2000**—Fuel tank noise is caused by fuel moving in the tank. • Exhaust fumes enter the interior of the vehicle. **2001**—Parking light assembly fell out of its socket. • Noisy front suspension.

Secret Warranties/Service Tips/TSBs

All models/years: Tips for finding and fixing windshield noise are outlined in TSB #841-15772. **900: 1993–94**—Binding ignition switch contacts can lead to electrical failures. **1994**—A-pillar wind noise is addressed in TSB #08194-0486. • TSB #88/94-0480 lists the causes and remedies of AC malfunctions. **1994–98**—Diagnostic procedures and correction for brake vibration are addressed in TSB #510-1919. • If you find your battery has died, it may have drained though the trunk light switch. • A Low Oil light may come on for no apparent reason; fix the problem by reprogramming the SID module. **1997–98**—Customer Satisfaction Campaign #443 calls for the free replacement of the fuel pump. Its durability is compromised by its lack of a carbide coating on the pump spindle. **9000: All years**—Saab offers a pedal raising kit free of charge to short drivers wishing to sit farther away from the airbag housing. **1992–94**—A noisy climate control unit may have excess pressure building up at the fresh air intake. **1993–94**—A stuck shift lever may be caused by a blown #3 fuse. A faulty sun visor/vanity mirror causes the short circuit. **1994–98**—Noise or vibrations from the gear shift lever when accelerating are addressed in TSB #471-1937. **1995–98**—Sunroof rattling can be silenced following TSB #812-1983. **1998**—Poor AM/FM reception is a common problem addressed in TSB #367-2015. **1997–98**—If the hood is difficult to open, install an upgraded lock. **9-3: 2000**—Noise emanating from the right-side wheel housing is likely caused by a faulty bypass valve. • Water may drip on the floor from the lower air vents. • Inaccurate fuel consumption display. **9-5: 2000**—ACC panel display may light up brightly and then go out. • Moisture may degrade the trunk-mounted CD changer's operation. • The hydraulic hose on cars with automatic transmissions may be incorrectly positioned.

900, 9000, 9-3, 9-5 Profile

	1994	1995	1996	1997	1998	1999	2000	2001
Cost Price ($)								
900/9-3	27,000	26,995	28,500	29,901	30,700	33,800	34,100	35,465
9000/9-5	35,000	35,995	36,400	37,100	50,300	39,800	40,200	41,515
Used Values ($)								
900/9-3 ⋀	6,500	7,500	9,000	11,000	14,000	17,500	23,000	26,000
900/9-3 ⋁	5,500	6,500	7,500	9,000	12,000	15,000	21,000	24,000
9000/9-5 ⋀	8,500	10,000	11,000	15,000	19,000	21,000	26,000	30,000
9000/9-5 ⋁	7,500	8,500	9,500	13,500	17,000	18,500	24,000	28,000
Extended Warranty	Y	Y	Y	Y	Y	Y	Y	Y
Secret Warranty	N	N	N	N	N	N	N	N
Reliability	❷	❷	❷	❷	③	③	③	④
Crash Safety (900)	—	④	④	④	④	—	—	—
Off-set (900, 9-3)	—	❷	❷	❷	❷	③	③	③

9-5	—	—	—	—	—	③	③	③
Head Restraints (900)	—	③	—	③	—	—	—	—
9-3	—	—	—	—	—	⑤	—	⑤
9000, 9-5	—	❶	—	❶	—	⑤	—	⑤

Toyota

AVALON   ★★★★

RATING: Above Average (1995–2001). Surprisingly, the Avalon has generated an unusually large number of safety-related defects, in addition to charges that its engines are often sidelined by engine oil sludge. It's a good idea to make sure that headlight illumination is adequate for your driving needs, "green glow" dash reflections onto the windshield aren't too distracting, and windshield visibility is adequate for rainy weather. **Maintenance/Repair costs:** Average. **Parts:** Higher-than-average cost and limited availability. **Best alternatives:** A fully loaded Camry; if you want a more driver-involved experience in a Toyota, consider a Lexus ES 300 or GS 300. Other good choices: the Acura Integra, TL, and RL; BMW 3 Series; Infiniti I30 or I35; Mazda Millenia; and Nissan Maxima.

Strengths and weaknesses: This near-luxury four-door offers more value, interior space, and performance than do other cars in its class that cost thousands of dollars more. A front-engine, front-drive, mid-sized sedan based on a stretched Camry platform, the six-passenger Avalon is bigger than the rear-drive Cressida it replaced and similar in size to the Ford Taurus. Sure, there's a fair amount of Camry in the Avalon, but it's quicker on its feet than the Camry, better attuned to abrupt manoeuvres, and two inches longer. In fact, there's more rear-seat leg room than you'll find in either the Taurus or the new Chevrolet Lumina. It's close to the Dodge Intrepid in this respect.

Dual airbags are standard, along with power locks, windows, and mirrors. '97 models were given more power, torque, and standard features, while the '98s got seatbelt pretensioners, side airbags, new headlamps and taillights, and a new trunk lid and grille. The 1999 Avalon was carried over without any significant changes, but the re-styled year 2000 version was considerably improved. It's more powerful, roomier, and full of more high-tech safety and convenience features. 2001s were relatively unchanged, except for an emergency trunk release.

Quality control is better than average, though steering, suspension, and fuel system components are failure prone, and many owners have complained of engine sludge forcing them to spend thousands of dollars for engine repairs. Owners also have some performance gripes that include numerous electrical system glitches, premature front brake repairs and suspension strut failures, power steering that's a bit too light, hydroplaning, excessive body lean, and under-steer when cornering. Body construction and assembly are fairly good, although rattles are commonplace for all model years, trunk leaks have been reported on the '99 models, and paint flaking has afflicted some 2001 models.

Safety summary: All models: 1997—Airbags deployed while stopped at a light. • Airbags failed to deploy in an accident. • Sudden engine failure; engine leaks oil. • Engine cylinder failure. • Fuel damper and fuel pump failed twice; leaking fuel. • Brakes failed due to freezing vacuum hose. • ABS controller failure. • Frequent complaints of steering fluid leaks. • Many reports of premature failure of the steering assembly (upper steering knuckle) and front strut support. • Front suspension bar suddenly broke. • Transmission failure caused by loss of internal pressure. • Vehicle hydroplanes on the slightest wet pavement; Bridgestone tires don't help. • Early replacement of Bridgestone/Firestone tires due to hydroplaning, excessive wear, and substandard performance. • Several incidents of Bridgestone Potenza tire tread separation. • Driver's seat moves when vehicle turns. • Wind blew trunk lid shut on driver's neck. • Taillight bulbs have a short lifespan. **1998**—Many incidents where vehicle suddenly accelerated in Drive and in Reverse. • Vehicle caught fire at fuel filler neck when getting gas. • Gas tank fuel hose leaks fuel. • Front and side airbags fail to deploy in collisions. • Airbag deployment caused severe chest and chin injuries. • Front seat reclined suddenly when vehicle was hit from the rear. • Engine surges and drops rpms rapidly and unexpectedly when engaging cruise control or when taking foot off the gas pedal. • Power-steering pump failure and fluid reservoir leakage. • Early replacement of brake pads, calipers and rotors. • Dunlop Sport 4000 tread separation. • Premature tire wear. • Front suspension bangs and clanks when going over any size bump and rear suspension bottoms out. • Constant vibration in steering wheel and accelerator while driving caused by fuel pressure regulator. • Loose driver's seat. • Kick panel falls off repeatedly. **1999**—Vehicle suddenly accelerated; surges at intersections. • Airbag failed to deploy. • Airbag warning light comes on for no reason. • Cruise control operates erratically. • Brake pedal went to floor with little effect. • Car shifts poorly (hesitates and jerks) when you let off the gas and then accelerate, or do a rolling stop. **2000**—Sudden, unintended acceleration. • Engine sludge makes vehicle inoperable. • Automatic transmission slippage. • Brake pedal went to the floor with no braking effect. • Driver's seat rocks back and forth. • Steering wheel off-centre. • Airbag light stays lit. • Dash lights and gauges reflect onto windshield. • Inadequate headlight illumination. • Windshield is hard to see through in the rain due to water streaking. • Horn failure. **2001**—Airbags failed to deploy. • Fuel line pulled out of filter. • Excessive highway wandering. • Engine surging at idle. • Flex hose came off the charcoal canister, causing warning light to come on when refuelling. • Front and rear suspension bottoms out when carrying four adults. • Insufficient steering feedback • Jerky acceleration. • Sudden failure of the instrument and information panel lighting and headlights. • Driver's side-view mirror has a small viewing area. • At night, the instrument panel lights and gauges reflect a green glow onto the windshield.

Secret Warranties/Service Tips/TSBs

All models: 1990–2000—Brake pad clicking may be corrected by use of a special Toyota-recommended grease; however, some owners say it's not very effective. **1995–96**—Use an upgraded rear brake pad material to eliminate rear brake moan. • To reduce wind noise from the front door A-pillar area, consult TSB #B0010-97. **1995–97**—Countermeasures are listed to reduce front suspension groan under the base warranty. **1995–2000**—A power-steering squeak can be silenced by installing a new rack end shaft. **1996**—Tips on reducing engine noise, front door wind noise, and front suspension and rear popping noise. • Upgraded hazard switch. **1997**—AC odour troubleshooting. • Fixing front suspension crunch. **1997–99**—A front brake grind or groan can be silenced by installing a new front brake pad kit under warranty. • Front suspension noise can be eliminated by changing the suspension support. **1998–99**—Door weather stripping improvements are detailed in TSB #B0-009-99. **2000**—Roof water leaks. • Sliding roof and door mirror noise. • Loose rear door garnish. **2000–01**—Measures to reduce instrument panel luminosity. • Wheel bearing ticking noise. • Door popping and creaking.

Avalon Profile

	1995	1996	1997	1998	1999	2000	2001
Cost Price ($)							
XL	31,058	33,368	33,718	34,688	35,605	36,595	36,370
XLS	34,458	35,778	36,188	37,868	42,515	43,800	44,710
Used Values ($)							
XL Λ	10,500	12,500	14,500	17,000	22,000	27,000	30,000
XL V	9,000	10,000	13,000	15,000	20,000	25,000	28,000
XLS Λ	12,500	13,500	15,500	20,000	24,000	30,000	34,000
XLS V	11,000	12,000	14,000	18,000	22,000	28,000	32,000
Extended Warranty	N	N	N	N	N	N	N
Secret Warranty	N	N	N	N	N	N	N
Reliability	⑤	⑤	⑤	⑤	⑤	⑤	⑤
Crash Safety	—	④	④	④	④	—	③
Side Impact	—	—	—	⑤	⑤	—	④
Off-set	❷	❷	❷	③	③	⑤	⑤
Head Restraints (F)	❶	❶	❶	③	③	③	③
Rear	—	—	—	❶	❶	—	—

Volvo

850, C70, S40, S70, V40, V70   ★★★★

RATING: Above Average (1993–2001). Surprisingly, for a car company that emphasizes its commitment to safe cars, the 850 and 70 series have quite a few safety-related defects reported by owners, including engine and seat fires, loss of steering, sudden acceleration, transmission failures, electrical shorts, light failures, and tire blowouts. **Maintenance/Repair costs:** Higher than average, and repairs must be done by a Volvo dealer. **Parts:** Higher-than-average cost and limited availability. **Best alternatives:** Don't waste your money on a 1997 850; the 1996 models are virtually identical to the more expensive 1997 versions and are a real bargain if the selling price has been reduced sufficiently. The 1998 model 850s were renamed the C70, S70, and V70; they also have a disappointingly high number of safety-related deficiencies reported to the federal government. Other choices: Acura Integra, TL, and RL; BMW 3 and 5 Series; Infiniti I30 or I35; Lexus ES 300; Mazda Millenia; Nissan Maxima; and Toyota Avalon.

Strengths and weaknesses: Bland, but practical to the extreme, with plenty of power, good handling, and lots of capacity. For 1997, the 850 GLT got a bit more lower-end torque, while the turbo version was upgraded with electrically adjusted front passenger seats and an in-dash CD player. The base 850 sedan uses a 2.4L 24-valve, 168-hp 5-cylinder engine hooked to a front-drive powertrain. (An all-wheel-drive version is available in only Canada and Europe.) Wagons use the same base powerplant, hooked to a 5-speed manual or optional 4-speed electronic automatic. GLTs have a torquier, turbo variant of the same powerplant that boosts horsepower to 190.

The "sports" sedan T5 is a rounder, sportier-looking Volvo that delivers honest, predictable performance but comes up a bit short on the "sport" side. Volvo's base turbo boosts horsepower to 222, but its new T-5R variant uses an upgraded turbocharger that boosts power to 240 horses—for up to seven seconds.

Passenger space, seating comfort, and trunk and cargo space are unmatched by the competition. Braking on dry and wet pavement is also exemplary. The ride of both the sedan and the wagon deteriorates progressively as the road gets rougher and passengers are added. Turbo versions are particularly stiff, and passengers are constantly bumped and thumped.

The 850 hasn't escaped the traditional AC, electrical system, and brake problems that afflict its predecessors. Additionally, owners have complained that the early models have uncomfortable seatbelts, insufficient rear travel for the front seats, and some body hardware deficiencies, resulting in excess noise invading the interior.

70 series and 90 series

Making its debut for the 1998 model year, the 70 series is basically the discontinued 850 using a *nom de plume*. The letters S, V, and C preceding the numerical designation stand for sedans, wagons, and coupes. The 90 series is a redesignated rear-drive 960, and, as with the 70 series, sedans are indicated by an S and wagons by a V. Both the 70 and 90 series are carried over relatively unchanged, except for their names.

With the front-drive 70 series, all-wheel drive is offered with the wagons, and the base 2.4L 5-cylinder engine comes with three horsepower ratings: 168, 190, and 236. Only two transmissions are available: a manual 5-speed (relatively rare) and an automatic 4-speed.

Handling is superb, with the suspension dampened somewhat for a more comfortable ride than what many European imports offer. AWD performs flawlessly, road and body noise are muted, and the cars are well appointed with a full array of standard safety features, with the exception of traction control, which is optional.

On the downside, rear seating is cramped for three adults, and the instrument panel appears to be overly busy, with a confusing array of gauges, instruments and controls on the centre console. Plus, the three rear head restraints induce claustrophobia while severely restricting rear visibility.

The 90 series has plenty of room for three rear seat passengers and its 181-hp V6 performs very smoothly and fairly quietly, providing plenty of power for passing and merging. The car's tight turning circle makes parking a snap, and the suspension has been tuned for comfort rather than performance. Still, handling is quite good. Once again, the large rear head restraints obstruct rear visibility.

As far as quality control and dealer servicing are concerned, Volvo technical service bulletins and owner complaints indicate that factory defects on all models have been on the rise for the past several years. For example, the cars' electrical system may shut down in rainy weather or when passing over puddles; headlights, turn signal lights, and other bulbs burn out monthly; dash lights suddenly go berserk when passing through puddles; power window switches fail; wheels are easily bent; the turn signal lever doesn't return; airbags deploy for no reason; and springs are noisy.

The above defects clearly show that there's less stringent quality control at the factory level since Ford acquired the company and that Volvo is counting on Ford and Volvo dealers to repair their engineering mistakes. On the other hand, Volvo *has* improved service and warranty relations by accelerating service training programs and allowing its dealers to carry out most warranty and extra-warranty repairs without obtaining prior authorization from the company. Ford's impact upon the dealer network has been minimal and is likely to stay that way as long as Volvo products continue to be hot sellers.

C70

The C70's strong points: good acceleration with lots of torque, exceptional steering and handling, first-class body construction and finish, and predicted better-than-average reliability. It's weak points: difficult rear seat entry/exit, some engine turbo lag, excessive engine noise, a jarring suspension, and an uncertain future.

Seating four comfortably, this luxury coupe and convertible is based on the 850 (pardon, S70) platform, and marketed as a high-performance Volvo. It comes with two turbocharged engines: a base 2.4L 190-hp inline 5-cylinder and a 2.3L 236-hp variant. Either engine can be hooked to a 5-speed manual or a 4-speed automatic transmission. Of the two engines, the 190-hp appears to offer the best response and smoothest performance.

Acceleration is impressive, despite the fact that the car feels underpowered until the turbo kicks in at around 1500 rpm—a feature that drivers will find more frustrating with a manual shifter than with an automatic. Steering and handling are first class, fit and finish above reproach, and mechanical and body components are top quality.

The only things not to like are a high resale price, turbo lag, tire thumping caused by the high-performance tires, excessive engine and wind noise, and power sliding rear seats that require lots of skill and patience.

S40 and V40

Volvo's latest small sedan and wagon come with a 1.9L 150-hp turbocharged 4-cylinder engine coupled to an automatic transmission. Two side airbags, anti-lock brakes, air conditioning, cruise control, and power windows are also standard.

Safety summary: All models: 1996—A handful of reports that while vehicle was being driven, it suddenly lost all power and the engine compartment caught fire. • Inadvertent airbag deployment injured driver. • ABS brake failures. • Vehicle suddenly downshifts while cruising on the highway. • Transmission slipped out of Park, rolled down incline, and hit a house. • During rainy periods, the steering wheel locks up or the dashboard suddenly lights up. • Repeated tire blowouts. • Premature failure of the engine cooling fan and the evaporator pump fan relay for the exhaust manifold. Owners also cite cruise control, power-steering pump, and front seatbelt failures. • Electrical glitches affect the speedometer, radio cassette player, and battery. • Broken driver-side door hinge. **1997**—Heated seat caught on fire. • Driver's seatback frame broke when vehicle accelerated. • Sudden acceleration, spinning wildly, when backing up. • Pirelli (205/45-17) tires blew out; the design and size is inappropriate for this vehicle. • Original equipment tires bubble. • Total brake loss in rainy weather. • Rain also causes vehicle to shut down, without steering control. • Vehicle drifts left when being driven, even after the steering mechanism was replaced. • Gas odour in the interior after driving a short distance. • Driver's seatbelt retractor locks up. • Steering locks up in rainy weather. • Air pump and AC compressor failures. 1998—Passenger-side airbag suddenly deployed while vehicle was parked. • Frontal and side airbags failed to deploy in a collision. • Right front wheel assembly disengaged from car while vehicle was underway, causing loss of control and an accident. • Vehicle suddenly accelerated; brakes locked up. • Stalling while underway caused by defective air mass sensor. • A piece of the vacuum brake system came loose, causing engine rpms to surge and spontaneously locking up the brakes. • Transmission randomly fails to engage in Reverse gear, or kicks strongly when going into Reverse. • Frequent battery failures due to battery not holding its charge. • Headlights and other lights burn out frequently. • Two incidents where the front turn signal socket smouldered and charred. • Driver's seatbelt doesn't retract when disconnected. • Continental tires tread separation. • Frequent tire blowouts. • Wheels are easily bent, causing excessive vibration. • Defective door lock pin makes it difficult to open or close door. • Weak trunk lid struts allow lid to fall. • Dashboard causes excessive glare on windshield. • Tall front seats and head restraints obstruct visibility. 1999—Sudden acceleration when applying brakes. • Vehicle shuts down when making a left turn. • Airbags failed to deploy. • While underway, driver seat suddenly moved backward. • Fuel fumes leak into interior. • Brake pedal locks up. • Chronic light failures. • Automatic door locks and trunk lock fail to open. • Automatic gas tank door jams shut. • Tailpipe extends beyond bumper, burning occupant. • Inside door handles pinch fingers. S40, V40: 2001— When applying the brakes in cold weather, pedal won't depress, causing extended stopping distance (dealer confirmed vacuum pump motor was defective). • Vehicle pulls to the left when accelerating or coming to a stop. • Premature wearout of the front brake pads (around 20,000 km). • A new wiring harness is available to extend the life of low-beam headlight bulbs. • Under a special program, Volvo will replace the front door window to prevent excessive noise. This replacement is contingent upon a customer complaint. • Correction for front seat whining or creaking. S70, V70: 2000—Airbags failed to deploy. • Vehicle suddenly pulls to one side while cruising. • Unexpected total loss of power. • Engine sputters and then shuts off. • Prematurely worn front stabilizer link rod. • Considerable brake fade at start-up. • Driver's window stuck in the down position. • AC allows exhaust fumes into the vehicle. • Chronic light failures. V70: 2001—Excessive reflection of beige dash onto windshield. • Engine stalls in traffic; dealer says problem is caused by a "weak" fuel pump. • Engine mounts broke. • Manual transmission clutch sticks in cold weather. • Vehicle can roll away when parked on an incline. • Brake pedal is too close to gas pedal. • Front door indent doesn't hold door open. • Sunroof blew in while going through a car wash. • Rear tailgate door won't lock. • Coffee spilled from cupholder and shorted airbag computer. • Frequent bulb failures.

Secret Warranties/Service Tips/TSBs

All models/years: Check the valve cover nuts at every servicing interval to prevent oil leakage. • Availability of free front seatbelt extenders. **All models: 1992–97**—Upgraded parts have been produced to correct a steering column knocking noise. • Tips on silencing an automatic transmission whining noise. **1993–97**—A number of bulletins have been issued to reduce cargo compartment and interior noise and trim rattles. **1995**—If the cruise control won't engage, check the vacuum supply and vacuum supply pipe first. **1996**—An upgraded engine control module (ECM) has been released to improve engine function. **1996–99**—Automatic transmission final drive whining sound can be eliminated by putting a damper on the driveshaft. This is covered under warranty, under "claim type 01." **1997**—Correct high oil consumption. • New shims will minimize low-speed braking vibrations. • Tips on correcting hard starting. • AC odour troubleshooting tips. • Measures for improved ventilation and defrosting. • Engine may run too lean. **1997–99**—Rear axle whining countermeasures. • Automatic transmission final drive whining correction tips. **1998–2000**—Installation of protective door lock covers. **1999**—Measures to reduce upper windshield moulding noise. **2000**—Special service campaign to service the engine oil filler grate. **850, S70, V70: 1997**—Tips for eliminating upper windshield moulding noise. **1997–99**—There are at least a half-dozen bulletins addressing water leaks affecting the C70. • Rear axle whining countermeasures. **1997–2000**—Automatic transmission final drive whining correction tips. • **1998–2000**—Power window noise can be silenced by following the procedures outlined in TSB #8330033. • Poor FM reception (static) can be improved by modifying the ground strap. This gives the additional benefit of bringing in more stations in scan mode. **1998–2001**—Upgraded rear brake pads will be installed under warranty for more efficient and quieter braking. • Service campaign provides for the free replacement of the headlight wiper stop lug. **2001**—Special service campaign to upgrade service life of headlights; free bulb replacement. **S40, V40: 2001**—Exhaust manifold retaining nuts may be loose or missing. • Engine oil filler neck may be faulty. • A ticking noise may be heard from the canister purge valve. • The malfunction indicator light (MIL) stays on while driving. **S70, V70, C70: 1997–2000**—Reducing power seat lateral movement. **1998–2000**—Special service campaign to upgrade service life of headlights; free bulb replacement. • Another campaign provides for the free replacement of the headlight wiper stop lug.

850, C70, S40, S70, V40, V70 Profile

	1994	1995	1996	1997	1998	1999	2000	2001
Cost Price ($)								
850	29,095	29,995	31,995	32,995	—	—	—	—
Turbo	37,495	40,640	41,695	43,995	—	—	—	—
TLA/AWD	—	—	48,695	48,495	—	—	—	—
C70	—	—	—	—	54,675	49,995	50,595	52,995
S40	—	—	—	—	—	—	—	31,400
S70	—	—	—	—	33,995	34,994	35,195	—
V40	—	—	—	—	—	—	—	32,400
V70	—	—	—	—	33,295	36,295	36,495	37,495
Used Values ($)								
850 ▲	8,000	10,000	11,500	15,000	—	—	—	—
850 ▼	7,000	8,000	10,000	13,000	—	—	—	—
Turbo ▲	9,500	11,000	13,500	16,000	—	—	—	—
Turbo ▼	8,500	9,000	12,000	14,500	—	—	—	—
TLA/AWD ▲	—	—	15,000	18,000	—	—	—	—
TLA/AWD ▼	—	—	13,000	16,500	—	—	—	—
C70 ▲	—	—	—	—	28,000	32,000	38,000	43,000
C70 ▼	—	—	—	—	26,000	30,000	36,000	40,000
S40 ▲	—	—	—	—	—	—	—	25,500
S40 ▼	—	—	—	—	—	—	—	23,500
S70 ▲	—	—	—	—	18,500	23,000	26,000	—
S70 ▼	—	—	—	—	17,000	21,000	24,000	—
V40 ▲	—	—	—	—	—	—	—	26,000
V40 ▼	—	—	—	—	—	—	—	24,000
V70 ▲	—	—	—	—	19,000	23,500	26,000	30,000
V70 ▼	—	—	—	—	17,000	21,500	24,500	28,000
Extended Warranty	Y	Y	Y	Y	Y	Y	Y	Y
Secret Warranty	N	N	N	N	N	N	N	N
Reliability	④	⑤	⑤	⑤	④	④	④	④
Crash Safety								
850	⑤	⑤	⑤	⑤	—	—	—	—
S70	—	—	—	—	⑤	⑤	⑤	—
Side Impact								
850	—	—	—	④	—	—	—	—
S70	—	—	—	—	④	④	④	—
Off-set (850/S70)	⑤	⑤	⑤	⑤	⑤	⑤	⑤	—
Head Restraints								
850	—	⑤	—	⑤	—	—	—	—
C70	—	—	—	—	—	⑤	—	⑤
S70	—	—	—	—	—	⑤	—	—

900 SERIES, S80, S90, V90   ★★★

RATING: Average (1997–2001); Above Average (1989–96). The 1998 model 900s were renamed the S90 and V90, and have apparently inherited similar brake and electrical deficiencies. The model was renamed the S80 for the 1999 model year. It's interesting to note that the 960 series becomes cheaper to acquire than the 940 as the years progress. Unfortunately, as the revamped Volvos have gotten more popular during the past few years, their reliability and safety have become more problematic. **Maintenance/Repair costs:** Higher than average, and repairs must be done by a Volvo dealer. **Parts:** Higher-than-average cost and limited availability. **Best alternatives:** Acura Integra, TL, and RL; BMW 3 Series; Infiniti I30 or I35; Lexus ES 300; Mazda Millenia; Nissan Maxima; and Toyota Avalon.

Strengths and weaknesses: Practical to the extreme, with plenty of power, good handling, lots of carrying capacity, many standard safety features, and impressive crashworthiness ratings and accident injury claim data. On the other hand, weak points include a jarring ride with vehicles equipped with 16- and 17-inch wheels; limited rear visibility; excessive engine, wind, and road noise; fuel-thirstiness (turbo models); declining quality control and increased frequency of safety-related deficiencies; and limited availability, causing soaring resale prices for recent reworked models, with little room for negotiating.

Having debuted as essentially repackaged 760s, the flagship 900 series rear-drive sedans and wagons have a much better reliability record than do the 240 and 700 series, and have been on par with the 850, S70, and V70 over the last few model years. Both the 940 and 960 offer exceptional roominess and comfort, and are capable of carrying six people with ease. The wagon provides lots of cargo space and manages to do it in great style. Some owner gripes: the base 114-hp 2.3L engine is overpowered by the car's weight, excessive fuel consumption with the turbo option, and excessive road and wind noise at highway speeds.

Most of the 900 and 90 series' deficiencies are identical to the S70's, with some exceptions, like miscalibrated engine computer modules that cause random misfiring; rotten-egg and other exhaust odours that permeate the interior even after the catalytic converter is replaced; ignition switch, rear spring, and climate control unit failures; excessive on-road shudder/vibration, drifting, and hard steering; frequent fuel leaks; children suffering burns from the extended tailpipe; battery boiling over, causing acid to spray into engine compartment; and seatbelts that catch in the door after failing to retract properly. Drivers also report that the front bumper is too low; it hits the wheel stop in parking lots, causing extensive bumper and wheelwell damage. Also, brakes continue to require frequent and expensive maintenance due to the poor durability of front and rear pads and the premature warpage of the brake rotors (15,000–30,000 km).

The S80 is a redesign of the S90 and offers several interesting new features like a powerful 268-hp, transverse inline 6-cylinder engine and a sophisticated automatic transmission called the Geartronic—a 4-speed automatic with a feature for manually changing gears, if one so desires. Additionally, the car is chock-full of safety features, has the largest interior of any Volvo, gives impressive performance and handling, and is attractively styled.

Unfortunately, the S80s' defects closely resemble the problems reported on prior years' models (see "Safety summary") and seriously undermine Volvo's much-touted safety claims.

Safety summary: All models: 1991–95—Airbags deploy for no reason. **1998**—Engine fire. • Airbags didn't deploy in a collision. • Fuel system leak (T-junctions and clamps replaced). • Other fuel leaks reported where owners claim problem may relate to the fuel expansion tank or its hoses. • Vehicle suddenly accelerated. • Tire tread separation. Premature failure of the headlight, taillight, turning signal, driveshaft, front and rear brake pad and rotor, tailgate struts, window switches, and door locks. • Turn signal bulbs are scorched and plastic melted. • Total loss of braking ability. • Inappropriate placement of the tailgate handle causes one to pull the tailgate close to one's face, causing nose injury. • Brakes didn't work on an incline after vehicle stalled out. **1999**—Electrical short caused under-hood fire. • Another fire occurred as vehicle was backing into a parking space. • Airbags deployed inadvertently while car was in Park. • Vehicle suddenly accelerated while parking. • Accelerator pedal became stuck when passing another vehicle on the highway. • Several incidents where electrical switches continually malfunction, console and console knobs are hot to the touch, and tapes have melted in the tape deck. • Chronic short circuits of headlights and turn signal lights, leading to lights constantly burning out; wires melted in turn signal socket. • Engine wire harness cracked and fell apart; shorted out near engine and radiator. • Fuel pump leaks and other unspecified leaks from the gas tank area. • Fuel tank wouldn't accept fuel. • Fuel line sprayed small amounts of fuel from impact with a rock. It should have some kind of protective shield. • Tire tread separation. • Transmission grinding and vibration when underway. • Suddenly stalled while turning. • Steering wheel locks up when making a left turn. • Total brake failure and excessive brake fade after successive braking. • Defective steering rack replaced by dealer. • Front wheel fell off the axle. • Sudden ball joint failure also causes premature tire wear. • Chronic front end shimmy. • Subframe bushing problem. • Clunking sound when automatic transmission is put into Reverse. • Power windows operate erratically. **2000**—Severe glare onto windshield from beige dash. • Airbags failed to deploy. • Chronic stalling; refuses to accelerate on turns. • Signal light blown; housing melted. • Excessive front end vibration, accompanied by a thumping or humming sound. • Broken right front ball bearing. • Brakes fail to stop car when applied shortly after start-up. • When stopped on an incline, vehicle will roll back even though transmission is set in Drive. • Front head restraints block view, and front seatbelt retractor locks unexpectedly. • Poorly anchored fuel filler could spill fuel in an accident. 2001—Engine compartment electrical fire. • Fuel tank leakage. • Vehicle doesn't track in a straight line. • Rough terrain causes vehicle to bounce and veer off in one direction. • Vehicle jolts forward when accelerator pedal is depressed.

Secret Warranties/Service Tips/TSBs

All models/years: Check the valve cover nuts at every servicing interval to prevent oil leakage. • New steering components will reduce power steering knocking. • AC evaporator odours can be controlled by installing a new fan control module. • Tips on silencing noise from the manual front seats. **All models: 1992–98**—Oil pump leaks are usually due to loose pump retaining screws. **1997–99**—Rear axle whining countermeasures. • Automatic transmission final drive whining correction tips. • Upgraded rear brake pads to reduce grinding. • Upgraded weather stripping to reduce upper windshield moulding noise. • Installation of protective covers for door locks. • Improvements for door handle operation in cold weather. **1998**—Service Campaign #83 provides for the free replacement of faulty AC compressors. Service Campaign #83A and 83B provide for the free replacement of the front panel to prevent it from interfering with the AC. **S80: 1999–2000**—Automatic transmission shudder during upshift. **1999–2001**—New rear brake pads have been developed to reduce vibration. • Power seat movement on acceleration and deceleration. • Loose A-pillar trim. • Subframe bushing knocking noise. **2000**—Free engine oil grate inspection.

900 series, S80, S90, V90 Profile

	1994	1995	1996	1997	1998	1999	2000	2001
Cost Price ($)								
940 GLE	26,995	28,460	—	—	—	—	—	—
Wagon	27,995	29,490	—	—	—	—	—	—
960	35,495	41,300	46,400	47,400	—	—	—	—
S90	—	—	—	—	47,400	—	—	—
V90	—	—	—	—	49,075	—	—	—
S80	—	—	—	—	—	49,995	55,995	54,395
Used Values ($)								
940 GLE ⋀	8,000	9,000	—	—	—	—	—	—
940 GLE ⋁	7,000	7,500	—	—	—	—	—	—
Wagon ⋀	8,500	9,500	—	—	—	—	—	—
Wagon ⋁	7,500	8,000	—	—	—	—	—	—
960 ⋀	9,500	11,000	14,500	17,500	—	—	—	—
960 ⋁	8,000	9,500	12,500	16,000	—	—	—	—

S90 ▲	—	—	—	—	23,000	—	—	—
S90 ▼	—	—	—	—	21,000	—	—	—
V90 ▲	—	—	—	—	24,000	—	—	—
V90 ▼	—	—	—	—	22,000	—	—	—
S80 ▲	—	—	—	—	—	30,000	35,000	40,000
S80 ▼	—	—	—	—	—	28,000	33,000	38,000
Extended Warranty	Y	Y	Y	Y	Y	Y	N	N
Secret Warranty	N	N	N	N	N	Y	Y	Y
Reliability	④	⑤	⑤	③	③	③	④	④
Crash Safety								
960	—	—	—	④	—	—	—	—
S80	—	—	—	—	—	—	—	⑤
Side Impact (S80)	—	—	—	—	—	—	—	⑤
Off-set (S80)	—	—	—	—	—	—	⑤	⑤
Head Restraints								
940	—	⑤	—	—	—	—	—	—
960/S90	—	⑤	—	⑤	—	—	—	—
S80	—	—	—	—	—	⑤	⑤	⑤

SPORTS CARS

There are two kinds of cars in this category: the traditional two-seater roadster, styled much like the MGB of the early '70s, Mazda's Miata, or, in the extreme, the Chevrolet Corvette; and sporty cars, such as coupes and hatchbacks, that offer sportier styling, performance and handling than their entry-level versions. Honda's Si and the Ford Mustang GT are two examples of this more practical and reasonably priced sporty car.

The Miata is more like an early British roadster than a sporty wannabe. Its credo is less hardware, weight, and size equals more performance.

Most sports cars, or "high-performance vehicles" as they're euphemistically named, don't offer the comfort or reliability of a Hyundai Tiburon or Toyota Celica. Instead, they sacrifice reliability, interior space, and a comfortable suspension for speed, superior road handling, and attractive styling. They also need a whole slew of expensive high-performance packages, because many entry-level sports cars aren't very sporty in their basic form. Keep in mind, as well, that sports cars often have serious accident damage that may not have been repaired properly, resulting in serious tracking problems because of a bent chassis. This risk can be attenuated only by a thorough check-up by a body shop before you purchase.

The Corvette's basic premise is that more hardware equals more performance. Unfortunately, it also means more costs and less reliability.

By carefully browsing through classified ads and dealer car lots, you should find many fully loaded sporty cars at a fraction of their original cost. Sports cars, on the other hand, will probably still cost much more than they're worth. Remember, most models that have been taken off the market, like the Toyota Supra, Nissan 300ZX, and Chevrolet Corvette ZR1, aren't likely to become collectors' cars with soaring resale values. In fact, discontinued Japanese sports cars like the Nissan 1600 haven't done nearly as well as some of the British roadsters taken off the market at about the same time.

SPORTS CAR RATINGS

Recommended

Ford Probe (1995–97)
General Motors Camaro, Firebird,
  Trans Am (1997–2001)
Honda Prelude (1993–2001)
Hyundai Tiburon (2000–2001)

Mazda Miata (1996–2001)
Mazda MX-3 (1994–96)
Nissan 240SX (1995–98)
Toyota Celica (1995–2001)

Above Average

DaimlerChrysler Laser, Talon
  (1997–99)
Ford Mustang (1996–2001)
General Motors Corvette (1996–2001)
Honda Prelude (1985–92)
Hyundai Tiburon (1997–99)

Mazda Miata (1990–95)
Mazda MX-3, Precidia (1992–93)
Nissan 200SX (1995–98)
Nissan 240SX (1989–94)
Toyota Celica (1986–94)

Average

DaimlerChrysler Avenger, Sebring (2000–01)	General Motors Camaro, Firebird, Trans Am (1994–96)
Ford Probe (1993–94)	General Motors Corvette (1994–95)

Below Average

DaimlerChrysler Avenger, Sebring (1995–99)	Ford Probe (1989–92)
Ford Mustang (1980–95)	General Motors Camaro, Firebird, Trans Am (1992–93)

Not Recommended

DaimlerChrysler Laser, Talon (1990–96)	General Motors Camaro, Firebird, Trans Am (1982–91)
	General Motors Corvette (1977–93)

DaimlerChrysler

AVENGER, SEBRING

RATING: Average (2000–01); Below Average (1995–99). The Avenger and its more luxuriously appointed Sebring twin have had fewer factory-related defects than other new Chrysler designs, though this is faint praise indeed. Drive a hard bargain, because the money you save will be eaten up in transmission, engine head gasket, and AC evaporator repair bills, unless you threaten small claims court action. Interestingly, the Avenger has had fewer factory-related defects than the Sebring. **Maintenance/Repair costs:** Average. Avenger repairs must be done by a Chrysler dealer. **Parts:** Average cost and availability. **Best alternatives:** Ford Mustang and Probe, GM Camaro and Firebird, Hyundai Tiburon, Mazda Miata, Nissan 240SX, or Toyota Celica.

Strengths and weaknesses: The Avenger and Sebring, designed by Chrysler and built by Mitsubishi in Illinois, are both surprisingly agile—which isn't actually that surprising, considering they share the same components, except for the grille and taillights. Since Avengers come with fewer standard features, they're usually priced a bit lower than Sebrings. The convertible, made in Mexico, is six inches longer than the Sebring coupe and is powered by a standard 2.0L twin cam, while the upscale JXi gets a performance injection with the 2.5L 6-cylinder power-plant. ABS was standard on ES versions and optional on base Avengers; dual airbags were standard on all models.

From 1995 through the 1999 model, neither the Avenger nor the Sebring have changed much, except for minor re-styling touches and the

dropping of the 4-cylinder engine in mid-1999. The 2000 Sebring convertible's suspension was retuned to give a more comfortable ride, and
the same year's base Avenger was given additional standard equipment—
notably, the ES's 2.5L V6 and automatic transmission. The redesigned
2001 Sebring added a sedan, a more powerful V6, and a premium sound
system. The Avenger is no more.

Acceleration is fairly good, though noisy, with the base 140-hp engine
and a manual transmission; however, the optional V6 powerplant is the
engine of choice to overcome the power-hungry automatic transmission
and to avoid a persistent 4-cylinder engine head gasket defect affecting
all model years through 1999. Handling is better than average, and the
ride is generally comfortable, except for a bit of choppiness due to the
firm suspension.

Mitsubishi quality control, although much better than Chrysler, has
slipped a bit as of late and is compounded by the increased use of poor-
quality generic Chrysler parts. Hopefully, now that Mitsubishi has set up
its own dealer network in Canada for 2002, parts availability and servicing will improve.

Owners single out the automatic transmission failures, grinding
when shifting, shuddering from a stop, and defaulting to Second gear;
4-cylinder engine head gasket failures; engine oil leaks caused by broken
plastic guard; loss of steering and a clanking or rattling heard when
turning over rough pavement; premature brake wear and brake failures;
ignition, electrical system, and power control module (PCM) glitches;
sunroof malfunctions; and sloppy body construction as the areas most
needing attention. Would you believe the driver's seat motor burns out
because it doesn't have a fuse? Replacement cost: $2,000!

The convertible top is prone to fly off on early models, leaks water
and air, and operates erratically. A faulty window regulator allows the
window to run off its track. Poor design and sloppy construction allows
water into the vehicle when window is partly opened; rear windshield
sealant lets water leak into vehicle; wheel rims are easily bent and leak
air from normal driving; there's excessive brake dust; a black goo oozes
from body panels and the undercarriage; side door mouldings melt; and
the airbag coating peels.

Safety summary: All models: 1995–99—Mitsubishi-built Avengers have
had few safety-related incidents reported to NHTSA. Sebring safety failures over the same period were frequent and serious. **Sebring:
1995**—Fuel line connection fire. • Rear window explosion from defroster
short circuit. • No airbag deployment. • Premature transmission failure;
sticks in Second gear or won't go into Park or Reverse. • ABS brake failures. • Premature brake wear, due to a defective sensor relay, forces rotor
and pad replacement every 10,000–20,000 km and makes the car jerk and
vibrate when braking. • Faulty seatbelts. • Anti-theft alarm self-activates. •
Front windshield moulding peels away. • Trunk supports gave out,

causing lid to slam down. • The low front end causes the front bumper to hit the pavement whenever passing over a speed bump. • Annoying engine ticking noise and head gasket failure. **1996**—Same problems generally as '95 models, except for more frequent reports of the convertible top flying off, fires igniting inside the driver and passenger doors and shift console, key trapped in ignition, and transmission jumping out of gear while in Park with key removed. • Engine head gasket failure reports are more frequent, as are transmission defects, ABS failures, brake rotor warpage, and sudden failure of suspension and steering components. • New problems: water leaks into the interior and collects under the back seat cushion and on the floor; carpeting may cause the steering to lock up; horn doesn't blow; digital mileage and gear shift screen goes blank; rotten-egg smell; electrical shorts cause the car to suddenly shut down. **1997**—As unbelievable as it seems, Chrysler still carries on with safety problems almost identical to those reported earlier. For example, reports of transmission failures have increased, sudden acceleration due to the throttle jamming is still a danger, brake failures and frequent rotor and pad replacement continue, seatbelts frequently lock up, and owners report the transmission still permits the vehicle to roll away even though the lever was put into Park. • Trunk leaks, noisy steering, and an inadequate and hard-to-find spare tire also make this year's list. • Interestingly, head gasket failure reports have tapered off (too early to tell?). **1998**— After only two years on the market, you'd expect few complaints, right? Wrong! More of the same old, same old. However, virtually no engine failures have been reported, but most of the same electrical short circuits, brake, and airbag complaints, as enumerated above, have continued. • There have also been a greater number of reports concerning sudden acceleration, loss of steering control due to the floor mat blocking the steering column, bent wheel rims causing tire blowouts, seatbelt lockup, and alternator/battery failures. • One new item: an unusually large number of complaints that the side door panel cladding falls off while cruising. **1999**—Vehicle caught fire after hitting bumper of other car at 5 mph (8 km/h). • Other fire reported from a leaking fuel hose. • Front airbags failed to deploy upon impact. • Many incidents where the throttle stuck while engaging Reverse. • Premature replacement of the lower lateral sway bar. • Automatic transmission rebuild after 38,000 miles (61,000 km). • Split transmission line. • Delayed, noisy transmission shifting. • Slipped into Reverse and rolled downhill, despite being in Park with ignition off. • Constant velocity joint flew off in heavy traffic on interstate. • Brakes don't grab sufficiently; complete loss of braking due to loss of vacuum. • Defective rear defroster clip. • Windshield wipers suddenly stop working. • Toxic (?) tar substance leaks out of the doors and body cladding (door panels) falls off on the highway. • Convertible boot flew off while vehicle underway. • Replaced ignition switch because key couldn't be inserted. • Front end too low. **2000**—Vehicle hydroplaned out of control at 90 km/h. • Brake failure and extended

stopping distance caused by defective wheel speed sensor, modulator, or
master cylinder and brake pad disintegrating, causing rotor scoring. •
Automatic transmission slipped out of gear while vehicle was cruising at
120 km/h; suddenly went to 50 km/h. • Transmission fluid leakage
through a crack in the transmission case. • Driver's seatbelt often
unlatches and seatback side latch may fail. 2001—Brake failure accompanied by sudden, unintended acceleration. • Brake caliper bolt fell off. •
Brake and accelerator pedals are too close to each other. • Window shattered when convertible top was lowered.

Secret Warranties/Service Tips/TSBs

All models: 1995—One of the causes of premature brake wear, shudder,
and noise is a misadjusted brake light switch. **1995–96**—Engine compartment ticking can be silenced by replacing the duty cycle purge
solenoid with a quieter solenoid assembly. **1995–97**—Engine compartment popping or knocking may require an upgraded EGR valve.
1995–98—Delayed transaxle engagement can be corrected by installing
an upgraded trailing arm bushing. **1995–99**—Front coil spring creak,
pop, or squeak can be silenced by putting in coil spring insulators. •
Intermittent loss of speed control can be prevented by installing new
speed sensors. • Wind noise coming from the front windshield area is
caused by wind lifting the windshield moulding at the glass. • Tips on
reducing excessive front brake pulsation or shudder. • Paint delamination, peeling, or fading (see Part Two). **1997–99**—A light knocking noise
from the rear shock area may mean you need to install various upgraded
rear shock components. • New software will prevent the transmission
from shifting erratically or falling into a Second gear "limp" mode.
1997–2000—To prevent the door cladding from falling off, Chrysler recommends replacing the lower mounting clips under warranty (TSB
#23-40-99). **1999–2000**—A black, tar-like residue can be cleaned under
warranty by following guidelines found in TSB #23-56-99. **Sebring:**
1996–2000—Steering wheel clunk or rattle. • Wet carpet (convertible).
1996–2001—Inoperative rear window defogger.

Avenger, Sebring Profile

	1995	1996	1997	1998	1999	2000	2001
Cost Price ($)							
Avenger	17,175	18,954	18,780	19,280	20,360	—	—
Avenger V6	21,275	22,544	23,820	24,320	23,545	—	—
Sebring	18,155	19,514	21,420	21,500	23,380	26,525	—
Sebring V6	24,025	25,538	24,135	24,360	28,675	26,525	30,095
Convertible	—	25,210	27,030	27,530	—	32,585	33,595
Used Values ($)							
Avenger ▲	6,500	7,500	9,000	10,500	13,000	—	—
Avenger ▼	5,000	6,000	7,000	9,000	11,000	—	—

Avenger V6 ▲	7,500	9,000	11,000	12,000	14,500	—	—
Avenger V6 ▼	6,000	7,500	9,500	10,500	13,000	—	—
Sebring ▲	7,000	8,000	11,500	14,000	16,500	19,500	—
Sebring ▼	6,500	9,000	10,000	12,500	15,000	17,500	—
Sebring V6 ▲	7,000	8,000	11,000	13,000	14,500	16,500	21,000
Sebring V6 ▼	5,500	7,000	9,500	11,500	13,000	15,500	19,500
Convertible ▲	—	11,000	13,000	16,000	—	21,000	24,500
Convertible ▼	—	9,500	11,500	14,500	—	19,000	22,500
Extended Warranty	Y	Y	Y	Y	Y	Y	Y
Secret Warranty	Y	Y	Y	Y	Y	Y	Y
Reliability	❷	❷	❷	③	③	③	③
Crash Safety (Avenger)	—	⑤	⑤	—	—	—	—
Sebring	—	—	⑤	—	—	—	④
Sebring 4d	—	—	—	—	—	—	⑤
Sebring conv.	—	—	④	—	—	—	③
Side Impact (Sebring)	—	—	—	—	—	—	③
Sebring 4d	—	—	—	—	—	—	③
Sebring conv.	—	—	—	—	—	—	③
Off-set	—	—	—	—	—	—	⑤
Head Restraints (Avenger)	❶	—	❷	—	❷	—	—
Sebring (F)	❶	—	❶	—	③	—	❷
Sebring (Rear)	—	—	—	—	❷	—	❶
Rollover Resistance (Sebring 4d)	—	—	—	—	—	—	⑤

LASER, TALON ★★★★

RATING: Above Average (1997–99); Not Recommended (1990–96). The '95 models offered fresh styling, dual airbags, and a more powerful engine. The 1997 versions are identical to the more expensive, re-styled '98 models (the Talon's last year), and are the better buy since they're substantially cheaper and don't have the first-year glitches found on earlier offerings. **Maintenance/Repair costs:** Higher than average, but routine repairs can be done practically anywhere. Make sure the engine timing chain is inspected regularly and check for head gasket failures—I've received about a dozen reports of owners having to pay huge repair bills for new engines. **Parts:** Good parts availability. Dealers have had some trouble adequately servicing high-tech components, and parts are a bit more expensive than other cars in this class. **Best alternatives:** Ford Mustang and Probe, GM Camaro and Firebird, Hyundai Tiburon, Mazda Miata, or Toyota Celica.

Strengths and weaknesses: These sporty Mitsubishi-made cars combine high performance, low price, and reasonable durability. The base 1.8L engine is adequate and the suspension is comfortable, although a bit soft. The optional 16-valve, turbocharged 2.0L comes with a firmer suspension and gives more horsepower for the dollar than most other front-drive sports coupes, without much turbo lag. The 5-speed manual is the gearbox of choice. Torque steer makes the car appear to try to twist out of your hands when all 195 turbocharged horses are unleashed. The 4-speed automatic transmission cuts into the Laser's highway performance. Overall handling is impressive, with the 4X4 system giving sure-footed foul-weather stability. Keep in mind that the all-wheel-drive (AWD) model has a smaller trunk area than the front-drive.

All high-performance models cost thousands of dollars less than their Japanese competitors, without compromising quality or performance. The 16-valve Talon and its 4X4 variant are at the top of the trim list and provide five more horses than the turbocharged TSi.

Beginning with the 1990–94 models, owners report glitches with the 1.8L engine and electrical system, driveline vibrations, premature brake wear and excessive noise, and poor fit and finish that includes water leakage into the interior and paint delamination. Some problems reported with 1995–98 versions were unstable idling, poor idling, and reduced rpm when the AC is running; hard starts and stalling in cold weather; cold weather transmission shift delays (2–3 and 3–4) that take up to two minutes; transmission defaults into Second gear (limp-in mode); frequent wheel alignments; a tendency to drift or lead to the right; speed control undershoot or overshoot; chronic electrical system, brake, and transmission failures; false theft alarm; centre exhaust pipe heat shield buzz; door buzz and rattle; misadjusted door glass and poor windshield sealing, causing water leaks and wind noise; noisy clutch pedal; interior window film buildup; headliner sagging; power seat switch sticking; stress marks on the quarter trim panel; buzz or rattle from the rear quarter trim; inoperative, noisy, and jerky sunroof operation; faulty lever latch pin; and the sunroof may open by itself.

Safety summary: All models/years: Standard brakes often lock up or require long stopping distances. Choose the optional ABS. • Head restraints block rear visibility. • Airbags often fail to deploy. **All models: 1995–98**—Most of the following problems reappear each year in NHTSA records: engine and fuel tank fires; fuel leakage after recall repairs; sudden acceleration due to jammed throttle; chronic transmission failures that include transfer case leakage after recall repairs (automatic and manual transaxles), causing sudden wheel lockup; wheels fall off; engine timing belt breakage (100,000–120,000 km); loss of steering caused by going through a puddle of water or the steering belt slipping off the pulley; collapse of suspension and steering components (front control arms and ball joints); frequent replacement of brake pads and warped rotors; electrical system failures; faulty door locks and windows; water leakage into interior; horn won't work or self-activates; ABS and Check Engine lights come on for no reason.

Secret Warranties/Service Tips/TSBs

All models: 1993–99—Paint delamination, peeling, or fading (see Part Two). • A rotten-egg odour coming from the exhaust may be the result of a malfunctioning catalytic converter, which may be covered by the emissions warranty. **1995–96**—Engine compartment ticking can be silenced by replacing the duty cycle purge solenoid with a quieter solenoid assembly. **1995–97**—Engine compartment popping or knocking may require an upgraded EGR valve. **1995–98**—Front coil spring creak, pop, or squeak can be silenced by putting in coil spring insulators. • Delayed transaxle engagement can be corrected by installing an upgraded trailing arm bushing. **1995–99**—Intermittent loss of speed control can be prevented by installing new speed sensors. • Wind noise coming from the front windshield area is caused by wind lifting the windshield moulding at the glass. • Tips on reducing excessive front brake pulsation or shudder. **1997–99**—A light knocking noise from the rear shock area may mean you need to install various upgraded rear shock components. • New software will prevent the transmission from shifting erratically or falling into a Second-gear "limp" mode. **1998**—Erratic automatic transmission performance can be corrected by installing new software.

Laser, Talon Profile

	1991	1992	1993	1994	1995	1996	1997	1998
Cost Price ($)								
Laser	13,000	13,735	14,145	14,145	—	—	—	—
Turbo RS	14,900	15,820	16,310	16,310	—	—	—	—
Talon	15,505	16,205	14,475	16,000	19,425	20,695	19,885	20,290
Talon TSI	18,100	19,365	19,365	19,975	28,360	29,985	30,225	30,675
Used Values ($)								
Laser ⋀	2,500	3,000	4,000	4,000	—	—	—	—
Laser ⋁	2,000	2,500	3,500	4,500	—	—	—	—
Turbo RS ⋀	3,000	3,500	4,000	5,000	—	—	—	—
Turbo RS ⋁	2,500	3,000	3,500	4,500	—	—	—	—
Talon ⋀	3,000	4,000	4,500	5,000	6,000	8,000	9,000	11,000
Talon ⋁	2,500	3,500	4,000	4,400	5,500	6,500	7,000	9,000
Talon TSI ⋀	4,500	5,000	6,500	8,000	9,500	11,000	13,500	16,500
Talon TSI ⋁	4,000	4,500	5,500	7,000	8,000	9,000	12,000	14,500
Extended Warranty	Y	Y	Y	Y	Y	Y	Y	Y
Secret Warranty	N	Y	Y	Y	Y	Y	Y	Y
Reliability	❷	❷	❷	❷	❷	❷	④	⑤
Crash Safety	—	—	—	—	—	—	④	—
Side Impact	—	—	—	—	—	—	—	❶

Ford

MUSTANG ★★★★

RATING: Above Average (1996–2001); Below Average (1980–95). Unfortunately, Mustangs don't perform well in rough weather and they have had a frighteningly high number of safety-related mechanical failures. Additionally, new crash data indicates the vehicles may be fire prone following a collision at moderate speeds (see *www.bonforums.com/mustang_safety*). GM's Camaro and Firebird are the Mustang's traditional competition as far as performance is concerned. Ford has the price advantage, with a base Mustang costing a bit less than the cheapest Camaro, but it lags from a performance standpoint—10 fewer horses with the V6 and only 60 more horses with the V8. The GM models also offer more sure-footed acceleration, crisper handling, standard ABS, a 6-speed transmission, and more comfortable rear seats. All 4-cylinder Mustangs should be shunned. **Maintenance/Repair costs:** Average, particularly because repairs can be done anywhere. **Parts:** Average cost, and parts are often sold for much less through independent suppliers. Some parts are continually back-ordered, particularly if involved in recall repairs (cruise control components, for example). **Best alternatives:** Ford Probe, GM Camaro and Firebird, Hyundai Tiburon, Mazda Miata, or Toyota Celica.

Strengths and weaknesses: This is definitely not a family car. For example, a light rear end makes the car dangerously unstable on wet roads or when cornering at high speeds. But for those who want a sturdy and stylish second car, or who don't need room in the back or standard ABS, the 1996–98 Mustang is a pretty good sports car buy. And if GM carries out its threat to drop its rear-drive Camaro and Firebird after 2001, the Mustang will be the main alternative for rear-drive sports car enthusiasts. As stated earlier, Mustangs remain popular because they offer sporty styling and high-performance thrills, usually for less money than GM's Camaro and Firebird, the Mustang's main domestic rivals.

Base models come equipped with a host of luxury and convenience items, which can be a real bargain once the base price has sufficiently depreciated—say, after the first three or four years. Off-lease models are particularly good buys these days.

1990–93
There are three body styles to choose from—a coupe, a coupe hatchback, and a ragtop—and two engines were offered—a wimpy 2.3L 4-banger and a 5.0L V8. A driver-side airbag was a standard feature. 1991 models added 15 more horses to the base engine (105 hp), upgraded convertible tops, and a brake/shift interlock. The following year's models were

unchanged carryovers; however, the '93 model year saw the debut of the high-performance Mustang Cobra, sporting a 245-hp V8 and marketed in limited numbers in Canada.

Mustangs have never been very reliable cars, and the 1990–93 models were particularly troublesome. Yet when failures do occur, they aren't difficult or expensive to fix (engine head gaskets excepted). The first Mustang, launched in 1964 and now worth more than $30,000, had serious rusting, electrical, and suspension problems. And guess what? Thirty-eight years later, later Mustangs still have electrical systems and electronic modules that are constantly breaking down, transmissions that jump from Park to Reverse, and a base suspension and front brakes that wear out in the blink of an eye.

The less said about the infamous 2.3L 4-cylinder engine, the better. The V6 is also failure prone (head gaskets, again), leaving the V8 engine with a definite performance and reliability edge. Turbocharged models aren't recommended because of their frequent and expensive mechanical breakdowns. If you want high-performance action, you'll have to pay a premium—and be prepared for some monstrous repair bills and white-knuckle acceleration on wet roadways. Sport trim models feature an upgraded suspension and wheel package that improves handling considerably.

Keep in mind that the electronic modules that govern engine and transmission performance are often on the fritz, producing chronic hard starts, stalling, and overall poor city and highway performance. Furthermore, the 3.8L 6-cylinder engine has begun to tally up a record number of head gasket failures around the 150,000 km mark. Other problem areas: the front brakes, fuel pumps, and front suspension remain consistent weak spots, and MacPherson struts and various steering components are likely to wear out before their time. The parking brake cable also seizes easily. The EEC IV engine computer can be temperamental, and electrical problems are common. Assembly quality is still not on par with Japanese vehicles.

The 4-cylinder engine, used through 1993, isn't just failure prone—it also doesn't carry half the horses of the 5.0L V8 and has no redeeming qualities. Unfortunately, the 1993 Mustang fell behind the GM competition when the Camaro and Firebird were radically re-styled that year, gaining additional safety features, a more rigid and dent-resistant body, better body fit and finish, and a more powerful base engine.

1994–2001

Ford fought back with its own redesign of its 1994 model, replacing the 4-banger with a V6, adding four-wheel disc brakes and dual airbags, making the chassis more rigid (especially the convertible version), and dropping the hatchback. Mustangs now carry a base 3.8L V6 and an optional 4.6L V8. In addition, the high-performance limited edition Cobra variation delivers 90 more horses than the stock 4.6L V8 offers.

The single and twin cam V8 options make the Mustang a powerful—if a bit unsophisticated—street machine. V6 models are an acceptable compromise, even though the engines fail to deliver the gobs of power most performance enthusiasts expect.

1995 models were simply carried over unchanged. The '96s got a 4.6L V8 with upgraded spark plugs, and the Cobra received a 305-hp variant of the same powerplant; '97s returned mostly unchanged, except for new colours and option upgrades. For 1998, the GT version got a 10-hp performance boost; the '99s got fresh styling and another horsepower boost. That year, the V6 models also got suspension and steering gear upgrades. Year 2000 models returned unchanged, except for improved child safety seat anchoring. The following model year, 2001 GT models received hood and side scoops and larger wheels. All models got an upgraded centre console, blacked-out headlights, and spoilers.

Unfortunately, Ford's safety-related problems continue to be carried over as well (see "Safety summary"). Additionally, both the V6 and V8 engines have a propensity for chronic surging and stalling; blowing engine intake manifold and head gaskets; failed motor mounts; ticking and rattling at 3,000 rpm until car shifts into Second gear; automatic transmission shifts poorly, especially from First to Second gear; differential howling or whining (ring and pinion failure); engine dies when decelerating; fuel system glitches, highlighted by frequent fuel injector malfunctions; faulty differential carrier bearings; prematurely worn clutch pressure plates; electrical short circuits causing instrument panel shutdown; early replacement of brake rotors, pads, and calipers; seat material deteriorates quickly; paint defects and premature rusting.

Safety summary: All models/years: Regularly equipped Mustangs, like most rear-drive Fords, don't handle sharp curves or wet pavement very well. The rear end swings out suddenly, and the car tends to spin uncontrollably. Furthermore, the car loses traction easily on wet roads and braking is barely adequate. • Serious doubts have also been raised regarding the Mustang's fuel system failing safety integrity standards and the convertible's doors tendency to jam shut in a 57 km/h frontal collision. • Transmission allows vehicle to roll away when parked on an incline; emergency brake disengages. • Airbag failed to deploy; inadvertent airbag deployment. • Sudden acceleration due to a stuck throttle. • Brake failure and premature replacement of the brake master cylinder. • Excessive vehicle vibration when accelerating. • Side windows fall off their tracks. **All models: 1995**—Fuel line failure caused several fires. • Front fan belt caught on fire with no warning. • Airbag deployment caused severe injuries. • Several reports that when driver applied the brakes, the airbag deployed. • ABS brake failures, warped rotors, and frequent pad replacement. • Engine head gasket failures. • Power steering fails; steering wheel is off-centre or locks up. • Chronic stalling thought to be caused by defective fuel pump. • Transmission failure while driving caused accident. • Torque converter failure causes transmission to slip. • Rear axle broke during normal driving conditions. • Front-end alignment doesn't hold, causing premature wear of steering and tie-rods. • On one occasion, tie-rods broke and caused vehicle to go out of control, resulting in several fatalities. • Front struts suddenly collapsed. • Weak rear struts allow vehicle to bottom out. • Front stabilizer bar rusted and cracked. • Driver's door hinge broke. • Fuel gauge is inoperative or gives an inaccurate reading. • Gas tank too small and requires frequent fillups. • Fog lights fill with water and blow their bulbs. • Frequent AC failures. • Seatbelt failed to restrain driver. **1996**—Carried-over defects include mostly braking, automatic transmission, and engine cooling problems (many allegations that the plastic intake manifold ruptures under pressure from the cooling system and may be a causative agent for an increase in head gasket failures). • Other repeats: airbag problems, stalling, sudden acceleration (now appears to be cruise control-related), ABS failures, frequent brake rotor and pad replacement, fuel tank leakage and fuel line fire, sudden steering loss, and water leaking into lights. • New problems: broken rear sway bar behind rear mounting bolt, excessive front-end vibrations, timing chain and fan belt failures, and Check Engine light coming on due to a defective evaporator canister solenoid. • Some airbag injuries traced to the use of sodium azide, the airbag propellent; apparently, it changes to the very toxic sodium hydroxide (caustic soda) when detonated. **1997**—Returning defects: engine overheating caused by a defective intake manifold; many more reports of manual and automatic transmission failures (popping out of gear, grinding, clutch vibrations, no reverse of 2–3 gear shift); ABS and parking brake failures; power-steering pump; seatbelt fails to retract; sway bar breakage; sudden acceleration; and fuel leakage at fuel tank connection. • New problems: differential rear ring and pinion gear; AC compressor; hood pops open; front brake line separation; and front lower control arm/ball joint separation. **1998–99**—Fuel tank leaks. • Engine compartment fires. • Hood flew up unexpectedly while underway. • Frequent stalling, hesitation, and loses power. • No airbag deployment; airbag-induced injuries. • Parking brake doesn't hold (traced to a broken ratchet assembly). • Brake pedal goes to floor without braking. • Steering system failure. • Right ball joint fractured, causing wheel to turn inward. • Tire sidewall tread separation. • Seatbelt tightens up continually. • Other repeats of '97 problems: transmission, braking, and engine failures. • New problems: fire ignited in the centre console and dash areas, defective seatbelt retractor and poor design allows belt to slip out of guide, stalling caused by fuel pump or fuel relay cut-off switch failure, and original equipment tire blowouts (sidewall splits). **2000**—There's an unusually large number of safety complaints recorded by NHTSA for year 2000 models. • Fumes from airbag deployment made passengers ill and temporarily blinded them. • Alternator melted battery wires; car caught on fire. • Automatic transmission sticks in Reverse. • Convertible top unlatches and flips up while underway. • Hood flew up. • Head restraints sit too low. • Many reports of rear axle failures. • Brake calipers and lines were replaced to correct brake fluid leakage. • Multiple function switch failure causes headlights to suddenly go out. 2001—Lower control arm came off. • Sudden brake lockup. • Loose brake rotor responsible for collision. • Foot hits fuse box when engaging clutch pedal. • Seatbelt retracted unexpectedly, nearly choking occupant, who had to be cut free. • Driver's seat rocks back when driving.

Secret Warranties/Service Tips/TSBs

All models/years: Paint delamination, peeling, or fading (see Part Two). • Ford "goodwill" warranty extensions usually cover engine and transmission components. • Cold hesitation when accelerating, rough idle, long crank times, and stalling may all signal the need to clean out excessive intake valve deposits. These problems also may result from the use of fuels that have low volatility, such as high-octane premium blends. • Excessive oil consumption is likely caused by leaking gaskets, poor sealing of the lower intake manifold, defective intake and exhaust valve stem seals, or worn piston rings; install new guide-mounted valve stem seals for a better fit, as well as new piston rings with improved oil control. • A buzz or rattle from the exhaust system may be caused by a loose heat shield. • A thumping or clacking heard from the front brakes signals the need to machine the front disc brake rotors. All models: 1985–2002—Repeated heater core failures. 1994—Automatic transmissions with delayed or no forward engagement, or a higher engine rpm than expected when coming to a stop, are covered in TSB #94-26-9. • A cracked cowl top vent grille should be replaced with an upgraded version. • A driveline boom can be silenced by replacing the rear upper control arms. • A noisy fuel pump needs to be replaced by an improved "guided check valve" fuel pump. • A ticking or tapping sound coming from the engine at idle can be silenced by installing an improved fuel hose/damper assembly. • Loss of torque during or just after 3–4 shift may be caused by a hydraulic condition in the transmission or an intermittent signal from one of the powertrain system sensors. 1994–97—An erratic or prolonged 1–2 shift is likely caused by a defective aluminum piston. 1994–98—Loose rocker panel mouldings will be fixed under the bumper-to-bumper warranty; out-of-warranty claims will be reviewed on a case-by-case basis. 1994–2000—Hood may be difficult to close. 1996—Stalling or hard starts may be due to the idle air control valve sticking. 1996–97—The engine's lower intake manifold side and front cover gaskets might leak coolant, a problem that can cause overheating and severe engine damage (see following letter).

A.R. O'Neill
Director
Vehicle Services and Programs
Ford Customer Service Division

Ford Motor Company
P.O. Box 1904
Dearborn, MI 48121-1904

January, 2000

Ford Motor Company is providing a no-charge Service Program, Number 99B29, to owners of certain 1996 and 1997 model year Mustang, Thunderbird, Cougar, and 1997 F-Series vehicles equipped with 3.8L or 4.2L engines.

What Is The Reason For This Program?	The affected vehicles may experience engine coolant leaks at the engine front cover gasket; this could cause severe engine damage if not corrected. To avoid engine damage, you should make an appointment to have this service performed on your vehicle at your Ford or Lincoln Mercury Dealer as soon as possible.
No Charge Service:	At no charge to you, your dealer will replace the engine from cover gasket with a redesigned gasket and change the engine oil and filter. This service will reduce the likelihood of coolant leaks at the engine front cover, and will help avoid the potential inconvenience of breakdowns and costly engine repairs.
	Your vehicle is eligible for this program until March 31, 2001, regardless of mileage.

Ford asks owners to call their dealers immediately to have the gasket replaced, even if they have not experienced any problem. Consumers who have already had the repair will be reimbursed for their expenses.

1997–99—Delayed or no 2–3 upshift may be caused by a leaking accumulator seal. • Road noise or dust/water leaks in the luggage compartment can be fixed by sealing the wheelhouse flange. 1997–2000—Automatic transmission fluid leaks at the radiator can be stopped by installing an O-ring on the transmission oil cooler fitting. 1998–99—Tips for spotting abnormal ABS braking noise. 1999–2000—An erratically operating front windshield wiper probably has a faulty multifunction switch. Replace it under warranty, says TSB #00-9-6. • Same thing goes for an inaccurate speedometer. 1999–2001—Troubleshooting a downshift clunk and a driveline whine upon coastdown. 2000–01—First gear ticking.

Mustang Profile

	1994	1995	1996	1997	1998	1999	2000	2001
Cost Price ($)								
Mustang LX/Coupe	15,595	17,595	18,595	19,795	22,595	20,995	21,195	22,275
Convertible	24,995	26,095	25,895	26,795	29,295	24,995	25,195	26,945
Used Values ($)								
Mustang LX/Coupe ▲	5,500	7,000	8,500	10,000	12,000	13,500	15,000	17,000
Mustang LX/Coupe ▼	4,000	5,500	7,000	8,500	10,000	12,000	13,000	15,000
Convertible ▲	8,500	10,000	12,000	13,500	16,500	18,500	20,000	22,000
Convertible ▼	7,000	8,500	10,500	12,000	14,000	17,000	18,500	20,500
Extended Warranty	Y	Y	Y	Y	Y	Y	N	N
Secret Warranty	Y	Y	Y	Y	Y	Y	Y	Y
Reliability	❷	❶	❷	❷	③	③	④	④
Crash Safety	④	④	④	④	⑤	④	④	⑤
Convertible	—	—	⑤	⑤	—	—	—	—
Side Impact	—	—	—	—	③	③	③	③
Convertible	—	—	—	—	—	—	—	❷
Head restraints	—	❶	—	❶	—	❶	—	❶

PROBE ★★★★★

RATING: Recommended (1995–97); Average (1993–94); Below Average (1989–92). **Maintenance/Repair costs:** Average, and repairs can be done by independent garages or Mazda dealers. Nevertheless, the under-hood layout is crowded, making for high routine maintenance costs. **Parts:** Despite the fact that 1997 was the Probe's last model year (Mazda's MX-6 bit the dust as well), parts should remain plentiful and reasonably priced. **Best alternatives:** Ford Mustang, GM Camaro and Firebird, Hyundai Tiburon, Mazda Miata, or Toyota Celica.

Strengths and weaknesses: The four-seater Probe sporty coupe was launched in May 1988 as the front-drive replacement for the aging Mustang. Don't get the impression that the Mazda MX-6 and Probe are twins because they share most mechanical features. In fact, they differ markedly in handling and appearance. Ford engineers took more control of the chassis tuning and suspension geometry to give the Probe a smoother and firmer sporty demeanor, and its stylists chopped and pulled the body to give it a more aerodynamic, aggressive personality.

Available only as a two-door hatchback, there are two models, each with its own powerplant: a 2.0L 4-cylinder and a 2.5L V6 engine. These engines give the car much-needed power and smoothness not found in the anemic and brutish powertrains used in the past.

Mazda's mechanicals are above reproach, but despite gobs of torque, the GT doesn't give the muscle-car performance found in the less refined

5.0L Mustang GT. Performance is sapped considerably by the automatic transmission. Early models are beset by severe "torque steer," a tendency for the chassis to twist when the vehicle accelerates. Nevertheless, overall handling is precise and predictable on all models without sacrificing ride quality, which is a bit on the hard side.

Refinements of the 1993 and later versions include two new Mazda-designed engines that give the car a small horsepower boost, more interior room, all-wheel disc brakes on the GT, and less torque steer. '94s were the first to get dual airbags.

The Probe's overall mechanical reliability is fairly good, but like its Mustang cousin, body assembly is the pits (no surprise here—Mazda did the mechanicals; Ford did the body work). Paint quality and rust protection are mediocre at best. The turbocharged engine has been relatively trouble-free, but owners have complained of frequent stalling and stumbling with the base powerplant. Many experience excessive ABS noise and vibrations when braking, and the front brakes tend to wear out very quickly. AC components have a short life span of three to five years and are outrageously expensive to troubleshoot and repair.

The car is essentially a 2+2, with the rear reserved for children or cargo. The interior is short on head room for tall drivers (especially on vehicles equipped with a sunroof), but cargo room is increased with the folding rear seatbacks. Multiple squeaks and rattles, wind and water leaks, and cheap interior appointments are the most common body complaints. The digital read-outs are distracting and often incorrect.

Safety summary: All models/years: The driver's motorized shoulder belt is literally a pain in the neck. It rides high on the neck, fails to retract properly, tangles easily, and often hangs too loose. It also requires that the driver attach the lapbelt separately, which isn't done very often, resulting in decapitation in high-speed collisions. • Beware of coil spring corrosion, causing the spring to suddenly break. Ford will pay for the repair on a case-by-case basis. • There are far fewer and less dramatic safety-related complaints on the Probe than one finds with the Mustang. For example, the '95 Probe has about half as many incidents reported to NHTSA as does the '95 Mustang. **All models: 1995**—Engine fire. • Leaking fuel tank connection. • Sudden acceleration. • No airbag deployment. • Windshield cracks near the outside moulding. • Hatchback collapses. • Driver's door pops open. **1995–97**—Three repeated problems for these years are chronic stalling, possibly due to a defective catalytic converter, wiring harness, spark-plug wiring, or throttle valve; Check Engine light coming on for no apparent reason; and poor brake performance and lockup. **1996**—Engine failure. • Seatbelt fails to retract. • Wind noise around glass. • Cruise control won't disengage. • Strong odour emitted by the ventilation system. **1996–97**—Sudden loss of steering, lockup, and premature rack-and-pinion failure. • Transmission failures and stalling. • Loose outside door handles (defective retention rings). •

Engine misses, stalls, runs rough, or has reduced power. • Excessive engine noise. • Upper engine noise service tip. • Hesitation, low power, rough idle. • 3–4 shift hunt. • CD4E transmission shifts harshly, seeps fluid from the vent, and produces a buzz or a clicking vibration. It may also make a whistling noise in Park. • Fluid leaks at axle shaft. • Inaccurate fuel gauge reading when the tank is full. • Loose catalyst or muffler heat shields. • Fog or film on windshield/interior glass. • Door glass makes a pop or snap noise when rolled up or down. • Musty and mildew-type odours. 1997—Airbags failed to deploy. • Engine fire. • Sudden stalling in traffic. • Engine timing chain failure. • Metal bar protrudes through the driver's seatback.

Secret Warranties/Service Tips/TSBs

All models: 1989–94—A no-start condition or inoperative heater or lights may be caused by water and corrosion in the wiring connector, or a short-to-ground at splice 102 (circuit 9). 1990–94—A speaker whine or buzz caused by the fuel pump can be stopped by installing an electronic noise RFI filter. 1993–94—A clunk or knock from the steering assembly when turning the steering wheel is likely due to an insufficient yoke plug (pinion) preload. • Wind/water leaks require the readjustment of the front door glass, as outlined in TSB #994-5-4. • Inoperative power door locks may have a corroded wiring harness connection. • Frozen door locks, a common problem, are addressed in TSB #94-8-6. • A ticking noise coming from the 2.0L engine's hydraulic lash adjusters can be stopped by a longer oil pump control plunger that prevents air from passing through to the oil pump. 1993–97—Ford "goodwill" warranty extensions often cover powertrain components, catalytic converters, and computer modules. If Ford balks at refunding your money, apply the emissions warranty for a full or partial refund. • Paint delamination, peeling, or fading (see Part Two). 1994—A rough idle affecting 2.0L engines could be caused by spark leakage from a damaged number 1 or number 2 spark plug wire. 1994–97—Transaxle fluid seepage can be corrected by servicing with a remote vent kit or by replacing the main control cover.

Probe Profile

	1990	1991	1992	1993	1994	1995	1996	1997
Cost Price ($)								
GL	14,972	13,795	14,795	15,165	16,495	17,895	18,395	19,095
GT	21,760	19,895	17,795	18,240	20,195	21,595	22,195	22,995
Used Values ($)								
GL ʌ	2,500	3,000	3,500	4,000	4,500	6,000	6,500	9,500
GL v	2,000	2,700	3,000	3,500	4,000	4,500	6,000	8,000
GT ʌ	3,500	4,000	4,500	5,500	6,500	7,500	8,500	11,000
GT v	3,000	3,500	4,000	4,500	5,500	6,500	7,500	9,000

Extended Warranty	Y	Y	Y	Y	Y	N	N	N
Secret Warranty	N	N	N	Y	Y	Y	Y	Y
Reliability	③	③	③	③	④	④	⑤	⑤
Crash Safety	—	④	④	③	⑤	⑤	⑤	⑤

Note: Although the 1990 Probe wasn't crash-tested, the 1989 crash test results showed minimal injury would be sustained by the driver and front-seat passenger.

General Motors

CAMARO, FIREBIRD, TRANS AM   ★★★★★

RATING: Recommended (1997–2001); Average (1994–96); Below Average (1992–93); Not Recommended (1982–91). As with the Mustang, the Camaro and Firebird have elicited many safety-related complaints, including airbag deployment injuries, sudden acceleration, brake failures, and steering loss. Be especially wary of brake rotor warpage, requiring rotor replacement every two years (about a $300 job). The 1996 Camaro and Firebird are essentially the same as the more expensive 1997 versions. A V8-equipped Camaro or convertible is the best choice for retained value a few years down the road. But you can do quite well with a used base coupe equipped with the performance handling package and high-performance tires. GM has announced it will drop the Camaro and Firebird after the year 2002. If it does, this move is unlikely to affect the cars' resale values or parts supply. **Maintenance/Repair costs:** Average, and repairs can be done by any independent garage. **Parts:** Reasonably priced and easy to find. **Best alternatives:** Ford Mustang and Probe, Hyundai Tiburon, Mazda Miata, or Toyota Celica.

Strengths and weaknesses: When compared with the Mustang, Camaros and Firebirds are better performing rear-drive muscle cars that produce excellent crash protection scores and high resale values. They also take the lead over the Mustang with their standard ABS and slightly better reliability record. The Camaro's and Firebird's overall performance varies a great deal depending on the engine, transmission, and suspension combination in each particular car. Base models equipped with the V6 powerplant accelerate reasonably well, but high-performance enthusiasts will find them slow for sporty cars. Handling is compromised by poor traction on wet roads, minimal comfort, and a suspension that's too soft for high-speed cornering and too bone-jarring for smooth cruising. The Z28, IROC-Z, and Trans Am provide smart acceleration and handling, but at the expense of fuel economy.

1982–92

Relatively unchanged since its last redesign in 1982, a convertible was added in 1987. In 1990 GM offered a standard driver-side airbag, tilt steering wheel, tinted glass, intermittent wipers, and halogen headlamps. That same year, the IROC-Z debuted with a standard limited-slip differential and 16-inch alloy wheels.

For 1991, the V8-equipped Z-28 returned after a 3-year hiatus and the IROC-Z was axed; '92 models were carried over unchanged.

During this period, performance and reliability problems are commonplace. Much like Ford's embarrassing 4-banger, the puny and failure-prone 2.5L 4-cylinder powerplant was the standard engine up to 1986—part of the legacy of an earlier fuel crisis and the subsequent downsizing binge. The turbocharged V8 offered on some Trans Am models should be viewed with caution because of its many durability problems.

Body hardware is fragile, poor paint quality and application are common and lead to premature rusting, and squeaks and rattles are legion. Body integrity is especially poor on cars equipped with a T-roof. Areas particularly vulnerable to rusting are the windshield and rear wheel openings, door bottoms, and rear quarter panels. The assorted add-on plastic body parts found on sporty versions promote corrosion by trapping moisture along with road salt and grime. Also note that the Camaro's flat seats don't offer as much support as the better-contoured Firebird seats.

These cars are also plagued by chronic fuel-system problems, especially on the Cross-Fire and multi-port fuel-injection controls. Automatic transmissions, especially the 4-speed, aren't durable. The standard 5-speed manual gearbox has a stiff shifter and a heavy clutch. Clutches fail frequently and don't stand up to hard use. The 2.8L V6, used through 1989, suffers from leaky gaskets and seals and premature camshaft wear. The larger 3.1L 6-cylinder has fewer problems. However, malfunctioning dash gauges and electrical problems are common, and exhaust parts rust quickly. Dual outlet exhaust systems on V8 engines are expensive to replace. Front suspension components and shock absorbers wear out very quickly.

1993–2001

1993s were totally redesigned and given a more aerodynamic body style. Dimensions were slightly enlarged, weight was added, power boosted, and the dashboard was reworked. Dual airbags and ABS also became standard safety features. There was no '93 convertible.

For the '94 model year, the convertible returned with an upgraded top and 6-speed gearbox. '95s added a 3.8L V6 engine and optional traction control. '96 models carried the 3.8L engine as the base powerplant, the 5.7L V8 gained 10 extra horses, and a new high-performance SS option was offered for the first time on the Z28. On 1997 models, GM offered a

30th birthday styling package for the Camaro and some interior upgrades, V6 engine dampening for smoother running at high speeds, optional Ram Air induction, and racier-looking ground-effects body trim for the Firebird. The '98 model got a minor facelift, and the Z28 and SS both received a slight horsepower boost. Optional traction control became available on the '99s, along with standard electronic throttle control on V6-equipped versions and a new Zexel Torsion differential used in the limited-slip rear axle. Year 2000 Camaros and Firebirds got alloy wheels and an improved throttle response for cars equipped with the manual transmission. 2001 Z28 and SS models were given five more horses and re-styled chrome wheels.

Of this grouping, you should stick with the 1996–99 models for the best performance and price. All of these cars are much better overall per-formers than previous models, and additional standard safety features are a plus.

These sporty convertibles and coupes are almost identical in their pricing and in the features they offer (the Firebird has pop-up headlights, a more pointed front end, a narrower middle, and a rear spoiler). As noted above, both cars got a complete make-over in 1995, making them more powerful and aerodynamic, with less spine-jarring performance.

As one moves up the scale, overall performance improves consider-ably. The V8 engine gives these cars lots of sparkle and tire-spinning torque, but there's a fuel penalty to pay. A 4-speed automatic transmis-sion is standard on the 5.7L-equipped Z28; other versions come with a standard 5-speed manual gearbox or an optional 6-speed. Many of these cars are likely to have been ordered with lots of extra performance and luxury options, including a T-roof package guaranteed to include a full assortment of creaks and groans.

Both the Camaro and the Firebird may be equipped with an impres-sively effective PASS KEY theft deterrent system, similar to the one used successfully in the Corvette. A resistor pellet in the ignition disables the starter and fuel system when the key code doesn't match the ignition lock.

Not everything is perfect, however. Owners report that the base engine is noisy, though the 3.8L doesn't have the head gasket failures seen with Ford's 3.8L powerplant. Fuel economy is unimpressive, the air conditioner malfunctions (but not to the same extent as Ford-produced units), front brakes and MacPherson struts wear out quickly, servicing the fuel-injection system is an exercise in frustration, electrical problems are common, gauges operate erratically, and body problems are worse than with the Mustang and just won't go away.

These cars are still afflicted by door rattles, misaligned doors and hatch, a sticking hatch power release, and poor fit and finish. Owners also complain that the steering wheel is positioned too close to the driver's chest, the low seats create a feeling of claustrophobia, visibility is limited by wide side pillars, and trunk space is sparse with a high liftover.

Safety summary: All models/years: Early brake rotor warpage and pad replacement. One dealer mechanic who wishes to remain anonymous explains the problem this way:

> The rotors are not thick enough and have insufficient air to cool them. ASE-certified Independent mechanics and dealership employees (unofficially) buy slotted "racing" rotors or use ceramic non-metal pads from other sources. This has apparently gone on since 1998 on both Firebirds and Camaros.

• Airbag malfunctions. • Seatbelts fail to lock up. **All models: 1995—** Severe injuries caused by airbag deployment. • Airbag deployed, projecting dash panel into the passenger's face. • Airbag deployed and caught fire. • Rear brakes rusted out. • Left rear caliper grabs when making turns. • Faulty cruise control. • The tie-rod broke while driving, forcing the car off the road. • Broken gas tank weld. • Stabilizer bar failure. • Transmission bolts came off. • Trunk latch failure allows trunk to open while driving. • Two reports that double-locking T-top flew off from passenger side while driving with both locks engaged. • In another incident, the sunroof flew off. • Convertible top latch failure. • Door windows leak. • Inadequate defroster causes windows to fog. • Headlight dimmer switch failures. • Driver's seatbelt failed during accident. **1995–96**—Many reports that car caught fire near the fuel tank. • Fuel line retaining clamp could fail, causing the plastic fuel lines to come into contact with the exhaust manifold cover. • Other fires ignited near the radio and in the engine compartment. • Many reports claiming sudden acceleration. • Airbag failed to deploy. • Frequent ABS brake failures; pedal goes to the floor. • ABS is particularly ineffective in rainy weather. • Rear brake caliper failure. • Emergency brake fails frequently, allowing car to roll away even though shift lever is placed in Park. • In wet conditions or when passing over a puddle, the power-steering pump fails, resulting in steering lockup. • Frequent transmission failures while driving. **1996**—Transmission jumps out of gear. • Traction control fails in cold weather. • Right rear axle broke. • Rear main oil seal leakage and failure. • ABS light remains lit due to defective jumper. • Seatbelts slip off their guides and their anchorages may break. • Faulty ignition control module. • Windshield wipers stay on one speed, don't clean enough of the right side, and their placement blocks right-side visibility. **1997**—Fire caused by a short in the defroster wiring. • Engine intake manifold gasket and valve cover failure. • Faulty power-steering pumps. • Stalling in the rain. **1997–98**—Four recurring problems are: prematurely worn brake pads and warped or cracked rotors, sudden acceleration, no airbag deployment, and failure of the emergency brake to hold. **1998**—Dash fire. • Axle seal, tie-rod, serpentine belt, fuel pump, brake caliper bolt, AC blower motor, fuel gauge, and wiper failures. **1999**—Interestingly, both the Camaro and Firebird have about one-third fewer safety-related complaints registered against them by NHTSA than does the Ford Mustang. • Airbags failed to deploy upon impact. • Cracked fuel tank leaks fuel. • Accelerator pedal sticks. • Prematurely warped front brake rotors jerk to one side when brakes are applied and cause pulsation, excessive noise, and extended stopping distance. • Many incidents of clutch slippage at low mileage. • Frequent complaints that the stock shifter causes mis-shifts. • Electrical system shorts cause instrument panel and assorted gauges and lights to operate erratically. • Turn signal lights don't flash, headlights often dim to about 50 percent of their intended brightness, heater slows down, and power windows run slowly. **2000**—Again, these cars only have one-third of the safety complaints registered for year 2000 Mustangs. • Engine surging and stalling. • Electrical wires melted. • Emergency brake failed to hold vehicle; came off in driver's hand. • Noisy manual transmission shifting (First to Reverse). • Rear brake lockups and chronic pad and rotor failures. • T-top flew off vehicle. • Seatbelt failed to retract in an emergency stop. • Headlights flicker or suddenly go out. • Horn collects water which muffles sound. • Front end pulls to the right. • Headrests are set too low (same complaint heard from Mustang owners). • Replacement windshields are seriously distorted along the bottom edge. • Windows leak water. • Premature power window motor failures. • Severe vibration when accelerating. **2001**—Premature automatic transmission failure.

Secret Warranties/Service Tips/TSBs

All models/years: Eliminate AC odours by applying an evaporator core cooling coil coating. • A rotten-egg odour coming from the exhaust is probably the result of a malfunctioning catalytic converter, which may be covered by the emissions warranty. • Paint delamination, peeling, or fading (see Part Two). • GM guidelines to dealers on troubleshooting exterior lamp condensation complaints. • Oil leaks between the intake manifold and engine block are most often caused by insufficient RTV bonding between the intake manifold and cylinder block. **All models: 1993–96**—Uneven rear brake pad wear or premature wear can be corrected by replacing the caliper anchor bracket, guide pins, and the brake pads with upgraded parts. **1993–2002**—GM has a special kit to prevent AC odours in warm weather. **1994**—Excessive oil consumption is likely due to delaminated intake manifold gaskets. Install an upgraded intake manifold gasket kit. • Delayed automatic transmission shift engagement is a common problem, addressed in TSB #47-71-20A. • Install a new "flash" PROM to cure engine surging or hesitation and stalling upon acceleration for cars with automatic transmissions. **1994–98**—GM guidelines for repairing front brake problems. **1995–96**—Delayed automatic transmission shift engagement may require the replacement of the pump cover assembly. **1997**—New switches will fix inoperative door locks. • Fixing automatic transmission slippage. • Engine oil leak diagnosis. • Theft alarm sounds when vehicle gets wet. • Diagnosing engine miss and poor driveability. **1998**—Tips on eliminating roof panel ticking. **1998–2000**—An engine that loses coolant or runs hot may simply need a new radiator cap or the radiator filler neck polished. • Install upgraded disc pads to eliminate rear brake chirp or groan and front brake squeal when braking. • Silence accessory drive belt chirping or squeaking by installing a new double row idler pulley, generator bracket, and serpentine belt. **1998–2001**—Water runs out of front lower corners of rear hatch. **1999**—If the convertible top closes with difficulty it may be because the headliner is too short. **1999–2001**—Steering wheel squeaks when turning. • Windshield moulding squeaks. **2000**—Repair tips for fixing an inoperative or an erratically operating antenna. **Models with 2.5L engines/all years**—Spark knock can be fixed with a new PROM module (#12269198), if the emissions warranty applies. • Frequent stalling may require a new MAP sensor (TSB #90-142-8A). **3.8L V6: 1996–98**—These engines have a history of low oil pressure caused by a failure-prone oil pump. A temporary remedy is to avoid low-viscosity oils and use 10W-40 in the winter and 20W-50 for summer driving.

Camaro, Firebird, Trans Am Profile

	1994	1995	1996	1997	1998	1999	2000	2001
Cost Price ($)								
Camaro/RS	16,498	18,995	20,195	22,075	22,790	23,100	26,065	26,120
Z28	20,498	23,650	25,530	27,270	27,840	28,670	31,630	29,540
Convertible	24,370	26,045	28,365	29,080	29,795	30,105	38,270	38,585
Firebird	17,198	19,795	20,955	23,120	24,580	24,865	27,605	26,915
Trans Am	24,500	27,390	28,755	30,780	34,080	34,750	35,505	35,815
Used Values ($)								
Camaro/RS ⋀	5,000	7,000	9,000	10,000	13,000	15,000	17,000	20,000
Camaro/RS ⋁	4,000	5,500	7,000	8,500	11,000	13,000	16,000	18,000
Z28 ⋀	7,500	8,500	11,500	13,000	15,500	18,500	21,500	24,000
Z28 ⋁	6,500	7,000	9,500	11,000	14,000	17,000	19,500	22,000
Convertible ⋀	10,500	12,500	15,000	17,000	20,000	23,000	27,000	31,000
Convertible ⋁	9,000	11,000	13,000	15,000	18,000	21,000	25,000	28,500
Firebird ⋀	6,000	7,500	9,000	11,000	13,000	15,500	18,500	20,000
Firebird ⋁	5,000	6,500	7,500	9,500	11,000	13,500	17,500	18,000
Trans Am ⋀	8,500	10,000	12,000	13,500	17,000	21,000	24,000	28,000
Trans Am ⋁	8,000	8,500	10,000	12,500	15,000	19,000	22,000	26,000
Extended Warranty	Y	N	N	N	N	N	N	N
Secret Warranty	Y	Y	Y	Y	Y	Y	N	N
Reliability	❷	③	③	④	④	⑤	⑤	⑤
Crash Safety (Camaro)	⑤	⑤	⑤	⑤	④	④	④	④
Side Impact (Camaro)	—	—	—	③	③	③	③	③
Head Restraints	—	❶	—	❶	—	❶	—	❶

CORVETTE   ★★★★

RATING: Above Average (1996–2001); Average (1994–95); Not Recommended (1977–93). The cheaper 1996 Corvette won't have the cachet or the mechanical and body refinements of the redesigned 1997 version. If you choose the 1997 model, try to get a second-series car that was made after June 1997. Keep in mind that premium fuel and astronomical insurance rates will further drive up your operating costs. Plus, don't discount the serious safety-related problems you're likely to experience on 1997–99 models. They run the gamut of sudden steering lockup when underway, electrical shorts causing vehicle shutdown, a non-functioning parking brake, brake failures due to premature rotor warpage (around 16,000 km), and seatbelts that jam in the retractor. The locked-up steering is particularly scary because it apparently has carried over to year 2000 models, and traffic accident investigators may simply conclude that a resulting accident was due to driver inexperience or unsafe driving. **Maintenance/Repair costs:** Higher than average, although most repairs can be done by any independent garage. Long waits for recall repairs. **Parts:** Pricey, but easy to find. Surprisingly, it is often easier to find parts for older Corvettes, through collectors' clubs, than to find many of the high-tech components used today. **Best alternatives:** Ford Mustang and Probe, GM Camaro and Firebird, Mazda Miata, or Toyota Supra.

Strengths and weaknesses: Corvettes made in the late '60s and early '70s are acceptable buys, due mainly to their value as collector cars and their uncomplicated repairs. Unfortunately, the Corvette's overall reliability and safety have declined over the years as its price and complexity have increased. This is due in large part to GM's updating its antiquated design with high-tech, complicated add-ons rather than coming up with something original. Consequently, the car has been gutted and then retuned using failure-prone electronic circuitry. Complicated emissions plumbing and braking and suspension systems have also been added in an attempt to make the Corvette a fuel-efficient, user-friendly, high-performance vehicle—a goal that General Motors has missed by a large margin.

The electronically controlled suspension systems have always been plagued by glitches. Servicing the different sophisticated fuel-injection systems is a nightmare—even (especially) for GM mechanics. The noisy 5.7L engine frequently hesitates and stalls, there's lots of transmission buzz and whine, the rear tires produce excessive noise, and wind whistles through the A- and C-pillars. These, and the all-too-familiar fibreglass body squeaks and paint delamination, continue to be unwanted standard features throughout all model years. The electronic dash never works quite right (speedometer lag, for example).

On the other hand, Corvette ownership of more recent models does have its positive side. For example, the ABS vented disc brakes, available since 1986, are easy to modulate and fade-free. The standard European-made Bilstein FX-3 Selective Ride Control suspension can be preset for touring, sport, or performance. Under speed, an electronic module automatically varies the suspension setting, finally curing these cars of their earlier endemic over-steering, wheel spinning, breakaway rear ends, and other nasty surprises.

All used Corvettes are high-risk buys, but the 1977–93 models have been particularly troublesome. These models are notorious for experimenting with complicated and failure-prone safety, emissions, and performance "innovations" that were routinely brought in one year and dropped shortly thereafter—making for difficult troubleshooting and hard-to-find parts. There's also a greater chance you'll get stuck with a turned-back odometer or an accident-damaged car, written off by the insurance company and then resold through wholesalers, auctions, body shops, or their employees.

To protect yourself from these scams, all you need to do is give the Corvette's VIN (vehicle identification number) to any GM garage and you'll get a printout of the previous owners' names and all the repairs carried out and at what mileage. As far as body damage is concerned, this too should be checked out by a Chevrolet dealer's body shop.

There is one other precaution you should take when buying a Corvette: get a GM-backed supplementary warranty, or look for a recent model that has some of the original warranty left. The frequency of repairs and the high repair costs make maintenance outrageously expensive. Following are some of the things that can put a large dent in your wallet if they haven't been fixed already.

1977–83
Major mechanical failings affect the fuel and emissions systems, air conditioning, transmission, clutch, shift linkage, camshaft lifters and rear half-shaft soft yokes, carburetor, steering, brakes, and starter and electrical systems, including the lights. As far as body assembly goes, the major deficiencies are poor panel fits, faulty and fragile interior/exterior parts and trim items, quirky instruments, cheap upholstery, and defective window lifts. Owners also complain of poor workmanship/shoddy assembly causing a cacophony of squeaks and rattles, poor dealer servicing, unavailable and expensive parts, and excessive labour charges.

1984–90
These model years are incredibly difficult to service. One *Lemon-Aid* reader had a faulty engine bearing at 16,000 km and spent $2,500 to remove the engine. It takes half a day to change the spark plugs on the passenger side. Likely mechanical problem areas are the emission control system (injectors, computer-controlled sensors, fuel injection, and engine gaskets), air conditioning, and ignition/distributor. Owners also experience engine and drivetrain failures, Bosch radio malfunctions, and

the need to make frequent wheel alignments. Fragile body hardware, poor fit and finish, wind/road noise, and water intrusion into the interior are still major weaknesses. Owners complain of faulty controls and window lifts, defective paint (base coat comes through the finish), interior/exterior parts and trim, glass and weather stripping, instruments, lights, door locks, upholstery, and carpeting.

1991–2001

Though the re-styled 1991 Corvette remained the same mechanically, all models got the convex tail and square taillights previously used only on the upscale ZR-1 coupe. Acceleration Slip Regulation on 1992–96 models effectively reduces the horrendous wheel spin that threw many Corvettes out of control when accelerating on slippery surfaces. A new LTI engine with 55 more horses came on the scene with the 1992 'Vette, and the following year the ZR-1 got a 405-hp variant of the same powerplant, shortly before the model was replaced in the spring of 1995 by the Grand Sport. Incidentally, the super-powered ZR-1's depreciated price makes the car a bargain when one totes up the cost of its standard performance features.

A more substantial redesign was carried out in mid-1997. Although styling remained practically unchanged, the transmission was moved back, creating a roomier cockpit; the interior was made much more user-friendly; structural improvements reduced body flexing (a problem with most convertibles) and made for a more rigid hatchback; and a new aluminum 340-hp LSI V8 engine arrived on the scene. The '98 and '99 versions are pretty much carryovers of the redesigned '97 and aren't worth a higher price. A high-performance hardtop model was launched for the '99 model year. Year 2000 models returned unchanged; however, the 2001 Corvette got a horsepower boost, an Active Handling performance upgrade, and was joined by a high-performance Z06 variant.

Owners rave about the redesigned '97 models' improved performance, better handling, and additional safety features, but they still find fault with the stiff ride, poor fuel economy, and excessive interior noise. From a reliability standpoint, these 1997 and later models are much improved, with the most serious problems being excessive engine oil consumption (rings are suspected), which causes an oily black buildup on the exhaust tips and catalytic converter failure. Defective steering columns lock while underway or parked, a problem since 1997, says the following Corvette owner:

This item has failed on an estimated 3000 Corvettes throughout the USA. Please see Internet site *www.corvetteforum.com*. As a safety professional, I see this as a hazard that Chevrolet needs to address with more severity. The loss of steering control because the steering wheel locks can lead to property loss, as well as death.

Owners report the active handling system malfunctions and makes their car veer into traffic or spin out of control; problems with the electronic and electrical systems; brakes sticking (brake booster is the suspected culprit); poor body hardware; fit and finish; suspension; and air conditioning.

Safety summary: All models: 1995—Fire ignited in the wiring harness. • Sudden acceleration. • Electrical system failure. • Defective convertible top, fuel gauge, and ABS brakes. **1996**—Fire started in the engine computer system. • Faulty front wheel bearing hub, fuel pump, intake manifold, and tire pressure sensor (no parts available). • Transmission failures and fluid leakage. • Excessive vibration when top is taken off. **1997–98**—Sudden loss of power, engine shuts down, and warning lights come on everywhere. • Defective throttle control module, parking brake, brake rotors and pads, seatbelt retractors, fuel line clips, and Check Engine light. **1997–99**—NHTSA is looking into complaints of steering column lock module failures, non-functional parking brake, and jammed seatbelts. • **1998**—Fuel tank leakage. • No airbag deployment. • Transmission failure, leaks. • Emergency brake won't hold. • Excessive vibrations when driving. • Poor headlight illumination. **1999**—Epidemic of complaints relating to sudden steering column lockup. • Also, frequent complaints that the steering wheel won't unlock with ignition key. • Sudden, unintended acceleration. • Fuel tank leaks when gassing up; vehicle caught fire as raw fuel was ignited by the catalytic converter. • Fuel pump failures. • Parking brake won't hold car. • Chronic premature warpage of the brake rotors. • Front lapbelts jam in the retractor. • Electrical shorts caused headlights to stick open, melted rear-view mirror assembly, and a plethora of other electronic glitches, leading to vehicle shutdown. • Engine serpentine belt and tensioner failures. • Poorly anchored driver's seat and warped trunk door. **2000–01**—Excessive heat buildup from catalytic converters deforms rear bumper assembly and makes interior unbearable. • Seatbelt doesn't retract properly when reeling it out and tightens up progressively when driving. • Fuel leaks from the fuel lines near the firewall inside the engine compartment. • Driver's seat rocks. • Foot easily slips off clutch and brake pedals.

Secret Warranties/Service Tips/TSBs

All models/years: A rotten-egg odour coming from the exhaust is probably caused by a defective catalytic converter, which may be covered by the emissions warranty. • Clearcoat paint degradation, whitening, and chalking, long a problem with GM's other cars, is also a serious problem with the fibreglass-bodied Corvette, says TSB #331708. It too is covered by a secret warranty for up to six years (see Part Two). **All models: 1992–96**—Oil leaks between the intake manifold and engine block are most often caused by insufficient RTV bonding between the intake manifold and cylinder block. **1993–2002**—GM has a special kit to prevent AC odours in warm weather. **1995–96**—Delayed automatic transmission shift engagement may require the replacement of the pump cover assembly. **1995–2000**—Guidelines for repairing brake rotor warpage under warranty. **1997**—Correcting water leaks into the rear compartment. • Inadequate heating, defrosting. • Correcting drivebelt noise. **1997–98**—What to do when the Low Engine Coolant light comes on. • A poor front-fender-to-door fit can be fixed by installing an additional front fender clip. • Silence a muffler insulator rumble noise by installing upgraded insulators. • Countermeasures to eliminate water leaks above the door glass and door glass rattles. **1997–99**—A no-start condition can be corrected by reprogramming the power control module (PCM). • TSB #99-06-02-016 has the remedy for a low coolant light that comes on at start-up. • Shift boot squeaking can be silenced by installing a new shift boot assembly. • Accessory drive squeaks can be corrected by installing a new idler pulley assembly. **1997–2000**—Repair tips for an inaccurate fuel gauge. **1997–2001**—Sound system speakers make the door panel rattle or buzz. **1998**—Tips on correcting a faulty rear window defogger. **1998–2000**—An inoperative or noisy window motor can be corrected by replacing the window regulator and motor assembly. **1999**—Rattling from the left fuel tank area can be silenced by installing a fuel tank foam insulator pad. **1999–2000**—An engine that runs hot or loses coolant may simply need a new radiator cap or polishing of the radiator filler neck. **1999–2001**—Wind noise around the B-pillar. **2000**—Reducing exhaust boom. • Repair tips on fixing an inoperative or erratically operating antenna. • Left headlamp door may not remain closed. **2001**—Incomplete brake pedal return can be fixed by replacing the vacuum brake booster.

Corvette Profile

	1994	1995	1996	1997	1998	1999	2000	2001
Cost Price ($)								
Base	43,398	47,580	48,080	48,895	50,430	53,870	60,050	61,400
Convertible	50,498	55,020	56,335	—	58,430	60,850	66,965	68,315
ZR-1	80,798	86,765	—	—	—	—	—	—
Used Values ($)								
Base Λ	18,000	21,500	24,500	34,000	40,000	45,000	50,000	55,000
Base V	16,000	18,000	21,500	31,000	36,000	41,000	46,000	52,000
Convertible Λ	21,000	23,500	27,000	—	44,000	49,000	53,000	60,000
Convertible V	19,000	20,500	24,000	—	41,000	45,000	50,000	55,000
ZR-1 Λ	23,000	26,000	—	—	—	—	—	—
ZR-1 V	21,000	24,000	—	—	—	—	—	—
Extended Warranty	Y	Y	Y	Y	Y	Y	Y	Y
Secret Warranty	Y	Y	Y	Y	Y	Y	V	N

Reliability	❷	③	③	③	③	③	③	③
Head Restraints (F)	—	❷	—	—	—	③	—	③
Rear	—	—	—	—	—	—	—	❷

Note: The Corvette hasn't been crash-tested.

Honda

PRELUDE ★★★★★

RATING: Recommended (1993–2001); Above Average (1985–92). These are reliable used sporty cars that cost far too much; cheaper, almost as reliable makes should be checked out first. **Maintenance/Repair costs:** Average. Repairs aren't dealer dependent. To avoid costly engine repairs, check the engine timing belt every 2 years/40,000 km and replace it every 96,000 km ($300). **Parts:** Higher-than-average cost, but independent suppliers sell parts for much less. **Best alternatives:** Ford Mustang and Probe, GM Camaro and Firebird, Mazda Miata, or Toyota Celica.

Strengths and weaknesses: Unimpressive as a high-performance sports car, the Prelude instead delivers a stylish exterior, legendary reliability, and excellent resale value.

The 1978–87 first-generation Preludes were described as luxury sporty cars, but didn't offer much of either. They should be inspected carefully for engine problems and severe underbody corrosion, particularly near the fuel tank. They're also prone to extensive rusting around wheel openings, door bottoms, the trunk lid, fenders, rear taillights, bumper supports, chassis members, and suspension components. Noisy front brakes, premature disc warpage, high oil consumption, and worn engine crankshaft/camshaft lobes are the main problem areas with these models.

The 1988–91 models offer more and smoother engine power, excellent handling, and improved reliability. There are some generic complaints that continue to crop up, including rapid front brake wear, scored and warped front brake rotors, automatic transmission failures, defective constant velocity joints, premature exhaust system rust-out, and a warping hood.

The 1992–96 models are shorter, wider, and heavier. They're not very fast. The four-wheel steering found on the 1992 4WS version is more gimmick than anything else. It was dropped after 1994. The automatic transmission is smoother, although it still saps some of the Prelude's power. Both the rear seating and tiny trunk are inadequate for most people. You can expect fewer but all-too-familiar glitches, including engine oil leaks (covered by a secret warranty), minor electrical problems, body and accessory defects, brake squealing, and prematurely warped front brake rotors. Most independent mechanics can now service these cars because Preludes haven't changed that much over the years.

1997–2001

The year for big Prelude changes was 1997, while 1998–2001 models just coasted along with minor improvements. The '97 was re-styled, re-powered, and given handling upgrades that make it a better performing, more comfortably riding sports coupe. It got an additional five horses for the base 2.2L VTEC engine, a new Automatic Torque Transfer System (ATTS), an upgraded suspension, and standard ABS, air conditioning, 16-inch wheels, and a CD player with six speakers. The Sequential SportShift automatic transmission (a variation of the one used in the NSX) equips the base Prelude. Overall, the car is roomier (the extended wheelbase gives added stability and provides more room in the rear seating area), has a more solid body structure, and includes a totally redesigned, user-friendly dash with analogue gauges.

On these more recent models, owners report that the engine tends to leak oil and air conditioner condensers frequently fail after a few years and often need cleaning to eliminate disagreeable odours. Other problems include minor electrical glitches, brake squealing, and prematurely warped front brake rotors. A host of new technical features adds to the Prelude's complexity and guarantees that you'll never stray far from the dealer's service bay. In fact, most corner mechanics are poorly equipped to service these cars, and the Automatic Torque Transfer System (ATTS) won't make their job any easier.

Safety summary: All models: 1999—Sudden tire tread separation. • Power-steering loss; steering failure after steering pump replaced. • Airbags failed to deploy upon impact. • Engine loses power in cold weather or at cruising speeds. **2000**—Poor throttle response on hot days with AC engaged while passing through the lower gears. • Airbag deployed three seconds after collision. • Premature failure of Fifth gear. • Excessive carbon buildup leads to chronic stalling. **2001**—Sudden brake failure caused collision.

Secret Warranties/Service Tips/TSBs

All models/years: Steering wheel shimmy can be reduced by rebalancing the wheel/tire/hub/rotor assembly in the front end. • Seatbelts that fail to function properly during normal use will be replaced for free under Honda's lifetime seatbelt warranty. • Honda will also repair or replace defective steering assemblies, constant velocity joints, and catalytic converters free of charge up to 5 years/80,000 km on a case-by-case basis. • Honda TSBs allow for special warranty consideration on a "goodwill" basis for most problems even after the warranty has expired or the car has changed hands. **All models: 1992–97**—You may have to change the Fifth gear shift fork if the transmission grinds when going into Fifth gear. **1994–96**—Silence rear headliner rattling by applying EPT sealer 5T to the rear headliner where it contacts the wiring harness. **1994–97**—Engine oil leaks will be fixed for free under a Honda "goodwill" program. **1997**—A squeaking seat may need a new seat pivot bushing. **1997–98**—Power window clunking can be stopped by changing the motor. **1997–99**—A rear suspension clunk can be fixed by replacing the coil springs under Honda's "goodwill" policies. • Doors that are hard to open from the inside may simply require a new inner door handle rod (a "goodwill" repair). • A rattling moon roof may need new guide rails and a re-adjustment of the glass brackets ("goodwill"). • A trunk clunking noise may be silenced by replacing the trunk spring clip. **1997–2000**—Deformed upper windshield mouldings are addressed in TSB #00-064. **1997–2001**—Rear suspension clunks may be silenced by replacing the upper collars in both rear damper assemblies. **1998–2000**—Corrective measures to apply to a warped or deformed windshield moulding. **1999–2000**—Try replacing the power-steering pump bearing and seals to silence a noisy power-steering pump.

Prelude Profile

	1994	1995	1996	1997	1998	1999	2000	2001
Cost Price ($)								
Base/SR	21,895	26,995	27,395	27,300	27,600	27,800	27,900	28,300
VTEC	28,295	29,695	29,995	—	—	—	—	—
Used Values ($)								
Base/SR ▲	8,500	10,000	11,500	14,000	17,000	19,500	21,500	24,000
Base/SR ▼	7,000	8,500	10,000	12,500	15,500	17,500	19,500	22,000
VTEC ▲	9,500	10,500	12,500	—	—	—	—	—
VTEC ▼	8,500	9,500	11,000	—	—	—	—	—
Extended Warranty	N	N	N	N	N	N	N	N
Secret Warranty	Y	Y	Y	Y	Y	Y	Y	Y
Reliability	⑤	⑤	⑤	⑤	⑤	⑤	⑤	⑤
Head Restraints	—	❷	—	❷	—	❷	—	❷

Note: The Prelude hasn't been crash-tested.

Hyundai

TIBURON ★★★★★

RATING: Recommended (2000–01); Above Average (1997–99). A high-performance Elantra. Keep in mind that for about $1,000–$1,500 more you can get the better-performing FX model. **Maintenance/Repair costs:** Higher than average, although most repairs can be done by any independent garage. **Parts:** Average cost and good availability. **Best alternatives:** Ford Mustang and Probe, GM Camaro and Firebird, Mazda Miata, Nissan 200SX, or Toyota Celica.

Strengths and weaknesses: This is a fun-to-drive, budget sport coupe that's based on the Elantra sedan. Although it's too early to have a definitive opinion, overall reliability looks promising. On early models, the base 16-valve 1.8L 4-cylinder engine is smooth, efficient, and adequate when mated to the 5-speed manual transmission. Put in an automatic transmission and performance heads south, and engine noise increases proportionally. Overall handling is crisp and predictable, due mainly to the Tiburon's long wheelbase and sophisticated suspension.

Since its debut as a '97 model, the Tiburon has changed little. The '97 FX got the more sprightly 2.0L engine along with optional ABS. Standard brakes are adequate though sometimes difficult to modulate. As with most sporty cars, interior room is cramped for average-sized occupants. Tall drivers, especially, might find rearward seat travel insufficient, making head room a bit tight. The 145-hp 2.0L engine became a standard feature with the '98 versions. '99 models were carried over unchanged; however, the year 2000 Tiburon got four-wheel disc brakes and a re-styled interior and exterior. The following year's model got redesigned wheels and a rear spoiler.

Although no serious defects have been reported, be on the lookout for body deficiencies (fit, finish, and assembly), harsh shifting, slipping with the automatic transmission, oil leaks, minor brake glitches, and seatbelt twisting and jamming in its housing.

Safety summary: All models: 1999—Brake failure on wet pavement. • Car jolts when accelerating. • Transmission slippage. • Tires won't hold air. • Original equipment jack won't support vehicle. • Seatbelt webbing jams in retractor. **2000**—No airbag deployment or inadvertent airbag deployment. • Sudden acceleration caused by faulty cruise control. • Shoulder belt twists and jams at door post and is hard to latch. • Premature wheel bearing failure. • Headlight illumination is inadequate with low beams; hard to adjust. • Headlights and tires fail prematurely. **2001**—No airbag deployment. • Seatback failure from rear-end collision. • Seatbelts are hard to latch.

Secret Warranties/Service Tips/TSBs

All models/years: Hyundai has a new brake pad kit (#58101-28A00) that the company says will eliminate squeaks and squeals during light brake application. • Hyundai suggests that you replace the oil pump assembly if the engine rpm increases as the automatic transmission engages abruptly during a cold start. • Harsh automatic transmission shifting, no Fourth gear engagement, and a lit MIL light may all point to the need for a new automatic transaxle oil temperature sensor or transaxle solenoid. **All models: 1997**—A tip on eliminating clutch pedal squeaking is offered. • Tips on eliminating clutch drag. **1997–98**—DOHC timing chain noise can be stopped by installing an upgraded timing chain. • Park–Reverse or Park–Drive harsh shifting may require an upgraded TCM. **1997–99**—Poor automatic transmission performance is addressed in TSB #97-40-031. • Automatic transmission drain hole oil leak and fluid leak behind the torque converter. • Delayed engagement into Drive or Reverse is addressed in TSB #99-40-006. **1997–2001**—Correction for an erratic-shifting or slipping automatic transmission that often sticks in Third gear. **1999**—Tips on dealing with a hard-to-fill fuel tank. **1999–2000**—Timing belt noise may be caused by the belt rubbing against the front dust cover.

Tiburon Profile

	1997	1998	1999	2000	2001
Cost Price ($)					
Base	16,996	17,895	17,895	18,995	19,195
FX/SE	18,895	19,895	19,895	21,295	21,495
Used Values ($)					
Base ⋀	7,500	9,000	10,500	12,000	14,000
Base ⋁	6,500	7,500	9,000	10,500	12,500
FX/SE ⋀	8,000	10,000	12,000	13,500	15,500
FX/SE ⋁	6,500	8,500	10,500	12,500	14,500
Extended Warranty	N	N	N	N	N
Secret Warranty	Y	Y	Y	N	N
Reliability	④	④	⑤	⑤	⑤
Head Restraints (F)	❶	—	❷	—	③
Rear	—	—	❶	—	—

Note: Tiburon has not been crash-tested by NHTSA; Elantra scores should be indicative of what the Tiburon would do.

Mazda

MIATA   ★★★★★

RATING: Recommended (1996–2001); Above Average (1990–95). There was no 1998 model. An almost-perfect sports car, except for its poor braking performance on rain-slicked roadways. **Maintenance/Repair costs:** Higher than average, and dealer dependent. **Parts:** Higher-than-average cost, with limited availability. **Best alternatives:** Ford Mustang and Probe, GM Camaro and Firebird, Hyundai Tiburon, Nissan 200SX, or Toyota Celica.

Strengths and weaknesses: The base 1.6L engine delivers adequate power and accelerates smoothly. Acceleration from 0 to 100 km/h is in the high 8-second range. The 5-speed manual transmission shifts easily and has well-spaced gears. The vehicle's lightness and 50/50 weight distribution make this an easy car to toss around corners, but it's quite jittery on uneven roads.

The Miata changed very little during 1995–1998. '99 models received some handling upgrades and additional standard features; year 2000 Miatas returned unchanged; and the 2001s were given a slight horsepower boost, a re-styled interior and exterior, 15-inch wheels, seatbelt pretensioners, improved ABS, and an emergency trunk release.

Owners' top performance gripes target the same characteristics that make other sports car enthusiasts swoon: inadequate cargo space, cramped interior for large adults, excessive interior noise, and limited low-end torque, which makes for frequent shifting.

Owners also say it's important to change the engine timing chain every 100,000 km. Other reported problems: crankshaft failures, leaky rear end seals and valve cover gaskets, rear differential seal failure, a leaking or squeaky clutch, hard starts and stalling, torn drive boots, transmission whining in upper gear ranges, engine and exhaust system rattles, electrical system glitches, brake pulsation, valvetrain clatter on start-up (changing oil may help), prematurely worn-out shock absorbers and catalytic converter, the softtop cover comes off or breaks, and minor body and trim deficiencies.

Safety summary: All models/years: Used Miatas will likely have some collision damage. **All models: 1995**—NHTSA is probing inadvertent airbag deployment. • An unusually large number of reports that the airbag deployed for no reason, causing severe injuries. In one instance, a bolt in the convertible roof hinge assembly impaled the driver's skull when the airbag deployed. • Airbag failed to deploy. • Fire ignited in the engine compartment wiring. • Small triangular window exploded while driving. **1995–97**—Engine and horn failures. • Roof leaks. • Accelerator pedal cut a slit in the carpet, allowing the gas pedal to jam. **1997**—Airbag failed to deploy. • Convertible hard top flew off. • Cell phone usage caused battery failure. • Gas tank expansion puts too much stress on the metal. **1999**—Airbags failed to deploy upon impact. • While passing another car on the highway, accelerator cable and the cable adjuster assembly disengaged from the horseshoe bracket that holds the cable. • Transmission suddenly failed, causing both rear wheels to seize. • Keizer aluminum wheel cracked, damaging brake caliper, rotor, and fender. • Car stalls whenever the clutch is released. • Miata performs poorly on wet roads. • At highway speeds, vehicle tends to wander all over the roadway. • Premature wearout of Yokohama tires. **2000**—In heavy rain, stepping on the brakes results in a 2-second delay before braking; must continually pump the brakes. • Airbags deployed two minutes after collision. • Convertible top latches may inadvertently open while vehicle is underway. • Hard shifting and stiff shifter at Neutral causes gear "hunting," grinding, and rattling. • Gas pump shuts off before tank is filled. **2001**—Vehicle rolled down hill despite being parked with emergency brake engaged.

Secret Warranties/Service Tips/TSBs

All models/years: TSB #006/94 gives all of the possible causes and remedies for brake vibration. • TSB #N00198 addresses complaints that the steering wheel is off-centre. • Other bulletins address the issue of musty AC odours. • Coated evaporator core (#NA0J 61II0A). **All models: 1990–95**—Dirt and debris can clog up side sill drain holes, allowing water to collect and corrosion to occur; drill larger drain holes. **1990–99**—Paint damage caused by the trunk rubber cushions will be repaired under the base warranty. Ask for pro-rata compensation if the warranty has expired. **1992–94**—If the window won't open fully, install a new cable fastener. **1994**—Timing belt noise can be silenced by replacing the tensioner pulley with an upgraded part. **1996**—Softtop water leakage may require a new softtop link assembly. **1996–97**—An inoperative AC may need a new power-steering pressure switch; believe it or not, they are related. • Tips for troubleshooting power window glitches. **1999**—A hard-to-start engine may have debris accumulated at the fuel pressure regulator valve area, causing the valve to stick open. • Engine rattling may be caused by premature wear of the engine thrust bearing or the engine harness clips rubbing against the car's frame. • Muffler rattling may be silenced by installing an upgraded unit, under warranty. **1999–2000**—Additional tips on reducing AC odours.

Miata Profile

	1993	1994	1995	1996	1997	1999	2000	2001
Cost Price ($)								
Base	18,895	20,165	21,820	24,210	24,695	26,025	26,995	27,605
Used Values ($)								
Base ▲	6,500	8,500	10,500	11,500	13,500	16,500	18,500	21,500
Base ▼	6,000	7,000	9,000	10,000	12,000	14,500	16,500	19,500
Extended Warranty	N	N	N	N	N	N	N	N
Secret Warranty	N	N	N	N	N	N	N	N
Reliability	④	④	④	⑤	⑤	⑤	⑤	⑤
Crash Safety	—	—	④	④	—	—	—	④
Side Impact	—	—	—	—	—	—	—	③
Head Restraints (F)	—	❶	—	❶	—	❶	—	③
Rear	—	—	—	—	—	—	—	❷

MX-3, PRECIDIA ★★★★★

RATING: Recommended (1994–96); Above Average (1992–93). **Maintenance/Repair costs:** Higher than average, and most repairs have to be done by a Mazda dealer. **Parts:** Higher-than-average cost, with limited availability. **Best alternatives:** Ford Mustang and Probe, GM Camaro and Firebird, Hyundai Tiburon, Nissan 200SX, or Toyota Celica.

Strengths and weaknesses: The base 1.6L engine supplies plenty of power for most driving situations. When equipped with the optional 1.8L V6 powerplant (the smallest V6 on the market at the time) and high-performance options, the MX-3 (also known as the Precidia in the U.S.) transforms itself into a 130-hp pocket rocket. In fact, the MX-3 GS sports coupe easily outperforms the 4-cylinder Honda del Sol, Toyota Paseo, and Geo Storm for comfort and high-performance thrills. It does fall a bit short of the Saturn SC due to its limited low-end torque, and fuel economy is disappointing. Reverse gear is sometimes hard to engage.

Brake and wheel bearing problems are commonplace. Most of the MX-3's parts are used on other Mazda cars, so their overall reliability should be outstanding.

Body assembly is average and rattles/squeaks are common. Owners have complained of paint defects and sheet metal that's too thin above the door handles (dents in the metal appear where you would ordinarily place your thumb when closing the door). Some owners report wind and water leaks around the doors and windows. Moderate engine noise increases dramatically above 100 km/h.

Safety summary: All models/years: Airbags fail to deploy. **All models: 1994**—Throttle stuck in open position. • Driver burned from airbag deployment. • Cracked coil springs caused tire to blow and front end to collapse. • Excessive brake fade. • Broken tie-rod end. • If there's a low level of fuel in tank, vehicle shuts off when cornering. • Hood suddenly unlatched and smashed the windshield. • Window falls off its track and has to be pulled up by hand. **1995**—Brakes lock up in the rain. • Interior and exterior lights dim when brakes are applied.

Secret Warranties/Service Tips/TSBs

All models/years: TSB #006/94 gives all of the possible causes and remedies for brake vibrations. **All models: 1992–94**—Freezing door and hatch lock cylinders are addressed in TSB #021/94. • Clutch squealing can be silenced by installing an upgraded part with a thicker clutch cushioning plate. **1992–95**—A hard-to-operate automatic transmission selector lever may need a new modified manual shaft. • A popping noise from the front brakes may indicate a warped rotor and/or brake caliper main sleeve wear. **1992–96**—Wind noise around the door is addressed in TSB #S0901898. **1994**—Timing belt noise can be silenced by replacing the tensioner pulley with an upgraded part.

MX-3, Precidia Profile

	1992	1993	1994	1995	1996
Cost Price ($)					
Base	13,725	13,995	15,175	16,070	16,580
GS	16,725	17,065	17,495	18,505	19,240
Used Values ($)					
Base Λ	3,000	3,500	4,500	5,500	6,500
Base V	2,500	3,000	3,500	4,500	5,500
GS Λ	4,000	4,500	5,500	6,500	7,500
GS V	3,500	4,000	4,500	5,500	7,000
Extended Warranty	N	N	N	N	N
Secret Warranty	N	N	N	N	N
Reliability	③	③	④	⑤	⑤
Crash Safety	③	③	—	—	—

Nissan

200SX   ★★★★

RATING: Above Average (1995–98), if you're not a real high-performance enthusiast. The '98 SE-R offered standard AC and ABS in addition to its peppy 140-hp 2.0L engine. **Maintenance/Repair costs:** Average, and most repairs can be done by any garage. **Parts:** Reasonably priced, but hard to find. **Best alternatives:** Ford Mustang and Probe, GM Camaro and Firebird, Hyundai Tiburon, Mazda Miata, or Toyota Celica.

Strengths and weaknesses: Nissan calls this front-drive compact its sporty coupe class leader, but the 200SX is merely a Chrysler Neon fighter that has a sports-car flair without the substance. The interior is unnecessarily cramped, and you get only average power and handling with the base powerplant. Later models are much sportier and have more passenger room. Prices are reasonable, though, and the repair history for these cars is average.

All engines have performed reasonably well, although the SE-R's 2.0L has been the most suitable for hard-driving thrills. The clutch and clutch cable, axle seal assembly, and AC pressure hose connector have been the source of some complaints, along with occasional electrical malfunctions. Rapid front brake wear and rotor damage are common problems. Body construction is much better than average.

Safety summary: All models: 1996—Inadvertent airbag deployment. • Dual airbags failed to deploy. • Airbag indicator and Check Engine lights come on intermittently for no reason. • Shoulder seatbelt retractors lock up whenever occupant makes the slightest movement. • Clutch makes grinding, chattering noise when fully depressed. • When the weather turns cold, the emergency brake freezes and won't release. • Faulty sunroof. **1997**—Inadvertent airbag deployment. • Hit curb, airbag deployed, two fingers broken. • Cruise control wouldn't disengage when the brakes were applied. • Airbag warning light comes on constantly. • Brake warning light comes on when brakes are wet. **1998**—Airbag failed to deploy upon impact. • Engine fire. • When you hit the brakes, you will hit the gas pedal at the same time if your foot isn't square on the brake pedal. • Vehicle veers to the left when accelerating.

Secret Warranties/Service Tips/TSBs

All models/years: TSB #006/94 gives all of the possible causes and remedies for brake vibration. • 1994 and earlier models equipped with RE4RO1A transmissions may experience repeated planetary failure due to poor cooler flow in the fin-type cooler. Apparently, cooler line flushing machines can't flush clear this type of cooler. In the past, the entire radiator would need to be replaced to upgrade the cooling system. Nissan has a spiral cooler replacement kit (#21606-15V25) that can be used instead. **All models: 1995**—AC system shuts off. • AC compressor leakage. • Brake noise. • Cold-weather starting tips. • C-pillar finisher lifting. • Engine cranks but won't start. • Front window misalignment. • Fuel gauge not indicating full tank. • Horn activates randomly. • Squeak and rattle troubleshooting tips. • Wind noise field fix procedure. **1995–98**—Tips for curing interior squeaks and rattles. • Guide to fixing shoulder belts that retract slowly. • Diagnostic help and repair procedures for an engine that won't start or is hard to start. • A self-activating horn will likely need a new horn spring and spring insulators.

200SX Profile

	1995	1996	1997	1998
Cost Price ($)				
Base	14,590	15,598	16,128	17,998
SE-R	18,191	20,698	21,228	22,998
Used Values ($)				
Base Λ	5,000	6,500	8,000	10,500
Base V	4,000	5,000	6,500	9,000
SE-R Λ	6,500	8,000	10,000	13,000
SE-R V	5,000	7,000	8,500	11,000
Extended Warranty	N	N	N	N
Secret Warranty	N	N	N	N
Reliability	⑤	⑤	⑤	⑤
Crash Safety	—	—	⑤	—

240SX   ★★★★★

RATING: Recommended (1995–98); Above Average (1989–94). Only the convertible version was carried over in 1994. **Maintenance/Repair costs:** Average. Most repairs can be done by any garage. **Parts:** Reasonably priced and easy to find. **Best alternatives:** Ford Mustang and Probe, GM Camaro and Firebird, Hyundai Tiburon, Nissan 200SX, or Toyota Celica.

Strengths and weaknesses: Although this rear-drive sport coupe carried a 2.4L 4-cylinder engine to differentiate it from its 2.0L weaker cousin, the 200SX, it still falls far short of producing high-performance thrills. Its 140-hp base engine provides more than enough torque to handle most driving needs—just don't expect fast acceleration times or a comfortable ride. Handling is impressive, though, thanks to the car's independent suspension. The redesigned 1995 coupe features a longer wheelbase, 15 additional horses, and optional ABS/traction control. It still provides a harsh ride and poor traction on slippery roadways. Head room remains limited, cargo space is practically nil, and the trunk is barely large enough to carry your lunch—as long as you eat light and can fit it through the small opening.

'97 models got extensive exterior re-styling, while 1998 models were carried over practically unchanged.

This car doesn't have any serious shortcomings, apart from a cramped interior and excessive engine noise. The few deficiencies reported concern electrical malfunctions, early AC burnout, premature clutch wear, noisy brakes that wear out quickly, early exhaust system rust-out, and fit and finish deficiencies.

Safety summary: All models: 1996—ABS brake failure; pedal went to the floor and brakes failed to stop the vehicle. **1997**—When making a left turn into a driveway, both airbags deployed for no reason. **1998**—Brakes lock up when applied.

Secret Warranties/Service Tips/TSBs

All models/years: TSB #006/94 gives all of the possible causes and remedies for brake vibration. • Engine overheating and poor driveability (Code 45). • AC compressor leaks or is noisy. • Excessive brake noise. • Some windshield cracks are covered under warranty. **All models: 1995–98**—Tips for curing interior squeaks and rattles. • Guide to fixing shoulder belts that retract slowly. • Diagnostic help and repair procedures for an engine that won't start or is hard to start. • Extended-life front brake pads. • A self-activating horn will likely need a new horn spring and spring insulators.

240SX Profile

	1991	1992	1993	1995	1996	1997	1998
Cost Price ($)							
Base	17,890	22,090	22,890	26,990	25,598	26,398	26,698
Used Values ($)							
Base Λ	3,500	4,500	5,500	8,500	10,000	11,000	13,000
Base V	3,000	4,000	4,500	7,000	8,000	9,000	11,000
Extended Warranty	N	N	N	N	N	N	N
Secret Warranty	N	N	N	N	N	N	N
Reliability	③	③	③	④	④	④	⑤
Crash Safety	⑤	⑤	⑤	—	③	③	③

Note: A high-priced convertible was the only '94 model available.

Toyota

CELICA   ★★★★★

RATING: Recommended (1995–2001); Above Average (1986–94). The 1996 and 1997 models are practically identical; choose the cheaper version. With its upgrades, the 2000 model is also a very good deal. Keep in mind that the 1989–96 GTS is far superior to the GT, with its 135-hp DOHC 2.0L engine, firmer suspension, better-equipped interior, ABS, and a more sporting feel. All handle competently and provide the kind of sporting performance expected from a car of this class. The extra performance in the higher-line versions does come at a price, but this isn't a problem, given the high resale value and excellent reliability for which

Celicas are known. Few safety-related complaints or recalls. **Maintenance/Repair costs:** Average, and most repairs can be done at any garage. **Parts:** Reasonably priced and easy to find. **Best alternatives:** Ford Mustang and Probe, GM Camaro and Firebird, Hyundai Tiburon, or Nissan 200SX.

Strengths and weaknesses: The pre-1986 Celicas weren't very sporty. Their excessive weight and soft suspension compromised handling and added a high fuel penalty. With the 1986 make-over, Celicas gained more power and much better handling—especially in the GT and GTS versions—but the GT is still more show than go, with limited rear passenger room.

Redesigned 1994 models are full of both show and go, with more aero-dynamic styling, an enhanced 1.8L that gives more pickup than the ST's 1.6L, and better fuel economy. Among the upgraded models available, smart buyers should choose a used 1994 ST for its more reasonable price, smooth performance, quiet running, and high fuel economy.

Owner gripes target the excessive engine noise, limited rear seat room, and inadequate cargo space. Pre-1994 models get the most complaints regarding brakes, electrical problems, AC malfunctions, and premature exhaust wearout. The 1994 models may have a manual transmission that slips out of Second gear, as well as hard starts caused by a faulty air flow meter (#22250-74200). Areas vulnerable to early rusting include rear wheel openings, suspension components, the area surrounding the fuel-filler cap, door bottoms, and trunk or hatchback lids.

1995-2001
A GT convertible joined the lineup for the '95 model year; everything else was carried over practically unchanged. '96s got extra sound insula-tion and add-on skirts for a sportier appearance; '97s were mostly unchanged, except for the GT's five extra horses and the notchback GT getting axed. The 1998 Celica lineup dropped the ST and gave more standard features to the GT. In the '99 model year, the GT Sport Coupe was dropped. The re-styled 2000 Celica was redesigned with the accent on high performance. It has crisper handling, a new 180-hp engine, and a 6-speed gearbox (GT-S). The 2001 returned unchanged.

All late-model Celicas offer exceptional reliability and durability, with the only exception being engine sludging and brake vibration/pulsation. Servicing and repair are straightforward, and parts are easily found. The front-drive series performs very well and hasn't presented any major problems to owners. Prices are high for Celicas in good condition, but some bargains are available with the base ST model.

Some common problems over the years include engine failure caused by engine oil sludge (1997–2001 models), a problem covered by Toyota "goodwill" (see Sienna); brake pulsation and pulling to one side; rear defroster terminals breaking on convertibles; sunroof leaks; erratic CD changer performance; and smelly AC emissions.

Safety summary: All models/years: Even if your vehicle has 4X4 capability, it's imperative that snow tires be fitted in order to avoid dangerous control problems on snow and ice. **All models: 1996**—Sudden brake failure. • Broken brake caliper bolt. • Clogged-up idle control valve makes for hard starts. **1997**—Convertible rear window glass shattered as top was lowered. • Headlights and instrument lights dim when brakes are applied.

Secret Warranties/Service Tips/TSBs

All models/years: Older Toyotas with stalling problems should have the engine checked for excessive carbon buildup on the valves before any more extensive repairs are authorized. Oil sludging can be prevented by cleaning the throttle body, unplugging the PCU hose, plugging the hole in the throttle body, and then putting a crankcase vent (such as KEN) on the end of the hose. • Owner feedback and dealer service managers (who wish to remain anonymous) confirm the existence of Toyota's secret warranty that will pay for replacing front disc brake components that wear out before 2 years/40,000 km. • The decade-old problem of brake pulsation/vibration is fully outlined and corrective measures are detailed in TSB #BR94-002, issued February 7, 1994. • To reduce front brake squeaks on ABS-equipped vehicles, ask the dealer to install new, upgraded rotors (#43517-32020). **All models: 1990–2000**—Toyota has put out a special grease to minimize brake clicking. **1994–96**—Rear brake squeaks can be silenced by installing countermeasure rear brake pads. **1995–97**—Convertible top chafing may require a new convertible top, covered by the base warranty. If that warranty has expired, ask for partial "goodwill" compensation. **2000**—Loose outer door handle. • Sunshade improvements. • Cruise control shock can be attenuated by replacing the ECU. • Squeak and rattle service tips.

Celica Profile

	1994	1995	1996	1997	1998	1999	2000	2001
Cost Price ($)								
Base	21,438	23,878	27,968	28,528	34,138	34,475	23,980	24,140
Used Values ($)								
Base Λ	8,000	9,500	13,500	15,500	18,500	22,500	18,500	21,000
Base V	7,000	8,000	11,500	14,500	16,500	20,000	16,500	19,000
Extended Warranty	N	N	N	N	N	N	N	N
Secret Warranty	N	N	Y	Y	Y	Y	Y	Y
Reliability	④	④	④	⑤	⑤	⑤	⑤	⑤
Crash Safety	—	—	—	—	—	—	—	④
Side Impact	—	—	—	—	—	—	—	③
Head Restraints (F)	—	❶	—	❷	—	③	—	⑤
Rear	—	—	—	—	—	❷	—	—

MINIVANS

From "flower power" to horsepower

Volkswagen, not Chrysler, was the first automaker to mass produce a minivan for the North American market. Its design, used since the 1950s, morphed into the EuroVan in the early '90s, and is now scheduled to be dropped during the 2002 model year. Used mostly as a camper or a cheap commuter to Grateful Dead concerts, VW's minivan suffered from decades-old styling, poor dealer support, insufficient heating, glacial acceleration, and a reputation for being reliably unreliable. Warranty protection was as elusive as finding a competent VW mechanic.

VW's Camper minivan: all the comforts of home during those long roadside waits for Helmut and Franz to come along with a tow truck.

Chrysler succeeded where VW failed when it launched the modern minivan concept with its 1984 Caravan and Voyager. Although poorly assembled and riddled with deficiencies affecting the automatic transmission, brake, AC, body, and paint, the tall, boxy styling was an instant success. Buyers appreciated the reasonable base price, fuel efficiency, car-like manoeuvrability, tons of convenience features, and increased cargo/passenger space. Since the mid-'90s, though, Chrysler minivan sales have waned as buyers look to more versatile and reliable SUVs that don't project a "soccer Mom" cachet.

Enter the Japanese. Granted, the early Toyota and Honda minivans were underpowered and poorly configured for passengers and cargo, yet Nissan's small Axxess minivan did provide the space and reliability most buyers wanted and was an immediate hit. Unfortunately, the Axxess' small volume and high production costs forced Nissan to abandon it in 1995 for the Quest, a co-production with Ford and its Villager minivan.

Honda and Toyota quickly recovered from their first missteps and now offer minivans that provide all the performance, interior space, and convenience features of the Detroit Big Three. But these Asian competitors aren't perfect machines, as a quick perusal of NHTSA-registered safety complaints, service bulletins, and on-line complaint forums will quickly confirm. Both companies have been bedevilled by chronic automatic transmission failures, sliding door failures, catastrophic tire blowouts, and electrical malfunctions. In fact, engine "sludge" buildup in 1997–2000 Siennas, Avalons, and Camrys can cause up to $7,000 in damage.

"Oh, what a feeling!" when you get a $7,000 repair bill for your Sienna's engine sludge buildup and are told it was due to poor maintenance (see *www.minivanreview.com/MiniCans*).

Interestingly, Honda and Toyota's quality woes and high MSRP over the past few years have actually boosted the attractiveness of GM, Nissan, and Mazda minivans—until recently, only mediocre contenders.

Rear-drives brawnier, front-drives less thirsty

If you must buy a minivan, remember that, much like sport-utilities, they usually fall into two categories: upsized cars and downsized trucks. The upsized cars are "people movers." They're mostly front-drives, handle like a car, and get great fuel economy. The Honda Odyssey and Toyota Sienna are the best examples of this kind of minivan. In fact, their road performance and reliability surpass the front- and rear-drive minivans built by Chrysler, Ford, and General Motors.

GM's Astro and Safari and Ford's Aerostar, on the other hand, are downsized trucks. Using rear-drive, 6-cylinder engines, and heavier mechanical components, these minivans handle cargo as well as passengers. On the negative side, fuel economy is no match for the front-drives, and highway handling is also more trucklike. Interestingly, rear-drive GM and Ford minivans are much more reliable performers than the front-drive Ford Windstar or Chrysler minivans.

Rear-drive vans are also better suited for towing trailers in the 3,500–6,500 lb. (1,600–2,950 kg) range. Most automakers say their front-drive minivans can pull up to 3,500 lb. with an optional towing package (often costing almost $1,000 extra), but don't you believe it. Owners report white-knuckle driving and premature powertrain failures caused by the extra load. It just stands to reason that Ford and Chrysler front-drives equipped with engines and transmissions that blow out at 60,000–100,000 km under normal driving conditions are going to meet their demise much earlier under a full load.

Getting more for less

Most minivans are overpriced for what is essentially an upgraded car or downsized truck, and motorists needing a vehicle with large cargo- and passenger-carrying capacity should consider a cheaper GM Vandura or Chevy Van, even if it means sacrificing some fuel economy and convenience features (they can be added by most conversion shops at competitive prices). You just can't beat the excellent forward vision and easy-to-customize interiors that these large vans provide. Furthermore, parts are easily found and are competitively priced due to the large number of independent suppliers.

Please remember that the following minivan ratings may differ somewhat from those in *Lemon-Aid SUVs, Vans, and Trucks 2002* due to the use of more current data and an additional review of the ratings by the author. The VW EuroVan and Camper have also been moved to Appendix II, "Good Buys for a Bad Economy: 'Beaters,' 'Orphans,' and 'Chick Magnets.'"

MINIVAN RATINGS

Recommended
No models are recommended.

Above Average
Ford Villager/Nissan Quest
(1997–2001)
General Motors Astro, Safari
(2001)

General Motors Montana, Silhouette,
Trans Sport, Venture (1997–2001)
Honda Odyssey (1999–2001)
Toyota Sienna (1998–2001)

Average
DaimlerChrysler PT Cruiser (2001)
DaimlerChrysler Caravan, Voyager,
Grand Caravan, Grand Voyager,
Town & Country (2001)
Ford Villager/Nissan Quest
(1995–96)
General Motors Astro, Safari
(1996–2000)

General Motors Lumina, Lumina APV,
Trans Sport (1995–96)
Honda Odyssey (1996–98)
Mazda MPV (1996–98)
Toyota Previa (1991–97)

Below Average

DaimlerChrysler Caravan, Voyager,
   Grand Caravan, Grand Voyager,
   Town & Country (1998–2000)

Ford Windstar (2000–01)
Mazda MPV (1988–95, 2000–01)

Not Recommended

DaimlerChrysler Caravan, Voyager,
   Grand Caravan, Grand Voyager,
   Town & Country (1984–97)
Ford Villager/Nissan
   Quest (1993–94)

Ford Windstar (1995–99)
General Motors Astro, Safari
   (1985–95)
General Motors Lumina, Lumina APV,
   Trans Sport (1990–94)

DaimlerChrysler

CARAVAN, VOYAGER, GRAND CARAVAN, GRAND VOYAGER, TOWN & COUNTRY ★★★

RATING: Average (2001); Below Average (1998–2000); Not
Recommended (1984–97). Not to be bought without an extended warranty, which should be bargained down to about one-third the $1,200
asking price for a 7-year powertrain warranty (the bumper-to-bumper
extended warranty is simply too expensive). Major generic defects make
the 1984–2000 models very risky buys. Chrysler's lineup has been particularly compromised by a history of poor quality control and unreliable
powertrain components (especially since 1991). Strong points: Lots of
innovative convenience features, user-friendly instruments and controls,
driver-side sliding door, and plenty of interior room. Depreciation is
slower than average, but much faster than pickups, SUVs, and Japanese
minivans. Weak points: Poor acceleration with the base engines and
mediocre handling with the extended versions. Both automatic transmissions perform poorly in different ways, but the 3-speed is decidedly
the worst of the two. Headlight illumination is inadequate. Get used to a
cacophony of rattles, squeals, moans, and groans, caused by the vehicle's
poor construction and subpar components. Crashworthiness has
declined as of late. A chintzy 5-year base warranty (Americans get 7-year
protection) is inadequate to deal with serious powertrain, ABS, and body
defects, and is exacerbated by the automaker's hard-nosed attitude in
interpreting its warranty obligations in Canada. **Maintenance/Repair
costs:** Repair costs are average during the warranty period and rise dramatically after the warranty expires. Chrysler says that its 3.3L and 3.8L
engines won't require tune-ups before 160,000 kilometres. Prepare to be

disappointed; many owners have had to tune up their minivans way before then. The ABS control unit is located behind a front wheel, where it's susceptible to contamination by road salt and dirt. **Parts:** Higher-than-average costs, especially for paint, AC, transmission, and ABS components, which are covered under a number of "goodwill" warranty programs and numerous recall campaigns. Independent garages offer cheaper parts, provide longer warranties, and will often give expert testimony when the replaced component is found to be poorly manufactured. **Best alternatives:** Go for the top-rated Honda Odyssey or Toyota Sienna. Other acceptable choices: Ford's Villager, recent GM front-drives or the Astro and Safari, Mazda's MPV, and the discontinued Nissan Axxess and Quest (see Appendix II). Some full-sized GM or Chrysler rear-drive cargo vans, ripe for conversion, might be a more affordable and practical buy if you intend to haul a full passenger load, do some regular heavy hauling, use lots of accessories, or take frequent motoring excursions. Remember, as you increase body length you lose manoeuvrability and fuel economy.

Strengths and weaknesses: Cheap and plentiful, Chrysler's minivans continue to dominate the new- and used-minivan market, though they're quickly losing steam, due to a cooling of the market and better product quality from the Japanese automakers and General Motors. They can carry up to seven passengers in comfort and also ride and handle better than most truck-based minivans. The shorter-wheelbase minivans also offer better rear visibility and good ride quality, and are more nimble and easier to park than truck-based minivans and larger front-drive versions. Cargo hauling capability is more than adequate, with a 1,225–1,600 kg (2,700–3,500 lb.) maximum towing range.

On the downside, these minivans are unreliable, expensive to repair, and pose serious safety risks, due to the chronic electronic, mechanical, and body component failures affecting both the top- and bottom-rung versions. Owners report frightening and bizarre "happenings" that include seatbelts that may strangle children, airbags that explode when the ignition is turned on, stuck doors and hatches that may suddenly open, fuel leakage, and sudden acceleration or stalling on the highway when within radar range of airports or military installations (see following bulletin).

Chrysler's "Radar" Stalling

NO: 18-16-96   GROUP: Vehicle Performance   DATE: May 3, 1996

SUBJECT: Intermittent Driveability Problems When Driving Near Radar

MODELS:

1996 (NS) Town & Country/Caravan/Voyager

SYMPTOM/CONDITION:

Some vehicles may experience intermittent driveability concerns or problems when driven in close proximity to military or air traffic control radar installations.

REPAIR PROCEDURE:

This bulletin involves installing a new "hardened" crankshaft position sensor and/or reprogramming (flashing) the PCM with new software calibrations.

POLICY: Reimbursable within the provisions of the warranty.

TIME ALLOWANCE:

Labor Operation No: 08-19-43-94 0.5 hrs.

FAILURE CODE: FM – Flash Module

A Chrysler official tells me that "driveability problems" is a euphemism for engine stumbling and stalling. CLOG (Chrysler Lemon Owners Group) members tell me this is a common problem.

The sudden acceleration problem can be a harrowing experience, as the following email from Canning, Nova Scotia, relates:

This fall my daughter was driving the family '97 Caravan when the accelerator cable stuck. Having recently received her license, she did not know what to do, other than apply the brakes. For 5 kms she did this through the country and a small town, almost striking several pedestrians and cars, and finally brought the runaway van to a halt against a concrete wall.

The accelerator cables were found to be seriously flawed, which caused the cables to stick inside the tube, making the van a very dangerous, out of control, 80 km/hr projectile.

I have the cables in my possession, but the response from DaimlerChrysler has been astonishing. Quite frankly, they don't want to talk to me, and furthermore, a service rep suggested, after "consulting with an engineer" that it must have been conditions or maintenance that led to the deterioration of the cables.

My service manager, at the dealership where the van is always serviced, said this was not the case. The bottom line is that my daughter came close to seriously hurting herself and others due to a serious mechanical defect. There are many other Caravans like mine on the road. Chrysler is not even interested in looking at the faulty part. The accident bill was just under $5,000, with $450 deductible. The insurance company treats it like the driver's fault...they are not interested in mechanical faults, in fact said if it was that, the insurance would be "voided."

To add insult to injury, my rates are going up for 6 years due to this "accident."

1984–90 models were bad, but at least the engine head gasket, brakes, suspension, and electrical repairs were relatively inexpensive. But that all changed when automatic transmission, ABS, and paint delamination problems became commonplace on 1991–97 models. Since then, complaints have trailed off somewhat—perhaps due to a shorter time on the market and the availability of warranty coverage. Although Chrysler's V6 engines have always performed quite well—far better than the similar 3.0L and 3.8L engines equipping Ford's Taurus, Sable, and Windstar— owners have reported 4-cylinder engine head gasket failures, hard starts, stalling, and serpentine belt failures (causing loss of power steering). Most of Chrysler's 41TE and 42LE automatic transmissions built over the past decade are a nightmare from a reliability and performance standpoint: imagine having to count to three in traffic before Drive or Reverse will engage, or "limping" home on the highway in Second gear at 50 km/h.

Powertrain failures are increasingly found to be caused by defective or poorly calibrated computer modules, rather than the hardware deficiencies seen a decade ago. Nevertheless, some components do have a short lifespan. They include the engine tensioner pulley, 4-cylinder engine head gaskets, motor mounts, oil pan (premature cracking), fuel-injectors, automatic transmission speed sensors, and a differential pin that breaks through the casing.

Other parts that have a high failure rate are the starter motor, steering column assembly (the power-steering pump frequently leaks and tie-rods may suddenly break), front brake discs and pads (the brake pad material crumbles in your hands), front rotors and rear drums, brake master cylinder, suspension components, exhaust system, ball joints, wheel bearings, water pumps, fuel pumps and pump wiring harnesses, radiators, heater cores, and AC units. Factory-installed Goodyear tires frequently fail prematurely at 40,000–65,000 km.

Over the past decade, fit and finish has gotten worse, not better, and Chrysler often expects dealers to repair the factory's mistakes. For example, some of the 1996–2000 models were delivered with wavy roof panels and assorted panel dents, which dealers were asked to repair (see "Secret Warranties/Service Tips/TSBs"). Body hardware and interior trim are fragile and tend to break, warp, or fall off (door handles are an example). Sliding doors are notoriously glitch-ridden.

Sloppy assembly and poor quality components transform these minivans into self-contained orchestras of clicks, clunks, rattles, squeaks, and squeals, with noisy brakes, suspensions, steering assemblies, bench seats, and body panels providing backup. Finish problems can be summed up in three words: paint, paint, paint. The paint will likely discolour or delaminate on horizontal panels (roof and hood) after the third year. Chrysler knows about this problem and often tries to get the owner to pay half the cost of a repainting job (about $1,500 on a $3,000 job), but will eventually agree to pay the total cost if the owner stands fast, threatens small claims court action, cites *Frank vs. GM* (see Part Two), or belongs to a consumer protection group like the Alberta- or Saskatchewan-based CLOG associations (Chrysler Lemon Owners Groups).

These vehicles were redesigned in 1996, with more aerodynamic styling, driver-side sliding door, roll-out centre and rear seats, a longer wheelbase, standard dual airbags and ABS (ABS later became optional on base models), and a more powerful 150-hp 2.4L, 4-cylinder engine. In 1998, Grand models got optional AWD along with four-wheel disc brakes; LE models got optional traction control. The 3.0L V6 engine was paired with a better-performing 4-speed automatic transmission for 1998, and the 3.8L V6 got 14 additional horses. Year 2000 changes included more standard equipment, an AWD Sport model (it was a sales flop), and additional colours. 2001 models got a small horsepower boost for the V6s, front side airbags, adjustable pedals, upgraded headlights, and a power-operated rear liftgate for easier cargo handling.

True, there's an abundance of used Chrysler minivans on the market selling at bargain prices; however, very few have any of their original warranty coverage left, and "goodwill" repair refunds are spotty and guidelines are vague. Don't even consider the 4-cylinder engine—it has no place in a minivan, especially when hooked to the inadequate 3-speed automatic transmission. It lacks an Overdrive and will shift back and forth as speed varies, and it's slower and noisier than the other choices. The 3.3L V6 is a better choice for most city-driving situations, but don't hesitate to get the 3.8L if you're planning lots of highway travel or carrying four or more passengers. Since its introduction, it's been relatively trouble-free, and it's more economical on the highway than the 3.3L, which strains to maintain speed. The sliding side doors make it easy to load and unload children, install a child safety seat in the middle, or remove the rear seat. On the downside, they expose kids to traffic and are a costly, failure-prone option. Child safety seats integrated into the rear seatbacks are convenient and reasonably priced, but Chrysler's versions have had a history of tightening up excessively or not tightening enough, allowing the child to slip out. Try the seat with your child before buying it. You may wish to pass on the tinted windshields; they seriously reduce visibility. Be wary of models featuring all-wheel drive and ABS brakes: the powertrain isn't reliable and is horrendously expensive to repair, and Chrysler's large number of ABS failures is worrisome. Ditch the failure-prone Goodyear original equipment tires and remember that a night drive is a prerequisite to check out headlight illumination, called inadequate by many.

Safety summary: All models/years: Chrysler downplays the safety implications of its minivan safety defects, whether in the case of ABS failures, inadvertent airbag deployments, or sudden transmission break-downs. Chrysler is particularly slow in getting parts to dealers to carry out recall compaigns. For example, in September 2000, the automaker said it would recall minivans built between 1996 and 2000 to install a fuel line clamp to prevent fuel leakage and fire. In January 2002 the parts till hadn't arrived at the dealers. Federal officials said 19 fires had been reported before the recall, and six had been reported since, with 56 injuries linked to the minivans. Chrysler says the first stage of the recall will target 1996 model year minivans, since the frequency of the problem increases with vehicle age. Company spokespersons say they hope to notify all affected owners by March 2002. We're talking about a fuel line clamp here—not rocket science. Seatbelts are another recurring problem: they may become unhooked from the floor anchor, buckles jam or suddenly release, and the child safety seat harness easily pulls out or over-retracts, trapping children. NHTSA has also recorded numerous complaints of airbags failing to deploy in an accident or deploying unexpectedly—when passing over a bump in the road, or simply turning on the vehicle. Owners report that cruise control units often malfunction, accelerating or decelerating the vehicle without any warning, and that sudden stalling and transmission failures also create life-threatening situations. **All models: 1995**—Engine fires. • Thieves love the door lock design. • Broken spare tire suspension cable allows tire to fall away while driving. • Right-side rear door suddenly flies open when vehicle passes over a small bump. • Roof drip rails allow water to leak inside. • Open glove-box back section allows papers to be sucked into the AC blower. • Inoperative horn. **1995–96**—Brake failures, lockup, excessive noise, and premature wear. • Sudden acceleration, stalling. • No steering. • Seatbacks fall backward. • Fuel tank is easily damaged. • Park won't hold vehicle. • Transmission fails, suddenly drops into low gear, won't go into Reverse, delays engagement, or jumps out of gear. • Rear windows fall out or shatter. • Power window and door lock failures. • Sliding door jams, trapping occupants. • Weak headlights. **1996**—3.3L and 3.8L lower engine oil leaks. • Coolant seepage from rear heater hose connections. • Cold-start stumble. • Rough idle, hesitation, or sags after fuel tank is filled (see "Secret Warranties/Service Tips/TSBs"). • Intermittent driveability problem near radar (again, explained more fully in "Secret Warranties/Service Tips/TSBs"). • Intermittent powertrain shudder. • Transmission limp-in caused by a faulty speed sensor. • Reduced limp-in default sensitivity. • Excessive transmission down-shifting/upshifting in cruise control; dealers will install an upgraded overdrive clutch hub. • Difficulty going into Second gear or Reverse after a cold start. • Upshift shuddering. • ABS activates below 16 km/h. • Front wipers activate while driving or will not turn off. • Vehicle drifts or leads at high speeds. • Underbody squeaks, buzzes, and rattles. • Exhaust drone at 2500–2800 rpm. • B-pillar area rattling. • Blower motor whine and AC-related moan/whine. • Power steering produces a clunk or popping noise at highway speeds. • Steering noise during parking lot manoeuvres. • Front door squeak/creak noise. • Ratcheting sound when coming to a stop. • Rear wheel rattle or click noise. • Rattling rear bench seat. • Rear brake noise (see "Secret Warranties/Service Tips/TSBs"). • Integrated child safety seat seatbelt retractor may restrict seatbelt travel; dealer will replace assembly at no charge under Customer Satisfaction Note #650. • Child seat shoulder harness won't pull out. • Discoloured outside rear-view mirrors or cowl grille. • Poor cowl cover fit. • Dust intrusion into rear of vehicle. • False info on fuel tank capacity and inaccurate fuel gauge. • Hard to unlatch rear bench seats. • HVAC control knobs or buttons may stick. • Interior window film buildup. • Intermittent operation of sliding door locks. • Gap between liftgate and rear fascia is too small. • Paint chips at the upper front corner of the sliding doors. • Poor AM radio reception and RAS radio cassette malfunctions. • Faulty power vent windows. • Loose quad seats. • Inoperative sliding door and liftgate power lock motor; the sliding door may be difficult to open from the outside. • Suction-cup marks on door glass. • Unexplained theft alarm activation or dead battery. • Water leaks onto carpet from HVAC housing. • White stress marks on interior trim panel. • Flying hubcaps (see "Secret Warranties/Service Tips/TSBs"). • Broken steering belt tensioner causes the sudden loss of power steering and power brakes. • Wipers self-activate. • Sliding door falls off. • Faulty power door locks. • Cracked axle/drive shaft. • Cruise control drops speed and then surges to former setting. • With AC engaged, vehicle stalls, then surges forward. • Power-steering failure, excessive noise. • Vehicle, parked with gear in Park and with emergency brake applied, rolled into a lake. **1996–97—** Dashboard interior light switch started burning when ignition switch was turned on. • Numerous complaints of 4-cylinder head gasket failures. • When driving through water, air breather intake ingests water and engine seizes. • Sluggish acceleration after cold starts. • Check Engine light comes on for no reason. • Slipping engine serpentine belt causes immediate steering loss. • Transmission hesitates and stumbles at highway speeds. • Constant stalling, often due to failure of the power control module (PCM) and oxygen sensor. • Chronic transmission failures. • Transmission allows vehicle to roll away when in Park. • One can move automatic transmission shift lever without applying brakes. • Several incidents where ignition was turned and vehicle went into Reverse at full throttle, although transmission was set in Park. • PRNDL indicator suddenly goes blank, comes back on only after vehicle restart. • ABS failure caused an accident. • Brakes activated by themselves while driving. • Prematurely warped rotors and worn-out pads cause excessive vibrations when stopping. • Rear drums often need replacing; often the rotors are rusted and pitted. • Steering may suddenly lock up. • Loss of steering control after running through a puddle. • No standard head restraints on the second- and third-row seats. • Seatback collapsed in collision. • Right front door latch failures, and sliding door often opens while vehicle is underway. • Driver- and passenger-side locks failed on sliding doors. • Headlights are too dim. • Distorted windshields and exterior rear-view mirror. • Inadequate windshield defrosting caused by poor design. • Early burnout of the AC compressor clutch. • Inoperative blower motors caused by a defective resistor. • Chronic wiper failure or self-activation. • Frequent battery failures. • Vehicle must be lifted by a straight flat bed or the windows will pop out and the gas tank could blow out. 1997—1–2 shift shudder fix. • Delayed transaxle engagement. • 3.8L engine idle vibration. • Engine sags, hesitates, stumbles, stalls, or is hard to start. • Faulty speed control. • Engine misses or bucks. • Momentary loss of power steering. • Steering system honking or squealing during parking lot manoeuvres. • Rattling sliding door and B-pillar, quad seat latch, and roof rack. • Front-end popping. • Underbody creak or knock. • Thumping noise coming from the rear. • Rear brake cyclic rubbing noise, moaning, or howling. • Power door lock motor noise. • Ticking noise from left B-pillar. • Low-speed tire wobble. • Smooth-road shake, vibration, or wobble. • Loose or detached seatback assist handle. • High effort needed to unlatch rear bench seats. • Poor fit at rear of sliding door. • CV boot grease seepage. • Coolant seepage at rear heater line. • Inoperative radiator fans. • Self-activating front wipers. • Wipers won't park or wipe in intermittent mode. • Inoperative CD player. • AC evaporator odours. • Water leaks onto floor from HVAC housing. 1998— Engine overheating. • Delayed transaxle engagement. • Transmission desensitization. • Intermittent loss of speed control or power-assisted steering. • Sags, hesitation, stumble, hard starts, or stalling. • Snow/water ingestion into rear brake drums. • AC compressor lockup. • Ignition key stuck or won't turn. • Whistling when accelerating. • Exhaust drone. • Steering wheel clicks and rattles. • Quad seat latch, roof rack, and sliding door rattling. • Front-door glass wind noise. • Power door lock motor whirling noise. • Left B-pillar ticking. • Suspension strut bearing squeaks. • Poor radio reception (AM). • Backlight and HVAC housing water leaks. • Smooth road vibration, shake, or wobble. • Low-speed tire wobble. • CV boot grease seepage. • Right rear taillight caught fire. • Slipping engine serpentine belt causes immediate steering loss. • Defective engine head gaskets, rocker arm gaskets, and engine mounts. • Chronic stalling caused by camshaft or oxygen sensor failures. • Surging and hesitation at highway speeds, especially with AC engaged. • Multiple transmission failures. • Vehicle rolled away while parked. • Many reports of vehicle suddenly jumping from Park into Reverse and speeding away. • Transmission fluid leaks due to defective front pump housing oil seal. • Sudden steering or brake loss. In one incident, the steering wheel separated from the steering column. • Frequent replacement of the steering column and rack and pinion. • Front suspension strut failure. • Many reports of defective liftgate gas shocks. • Many incidents reported of electrical short circuits and total electrical system failure. • Water leaks from the passenger-side dash. • Difficult to see through windshield in direct sunlight. • Defroster vent reflects in the windshield, obscuring driver's vision. • Poor steering wheel design blocks the view of instruments and indicators. • Rear-view mirror often falls off. • Door cannot be unlocked with remote entry system. • Horn hard to find on steering hub. • Battery failures. **1999**—Van rolled away while in Park. • Transmission failures. • When put into Reverse, vehicle may accelerate or brakes may lock up. • Headlights aimed too low; not bright enough. • Sliding power door opens when vehicle passes over a bump. • Instrument panel fire. • Sudden, unintended acceleration. • When cruising on the highway, vehicle will suddenly shut down completely; problem also occurs at traffic lights. • Premature engine head gasket and automatic transmission failures. • Faulty speed sensors cause the automatic transmission to shift erratically and harshly. • With cruise control engaged, transmission won't downshift when going uphill. • 5-year-old was able to pull shift lever out of Park into Drive without engaging brakes. • Sudden tie-rod breakage, causing loss of vehicle control. • Chronic steering pump and rack failures. • Poor braking performance; brake pedal depressed to the floor with little or no effect; also excessive vibrations or shuddering when braking. • Rusted-through front brake rotors and rear brake drums. • Original-equipment Goodyear Conquest tires leak air or fail prematurely, with sidewall defects most evident; don't last half of their expected mileage rating. • Sudden Goodyear Conquest blowout and split wheel after passing over a small bump in the road. • Sliding power door opens when vehicle passes over a bump. • Power side windows fail to roll up. • Horn often doesn't work. • Dash gauges all go dead intermittently. • Windshield wiper bumps into other wiper. **2000**—Gas tank rupture. • Engine camshaft failure. • Sudden acceleration as vehicle being parked; no airbag deployed in ensuing collision. • Many incidents where children were able to shift transmission without applying brakes. Although the owner's manual says vehicle should have a transmission/brake interlock, the feature is lacking (see "Secret Warranties/Service Tips/TSBs"). • Excessive transmission noise, fluid leak, and then premature transmission failure. • Cruise control malfunctions. • ABS brake failure. • Frequent premature rotor and pad replacements; brake rotors often found to be out-of-round and pads show signs of heat damage. Both components are usually replaced under a secret warranty. • Parking brake lockup. • Metal-to-metal brake noise when braking. • Sudden blowout, premature wear, and sidewall bulging of Goodyear tires (often replaced under a secret warranty). • Sudden steering lockup. • Steering column replacement. • Two front seatbacks collapsed from rear impact. • In a collision, third rear seat flew forward, injuring children seated on it. • Broken door latch. • Several incidents where side windows exploded for no apparent reason. • Carbon monoxide intrudes into the cabin area. • Front passenger seat metal bar heated by sun radiation may cause leg burns. **2000–01**—Sudden loss of engine power, accompanied by fuel leakage from the engine compartment. • Emergency parking brake may not release, due to premature corrosion. • Right front brake locked up while driving, causing the vehicle to suddenly turn 90 degrees to the right; same phenomenon when braking. • Vehicle pulls to the left or right while driving. • When driving about 60 km/h up an incline, transmission suddenly slips into low gear and the vehicle stops. • Defective clock spring causes airbag light to remain lit. • Transmission shift lever blocks the driver's right knee when braking. • Excessive engine and steering wheel noise. • Carbon monoxide comes through air vents. • Fifth-wheel assembly fell off while vehicle was underway. • Back sliding door popped open while cruising. • Instruments are recessed too deep into the dash, making it hard to read the fuel gauge and speedometer, especially at night.

Secret Warranties/Service Tips/TSBs

All models/years: If pressed, Chrysler will replace the AC evaporator for free up to seven years (see Introdcution). Other AC component costs are negotiable. **All models: 1989–95**—An excellent summary of Chrysler's transmission glitches and corrections covering these seven model years can be found in TSB #18-24-95. **1989–96**—Acceleration shudder that may be accompanied by a whine is likely the result of leakage in the transmission front pump, caused by a worn pump bushing. **1991–95**—TSB #24-05-94 looks at all the causes of, and remedies for, poor heater performance. • If the vehicle tends to drift left, cross-switch the tire and wheel assemblies, readjust the alignment, or reposition the front cross-member. **1993–95**—Delayed automatic transmission engagement may be due to low fluid, a stuck or frozen PRNDL switch, or a transaxle front pump with excessive ground clearance. • Harsh low-speed automatic transmission shifting, accompanied by a fluctuating digital speedometer reading, may be corrected by covering the wiring harness with aluminum wire, which prevents the spark plug wires from sending false signals to the outport speed sensor wiring that connects to the TCM. • Constant upshifting/downshifting on vehicles equipped with cruise control has a variety of causes, as set out in TSB #08-15-95. **1993–2000**—Paint delamination, peeling, or fading (see Part Two). • A rotten-egg odour coming from the exhaust may be the result of a malfunctioning catalytic converter, probably covered under the emissions warranty. **1994–95**—Intake valve deposits are frequently the cause of poor driveability complaints. • Intermittent no-cranks can be corrected by modifying the battery-to-starter-cable terminal insulator at the starter connection. • A front suspension rapping noise heard when going over bumps can be corrected by providing additional clearance between the front coil springs and strut towers. **1996**—Poor engine performance near military installations or airports is caused by radar interference. Correct by installing a "hardened" crankshaft position sensor and/or reprogramming (flashing) the PCM with new software calibrations. • Rear brake noise that occurs at any time can be silenced by replacing the rear brake shoes and rear wheel cylinders. Another possibility is the addition of rear brake shoe springs. • Rough idle, hesitation, or sags after the fuel tank is filled can only be corrected by the installation of a new fuel tank, according to TSB #18-28-95. The repair is covered under warranty and should take about an hour. • Steering noise during parking lot manoeuvres may be fixed by installing a new power-steering gear and left-side attaching bolt. • Chrysler minivan wheel covers tend to take flight (and I thought that was only a Chevy Caprice problem). Chrysler will install upgraded covers under warranty. **1996–99**—A serpentine belt that slips off the idler pulley requires an upgraded bracket. **1996–2000**—Cruise control that won't hold the vehicle's speed when going uphill may have a faulty check valve. • Snow or water ingestion into the rear brake drum calls for the installation of a revised rear drum brake support (backing) plate and the possible replacement of the rear brake shoes and drums under warranty (Failure Code: P8-New Part). • Roof panel wavy or has depressions. • Countermeasures detailed to correct a steering column click or rattle. **1996–2001**—AWD models *must* be equipped with identical tires; otherwise, the power transfer unit may self-destruct. • A suspension squawk or knock probably means the sway bar link needs replacing under Chrysler's "goodwill" policy (5 years/100,000 km).

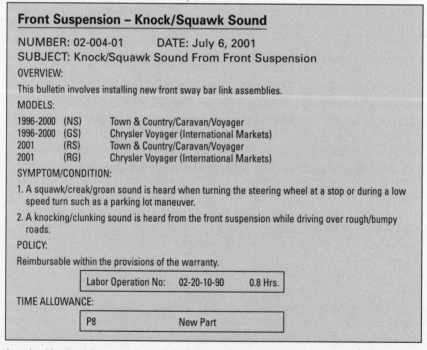

Front Suspension – Knock/Squawk Sound

NUMBER: 02-004-01   DATE: July 6, 2001
SUBJECT: Knock/Squawk Sound From Front Suspension
OVERVIEW:
This bulletin involves installing new front sway bar link assemblies.
MODELS:

1996-2000	(NS)	Town & Country/Caravan/Voyager
1996-2000	(GS)	Chrysler Voyager (International Markets)
2001	(RS)	Town & Country/Caravan/Voyager
2001	(RG)	Chrysler Voyager (International Markets)

SYMPTOM/CONDITION:

1. A squawk/creak/groan sound is heard when turning the steering wheel at a stop or during a low speed turn such as a parking lot maneuver.
2. A knocking/clunking sound is heard from the front suspension while driving over rough/bumpy roads.

POLICY:
Reimbursable within the provisions of the warranty.

Labor Operation No:	02-20-10-90	0.8 Hrs.

TIME ALLOWANCE:

P8	New Part

Anecdotal feedback from owners confirms Chrysler will pay for much of this repair *only* if the dealer backs up your claim.

1997–98—Engines that run poorly or stall may need the PCM reprogrammed under the emissions warranty. 1997–2000—If the ignition key
can't be turned or cannot be removed, TSB #23-23-00 proposes four possible corrections. 1998—A faulty radiator fan relay may cause the engine
to overheat; replace it with a new relay and reprogram the powertrain
control module under Customer Satisfaction Notice #771. 1998–99—
Front brakes continue to wear out quickly on front-drive minivans.
Owners report that Chrysler pays half the cost of brake repairs for up to
2 years/40,000 km. • Silence a chronic squeaking noise coming from
underneath the vehicle by installing a new strut pivot bearing.
1999–2000—Measures to prevent the right side sliding door trim panel
from hitting the quarter panel when the door is opened. • Tips for eliminating radio speaker static. 2000—In Technical Service Bulletin Number:
856, Bulletin sequence number: 106, dated: 0003; and NHTSA Item
Number: SB610643, Chrysler admits that its owner's manual mistakenly
states vehicle is equipped with a transmission/brake interlock safety feature. • Delayed transmission engagement after a cold start. •
Countermeasure to eliminate accelerator pedal buzz or vibration. • Front
sway bar link knock or clunk when passing over rough roads. • Sliding
door power lock chattering. 2000–01—Poor starting, engine sag, and hesitation caused by a faulty throttle position sensor (TPS). • Rusted, frozen
rear brake drums (see following bulletin).

Rear Brake Drum - Rusted/Frozen

NUMBER: 05-001-01   DATE: Feb. 9. 2001
SUBJECT: Snow/Water Ingestion Into Rear Brake Drum
OVERVIEW:
This bulletin involves installing a revised rear drum brake support (backing) plate and possible
replacement of the rear brake shoes and drums.
MODELS:
2001   (RS) Town & Country/Caravan/Voyager
1996–2000 (NS) Town & Country/Caravan/Voyager
SYMPTOM/CONDITION:
While driving through deep or blowing snow/water, the snow/water may enter the rear brake
drums, causing rust to develop on the rear brake drum and shoe friction surfaces. This condition
can lead to temporary freezing of the rear brake linings to the drums. This symptom is experienced
after the vehicle has been parked in below freezing temperatures long enough for the snow/water
to freeze inside of the rear brake drums. If the parking brake has been applied, the symptom is
more likely to occur.

DIAGNOSIS/REPAIR PROCEDURES:

If the vehicle operator describes the symptom/condition above, perform the following Repair Procedure.

Qty.	Part No.	Description
1	05016612AA	Plate, Rear Drum Brake Support, Right
1	05016613AA	Plate, Rear Drum Brake Support, Left
1	04796269	Lubricant, Special Brake
AR (1)	04883833AA	Kit, Rear Brake Shoe and Lining (NS/RS)
**AR (2)	04883830AA	Cylinder, Wheel 13/16 in. (NS)**

Qty.	Part No.	Description
AR(2)	04877262	Drum, Rear Brake with 14 in. Wheels
**AR(2)	05019407AA	Drum, Rear Brake with 15 in. Wheels**
AR	04318080	Fluid, Brake DOT3
**AR	05010884AA	Sealer, RTV**

Yikes! Water can be ingested into the rear brake drums, causing them to freeze or corrode. Repairs are covered by the base warranty. Problem started with the 1996 models.

• Rear brake howl or moan (see following bulletin).

Brakes - Howl/Moan From The Rear

Bulletin No.: 05-003-01   Date: Apr. 20, 2001
Subject: Off pedal rear brake howl/moan

Overview: This bulletin involves replacing the rear disc brake adapters.

Models: 1997-2000 (NS)   Voyager/Caravan/Town & Country

1997-2000 (GS)   Chrysler Voyager (International Markets)

2001   (RS)   Voyager/Caravan/Town & Country

2001   (RG)   Chrysler Voyager (International Markets)

NOTE: THIS BULLETIN APPLIES TO VEHICLES EQUIPPED WITH ALL WHEEL DRIVE (AWD).

Symptom/Condition: During low speed and/or low speed turns such as a parking lot maneuver, with no brake pedal pressure applied, a low frequency howl/moan noise is heard from the rear brake area.

Diagnosis: If the vehicle operator describes the Symptom/Condition above, perform the Repair Procedure.

Qty.	Part No.	Description
1	05073640AA	Adapter, Right
1	05073641AA	Adapter, Left
2	02207919	Clip (NS/GS vehicles only)
2	NPN	Cotter Pin
AR	J8993704	Brake Grease

Parts Required:

| 8214-1 | Remover, Hub/Bearing |
| C-3919 | Gauge, Brake Shoe |

Policy: Reimbursable within the provisions of the warranty.

These brakes have been moaning since 1997. C'mon Chrysler, fix them on the assembly line once and for all! Until then, this hour-and-a-half job is covered by the base warranty on AWD vehicles. The same parameters can be applied to getting warranty coverage for all complaints of excessive brake noise.

• Rear disc brake squeal. • AC compressor failure, loss of engine power when switching on the AC, serpentine belt chirping, and spark knock can all be traced to a miscalibrated PCM. • No heat on front right side, due to a defective blend air door. • AC compressor squeal. • Rear bench seat rattle or groan. • Hood hinge rattle. • Noisy Michelin tires (for a free replacement, dealer must refer to Chrysler TSB #22-003-01 and call Michelin Canada Public Relations at 1-888-871-4444, or for Quebec: 1-800-565-7638). • Centre console won't hold a cellular phone. • Inoperative overhead reading lamp and rear wiper. Noisy roof rack. • Noisy power sliding door. 2001—Power steering hiss or "swoosh" sound can be silenced by installing a hose kit. • Accessory drivebelt squeals or jumps off the pulleys. • Loose or missing sliding door weatherstrip. • Inoperative seat heating element.

Caravan, Voyager, Grand Caravan, Grand Voyager, Town & Country Profile

	1994	1995	1996	1997	1998	1999	2000	2001
Cost Price ($)								
Caravan	16,860	18,840	18,840	19,885	20,255	24,230	24,970	25,430
Grand Caravan	20,425	22,120	20,320	21,465	23,160	26,665	29,505	28,875
Town & Country	34,874	35,980	38,280	40,350	41,040	41,815	41,150	40,815
Used Values ($)								
Caravan ▲	5,000	6,000	8,500	10,500	13,500	16,000	18,500	20,000
Caravan ▼	4,000	5,000	7,000	9,000	12,000	14,500	17,500	19,000
Grand Caravan ▲	6,000	7,000	9,000	11,500	14,500	17,000	20,000	23,000
Grand Caravan ▼	5,000	6,000	7,500	10,000	13,000	15,500	18,500	21,500
Town & Country ▲	9,000	10,500	14,500	17,500	21,500	25,000	29,00	34,000
Town & Country ▼	8,000	9,000	13,000	16,000	19,000	23,500	27,000	32,000
Extended Warranty	Y	Y	Y	Y	Y	Y	Y	Y
Secret Warranty	Y	Y	Y	Y	Y	Y	N	N
Reliability	❶	❶	❶	❶	❷	❷	❷	③
Crash Safety (F)								
Caravan	④	④	—	④	③	—	④	③
Grand Caravan	—	—	③	③	③	④	④	④

Town & Country	④	④	—	④	③	—	—	—
Town & Country LX	—	—	③	③	③	④	④	④
Side								
Caravan	—	—	—	—	—	⑤	⑤	—
Grand Caravan	—	—	—	—	—	⑤	⑤	④
Town & Country LX	—	—	—	—	—	⑤	⑤	④
Off-set	—	—	—	—	—	—	—	❷
Rollover Resistance	—	—	—	—	—	—	—	③
Head Restraints (F)	—	❷	❷	❷	❷	❷	❷	④
Rear	—	❶	❶	❶	❶	❶	❶	③

Note: Voyager and Grand Voyager prices and ratings are almost identical to those of the Caravan and Grand Caravan. No crash test data available for 2002.

PT CRUISER ★★★

RATING: Average (2001). If you regret your choice, a Cruiser can be sold for almost as much as you paid. Strong points: Excellent fuel economy (regular fuel), nimble handling around town, good braking, lots of interior space, easy access, versatile cargo area, many thoughtful interior amenities, slow depreciation (about 10 percent a year), and unforgettable styling. Weak points: Outrageously high used prices; failure-prone Neon DNA; lethargic engine (especially with the automatic transmission); rough downshifts; poor crashworthiness rating (driver); mediocre highway performance and handling; a firm ride; lots of engine, wind and road noise in cabin area; and unforgettable styling. Log on to *www.ptcruiser.org* for the latest owners' comments. **Maintenance/Repair costs:** Average, until the 5-year mark, when poor durability, first-year glitches, and the warranty's expiration will hike maintenance and repair costs. **Parts:** Below average; one fuel line part took two months to arrive. Body parts are another matter. Expect long delays and high costs until independent suppliers and Chrysler's own distribution network come up to speed in 2003. **Best alternatives:** In a pinch, you may wish to consider the Kia Sedona minivan (first year on the market), or the following wagons: VW's Jetta wagon and Passat GLS 4, the Subaru Legacy Outback Limited, or the Volvo V40. Sport-utilities worth considering are the Subaru Forester, Honda CR-V EX, GM Tracker, Hyundai Santa Fe, Suzuki Grand Vitara, and Isuzu Rodeo S. Both Ford's Escape and Jeep's Liberty are risky first-year SUV alternatives. The Escape is unproven and the Liberty is both unproven and rollover prone, say *Autoweek* and Germany's *Auto Bild* magazine ("Wie gefahrlich ist der Jeep," or "How dangerous is the Jeep?").

Strengths and weaknesses: A Neon clone, cobbled together with Neon parts and engineering and assembly processes, the PT Cruiser is essentially a fuel- and space-efficient hatchback mini-minivan that uses the same nostalgic hot-rod flair that's been so successful with the Prowler.

And it doesn't look like any other vehicle on the market. Even the U.S. federal government can't agree upon whether it's a truck or a car. This confusion is presently playing out in underground parking lots and condo associations, where trucks pay additional fees or are simply banned.

Reliability is predicted to be below average. Major drivetrain complaints include excessive oil consumption due to a faulty valve cover gasket, and automatic transmission failures or erratic transmission performance (gears down to "limp mode") due to a faulty transmission control module:

I have had my transmission go out 2 times now, The first time the whole tranny had to be replaced, second time, it just lost all its fluid. The 41TE transmission is one of the worst transmissions ever made. Go to any search engine and type in 41TE and all the websites talking about the problems with the tranny will come up. DC has known of the problems since 1989 and doesn't care.

Writes another owner of a 2001 PT Cruiser:

Transmission control unit went out on the freeway in stop and go traffic. Tranny went into failsafe (2nd gear) so I drove it to the dealership for repairs. Took one day (they had the part in stock). Two days later, my wife's Dodge Caravan had the SAME part go out on her.

Premature failure of the power-steering pump and the steering unit are also frequent problems that can result in costly repairs once the warranty expires:

My power steering pump had to be replaced at about 10,000 miles [16,000 km]. Took 7 hours in the service department to replace it. I was originally told about 1 hour or so. It was their first time with this problem at this dealer and they had no clue. Everything in the engine compartment is so tight that it takes a full day to do this simple pump replacement. God forbid it happens again after warranty. 7 hours of labor sure would hurt the wallet.

Windshield stress cracks are another PT Cruiser specialty reported on the Internet by owners in Australia, Canada, and the United States. Chrysler is replacing the windshields under a "goodwill" program, while insisting that the poor windshields just happen to be "rock prone":

I had a stress crack within 3 weeks of taking delivery (July 2000). Started on the top passenger side and was about 5" long. It happened while I was washing the car on a hot day. Mine was covered under warranty but the dealer said it was the first legitimate stress crack they had ever seen.

It started on what you guys call the passenger side at the bottom about mid way through the wiper blade and moved up and across to the centre of the driver's side.

Rental car company in Brisbane has a fleet of 17 PT's – 3 of them have had cracked windscreens all starting under the "passenger" side wiper. Coincidence? I think not!

Other owner concerns: annoying wind noise when driving with the rear window or sunroof open; drivetrain whine; moisture between clearcoat and paint turns the hood a chalky white colour; and water leaks through the side passenger window.

Forget about hot-rod power. The 2.4L 150-hp, 4-cylinder engine is not very smooth running and, when matched to the automatic transmission, struggles when going uphill or merging with freeway traffic. This requires frequent downshifting and lots of patience—accelerating to 100 km/h takes about nine seconds. The automatic transmission doesn't have much low-end torque, forcing early kickdown shifting and deft manipulation of the accelerator pedal, but the manual shifter is precise. The optional automatic gearbox has four forward gears, rather than the Neon's primitive 3-speed automatic. Steering provides good road feedback and easy manoeuvrability around town. Emergency handling, though, is slow and sloppy, and the turning diameter seems excessive for such a short vehicle. Hard cornering produces an unsteady, wobbly ride due to the car's height. ABS braking is acceptable, when the system functions as it should.

About 800 lb. (1,280 km) heavier than a Neon, the Cruiser uses larger brake rotors and drums to carry the extra weight. Head restraints have a locking feature for added protection during a crash. There are three-point safety belts for four passengers and a rear lap belt for the centre rear passenger.

Safety summary: All models: 2001—NHTSA crash tests have determined the driver would possibly sustain severe or fatal injuries in a frontal collision. • Some side wind instability. • Tall drivers beware: the windshield is uncomfortably close, and its styling makes it difficult to see overhead traffic lights. • The three small, recessed instrument pods are difficult to read in the daylight. • Wide pillars obstruct one's view. • When parked, transmission slipped out of gear and vehicle rolled down driveway. • Hot exhaust may melt the rear bumper. • Oil blows through tailpipe. • Engine suddenly shuts down when vehicle passes over a large puddle. • Sudden loss of all electrical power. • Chronic stalling due to a faulty ignition coil. • Defective powertrain control module (PCM). • Steering wheel loosens on its shaft. • Excessive vibration caused by out-of-round tires or a too-loose suspension. • Steering column popping or cracking sound. • Head restraints won't stay in position; tend to drift up. • Headlights flicker from bright to dim. • Low-beam headlight may suddenly go out. • Only part of the headlight beam illuminates the roadway.

Secret Warranties/Service Tips/TSBs

All models: 2001—Hard starting due to a faulty fuel pump module. •
Hard starting in cold weather due to failure of the 5-volt regulator in the
SBEC PCM. • An incorrectly calibrated transmission control module
(TCM) may cause harsh shifting, surging, or shift hesitation (see fol-
lowing bulletin).

A/T – Surge/Sag/Shift Bump

NUMBER: 18-007-01   DATE: Feb. 23, 2001

SUBJECT: Transaxle Shift Quality Improvements

OVERVIEW:

This bulletin involves reprogramming the Transmission Control Module (TCM).

MODELS:

2001	(JR)	Sebring/Stratus Sedan/Sebring Convertible
2001	(LH)	Intrepid/Concorde/LHS/300M
2001	(PT)	PT Cruiser

This correction is a warranty repair that also applies to the 2001 Sebring, Stratus, Intrepid,
Concorde, LHS, and 300M.

• MIL (malfunction indicator light) comes on due to a faulty TCM harness connector or a defective evaporator purge flow monitor. • Poor
acceleration and spark knock. • Due to a delamination problem, the
accessory drive belt for the power steering pump and AC compressor may
need replacement. • Left or right floor latch on rear seat won't release. •
Fuel gauge won't indicate full. • Missing or loose roof luggage rack stan-
chion. • Airbag pads fall off. • Airbag rattles. • Ticking noise caused by
faulty rear body exhauster. • Discoloured B- and C-pillar door appliqués.
• Wind buffeting with the windows and/or sunroof open or partially
opened. • The front door water dam may contact the speaker and create
a buzzing or humming. • Don't make an insurance claim for a windshield stress crack (Chrysler is replacing the windshield under a
little-publicized "goodwill" program).

PT Cruiser Profile

	2001
Cost Price ($)	
PT Cruiser	23,665
Limited	27,180
Used Values ($)	
PT Cruiser Λ	22,000
PT Cruiser V	21,000
Limited Λ	24,000
Limited V	23,000

Extended Warranty	N
Secret Warranty	Y
Reliability	④
Crash Safety (F)	❷
Side	④
Rollover Resistance	④
Head Restraints (F)	❷
Rear	④

Ford

WINDSTAR   ★★

RATING: Below Average (2000–01); Not Recommended (1995–99). Another bad minivan choice, noted for poor quality control at the factory and supplier level. The Windstar has similar automatic transmission, brake, and AC problems to the Chrysler competition, and its engines eat head gaskets regularly. On the plus side, however, the Windstar has fewer paint delamination reports (not surprising, since its lineup is younger). Strong points: Comfortable and well-appointed interior; pleasant ride; good instrument/controls layout; plenty of passenger space; lots of small storage spaces, in addition to the large amount of space for larger items; low floor improves cargo handling; and a five-star crashworthiness rating. Weak points: Mediocre handling and restricted side and rear visibility. Driver's seat isn't comfortable for big, tall drivers, who complain of the lack of leg room, seat contouring, and lower back support. "Goodwill" payouts, with owners paying over one-third the cost, have been used as a substitute for better quality control. An abundance of clunks, rattles, and wind and road noise. Failure-prone engines, transmissions, brakes, electrical systems, and suspension components. Sure, the Windstar combines an impressive five-star safety rating, plenty of raw power, an exceptional ride, and impressive cargo capacity. But self-destructing automatic transmissions, defective engine head gaskets and bearings, and "do you feel lucky today?" brakes can quickly transform your dream machine into a nightmare. And, as a counterpoint to Ford's well-earned Windstar crashworthiness boasting, take a look at the summary of safety-related complaints recorded by the U.S. Department of Transportation: coil spring breakage blowing the front tire, sudden acceleration, stalling, steering loss, windows exploding, wheels falling off, horn failures, sliding doors that open and close on their own, and vehicles rolling away while parked. **Maintenance/Repair costs:** Average while under warranty; outrageously higher than average thereafter, due primarily to powertrain breakdowns not covered by warranty or insufficiently covered by parsimonious "goodwill" gestures. **Parts:** Reasonably priced parts are easy to find, mainly due to the entry of independent suppliers, lured by attractive profits sustained by parts that apparently have a high failure rate, like engine head gaskets, brake master cylinders, and speedometers. Digital speedometers are particularly failure prone and can be exceptionally expensive when replaced by the dealer. Parts needed for recall repairs are often back-ordered for months at a time. **Best alternatives:** Still can't beat the Japanese for minivan reliability and performance. Honda's Odyssey and the Toyota Sienna are the best choice if you don't mind spending a few thousand dollars more. You can cut costs and get fairly good reliability from the Ford Villager, recent GM Venture and Montana front-drives or the Astro and Safari, Mazda's MPV, and the discontinued Nissan Axxess and Quest (see Appendix II). Some full-sized GM (Chevy Van and Vandura) or Chrysler rear-drive cargo vans might be a more affordable and practical buy if you intend to haul a full passenger load, do some regular heavy hauling, use lots of accessories, or take frequent motoring excursions. Even an older Ford Aerostar rear-drive minivan may fill the bill if the automatic transmission, electrical system, and brakes check out OK.

Strengths and weaknesses: The Windstar is longer, larger, and lower than most other minivans. It's also one of the few minivans not built on a truck platform (it uses the Taurus platform instead), and as such it has some of the carlike handling characteristics of Chrysler's minivans and many of the engine and automatic transmission problems experienced by Taurus and Sable owners. It's offered in two body styles—a seven-passenger people-hauler and the less expensive basic cargo van.

The Windstar was launched as a 1995 model in March 1994. The 1996 version got 45 more horses added to the 3.8L engine, upgraded seatbelts, and a tilt-slide driver-side seat to improve rear seat access. A fully equipped Limited version was introduced in 1998, and 1999 models came with a host of new features, including optional seat-mounted side airbags, optional rear-bumper sonar sensors, improved steering and brakes, standard ABS, an anti-theft system, new side panels, a new liftgate, larger headlights and taillights, and a revised instrument panel. 2000 models returned relatively unchanged; however, the 2001s got an upgraded automatic transmission, "smart" airbags, adjustable pedals, and an optional traction-control system. Buyers now get a standard 200-hp 3.8L V6, hooked to a 4-speed automatic transmission.

Transmission failures
There are a number of transmission and engine deficiencies through year 2000 models that cut dramatically into the Windstar's performance and overall reliability. This is in contrast to Chrysler, where the engines are

mostly fairly durable. Ford's automatic transmission, for example, is anything but smooth and has a history of running away when unattended (also a Jeep Grand Cherokee problem) or simply self-destructing due to a failure-prone forward clutch piston, among other defective components ('99 Windstars are covered by an extended warranty). Early warning signs are few and benign: the transmission pauses before downshifting or shifts roughly into a higher gear. Owners may also hear a transmission whining or groaning sound, accompanied by driveline vibrations. There is no other prior warning before the transmission breaks down completely and the minivan comes to a sudden banging, clanging halt.

> I just want to thank you for saving us at least $1,500. The transmission in our '98 Windstar went BANG with only 47,300 miles [75,700 km]. After reading about Ford's goodwill adjustment on your site, we were told by our local Ford dealer that owner participation would be $495. We received a new rebuilt Ford unit installed. Believe it or not, I am a fairly good mechanic myself and this came with no warning! We even serviced the transmission at 42,000 miles [67,200 km] and found no debris or evidence of a problem.

As this edition of Lemon-Aid went to press, we got additional information that automatic transmission glitches now affect Ford's 2001 Taurus, Sable, Windstar, and Continental. In a March 2001 Special Service Instruction (SSI) #01T01, Ford authorized its dealers to replace all defective transaxles listed in its TSB, which describes the defect in the following manner:

> The driver may initially experience a transaxle "slip" or "neutral" condition during a 2–3 shift event. Extended driving may result in loss of 3rd gear function and ulitmately loss of 2nd gear function. The driver will still be able to operate the vehicle, but at a reduced level of perfromance.

Ford states that owners won't be notified of the potential problem.

Getting compensation
Over the past four years, I've been lobbying Ford executives to get the company to stop playing cat and mouse with its customers and set up a 7-year/160,000 km extended transmission warranty Owner Notification Program to fully compensate Windstar, Taurus, and Sable owners without their having to file small claims court lawsuits. As of March 2000, Ford of Canada was in favour of the program, but Ford USA (thanks to former U.S. CEO Jac Nasser) squashed the whole idea, saying there was insufficient proof the transmissions are that failure prone. I disagree, and urge afflicted owners to file a small claims lawsuit requesting a refund under *Frank vs. GM* and *Dufour vs. Ford* (see Part Two). That action should force

Ford to review your case and settle during mediation or just before trial. Whether you settle for half or 100 percent depends upon how much additional time you wish to invest in your claim, as the following '96 Windstar owner explains:

Hi Phil: I just wanted to let you know that I did have to go to small claims court to nudge Ford into action. In pre-trial, settlement proceedings, the Ford representative at first gave me an offer of $980 for my troubles. I countered with the actual cost of $2190 to replace my transmission. He did not like that idea, and we went back into the court setting. After instruction from the judge, I began to copy my 200+ pages (for the judge as evidence) of documentation for why this is a recurring problem with Ford transmissions (thank you, by the way, for all the great info).

I think it made him a little scared, so I asked if he would settle for $1600 (a middle ground of our original proposals) to which he accepted. My transmission costs were $2190, so I basically paid about $600 for a new transmission (NOT a Ford replacement, either).

Anyway, I figured a guaranteed $1600 was better than not knowing what would happen in court. Thanks for your help!

Also, his whole defense (I asked what it would have been after we had signed the paperwork for our settlement) rested on the fact that the vehicle was out of warranty. This aggravated me so much that I almost marched back into the courtroom. Just because something is out of warranty, does it cease to function in the purpose it was meant to fulfill? Ford knows its product should last much longer than the 60,000 miles [96,000 km] it did for me. And with it being a constant problem, they should take the initiative to solve it! However, I'm happy to be through with it all. Thanks again, Phil!

But, what about cases where the company repairs the transmission and it breaks again? Or, Ford settles, but the dealer won't, forcing you to actually go to trial? Here are some tips from Alan MacDonald, a *Lemon-Aid* reader who won his case in small claims court after a short trial:

I want to thank you for the advice you provided in my dealings with the Ford Motor Company of Canada, Limited and Highbury Ford Sales Limited regarding my 1994 Ford Taurus wagon and the problems with the automatic transmission (Taurus and Windstar transmissions are identical). I also wish to apologize for not sending you a copy of this judgement earlier that may be beneficial to your readers. (*MacDonald v. Highbury Ford Sales Limited*, Ontario Superior Court of Justice in the Small Claims Court London, June 6, 2000, Court File #0001/00, Judge J. D. Searle).

As the judgement is self-explanatory, I will just very briefly sum up and explain my observations in going through the small claims court process.

In 1999 after only 105,000 km the automatic transmission went. I took the car to Highbury Ford to have it repaired. We paid $2,070.00 to have the transmission fixed, but protested and felt the transmission failed prematurely. We contacted Ford, but to no avail: their reply was we were out of warranty period. The transmission was so poorly repaired (and we went back to Highbury Ford several times) that we had to go to Mr. Transmission to have the transmission fixed again 9 months later at a further $1,906.02.

It is at that point that I contacted you, and I was surprised, and somewhat speechless (which you noticed) when you personally called me to provide advice and encouragement. I am very grateful for your call. My observations with going through small claims court involved the following: I filed in January of 2000, the trial took place on June 1 and the judgement was issued June 6.

At pre-trial, a representative of Ford (Ann Sroda) and a representative from Highbury Ford were present. I came with one binder for each of the defendants, the court and one for myself (each binder was about 3 inches thick—containing your reports on Ford Taurus automatic transmissions, Alldata Service Bulletins, Taurus Transmissions Victims (Bradley web site), Center for Auto Safety (web site), Read This Before Buying a Taurus (web site), and the Ford Vent Page (web site)).

The representative from Ford asked a lot of questions (I think she was trying to find out if I had read the contents of the information I was relying on). The Ford representative then offered a 50% settlement based on the initial transmission work done at Highbury Ford. The release allowed me to still sue Highbury Ford with regards to the necessity of going to Mr. Transmission because of the faulty repair done by the dealer. Highbury Ford displayed no interest in settling the case, and so I had to go to court.

For court, I prepared by issuing a summons to the manager at Mr. Transmission who did the second transmission repair, as an expert witness. I was advised that unless you produce an expert witness you won't win in a car repair case in small claims court. Next, I went to the law school library in London and received a great deal of assistance in researching cases pertinent to car repairs. I was told that judgments in your home province (in my case Ontario) were binding on the court; that cases outside of the home province could be considered, but not binding, on the judge.

The cases I used for trial involved *Pelleray v. Heritage Ford Sales Ltd.*, Ontario Small Claims Court (Scarborough) SC7688/91 March 22, 1993.; *Phillips et al. v. Ford Motor Co. of Canada Ltd. et al.*, Ontario Reports 1970, 15th January 1970; *Gregorio v. Intrans-Corp.*, Ontario Court of Appeal, May 19, 1994; *Collier v. MacMaster's Auto Sales*, New Brunswick Court of Queen's Bench, April 26, 1991; *Sigurdson v. Hillcrest Service & Acklands* (1977), Saskatchewan Queen's Bench; *White v. Sweetland*, Newfoundland District Court, Judicial Centre of

Gander, November 8, 1978; *Raiches Steel Works v. J. Clark & Son*, New
Brunswick Supreme Court, March 7, 1977; *Mudge v. Corner Brook
Garage Ltd.*, Newfoundland Supreme Court, July 17, 1975; *Sylvain v.
Carroseries d'Automobiles Guy Inc. (1981)*, C.P. 333, Judge Page;
*Gagnon v. Ford Motor Company of Canada, Limited et Marineau
Automobile Co. Ltée.* (1974), C.S. 422-423.

In court, I had prepared the case, as indicated above, had my expert
witness and two other witnesses who had driven the vehicle (my wife
and my 18-year-old son). As you can see by the judgement, we won
our case and I was awarded $1,756.52, including prejudgment interest
and costs.

My recommendation to anyone considering suing over improper
car repairs is the following: 1) make sure the amount of money is worth
the time spent to go to court. In my case, not only was there a lot of
research time and letters sent to the car manufacturer and dealer, but
also a day off work to go to court (pre-trial was done after my regular
work hours). You need an expert witness to testify. Surf the internet to
find other owners who have experienced the same problems you have
and follow the *Lemon-Aid* guides.

But, Mr. Edmonston, I have to admit that this isn't for everybody—
which is why the words "judging on a case-by-case basis" stack the
deck completely in favour of the car manufacturer or dealer.

They know only a few will come forward and challenge. The people
who do will have to go the limit and will be compensated; but they
know that for one dissatisfied customer who comes forward, probably
ten in the same situation won't.

Ford insiders and service bulletins confirm that this transmission
problem is both hardware- and software-related and affects much of
Ford's front-drive model lineup over the past decade.

Engine and other Windstar failures

The 3.0L engine is overwhelmed by the Windstar's heft and struggles to
keep up, but opting for the 3.8L V6 may get you into worse trouble.
Owners report that the 3.8L engine head gaskets on '95 and '96 models
need replacing shortly after the 60,000 km mark, but Ford's 7-year/
160,000 km Owner Notification Program only covers '95s. Even when
it's running properly, the 3.8L knocks loudly when under load and pings
at other times.

Brakes are another sore point with Windstar owners. They aren't reliable, and calipers, rotors, and the master cylinder often need replacing. If
left unattended, your drive will be punctuated by pedal-to-the-floor brake
loss, jerking from side to side when the brakes are applied, excessive
vibrations when braking, or brake fading after successive stops. Plus,
major brake repairs will keep you on a first-name basis with your bank
manager.

Other frequent Windstar problems concern no-starts and chronic stalling, believed to be caused by a faulty fuel pump or powertrain control module (PCM); electrical system power-steering failures; hard steering at slow speeds; excessive steering wheel vibrations; sudden tire tread separation and premature tread wear; advanced coil spring corrosion, leading to spring collapse and puncturing of the front tire (only 1997–98 models were recalled); rear shock failures at 110 km/h; left side axle breakage while underway; exploding rear windshields; power sliding door malfunctions, and failure-prone digital speedometers that are horrendously expensive to replace. There have also been many complaints concerning faulty computer modules, engine oil leaks, AC failures, and early replacement of engine camshafts, tie-rods, and brake rotors and calipers.

Safety summary: All models/years: I'm both amazed and disgusted at the large number of safety complaints registered against recent-model Windstars; '98 Windstars, for example, have 616 complaints in the NHTSA database, compared to 100 or so for the imported competition. And it gets worse the further back you go. • Base models may not have head restraints for all seats, and the digital dash can be confusing. • Optional adjustable pedals help protect drivers from airbag injuries. Be careful, though; some drivers have found that they are set too close together and say they often felt loose. • Other nice safety features: airbags that adjust deployment speed according to occupant weight and a sliding door warning light. **All models: 1995–98**—The following is a short summary of problems carried over year after year; unfortunately, I don't have the space to list many other reported defects. Nevertheless, you can easily access NHTSA's website (see Appendix I) for the details of thousands of other Windstar complaints: Airbag failed to deploy. • Severe injuries caused by airbag deployment. • Sudden acceleration and chronic stalling. • Control arm and inner tie-rod failures cause the wheel to fall off. • Sudden steering lockup or loss of steering ability. • Engine head gasket failures. • Loose or missing front brake bolts could cause the wheels to lock up or a loss of vehicle control. • Chronic ABS and transmission failures. Roger McCoy, a tenacious and persistent Columbus, Ohio, CBS investigative reporter, discovered that '95 Windstar sales represented 17 percent of the market, but 77 percent of NHTSA's combined '95 minivan transmission complaints. He interviewed an NHTSA spokesman in early 2001 and was told that NHTSA knew Windstar transmissions were "less robust and more failure-prone than the competition." McCoy's analysis is bolstered by *Consumer Reports* and CAA member surveys highlighting the tranny problem. ALLDATA service bulletins show the same automatic transmission defect is factory-related and is a widespread problem for Windstar, Taurus, and Sable. • Almost a dozen reports that the vehicle jumps out of Park and rolls away when on an incline, or slips into Reverse with the engine idling. • Transmission and axle separation. • Faulty fuel pump, sensor, and gauge. • Built-in child safety seat is easy to get out of, yet securing seatbelts are too tight; child almost strangled. • Faulty rear liftgate latches; trunk lid can fall on one's head. • Horn doesn't work properly. **1999**—This is a faithful summary of the 230 complaints in the NHTSA database. Keep in mind that many of these defects have been found in previous model year Windstars, but may not have been included due to space limitations: Airbag failed to deploy. • While parked, cruising, turning on the ignition, or when brakes are applied, vehicle suddenly accelerates. • Stuck accelerator causes unintended acceleration. • Chronic stalling caused by fuel vapour lock or faulty fuel pump. • Check Engine light constantly comes on, due to a faulty gas cap or over-sensitive warning system. • Front passenger-side wheel fell off when turning at a traffic light; in another reported incident, dealer found the five lug nuts had broken in half. • Vehicle pops out of gear while parked and rolls away. • Frequent transmission failures, including noisy engagement, won't engage forward or Reverse, slips, or jerks into gear. • Transmission jumped from Park to Reverse (this is a common problem affecting Ford vehicles for almost three decades) and pinned driver against tree. • Sudden loss of power steering, chronic leakage of fluid, and early replacement of steering components, like the pump and hoses. • Excessive brake fade after successive stops. • When brake pedal is depressed, it sinks below the accelerator pedal level, causing the accelerator to be pressed as well, particularly annoying for drivers with large feet. • ABS module wire burned out. • Complete electrical failure during rainstorm. • Horn button "sweet spot" is too small and takes too much pressure to activate; one owner says, "Horn doesn't work, unless you hit it with a sledgehammer." • Windshield suddenly exploded when car was slowly accelerating. • Sliding door opens and closes on its own, sticks open or closed, or suddenly slams shut on a downgrade. • Sliding door closed on child's arm. • Door locks don't stay locked; passenger-side door opened when turning, causing passenger to fall out. • Many complaints that the side or rear windows suddenly exploded. • Rear defogger isn't operable (lower part of windshield isn't clear) in inclement weather when windshield wipers are activated. • Windshield wipers fail to clear windshield. • Water pours from dash onto front passenger floor. • Floor cupholder trips passengers. • Continental General tires lose air and crack between the treads. • Unspecified original-equipment tires have sudden tread separation. • Large A-pillar (where windshield attaches to door) seriously impairs forward visibility, hiding pedestrians. • Seatbelts aren't as described in owner's manual (supposed to be automatic retractable). • Two incidents where flames shot up out of fuel tank filler spout when when car was being gassed up. **2000**—Vehicle caught on fire while parked. • Sudden, unintended acceleration while stopped. • Chronic stalling; engine shuts down when turning. • Sometimes cruise control won't engage or engages on its own. • Passenger-side wheel came off due to lug nut failure. • One

Ingersoll, Ontario, owner of a year 2000 Windstar recounts the following
harrowing experience:

> Last week, as my wife was running errands, the support arm that goes
> from the rear crossmember (not an axle anymore) up under the floor,
> broke in half. The dealer replaced the whole rear end as it is one
> welded assembly. If she had been on the highway going 80 km/h she
> would probably have been in a bad accident.

• Check Engine light constantly comes on for no reason. • Driver heard a
banging noise and Windstar suddenly went into a tailspin; dealer blamed
pins that "fell out of spindle." • Transmission jumped out of gear while
on highway. • Many reports of premature transmission replacements. •
Transmission lever can be shifted without depressing brake pedal (unsafe
for children). • After several dealer visits, brakes still spongy, pedal goes
to floor without braking, and emergency brake has almost no effect. •
When braking, foot also contacts the accelerator pedal. • Emergency
brake is inadequate to hold the vehicle. • Dealers acknowledge that brake
master cylinders are problematic. • Joints aren't connected under quarter
wheel weld; one weld is missing and three aren't properly connected. •
Passenger door opened when vehicle hit a pothole. • While vehicle is
underway, right-side sliding door opens on its own and won't close. •
When vehicle was parked on an incline, sliding door released and came
crashing down on child. • Hood suddenly flew up on the freeway. •
Steering failed three times. • Power-steering pump whines and lurches. •
Steering wheel is noisy and hard to turn. • Excessive suspension wallow.
• Rear side windows, liftgate window, and windshield often explode suddenly. • When the interior rear-view mirror is set for night vision, images
become distorted and hard to see. • Windshield wipers are unreliable. •
Second-row driver-side seatbelt buckle wouldn't latch. • Original equipment tire blowouts and sidewall bulging. • Driver must hunt for right
place to push for horn to work. **2000–01**—Harsh 2–3 shifting when
coasting then accelerating. • Transmission fluid leakage. • 3.8L engine
hum, moan, drone, spark knock, and vibration. • Vibration under light
acceleration. • Power-steering grunt or shudder during slow turns. •
Power steering fluid leaks. • Instrument panel popping. • Snapping at
the lower centre bin area. • Rattling, clunking noise from front of
vehicle. • Suspension noise, squeaks, and rattles from the exterior right
rear and liftgate areas. • Fuel pump whine heard in speakers. • Faulty
self-activating wipers and door, trunk, and ignition locks. • Centre
storage bin binds, and door glass may bind or travel slowly. •
Discharged battery after extended parking. • Instrument panel chimes
continually. • Malfunctioning indicator lights. • Dust enters into AC
auxiliary air distribution system. • Vehicles equipped with PATS anti-
theft device may not crank or start. **2001**—Faulty fuel tank ceramic plug
causes sudden, rapid fuel loss. • Airbag failed to deploy and seatbelts

failed to lock upon impact. • Sudden brake failure. • Automatic transmission allows vehicle to roll away on an incline. • Defective tie-rods noted after inspecting for undercarriage noise. • Both rear shocks broke at 110 km/h; left-side axle broke at 40 km/h. • Many reports of the rear window shattering, particularly after activating the defogger. • Engine warning light remains lit. • Sudden acceleration, vehicle lurches forward, and engine revs at high speeds (defective idle control suspected). • Chronic stalling at all speeds. • Sliding side door fails intermittently. • Tailpipe sticks out too far; cut child's knee.

Secret Warranties/Service Tips/TSBs

All models/years: Paint delamination, peeling, or fading (see Part Two). **All models: 1995**—Blower motor squeaking or chirping can be silenced by installing an upgraded blower motor. **1995–96**—Intermittent no-starts may be caused by microscopic cracks on the fuel pump relay cover located inside the Constant Control Relay Module (CCRM); install a new CCRM. **1995–98**—Replace the seatbelt retractor if the integrated child safety seat's belt twists or binds. • A driver's seat that chucks or squeaks may need a seat track repair kit. • Ford says a clunking noise when shifting out of Park is normal. • A parking brake that won't release needs a new parking pawl actuating rod. • Power door locks that grind or won't work may need a new front door lock actuator. • Tips on finding and silencing instrument panel buzzing, rattling, squeaking, chirping, and ticking. • The front-end accessory drive belt (FEAD) slips in wet weather, causing a reduction in steering power-assist; Ford suggests the belt be replaced. • A whistling noise from the front AC heater plenum requires a tighter seal. • Getting rid of AC odours requires a new moisture purge module and "disodorizer." • Water leakage onto carpet or headliner in rear cargo area is a factory-related defect covered in TSB #98-5-5. **1995–99**—Tips for correcting excessive noise, vibration, and harshness while driving; side door wind noise; and windshield water leaks. • An exhaust buzz or rattle may be caused by a loose catalyst or heat shield. **1995–2000**—A harsh 3–2 downshift/shudder when accelerating or turning may simply mean the transmission is low on fluid. • Diagnostic tips on brake vibration, inspection, and friction material replacement. **1995–2001**—Owner Notification Program 97B17 calls for the free replacement of the fuel gauge/sender assembly. • Engine oil leak at the oil pan, front cover, or the front and rear crankshaft oil seal (TSB #BC5181961001). • EEC/PCM recalibration for vehicles that lack power due to torque converter engagement scheduling, catalytic converter failures, or rough idle and hard starts. • Automatic transmission whistling. • Light to moderate axle whine (above 80–110 km/h). • Rattling door glass. • Wind noise and water leaks at the lower passenger door area and third door. • A revised hood seal will eliminate high-speed wind whistling. • Excessive speedometer needle fluctuation. • Improved parking brake cables and revised rear linings will reduce rear brake drag. •

AC goes to defrost mode when climbing grades or accelerating. • Liftgate may be hard to open or won't stay open during cold weather. **1995–2002**—Repeat heater core failure, a problem with all 1985–2002 Ford vehicles, is likely caused by electrolysis, says TSB #01-15-06. Adding a restrictor on the inlet hose should solve the problem. **1996–98**—Harsh automatic 1–2 shifting may be caused by a malfunctioning electronic pressure control or the main control valves sticking in the valve body. • Unwanted airflow from the AC vents can be stopped by replacing the evaporator case baffle. • An intermittent Neutral condition when coming to a stop signals the need to replace the forward clutch piston and the forward clutch cylinder. • Engine oil mixed with coolant or coolant loss signals the need for revised 3.8L engine lower intake manifold side gaskets and/or front cover gaskets. This is a little-known free repair under the emissions warranty and can be used as a benchmark for other engines and years. **1997–98**—A rattling or clunking noise coming from the front of the vehicle may be caused by a loose front tension strut bushing retainer. **1998**—Lack of AC cooling may be caused by refrigerant leak at the P-nut fitting. • AC may have a loose auxiliary climate control fan switch. • A Low Fuel light lit for no reason signals the need for an upgraded fuel tank and sender assembly. • A malfunction indicator light (MIL) lit for no reason may simply show that the gas cap is loose. • An inaccurate metric speedometer requires a new speedometer gear. • An overhead console that's loose or hangs down needs a revised bracket. • Sliding-door rattles and squeaks when passing over bumps require adjusting and silicone. • Squeaks and creaks from the left rear of the driver's seat can be silenced by lubricating the lateral stability bracket. • Stalling when stopping, parking, coasting, or during slow turns can be corrected by reprogramming the PCM. • An upper radiator hose leak requires an upgraded hose or protective sleeve. • Excessive vibration at highway speeds may require new rear brake drums. **1998–99**—Tips on spotting abnormal ABS braking noise, although Ford says some noise is inevitable. **1998–2001**—Power-steering fluid leaks call for an upgraded steering rack (3504), installed under warranty. **1999**—No Reverse engagement may be caused by torn Reverse clutch lip seals. • To improve the defogging of the driver-side door glass, install a revised window demister vent. • A squeaking or rattling noise coming from the rear of the vehicles is likely caused by a poorly insulated parking brake cable. **1999–2000**—Spark knock upon acceleration will be corrected under the emissions warranty (see following bulletin).

Driveability – Spark Knock on Acceleration

Article No. 00-21-8   10/16/00
SPARK KNOCK – SPARK KNOCK ON ACCELERATION –
VEHICLES EQUIPEED WITH 3.8L ENGINE ONLY

FORD:

1999-2000 WINDSTAR

ISSUE:

Some vehicles equipped with a 3.8L engine may exhibit a spark knock condition on heavy acceleration with 87 octane gasoline. Hot weather and lower octane gasoline may contribute to the concern. This may also be caused by excessive carbon deposits in the combustion chamber due to oil migration into the upper intake manifold.

ACTION:

If the spark knock condition is still present after performing normal diagnostics, reprogram Powertrain Control Module (PCM), perform engine octane adjustment, decarbonize engine, clean upper intake manifold and install new design left side valve cover.

• If the power sliding door won't close, replace the door controller; if it pops or disengages when fully closed, adjust the door and rear striker to reduce closing resistance. • Front wipers that operate when switched off need a revised multifunction switch (service program and recall). • Special Service Instruction #00T07 concerning free Powertrain Control Module recalibration to correct reduced battery charging perfomance (it's an emissions warranty fix). **1999–2001**—Tips to eliminate a grunt noise when turning (3.8L-equipped vehicles). **2001**—Special Service Instruction allows for the free inspection and replacement of the AX4N transaxle. • Ford engineers are investigating reports of excessive brake noise and pulling or drifting at highway speeds on low-mileage Windstars. • Some vehicles may produce a rough ride. • Uneven or notchy steering feel when turning. • Rear drum brakes may drag or won't release properly when operated in wet, or below freezing conditions. • Constant MIL warning lamp illumination—automatic transmission-induced. • AX4N or 4F50N transaxles may leak fluid from the main control cover area or shudder during a 3–4 shift. • Power steering fluid leaks. • Excessive window fogging. • High-back front seats may have a twisted seatback frame. • A faulty vacuum management valve may produce a hooting sound. • Loose front door window moulding belt. • AC grunt or grind on initial startup. • Rear creaking noise. • AC compressor rattling.

Windstar Profile

	1995	1996	1997	1998	1999	2000	2001
Cost Price ($)							
GL/Base	23,095	22,495	23,495	24,495	24,295	24,295	—
LX	27,195	27,495	28,995	28,995	28,195	25,995	26,750
SEL	—	—	—	—	36,195	36,195	33,190
Used Values ($)							
GL/Base ▲	7,000	9,000	11,500	14,000	15,000	17,000	—
GL/Base ▼	5,500	7,500	10,000	12,500	13,500	16,000	—
LX ▲	7,500	9,500	13,500	16,000	17,500	19,500	20,500
LX ▼	6,000	8,000	12,000	14,500	16,000	17,500	19,000

SEL ⋀	—	—	—	—	21,500	24,000	26,000
SEL ⋁	—	—	—	—	20,000	23,000	24,500
Extended Warranty	Y	Y	Y	Y	Y	Y	Y
Secret Warranty	Y	Y	Y	Y	Y	Y	Y
Reliability	❶	❶	❶	❶	❶	❷	❷
Crash Safety (F)	⑤	⑤	⑤	⑤	⑤	⑤	⑤
Side	—	—	—	—	⑤	④	⑤
Off-set	—	—	—	—	—	—	⑤
Head Restraints (F)	④	④	④	④	④	④	④
Rear	❶	❶	❶	❶	❶	❶	❶

Ford/Nissan

VILLAGER, QUEST ★★★★

RATING: Above Average (1997–2001); Average (1995–96); Not Recommended (1993–94). Best used for city commuting, rather than long highway journeys. Still sold in the States, the Villager was dropped in Canada (along with the Mercury franchise) after the 2000 model year. The Quest will be dropped for 2002. Strong points: Impressive highway performance (as long as you're not carrying a full load) and easy, no-surprise, carlike handling; highway stability is above reproach; occupants get a comfortable ride with lots of seating choices; the 4-speed automatic transmission is particularly smooth and quiet; braking performance is quite good (when it's working properly); plenty of passenger and cargo room: these vans are nearly a foot longer and two inches wider and higher than Chrysler's short-wheelbase minivans; and mechanical components have been tested for years on the Maxima. Weak points: These fuel-thirsty minivans are quite heavy, and the 3.0L and 3.3L engines have to go all out to carry the extra weight. Surprisingly, GM's 2.8L engines produce more torque than what the Villager and Quest can deliver. Powertrain setup trails the Odyssey in acceleration and passing. Other minuses: a cheap-looking interior; the control layout can be a bit confusing; suspension is too soft; and rear-seat access can be difficult. Some wind and road noise, and excessive engine noise under heavy throttle. **Maintenance/Repair costs:** Higher than average. Costs can be kept down by frequenting independent repair agencies. **Parts:** Both Ford (Mercury dealers were closed down) and Nissan dealers carry parts, and parts are less expensive than those of most other minivans in this class. The exception to this rule: broken engine exhaust manifold studs (a frequent problem through 1995), AC, and electrical components. **Best alternatives:** The Quest, engineered by Nissan and built by Ford, is practically identical to the Villager, except for some slight styling differences, more standard equipment, and a slightly lower rate of depreciation. Look for used models with a separate rear air conditioner/heater and power side windows. The optional performance handling equipment makes little improvement to the standard suspension; don't pay anything extra for it. Other minivans worth considering are the GM Venture and Express, Honda Odyssey, Toyota Sienna, or Nissan Axxess.

Strengths and weaknesses: Smaller and more carlike than most mini-vans, the Villager and Quest are built by Ford at its truck factory in Avon Lake, Ohio, and sized comfortably between the regular and extended Chrysler minivans. These front-drive, five- or seven-passenger minivans are the most fun to whip around the city in.

These minivans' strongest assets are a 170-hp 3.3L V6 engine that gives them carlike handling, ride, and cornering; modular seating; and reliable mechanical components. Nissan borrowed the powertrain, sus-pension, and steering assembly from the Maxima, mixed in some creative sheet metal, and left the job of outfitting the sound system, cli-mate control, dashboard, steering column, and wheels to Ford. This has resulted in an attractive and not overly aero-styled minivan.

Most owner-reported problems involve excessive brake noise and pre-mature brake wear, door lock malfunctions, interior noise, and driveline vibrations. There have also been many reports of engine exhaust mani-fold stud and crankshaft failures (through 1995); electrical problems; brake failures due to vibration, binding, or overheating; premature wear of the front discs, rotors, and pads; chronic stalling, possibly due to faulty fuel pumps or a shorted electrical system; and loose steering and veering at highway speeds. Other common problems include film buildup on windshield and interior glass; a sulfur smell from the exhaust system; poor AC performance or compressor failures, accompanied by musty, mildew-type AC odours; and recurring fuel pump buzzing heard through the radio speakers. Body integrity is subpar, with doors opening and closing on their own and poor fit and finish, allowing lots of wind noise to enter the interior. (Yes, Ford did the body work, while Nissan handled the mechanicals. You can tell, can't you?) There have also been some reports of panel and paint defects, as well as premature rusting on the inside sliding door track. Post-'98 models have improved quality con-trol and better fit and finish.

In 1996, motorized shoulder belts were dropped, a passenger-side airbag was added, and the dash and exterior were slightly restyled. 1997 buyers of the entry-level GS model could order captain's chairs. '98s carried over unchanged in preparation for the redesigned '99 ver-sion. For 1999, the Pathfinder's 3.3L V6 replaced the 3.0L V6, giving the Villager and Quest an additional 19 horses. The Villager gained a fourth door; more interior room; a revised instrument panel that's easier to reach; restyled front and rear ends; and improved shifting, acceleration, and braking (ABS takes less effort and is supposedly more durable). The suspension was re-tuned to give a more carlike ride and handling, the old climate control system was ditched for a more sophisticated version with air filtration, and optional ABS was made available with all models. Mercury's top-of-the-line model, the Nautica, was dropped. For the same model year, the Quest has an additional 4.6 inches in length and 1.2 inches in width, standard ABS brakes, a driver-side sliding rear door, upgraded headlights, and rear leaf springs. The second row of seats can now be removed and the third row is set on tracks. Owners gain an extra 10 cubic feet of storage space, due to the addition of a cargo shelf behind the rear seats. 2000–02 models carried over without any significant changes, except for an improved child safety seat anchoring system. An entertainment centre with a larger screen is standard on all Quest models, as well as a stabilizer bar on the GLE.

Safety summary: All models/years: Plenty of glass provides excellent front and rear visibility. • Interestingly, front passenger protection in a frontal collision for the 1999–2000 models only rated three stars, compared to the Windstar, Odyssey, and Toyota five-star awards. **All models: 1993–98**—NHTSA is looking into fuel leaks into the engine compartment or from cracked fuel tank vent hoses that allow gas fumes to infiltrate the interior. **1994–96**—Vehicle suddenly accelerated forward. • Inadvertent airbag deployment. • Sudden stalling due to faulty fuel pump. • Both steering and brakes failed when turning into an intersection. • Steering wheel locked up while making a right turn. • Chronic ABS failures; brake pads and rotors need replacing every 5,000 km, and drums often need turning. • Alarm system will lock and unlock the doors on its own. • Remote-control door locks often won't respond, trapping occupants inside. • Faulty rear door latch and lock allow the door to come open while driving. • The sliding door opens for no apparent reason. • Power windows often jam. • Seatbelts don't retract properly and ratchet too tightly. • Shoulder belt got caught around child's neck and had to be cut away. • Frequent rear windshield wiper failures. • Solar window distorts vision by reflecting images at certain angles. **1997–99**—Airbags fail to deploy. • Power door locks self-activate. • Gas fumes leak into the interior. • Gas pedal sticks. • Sudden acceleration. • Brake failures (extended stopping distance, noisy when applied). **2000**—Gas and brake pedals are too close together. • Frequent brake repairs and failures. • Some steering wander and excessive vibration. • Vehicle tends to lurch forward when the AC is first engaged. • Weak tailgate hydraulic cylinders. • Instrument panel's white face hard to read in daylight hours. **2000–01**—Front brake groan. • Grinding noise when braking. • Rear suspension rattling. • Cycling or self-activating front door locks. • Missing seatbelt latch plate stopper button. • Broken shift lock cable plate causes shift indicator to be misaligned. • ABS failures. • Complete brake loss. • Brake and accelerator pedals are the same height, so driver's foot can easily slip and step on both at the same time. •22-month-old child was able to pull the clasp apart on integrated child safety seat. • Seatbelts don't retract properly. • Many complaints that the mid-row passenger bench seat vibrates uncomfortably. • Rear window on liftgate door shattered for unknown reason (dealer was aware of problem and replaced window under warranty). • Power steering fluid leakage due to O-ring at rack gear splitting. • Door hinge allows the door to damage the fender during average windstorms. • Windshield wipers are noisy when put in the "high" mode. • Safety investigators are also looking into reports of electric door lock and power window failures that have trapped occupants in their vehicles. **2001**— Excessive vehicle vibration causes loss of steering control. • Vehicle began vibrating and brakes failed. • Seatbelts don't retract properly. • The automatic transmission shift cable lock plate breaks, causing the shift indicator to give an incorrect reading.

Secret Warranties/Service Tips/TSBs

All models/years: Many of the Windstar service bulletins also apply to the Villager and Quest, so check the Windstar entries, as well. **All models: 1993–95**—Ford has refunded repair costs for defective engine exhaust manifold studs on a case-by-case basis up to 5 years/100,000 km; owners exceeding these parameters should seek partial compensation. • The rear wiper motor may quit or stop intermittently because water has gotten into the motor printed circuit board. • Replace front brake pads that cause excessive brake squeaking or groaning with upgraded pads. **1993–96**—A crunch/grunt noise from the rear suspension may be caused by rear shackle bushings that need lubrication. **1993–97**—Front door windows that bind may have the glass rubber improperly installed in the door sheet metal channel. **1993–98**—Automatic transmission whining when accelerating may be caused by a faulty transaxle support bracket and insulators. **1993–99**—Inadvertent disabling of the brake shift interlock may occur when emergency vehicles have their brake lights and flashers modified. • Fuel pump may be cause of radio speaker noise. • **1993–2000**—Paint delamination, peeling, or fading (see Part Two). **1993–2001**—Shudder from the transmission torque converter clutch in Third or Fourth gear, or during a 3–4 shift. • Vehicle may not start due to moisture freeezing in the fuel pump relay contained within the CCRM (constant control relay module). • Cold start stalling. • Engine oil leak at the oil pan, front cover, or the front and rear crankshaft oil seal (TSB #BC5181961001). • EEC/PCM recalibration for vehicles that lack power due to torque converter engagement scheduling, catalytic converter failures, or rough idle and hard starts. • Remedy for excessive front or rear brake squeal or grinding. • Front door window binding. • Liftgate may be hard to open or won't stay raised in cold weather. • Side window latch may not stay in the open or closed position. • Rear leaf spring squeaks. • Lightbar bulbs have a short life span. **1993–2002**— Remedy for repeat heater core failures. **1994–98**—If there's a strong fuel odour in the passenger compartment when refuelling, it's likely there's a missing sealer between the fuel-filler opening upper flange and the fuel-filler base assembly. • Poor AC performance may be due to a faulty high-pressure cut-off switch. **1995–96**—Ford has replaced, at no charge, 3.0L V6 engine blocks that produce excessive engine knock following a cold start. Refer to Service Program 96M89. **1995–99**—Tips for correcting windshield water leaks and excessive noise, vibration, and harshness. **1996–98**—Power door locks that intermittently self-activate (help, let me out!) are a common occurrence that's covered in TSB #98-22-5. **1997–98**—Tips on silencing rattles and creaks. • Hard starts, no-starts, stalling, or an exhaust rotten-egg smell can all be corrected by replacing the power control module (PCM) under the emissions warranty. **1997–99**—An exhaust buzz or rattle may be caused by a loose catalyst or muffler heat shield. **1999–2000**—Self-activating power door locks may be caused by a misadjustment of the front door lock linkage, excess solder in the front door power window switch, or water infiltration of a potential open wire harness connection inside the front doors. • Excessive highway vibration or shaking has been traced to defective original-equipment Goodyear Eagle tires. Ford will replace the tires under a "goodwill" program, says TSB #00-18-1. • Latest Ford guidelines for correcting brake vibration. • Second-row seats rattle and shake. **1999–2001**—Automatic transmission gear whine correction. **2001**—Steering pull or drifting while driving. • Transmission may perform erratically. • Upper windshield outside trim piece may loosen.

Villager, Quest Profile

	1994	1995	1996	1997	1998	1999	2000	2001
Cost Price ($)								
Villager GS	21,195	22,595	23,695	24,295	24,595	24,595	24,595	—
Villager LS	26,195	27,095	28,095	29,195	29,495	29,495	29,495	—
Quest XE/SE	23,490	24,598	25,598	25,598	25,598	32,498	35,198	35,198
Quest GXE	27,290	29,598	30,598	30,898	30,898	27,798	30,498	30,698
Used Values ($)								
Villager GS ▲	6,500	7,500	9,500	11,000	14,000	16,000	19,000	—
Villager GS ▼	5,000	6,000	9,000	9,500	12,000	14,500	17,500	—
Villager LS ▲	7,000	8,000	11,000	13,000	15,500	19,000	22,000	—
Villager LS ▼	5,500	6,500	9,500	11,500	13,500	17,000	20,000	—
Quest XE/SE ▲	7,500	8,500	12,000	15,500	17,500	20,500	23,000	25,000
Quest XE/SE ▼	6,500	7,500	10,500	14,500	16,500	18,500	21,500	23,500
Quest GXE ▲	8,000	11,500	14,000	17,000	19,500	22,000	26,500	28,000
Quest GXE ▼	6,500	8,500	12,500	15,000	17,500	20,000	25,000	27,000
Extended Warranty	Y	Y	Y	N	N	N	N	N
Secret Warranty	Y	Y	Y	Y	Y	Y	N	N
Reliability	❷	③	④	④	④	④	⑤	④
Crash Safety (F)	④	④	④	④	—	—	④	④
Side	—	—	—	—	—	—	⑤	④

Off-set	—	—	②	②	②	①	①	①
Rollover Resistance	—	—	—	—	—	—	—	④
Head Restraints	—	③	—	②	—	①	①	①

General Motors

ASTRO, SAFARI ★★★★

RATING: Above Average (2001); Average (1996–2000); Not Recommended (1985–95). These vehicles are more mini-truck than minivan. Believe it or not, these run-of-the-mill minivans are beginning to look quite good when compared to the problem-plagued Chrysler and Ford minivans and the overpriced Asian competition (VW? Not even in the running). They have fewer safety-related problems reported to the government, are easy to repair, and cost little to acquire. Stay away from the unreliable AWD models; they're expensive to repair and not very durable. Strong points: Brisk acceleration, trailer-towing capability, lots of passenger room and cargo space, and well laid-out instrument panel with easy-to-read gauges. The optional Dutch doors provide better rear-view visibility and include a convenient lift-open glass and defroster. Very low ground clearance enhances this minivan's handling, but precludes most off-roading. Good brakes. Reasonable price, and improved reliability and quality control. Weak points: Driving position is awkward for most drivers; tall drivers will find the pedals too close; obtrusive engine makes for very narrow front footwells that give little room for the driver's left foot to rest. Difficult entry/exit due to the high step-up and the intruding wheelwell. Harsh ride, limited front seat room, interior noise levels rise sharply at highway speeds, and excessive fuel consumption made worse by the AWD option. **Maintenance/Repair costs:** Average. Most of the Astro's and Safari's defects are easy to diagnose by independent repairers, leading to cheaper repairs and a minimum of downtime. **Parts:** Good supply of cheap parts. A large contingent of independent parts suppliers keeps repair costs down. Parts are less expensive than they are for other vehicles in this class. **Best alternatives:** Front-drive minivans made by Nissan and Toyota have better handling and are more reliable and economical people carriers; unfortunately, they lack the Astro's considerable grunt, essential for cargo hauling and trailer towing. Also consider getting a later-model Ford Aerostar (watch the tranny, though), or a GM Montana or Venture, if hauling isn't a high priority.

Strengths and weaknesses: More a utility truck than a comfortable minivan, these boxy, rear-drive minivans are built on a reworked S-10 pickup chassis. As such, they offer uninspiring handling and relatively high fuel consumption. Both Astro and Safari come in a choice of either cargo or passenger van. The cargo van is used either commercially or as an inexpensive starting point for a fully customized vehicle. The Safari is identical to the Astro, except for a slightly higher base price.

With the right options, the Astro and Safari have the advantage of being versatile cargo haulers when equipped with a heavy-duty suspension. In fact, Astro's 5,500 lb. (2,500 kg) trailer-towing capability is 2,000 lb. (900 kg) more than that of the front-drive Venture. The base 4.3L V6 gives acceptable acceleration, but the High Output variant of the same engine (first available in the 1991 model) is a far better choice, particularly when it's mated to a manual gearbox. The full-time AWD versions aren't very refined, have a high failure rate, and are expensive to diagnose and repair.

The 1985–95 versions suffer from failure-prone automatic transmissions, poor braking systems, failure-prone AC compressors, and fragile steering components. The early base V6 provides ample power, but also produces lots of noise, consumes excessive amounts of fuel, and tends to have leaking head gaskets and failure-prone oxygen sensors. These computer-related problems often rob the engine of sufficient power to keep up in traffic. While the 5-speed manual transmission shifts fairly easily, the automatic takes forever to downshift on the highway. Handling isn't particularly agile on these minivans, and the power steering doesn't provide the driver with enough road feel. Unloaded, the Astro provides very poor traction, the ride isn't comfortable on poor road surfaces, and interior noise is rampant. Many drivers find the driving position awkward (no left-leg room) and the heating/defrosting system inadequate. Many engine components are hidden under the dashboard, making repair or maintenance awkward. Even on more recent models, highway performance and overall reliability aren't impressive. Through the 2000 model year, the 4-speed automatic transmissions are clunky and hard shifting, though they're much more reliable than Ford or Chrysler gearboxes.

Other owners report that the front suspension, steering components, computer modules, and catalytic converter can wear out within as little as 60,000 km. There have also been lots of complaints about electrical, exhaust, cooling, and fuel system bugs; inadequate heating/defrosting; failure-prone wiper motors; and axle seals wearing out every 12–18 months.

Body hardware is fragile, and fit and finish is the pits. Water leaks from windows and doors are common, yet hard to diagnose. Squeaks and rattles are legion and hard to locate. Sliding-door handles often break off and the sliding door frequently jams in cold temperatures. The hatch release for the Dutch doors occasionally doesn't work, and the driver-side vinyl seat lining tears apart. Premature paint peeling, delamination, and surface rust are fairly common.

The 1995–99 models are a bit improved, but they still have problems carried over from earlier years, with stalling, hard starts, and expensive and frequent automatic transmission, power-steering, wheel bearing, brake pad, caliper, and rotor repairs heading the list. Year 2000–01 models are more reliable and better performing, inasmuch as they underwent considerable upgrading by GM. Nevertheless, buyers should be aware that extra attention is merited in the following areas: excessive vibration transmitted through the AWD; automatic transmission clunk; poor braking performance (brake pedal hardens and brakes don't work after going over bumps or rough roads) and expensive brake maintenance; electronic computer modules and fuel system glitches that cause the Check Engine light to remain lit; hard starts, no-starts, or chronic stalling, especially when going downhill; heating and AC performance hampered by poor air distribution; electrical system shorts; and sliding door misalignment and broken hinges.

Safety summary: All models/years: NHTSA has recorded numerous complaints of dashboard fires. • Power steering locks up or fails unexpectedly, components wear out quickly, and steering may bind when turning. • Seatbelt complaints are also common: seatbelts tighten up unexpectedly, cannot be adjusted, or have nowhere to latch. • Reports of ABS failure, brakes hesitating when applied, brakes engaging for no reason, and premature brake wear. **All models: 1995–98**—Vehicle continues to accelerate after foot is removed from accelerator. • Frequent stalling. • Erratic engine performance due to blocked catalytic converter. • Engine leaks oil. • Power-steering fluid leaks. • Vehicle jerks to one side when braking. • Front wheels lock up when turning the steering wheel to the right from a stop while in gear. • Steering stuck when turning. • Fresh-air ventilation system allows fumes from other vehicles to enter interior compartment. • With jack almost fully extended, wheel doesn't lift off ground. • Spare tire not safe for driving over 60 km/h. • Design of horn makes it difficult to use. • Horn buttons require excessive pressure to activate them. • Driver-side window failure. • Sliding door suddenly fell off. • Faulty door hinges allow the door to fall off. • Sliding door rattles. • Front passenger door won't close. • Passenger-side door glass fell out. • Rear hatch latch release failed. • Rear hatch hydraulic rods are too weak to support hatch. • Front passenger's seat reclining mechanism failed. • Poor traction. • Parked in gear and rolled downhill. • Transmission failures. • Left rear axle seal leaks, causing lubricant to burn on brake lining. • Excessive rear-end axle noise. • Sudden wheel bearing failure. • AC clutch fell apart. • Alternator bearing failure. **1999**—Only 58 safety-related complaints, compared with an average of a few hundred for most vehicles. Many of the 1999 model problems have been reported by owners of earlier model years, which isn't surprising, since these vehicles have changed little over the years. • Chronic stalling can't be remedied by dealers. • Check Engine light is constantly lit and engine continues to misfire. • Difficult starting. • Hard shifting between First and Second gear; transmission slippage. • Delayed shifting or stalling when passing from Drive to Reverse. • Leaking axle seals. • Rear cargo door hinge and latch slipped off, and door opened 180 degrees. • Floor mat moves under brake and accelerator pedals. • Brake pedal set too close to the accelerator. • Fuel gauge failure caused by faulty sending unit. 2000—Brake and gas pedals are too close together. • When brakes are applied, rear wheels tend to lock up while front wheels continue to turn. • Vehicle stalls when accelerating or turning. • Astro rolls back when stopped on an incline in Drive. • Sliding door slams shut on an incline or hinges break. • Extensive damage caused to bumper and undercarriage by driving over gravel roads. 2001—Sudden acceleration. • Chronic stalling. • Hard starts. • Cranks, but would not start, due to broken electrical connection. • Sudden total electrical failure, especially when going into Reverse. • Brake pedal set too high. • Differential in transfer case locked up while driving; defective axle seals. • Vehicle rolls backward on an incline while in Drive (dealer adjusted transfer case, to no avail). • Fuel gauge failure. • Faulty AC vents. • Water can be trapped inside the wheels and freeze, causing the wheels to be out of balance.

Secret Warranties/Service Tips/TSBs

All models: 1993–99—Tips on getting rid of AC odours. • Defective catalytic converters that cause a rotten-egg smell may be replaced free of charge under the vehicle's emissions warranty. **1993–2000**—GM says that a chronic driveline clunk can't be silenced and is a normal characteristic of its vehicles. • Paint delamination, peeling, or fading (see Part Two). **1995–2000**—Dealer guidelines for brake servicing under warranty. **1996–97**—Excessive engine noise can be curtailed by installing an upgraded valve stem oil seal. **1996–98**—Rough engine performance may be caused by a water-contaminated oxygen sensor, and a rough idle shortly after starting may be caused by sticking poppet valves. • Accessory drivebelt noise is likely caused by a misaligned power-steering pump pulley. **1996–2000**—Hard start, no-start, backfire, and kickback when starting may be corrected by replacing the crankshaft position sensor. • Silence a boom-type noise heard during engine warm-up by installing an exhaust dampener assembly. • A rough idle after start and/or a Service Engine light that stays lit may mean you have a stuck injector poppet valve ball that needs cleaning. **1996–2001**—Poor heat distribution in driver's area of vehicle (install new heat ducts). • Exhaust rattle noise. **1997–98**—An engine ticking noise that appears when the temperature falls may require an EVAP purge solenoid valve. **1997–99**—A hard start, no-start, and rough idle can be fixed by replacing the fuel tank fill pipe assembly and cleaning the SCPI poppet valves. **1999**—Steering column squeaking can be silenced by replacing the steering wheel SIR module coil assembly. **1999–2000**—If the engine runs hot, overheats, or loses coolant, try polishing the radiator filler neck or replacing the radiator cap before letting any mechanic convince you that more expensive repairs are needed. **2001**—Harsh automatic transmission shifts. • 2–4 band and 3–4 clutch damage. • Steering shudder felt when making low-speed turns. • Excessive brake squeal. • Wet carpet/odour in passenger footwell area (repair evaporator case drain to cowl seal/open evaporator case drain). • Delayed shifts, slips, flares or extended shifts during cold operation (replace shift solenoid valve assembly).

Astro, Safari Profile

	1994	1995	1996	1997	1998	1999	2000	2001
Cost Price ($)								
Cargo	18,198	22,640	23,475	25,110	25,110	23,290	24,015	24,665
CS/base	19,998	23,295	25,285	26,920	26,920	23,839	25,675	26,440
Used Values ($)								
Cargo Λ	3,500	4,500	7,000	9,000	12,500	15,000	18,000	20,000
Cargo V	2,800	3,000	6,000	7,500	11,000	14,000	16,500	19,000
CS/base Λ	5,000	6,000	8,000	10,000	13,500	16,500	19,000	21,500
CS/base V	3,800	4,500	7,000	9,000	12,500	15,000	17,500	20,000
Extended Warranty	Y	Y	Y	Y	N	N	N	N
Secret Warranty	Y	Y	Y	Y	Y	Y	N	N
Reliability	❷	❷	❷	❷	③	③	③	③
Crash Safety (F)	❶	—	③	③	③	③	③	③
Off-set	—	—	❶	❶	❶	❶	❶	❶
Head Restraints (F)	—	❶	❷	❷	—	❷	—	❷
Rear	—	—	❶	❶	—	—	—	—

LUMINA, LUMINA APV, MONTANA, SILHOUETTE, TRANS SPORT, VENTURE   ★★★★

RATING: Above Average (1997–2001); Average (1995–96); Not Recommended (1990–94). **Strong points:** A comfortable ride, easy handling, dual sliding doors, plenty of comfort and convenience features, flexible seating arrangements, good visibility fore and aft, lots of storage bins and compartments, and good crash scores. Some of the quietest minivans in their class. **Weak points:** Average acceleration with a light load; unproven AWD; less effective rear drum brakes and excessive brake fading; tall drivers will find insufficient head room, and short drivers may find it hard to see where the front ends; low rear seats force passengers into an uncomfortable knees-up position; narrow cabin makes front-to-rear access a bit difficult; seat cushions on the centre and rear bench seats are hard, flat, and too short, and the seatbacks lack sufficient lower back support; cargo may not slide out easily, due to the rear sill sticking up a few inches; a high number of safety-related failures; and disappointing fuel economy. **Maintenance/Repair costs:** Average. Transmission, ABS, and electrical malfunctions will likely cause maintenance costs to rise after the third year of ownership. **Parts:** Engine parts are generic to GM's other models, so they should be reasonably priced and not hard to find. Body parts are likely to be more problematic and costly. **Best alternatives:** Honda Odyssey, Nissan Quest or Axxess, and Toyota Sienna. Many of these vans are equipped with Firestone tires—replace them with Michelins or Pirellis and ask for a $200 rebate.

Strengths and weaknesses: GM's plastic-bodied, front-drive minivans resemble a swoopy station wagon more than the traditional minivan. These vehicles use the Chevrolet Lumina platform and therefore have more carlike handling than GM's Astro and Safari. Seating is limited to five adults in the standard models (two up front and three on a removable bench seat), but this can be increased to seven if you find a vehicle equipped with optional modular seats. Seats can be folded down flat, creating additional storage space. Incidentally, be careful not to drop your keys between the windshield and the dash, because you'll need a fishing rod to get them back.

Be wary of vehicles equipped with a power-assisted passenger-side sliding door; it's both convenient and dangerous—despite its override circuit that prevents the door from closing on a hand, a number of injuries have been reported. Furthermore, with most sliding doors, mechanical and electronic glitches allow the doors to open when they shouldn't, and they are difficult to close. Overall, this convenience feature is overpriced, failure prone, and a bit slow in operation.

Pre-1997 models had serious reliability problems—notably, electronic module (PROM) and starter failures; premature front brake component wear, brake fluid leakage, and noisy braking; short circuits that burn out alternators, batteries, power door lock activators, and the blower motor; AC evaporator core failures; premature wearout of the inner and outer tie-rods; automatic transmission breakdowns; abysmal fit and finish; chronic sliding door malfunctions; and faulty rear seat latches. Other problems include a fuel-thirsty and poor-performing 3-speed automatic transmission; a poorly mounted sliding door; side door glass that pops open; squeaks, rattles, and clunks in the instrument panel cluster area and suspension; and a wind buffeting noise around the front doors. The large dent- and rust-resistant plastic panels are robot-bonded to the frame, and they absorb engine and road noise very well, in addition to having an impressive record for durability.

By the way, don't trust the towing limit listed in GM's owner's manual. Automakers publish tow ratings that are on the optimistic side—and sometimes they even lie. Also, don't be surprised to find that the base 3.1L engine doesn't handle a full load of passenger and cargo, especially when mated to the 3-speed automatic transmission. The ideal powertrain combo would be the 4-speed automatic coupled to the optional "3800" V6 (first used on the 1996 versions). These minivans use the same quiet-running V6 powerplant that harnesses a few more horses than the Chrysler minivans' top-line 3.8L 6-cylinder, providing good mid-range and top-end power. The GM engine is hampered by less torque, however, making for less grunt when accelerating, and frequently downshifting out of Overdrive when climbing moderate grades. The electronically controlled 4-speed automatic transmission shifts smoothly and quietly—a clear advantage over Chrysler and Ford.

1997 and later models are less rattle prone, due to a more rigid body structure than that of their predecessors. However, fit and finish is still not up to the Asian competition. Chassis could still use reinforcing to mute the rattles heard when passing over rough roads. Owner-reported problems on post-'97s include chronic plastic intake manifold gasket failures (covered by a 6-year/100,000 km secret warranty), EGR valve failures, transmission fluid leaks, electrical glitches shorting out dash gauges and causing difficult starting, excessive front brake noise and frequent repairs (rotors and pads), and assorted body deficiencies, including water leaks in the jack well.

1994 model year changes included a shortened nose, APV designation dropped, a standard driver-side airbag, length cut by three inches, integrated child safety seats offered on seven-passenger versions, and optional traction control. 1995 models were carried over unchanged. 1996 brought a new standard 3.4L V6, and the Lumina was replaced by the Venture at the end of the model year. Changes in 1997: an optional driver-side sliding door on extended versions, and standard dual airbags and ABS; in 1998 the sliding driver-side door was available on more models, and side airbags were offered for the first time. In 1999 there was 5-hp boost to the base V6 engine (185 hp), heated rear-view mirrors, and the debut of a Premiere model, which offers a mobile entertainment centre that includes a videocassette player and colour monitor. The Venture got de-powered airbags, upgraded electronically controlled automatic transmission, and a standard rear-window defogger. 2000 models have dual sliding rear side doors; 2001 vehicles got a slight re-styling of the front and rear end and a fold-flat third-row seat.

Safety summary: All models/years: Watch out for excessive brake fading; the brakes progressively lose their effectiveness after repeated application. • Other common problems: sudden steering loss in rainy weather or when passing over a puddle (serpentine belt slippage); ABS brake failures; ABS light stays on for no reason; airbags fail to deploy; sliding doors suddenly open, close, come off their tracks, jam shut, stick open, injure children, and rattle (1997–2001 models recalled); fire may ignite around the fuel filler nozzle or within the ignition switch; tie-rod failures may cause loss of control; during highway driving, transmission slips from Drive into Neutral. • Some front door-mounted seatbelts cross uncomfortably at the neck, and there's a nasty blind spot on the driver's side that requires a small stick-on convex mirror to correct. **All models: 1995–99**—Transmission won't hold gear on a grade. • Headlight assembly collects moisture, burns bulb, or falls out. • Seatback suddenly collapses. • Windshield wipers fail intermittently. • Accelerator and brake pedals are too close together. • Fuel slosh/clunk when vehicle stops or accelerates (new tank useless). • Self-activating door locks lock occupants out or in. • Door handles break inside the door assembly. • Horn is hard to access. • Window latch failures. **2000**—The 2000 models still have scattered automatic transmission failures and hard, noisy shifting; AC glitches; frequent replacement of front brake calipers, pads, and rotors; and sliding door and window problems. Other problems: fuel leakage from the fuel regulator; fire ignited under passenger seat due to "hot" wires shorting out; automatic transmission won't hold vehicle stopped on an incline; steering column locked up while vehicle was underway; Service Engine light stays lit; electrical cluster module shorts, causing temperature gauge, speedometer, ABS, seatbelt, and coolant malfunctions, and engine surging, stalling, or no-starts. **2001**—Fire ignited under driver's seat. • Windshield suddenly exploded outward while driving with wipers activated. • Firestone tire blowout. • Brakes activate on their own, making it appear as if van is pulling a load. • Steering idler arm fell off due to missing bolt. • Loose fuel tank due to loose bolts/bracket. • Fuel tank cracked when passing over a tree branch. • Plastic tube within heating system fell off and wedged behind the accelerator pedal. • Bracket weld pin that secures the rear split seat sheared off. • Faulty fuel pump causes chronic stalling, no-starts, surging, and sudden acceleration. • Vehicle suddenly lost power while going uphill, slid back, and stalled. • Van will roll back while in gear on an incline. • Service Engine light comes on constantly. • Service Engine light remains on, due to transmission bearing assembled backward in the transmission box. • Premature transmission failures. • Centre rear lap seatbelt isn't long enough to secure a rear-facing child safety seat. • Children can slide out of the integrated child safety seat. • Electrical harness failures result in complete electrical shutdown. • Headlights, interior lights, gauges, and instruments fail intermittently (electrical cluster module is the prime suspect). • Excess padding around horn makes it difficult to depress horn button in an emergency. • Weak-sounding horn. • Loud noise emanating from under the vehicle. • Frequent windshield wiper motor failures. • Heater doesn't warm up vehicle sufficiently. • Antifreeze smell intrudes into interior. • Intermittent no-starts or hard starts. • Premature failure of the transmission's Fourth clutch. • Some transmissions may produce a grinding or growling noise when engaged on an incline with the engine running and the parking brake not applied. • Delayed shifts, slips, flares, or extended shifts in cold weather. • Poorly performing rear AC. • Flickering interior and exterior lights. • Airbag warning lamp stays lit. • Windshield glass distortion. • Exterior light condensation.

Secret Warranties/Service Tips/TSBs

All models: 1990–98—An oil odour coming from the engine compartment may be eliminated by changing the crankshaft rear main oil seal.

1993–95—An engine coolant leak from the throttle body assembly may require an upgraded service seal kit. **1993–99**—Tips on eliminating AC odours. • Defective catalytic converters that cause a rotten-egg smell in the interior may be replaced free of charge under the emissions warranty. **1993–2000**—GM says that a chronic driveline clunk can't be silenced and is a normal characteristic of its vehicles. • Paint delamination, peeling, or fading (see Part Two). **1993–2002**—Tips on eliminating AC odours during start-up in hot, humid climates. • Delayed shifting during cold weather. **1995**—A thud/clunk noise occurs when the fuel tank is more than three-quarters full; GM will replace the fuel tank and sender assembly. **1995–96**—Intermittent Neutral/loss of Drive at highway speeds can be fixed by replacing the control valve body assembly. **1995–2000**—Dealer guidelines for brake servicing under warranty. **1996–98**—A cold-engine tick or rattle after start-up can be silenced by installing all six pistons with pin assemblies. **1996–2001**—Poor heat distribution in driver's area of vehicle (install new heat ducts). **1997**—Rear brake clicking or squealing may be caused by a misadjusted parking brake cable. • Brakes that don't work, drag, heat up, or wear out early may have a variety of causes, all outlined in TSB #73-50-27. • A rear suspension thud or clunk may be silenced by installing upgraded rear springs. **1997–98**—A fuel tank thud or clunk noise may require new fuel tank straps and insulators. • Loose lumber noise coming from the rear of the vehicle when it passes over bumps means upgraded rear shock absorbers are required. • Poor rear windshield wiper performance may require that the fluid line be purged. • Windshield wiper blade chatter can be reduced by changing the wiper arm. • Insufficient windshield clearing in defrost mode requires the installation of new seals. **1997–99**—Upgraded front disc pads will reduce brake squeal. **1997–2000**—Front door windows that are inoperative, slow, or noisy may need the window run channel adjusted or replaced, in addition to new weather stripping. **1997–2001**—Grinding or growling noise in Park on an incline. **1998**—No-start, engine miss, and rough idle may indicate that melted slush has contaminated the fuel system. **1998–99**—An inoperative sliding door may have a defective control module. **1998–2000**—Poor AC performance in humid weather may be caused by an undercharged AC system. **1999**—Diagnostic tips for an automatic transmission that slips, produces a harsh upshift and garage shifts, or causes acceleration shudders. **1999–2000**—If the engine runs hot, overheats, or loses coolant, try polishing the radiator filler neck or replacing the radiator cap before considering more expensive repairs. • Before taking on more expensive repairs to correct hard starts or no-starts, check the fuel pump. • An automatic transmission that whines in Park or Neutral, or a Service Engine light that stays on, may signal the need for a new drive sprocket support bearing. **1999–2001**—Transmission shudder when accelerating. **1999–2002**—Excessive engine knocking on start-up (TSB #01-06-01-028). **2000–01**—Flickering exterior and interior lights (replace generator voltage regulator ground screw). **2001**—Customer Satisfaction Program (read: secret warranty) to correct the rear HVAC control switch. • Delayed automatic transmission shifts, slips, flares, or extended shifts (see Century, Ciera). • Free seatbelt buckle correction (product safety campaign). • Remedies for MIL or airbag lights staying lit. • Wet carpet and odour in passenger footwell area.

Lumina, Lumina APV, Montana, Silhouette, Trans Sport, Venture Profile

	1994	1995	1996	1997	1998	1999	2000	2001
Cost Price ($)								
Lumina Cargo	17,998	20,110	20,110	—	—	—	—	—
Passenger	19,598	22,730	22,730	—	—	—	—	—
Montana	—	—	—	—	—	25,130	26,625	26,755
Silhouette	—	—	—	—	—	—	—	31,105
Trans Sport/SE	20,298	23,475	23,475	23,690	24,650	—	—	—
Venture	—	—	—	23,185	24,145	24,725	24,895	25,230
Used Values ($)								
Lumina Cargo ▲	3,500	4,000	6,000	—	—	—	—	—
Lumina Cargo ▼	2,500	3,000	4,500	—	—	—	—	—
Passenger ▲	6,000	7,000	8,500	—	—	—	—	—
Passenger ▼	5,000	6,000	7,500	—	—	—	—	—
Montana ▲	—	—	—	—	—	16,000	19,000	22,000
Montana ▼	—	—	—	—	—	14,500	17,500	20,000
Silhouette ▲	—	—	—	—	—	—	—	24,500
Silhouette ▼	—	—	—	—	—	—	—	23,000
Trans Sport/SE ▲	6,000	7,000	9,000	11,500	14,500	—	—	—
Trans Sport/SE ▼	4,500	5,500	7,500	10,000	13,000	—	—	—
Venture ▲	—	—	—	11,500	14,500	17,000	19,000	21,000
Venture ▼	—	—	—	10,000	13,000	15,000	17,500	20,000
Extended Warranty	Y	Y	Y	Y	N	N	N	N
Secret Warranty	Y	Y	Y	Y	Y	Y	Y	Y
Reliability	❷	❷	❷	③	④	④	④	④
Crash Safety (F)	⑤	⑤	⑤	④	④	④	④	④
Side	—	—	—	—	—	⑤	⑤	⑤
Off-set	—	—	—	❶	❶	❶	❶	❶
Rollover Resistance	—	—	—	—	—	—	—	③
Head Restraints (F)	—	—	—	❶	—	③	—	③
Rear	—	—	—	—	—	❶	—	—

Honda

ODYSSEY ★★★★

RATING: Above Average (1999–2001); Average (1996–98). A slightly better buy than the Toyota Sienna, thanks to the Odyssey's extra horse-power, more comfortable ride, and better use of interior space. The Sienna, on the other hand, has a bit more mid-range torque for passing or merging. On both minivans, quality has slipped in recent years, as evidenced by the disturbingly frequent reports of safety- and performance-related failures. Of particular concern are airbag malfunctions, automatic sliding door failures, transmission breakdowns and erratic shifting, and sudden brake loss. Early Odysseys get only an Average rating due to their small engine and interior—identical shortcomings to those of Mazda's recently revised MPV minivan. If you consider these early, fuel-efficient vehicles as full-sized, urban station wagons rather than highway-hauling minivans, you'll be much happier with your choice. The redesigned '99 model offers better performance and a larger interior, but it suffers from many first-year glitches. **Strong points:** Strong engine performance on recent models; carlike ride and handling; easy entry/exit; second driver-side door; quiet interior; most controls and displays are easy to reach and read; lots of passenger and cargo room; low step-up facilitates entry/exit; and an extensive list of standard equipment. **Weak points:** High-priced; early models equipped with weak engines; front-seat passenger leg room is marginal due to the restricted seat travel; the narrow back bench seat provides little leg room; radio control access is blocked by the shift lever, and it's difficult to calibrate the radio without taking your eyes off the road; power-sliding doors are slow to retract; some tire rumble and body drumming at highway speeds; premium fuel is required for optimum performance; a decline in quality; poor head restraint crashworthiness rating; and rear-seat head restraints impede side and rear visibility. The storage well won't take any tire larger than a "space saver"—meaning you'll carry your flat in the back. **Maintenance/Repair costs:** Higher than average, but any garage can repair these minivans. **Parts:** Moderately priced parts; availability is better than average because the Odyssey uses many generic Accord parts. Parts used in recall campaigns, though, are often back-ordered. **Best alternatives:** if you want something cheap, but still reliable, consider a Mercury Villager or Nissan Axxess and Quest (see Appendix II). If you want better handling and reliability, the closest competitor to the Odyssey is Toyota's Sienna minivan. The Pontiac Montana and Chevrolet Venture from GM are good front-drive choices—they're only a bit less reliable, but are still acceptable. If you're looking for lots of towing "grunt," then the rear-drive GM Astro, Safari, or full-sized vans would be good buys. Ditch the original equipment Firestone tires: you don't need the extra risk.

Strengths and weaknesses: When it was first launched in 1995, the Odyssey was a sales dud, simply because Canadians and *Lemon-Aid* saw through Honda's ruse in trying to pass off an underpowered, mid-sized, four-door station wagon with a raised roof as a minivan. However, several years ago the Odyssey was redesigned, and it now represents one of the better minivans on the Canadian market.

One can sum up the strengths and weaknesses of the 1996–98 Odyssey (and its American twin through the 1998 model, the Isuzu Oasis) in three words: performance, performance, performance. You get carlike performance and handling, responsive steering, and a comfortable ride, off-set by slow-as-molasses-in-January acceleration with a full load, a raucous engine, and limited passenger/cargo space due to the narrow body.

Despite the above-mentioned drawbacks, the 1996–98 Odysseys have proven to be more reliable and offer better handling than American rear-drive, truck-inspired minivans. But their high price on the used-car market, weak 2.2L 4-cylinder engine (given 10 extra horses in the '98 version), and small dimensions can't compete with GM's front-drives or most rear-drive competitors. The upgraded 1999 models have powerful 6-cylinder engines and a larger interior, wiping out most of the previous model's deficiencies. The drivetrain, though, is lots rougher than Toyota's Sienna and doesn't feel capable of handling as heavy a load. The timing chain may also have to be replaced frequently.

Reliability is much better than average, but Honda still has a few problems to work out. One notable and hazardous example: failure-prone sliding doors. Imagine, they open when they shouldn't, won't close when they should, catch fingers and arms, get stuck open or closed, are noisy, and frequently require expensive servicing. The Check Engine light may stay lit due to a defective fuel filler neck. There's a fuel sloshing noise when accelerating or coming to a stop, and the transmission clunks or bangs when backing uphill or when shifted into Reverse. There are also reports of rattling and chattering in forward gear. Owners note a loud wind noise and vibration from the left side of the front windshield, along with a constant vibration felt through the steering assembly and front wheels. Passenger doors may also require excessive force to open. And owners have complained of severe static electricity shocks when exiting. Expect frequent and high-cost front brake maintenance (see "Secret Warranties/Service Tips/TSBs"), and trim and accessory items that come loose, break away, or malfunction. Automatic transmission failures continue to be a major and shameful Odyssey shortcoming that should tilt one's choice in favour of the Toyota Sienna or GM front- or rear-drives. Interestingly, there is only one mention of the problem in Honda service bulletins, leading one to conclude that Honda doesn't know what to do, or doesn't care.

Other owner-reported problems: transmission breakdowns; when shifting into Fourth gear, engine almost stalls out and produces a noise like valve clattering; transmission gear whine at 90 km/h or when in

Fourth gear (transmission replaced); front-end clunking caused by welding breaks in the front sub-frame; vehicle pulls to the right when underway; premature front brake wear; excessive front brake noise; and sliding side door frequently malfunctions. Plastic interior panels have rough edges and are often misaligned.

The comprehensive base warranty has lots of "wiggle room" that the service manager can use to apply "goodwill" adjustments for post-warranty problems. However, dealer servicing has come in for a great deal of criticism from Lemon-Aid readers. Owners complain that recall repairs take an eternity to perform due to parts shortages, and dealers may be reluctant or unable to perform the required tasks competently.

In 1996, Isuzu began marketing the Odyssey as its own Oasis in the U.S. 1997 models have small improvements that include intermittent windshield wipers; '98s have a new 2.3L engine that boosts horsepower by 10 more horses (not enough!), and a restyled grille and instrument panel make their debut. In 1999, a new, powerful engine and increased size make this Average-rated minivan an Above Average buy. Nevertheless, seats are still too firm, steering requires fully extended arms, power sliding doors operate slowly, and the cupholder under the radio is useless. 2001 models have user-friendly child safety seat tether anchors, upgraded stereo speakers, and an intermittent rear window wiper.

Safety summary: All models/years: NHTSA reports that Honda USA is actively investigating reports of transmission banging when put into Reverse, severe pulling to right at highway speeds, and excessive front brake noise. • The power sliding door is another common problem: it opens and closes on its own, often pinning passengers' fingers, or fails to open and close properly. • There have been numerous reports of total brake failure, as well as brake noise caused by premature wear of the brake pads and rotors. **All models: 1995**—Front two wheels separated from car while driving. • When vehicle is going over a hill, the cruise control has a tendency to overshoot the set speed by almost 10 km/h. • AC doesn't cool the vehicle sufficiently and puts out a nasty odour. • Defroster can't clear up fogged windows. • Due to its design, the muffler can suddenly fly off while the vehicle is underway. • Far rear restraint retracted so tightly that it had to be cut to free the passenger. • Rear middle seatbelt slips and won't stay snug around the lap. **1996**—While backing out the vehicle, occupant turned AC on, and vehicle shot forward with no brakes. • Cruise control failed while vehicle was going uphill. **1997–98**—Sudden acceleration upon brake application. • Minivan was put in Drive, and AC was turned on; vehicle suddenly accelerated, brakes failed, and the minivan hit a brick wall. **1999**—Sudden, unintended acceleration due to stuck accelerator. • Fire erupted in the electrical harness. • Another fire erupted as vehicle was being fuelled. • Plastic gas tank cracks, leaks fuel. • Gasoline smell when transmission is put into Reverse. • Side window exploded while driving. • Check Engine light comes on and vehicle loses all power. • Engine and electrical shutdown when coming to a stop. • When driving, all the instrument panel lights will suddenly go out (faulty multiplex controller suspected). • When parked on a hill, vehicle may roll backward; transmission doesn't hold vehicle when stopped at a light on a hill and foot is taken off accelerator or brake. • Complete loss of power steering due to a pinhole in the power-steering return hose. • Poor power-steering performance in cold weather. • Many incidents of sudden tire tread separation (Firestone). • Power door locks lock and unlock on their own. • Design of the gear shifter interferes with the radio controls. • Child unable to get out of seatbelt due to buckle lockup. • Faulty fuel gauge. • Inconvenient cell phone jack location. 2000—During fuelling, fuel tank burst into flames. • Many incidents where driver-side sliding door opened onto fuel hose while fuelling, damaging gas flap hinge and tank. • Sudden, unintended acceleration when slowing for a stop sign. • On cold days, accelerator pedal is hard to depress. • Catastrophic failure of the right side suspension, causing wheel to buckle. • Vehicle continually pulls to the right; dealers unable to correct problem. • Excessive steering wheel vibration at 105+ km/h. • Electric doors often inoperative. • As child slept in safety seat, seatbelt tightened progressively to point that fire department had to be called; other similar incidents. • Chronic automatic transmission problems: won't shift into lower gears; suddenly loses power; torque converter failure; makes a loud popping sound when put into Reverse. • Two incidents where vehicle rear-ended due to transmission malfunction. • Van's transmission doesn't hold when stopped on a hill; gas or brakes have to be constantly applied. • Power seatback moves on its own. • Dash lights don't adequately illuminate the dash panel. • Driver's seatback suddenly reclines, hitting rear passenger's legs, even though power switch is off. • Protruding bolts in the door assembly are hazardous. • Seatbelt buckle fails to latch. • Driver-side mirror breaks away; mirror glass fell out due to poor design. 2001—While fuelling, fuel tank exploded. • In a frontal collision, van caught fire due to a cracked brake fluid reservoir. • Sudden acceleration when approaching a stop sign. • While travelling at 90 km/h, accelerator jammed. • Chronic stalling (transmission replaced). • Many reports of sudden transmission and torque converter failure. • While stopped on an incline of about 35 degrees, van rolled backward. • When Reverse is engaged, car makes a popping or clunking sound. • Cracked wheel rim. • Check Engine light constantly on (suspect faulty gasoline filler neck). • Engine knocks when vehicle reaches 90 km/h. • Entire vehicle shakes excessively at highway speeds and van pulls to the right (dealer said some type of bar adjustment was needed). • Passenger-side door window suddenly exploded while driving on the highway. • Driver's seatback collapsed from rear-end collision. • Driver's power seat will suddenly recline on its own, squeezing rear occupant's legs and falling on child. • Rear seatbelt tightened up so much that a child had to be cut free. • Too much play in rear lapbelts, which won't tighten adequately, making it difficult to install a child safety seat securely. • Inoperative driver seatbelt buckle. • Faulty speedometer and tachometer. • Remote wouldn't open or lock vehicle. • Placement of the gear shift lever interferes with the radio's controls. • Unable to depress accelerator pedal on cold days. • Can hear gasoline sloshing in tank while driving. • Frequent static electricity shocks. • Many owners report that the rear head restraints seriously hamper rear and forward visibility and that it was difficult to see vehicles coming from the right side.

Secret Warranties/Service Tips/TSBs

All models/years: Most of Honda's TSBs allow for special warranty consideration on a "goodwill" basis by the company's District Service Manager or Zone Office, even after the warranty has expired or the vehicle has changed hands. Referring to this euphemism will increase your chances of getting some kind of refund for repairs that are obviously factory defects. This is a big plus for Odyssey owners with automatic transmission and sliding door claims, and it has boosted owner loyalty. In fact, I don't know of a single Odyssey owner who has paid for the correction of the above defects. Chrysler, Ford, and GM, on the other hand, have identical transmission and door problems for which they demand owners pay some or all of the repair costs. This is one of the reasons why Honda and Toyota minivans are given preferred ratings, even though their vehicles have similar deficiencies. **All models: 1995–97**—In a settlement with the U.S. Environmental Protection Agency, Honda paid fines totalling $17.1 million (U.S.) and extended its emissions warranty on 1.6 million 1995–97 models to 14 years/150,000 miles (240,000 km). Canadian owners may wish to use this settlement as leverage for free repairs in Canada, or use the full terms of the settlement when visiting the United States. One thing is certain: Neither Transport Canada nor Environment Canada are sufficiently enthused to render any assistance. • Rear wheel bearing noise can be silenced by replacing the hub bearing assembly and hub caps. • If the driver's seat makes a clicking noise, you may need to install a stop in the rear seat rail. **1997**—The front balancer oil shaft may back out of the oil pump housing over time. If this happens, the oil can be rapidly pumped out of the engine without warning, resulting in serious engine damage. Free repairs are offered under a Product Update Campaign (NHTSA TSB #SB618907 and #SB618908). • Troubleshooting a leaky automatic transmission torque converter. • If the tailgate-open indicator light stays on, you may need to replace the tailgate latch assembly. • Distorted sound from the front speakers can be corrected only by installing new speakers. **1997–98**—If the blower motor works only on high speed, try replacing the blower motor and resistor. **1998**—Harsh or late upshifts and downshifts are likely caused by a faulty clutch pressure switch (eligible for "goodwill"

consideration). • More info on leaking transmission torque converters. •
Front brake growling and excessive vibration when braking.
1998–2001—Correcting a warped or deformed windshield moulding.
1999—Faulty clutch pressure switches may screw up automatic shifting,
and leaky torque converters are still a problem (both items are eligible for
"goodwill" consideration). • Suggested fix for an automatic transmis-
siomn that bangs into gear. • Insufficient EGR flow causing poor engine
performance or a DTC PO401 code reading has prompted Honda to carry
out a free service campaign whereby the company will replace, at no
charge, the rear intake manifold end plate and gasket, the PCV hose, and
the intake manifold cover. • Problems with the fuel tank pressure sensor
are covered in TSB #99-056 and could call for the installation of an inline orifice in the two-way valve vacuum hose. • Honda is investigating
complaints concerning pulling or drifting at moderate speeds. •
Excessive front brake noise will be silenced under a "goodwill" repair if
you get Honda's permission first, says TSB #99013. This correction
involves refinishing the front discs and installing new pads. • There's an
incredibly large number of sliding door problems covered by a recall and
a plethora of service bulletins that are simply too numerous to print
here. Ask Honda politely for the bulletins or "goodwill" assistance. If
refused, subpoena the documents through small claims court. Normally,
ALLDATA would supply the data for $25 (U.S.), but Honda USA has
enjoined the company from giving out bulletin information to its customers. Shameful! • AC knocking may require the installation of a new
compressor clutch set. • Heat may not be distributed through the ceiling
vents. • Front windows that bind or are noisy when activated require
that a mechanic inspect the window regulator guide rail for proper lubrication, and possibly replace the glass run channel and adjust the glass
channels. • An inaccurate fuel gauge is likely caused by a faulty sending
unit. • Some vehicles produce a groaning noise when coming to a stop. •
Dash clicking or ticking. **2000–01**—Clunk or bang when engaging
Reverse. • Bulletin confirms Honda USA is still investigating complaints
of pulling or drifting (Service Bulletin Number: 99165, Bulletin Sequence
Number: 802, Date of Bulletin: 9909, NHTSA Item Number: SB608030). •
Excessive front brake noise. • More reports of dash ticking or clicking. •
Additional sliding door bulletins. • Intermittent wiper operation. **2001**—
Harsh or late upshifts or downshifts may be due to faulty clutch pressure
switches. • Troubleshooting automatic transmission vibration. • Ceiling
vents may not distribute heat. • Sliding door latch problems. •
Temperature gauge sticks in the middle position. • Roof rack creates a
wind buffeting noise. • Third-row seat won't unlatch.

Odyssey Profile

	1996	1997	1998	1999	2000	2001
Cost Price ($)						
LX	28,796	28,995	29,800	30,600	30,600	30,800
EX	—	—	—	33,600	33,600	33,800
Used Values ($)						
LX ▲	11,500	13,500	17,500	20,000	22,500	26,500
LX ▼	9,500	12,000	16,000	19,000	21,000	24,500
EX ▲	—	—	—	21,000	24,000	28,000
EX ▼	—	—	—	20,000	22,000	26,500
Extended Warranty	N	N	N	N	N	N
Secret Warranty	Y	Y	Y	Y	Y	Y
Reliability	③	③	③	④	⑤	⑤
Crash Safety (F)	④	④	—	⑤	⑤	⑤
Side	—	—	—	—	⑤	⑤
Rollover Resistance	—	—	—	—	—	④
Head Restraints (F)	❷	❷	—	❷	—	❷
Rear	—	—	—	❶	—	—

Mazda

MPV ★★

RATING: Below Average (2000–01); Average (1996–98); Below Average (1988–95). This underpowered, lumbering, undersized, and overpriced minivan is an Odyssey wannabe that simply comes across as odd. It's hobbled by poor reliability and servicing, yet there are remarkably few safety-related complaints in NHTSA's database. The 1996–98 models have lots of potential, if they don't fall apart as they age. There was no '99 model. The redesigned 2000 model is hampered by a wimpy powertrain and is just too small for most tasks. Strong points: Well appointed (lots of gadgets), comfortable ride and easy handling, good driver's position, responsive steering, and innovative storage spots. Without a doubt, the MPV manages its limited interior space far better than the competition. Not many factory-related defects reported. Weak points: The small V6 engine is performance challenged; it gives the impression that there's nothing in reserve, with barely enough power for highway use and leisurely acceleration from a stop (like the first Odysseys). Mediocre automatic transmission performance. Smaller than most of the competition; don't believe for a minute that the MPV will hold seven passengers in comfort—six is more like it. Elbow room is at a premium, and it takes a lithe figure to move down the front- and middle-seat aisle. Excessive engine and road noise. Dealer servicing and head office support have been problematic in the past. **Maintenance/Repair costs:** Average; independent garages can service these minivans more cheaply than Mazda dealers. **Parts:** Likely to be back-ordered and cost more than average, despite Mazda's best efforts to cut prices. **Best alternatives:** a late-model GM front-drive, Honda Odyssey, Ford Mercury Villager, Nissan Axxess or Quest, or Toyota Sienna.

Strengths and weaknesses: Mazda's only minivan quickly became a bestseller when it first came on the market in 1989, then its popularity plummeted as the competition added more powerful engines and increased interior room. Mazda hoped to get a fresh start with the redesigned 2000 MPV, but that iteration embodied all the mistakes made by Honda's first Odyssey—a 170-hp engine not suitable for hauling a full load and a foot shorter than the Ford Windstar and a half foot shorter than the Toyota Sienna and Nissan Quest.

The base 2.6L 16-valve 121-hp 4-cylinder engine is a dog, especially when hooked up to the automatic 4-speed transmission, which robs it of what little power it has. Ford's Duratec V6 (essentially the same engine that powers the Mercury Cougar) has plenty of power for in-town use, but nothing in reserve for highway use. Slow acceleration makes merging with traffic and passing other cars a bit scary. Expect lots of engine whine and vibration when passing the 4500-rpm mark. The drivetrain is particularly rough when cold, and shifts roughly and constantly. It lumbers through First and Second gear, and then bangs when going from Second to Third. The 5-speed manual transmission shifts easily and has well-spaced gears, but it's relatively rare.

Mediocre quality control and high fuel and parts costs make pre-1996 versions below-average buys when it comes to overall operating costs. Overheating and head gasket failures are commonplace with the 4-banger, and the temperature gauge warns you only when it's too late. Some cases of chronic engine knocking in cold weather with the 3.0L have been fixed by installing tighter-fitting, Teflon-coated pistons. Valve lifter problems are also common with this engine. Winter driving is compromised by the MPV's light rear end and mediocre traction, and low ground clearance means that off-road excursions shouldn't be too adventurous. 1996–98 models feature improved workmanship and more rugged construction. Nevertheless, expect engine oil leaks, transmission failures, ABS malfunctions, and premature wearout of the front and rear brakes.

Owners of more recent models report that the electronic computer module (ECU), automatic transmission driveshaft, upper shock mounts, front 4X4 drive axles and lash adjusters, AC core, and radiator fail within the first three years. Cold temperatures tend to "fry" the automatic window motor, and the paint is easily chipped and flakes off early, especially around the hood, tailgate, and front fenders. Premature brake caliper and rotor wear and excessive vibration/pulsation when braking continue to be a problem (rotor replacement every 12,000 km, premature rusting, and noisy when applied).

Safety summary: All models: 1998—Rear anti-sway bar brackets snapped off from rear axle housing. • Airbag failed to deploy. • ABS brake failure. • Defective gas cap causes the false activation of the Check Engine light. **2000**—Airbags failed to deploy. • Passenger-side seatbelt tightens up continually. • Fixed seatbelt anchors and buckle placement prevent the safe installation of child safety seats. • Shifter won't go into Park. • Vehicle windshield and side glass suddenly shattered while parked. • Excessive vibrations while cruising. • Vehicle constantly pulls to the left when underway. • Rear hatch door flew open when rear-ended. • Uneven springs. • Premature tire wear (incorrect coil springs and improperly aligned tie rods suspected). **2001**—Engine oil leaks. • Fuel smell emanating from the AC. • Sliding doors don't lock in place. • Brake caliper bolt fell off, causing vehicle to skid. • Excessive drivetrain vibration at 90 km/h. • Seatbelts lock up when vehicle is moving. • Seatbelts are too short. • Difficult keeping child safety seat secured properly, due to the anchor placement. • Rear visibility obstructed by high seatbacks.

Secret Warranties/Service Tips/TSBs

All models/years: TSB #006-94 looks into all the causes and remedies for excessive brake vibrations, and TSB #11-14-95 gives an excellent diagnostic flow chart for troubleshooting excessive engine noise. • Steering wheel slightly off-centre. • Serious paint peeling and delaminating will be fully covered for up to six years under a Mazda secret warranty, say owners. • Troubleshooting tips for correcting wind noise around doors and sunroof water leaks. • Servicing tips for an inoperative wiper motor. • Cigarette lighter may not work or stay in position. • Tips for eliminating a musty, mildew-type AC odour. **All models: 1995**—Brake pulsation repair. • Loose, rattling outer door handles. • Slightly off-centre steering wheel. • Tips for troubleshooting excessive engine noise. **1996–98**—Tips for correcting water leaks from the sliding sunroof. • Brake pulsation repair tips. • Front power window noise. • Wind noise around doors. **1997–98**—Front power window noise can be silenced by installing a modified window regulator. **2000**—Excessive front and rear brake noise. • Special Service Campaign to install, free of charge, bumper reinforcements to all MPVs made from March 13, 1999, to March 13, 2000. • Troubleshooting insufficient airflow. • Corroded or discoloured windshield wiper links inside the engine compartment caused by a poor seal between the cowl grille and the windshield, which allows excessive water to enter the engine compartment. • Spring height variance. **2000–01**—Hard starts caused by inadequate fuel system pressure, due to a fuel pressure regulator that's stuck open. • Door key difficult to insert or rotate. **2001**—Insufficient air flow at bi-level setting. • Rear brake popping, squealing, or clicking.

MPV Profile

	1994	1995	1996	1997	1998	1999	2000	2001
Cost Price ($)								
Bas	20,615	21,780	27,330	—	—	—	—	—
DX	—	—	—	—	—	—	—	25,095
LX	24,975	26,720	30,900	27,845	25,199	—	—	29,150
Used Values ($)								
Base ▲	7,500	9,500	10,500	—	—	—	—	—
Base ▼	6,500	8,500	9,500	—	—	—	—	—
DX ▲	—	—	—	—	—	—	—	20,000
DX ▼	—	—	—	—	—	—	—	18,500
LX ▲	9,000	10,000	11,000	12,000	15,000	—	—	22,000
LX ▼	8,000	9,000	10,000	10,500	14,000	—	—	21,000
Extended Warranty	Y	Y	Y	Y	Y	—	N	N
Secret Warranty	Y	Y	Y	Y	Y	—	N	N
Reliability	❷	❷	③	③	③	—	④	④
Crash Safety (F)	④	④	④	④	—	—	④	④
Side	—	—	❷	❷	❷	—	⑤	⑤
Rollover Resistance	—	—	—	—	—	—	—	③
Head Restraints (F)	—	❷	❷	❶	—	—	③	❷
Rear	—	—	—	—	—	—	—	❶

Note: 4X4 models cost about $500 more. No prices listed for 2000 models, and there was no 1999 model.

Toyota

SIENNA, PREVIA ★★★☆

RATING: *Sienna:* Above Average (1998–2001), but still outclassed by the brawnier, more innovative Odyssey. Plus, Mazda and Nissan's minivans are catching up to Honda and Toyota. On the other hand, the Sienna's transmission shifts more smoothly and has a bit more mid-range torque for passing and merging than its Honda competitor. *Previa:* Average (1991–97). As with the Honda Odyssey, Sienna owners also report some serious safety-related failures, including poor headlight illumination, transmission breakdowns, brake malfunctions, and faulty sliding doors. This said, the number of Toyota complaints is far lower than what one finds with Chrysler, Ford, GM, and Honda. The Previa has high-priced reliability, mediocre road performance, and limited interior amenities. Nevertheless, it's far better than any of Toyota's earlier LE minivans.

Strong points: Incredibly smooth powertrain; plenty of standard safety, performance, and convenience features; and a good amount of passenger and cargo room. **Weak points:** equipped with less-efficient rear drum brakes; rear visibility obstructed by middle roof pillars and rear head restraints; low head restraint crashworthiness rating; the wide centre pillars make for difficult access to the middle seats; radio speakers are set too low for acceptable acoustics; and an unusually large number of body rattles and safety-related complaints, including power sliding door dangers and automatic transmission defects. **Maintenance/Repair costs:** For the Sienna, like the Camry, much lower than average. The only exception is engine sludge requiring expensive repairs. Previas aren't afflicted by the sludge problem, but their maintenance costs are still higher than average. Only Toyota dealers can repair these minivans, particularly when it comes to troubleshooting the supercharged 2.4L engine and All Trac. Ditch the original-equipment Firestone tires, unless, paraphrasing Clint Eastwood, you feel "lucky." **Parts:** Excellent supply of reasonably priced Sienna parts taken from the Camry parts bin. Previa parts are in limited supply, but reasonably priced. Automatic transmission torque converters on 2000 models are frequently back-ordered due to their poor reliability. **Best alternatives:** GM front-drive minivans, Ford Mercury Villager, Honda Odyssey, and Nissan Quest or Axxess. As with most minivans and vans, you can save money by buying the cargo version, but you won't get as many features. Siennas equipped with 4X4 capability will cost about $1,000 more than the equivalent front-drive version. Be wary of the power sliding door. As with the Odyssey and GM minivans, these doors can injure children and pose unnecessary risks to other occupants.

Strengths and weaknesses: The Sienna, Toyota's Camry-based front-drive minivan, replaced the Previa for the 1998 model year and abandoned the Previa's futuristic look in favour of a more conservative Chevrolet Venture styling. The Sienna seats seven, and offers dual power sliding doors with optional remote controls and a V6 powerplant. It's built in the same Kentucky assembly plant as the Camry and comes with lots of safety and convenience features that include side airbags, anti-lock brakes, and a low-tire-pressure warning system.

Some of the Sienna's strong points: standard ABS and side airbags (LE, XLE); a smooth-running V6 engine and transmission that's a bit more refined and capable than what the Odyssey offers; a comfortable, stable ride; a fourth door; a quiet interior; easy entry/exit; and better-than-average fit and finish reliability. Its weak areas: V6 performance is compromised by AC and the automatic transmission powertrain; it lacks the trailer-towing brawn of rear-drive minivans; although the rear seats fold flat to accommodate the width of a 4' x 8' board, the tailgate won't close, plus the heavy seats are difficult to reinstall (a two-person job, and the centre seat barely fits through the door). There's also no traction control, fuel economy (premium fuel) isn't impressive, the low-mounted radio is hard to reach, and third-row seats lack a fore/aft adjustment to increase cargo space.

Reliability is better than average, but problematic on 1997–2001 models. Although mechanical and body components are generally reliable, there's been a disturbing increase in factory-related defects reported by owners during the past few years. The most serious reliability problems concern engines (1997–2001 models) and defective transmission torque converters on 2000 Siennas that cause the Check Engine light to remain lit and can lead to sudden transmission failure. Excessive engine sludge buildup requires expensive engine overhauls that some dealers try to pass off as normal maintenance (see Part Two, "Secret Warranties," and *www.toyotarepair.com/Sludge%20Zone.html*). To its credit, however, Toyota has stopped this "blame game" and has just announced a one-year "Customer Appreciation Program" to repair, free of charge, engines that have been afflicted by the oil sludge problem. An estimated 3,000 North American complaints have been received by the automaker. Here are the details taken from the February 11, 2002, edition of *Automotive News* and Toyota Canada's February 12, 2002, press release:

Engine Oil Sludge

What: 3.3 million Toyota engines built from 1996 to 2001
Problem: Sludge buildup that can ruin engine

Vehicles Affected

Toyota models equipped with 3.3 million 1MZ V-6 and 5SFE inline-four engines produced between July 1996 and July 2001.

- Camry, 4- and 6-cylinder, August 1996 to July 2001
- Camry Solara, 4- and 6-cylinder, June 1998 to May 2001
- Sienna, July 1997 to May 2001
- Avalon, July 1996 to May 2001
- Celica, 4-cylinder, August 1996 to April 1999
- Highlander, November 2000 to July 2001
- Lexus ES 300, August 1998 to July 2001
- Lexus RX 300, January 1998 to July 2001

Source: Toyota Motor Sales U.S.A.

Toyota Canada advises owners who notice the tell-tale signs of engine sludge formation to take their vehicle to their local dealer to have the engine inspected. These signs may include the emission of blue smoke from the tailpipe and/or excessive oil consumption, which may cause overheating, rough running, or the Check Engine light to come on.

Other problems reported by owners include stalling when the AC engages; electrical shorts; premature brake wear and excessive brake noise; distracting windshield reflections and distorted windshields; sliding door defects; and various other body glitches, including excessive creaks and rattles and paint that's easily chipped.

In 1995, DX models got a supercharged engine. As of 1996 the super-charged engine was the only powerplant offered. 1997 models got extra soundproofing; in 1998, the Sienna replaced the Previa. 1999 models have an optional, passenger-side power sliding door and a remote keyless locking/unlocking device that doubles as an engine-immobilizing anti-theft device. Year 2000 models were carried over practically unchanged, and 2001s have a driver-side sliding door and standard rear defroster.

Previa
The redesigned 1991 Previa's performance and reliability are so much improved over its LE predecessor that it almost seems like a different vehicle. Roomier and rendered more stable thanks to its longer wheel-base, equipped with a new 2.4L engine (supercharged as of the 1994 model year), and loaded with standard safety and convenience features, 1991–97 Previas are almost as driver-friendly as the Chrysler and Mazda competition. Still, they can't match Ford, GM, or Chrysler front-drive minivans for responsive handling and a comfortable ride, and Toyota's small engine is overworked and doesn't hesitate to tell you so. Previa owners have learned to live with engine noise, poor fuel economy, pre-mature front brake wear, excessive brake vibration and pulsation, electrical glitches, AC malfunctions, and fit and finish blemishes. The 4X4 models with automatic transmissions steal lots of power from the 4-cylinder powerplant, though they have fewer reliability problems than similar drivetrains found on competitors, especially Chrysler.

Safety summary: All models/years: Many complaints that the steering wheel locks up when making a turn, won't return to centre without extreme effort, or simply no longer responds. • Owners have also com-plained that the vehicle pulls sharply to one side or another when driving at moderate speeds. • Numerous reports of ABS failures, loud grinding or groaning noise when braking, and brake pedal going to the floor without braking effect. **Previa: 1996**—Poor, noisy AC compressor performance. • Windshield wipers suddenly stopped working. • Middle right bench seat lapbelt is impossible to adjust, due to its poor design. • Speed sensor failure. **Sienna: 1998**—Sudden acceleration, due to a defec-tive throttle cable; vehicle hit a wall. • Shape and design of the Sienna creates severe blind spots. • Headlights give poor illumination. • Windshields are distorted, exhibiting a "melted" image. • Rear door doesn't shut tightly. • Poor visibility due to the tinted window design. • Headrests and third-row seats are loose and vibrate. • Shoulder belts in the middle row lock up instantly when first put on and stay locked up, binding the passenger. **1999**—Wheel lug nuts broke and allowed wheel to fall off. • Window exploded at stoplight. • Many complaints of sudden tire tread separation (Firestone). • Severe vibration at cruising speeds. • Rear brake drums may overheat and warp. • Distracting dashboard reflec-tion into the windshield. • Windshield distortion. • Faulty fuel cap causes the Check Engine light to come on. 2000—Check Engine light continues to come on due to a defective transmission torque converter. • Sudden acceleration during rainstorm. • Premature tire blowouts (Dunlop and Firestone). • Chronic transmission failure due to faulty torque converter. • Wheel lug nuts sheared off. • Driver's seatbelt anchor bolt on door pillar unscrewed and fell to the floor. • Right rear passenger window suddenly exploded. • Annoying dash/windshield reflection also impairs visibility (very bad with black and beige colours). 2001—Automatic transmission suddenly went into Neutral while on the highway. • Defective transmission torque converter causes the engine warning light to come on. • Sudden, unintended acceleration. • Sudden stalling when the AC is turned on • Vehicle rolled away, with shifter in Park on a hill and ignition shut off. • Reflection of the dashboard on the windshield impairs visibility. • Rear seatbelts can't be adjusted. • Centre rear seatbelt doesn't tighten sufficiently when children are restrained. • Slope of the windshield makes it hard to gauge where the front end stops. • Excessive door rattling. • Rear window exploded as front door was closed. • Sunroof flew off when opened while Sienna was underway.

Secret Warranties/Service Tips/TSBs

All models/years: Owner feedback confirms that front brake pads and discs will be replaced under Toyota's "goodwill" policy if they wear out before 2 years/40,000 km. Improved disc brake pad kits are described in TSB #BR94-004. Brake pulsation/vibration, another generic Toyota problem, is fully addressed in TSB #BR94-002, "Cause and Repair of Vibration and Pulsation." **Previa: 1994–96**—Excessive brake vibration or pulsation can be corrected by installing upgraded front brake pads. **Sienna: 1998**—Upgraded brake pads and rotors should reduce brake groan and squeak noises. **1998–99**—To reduce sliding door creaks, the control junction materials have been upgraded. **1998–2000**—Outline of various diagnostic procedures and fixes to correct vehicle pulling to one side. • Power-steering squeaks can be silenced by installing a counter-measure steering rack end under warranty. • Power-steering "feel" can be improved by replacing the steering rack guide. • False activation of the security alarm can be fixed by modifying the hood latch switch. • Power window rattles can be corrected by installing a revised lower window frame mounting bracket. **1998–2001**—One-year warranty extension for engine sludge claims. **1999–2000**—If the power sliding door is inoperative or won't close properly, Toyota says the cable should be adjusted. **2000**—Toyota has field fixes to correct washer fluid leakage from the rear washer nozzle and eliminate moisture and odours permeating the vehicle interior. • Correction for an inoperative spare tire lift. • Speedometer or tachometer troubleshooting. **2001**—Power sliding door malfunctions (troubleshooting tips). • False activation of the security alarm. • Power windows rattling. • Entertainment system hum. • Faulty speedometer and tachometer. • Inoperative third-row sliding seat. • Special service campaign to inspect or replace the front subframe assembly on 2001 models. • Water leaking into the trunk area (see following bulletin).

Trunk – Water Leaks

BODY   BO028-00   November 3, 2000

Title: LEAKS INTO TRUNK

Models:

'97-'01 Camry (U.S.), '98-'01 Sienna,
'99-'01 Solara & '01 Avalon

Introduction:

A field fix is available for incidents of moisture and odors permeating into the vehicle. The Quarter Panel Air Duct flaps may have become loose or missing. Replacing the Quarter Panel Air Duct will remedy the condition.

Applicable Vehicles:

1997-2001 model year Camry (U.S. produced)
1998-2001 model year Sienna
1999-2001 model year Solara
2001 model year Avalon

Sienna, Previa Profile

	1994	1995	1996	1997	1998	1999	2000	2001
Cost Price ($)								
Previa	24,748	28,578	35,908	36,998	—	—	—	—
Sienna CE 3d	—	—	—	—	24,438	24,570	24,570	—
Sienna CE 4d	—	—	—	—	26,808	26,940	27,770	29,535
Sienna LE 4d	—	—	—	—	29,558	29,980	30,705	31,900
Used Values ($)								
Previa Λ	7,500	8,500	11,000	14,000	—	—	—	—
Previa V	6,000	7,000	10,000	13,000	—	—	—	—
Sienna CE 3d Λ	—	—	—	—	16,000	19,000	22,000	—
Sienna CE 3d V	—	—	—	—	14,500	17,500	20,000	—
Sienna CE 4d Λ	—	—	—	—	16,500	19,500	22,000	25,000
Sienna CE 4d V	—	—	—	—	15,000	18,000	20,000	23,000
Sienna LE 4d Λ	—	—	—	—	18,000	21,000	24,000	27,000
Sienna LE 4d V	—	—	—	—	16,500	19,000	22,000	25,000
Extended Warranty	Y	Y	Y	Y	Y	Y	Y	Y
Secret Warranty	N	N	N	Y	Y	Y	Y	Y
Reliability	③	③	④	④	④	④	⑤	⑤
Crash Safety (F)	④	④	④	⑤	⑤	⑤	⑤	—
Side	—	—	—	—	④	④	④	—
Off-set	—	—	—	⑤	⑤	⑤	⑤	—
Rollover Resistance	—	—	—	—	—	—	—	④
Head Restraints	—	—	—	—	❶	❶	—	❷

Helpful Internet Info Sites

Look up these sites to find current MSRP, invoice prices, insurance ratings, service bulletins, independent auto tests, complaint tactics, jurisprudence and tips on how to set up your own protest/gripe site if things go wrong.

Consumer Protection

Automobile Consumer Coalition (*www.carhelpcanada.com*)
Founded by the former director of the Toronto Automobile Protection Association, Mohamed Bouchama, the ACC provides many of the same services as the APA (see below); however, it has been refined for its Ontario members.

Automobile Protection Association (*www.apa.ca*)
This Montreal-based consumer group fights for safer vehicles and has exposed many scams associated with new-vehicle sales, leasing, and repairs; for a small fee it will send you the invoice price for most new vehicles.

BBC TV's *Top Gear* Car Reviews (*www.topgear.beeb.com*)
Britain's automotive equivalent to Canada's CBC *Marketplace*, *Top Gear* blows the whistle on the best and worst European-sold vehicles, auto products, and industry practices.

CBC *Marketplace* (*cbc.ca/consumers/market/files/cars/index.html*)
Marketplace has been the Canadian Broadcasting Corporation's premier national consumer show for almost three decades. Its site has extensive links and in-depth reports on Chrysler paint delamination, ABS brake failures, airbag dangers, and a host of other automotive topics.

***Consumer Reports* and Consumers Union** (*consumerreports.org*)
It costs $3.95 a month to subscribe on-line, but *CR*'s database is chock full of comparison tests and in-depth stories on products and services.

Metro Credit Union (*www.metrocu.com*)
A unique credit union that puts a car broker at its members' disposition to negotiate new- or used-vehicle sales.

Supreme Court of Canada (*www.lexum.umontreal.ca/csc-scc/en/rec/index.html*)
It's not enough to have a solid claim against a company or the government. Supporting your position with a Supreme Court decision also helps. This website gives you a user-friendly database where you can

look for most kinds of claims you're likely to file. There were three pro-consumer judgments rendered in February 2002 that are particularly useful:

- *Whiten v. Pilot Insurance Co.* The insured's home burned down and the insurance company refused to pay the claim. The jury was outraged and ordered the company to pay the $345,000 claim, plus $320,000 for legal costs and $1 million in punitive damages, making it the largest punitive damage award in Canadian history. The Supreme Court maintained the jury's decision, calling Pilot "the insurer from hell." This judgment scares the dickens out of insurers, who fear that they face huge punitive damage awards if they don't pay promptly.
- *Bannon v. The Corporation of the City of Thunder Bay.* An injured resident missed the deadline to file a claim against Thunder Bay; however, the Supreme Court maintained that extenuating factors, such as being under the effects of medication, extended her time to file. A good case to remember next time your vehicle is damaged by a pothole or you are injured by a municipality's negligence.
- *R. v. Guinard.* An insured posted a sign on his barn claiming the Commerce Insurance Company was unfairly refusing his claim. The municipality of St-Hyacinthe told him to take the sign down. He refused, maintaining that he had the right to state his opinion. The Supreme Court agreed. This judgment means that consumer protests, signs, and Internet websites that criticize the actions of corporations cannot be shut up or taken down simply because they say unpleasant things.

Auto Safety

Center for Auto Safety (*www.autosafety.org*)
Consumers Union and Ralph Nader founded the Center for Auto Safety (CAS) to provide consumers with a voice for auto safety and quality in Washington and to help lemon owners fight back across the U.S.

Transport Canada (*www.tc.gc.ca/roadsafety/Recalls/search_e.asp*)
You can access the recall database for 1970–2002 model vehicles, but, unlike NHTSA's website (see below), owner complaints aren't listed, defect investigations aren't disclosed, and service bulletin summaries aren't provided. A list of vehicles admissable for import is available at *www.tc.gc.ca/roadsafety/importusa/impusae.htm*, or by calling the Registrar of Imported Vehicles at 1-800-511-7755.

U.S. National Highway Traffic Safety Administration
(*www.nhtsa.dot.gov/cars/problems*)
This site has a comprehensive, free database covering owner complaints, recall campaigns, crashworthiness and rollover ratings, defect investigations, service bulletin summaries, and safety research papers.

Insurance Institute for Highway Safety (*www.hwysafety.org*)
A dazzling site that's long on crash photos and graphs that show which vehicles are the most crashworthy.

The Safety Forum (*www.safetyforum.com*)
The Forum contains comprehensive news archives and links to useful sites, plus names of court-recognized experts on everything from unsafe Chrysler minivan latches to dangerous van conversions.

Strategic Safety (*www.strategicsafety.com/mainindex.html*)
The people who blew the whistle on dangerous Firestone tires. Provides research, investigation, analysis, and education on safety issues.

Airbag Killer Sites (*www.plescia.org/indexair.htm, www.gov.on.ca/health/ english/program/pubhealth/phero/phero_199906.html*)
Anecdotal evidence of airbag injuries and fatalities in low-speed collisions, as well as a compendium of independent research studies.

Information/Mediation/Protest

BMW, Mini Cooper, and Porsche Message Boards (*www.roadfly.com*)
This website provides useful info relating to problems (BMW fan fires), upgrades, and performance comparisons.

British Columbia Dead Ford Owners' Page
(*modena.intergate.ca/ personal/djk/*)
Dead Ford is a play on the acronym F.O.R.D.: "Found On the Road, Dead," or, when read backward, "Driver Returns On Foot." The site is a useful gathering place for Ford car, truck, sport-utility, minivan, and van owners, who discuss problems and solutions.

Chrysler Peeling Paint Page (*peelingpaint.homestead.com*)
This site must be your starting point in dealing with Chrysler for paint or any other problem. Helpful bulletins and sample claim letters.

Chrysler Products' Problem Web Page
(*www.wam.umd.edu/~gluckman/Chrysler/*)
A resource for Chrysler owners who have had problems in dealing with Chrysler, including issues with peeling paint, transmission failure, the Chrysler-installed Bendix-10 ABS, and other maladies.

Chrysler, Plymouth, and Dodge Car Information (*www.allpar.com*)
This is an excellent website that's jam-packed with historical information, tips on fixing common problems inexpensively, and advice on how to deal with Chrysler representatives and dealer service managers.

Diesel Central.com (*www.diesel-central.com/*)
A comprehensive site for all Chrysler, GM, and Ford diesel owners looking for service tips and general owner information. Check out the following three sites, as well (the GM site charges a $15.95 membership fee):

- Chrysler: *dodgeram.org/links/diesel_links.htm*
- Ford: *www.ford-diesel.com*
- GM: *www.62-65-dieselpage.com/*

Dodge Caravan Transmission Problems
(*www.aei.ca/%7egregoire/claude.html*)
Complaints in French accepted.

Ford Insider Info (*www.blueovalnews.com*)
This website is the place to go for all the latest insider info on Ford's quality problems.

Ford Paint Peel Information (*www.ihs2000.com/~peel*)
Everything you should know about the cause and treatment of Ford paint delamination, so common on its trucks, vans, and sport-utilities over the past decade. Useful links to other sites, and tips on resolving Ford and GM paint problems.

Ford Windstar Customer Action Information
(*home.att.net/~ccatanese/ford/*)
This is the most comprehensive site relating to faulty engine gaskets on Ford's 3.8L and 4.2L engines. Plenty of technical help, supported by internal service bulletins and extended warranties you can download. Many links to other helpful sites.

GM Paint Delamination/Peeling
Unfortunately, there's no longer a single website that relates to all the GM cars, trucks, minivans, and vans afflicted by this defect. Nevertheless, there are many sites where the problem is discussed for specific vehicles. Simply access AltaVista or any other search engine and type in "GM paint delamination" or "GM peeling paint."

Neon Enthusiasts (*www.neons.org*)
Lots of technical info and service tips from owners and mechanics. A good place to find Chrysler TSBs relating to engine head gasket failures and other problems afflicting Neons.

Taurus Transmission Victims (*members.aol.com/MKBradley/index.html*)
A great site for learning about Ford's biodegradable automatic transmissions (1991–99) from Lincoln Continental, Taurus, Sable, and Windstar owners. Expert mechanics give the why and how.

Toyota Celica Page (*www.celica.net/main.asp*)
A useful site for technical advice and owner reviews.

VW Lemon Page (*www.myvwlemon.com*)
Another owner's site that lists the pros and cons associated with VW products.

Information/Services

Alberta Vehicle Cost Calculator (*www1.agric.gov.ab.ca/app09/carcostcalc*)
This government-sponsored site allows you to estimate and compare the ownership and operating costs of vehicles with variations in purchase price, options, fuel type, interest rates, or length of ownership.

ALLDATA Service Bulletins (*www.alldata.com/consumer/TSB/yr.html*)
No more "he said," "she said." Technical service bulletins tell you about factory defects, upgraded parts, diagnostic and repair shortcuts, and secret warranties. TSBs that are summarized in Part Three, as well as others going back to 1970, are listed by year, make, model, and engine option. For $25 (U.S.), ALLDATA will send you a DVD containing all bulletins that are applicable to your vehicle (exception: BMW, Acura, and Honda). For the same price, you may also download the bulletins from the Internet.

The Auto Channel (*www.theautochannel.com*)
This website gives you comprehensive information that's useful when choosing a new or used vehicle, filing a claim for compensation, or linking up with other owners.

The Auto Extremist (*www.autoextremist.com*)
Rantings and ravings from a Detroit insider.

Canadian Driver (*www.canadiandriver.com/reviews/index.htm*)
An exceptionally well structured and current Canadian website for new- and used-vehicle reviews, MSRP prices, and consumer reports prepared by Canadian journalists. Other websites for car magazines:

- *World of Wheels* (*www.autonet.ca/WoW/Search.cfm*)
- *Automotive News* (*www.automotivenews.com*)
- *Car & Driver* (*www.caranddriver.com*)
- *Motor Trend* (*www.motortrend.com*)
- *Road and Track* (*www.roadandtrack.com*)
- *Motorage* (*www.motorage.com*)

CARFAX (*www.carfax.com*)
If you suspect a used vehicle is a rebuilt wreck, use CARFAX (tel.: 1-888-422-7329) to carry out a background check to see if the vehicle has been

"scrapped," had flood damage, is stolen, or shows incorrect mileage on the odometer. There's a fee of $14.95 U.S. ($23.39 Cdn.) if the order is placed via the Internet. An initial, free search on the Internet will confirm whether or not your vehicle is listed in the database.

Cartrackers (*www.cartrackers.com*)
This is a large site that has a nice balance of the pros and cons of vehicle ownership. Its technical resources are impressive, and there are experts to advise you on everything from secret warranties to simple maintenance.

Consumer's Guide to Insurance *(www.insurancehotline.com*)
This free service can yield big savings by giving you comparison quotes for a wide range of insurance plans through its website and 24-hour telephone number (416-686-0531).

Kelley Blue Book and Edmunds (*www.kbb.com, www.edmunds.com*)
Good reviews of almost every vehicle sold in North America, plus an informative readers' forum.

Phil Bailey's Auto World (*www.baileycar.com*)
Phil Bailey owns his own garage and specializes in the diagnosis and repair of foreign cars, particularly British ones. He's been advising Montreal motorists for years on local radio shows and has an exceptionally well written and comprehensive website.

Vehicle Information Centre of Canada (*www.vicc.com/index2.htm*)
Part of the Insurance Bureau of Canada. VICC's "How Cars Measure Up" compares the insurance claims experience of 1998–99 model vehicles for collision, personal injury, and theft losses.

Women's Garage (*www.womensgarage.com*)
Three Canadian mechanics with a combined 100 years' experience set up this site to take the mystery out of maintaining and repairing vehicles. Don't be confused by the site title—males will learn a lot.

Automobile News Groups
These news groups are compilations of email raves and gripes and cover all makes and models. They fall into four distinct areas: *rec.autos.makers.chrysler* (you can substitute any automaker's name at the end); *rec.autos.tech*; *rec.autos.driving*; and *rec.autos.misc*.

GOOD BUYS FOR A BAD ECONOMY:
"Beaters," "Orphans," and "Chick Magnets"

The North American economy is almost in a recession, and now's not the time to invest heavily in a car or minivan that's more than you need or priced far more than it's worth. Yet millions of Canadian teens and homemakers have no choice: they must have a vehicle that's safe, cheap and reliable, capable of taking them to school or the shopping mall.

Crashworthiness and reliability are two factors that are particularly important to teen drivers, who have greater exposure to highway dangers and mechanical breakdowns than most of us. Also, young drivers want vehicles they can work on themselves and that project a certain "cool" cachet to their peers. Fortunately, there are plenty of cheap used choices that will fill the bill.

First, consider the following 10 rules:

1. First and foremost, try to buy a vehicle that's presently being used by one of your family members. Although you may risk a family squabble somewhere down the road, you'll likely get a good buy for next to nothing, you will have a good idea of how it was driven and maintained, and you can use the same repair facilities that have been repairing your family's vehicles for years. Don't worry if a vehicle is almost 10 years old—that's becoming the norm for Canadian ownership, particularly the farther west you go.
2. Delay your purchase from a dealer until mid-2002, when automaker and dealer clearance rebates bring lots of inexpensive trade-ins on the market.
3. Look for high-mileage vehicles sold by rental agencies like Budget—a company that offers honest, money-back guarantees and reasonably-priced extended warranties.
4. Refuse all preparation or "administration" charges.
5. Stay away from most American front-drives—more frequent failures and costlier repairs.
6. Be wary of cheap, discontinued American models like the Lincoln Continental or Plymouth minivans.
7. Don't buy any European models—parts and servicing can be a problem, and quality control is declining.
8. Buy 3-year-old Hyundais, but stay away from Excels, early Sonatas, and all Kias and Daewoos. Also look for 5- to 10-year-old, one-owner Japanese models.
9. Shop for used, rear-drive, full-sized wagons or vans, instead of American minivans.
10. Don't buy for fuel economy alone: a 4-cylinder minivan is cheap to run, but highway merging will be a white-knuckle affair.

Used but not abused

It's getting pretty hard to find a vehicle 10 years old or more that's safe and reliable. Personally, I'd be reluctant to buy any decade-old vehicle anywhere east of Manitoba. Apart from salt being a real body killer, it's just too easy to fall prey to scam artists who cover up major mechanical or body problems resulting from accidents or environmental damage. As an alternative, I'd look for an orphaned vehicle, recently axed only because its popularity waned or because it didn't fit the automaker's long-term plans, like Nissan's Axxess or the Ford Escort, for example.

Nevertheless, if an independent mechanic gives you the green light, and if you have the time, knowledge, and parts suppliers to do your own maintenance and repairs, you're in better shape. In this case, you might seriously consider a 15- to 20-year-old, beat-up-looking car or minivan. Look for one of the following Recommended vehicles, avoid those that are Not Recommended, and take your time. Get an independent check-up and pay close attention to the trouble areas.

If you have a bit more money to spend and want to take less of a risk, look up the Recommended vehicles found at the beginning of each vehicle category in Part Three.

Recommended '80s to Mid-'90s Vehicles ($500–$5,000)

Ford—All rear-drives; Escort ('91 and later) and Probe
Chrysler—All rear-drives; Colt, Reliant, and Acclaim
GM—All rear-drives; Caprice, Roadmaster, Malibu, Astro, Safari, Venture, and Montana
Honda—Civic, Accord, and Odyssey
Hyundai—Accent, Elantra, and Tiburon
Mazda—MX-3, Precidia, MX-6, Miata, and 929
Mercury—Grand Marquis and Villager
Nissan—Sentra, Stanza, Axxess, and Quest
Subaru—All front-drives, Justy, and post-'95 Impreza, Legacy, and Forester
Toyota—Celica, Corolla, Supra, Avalon, Camry, and Sienna

Very Used Choices

Acura—The 5-cylinder **Vigor**, a spin-off of the Honda Accord sedan, sells for $7,000–$8,500. It went through only three model years (1992–94). This compact has power to spare, handles well, and has an impressive reliability/durability record. Problem areas: excessive brake noise and premature brake wear, in addition to fit and finish deficiencies. The 1992 Vigor turned in below-average crash test scores.

Checker—The quintessential taxi, last made in 1982, **Checker** is the poor man's Bentley. Its rear-drive configuration; sturdy, off-the-shelf GM mechanicals; and thick body panels all add up to bulletproof reliability. Beware of corrosion along door rocker panels and wheelwells, and badly repaired collision repairs.

Chrysler—**Dart**, **Valiant**, **Duster**, **Scamp**, **Diplomat**, **Caravelle**, **Newport**, rear-drive **New Yorker Fifth Avenue**, and **Gran Fury**. Problem areas: electrical system, suspension, brakes, body and frame rust, plus constant stalling when humidity is high). The **Caravelle**, **Diplomat**, and **New Yorker Fifth Avenue** are reasonably reliable and simple-to-repair throwbacks to a time when rear-drive land yachts ruled the highways. Powered with 6- and 8-cylinder engines, they will practically run forever with minimal care. The fuel-efficient "slant 6" powerplant was too small for this type of car and was changed to a gas-guzzling but smooth and reliable V8 after 1983. Handling is vague and sloppy, though, and emergency braking is often accompanied by rear-wheel lockup. Still, what do you want for $1,500–$2,500 for a 1984–89 "retro rocket"? Problem areas are the carburetor, ignition, electrical system, brake, and suspension (premature idler-arm wear). It's a good idea to adjust the torsion bars frequently for better suspension performance. Doors, windshield pillars, the bottoms of both front and rear fenders, and the trunk lid rust through more quickly than average.

Chrysler's 1991–93 **2000GTX** is an above-average buy that may cost $3,500–$4,000, depending upon the model year. It's a reliable Japanese-built sedan that was discontinued in 1994. It has a competitive price, modern styling, and high-performance options that put it on par with such benchmark cars as the Honda Accord and Toyota Camry. Problem areas are the front brakes, which need more attention than average. The car hasn't been crash-tested.

The Chrysler **Stealth** is a serious, reasonably priced sports car that's as much go as show. Although 1995 was its last model year in Canada, it's still sold in the United States as the Mitsubishi 3000GT. Prices range from $5,000 to $7,000 for the 1991–93 base or ES model. A '95 high-performance R/T will go for about $10,000—not a bad price for an "orphan" sports car, eh? Problem areas: engine, transmission, front brake, and electrical failures. The 1993 model excelled in crash tests.

Ford—**Maverick**, **Comet**, **Fairmont**, **Zephyr**, **Tracer**, **Mustang**, **Capri**, **Cougar**, **Thunderbird V6**, **Torino**, **Marquis**, **Grand Marquis**, **LTD**, and **LTD Crown Victoria**. Problem areas: trunk, wheelwell, and rocker panel rusting; brakes; steering; and electrical system failures. The 1993 **Festiva** is marginally acceptable for city use as long as you check out the brakes, exhaust system, and body panels for rust. The 1990–97 **Probe** is essentially a Mazda MX-6 sporty two-door coupe in Ford garb. It's quite reliable and gives better-than-average highway performance. Problem areas: AC, CV joints, electrical and body glitches. Good crashworthiness rating.

General Motors—**Chevette** and **Acadian** are inexpensive, rear-drive city runabouts. Problem areas: steering system defects, and brakes you have to stand on to stop. Rear-drive **Nova**, **Ventura**, **Skylark**, and **Phoenix**. Problem areas: undercarriage, steering system, and suspension rustout. Front-wheel drive **Nova** and **Spectrum**, **Camaro**, **Firebird**, **Malibu**, **LeMans**, **Century**, **Regal**, **Cutlass**, **Monte Carlo**, and **Grand Prix**. Problem areas: rear brake backing plate rust-out and steering failures. **Bel Air**, **Impala**, **Caprice**, **Roadmaster**, **Laurentian**, **Catalina**, **Parisienne**, **LeSabre**, **Bonneville**, and **Delta 88**. Be wary of undercarriage, suspension component, and rear brake backing plate rustout.

Mazda—Sports car thrills, minus the bills: the 1992–96 **MX-3**'s base 1.6L engine supplies plenty of power for most driving situations, plus it's reasonably priced at $3,500–$6,500. When equipped with the optional 1.8L V6 powerplant (the smallest V6 on the market at the time) and high-performance options, the car transforms itself into a 130-hp pocket rocket. In fact, the MX-3 GS easily outperforms the Honda del Sol, Toyota Paseo, and Geo Storm on comfort and high-performance acumen. It does fall a bit short of the Saturn SC due to its limited low-end torque, and fuel economy is disappointing. Reverse gear is sometimes hard to engage. Brake and wheel bearing problems are commonplace. Most of the MX-3's parts are used on other Mazda cars, so their overall reliability should be outstanding. Crash safety ratings have been average. Also consider the **MX-6** (see Ford Probe review).

The key word for the 1988–95 **929** is understatement: the engine is unobtrusive, the exterior is anonymous, and the interior is far from flashy. In spite of its lack of pizzazz and imprecise power steering, the 929 will accelerate and handle curves as well as the best large European sedans, and it has proven to be fairly reliable. For these advantages, you can expect to pay $3,500–$6,500 for a 1988–93 model. The '94s and '95s are priced in the $9,500–$12,000 range. Owners report some problems with premature disc brake wear, electrical glitches, exhaust system rust-out, electronic shock absorber durability (particularly with the 1989–91 models), and fit and finish deficiencies. The only real safety negative is the 929's consistently poor crash test scores since the '88 model was first tested.

Selling for $3,000–$4,500 for a base 1988–91 model, the **RX-7** is an impressive performer with a ride that can be painful on bad roads, due primarily to the car's stiff suspension. The GSL and Turbo models are very well equipped and luxuriously finished. Except for some oil burning problems, apex seal failures, and leaking engine O-rings, the RX-7 has served to dispel any doubts concerning the durability of rotary engines.

Nevertheless, careful maintenance is in order, since contaminated oil or overheating will easily damage the rotary engine. Clutches wear quickly if used hard. Disc brakes need frequent attention paid to the calipers and rotors. The MacPherson struts get soft more quickly than average. Fuel, exhaust-system, and electrical glitches and AC malfunctions are also common. Be wary of leaky sunroofs. Radiators have a short life span. Rocker panels and body seams are prone to serious rusting. The underbody on older cars should also be inspected carefully for corrosion damage. Fuel economy has never been this car's strong suit and crash-test scores were below average.

For more info, check out the Mazda RX-7 Lemon Site on the Internet at *scuderiaciriani.com/rx7/lemon_site/sources.htm*. It's a treasure trove of maintenance tips, common defects, copies of service bulletins, and specific buying and selling information.

Nissan—The **Micra** is a subcompact commuter car that was sold during 1985–91. It uses generic Nissan parts that are fairly reliable and not difficult to find. Electrical shorts, premature front brake wear, and body rusting along the door rocker panels and wheelwells are the more common deficiencies.

Pulsar and **NX** models are good small-car buys ($1,500–$2,500, depending upon the year), as long as you pick the right years and stay away from failure-prone and expensive-to-repair turbo models. The **Pulsar** was replaced by the 1991 **NX**, a similar small car that also shares Sentra components. For 1983–86 models, overall reliability is poor to very poor. As with other discontinued Nissans, the 1987–93 models have shown remarkable performance improvement and are all the more attractive due to their depreciated prices. Crash test scores were below average for the 1990 and earlier models, while the 1991 and later versions scored quite well. All Pulsars built before 1991 are prone to premature wear on the front brake pads and discs and faulty air conditioners. From 1991 on, the only problems reported concern minor AC malfunctions, premature wearout of front brakes and suspension components, and exhaust systems that don't last very long (two years, tops).

1990–92 **Stanzas** are roomy, reasonably priced ($2,500–$3,000), four-passenger compacts that offer peppy performance, more responsive steering, nimble handling, and good fuel economy. Overall reliability has been fairly good over the years. Except for some road noise, suspension thumps, starting difficulties, transmission malfunctions, and a biodegradable exhaust system, no major problems have been reported on 1988–92 Stanzas.

Owners complain of premature front brake wear and rust perforations, problems that are common for all years. Especially prone to rust perforation are wheel openings, the front edge of the hood, the rear hatch, and door bottoms. 1990 models produced below-average crashworthiness scores, but the 1991 and 1992 models did better than average.

Nissan's answer to the Corvette, the 1989–96 **300ZX** has everything: high-performance capability, a heavy chassis, complicated electronics, and average depreciation resulting in a price range of $6,000–$15,000. Turbocharged 1990 and later models are much faster than previous versions and better overall buys. This weighty rear-drive offers a high degree of luxury equipment along with a potent 300-hp engine. Traction is poor on slippery surfaces, though, and the rear suspension hits hard when going over speed bumps. Crashworthiness scores have been average.

The complexity of all the bells and whistles on the 300ZX translates into a lot more problems than you'd experience with either a Mustang or a Camaro—two cars that have their own reliability problems, but are far easier and less costly to repair. The best example of this is the electrical system, long a source of recurring, hard-to-diagnose shorts. Fuel-injectors are a constant problem and lead to poor engine performance. The manual transmission has been failure prone, clutches don't last long, front and rear brakes are noisy and wear out quickly, and the aluminum wheels are easily damaged by corrosion and road hazards. The exhaust system is practically biodegradable. The glitzy digital dash, with three odometers, and weird spongy/stiff variable shock absorbers are more gimmicky than practical. Body assembly is mediocre.

Subaru—Sold 1988–95, the **Justy** does everything reasonably well for an entry-level Subaru. Pairing smooth and nimble handling with precise and predictable steering, the 4X4 system is a boon for people who often need easy-to-engage extra traction and an automatic transmission. Price range: $1,500–$3,000.

The **Justy**'s reliability record has been about average from the 1991 model onward. Some owners complain about poor engine idling and frequent cold-weather stalling, manual and automatic transmission malfunctions, premature exhaust system rust-out, catalytic converter failures, and paint peeling. With the exception of the CVT, servicing and repairs are made easy due to a very straightforward design.

Toyota (late '80s and early '90s)—All models, except the **LE Van**, which has a history of chronic brake, chassis, and body rusting problems). Chassis rusting and V6 engine head gasket failures are common problems with the 1988–95 sport-utilities and pickups (Toyota has paid for the engine repairs up to eight years). **Celicas** are an especially fine buy, combining smooth engine performance and bulletproof reliability with sports car thrills.

Selling for $3,000–$5,000, the 1987–93 **MR2** is a mid-engine, rear-drive, 4-cylinder sports car that's both reliable and fun to drive. On the downside, you have to put up with a cramped interior, quirky turbo handling, inflated insurance premiums, and undetermined crashworthiness. In order of frequency, the most common complaints on all MR2s are as follows: the brakes, transmission, electrical glitches, and body hardware (fit and finish) deficiencies.

The **Cressida** ages well and offers an excellent combination of dependable, no-surprise, rear-drive performance, comfort, and luxury. All this in a price range from $3,000 to $6,000 for a 1985–92 model. There is little to fault when it comes to overall reliability, and the engine is a model of smooth power. The 1990–93 models are more crashworthy, reliable, and trouble-free than earlier versions, but they're also much more expensive. Two complaints continue to surface throughout the years: premature front brake wear and excessive brake pulsation/vibration. AC glitches and electrical short circuits are also commonplace.

From its humble beginnings as a rear-drive, stretched Celica in 1979, the **Supra** became Toyota's flagship sports car when it switched to front-drive in 1986 and took on its own unique personality—with the help of a powerful 3.0L DOHC V6 powerplant. Supra prices range from a low of $11,000 for a '90 model up to $40,000 for a '97.

It's an attractively styled, high-performance sports car that had been quite reliable up until it caught the Corvette/Nissan 300ZX malady in 1993: cumulative add-ons that drove up the car's price and weight and drove down its reliability. The 6-cylinder engines are smooth and powerful, and handling is sure and precise—better than the Celica because of the independent rear suspension. Like most sports cars, the Supra has limited rear seating, fuel mileage is marginal around town, and insurance premiums are likely to be much higher than average. Additionally, crashworthiness has never been determined.

Early models (pre-'93) are more reasonably priced and are practically trouble free, except for some premature front brake wear and vibrations. On later models, owners report major turbocharger problems; frequent rear differential replacements; electrical short circuits; AC malfunctions; and premature brake, suspension, and exhaust system wear. The 3.0L engine is an oil-burner at times, and cornering is often accompanied by a rear-end growl. Seatbelt guides and the power antenna are failure prone. Body deficiencies are common.

Volvo—The 1989–93 **240 Series** is an average buy, costing $2,000–$3,000. Avoid the turbocharged 4-cylinder engine and failure-prone air conditioning systems. Diesels suffer from cooling system breakdowns and leaky cylinder head gaskets. The brakes on all model years need frequent and expensive servicing, and exhaust systems are notorious for their short life span.

Interestingly, when a '79 Volvo 240 was crash-tested, researchers concluded both the driver and passenger would have sustained severe head trauma. 1992–93 models produced excellent NHTSA crashworthiness scores.

Selling for $3,500–$4,500, the 1986–92 **700 Series** models are more spacious, luxurious, and complicated to service than the entry-level 240. The standard engine and transmission perform well, but aren't as refined as the 850. The 700 Series suffers from some brake, electrical, engine cooling, air conditioning, and body deficiencies. Brakes tend to wear rapidly and can require expensive servicing. The 1988 model performed poorly in crash tests, while the 1991–92 versions did quite well.

Pickups

As a general rule, old trucks aren't very collectible, unless they were utilized for a specific purpose like fire trucks, army vehicles, or commercial vehicles (milk trucks, etc.). For most small trucks made by the Detroit Big Three that are 15–20 years old, you can expect to pay $500–$1,000. Asian imports may cost about twice as much, due to their reputation for being better made and more reliable. If you're looking for a larger pickup, the price may vary from $2,000 to $3,500, with no Asian competition in sight.

Old trucks are bought for function, not appearance. For the first half of the '70s, the full-sized Chrysler, Ford, and GM pickups are all practically equal in performance and reliability (although Ford vehicles were extremely rust prone). After 1976, stringent emissions regulations mandated the use of failure-prone fuel-injectors, computer modules, and catalytic converters. As leaded fuel was phased out, vehicles became much more complicated to troubleshoot, more expensive to repair, and less reliable.

Post-'76 GM trucks are afflicted by poor-quality computer modules that make for hard starts and poor engine performance, early catalytic converter failures, unreliable diesel engines, and poorly engineered braking systems where the rear brakes are vulnerable to premature backing plate corrosion. GM's use of the "side-saddle" gas tank design also led to additional risk of fire in a collision.

From the late '70s to the early '90s, Ford's trucks became gas hogs; their fuel and ignition systems would often fail, causing fires and full-throttle stalling; and fuel pumps, the AC, and electrical systems were chronically dysfunctional. During that same period, Chrysler's early trucks were plagued by persistent brake, computer module, suspension, and automatic transmission failures.

Recommendation: Stick with the smallest Japanese-made truck you can find that will do the job. This means choosing a small pickup like the **Mazda B-series**, **Nissan King Cab**, or **Toyota Pickup** and **T100**. Even though these vehicles are recommended, they should be inspected for brake, steering, and engine head gasket problems. Also check for undercarriage corrosion, particularly with older Toyotas and Mazdas.

Avoid: Steer clear of Japanese pickups sold under an American label, like the Mitsubishi-built 1981–93 **Chrysler Ram 50** ($500–$2,000), plagued by poor NHTSA crash scores, weak engine piston rings, prematurely worn timing chains, failure-prone automatic transmissions, and a rust-prone body. The 1980–82 **Ford Courier** (a Mazda import now worth about $500) is another truck to avoid. Its main traps for the unwary are poor crashworthiness; excessive corrosion afflicting suspension, steering, and brake components; and failure-prone engine head gaskets, automatic transmission, front brakes, and electrical systems. And don't get caught with a 1980–82 **VW Rabbit Pickup** ($300–$500) due to its poor parts availability; lack of service support; unreliable electrical, fuel, and cooling systems; and troublesome brakes, front suspension components, and diesel engine head gaskets. Also, be wary of the 1982–84 **Dodge Rampage** pickup, which should cost no more than $500.

Sport-utilities

Anyone buying a decade-old or older sport-utility is asking for trouble. The danger of rollover is quite high (particularly with Ford, Isuzu, and Suzuki versions), overall quality control is very poor, and performance is mediocre. Furthermore, don't assume that European luxury SUVs are more reliable. To the contrary, **Land Rover** and **Mercedes-Benz** SUVs have garnered a reputation for poor-quality vehicles.

Recommendation: The **Jeeps** are the best of a bad lot. Their rollover tendency isn't as great as the above-mentioned models; parts are more easily obtainable; and servicing, if not given with a smile, at least isn't accompanied by a snarl or head scratching. Nevertheless, the early **CJs** and **Wagoneers** have been known for their rattle-prone bodies, air and water leaks, electrical glitches, and high-cost brake maintenance. Expect to spend $2,000 tops for the entry-level CJ and a few thousand more for a Wagoneer.

Of course, if price is no object, there's nothing wrong with a 1987–89 **Toyota Land Cruiser**, selling for $5,500–$6,000. Just be sure to pull the wheels to examine the brakes, check for undercarriage corrosion, and make sure the engine head gasket is okay.

Avoid: Ever heard of American Motors? Well, back in 1981 they came out with the first 4X4 passenger car/sport-utility called the **Eagle** (others called it the Turkey), which was basically a Concord equipped with 4X4. It now sells for about $1,500. Be wary of its failure-prone drivetrain, ignition system, and clutch master; slave cylinder leaks; low rust resistance; and marginal crash protection. But at least it didn't roll over, something that can't be said for Ford's Bronco II.

Don't buy Ford's 1981–90 **Bronco II**, even though its $500–$3,000 price may seem like a bargain. It's one of the most unreliable, rollover-prone, rust-attracting 4X4s ever built. Even though repair costs can be cut by using independent garages, parts aren't easily found and can be quite expensive (especially TFI ignition components and computer modules). Between 1985 and 1989, the Bronco II was the undisputed leader in rollover deaths in the U.S. According to internal memoranda, Ford released the Bronco II in 1981 with full knowledge of the stability dangers inherent in the design. Critics contend that the present-day Explorer's rollover problems can be traced back to its Bronco heritage.

This sport-utility suffers from worse-than-average reliability. The 4-speed automatic has been the worst contributor to owners' woes. The complicated electronic fuel-injection system is a headache to diagnose and has a bad repair history. Brakes and 4X4 components can also be included on the list of potential problems. Overall, body assembly and paint quality are mediocre.

Now discontinued, the **Lada Niva** is a cheap Russian import ($500–$2,500 for 1990–97 models) that uses poor-quality body and mechanical components on a 20-year-old 4X4 design. They're noisy and trucklike on the road, the dealer network is non-existent, and parts are hard to find. Defective fuel and ignition systems (particularly the ignition control module) and a poorly designed electrical system are the most common problems. Frequent carburetor replacements, at $325 plus tax (if you can find one), are rendered necessary due to the butterfly shaft warping or corroding—the result of an inherently defective design. Front brakes need to be replaced often; and transmissions, engine head gaskets, and differentials aren't durable either. Ladas were never crash-tested nor airbag-equipped.

The 1987–94 **Suzuki Samurai** is another orphan you shouldn't buy, despite its low cost ($800–$2,500). Its rollover history is almost as bad as Ford's. In fact, the 1987–88 models appear to be particularly prone to rolling over at almost any speed or in windy conditions. Parts costs are average. Some owners have complained about long delays in getting replacement parts. Crash tests of the 1986 model concluded that the driver and passenger would have sustained severe leg trauma. Unsteady road manners, coupled with a high centre of gravity, make the Samurai susceptible to sudden rollovers if the vehicle is not driven carefully, especially on rough terrain. This is particularly true of the 1987–88 models, where NHTSA records show the largest grouping of owner complaints and accident injury reports.

Minivans and wagons

Assuming you can't afford the big bucks for a Honda Odyssey or Toyota Sienna, you have a number of cheaper, old minivans to choose from: **Chrysler's Caravan**, **Voyager**, and **Colt/Summit/Vista wagons**; the **Ford Aerostar**; **GM's Astro** and **Safari**; **Nissan's Multi** and **Axxess**; and the **VW Camper**. Out of this group, the Colt/Summit/Vista, Aerostar, Astro and Safari, and Nissan offerings are your best bets.

Recommendation: Chrysler's Colt, Summit, and Vista. Priced from about $1,000 for an '88 version to about $2,500 for a '95 (wagons are worth about $500–$1,000 more), these are three of the best small cars and wagons that Chrysler doesn't make (they're all Mitsubishi imports). The only exceptions are the 1985–88 models, which were quite troublesome. The Summit and the Vista were sold under the Eagle moniker in Canada.

The Vista and the Summit wagon are small minivans with five- to seven-passenger seating. They have excellent crash ratings and are more reasonably priced, practical, and fuel efficient than many other small wagons. The five-passenger Colt wagon, like the Summit and Nissan Axxess, offers the extra versatility of a third seat in the back and a tall body. As such, it makes a great car for a small family with space to haul loads to the cottage. The wagon series is available in 4X4 (not recommended) and uses practically the same mechanical components as the other Colt models. The Summit wagon is essentially a wagon version of the Colt 200 and sells for a bit more.

On post-1990 Colts and Summits, the 2.4L head gasket may fail prematurely. Shocks aren't very durable, braking isn't impressive, and the front brakes have a short life span. Emission components, like the oxygen sensor, often fail after two years of use. A few owners have reported automatic transmission failures. Be especially wary of the troublesome 4X4 powertrain on 1989–91 wagons and the 16-valve turbo, dropped in 1990. Owners of the 1993 wagon complain of poor heating and defrosting. Surface rust is common, as are rust perforations on door bottoms, the front edge of the hood, and the rear hatch.

The 1995–97 **Ford Aerostar** isn't a bad choice, though 1986–94 models are risky buys. A 1992 XL would cost about $3,000, while a fully equipped 1997 version (the Aerostar's last year) should cost between $6,000 and $7,000. These primitive rear-drives are brawnier and more reliable than Chrysler's or Ford's front-drive minivans (exception made for the failure-prone 4X4 system), and they've posted impressive crashworthiness scores since 1992.

The 1986–94 models are at the bottom of the evolutionary scale as far as quality control is concerned. However, the last three model years showed lots of improvement. Repair costs are reasonable (except for high automatic transmission, AC and computer module costs), and many of the Aerostar's myriad mechanical and body defects can be fixed quite easily by independent garages. The Aerostar's modern, swoopy shape belies its limited performance capabilities: the 3.0L and 4.0L engines are unreliable through the 1991 model year, and the 3.0L is a sluggish performer. Older 2.3L and 2.8L engines can barely pull their own weight. The failure-prone 4-speed automatic transmission often has a hard time deciding which gear to choose, and the power steering transmits almost no road feel to the driver. The ride is bouncy, handling is sloppy, and braking performance is poor. Reliability problems on all models make early Aerostars risky buys, especially if the previous owner has been less than fastidious in maintenance and repairs.

Valve cover and rear main oil seal leaks are frequent, and leaks from the front axle vent tube often require the replacement of the front axle assembly. Even oil pans, which you wouldn't normally associate with leaks, tend to leak as a result of premature corrosion (a big-buck repair). Fuel-injectors are either faulty or plugged. A grinding/growling coming from the rear signals that the in-tank electric fuel pump is defective. Other problems include expensive electronic and electrical system glitches; power-steering, suspension, and brake defects; and premature and chronic air conditioner condenser and compressor breakdowns. Auto air conditioning experts refer to the problem as the "Black Death"—in reference to the sludge these Ford ACs produce in the FX-15 compressor that leads to massive internal component failures.

Nissan's 1991–95 **Axxess** minivan is an excellent choice. It's fairly reliable, easily serviced, and has posted respectable crash-safety ratings. You get carlike handling and ride comfort and as much space as the higher-priced Honda Odyssey. As with most minivans equipped with a full load and a small engine, acceleration isn't confidence inspiring on the highway. However, the Axxess is ideal for city-to-suburb commuting. What further sets the Axxess apart is its reasonable price and better-than-average reliability. Prices have remained stable, ranging from $3,000 to $5,000 for the top-of-the-line SE. You may have trouble finding one. But it's worth the wait.

Expect some electrical problems, premature wear of the front disc brakes, manual transmission malfunctions, and paint defects. Owners have also reported that the resonator (located just behind the muffler) fails around the 3-year mark and costs about $250 to replace. Windshield wipers are another rip-off. Nissan original equipment wipers are rare, aren't very durable, and they're way overpriced. Use regular blades that are shorter, easier to find, more durable, and less costly.

Nissan's Multi was sold in the late '80s as the Stanza Wagon in the States. It's a five-passenger little wagon *cum* mini-minivan that looks much like the Colt/Summit/Vista. In good condition, a 1988–89 Multi should cost about $1,500–$2,000.

Avoid: Stay away from bargain-priced minivans that require frequent and costly repairs. Chief among these are **Chrysler minivans, Ford Windstars**, and the **Mercury Villager/Nissan Quest** (1993–95). Chrysler models had engine, drivetrain, electrical and fuel system, AC, brake, and body deficiencies galore. Windstars are noted for engine, automatic transmission, brake, steering, suspension, and fuel system failures. Early Villagers and Quests had chronic engine exhaust manifold stud failures that could cost thousands of dollars to replace. **VW Campers** are a good idea poorly executed. These minivans are nicely laid-out, but they aren't reliable and servicing is practically non-existent. Plus, they are costly: $4,000–$5,000 for a 1985–89 model.

Lemon-Proofing Before You Buy

Now that you've chosen a vehicle that's priced right and seems to meet your needs, take some time to assess its interior, exterior, and highway performance by following the checklist below. If you're buying from a dealer, ask to take the vehicle home overnight in order to drive it over the same roads you would normally use in your daily activities. This will give you an important insight into how well the engine handles all of the convenience features, how comfortable the seats are during extended driving, and whether front and rear visibility is satisfactory without your having to double up like a pretzel or avoid dash glare upon the windshield (a Volvo problem, particularly). Of course, if you're buying privately, it's doubtful you will get the vehicle for an overnight test—you may have to rent a similar one from a dealer or rental agency.

Safety Check

1. Is outward visibility good in all directions? (You can't see the nose of the Lumina APV, so you'll have to park by ear.)
2. Are there large blind spots impeding vision (such as side pillars)?
3. Are the mirrors large enough for good side and rear views?
4. Does the rear-view mirror have a glare-reducing setting?
5. Is there a rear window washer and wiper?
6. Are all instrument displays clearly visible (not washed out in sunlight), is there daytime or night driving dash glare upon the windshield, and are the controls easily reached?
7. Is the handbrake easy to reach and use?
8. Does the front seat have sufficient rearward travel to put you a safe distance from the airbag's deployment (about a foot) and still allow you to reach the brake and accelerator pedals? Are the brake and accelerator pedals spaced far enough apart?
9. Are the head restraints adjustable or non-adjustable? (The latter is better if you often forget to set them.)
10. Are the head restraints designed to permit rear visibility? (Some are annoyingly obtrusive.)
11. Are there rear three-point shoulder belts similar to those on the front seats? Two-point belts aren't as good. (Some older minivans don't have three-point belts anywhere.)
12. Is the seatbelt latch plate easy to find and reach?
13. Does the seatbelt fit comfortably across the chest without rubbing against the face or falling off the shoulder?
14. Do you feel too much pressure against you from the shoulder belt?
15. Does the seatbelt release easily, retract smoothly, and use pretensioners for maximum effectiveness?

16. Are there user-friendly child seat anchorage locations?
17. Are there automatic door locks controlled by the driver or childproof rear door locks?
18. Do the rear windows roll only halfway down?
19. Are the airbags de-powered?
20. Are there side airbags (still unproven)?

Exterior Check

Rust

Rust is a four-letter word that means trouble. Don't buy any used vehicle with extensive corrosion around the rear hatch, wheelwells, door bottoms, or rocker panels. Body work in these areas is usually only a temporary solution.

Cosmetic rusting (rear hatch, exhaust system, front hood) is acceptable and can even help push the price way down, as long as the chassis and other major structural members aren't affected. Bumps, bubbles, or ripples under the paint may be due to repairs resulting from an accident or premature corrosion. Don't dismiss this as a mere cosmetic problem; the entire vehicle will have to be stripped down, reprimed, and repainted.

Knock gently on the front fenders, door bottoms, rear wheelwells, and rear doors—places where rust usually occurs first. Even if these areas have been repaired with plastic, lead, metal plates, or fibreglass, once rusting starts, it's difficult to stop. Use a small magnet to check which body panels have been repaired with non-metallic body fillers.

Use a flashlight to check for exhaust system and suspension component rust-out. Make sure the catalytic converter is present. In the past, many drivers removed this pollution control device in the mistaken belief that it would improve fuel economy. Police can fine you for not having the converter and force you to buy one ($300–$400) before certifying your vehicle.

Tires

Don't be concerned if the tires are worn, since retreads are inexpensive and easy to find. Look at tire wear for clues that the vehicle is out of alignment, needs suspension repairs, or has serious chassis problems. An alignment and new shocks and springs are part of routine maintenance and are relatively inexpensive in the aftermarket. However, if it's a 4X4 or the MacPherson struts have to be replaced, you're looking at a $1,000 repair bill.

Accident damage

Accident repairs require a further inspection by an independent body shop in order to determine if the frame is aligned and the vehicle is tracking correctly. Frameless minivans need extensive and expensive work to straighten them out, and proper frame and body repairs can often cost more than the vehicle is worth. In British Columbia, all accidents involving more than $2,000 in repairs must be reported to subsequent buyers.

Here are some tips on what you can do to avoid buying a damaged vehicle. First, ask the following questions about the vehicle's accident history:

- Has it ever been in an accident?
- If so, what was the damage and who fixed it?
- Is the auto body shop that repaired the vehicle registered with the provincial government? Is there any warranty outstanding? Can you have a copy of the work order?
- Has the vehicle's certificate of title been labeled "salvage"? ("Salvage" means that an expert has determined that the cost to properly repair the vehicle is more than its value. This usually happens after the vehicle has been in a serious accident.)

If the vehicle has been in an accident, you should either walk away from the sale or have it checked by a qualified auto body expert. Remember, not all salvage vehicles are bad—properly repaired ones can be a safe and sound investment if the price is low enough.

What to look for

1. If the vehicle has been repainted recently, check the quality of the job by inspecting the engine and trunk compartments and the inside door panels. Do it on a clear day so that you'll find any waves in the paint.
2. Check the paint—do all of the vehicle's panels match?
3. Inspect the paint for tiny bubbles. They may identify a poor priming job or premature rust.
4. Is there paint overspray or primer in the doorjambs, wheelwells, or engine compartment? These are signs that the vehicle has had body repairs.
5. Check the gaps between body panels—are they equal? Unequal gaps may indicate improper panel alignment or a bent frame.
6. Do the doors, hood, and rear hatch open and shut properly?
7. Have the bumpers been damaged or recently repaired? Check the bumper support struts for corrosion damage.
8. Test the shock absorbers by pushing hard on a corner of the vehicle. If it bounces around like a ship at sea, the shocks need replacing.
9. Look at the muffler and exhaust pipe to detect premature rust or displacement from a low-impact collision; this could channel deadly carbon monoxide into the passenger area.
10. Make sure there's a spare tire, a jack, and tools necessary for changing a flat. Can you get at the spare easily? Also look for premature rusting in the side wheelwells and for water in the rear hatch channel.

11. Look at how the vehicle sits. If one side or end is higher than the other, it could mean that the suspension is defective.
12. Ask the seller to turn on the headlights (low and high beams), turn signals, parking lights, emergency blinking lights, and to blow the horn. From the rear, check that the brake lights, back-up lights, turn indicators, taillights, and licence plate light all work.

Interior Check

The number of kilometres on the odometer isn't as important as how well the vehicle was driven and maintained. Still, high-mileage vehicles depreciate rapidly because most people consider them to be risky buys. Calculate 20,000 km per year as average and take off about $200 for each additional 10,000 km above this average. Be suspicious of the odometer reading. Confirm it by checking the vehicle's maintenance records.

The interior will often give you an idea of how the vehicle was used and maintained. For example, sagging rear seats and a front passenger seat in pristine condition indicate that your minivan may have been used as a minibus. Delivery vans will have the paint on the driver's door sill rubbed down to the metal, while the passenger door sill will look like new.

What to look for
1. Watch for excessive wear of the seats, dash, accelerator, brake pedal, armrests, and roof lining.
2. Check the dash and roof lining for radio or cellular phone mounting holes (police, taxi, delivery van). Is the radio tuned to local stations?
3. Turn the steering wheel: listen for unusual noises and watch for excessive play (more than an inch).
4. Test the emergency brake with the vehicle parked on a hill.
5. Inspect the seatbelts. Is the webbing in good condition? Do the belts retract easily?
6. Make sure that door latches and locks are in good working order. If rear doors have no handles or locks, or if they've just been installed, your minivan may have been used to transport prisoners.
7. Can the seats be moved into all the positions intended by the manufacturer? Look under them to make sure that the runners are functioning as they should.
8. Can head supports be adjusted easily?
9. Peel back the rugs and check the metal floor for signs of rust or dampness.

Road Test

1. Start the vehicle and listen for unusual noises. Shift automatics into Park and manuals into Neutral with the handbrake engaged. Open the

hood to check for fluid leaks. This test should be done with the engine running and be repeated 10 minutes after the engine has been shut down following the completion of the test-drive.

2. With the motor running, check out all dashboard controls: windshield wipers, heater and defroster, and radio.

3. If the engine stalls or races at idle, a simple adjustment may fix the trouble. Loud clanks or low oil pressure could mean potentially expensive repairs.

4. Check all ventilation systems. Do the rear side windows roll down? Are there excessive air leaks around the door handles?

5. While in Neutral, push down on the accelerator abruptly. Black exhaust smoke may require only a minor engine adjustment; blue smoke may signal major engine repairs.

6. Shift an automatic into Drive with the motor still idling. The vehicle should creep forward slowly without stalling or speeding. Listen for unusual noises when the transmission is engaged. Manual transmissions should engage as soon as the clutch is released. Slipping or stalling could require a new clutch. While driving, make absolutely sure that a four-wheel drive can be engaged without unusual noises or hesitation.

7. Shift an automatic transmission into Drive. While the motor is idling, apply the emergency brake. If the motor isn't racing and the brake is in good condition, the vehicle should stop.

8. Accelerate to 50 km/h while slowly moving through all gears. Listen for transmission noises. Step lightly on the brakes; the response should be immediate and equal for all wheels.

9. In a deserted parking lot, test the vehicle's steering and suspension by driving in figure eights at low speeds.

10. Make sure the road is clear of traffic and pedestrians. Drive at 30 km/h and take both hands off the steering wheel to see whether the vehicle veers from one side to the other. If it does, the alignment or suspension could be defective, or the vehicle could have been in an accident.

11. Test the suspension by driving over some rough terrain.

12. Stop at the foot of a small hill and see if the vehicle can climb it without difficulty.

13. On an expressway, it should take no longer than 20 seconds for most cars and minivans to accelerate from a standing start to 100 km/h.

14. Drive through a tunnel with the windows open. Try to detect any unusual motor, exhaust, or suspension sounds.

15. After the test-drive, verify the performance of the automatic transmission by shifting from Drive to Neutral to Reverse. Listen for clunking sounds during transmission engagement.

Many of these tests will undoubtedly turn up some defects, which may be major or minor (even new vehicles have an average of a half-dozen major and minor defects). Ask an independent mechanic for an estimate and try to convince the seller to pay part of the repair bill if you buy the vehicle. Keep in mind that many 3- to 5-year-old vehicles with 60,000–100,000 km run the risk of an engine timing belt or timing chain failure that can cause several thousand dollars worth of repairs. If the timing belt or chain hasn't been replaced, plan to do it and deduct about $300 from the purchase price for the repair.

It's important to eliminate as many duds as possible through your own cursory check, since you'll later invest two hours and about $100 for a thorough mechanical inspection of your choice. Garages approved by the Automobile Protection Association or members of the Canadian Automobile Association usually do a good job. CAA inspections run from $100 to $150 for non-members. Oil company–affiliated diagnostic clinics are recommended only if they don't do repairs. Remember, if you get a bum steer from an independent testing agency, you can get the inspection fee refunded and hold the garage responsible for your subsequent repairs and consequential damages, like towing, missed work, or a ruined vacation. See Part Two for details.